BY HUGH FORDIN

*The World of Entertainment! Hollywood's
Greatest Musicals*

Vocal Selections from That's Entertainment!

Jerome Kern: The Man and His Music

*Film TV Daily Yearbook of Motion Pictures
and Television (52nd Edition)*

THE MOVIES' GREATEST MUSICALS

Produced in Hollywood USA
by THE FREED UNIT

HUGH FORDIN

FREDERICK UNGAR PUBLISHING CO.

New York

For Nickey and Dick Fleischer

Grateful acknowledgment is made for the use of the following material:

"Dear Mister Gable," "Keep Your Seats" and "Palace Introduction" by Roger Edens; "The Interview" by Roger Edens and Kay Thompson. Used by permission of the Robert F. Kennedy Memorial Foundation.

"Have Yourself a Merry Little Christmas" W/M: Hugh Martin and Ralph Blane. Copyright © 1944; renewed 1972 by Leo Feist Inc. Used by permission.

"Doin' What Comes Natur'lly" by Irving Berlin. Copyright © 1946 Irving Berlin. Excerpt on pages 272–73 reprinted by permission of Irving Berlin Music Corporation.

"That's Entertainment!" by Howard Dietz and Arthur Schwartz. Copyright © 1953 by Chappell & Co., Inc. Used by permission of Chappell & Co., Inc.

"Triplets" by Howard Dietz and Arthur Schwartz. Copyright © 1937 by De Sylva, Brown and Henderson, Inc. Copyright renewed. Copyright assigned to Chappell & Co., Inc. Copyright © 1953 by Chappell & Co., Inc. Used by permission of Chappell & Co., Inc.

Excerpts from *The New Yorker* magazine, September 7, 1957, "Letter From Paris," by Janet Flanner, used by permission.

Extracts of this book first appeared in *Vocal Selections From That's Entertainment,* commentary by Hugh Fordin. Copyright © 1974 The Big Three Music Corporation. Published by The Big Three Music Corporation, New York, N.Y.

CONTENTS

During the past thirty-six years millions of people have filled movie theatres all over the world. They saw Judy Garland skipping down the yellow brick road. They celebrated the opening of the St. Louis Fair. They saw the "good girls" invading the Wild West and watched Judy falling in love with Mickey. They shared Margaret O'Brien's fright on Halloween night. Annie told them she can do anything better. With the changing times, millions looked for more substantial diversions. They had met Gene Kelly, in love with his "gal"; now he was an American in Paris. Fred Astaire was dancing on the ceiling, Kelly was dancing in the rain—after going on the town with Frank Sinatra. The Show Boat came down the Mississippi and Brigadoon came back to life. Gigi, the adolescent of fatherless ancestry, turned the tables and married her lover. And they learned that there is no business like show business.

Almost four decades have gone by. And still both young and old alike are enraptured watching the "oldies." Revivals have become so incredibly popular that even at this writing Metro-Goldwyn-Mayer is in the midst of assembling highlights from that Golden Age when they were the reigning king of the film musical. This motion picture, aptly titled *That's Entertainment!,* could never have been made had it not been for the presence of one man: Arthur Freed.

Only a few know his name. It would be utterly pointless to write the life story of Arthur Freed; this book is not his biography. Instead, it is a documentary of his work which *was* his life, to the exclusion of almost everything else.

I set out to meet, to investigate the man, who in my eyes single-handedly was responsible for the evolution of the film musical.

My appointment was for 2 P.M. on October 10, 1971, at his home, situated in the most exclusive section of Bel Air in Los Angeles.

Already as I was driving up the very long, winding approach to the house, I had the impression that I was leaving Hollywood behind rather than entering it. This impression deepened once inside, where nothing whatsoever reflected my host's profession. After taking stock of me he asked the pertinent question: "What is it you want to know?" I put it on the line. "I came to find out *how* you did it—not *that* you did it." My directness broke the ice and a lasting rapport was established. "Why don't you ask my people?" Freed said, with unaffected modesty. "How can I bring this off?" I thought. My anxiety must have been transparent. "I'll open all the doors for you!"

On the top of my list was Fred Astaire. My first interview with him lasted six hours.

Freed then put his archives at my disposal: interoffice memoranda, scripts and story notes, censorship reports, contracts, budgets, cast sheets, set renderings, wardrobe breakdowns, production reports, music notes, recording reports and prerecording discs, shooting schedules, progress reports, publicity and photographs, business and personal correspondence plus the actual cost and derived income from each of the films he produced.[1]

I want to state here and now that the story of Hollywood's royal family, the Freed Unit, is not embellished behind-the-scenes gossip; not the conjecture and half truths of people who weren't there, but the words, remarks, criticisms and documented facts transcribed from over five hundred hours of recorded tapes of those who made Freed's

[1] "Box office gross" is used whimsically in movie industry accounting. It means different things at different times in different contexts. However, for simplification in this book, quoted grosses are actually the net return to the studio for the given production.

The Freed family (bottom row left to right): Ralph, Max, Ruth, Rosa (nee Grossman), Clarence; (top row): Hugo, Victor, Arthur, Sydney and Walter. RALPH FREED COLLECTION

Photograph
by Man Ray.
ARTHUR FREED
ARCHIVES

films under his guidance. In short, it is my account of what made him
the uncontested master of the movie musical.

Arthur Freed was born in Charleston, South Carolina, on September
9, 1894, to Rosa and Max Freed. He grew up in Seattle and began
writing poetry at Phillips Academy in Exeter, New Hampshire. His
father was an art dealer traveling all over the world with his family,
staying occasionally in one place long enough for Rosa to give birth
to another child. Eventually there were eight of them. The last was
born after the family settled in a large house, filled with European
antiques, overlooking Lake Washington, amid acres of cherry orchards,
fruit trees and berry bushes.

Music played a vital role in the Freed household. As a sideline
Max Freed sold zithers and was blessed with a resounding tenor voice.
Arthur, the oldest, became a lyricist. Sydney and Clarence went
into the recording business in Hollywood. Walter became an organist.
Ralph, emulating Arthur, made songwriting his profession. And even
Ruth, the only female offspring, has written numerous songs. Only
Hugo was of a more pragmatic nature; he became an accountant.
(Victor died during World War I.)

At the death of his father, Arthur became the head of the family, the protector, a character quality which extends into all phases of his life. He worshiped and admired his mother, a highly intelligent, articulate, vibrant lady, until the very day of her death in 1957.

In 1923, Freed married Renee Klein, of Alsatian ancestry, born in Santa Barbara County, raised and schooled in San Francisco, a refined, distinguished beauty, gifted with intelligence and tolerance. Their only child, Barbara, happily married, gave them two grandchildren. At the time of this writing the Freeds had just celebrated their fiftieth wedding anniversary.

In the two years it took me to write this book I grew to know Arthur Freed very well. In summing up I want to draw a brief sketch of the man as I see him. His emotional scale is limited and uncomplicated: admiration for some, respect for a few, rejection of mediocrity. Secure within himself, he has the courage, the daring to venture toward the unexplored. He is inclined to let problems take care of themselves; if they don't he makes decisions swiftly and without panic. His lack of social polish is deliberate. His anger is short-lived and never vindictive. He is nonverbal and conveys his thoughts by implication. He idolizes the home and the morality of marriage. He is a romantic, a sentimental man, whose powers of imagination always lure him beyond the rainbow.

It is my hope that this short profile on Arthur Freed, the man, makes him if not the reader's friend at least an acquaintance before the first page is turned.

Hugh Fordin

Malibu, California
March 1, 1973

1

THE WIZARD OF OZ
BABES IN ARMS

Arthur Freed had been on the Metro-Goldwyn-Mayer lot for a number of years as a songwriter. He and his collaborator Nacio Herb Brown had written the scores for *The Broadway Melody* (1929), *Hollywood Revue* (1929) and *Going Hollywood* (1932), among many others. On the sound stages he watched his songs being staged, rehearsed and photographed. He watched intently, absorbed much and learned a great deal.

Even at this early stage Freed began to move away—consciously or not—from the limited field of lyric writing. His urge for a wider range of creative activity began to surface. With his almost uncanny instinct he recognized talent where others passed it by. And, ignoring the already established patterns of the early musicals, he never ceased to search for new forms.

During the fall of 1934, an agent asked Freed to listen to a singer, Patricia Ellis, who was under contract to Warner Brothers. Agents were always at his doorstep, but Freed knew the girl's father, Alexander Leftwich, a famous Broadway director, so he went to hear her. "She's very pleasant," he told the agent, "but who's the fellow who played piano for her and did he do her vocal arrangements?" The next day Freed was told that it was Roger Edens, who had done the

Going Hollywood: Nacio Herb Brown, Arthur Freed, with stars Bing Crosby and Marion Davies. M-G-M

vocal arrangements. "Does he want a job?" The answer was yes. Freed arranged for a contract.

Edens came to Hollywood via Broadway. (His southern charm came from Richmond, Virginia.) In 1930, Ethel Merman's piano player and vocal arranger, Al Siegal, was appearing with her in the musical sequence "Sam and Delilah," in *Girl Crazy.* On the night after that memorable opening, Siegal suffered a heart attack. Edens was playing in the pit with the group called the Red Nichols Orchestra, which consisted of Red Nichols, Jimmy and Tommy Dorsey, Gene Krupa, Jack Teagarden, Glenn Miller and Harry James. Edens jumped on the stage to pinch-hit. The show not only launched the brilliant career of Merman but also her friendship and association with Edens. Edens then became her arranger for *Take a Chance*[1] and accompanied her in her moonlighting appearances at the Central Park Casino and the Palace. When she was offered a part in *Kid Millions* (Samuel Goldwyn-UA), Edens went with her to Hollywood.

Edens was very much at home in Hollywood among many other New York-ophiles. He was tall and handsome and charming; his

[1] Originally called *Humpty Dumpty,* it had a score by Richard Whiting and Nacio Herb Brown. When it closed out of town for revisions, Edens wrote Merman's legendary song, "Eadie Was a Lady." The show reopened on Broadway on November 26, 1932, as *Take a Chance.* Interesting note: Although Freed didn't know it, Edens worked with Brown before he came to M-G-M.

2

Roger Edens. Taken on the occasion of Edens' screen appearance in *Broadway Melody of 1936* where he was seen accompanying Eleanor Powell in a reprise of "You Are My Lucky Star." ROGER EDENS ARCHIVES

friends included Margaret Sullavan, Henry Fonda, Claudette Colbert, Peggy Fears, Katharine Hepburn[2] and Jimmy Stewart, then a group of sparkling young people, just on the threshold of their brilliant careers.

Edens' first assignment at Metro was on a Jean Harlow picture called *Reckless,* as the film's musical supervisor. He said, "My first task was an adaptation of the title song written by Jerome Kern and Oscar Hammerstein II for Jean—and I tried to tell the whole thing without dialogue, just as a story sequence with music."

Then he worked on several nonmusicals where one song or special scoring was required. And in a very short time his screen credit read: "Musical Adaptation by Roger Edens."

In the spring of 1935, the studio announced *Broadway Melody of 1936* for immediate production. The film would be based on an original screen story by Moss Hart. There was an all-star cast, including Jack Benny, Robert Taylor, Eleanor Powell and Frances Langford. Because this was to be a big musical, naturally their top songwriting team, Nacio Herb Brown and Arthur Freed, would supply the songs.

Freed and Brown went to work and in three weeks' time came up with a score that included some new and recent hits from their ever-growing catalogue: "I've Gotta Feelin' You're Foolin'," "Sing Before Breakfast," "You Are My Lucky Star" and "Broadway Rhythm."

At the first production meeting for this musical, John Considine,

---

[2] Thirty-five years later (1969) Hepburn only consented to appear in the Broadway musical *Coco,* after Edens agreed to coach her.

Nacio Herb Brown and Arthur Freed with Eleanor Powell on the set of *Broadway Melody of 1936*. M-G-M

Jr., the producer, announced that Freed would also be musical supervisor.

In his capacity as musical adapter Edens met with Freed to discuss ideas for the presentation of the songs. "Arthur, I've got a fabulous idea for the 'Broadway Rhythm' number. Use it at the end of the picture—imagine it split up into five sections, all interwoven naturally. First have Frances Langford and the boys sing it, then Vilma and Buddy Ebsen dance to it, then a section for June Knight and one for Nick Long, Jr.—with everything building up to Eleanor Powell, coming out with a slam-bang finale!"

Freed was enthusiastic, and with that his and Edens' long and meaningful association began.

Freed wanted a new sound, a new style. In this he was unquestionably influenced by Edens' Broadway background. One of his moves in that direction shook the music department at the studio in its complacent and illiterate shoes: By a swift coup he succeeded in bringing over Alfred Newman[3] from Samuel Goldwyn Pictures as musical director

---

[3] Soon after his assignment on this picture, Newman was signed by Darryl F. Zanuck to become Twentieth Century-Fox's general music director, a post he held for over two decades. But on several occasions Freed arranged to have him loaned out to Metro on important musical productions.

4

and his orchestrator Edward Powell (both originally from Broadway), to work on the new film.

One day Freed got a call from Jack Robbins, head of Metro's music publishing firm.[4] "Arthur, I want you to hear a little girl. . . ." "A little girl?" Freed groaned. "What do you mean . . . little girl!?" "I'll bring her in tomorrow." The next day Robbins arrived on Stage 1 with Judy Garland to audition for Freed and Edens. Accompanied at the piano by her father, Frank Gumm, the thirteen-year-old girl proceeded to sing. "That guy is the worst piano player I ever heard," mumbled Freed. "Roger, go over and do a song with the little girl." Judy then sang "Zing! Went the Strings of My Heart." Edens fell off the piano bench and Freed ran out of the sound stage. He was out of breath by the time he reached L.B.'s office. Ignoring receptionists, he burst in as Mayer was dictating to his secretary. It took some doing to induce Mayer to walk from the Administration Building to Stage 1, two city blocks away. By the time Freed and Mayer arrived, a crowd had gathered (in a studio, news travels fast). Judy sang again and again. And then again for Mayer. When she finally sang "Eli, Eli," Mayer had tears in his eyes.[5] Freed walked back with him to his office. "What did I tell you, boss? She's going to be a big star!"

Judy's contract was signed on September 27, 1935. Rather than have her make a screen test, she was cast in a mediocre two-reeler, *Every Sunday,* teamed with another pretty young girl, Deanna Durbin, who was also under contract to the studio. Mayer decided to cast the two girls, as a team, in a full-length picture. With this news panic broke out—Durbin's contract had lapsed and Universal Pictures had grabbed her.

For Judy the months following were a time of waiting and growing disappointment. She was idle—a state of affairs which even at this age did not sit well with her frail nervous system. Her mother, a stage mother par excellence, asked Judy's agent to get her some work that wouldn't conflict with her studio contract. He was able to spot her on several radio programs, among them one hosted by Wallace Beery, where she plugged tunes from the *Broadway Melody of 1936.* The audience response was excellent, but the studio felt she needed more experience and more exposure, and sent her to New York with Roger Edens to appear in vaudeville at Loew's State Theatre.

Edens' faith in Judy never wavered. He was fond of her and became

---

[4] M-G-M owned what was considered "the big three" (in the music industry): Robbins Music, Leo Feist, Inc. and Miller Music, later acquiring Freed's two publishing firms, Walter Jacobs and Variety Music, along with Harry Warren's song catalogue.

[5] Whenever Ida Koverman, Mayer's executive secretary and a great music lover, would bring in one of her protégés to audition, she advised them to sing "Kol Nidre." It is a known fact that this inevitably would lead, at least, to a short-term contract.

her professional and personal adviser. Before leaving with her for appearances in New York, he discarded her dismally tasteless clothes and substituted a simple, elegant wardrobe, white cotton gloves and all. A disgruntled Mrs. Gumm went along, of course, unappreciated by everyone around her. Judy was a great success at Loew's and by now was thriving on it.

Edens returned to Hollywood to work on the musical arrangements for Jack Oakie's radio program, "The Camel Caravan." Judy returned with him and once again Metro seemed to have forgotten her. But Edens kept his eyes open and promoted a principal role for her on Oakie's weekly show. He coached her; he taught her to sing softly and from the heart; he dissuaded her from singing songs too sophisticated for a girl of her age. His artistic ingenuity and tasteful choice of material brought about Judy's extraordinary success with radio audiences. A talent scout from Twentieth Century-Fox heard Judy on the show and she was loaned out for Fox's *Pigskin Parade*. At the completion of this not very memorable venture, Judy came back to her "home lot." And—again—nothing happened. She became restless and unhappy.

Now an unrelated event set the wheels rolling. The studio was preparing an elaborate party for Clark Gable's thirty-sixth birthday. Gable was one of Metro's biggest box-office stars, and this event was going to be celebrated in style. Freed was asked to organize the entertainment and he delegated Edens to set up the musical end of it. Edens put Judy on the program. She would have a captive audience

During one of the regular Sunday occasions at the Mayer compound, Freed took this snapshot of Judy Garland. To her left, Mayer's daughter, Irene (then Mrs. David O. Selznick), Mayer's sister Ida, L.B., and in the background his son-in-law David. ARTHUR FREED ARCHIVES

composed of the most glamorous and influential people in Hollywood. Judy encapsulated her number "You Made Me Love You" with a fan letter set to music Edens had written for her, "Dear Mr. Gable":

(*Quasi Recitativo*)

Dear Mr. Gable, I am writing this to you, and I hope you read it so you'll know . . . my heart beats like a hammer, and I stutter and I stammer, ev'ry time I see you at the picture show. . . . I guess I'm just another fan of yours, and I thought I'd write and tell you so ho! ho! ho!
    "You Made Me Love You"—complete refrain.
    Ah, gee, Mr. Gable I don't want to bother you, I guess you got a lot of girls who tell you the same thing. If you don't want to read this, well—you don't have to. But I just had to tell you about the time I saw you in *It Happened One Night*. That was the first time I ever saw you and I knew right then that you were the nicest fella in the movies. I guess it was 'cause you acted so well, so natur-a-like; not like a real actor at all, but like any fella you meet at school or at a party. Then I saw you in a picture with Joan Crawford, and I had to cry a little, 'cause you loved her *so* much and you couldn't have her—not till the end of the picture, anyway; then one time I saw you in person—you were going to the Cocoanut Grove one night, and I was standing there, when you got out of your car, and you almost knocked me down, but it wasn't your fault—no—I was in the way, but you looked at me and you smiled, yeah, you smiled right at me, as if you meant it, and I cried all the way home. Just 'cause you smiled at me for being in your way. Oh, I'll never forget it, Mr. Gable. Honest Injun, you're my favorite actor. [Judy picks up refrain of "You Made Me Love You" at "I don't care what happens, let the whole world . . ." to end.]

The reaction of the audience was moist eyes and thunderous applause. The rest is history. Without her two godfathers, there might never have been a Judy Garland.

Judy was immediately cast in the *Broadway Melody of 1938* (1937), with yet another Brown and Freed score. After this assignment Nacio Herb Brown's contract with Metro came to an end. He left the studio to try his hand at serious composing. In years to come, Freed occasionally lured him back to write a song or two with him. The team of Nacio Herb Brown and Arthur Freed has become a byword in the world of songwriting. It was a happy and fruitful partnership.

One morning Freed was already halfway to the studio when he turned back and drove to L. B. Mayer's house. He had an open invitation for breakfast, an indication of a relationship that had grown closer over the years. The *Broadway Melody of 1938* had opened to rave notices and packed houses. "They love the kid!" Freed said. "I'd put my bet on her if I were a producer." In the past Freed had at times hinted at his wish to produce, and he and Mayer had begun recently to discuss it in more concrete terms.

"Well, Arthur, now is the time," Mayer said suddenly. "Find a property and make a picture."

Freed immediately set things in motion. He picked up the phone and called Frank Orsatti, one of the most powerful Hollywood agents, and asked him to meet for lunch. Orsatti and Mayer had already discussed Freed's aspirations. At lunch he told Orsatti he was looking for a story; in fact, a vehicle for Judy. In the course of their conversation, Freed mentioned the children's stories written by L. Frank Baum, especially *The Wizard of Oz,* which he remembered vividly. Orsatti told Freed that Sam Goldwyn owned them.[6] Freed instructed Orsatti to negotiate a deal.

Briefly, the history of *Oz* is this: The stories were written mostly in Hollywood from 1904 until 1919, when Lyman Frank Baum died. The first of the fourteen that Baum wrote entitled *The Wizard of Oz* was made into a Broadway musical in 1903 with Fred Stone and Dave Montgomery in the starring roles. Two movies had been made of *Wizard,* in 1910 and 1925, respectively—silent films, of course. Oliver Hardy starred in the 1925 version. And now, in 1938, it came to life once more. A deal was made: Loew's, Inc. (parent company of M-G-M) bought the rights from Samuel Goldwyn for $20,000.

Freed had had extensive discussions with L.B. concerning his conception for the picture. On January 31, 1938, he sent a list of casting suggestions to Mayer. Mayer was a shrewd, enterprising and, at the same time, a circumspect executive. He realized that this would be an enormous undertaking. Moreover, the story was a fantasy, and past experience had shown that fantasies didn't play well. Audiences were happier with the mirror-up-to-life formula. It was one thing to make a cartoon like *Snow White and the Seven Dwarfs,* for instance, but to make a fantasy with real people was a sensitive undertaking. In a sense, *The Wizard of Oz* was a new approach and well removed from what had so far been the Hollywood musical. It needed special care. Both as the responsible head of the studio and as Freed's friend, Mayer meant to safeguard the project. For this purpose he called on Mervyn LeRoy, who had made his reputation as a producer at Warner Brothers. Mayer wanted an experienced man to work with Freed and made him the executive producer[7]; Freed was to be his associate.

[6] Goldwyn had bought the majority of *Oz* stories from the estate of L. Frank Baum. In a contract dated January 26, 1934, assurances were given Goldwyn that assignments to earlier filmizations had been obtained. They included: Selig Polyscope's production (1910), the Oz Film Company (Baum's defunct studio), Larry Semon Company (1925). But Goldwyn had done nothing with the properties.

[7] LeRoy had just moved over to Metro, having been lured by Mayer's offer of $6,500 per week. A record contract for a producer in any day.

8

Edens had Maurice Seymour, famous theatrical photographer, take this portrait of Judy while she was appearing in New York.

And so LeRoy found Freed's casting notes on his desk, forwarded from Mayer's office. His first thought was: "We've got to have a box-office star." It wasn't imaginative, but it was insurance. He thought Shirley Temple would be ideal as Dorothy and he told Mayer so. Mayer approached Zanuck for a possible loan-out, and Freed seemingly played along with him. He dispatched Edens to sound out Shirley Temple. But he was determined. After all, he'd chosen this story with Judy in mind.

"What can I say, Arthur?" Edens reported, having auditioned Shirley Temple. "Her vocal limitations are insurmountable."

It had frequently been reported that Zanuck was willing to trade his child star for Mayer's Jean Harlow and Clark Gable. Except that Jean Harlow was already dead by this time. The deal for Temple never reached the negotiating table.[8]

LeRoy was still in search of a big-name star. He was strongly supported by Nicholas Schenck, president of Loew's Inc., whose ear was only receptive to the ringing of a cash register. One must remember the great distance between Culver City and Mr. Schenck's office at 1540 Broadway was not exactly paved with artistic aspiration.

Now LeRoy was reaching out for Deanna Durbin—so the gossip columns said. But Universal wouldn't even consider it. Eventually, Freed convinced Mayer to cast Judy in the part of Dorothy Gale.

---

[8] After hearing Mayer's idea for Shirley Temple, Zanuck resurrected Maeterlinck's fantasy *The Blue Bird* as Twentieth Century-Fox's answer to M-G-M's project. After *The Blue Bird* laid an egg at the box office, Temple and Zanuck parted company and, oddly enough, she signed a contract with M-G-M.

On February 24, 1938, *Daily Variety* carried a six-line article on the bottom of page 3: "M-G-M has acquired the screen rights for *The Wizard of Oz* from Samuel Goldwyn and has assigned Judy Garland to the role of Dorothy."

On the following day a meeting was held in Mayer's office to discuss the production. Present were LeRoy and Freed. In preparation for this meeting, Freed had made a list of creative personnel that he thought would be "good bets" to work on the film. (He also brought up suggestions for the development of the story):

Cast
Garland (set)
Ebsen (set)
Bolger (set)
May Robson (Auntie Em)
Charley Grapewin[9] (Uncle Henry)
The Wizard/Professor Marvel
Miss Gulch/the Wicked Witch of the West
Good Witch Glinda
Munchkins/Midgets/Animals (Leo Singer's midgets)
Get Judy a Dog

Scenery and Costumes
Norman Bel Geddes
Vincente Minnelli

Color
Technicolor Company

Drawings
Hugo Ballin

Book
Noel Langley
Herbert Fields
Herman Mankiewicz
Irving Brecher

Music
Jerome Kern
Harold Arlen
Herb Brown
Herb Stothart (musical director)
Roger Edens (over-all musical supervision/arrangements

Lyrics
Ira Gershwin
Yip Harburg
Dorothy Fields

Special Effects
Buddy Gillespie (re: Winged Monkeys, Tornado, Talking Trees)

The only decision that resulted from the meeting was to proceed with a story outline. Screenwriters Florence Ryerson and Edgar Allan Woolf were assigned to work on a treatment.

Shortly thereafter in a communication to Freed they documented their impressions of the assignment:

> . . . perhaps the terrific strain under which we are living—with its war alarms, strikes, horrors at home and abroad that are forced upon us hourly by the radio—has drained life of its old joyousness.
>
> Whatever the cause, it has resulted in a mental retreat which might almost be called a stampede back to the simple untroubled hours of childhood.
>
> When the drawing of a character in a child's fairy story—*Snow*

[9] Grapewin had collaborated with Freed as the book writer of the West Coast legitimate musical *Pair o' Fools*.

10

White—becomes the number one heroine of the year, topping the greatest of flesh and blood stars in box office appeal, it is time for the adult glamor girls to start worrying.

After *Snow White* a flood of letters began pouring into the different studios, asking for the screen dramatization of various childhood classics. And Baum's story concerning the adventures of Dorothy, a little Kansas girl who, with her mopsy dog, Toto, is blown away in a farmhouse by a tornado to a magical land, was the most in demand.

A whole generation of theatregoers cherished their memories of Montgomery and Stone as the Scarecrow and the Tin Man, and they were fierce in their demands that the stage version should be followed, rather than the original book.

Ryerson and Woolf made a treatment of twelve pages and it was decided that they would start on a script. Noel Langley was brought in from the outside. "He has a fey quality," said LeRoy. "He has written fantasy, and I feel we need him."

Freed made frequent visits to the writers and expressed very definite ideas:

> There is no tie-over from Kansas to Oz—there is no conflict, no drama or suspense—Dorothy should be a more imaginative person —"I am Oz the Great!" "I am Dorothy the small and meek!" Some characters are not funny at all. The Scarecrow without brains should be a philosopher like Robert Burns, . . . but it's home, I want to make Auntie Em love me like I love her! . . . Toto is stolen—scene with Wicked Witch; Winged Monkeys take Dorothy, Toto should escape and find the rescuers and lead them to Dorothy to rescue her. "To the spirit of childhood that lingers on in the

Harold Arlen at the time he was composing *The Wizard of Oz* score. The inscription reads "For Arthur—with high regard for his excellent contribution." ARTHUR FREED ARCHIVES

hearts of every grown-up, we dedicate the beloved story of *The Wizard of Oz.*" Which is better—a heart or a brain? would the world be ruled better by a heart or by a brain? . . . Dorothy must say: "There's no place like home" (three times) to get back to Kansas.

In six weeks' time a first draft of the screenplay was submitted and a meeting was held in LeRoy's office with everybody concerned. After the meeting, Freed wrote the following observations:

Date: 7/6/38

NOTES
from Arthur Freed
on
The Wizard of Oz

Kansas sequence:

The opening with the boys at the wind machine seems to be pointless. The dialogue is also long. Aunt Em should never say: "Dime to a doughnut," on page 3.

Page 4

When Dorothy says: "Now I skinned my other knee," it is a little distasteful and unpleasant physically.

"I guess that's the kind of a molehill the schoolma'ams are trying to make a mountain of" was a very good character line for Lunk in the original script and is now left out.

Page 11

Aunt Em is too melodramatic, especially in the speech of "I guess J did wrong to take you, Dorothy, etc." Dorothy gets over with Professor Marvel that she is an orphan and it would only be repetitious to have Em talk about it to Dorothy.

Page 22, scene 31

Uncle Henry should not ignore the danger to Dorothy but should be concerned about Aunt Em getting into the cyclone cellar and that he will find Dorothy.

Starting with the opening of Technicolor I like Langley's scene much the best, both for its dialogue and its crispness. I like the direct speeches of Dorothy and the Good Witch. Dorothy's line about "America and Canada" is very natural and charming. The new script has double the dialogue in this scene than Langley's and it has the feeling of being padded.

I don't like all the stuff with the Munchkins laughing or the superfluous speeches of the witches being hard and ugly. I believe the charm and novelty of this scene will be enhanced by the minimum of dialogue.

I don't think the Wicked Witch should make too big a point about the slippers in this spot as we find out on page 60, scene 112, why the Wicked Witch is so anxious for the slippers and the extra dialogue and Munchkin line just makes for more gab.

I still like the line from the Good Witch to Dorothy saying: "Have you got your broomstick with you?"

Page 40, scene 78

Dorothy's speech is too long and a bit precious.

Page 42

I like Langley's first two speeches with the Scarecrow and Dorothy better. (During the Scarecrow's dance he might get caught on the nail again for a cute piece of business.)

Page 51 and 52

This sequence also seems padded.

Page 58, scene 111

Dorothy should say: "Why you great big bully!" instead of using the words "scary cat."

I'd like to discuss again the merits of Bulbo and the monkey.

Page 69, scene 135

Take out "tea biscuit" line.

I believe that we should go through the whole script with the thought in mind of using the minimum amount of dialogue and that Langley would be of great help on this in getting a rhythm through the whole script in one flavor of writing.

Studio conferences are serious affairs, often carried on with the assistance of aspirin and bicarbonate of soda. In this instance, though, according to voluminous minutes on these conferences, a congenial and productive atmosphere seems to have prevailed.

The script was on its way. Now the score became preeminent in Freed's thoughts. And again, Freed reached for "the best." He talked to his close friend Jerome Kern and Kern was interested. However, after much deliberation, Freed became convinced that the style of Harold Arlen and E. Y. "Yip" Harburg had the right sparkle and lightness for this story. One of their songs kept cropping up in his mind: "In the Shade of the New Apple Tree."[10] It was fanciful and beguiling, yet unsentimental. They would be the ideal team to create a score integrated into the story. Freed used the example of "In the Shade of the New Apple Tree" and Arlen and Harburg were hired.

On May 1, 1938, *The Wizard of Oz* was assigned production No. 1060 and budgeted at $3,700,000, at that time an astounding amount.

[10] This song was used in the Broadway musical *Hooray for What?* The 1938 production was directed by Vincente Minnelli, musical numbers staged by Robert Alton. In the cast were Kay Thompson (who left during the out-of-town tryout) and chorus members Hugh Martin and Ralph Blane. All later came to M-G-M to work in the Freed Unit.

Schenck was so aghast when the budget sheet was put before him that he wanted to stop the production instantly! But Mayer put all his weight behind his two producers and Schenck reluctantly gave in.

In his quest for fantasy, Freed met with Ogden Nash, who submitted a four-page synopsis, which proved to be totally uncinematic.

Arlen and Harburg went to work immediately; there were only two months to turn out what was expected to be a unique film score. Although a veteran, Arlen was anxious. More than ever before, his aim was to weave his music into the texture of the story. While he worried and worked, Harburg collaborated on some sequences of the script.

Now it came to casting. Freed and LeRoy agreed on Ray Bolger for the Scarecrow and Buddy Ebsen for the Tin Man. As far as the dual role of the Professor and the Wizard was concerned, LeRoy was hoping that W. C. Fields would accept Metro's offer of $150,000, but he turned it down. Frank Morgan, under contract to the studio, stepped in.

The screenplay began to take shape and in the process, some characters were added and others deleted.[11] New to the scene would be the Cowardly Lion, and here Harburg would play an important part. Harburg had worked on two Broadway shows with Bert Lahr. When asked for a suggestion, the lyricist began quoting lines from the script: "Put up your dukes! Put up your paws!" Then he said, "Can you imagine Bert doing that?" LeRoy and Freed liked the idea. Lahr was a natural. The remaining characters would be decided upon when the final shooting script was finished.

LeRoy was in the midst of shooting *Dramatic School,* starring Luise Rainer. Therefore, it was Freed's responsibility as associate producer, to co-ordinate all the preliminary details on *Wizard.* No director had yet been assigned.

[11] The Prince and Princess were deleted from the original book.

INTER-OFFICE COMMUNICATION

To ____

Subject Suggested Cast for "WIZARD OF OZ"

From ARTHUR FREED   Date 1/31/38

JUDY GARLAND	An Orphan in Kansas who sings jazz.
RAY BOLGER	The Tin Woodman.
BUDDY EBSEN	The Scare Crow.
FRANK MORGAN	The Wizard of Oz.
FANNY BRICE	A Witch.
EDNA MAE OLIVER	Another Witch.
BETTY JAYNES	The Princess of Oz, who sings opera.
KENNY BAKER	The Prince.

To: Mervyn LeRoy
Subject: WIZARD OF OZ
From: Arthur Freed

Date: May 20, 1938

In order to start shooting *The Wizard of Oz* in July, I submit
the following notes for your immediate attention:

1. Leo Singer should be contacted at this time regarding his midgets. He suggested at the time I spoke to him that he could also
   get us other novelties such as midget animals, etc., if he were
   given time enough to gather these together. We must also figure
   on an early enough rehearsal date for the midgets because their
   contemplated number has more detail to it than any other we
   are planning at the present time.

2. Judy Garland should be delivered to us immediately upon her
   completion of the "Judge Hardy" picture. We would need all her
   time from then on for rehearsals, costumes, tests, etc.

3. We should reserve the services of Bolger and Ebsen for some
   time in June, if possible, for rehearsals and tests. The same
   applies to Bert Lahr.

4. I suggest that you make a decision on Edna May Oliver for the
   Wicked Witch, as she is usually in demand.

5. It is important that we organize the company for rehearsals in
   June so that once we have started our shooting schedule, the
   least amount of time will be lost in okaying specialties and numbers of the above-mentioned performers.

I presume that you are following through on your idea of getting
Buzz Berkeley to direct the musical sequences.

If one were to single out one of the most marked contributions
Freed made to the picture, it was his urging Arlen and Harburg to write
a ballad which would act as a transition from Kansas to Oz.

Arlen agreed, but Harburg was reluctant. Arlen went to work and
the song came to him literally out of the blue. Harburg wasn't as enthusiastic as Arlen had hoped. "It's full of crescendos! It's too lush! That's
for Nelson Eddy, not for a little girl from Kansas," Harburg said. When
Arlen next played it for Ira Gershwin, it was pure and simple: He loved
it. And what had emerged was "Over the Rainbow."

So far everything had been somewhat tentative. LeRoy and Freed
now had to meet with Cedric Gibbons, head of the art department, Bill
Horning, the film's art director, and sketch artist (later art director),
Jack Martin Smith.

Gibbons arrived with a pile of sketches and dozens of models.
"The biggest set will be Munchkinland," said Gibbons. "On it will be
122 structures, one fourth normal size. It will take a month to build."
Emerald City looked like a lot of test tubes, upside down, inspired

by a photo in a German publication. Munchkinland: mushroom-shaped dome houses, invented by Horning, Gibbons and Smith. The yellow-brick road: gold and yellow paint worked into the individual stenciled bricks.

Several color changes were required for the Horse of a Different Color. "The only way we can do this," said Gibbons, "is by getting six horses and painting each one a different color, because we don't have time to paint and wash, paint and wash. And, remember, we'll have to test them, because if you paint a gray horse green the color won't turn out too pleasing. We'll have to do this by trial and error, with detergents and such, until we get the right patina. The trees have to talk—well, we'll use the rubber-tree thing that Universal invented for those horror films of theirs. For Oz, we'll have to use our largest stage lighting; this will be quite something. . . ."

Eventually the art department covered acres of cloths with paint, over two thousand feet of backing, all about forty feet high. One hundred and fifty painters worked to blend the sixty-two color shades. There were sixty-five sets in Oz, and assembled one beside another, they would have covered twenty-five acres.

Adrian, head of the wardrobe department and designer for the production, went pleasantly mad, understandably so. He turned out four thousand costumes for the more than one thousand members of the cast. This necessitated closest co-ordination with the art department: colors clashed or blended into the background; materials had to be photographed beforehand in order to see how their texture would reflect the lights. There were the fur-mounted uniforms of the Winkies, the glittering robes of the Good Witch Glinda, the murky garments of the Wicked Witch of the West and the changes for the choruses. He

Bill Horning's method of constructing the movable talking trees. M-G-M

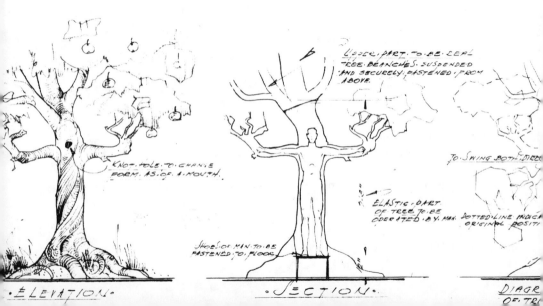

Bill Horning and Jack Martin Smith's conception of the exterior for the Munchkinland set. M-G-M

had to come up with "skins" and eagle wings for the flying monkeys, and two skins with a zipper for Bert Lahr, the Cowardly Lion. The sketch of the Tin Man was handed to the metalsmiths, who hammered and melted and molded and hinged it, so he could get in and out of it with relative ease.

The concerted activities of the art and costume departments can only be described as a sort of semiorganized bedlam.

Is it conceivable that all the elements in a tremendous undertaking such as this could ever be fused?

And where was a director?

July 12, 1939	No director
July 27	Norman Taurog set
August 16	Taurog off, Richard Thorpe set
August 29	Thorpe off, Taurog returns
September 2	Thorpe returns
September 16	Taurog returns for one day
September 17	Thorpe officially engaged to direct

On Wednesday, October 7, once again Freed joined L. B. Mayer in his palatial home in Santa Monica for breakfast. There was a tacit understanding between Mayer and Freed that these morning visits, in most instances, were not made just for ham and eggs. Usually some-

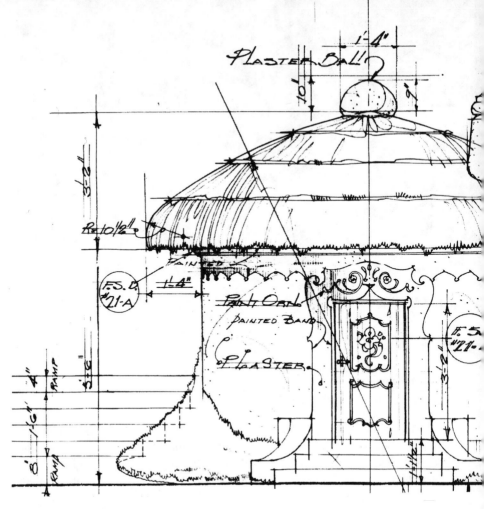

Jack Martin Smith's drawing of Munchkin houses.

thing was afoot. On this particular morning, Freed presented to L.B. with great zeal the idea for a new picture. A year ago he had seen *Babes in Arms* on Broadway, a musical with a marvelous score by Richard Rodgers and Lorenz Hart. He related to Mayer a synopsis of the story: A group of talented youngsters in a vaudeville milieu decide to put on a show to help their parents out of their difficulties. "It's ideal for Mickey and Judy, boss. And for the first time Mickey is going to sing and dance!" And to top it off, he told Mayer that just the night before Leland Hayward, the agent for the property, had told him that the motion-picture rights of the show were wide open—and for pennies!

"These are my aces back to back," Freed exclaimed. "What d'ye think, boss?"

18

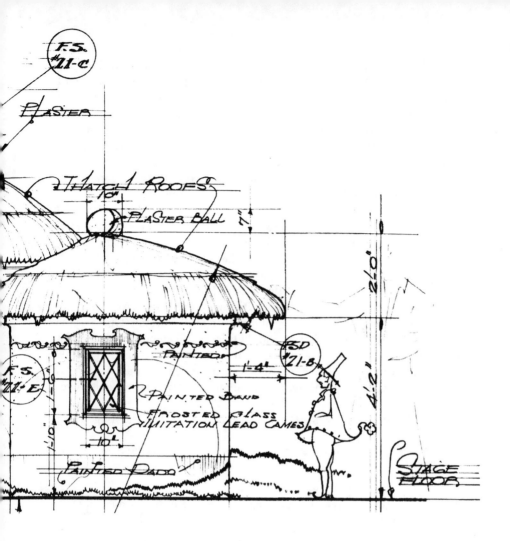

Mayer had listened attentively. "It sounds great!," he said. "Make a deal!"

Freed rushed back to his office, called Hayward in New York and made a deal of $21,000, lock, stock and barrel. As he hung up, Ryerson and Woolf walked in with their script changes on *Wizard*. But his mind was on his new brain child. "I'll see them later . . . right now I'm putting the two of you on my new picture, *Babes in Arms*. A copy of the Broadway script is coming over. Get to work!"

Ryerson and Woolf looked at each other, stunned, and exited.

With the acquisition of *Babes in Arms*, Freed turned an important corner of his career. He signed a producer's contract with M-G-M and moved out of the music department and into the Irving G. Thalberg (Administration) Building. As a producer he started at the bottom of the ladder, taking an enormous cut in salary; now he was working for $300 per week. But the move obviously wasn't for money. The row of "music bungalows," as they were called, separated by wire fences from the railroad tracks, were dilapidated little shacks. Although the office he moved into, taking his secretary Kathryn O'Brien with him, was not elegant, it meant a change in status. For many of those housed in the "Iron Lung," as the building was called, it meant simply being "in" and getting special service in the commissary. Nothing much came of it. For Freed, it meant the freedom to pursue his creative goals.

All the prerecordings of the musical numbers on *The Wizard of Oz* had been made under the supervision of Roger Edens: "If I Had a Heart" (Bolger-Ebsen), "If I Had Courage" (Lahr-Bolger-Ebsen), "If I Only Had a Brain" (Bolger), "The Jitterbug Dance" (Garland-Ebsen-Lahr-Bolger), "If I Were King of the Forest" (Lahr-Garland-Ebsen-Bolger), "Ding, Dong, the Witch Is Dead," "The Merry Old Land of Oz," "Come Out, Come Out Wherever You Are" (Burke and Munchkins), "You're Out of the Woods," "Watch Out for the Wicked Witch" (Munchkins) and "Over the Rainbow" (Garland). One last-minute change was made in the casting: Gale Sondergaard,[12] who had been signed to play the Wicked Witch of the West/Miss Gulch, was replaced by Margaret Hamilton, a Cleveland schoolteacher turned actress.

On October 13, 1938, *The Wizard of Oz* started shooting under

[12] Sondergaard was under contract to the studio but her contract was shortly dissolved.

Fleming positioning Jerry Maren during the shooting of the production number "We Welcome You to Munchkinland." M-G-M

Full view of Munchkinland after the Good Witch Glinda (Billie Burke) arrives. M-G-M

Richard Thorpe's direction with the studio's great cameraman Harold Rosson.

Trouble started at the outset. The scenes of the first week of shooting were lacking in fantasy and charm. LeRoy repeatedly had begged Mayer to let him direct. Now he went to him again pleading to let him have a go at it. But in vain. Instead L.B. brought in George Cukor, who was waiting in the wings to direct *Gone With the Wind*. Cukor lasted two days. Swiftly on his heels followed Victor Fleming.

Upon his take-over he scrapped the existing footage, recast the Tin Man with Jack Haley, but kept his favorite cameraman Rosson, with whom he had made many successful pictures (among them *Reckless* and *Bombshell*).

Fleming started on the picture with a crash schedule. He held meetings with Gibbons, Horning, Smith, and Adrian about modifications of sets and costumes; Edens prepared the re-recording of the numbers in view of the recasting; and Fleming told the casting department he wanted another busload of midgets.

"We have problems with the Munchkins," Rosson told Fleming. "They are so darn small and their costumes are all more or less the same. When they all mob together they are just a mass of

Judy and Toto during a break in the day's shooting under King Vidor's direction. M-G-M

nothing. . . ." Fleming was aware of these production problems, but his philosophy was: "Don't get excited! Obstacles make a better picture." He came up with a practical solution: The camera was never to be still. Fixed on a Chapman boom (crane) it should float in order to avoid the colors melting into each other or clashing.

These 350 midgets—where did they come from? Partly from Leo Singer, partly from Major Doyle. Wherever, they were the most deformed, unpleasant bunch of "adults" imaginable. Culver City and the Metro lot were crawling with them. They propositioned everybody; in the commissary, filled to capacity during lunchtime, they were constantly underfoot. This unholy assemblage of pimps, hookers and gamblers infested the Metro lot and all of the community.

In contrast; how enchanting to see Judy tripping down the Yellow Brick Road in her ruby slippers, with her little basket on her arm, and her little dog Toto at her heel!

Not only in the Land of Oz, but in the "real" world things were not without incidents. Judy came down with a cold. Her absence from the set cost the studio $150,000.

During these early years, Technicolor was going through various phases, trying to perfect its product, which included a new film, a new base of color. All this changing and experimenting were actually in preparation for the production of *Gone With the Wind*. In fact, David Selznick had bought into the Technicolor Corporation and exercised

22

great influence in this period of trial and error. So, *The Wizard of Oz* was the guinea pig for a lot of ideas by Selznick and Dr. Henry Kalmus, president of Technicolor.

The scenes in Kansas were to be in sepia tint and shot last. The Oz scenes, however, were to be photographed in color because it was highly important to heighten the effect of fantasy. At that time Technicolor cameras were at a premium, which made the setting up of shooting schedules a problem.

Ryerson and Woolf could barely have had the time to skim through the Broadway script of *Babes in Arms,* when they showed up in Freed's office with an outline. Now it was Freed who was stunned and, more than that, disappointed. After reading through their synopsis, Freed decided he needed a more experienced hand. He asked the studio to assign John (Jack) McGowan, recently put under contract. McGowan

(Right to Left). Bert Lahr, Frank Morgan, Jack Haley, Ray Bolger, Judy Garland and Toto in a publicity still. M-G-M

had been an actor on Broadway and had co-authored the book for the Gershwin musical *Girl Crazy*. At Metro, he wrote the screenplays for *Born to Dance* and *Broadway Melody of 1938*.

Before McGowan began to work, Freed told him how he wanted the original story expanded and how much he wanted to keep of the actual situation. "I just like the premise," Freed explained. "We keep that. In the play none of the older people appear. I want to change that and have the vaudevillians show that time has passed them by and that they couldn't catch up. . . . I got to thinking about George M. Cohan and his parents. He was always thinking about his father and mother, trying to do things for them. That's why in the last scene, when Mickey Rooney gets his big chance at success, I want him to send right away for his father. . . . I'm also considering two songs by Arlen: 'Let's Take a Walk Around the Block'[13] and 'God's Country.'"

Clearly Freed was eager to work with Edens. So, in this memo is the germ of what was to become the Freed Unit, in which Edens for two decades was the most essential factor.

The year 1939 found Freed occupied with getting *Babes in Arms* on the road. However, a chorus line of writers had fallen by the wayside: Ryerson and Woolf, Noel Langley, Anita Loos, Sid Silvers and Joe Laurie. Nonetheless, he built a casting list, using McGowan's final draft and sent it on to Mayer.

One week later, *Babes in Arms* was given a budget of $745,799. With this in hand, Freed believed it was time to sign a director. Busby Berkeley was his choice. He signed a one-picture contract and would receive $1,500 per week. Cast salaries amounted to: Rooney per term contract $900, plus a $7,500 bonus upon completion of the picture; Garland received $500 per; Charles Winninger and Guy Kibbee drew $4,000 and $1,600 respectively; ex-vaudevillian Grace Hayes received $150 per week.

Since he decided to bring in a seventh writer to polish up the shooting script, Freed chose Kay Van Riper, an old hand at this kind of work. Furthermore, he thought it important that Berkeley make some personal contributions to the script and set up a meeting for the two of them.

On February 14, Fleming was pulled off *Wizard*, ironically enough to replace George Cukor once again, this time on *Gone With the Wind* in which Metro had a financial stake and was going to release. At this time, *Wizard* was by no means completed. A fourth director, King Vidor, was brought in on twenty-four hours' notice. "At first I was not too happy with the chore," he remarked to LeRoy. "I feel that all the preparatory work done on the film gives Fleming a chance to establish, by building and rejecting, a solid foundation on which to operate. I'm a

[13] Written by Harold Arlen, Ira Gershwin and E. Y. Harburg for the Broadway show *Tonight at 8:40*.

little apprehensive, but after hearing the prerecording of Judy singing 'Over the Rainbow' . . ." He went on to say, "Many of the singing scenes photographed up to now are static and dull. This is my opportunity. I can move Judy around with complete freedom. . . ."

Important work remained to be done, including the sepia sequences and the tremendous task of devising technical tricks in order to make the Wicked Witch fly on her broomstick, Kansas to be blown away by a tornado, and the monkeys to fly.

After 136 days of shooting, *The Wizard of Oz* finally completed its principal photography on March 16, 1939.

The thousands of feet of film were neatly stacked in the cutting rooms, ready to be edited. From the outset, Freed told Margaret Booth, supervisor of film editors, that Fleming and Blanche Sewell were going to cut *Wizard*. The only way Fleming could do this was by moonlighting in the cutting rooms at M-G-M after a day's shooting of *GWTW*. Luckily the Selznick studio was only a few blocks away. "Editing is tedious, slow work," said Sewell, "especially on a picture with the visual complexities of *The Wizard of Oz*." And so the two came, night after night.

As Edens' work on *Wizard* was drawing to a close, he was deeply involved with the sorting out and laying in of all the musical numbers contemplated for *Babes*. Arrangements had to be made, orchestrations devised, all in order to proceed with the prerecordings. Among the songs chosen were: "Babes in Arms" (the torchlight marching number for the entire company); "Where or When" (Doug and Betty in the yard rehearsal); "I Wish I Were in Love Again" (Judy and Mickey—to be worked out) both from the Rodgers and Hart show; "Good Morning" (new song by Freed and Brown for Judy and Mickey in the music publisher's office); "I Cried for You" (old song by Freed-Gus Arnheim-Abe Lyman for Judy on the bus); "Opera vs. Jazz" (Edens' arrangement of popular and classical numbers for Judy and Betty); "My Daddy Was a Minstrel Man" (written by Edens with interpolations of old standards for Judy and Mickey); "God's Country" (Arlen and Harburg's song with an elaborate scene to be written by Edens as finale of picture for Judy, Mickey and the entire cast).

On May 12, 1939, Berkeley and his cameraman Ray June started shooting *Babes* on Stage 3 with Garland and Rooney. It was a different world for Berkeley than his days at Warner Brothers. No longer was a musical to be built around a backstage plot where the musical number is staged as a formal spectacle. In Freed's hands, the musical number became part and parcel of the story. The picture's budget was another factor and Berkeley, therefore, had to deal with a more intimate space since he didn't have at his disposal a huge area in which to display sixty or eighty girls. Moreover, he was now faced with the interplay of characters, woven into the texture of the musical picture.

The shooting of *Babes* rolled on without any problems. Still to come, though, was the "God's Country" finale. Edens was using all his inventiveness and talent. When he finished the number he turned it in to Freed. The legal department, always overburdened with clearances, copyrights and contractual obligation, had to be brought into play, as the finale contained an extracurricular implication.

Dear Mr. Mayer:

We have read the "God's Country" Finale (pages 1 through 4) dated July 3, 1939, for your proposed production titled *Babes in Arms,* and are happy to report that this material comes under the requirements of the Production Code.

However, on Page 3, Mickey used the word "shag." This should be changed since in England and the British colonies this word has a very objectionable sexual meaning which would cause its deletion by numerous political censor boards.

You understand, of course, that our final judgment will be based upon the finished picture.

Cordially yours,
Joseph I. Breen

"God's Country" occupied Stage 27 for the last ten days of production and it cost $32,970. It had five days to rehearse, one day to prerecord with the thirty-two-piece orchestra, twenty-five voices in the augmented chorus, and three days to shoot. In addition to the regulars for the number, Berkeley added ten boys and girls, nine children, twenty musicians on screen and sixty-one dancers.

Freed was in Projection Room A looking at the dailies from *Babes*. His secretary phoned to tell him that Fleming was anxious to have him take a look at his rough cut of *Wizard*. After the end title went off the screen and the lights went on, Freed turned to Fleming and said, "I don't know how you handled it—it's terrific! But one thing bothers me . . . I think you should cut out that whole scene where the jitterbug bites Lahr and they do the "Jitterbug dance" with Judy singing. It slows the picture down and it's irrelevant to the story. Maybe you can use it in *Gone With the Wind.*" Fleming was serious. "I want it in for the preview." Freed agreed.

Fleming turned the film over to Herbert Stothart and Georgie Stoll for the postscoring and he returned to finish *GWTW*. Stothart and Stoll had to compose and record the background score. Eighteen months had passed since the inception of the production, and, as always, suddenly everyone was in a hurry. The front office pressed for a preview while the orchestra was on Stage 1 day and night, and the dubbing rooms worked "golden hours."

On the occasion of the *Babes in Arms* première, Judy marks her rise to stardom by placing her hand and foot prints in the cement forecourt of Grauman's Chinese Theatre. Mickey and Judy's mother look on as she applies the finishing touches. M-G-M

A memorable day in Freed's career was July 18, 1939. On that day shooting was completed on *Babes in Arms*. And on the night of that same day, the first preview of *The Wizard of Oz* ran off at the Westwood Village Theatre.

The next morning, upon his arrival at the studio he learned that both "The Jitterbug" and "Over the Rainbow" would be cut from the film.

"The Jitterbug" number was laid to rest with no regrets. But a drama evolved about "Over the Rainbow."

Each time *The Wizard of Oz* was sneaked, "Over the Rainbow" was either cut out or put back. After each deletion Freed would storm into Mayer's office; it seemed everybody agreed that it should go except Arthur Freed. A meeting was called by Mayer to decide once and for all; there Sam Katz, executive producer of the musical division, remarked, "This score is above the heads of children." Jack Robbins put in his two cents: "Why, it's like a child's piano exercise. Nobody will sing it—who'll buy the sheet music?" Freed would have none of it, "The song stays—or I go! It's as simple as that."

The preview première took place on Thursday evening, August 17, 1939, at Grauman's Chinese Theatre in Hollywood. "Over the Rainbow" was in.

The next day, the picture opened officially at Loew's Capitol in New York. It did seven shows to better than thirty-seven thousand cash customers! "It was New Year's Eve on Broadway—the crowds were so large and so many people were turned away that the overflow filled almost all the other Broadway houses, jammed the restaurants, soft-drink parlors and candy stores," said *The Hollywood Reporter*. The Capitol management requested police protection and sixty policemen were sent to handle the mob. The lines started to form at five-thirty in the morning, and when the box office opened at eight o'clock there were fifteen thousand, four abreast, lined up clear around to Eighth Avenue. And that was the story all day long. The Capitol Theatre played nine shows on Saturday and nine on Sunday. And by the end of the week it grossed over $100,000.

On October 10, 1939, *Babes in Arms* premièred at Grauman's Chinese Theatre. The acclaim the picture received foreshadowed the emergence of a new cycle in motion-picture entertainment:

My dear Arthur,

No one would rather be with you on the night of your great success than I but I cannot get away from down here [St. Malo Beach, Oceanside, California] for at least another week.

That you have a smash hit picture on your hands is in no way a surprise to me as I know of many other ideas that have meant a lot of money to M-G-M in the past that originated with you. It only proves that talent and ability must come to the surface.

Mr. Mayer certainly lived up to his reputation as the smartest man in the picture business when he gave you an opportunity. Probably no one knows your capabilities more than I and I know you *are* the turning point for M-G-M on musicals.

The best of luck to you on Tuesday night and I know your picture will be a riot.

As ever,
Herb
(Nacio Herb Brown)

Thursday evening, February 29, 1940—twelfth annual Academy Award banquet, Cocoanut Grove, Ambassador Hotel, Los Angeles. In spite of the near sweep *Gone With the Wind* made, the one piece of film that the Metro hierarchy had condemned to the cutting-room floor —had it not been for Freed's tempestuous interception—took the Oscar for the best song, "Over the Rainbow." And the subtle handling by Freed and Edens of all the musical elements paid off, and *Wizard* took a second Oscar for the best original musical score.

Bob Hope, introduced as the "Rhett Butler of the air," started off his part of the proceedings with: "What a wonderful thing—this benefit for David Selznick." Then he introduced Mickey Rooney, who was called up to present the special juvenile award which he had won the previous year.[14] Nineteen-year-old Rooney handed the miniature Oscar to seventeen-year-old Judy Garland. Garland accepted it to a standing ovation, and then she obliged the audience with a rendition of "Over the Rainbow."

The final cost of *The Wizard of Oz* was $2,777,000. In its initial release it grossed $3,017,000. Its first re-release (1948–49) brought an additional $1,564,000; in 1954–55, $465,000 and two television sales: $1,000,000 (CBS) and $500,000 (NBC).

Babes in Arms cost $748,000 and grossed $3,335,000 in its initial release.

[14] Rooney was out of this category since he was a nominee for "Best Actor" for his performance in *Babes in Arms*.

2

STRIKE UP THE BAND

LITTLE NELLIE KELLY

LADY BE GOOD

BABES ON BROADWAY

PANAMA HATTIE

Hitler, the war, Mussolini in Ethiopia, Franco in Spain—none of these was a popular topic of conversation. Americans had not yet emerged from the disastrous Depression. They had already fought the "war to end all wars," and many wanted no more bad news.

So *Good News* was the title Metro announced for their next picture for the "kids," Judy Garland and Mickey Rooney. It is curious that in the otherwise overladen memo files of M-G-M no data can be found as to who actually rescued the story. Arthur Freed was assigned to produce and Roger Edens to adapt, arrange and supervise the musical score. Busby Berkeley was to be the director, thus completing the *Babes'* trinity. And with that, a new cycle of pictures began: the "kid pictures."

Following the Hollywood première of *Babes in Arms,* Edens flew east with Judy and Mickey for the New York opening. They were also there to appear together "live" for the first time, for the Capitol Theatre audiences.

Freed headed east the night before the opening. One of the main reasons for his trip, however, was to negotiate a new contract for himself with the executives at the home office, on special order of L. B. Mayer. *Babes in Arms* had catapulted Freed from a $300-a-week novice producer to the position of the Number One man for musicals on the Metro lot. A new contract was drawn up and signed which equaled the salaries of the high-priced old-time producers. His apprenticeship was over.

Also on Freed's agenda was a luncheon date with George M. Cohan at the Plaza Hotel. Ever since his teens, Freed had been in awe of Cohan's talent. When he entered the Oak Room and spotted Cohan at his legendary table, he had a momentary attack of stage fright. And what complicated matters was that Cohan had no interest in motion pictures whatsoever.

Cohan took Freed by surprise by opening the conversation with "You know—I haven't seen Louis Mayer in years, but he was awful nice to my mother . . . he always took care of her and got her theatre seats. . . ." There was an awkward silence. "What are you staring at me like that for?"

"All my life you've been an inspiration to me," Freed answered, "and if you were a dame I'd kiss you! . . ."

The luncheon ended with Cohan selling Freed *Little Nellie Kelly* for $35,000.

With one deal under his belt, he headed for Leland Hayward's agency. Freed was shopping for writers. In Hayward's office were two of his hottest clients, Fred Finklehoffe and John Monks, Jr., who had just made a tremendous hit on Broadway with their play *Brother Rat.*

Freed discussed his forthcoming revival of the musical *Good News.* "I want a different slant—we might use some new songs." Ideas were tossed around. Freed was quickly convinced that these two boys were right for him and they left on the next plane to go to work.

While this was a highly productive day for Freed, at the Capitol Theatre all was not well. In the middle of the show (they were doing seven a day), Judy collapsed. "Stall them, Mickey," somebody said. After about five minutes in which Rooney did everything from announcing a tennis match to a Joe Louis fight, including all the sound effects, Judy was back on stage.

Returning to his office after the weekend, Freed called Finklehoffe and Monks to come over with what they had accomplished so far. He then went to see Mayer.

In Mayer's office, holding court, were Messrs. Thau, Mannix and Katz, the top echelon. Mayer raised his hand in a grand gesture, pointing at Freed, and remarked, to his men-in-waiting, "There he is—I've taken this boy and I've made a great producer out of him!"

After the three had left, Mayer said, "Arthur, I've had second thoughts about *Good News.* I don't think we should go with it right now. Don't ask me why—I really don't know—it's just a hunch. Instead, I'd like you to go with *Strike Up the Band*—it sounds so patriotic."

Without hesitation, Freed said, "I guess you're right, boss—I'll get on it immediately."

In 1938, there was a tremendous resurgence in the popularity of the big bands. All of America was swept with swing fever. In small towns girls in saddle shoes tripped into ice-cream parlors with their boy friends, plugged nickels into the juke box and set the place rocking. Radio audiences clustered around their sets to hear their favorite band. The New York *Times* solemnly suggested that the craze was getting out of hand.

Actually, swing was nothing more than jazz under another signature, and the reigning king of jazz, at that time, was Paul Whiteman. Whiteman had been a big attraction in New York since 1921. That was also the year when the songwriting partnership of Brown and Freed began. With a few songs in their breast pockets they had headed east on a selling trip to Tin Pan Alley. Within a couple of days they had met Whiteman who had expressed great interest in their first song, "When Buddha Smiles." He made a recording, which sold over a million copies and with that their career was launched.

A year later, during another New York visit, Freed was walking along Broadway with his friend George Gershwin. They passed the Palais Royale where Whiteman was appearing. Gershwin said, "I think that Whiteman guy is fabulous."

"He's a good friend of mine," Freed said. "Let's go up and meet him." Eventually, it was Paul Whiteman who commissioned Gershwin to write "Rhapsody in Blue" and who conducted the first performance of it.

Freed called to Finklehoffe and Monks. "Boys—forget about *Good News,"* he said. "Do you know 'Strike Up the Band?' Forget the Broadway show; all we'll keep is Gershwin's title song. Get to work and come up with a story for Judy, Mickey and all those kids—and I'll get Paul Whiteman."

The box-office receipts on *Babes in Arms* came in hot and heavy. Wherever it played the critics were unanimous in their praise for the new singing and dancing team. This inspired Freed to immediately search for a sequel.

Freed then left his office and went to Romanoff's for lunch. During these years Romanoff's was more or less like a club. Everybody knew everybody else. Whoever was in the "business"—actors, directors, producers, agents, fringed by a few tourists—could be found there. This free-wheeling interaction in a neutral place was Freed's way of socializing—He could go from table to table, stay if he was entertained or informed, leave when the talk got stale. Chit-chat at cocktail parties, being trapped for endless formal dinners, was definitely not to his taste.

Some people are compelled to live in a state of constant nervous, and mostly useless activities. Freed, by contrast, was driven by his urge to seek out, to acquire—but he was not interested in the already established crop of Hollywood talent. He wanted those who had succeeded on the New York stage; they had had to make it the hard way. The limited talent of the Hollywood directors had worn thin, and he was convinced that their scope and style were rapidly becoming passé. And so, he went back to New York again.

He met with Yip Harburg whom he had hired as an associate within the emerging Freed Unit. Together they went to see a performance of the Jerome Kern-Oscar Hammerstein II musical *Very Warm for May*. After the show, Freed expressed his admiration for the score. "It was beautifully directed. By the way, do you know that fellow Minnelli?" Freed asked. "I want to meet him." In spite of the late hour they called Minnelli.

Vincente Minnelli was born in Delaware, Ohio, the son of circus performers. Even as a child he began to experiment with color and design. Soon he became a self-taught sketch artist and this landed him his first job as a window dresser at Marshall Field's in Chicago. After leaving Marshall Field's he became head of the costume department of Balaban and Katz's theatre chain; designer at the Paramount Theatre on Broadway; he designed costumes for Grace Moore in *Du Barry* (1932). He was appointed art director of the just opened Radio City Music Hall (1933–35); costume designer of *Ziegfeld Follies of 1936,* and director of *The Show Is On* (1936). It was while the last two were playing simultaneously that Paramount Pictures engaged Minnelli to come to Hollywood, an abortive experience indeed, which brought him back to New York.

Freed and Harburg arrived at Minnelli's studio and Freed shot right at his target: "How about coming to California?"

"I've been there," Minnelli answered, referring to his brief tenure in March of 1937 with Paramount. (All that he had been given to do was to stage "Public Enemy Number One," a number which featured Martha Raye and Louis Armstrong in the Jack Benny picture *Artists and Models*. After that nothing else seemed to be forthcoming and he quickly accepted a New York assignment as designer-director for the Broadway musical *Hooray for What?*)

"Don't put the blame on Hollywood because of one studio," said Freed. "What kind of salary were you getting?—$2,000? You see, they start noticing you if you get that kind of money and all you do is rehearse. They simply didn't understand you. Come on out for five or six months, take enough money for your expenses—no contract, nothing. If you don't like it at any time you can leave."

At the time Minnelli was trying to put together a musical with Lena Horne, based on the story *Serena Blandish*. When this did not materialize Minnelli took Freed up on his offer. His instinct told him that this opportunity in motion pictures might prove to be as creative as the theatre had been. Minnelli arrived in Hollywood on April 22, 1940.

Freed was on Stage 27 watching Berkeley rehearsing the kids for *Strike Up the Band* when he got a call from his secretary, telling him that Minnelli and Edens were in his office waiting to see him. Most important, she said, were the contracts the legal department had sent over, which neeeded his immediate attention.

Edens and Minnelli were in animated conversation when Freed walked in. "I'm glad you're here, boy," he greeted Minnelli. "Roger, take him to lunch, and by the time you come back we'll have you settled." "Gladly, Arthur," said Edens, "but before we go I'd like to show you what I did with your song 'My Wonderful One, Let's Dance.' You know, it's going into *Two Girls on Broadway*." Freed barely listened although this film was based on his *Broadway Melody of 1929;* this was not *his* production. Edens realized that Freed didn't care; he would proceed without him.

After Edens and Minnelli had left, Freed gave all his attention to the seven contracts on his desk. These specifically related to final agreements for seven projects which had previously been approved of and/or assigned to Freed: Jack McGowan, engaged for *Little Nellie Kelly,*[1] to star Judy Garland; followed by *Lady Be Good, Good News* and *Ziegfeld Follies;* Marguerite Roberts to develop a screenplay entitled *Twenty Little Working Girls,* based on the M-G-M film *Dancing Lady* (1933); Fred Finklehoffe (his *Strike Up the Band* work nearly completed) to work on *Babes on Broadway* as the sequel to *Babes in Arms.* McGowan was perplexed. These assignments were a surprise to him. He thought he was to develop a story for *Babes on Broadway*.

While all this was happening, Minnelli was visiting the stages, reading scripts and having lunches with Dorothy Parker, Lillian Hellman, S. J. Perelman and other writers. One lunch, though, he had to miss. Freed told him that Berkeley was having trouble thinking up an idea for the number "Our Love Affair." He dispatched Minnelli to the *Strike Up the Band* set and told him to be "inspired." When Berkeley put on the playback for him, Minnelli instantly remembered an article that had appeared in *Life* magazine[2] about various pieces of fruit that come to life as musicians.

"Take a bunch of grapes and make it the conductor's head; take a pear and a half, make the whole pear the head of a violinist and the half the violin; take a lemon and a pineapple—the lemon the head, the pineapple, half the bass fiddle; three halves of grapefruit, three kettledrums. . . ."

Strike Up the Band was based on the formula used in *Babes in*

[1] The George M. Cohan play was written for McGowan when he was an actor.
[2] The *Life* article displayed the work of the German sculptor Henri Rox.

In this set picture it seems Berkeley followed Minnelli's ideas explicitly. However, the slate indicates the director was already up to Take 8. The assistant director's report further indicates that seventeen takes were made before the number was completed. M-G-M

Arms. The story in this version finds Mickey and Judy, high school friends, organizing a modern swing band instead of the traditional school brass band, with Judy as soloist. The band is a success. Then they hear of a national radio contest for school bands. To raise money to go to Chicago to compete, they stage a benefit show.

One of the youngsters in the band becomes ill, and an immediate operation is necessary. His parents have no funds, so the kids use the band's money for the operation. The richest man in town hears of this and pays for their trip to Chicago. In a blaze of music and glory, they win the contest.

George and Ira Gershwin had been working on the score for the Broadway musical *Strike Up the Band* in the spring of 1927. Late one night George came into Ira's adjoining room. "I've got the march . . . I've finally got it!" He played it for Ira. "Do you like it?" he asked.

"Certainly I like it, but . . ."

"But what?"

"You're sure you won't change your mind again?" Ira said imploringly.

"No, this time I'm pretty sure. . . ."

During the preceding weeks George had "finally gotten" it four times. And each time it ended up with "No . . . not yet, not yet. . . ." Only the fifth try turned out to be it. The lyrics to the song were completely rewritten by Ira Gershwin in 1936, when he was asked to adapt

The trumpeter's head is an apple and part of the trumpet is an apple's stem.

The violinist has a pear for a head, pins for eyes and a wax nose; the violin is half a pear.

VINCENTE MINNELLI
COLLECTION

This grape-headed conductor reminded people of Leopold Stokowski.

A stringy-haired leek, wearing "tails," plays an asparagus organ.

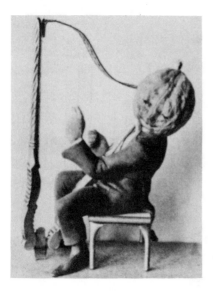

"Nutcracker Suite": A walnut head plays the harp, which is a nutcracker.

An orange-headed musician plays a pineapple double bass. His eyes are made by cutting the rind.

This mustachioed drummer, whose head is a tangerine, strikes resounding tones on his grapefruit timpani that are supported on miniature flower pots.

Jacques Kaprelick, M-G-M publicity artist noted for his caricatures of the studio's stars, began a series with *Strike Up the Band*. M-G-M

the song for the UCLA football games: It was and still is their marching song.

"Nell of New Rochelle," used in the benefit show, was a comical travesty on old-time melodramas. Staged as a play and supposedly produced by the youngsters, Judy, with the assistance of Edens' musical design, showed a great flair for parody in the skits.

With the exception of the title song, the musical additions were supplied by Freed and/or Edens. They included "Our Love Affair," sung as a duet by Mickey and Judy; "Drummer Boy," a swing novelty played by Mickey on drums with a vocal by Judy; "Nobody," a torrid torch number done by Judy; a medley of songs by Paul Whiteman and his orchestra; and "The La Conga."

"It started out simply as a song I had written for Judy to sing, based on the current dance craze, the conga," recalls Edens. "Then Berkeley got crazy and decided on blowing the whole number up into one of his 'typical finales,' using every possible camera angle he could think up. Judy was done up like someone out of a Persian carnival for what was to be the last scene needed to complete the film. Berkeley then decided to complicate matters even further by announcing that he would shoot the whole number in one take! With The Six Hits and a Miss as a vocal backup for Judy, Paul Whiteman and his orchestra, with Mickey on drums and 115 dancers (one of which was Marjorie Keeler, Ruby's sister), Berkeley rehearsed his cast and crew for thirteen days, and it was ready . . . it worked . . . and without a hitch." But it did increase the budget on the film by $93,980.65, upping the final cost of the picture to $838,661.40. Released on September 30, 1940, *Strike Up the Band* grossed $3,494,000.

Little Nellie Kelly went into production while *Strike Up the Band* was still shooting. Described as a romantic comedy with musical overtones, the film tells the story of a young Irish girl who marries and follows her husband to America. After a few years of happiness in the new land she dies, leaving behind her husband and an infant daughter. The character of Nellie Kelly was a distinct departure from Judy's previous roles. "This film," Edens said, "gave Judy her first opportunity to play an adult. But Mr. Mayer didn't like the idea of Garland growing up—'we simply can't have that baby have a child.'" In the end Mayer saw the value in presenting Judy as "a real actress."

Norman Taurog finally got a chance to direct a musical for Freed. He brought the picture in in forty-one days, at a cost of $665,300.28. *Little Nellie Kelly* was released on November 22, 1940, and grossed $2,046,000.

On October 1, 1940, after finishing her looping session for *Nellie Kelly,* Judy entered Cedars of Lebanon Hospital for a tonsilectomy. Although this usually is a routine operation, there was some apprehension in Judy's case, since she was eighteen years old. Her tonsils had plagued her for a long time and there was concern that her voice might be affected. Luckily everything went well.

Freed became nervous and edgy when Judy went to the hospital. He didn't want to wait around, so he went to San Francisco to attend an ASCAP dinner. Though not normally a party man and not keen on meetings, he did enjoy the ASCAP dinners. He met some of his peers, people he not only admired but liked; and it felt good to be one of the

Judy Garland as Nellie Kelly and George Murphy as her husband, Jerry. Judy dies in childbirth, but she "returns" as her daughter Little Nellie. It is the only film Judy Garland ever made in which she dies. M-G-M

top royalty earners on the ASCAP rostrum. He ran into Cohan, who said, "I hope you didn't keep any of my terrible play?" Freed grinned. "No, I just kept the title and little Nellie Kelly being a police captain's daughter." Cohan was satisfied.

Little Nellie Kelly and *Strike Up the Band* were both sensational hits.

Midway through 1940 to the chagrin of the public, a new admission tax was imposed on box-office prices. The Broadway prices went up to $.28, $.33, $.39 and $.44.

Once again Freed unearthed *Good News*.

Dear Jack:

Even though you will be back at the studio in two weeks time with your finished screenplay on *Lady Be Good,* I want to get your mind working on our next two projects; *Good News* and *Ziegfeld Follies.*

I think you know what I have in mind for *Good News*. It is to make it a fast collegiate musical, based on the original story. Of course, this should be a very free basis and I'm sure that you'll depart from the original substantially in your treatment. Judy Garland, of course, will be the lead and any other parts you will write we can cast with good people. I think the spirit of the piece should be comedy. Offhand, the songs we should retain from the old piece are "Good News," "The Best Things in Life Are Free" and "Just Imagine." We should get a new song in place of "Varsity Drag" that is more modern, along the lines of "The Conga" we did in *Strike Up the Band*. There is no objection to football as part of the plot, although I don't think there should be too many actual football scenes. Certainly the subject is good at present, because we are playing principally to an American market.

Judy Garland and Arthur Freed on the set. ARTHUR FREED ARCHIVES

I am positive that a good, healthy collegiate musical, with all the collegiate ingredients—sororities, fraternities, athletics, etc., as well as their varsity show stuff—filled with a lot of fair coeds, streamlined in the McGowan fashion—would be a hit. I do think this, Jack. *Good News* done in a good, fast tempo, with a lot of music and singing and youthful entertainment can be one of our big pictures!

And now to *The Ziegfeld Follies*. I have enclosed a synopsis of a treatment that was done. I know this is only a bare springboard and though it is in narrative fashion, still it has enough to give us an honest reason for calling the picture *The Ziegfeld Follies*. We intend to use all the stars in the studio for brief appearances in this picture. Naturally, there are some sketches and some songs that we can buy and readapt for our purposes, so don't get frightened that you have to write ten or fifteen sketches.

Kindest regards to both you McGowans.

Arthur

Here is McGowan's reply:

Dear Art:

I wanted to dash this note off to you in answer to your letter.

I'll be winding up on *Lady Be Good* at the end of the week, so you'll probably see my face first thing Monday. I was able to give some thought to *Good News*. I read the original Broadway book and believe I have found a plan that will give Judy a much better opportunity than the original sappy part of the girl. I am figuring on [Charles] Winninger also for a hoky part. He is not her father nor any relation.

I'll elaborate more on this when I see you, but I just wanted to let you know that I've done some homework.

As far as *Follies* is concerned let it lay for the moment. My limited brain capacity is at this point somewhat overburdened.

As Ever,
Jack

McGowan arrived and delivered his screenplay of *Lady Be Good*.[3] "That's fine, boy—it needs some polishing and a little rewrite," Freed said. "Right now I want you to take *Very Warm for May* and get to work on that."

Handing McGowan the book, Freed removed an attached note from Hammerstein:

Dear Arthur:

Have you gone any further into *Very Warm for May?* There is so much good material in the property. We had all the logs with

---

[3] Freed did not like the book of the Broadway musical. Instead he bought McGowan's original story "Feeling Like a Million."

which to build the fire but they were never properly piled on top of each other, nor the kindling properly placed. So the thing never took spark. With this brilliant simile I will finish this script.

With kindest regards to Mrs. Freed and yourself,

Sincerely,
Oscar

A meeting was called on the script of *Lady Be Good*. Three screenplay doctors were given the following instructions: Ralph Spence, John McClain and Kay Van Riper were to revamp McGowan's original script. Minnelli was told to think of an exciting way to lead into a musical number. Freed cast the picture before the shooting script was finished.

One of the two principal female characters was a sophisticated, wisecracking dance star. For this part Freed immediately thought of Eleanor Powell. He had seen her for the first time on the stage of the Paramount Theatre in New York. Then he visited her after the performance, and this led to her signing a contract with the studio.

He charmed Ann Sothern into accepting a singing role, the second female lead. Backing up these two ladies were Robert Young and John Carroll. Supporting actors were Red Skelton, Connie Russell, Virginia O'Brien, the Berry Brothers, two small parts played by Dan Dailey and Phil Silvers, plus a new dancing partner for Eleanor Powell, Buttons, a fox terrier.

Take the Reno, Nevada, divorce court files, mix them with those of the nearby wedding chapel, shake them with Tin Pan Alley, and you have the plot of *Lady Be Good*.

The property had been bought for $61,500 from Warner Brothers (some price to pay just for a title!), and in addition music licenses cost the studio $40,000. Two songs from the original Broadway show were retained: "Fascinating Rhythm" and "Lady Be Good" (George and Ira Gershwin). Edens and Freed were to supply several additional songs. But most important, Freed bought Kern and Hammerstein's most recent hit, "The Last Time I Saw Paris."

The creation of "The Last Time I Saw Paris" is a story in itself. The catastrophe had happened: Paris had fallen, Paris was dark (1940). Hammerstein was at work on the Broadway musical *Sunny River*, but his heart wasn't in it. Through his mind kept flashing impressions of his last trip to Paris. Words began to form and in less than an hour he had the verse for "The Last Time I Saw Paris."

Although his current project would have music written by Sigmund Romberg, he astutely knew that this ode to Paris should have Jerome Kern's melody. He phoned his long-time collaborator at his home on the Coast and read him his lyric, which Kern took down. Upon Hammerstein's arrival in Los Angeles, the following week, Kern had the song completed. The composition, incidentally, was not only their first

42

song that was written unconnected with any show, but it was a complete departure from their usual method of collaboration. Kern usually wrote the music before Hammerstein wrote the words. Freed asked Hammerstein to write the dialogue leading into the song.

```
OSCAR HAMMERSTEIN, 2ND

          INSERT.     Page 65


                    Max (Cont'd)
                 (Applause)
Whatever else has happened is none of  my business
- or yours!

              Max points out to the audience as he says
              that and there is a terrific yell of laugh-
              ter.

                    Max
What matters to us is that they have given the world
another great song.

          (A more serious note in his voice.)

And when you hear Dixie sing it ,I think you'll feel
as I do - that it isn't just the work of two song-
writers. It's as if they had a hundred million col-
laborators - the Americans who feel in their hearts
what Dixie and Eddie have said so beautifully in
their song...I refer to that tender and affectionate
salute to a lost city: "The Last Time I Saw Paris."

              Max takes Dixie's hand,and she rises t o
tremendous applause. Etc,etc.

          PROCEED AS NOW.
```

With the shooting script ready to go, director Norman McLeod and Busby Berkeley, demoted to dance director, took off.[4] McLeod kept to his timetable but lacked taste. Berkeley neither kept to his timetable nor to whatever taste he had.

The picture had closed production on April 11, after forty-six days of shooting, and yet to be rehearsed, recorded and shot was "Fascinating Rhythm." The number was to feature Eleanor Powell, the Berry Brothers, Connie Russell, eighty boys and five pianos. All this was to take place on two thousand square feet of shooting space with a chiffon curtain going up sixty-five feet to the ceiling. Freed had approved a budget of $80,965.86 for this sequence, even though the cost of the production was already $101,526.65 over budget (mostly due to Berkeley's delays). Freed gave Berkeley an ultimatum: "You've got three days to rehearse and one day to shoot." He started shooting at nine o'clock in the morning; at ten in the evening George Folsey, his cameraman, had to be replaced; and at two-thirty in the morning the crew walked off the set. Berkeley's total lack of discipline killed off any professionalism Eleanor Powell ever had.

[4] Berkeley had originally been announced to direct but Powell and Sothern were against it.

Ann Sothern, with Robert Young at the piano, singing what became the Academy Award-winning song, "The Last Time I Saw Paris." M-G-M

The production was finally completed on May 3, 1941; the total cost, $863,460.92. Released on September 12, 1941, it grossed $1,692,-000.

After the preview of *Lady Be Good,* Freed heard from Hammerstein. Kern had let him know how well it went and how much he enjoyed Ann Sothern's rendition of their song. But this was a call for more than one purpose. "Dick Rodgers and I were approached by the Theatre Guild to do a musical based on *Green Grow the Lilacs,*[5] said Hammerstein. "The Theatre Guild owns the stage rights,[6] but we want the screen rights; can you get them for us?"[7] "You know the studio never sells anything," Freed told Hammerstein, "but let me try." Freed knew that only one man could resolve this.

"Boss," he said to Mayer, "I came to buy—and I want you to sell." Mayer looked puzzled. Freed told him what it was all about. Mayer said no. "Oscar himself asked me." Mayer said, "If it's for Oscar—give him a six-month option for $50,000."[8]

[5] The musical was ultimately called *Oklahoma!*
[6] *Green Grow the Lilacs* was produced by the Theatre Guild in 1931.
[7] M-G-M acquired the motion-picture rights in 1932.
[8] Hammerstein bought the motion picture rights four days after the opening of *Oklahoma!*

So much for the selling. Now came the buying. "You know the battle we're having[9] with RKO over *Panama Hattie?* De Sylva and his Broadway partners are holding us up. If it were up to Cole Porter he'd go with us, but . . ." At the mention of Cole Porter, Mayer beamed.[10] "Let's offer them a package for *Hattie* and *Du Barry Was a Lady.*" Cole Porter was the magic word. The possible cost of this venture wasn't even discussed.[11]

Freed was now ready to proceed with *Babes on Broadway*. He had given Finklehoffe a springboard: the kids make their headquarters at the Pitt Astor drugstore, while waiting for a chance to land a role on Broadway. Growing discouraged, they decide the only way to win recognition is to produce their own show. Finklehoffe had taken Freed's suggestion and had developed a story. Freed found that it lacked scope and brought in Elaine Ryan to work with Finklehoffe.

Freed wanted to make it a film about *real* people. He engaged the legendary performer Elsie Janis as a technical adviser for the production,

[9] RKO wanted it for Ginger Rogers (hot off *Kitty Foyle*).

[10] Cole Porter and M-G-M's association began in 1935 when it rescued his show *Jubilee,* in trouble on the road, and acquired the motion-picture rights. In 1936, he wrote the original score to *Born to Dance; Rosalie* in 1937; *The Broadway Melody of 1940* in 1939.

[11] The M-G-M deal was $200,000—$140,000 for *Panama Hattie* and $60,000 for *Du Barry*.

"Fascinating Rhythm." Berkeley checks a close up of Eleanor Powell. M-G-M

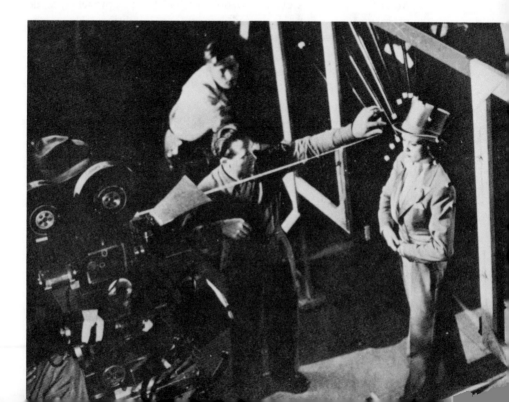

as well as a coach for Judy. He engaged Alexander Woollcott to appear on the screen as a prologue to the picture, similar to his "Town Crier" radio programs; he bought a sketch by Harry Kaufmann, "The Convicts Return," to be used as the play within the play the kids produce; and finally he asked Vincente Minnelli to use the expertise he had displayed on the Broadway stage.

Babes on Broadway was an original story, and Freed wanted an original score. He engaged three songwriters, Burton Lane, Yip Harburg and Ralph Freed, to give it the variance in style the story warranted. Lane and Harburg had been collaborators before.[12]

In addition to the kids, Judy and Mickey,[13] the studio announced that its new contract player Shirley Temple would also star in the musical. But this did not come to pass. She declined the role.

With Berkeley as director, production started on July 14, 1941, with Mickey, Ray McDonald and Richard Quine calling themselves "The Three Balls of Fire," singing and dancing to "Anything Can Happen in New York," written by Lane and Harburg. Virginia Weidler did another of their songs, "The Movies Are Going to Get You If You Don't Watch Out." In the sketch "The Convict's Return," which was bought for Mickey from the Broadway revue *Streets of Paris,* he played eight roles, making quick changes behind the scene in one take. The "Ghost Theatre" number that Minnelli created had Judy imitating Sarah Bernhardt, Blanche Ring and Fay Templeton, with Mickey doing Richard Mansfield as Cyrano de Bergerac, George M. Cohan and Harry Lauder. In another scene Mickey imitated the "Brazilian Bombshell" Carmen Miranda in her rendition of "Mama Yo Quiero."[14]

Author and critic Alexander Woollcott had been approached to do the prologue for the film. He agreed, but on three conditions: He wanted to see the film or a substantial part thereof, his price was a flat $5,000, he would only be available on one day, August 25.

Freed gave second-unit director George Sidney advice: "You don't know this guy, he's very strange. Make sure you get everything from him before you give him the check, because the minute you give him the check you'll never see him again. And, have lots of ice cream, quarts and quarts, because he loves the stuff."

Sidney followed the advice. "Young man," Woollcott remarked, "be nasty and knock people—that's the only way to get ahead." "He gave me all these Woollcottian philosophies," Sidney reported, "and I gave him the check, and he was gone. I sweated it out in New

---

[12] *Hold on to Your Hats* (1940), the Broadway musical starring Al Jolson had just opened. They later went on to write *Finian's Rainbow* (1947).

[13] Garland's contract had been renegotiated during the production of *Little Nellie Kelly,* and she was now receiving $2,000 per week; Rooney, for this picture, received $1,200 plus a $25,000 bonus on completion.

[14] Carmen Miranda, incidentally, appeared in *Streets of Paris.*

Judy and Mickey performing Burton Lane and Ralph Freed's "How About You." M-G-M

Freed caught Judy off guard in this photograph he took on the set of *Babes on Broadway*. ARTHUR FREED ARCHIVES

WESTERN UNION (29)

CLASS OF SERVICE

This is a full-rate Telegram or Cablegram unless its deferred character is indicated by a suitable symbol above or preceding the address.

R. B. WHITE
PRESIDENT

NEWCOMB CARLTON
CHAIRMAN OF THE BOARD

J. C. WILLEVER
FIRST VICE-PRESIDENT

SYMBOLS

DL = Day Letter

NT = Overnight Telegram

LC = Deferred Cable

NLT = Cable Night Letter

Ship Radiogram

The filing time shown in the date line on telegrams and day letters is STANDARD TIME at point of origin. Time of receipt is STANDARD TIME at point of destination

VS7 38 LAS VEGAS NEV 28 220A

ARTHUR FREED=

634 STONE CANYON RD =LOSA=

DEAR MR FREED. I AM SO VERY VERY HAPPY DAVE AND I WERE MARRIED THIS AM PLEASE GIVE ME A LITTLE TIME AND I WILL BE BACK AND FINISH THE PICTURE WITH ONE TAKE ON EACH SCENE LOVE=

JUDY.

Judy also sent the identical telegram to Louis B. Mayer announcing her marriage to conductor-composer David Rose. ARTHUR FREED ARCHIVES

York till the film came back from the studio lab—hoping that nothing was wrong with it."

Berkeley had finished the book part of the picture. What remained to be done were the four major musical numbers. "Chin-up! Cheerio! Carry On" (Lane and Harburg)[15] was done in the form of a musical radio message to their folks in London by scores of refugee children; "Hoe Down" (Edens and Ralph Freed) was an up-to-date twist on the old square dance, devised by Berkeley, Ray McDonald and seventy-five youngster with vocals by Judy, Mickey, Six Hits and a Miss and The

[15] Note from Burton Lane: "Yip and I wrote it as a kind of salute to the British, during the Dunkirk evacuation."

HIGHLAND FARM
DOYLESTOWN, PENNSYLVANIA
DOYLESTOWN 4818

January 8, 1942

Dear Arthur:

I saw BABES ON BROADWAY yesterday and feel impelled to write and tell you what a swell job I think it was. The Music Hall was packed and the large audience seemed to be with the picture every minute. There was spontaneous applause and the right kind of laughs, and now and then a handkerchief came out - including mine. But maybe I'm kind of a softy. I know I'm a pushover for Rooney and Garland. I think Buzz shot the picture superbly, and without straining too much, he built the numbers up to exciting peaks. Altogether it seemed to me to be one of the smartest and most well-rounded of all the musical productions that have come out of Hollywood, and I think you deserve congratulations. You are hereby getting mine.

All good wishes for a happy new year.

Oscar Hammerstein

Kaprelick's drawing for
Babes on Broadway. M-G-M

Five Musical Maids; the big minstrel show finale, imaginatively arranged by Roger Edens, in which Mickey did a banjo solo of "Swanee River" and "Alabama Bound"; Judy's specialty of "Franklin D. Roosevelt Jones," (Harold Rome)[16] and the entire cast doing a strut routine to "Waiting for the Robert E. Lee." This took nine days to rehearse, nine days to shoot, and shot the budget up another $107,422.62.

The production closed on November 7, 1941. All in all, *Babes on Broadway* cost $940,068.70. A lot of money for a comparatively small musical, but little in view of its incredible box-office success: $3,859,000. (Released January 2, 1942.)

As an afterthought it is worth mentioning that at the preview in Glendale, California, the minstrel number laid a terrible egg. "We tried to figure out why. As it turned out we realized there was no shot of Mickey and Judy making up in blackface, so the audience didn't know it was Judy and Mickey," Edens recalls. "And it was a very good lesson: If you ever are going to show someone in disguise, you better show them putting it on. So we did a retake showing Mickey and Judy getting into blackface so that the audience could tell it was them. And then the number went like a house on fire."

[16] Taken from the Broadway production *Sing Out the News* (1938).

Greta Garbo in a dress rehearsal with her partner-choreographer Robert Alton. Alton was soon to become an integral part of the Freed Unit. M-G-M and LELA SIMONE COLLECTION

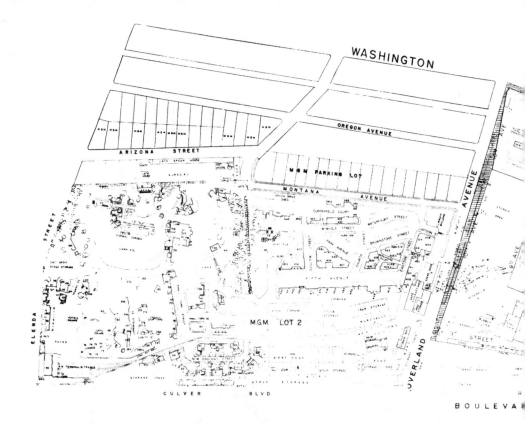

Let's pause and see what's going on at the studio at this time. On Stage 18, Greta Garbo and Robert Alton are dancing the "Chica Choca Rhumba" for *Two-Faced Woman;* W. S. Van Dyke was directing William Powell and Myrna Loy in *The Shadow of the Thin Man* on Stage 16; King Vidor was directing Hedy Lamarr, Robert Young and Charles Coburn in a scene for *H. M. Pulham Esq.* on Stage 22; Spencer Tracy and Katharine Hepburn were rehearsing *Woman of the Year* for George Stevens on Stage 3; in their first scene in *Johnny Eager* were Lana Turner and Robert Taylor on Stage 4, Mervyn LeRoy directing; on Stage 10 Walter Pidgeon and Rosalind Russell in *Miss Achilles Heel;* Nelson Eddy and Rise Stevens prerecording *The Chocolate Soldier* on Stage 1; Wallace Beery and Majorie Main on Lot 2 in *Steel Cavalry;* Norma Shearer in Rehearsal Hall A taking dancing lessons; Edward G. Robinson taking off in an airplane on Stage 30 for *Unholy Partners;* on Stage 12 Johnny Weissmuller swinging from tree to tree; and Eleanor Powell rehearsing a tap-dance routine for *I'll Take Manilla* in Rehearsal Hall B.

One can easily see that Metro-Goldwyn-Mayer was completely justified in coining their slogan "More Stars Than There Are in Heaven." Moreover, the opening signature of Leo, the Lion, roaring in the circle inscribed *Ars Gratia Artis* (Art for Art's Sake.)[17] defied anyone to prove its equal.

Panama Hattie was shot back to back with *Babes on Broadway.* While *Babes* went more or less without a hitch, *Hattie* was in trouble from the very beginning.

[17] Howard Dietz, a famous lyricist, had been the head of publicity since the inception of M-G-M. He invented the company's trade-mark by way of his alma mater, Columbia University, whose mascot is the lion.

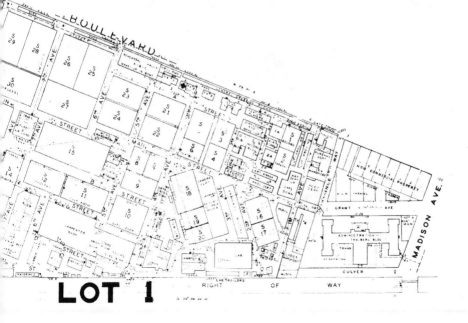

LOT 1

The screenplay of *Hattie* was in essence the book of the Broadway show, transferred to the screen without any cinematic development. Ann Sothern wasn't Ethel Merman; Virginia O'Brien wasn't Betty Hutton. Cole Porter's score was mutilated and the added new songs did not fit into the style in which the book originally was conceived. George Murphy was in one day and out another, and the role went to Dan Dailey, Jr. Shirley Temple's contract was bought out and she was replaced by Jackie Horner, an Ida Koverman protégé.

From the very beginning Sothern was not comfortable in the picture. She frequently reported ill; she was unhappy with the director, Norman McLeod; Freed and Mayer, on many occasions, were seen on the set, having long and supposedly encouraging talks with her. The film was just too overladen with dialogue and too light on entertainment.

There were ten songs in the picture, but with the exception of the three Cole Porter songs "Fresh as a Daisy," "What Say, Let's Be Buddies?" and "Make It Another Old-Fashioned, Please," none were memorable. Sothern was especially unhappy with the song "At the Savoy" by Walter Donaldson. One day she agreed to do it and the next day it was handed to O'Brien. Danny Dare's contribution as the dance director was unimaginative.

When the picture was previewed on November 15, 1941, the cost so far was $872,686.17.

Freed attended the Glendale sneak with trepidation. The picture moved along at a snail's pace. It seemed that Ann Sothern descended the staircase in her café a hundred times. The three sailors Red Skelton, "Rags" Ragland and Ben Blue came on, did slapstick bits and exited too many times. Virginia O'Brien's dead-pan delivery went unappreciated. In all, the picture lacked vitality.

Freed and Mayer left the theatre in a blue mood. During the ensuing

M-G-M

Between-the-scenes close-harmony group includes (from left) Joe Yule (Mickey Rooney's real father who played bits in many Freed films), Red Skelton, Ann Sothern, Ben Blue and Roger Edens. M-G-M

week Freed consulted daily with Edens, Minnelli, McGowan and Wilkie Mahoney, a new writer. There was much talk, few decisions and a lot of staring into space. But Freed held on to his belief that the film had the makings of good entertainment.

Then a catastrophe of gigantic proportions—Pearl Harbor—ironically brought welcome relief. Everything stopped. Roosevelt spoke to the nation. The United States was at war.

The whole nation was reshuffled—and so was the studio. Many employees joined the armed forces and were replaced by older people or women. After a remarkably short time things began to function again. And the fortunate who were not directly involved in the war effort were able to return to business as usual.

One day Louis "Doc" Shurr, an important Hollywood agent, came to Freed and told him about a great singer he wanted him to hear. A black girl. Freed said: "Here we go again. . . . I haven't any place for a girl like that right now. . . ." Shurr insisted. "Hear her sing a song or two. . . ." Freed gave in. "Bring her in for fifteen or twenty minutes." Shurr brought her in and Edens played for her. "Instead of fifteen minutes, we were in there for two hours listening to her," Freed recalls. "I called L.B. on the phone and took her up there—and Marion Davies was in the room when we came up. I had her sing a couple of songs and L.B. went crazy. So, instead of hiring her for one song in a picture, which Louis wanted, we put her under a long-term contract." And that, according to Freed, was the start of Lena Horne.

And here is Lena's version, as she wrote in her autobiography: "I was discovered for the movies by a man called Roger Edens. He came to hear me at the Little Troc."

As luck would have it—for Lena Horne—Freed, Edens and Minnelli went to see a performance of *Cabin in the Sky,* which was on tour in Los Angeles. One of the stars, Ethel Waters, had been in a Minnelli show, *At Home Abroad.* But this was not the reason they went to see the show. It had a score by Vernon Duke and John LaTouche, and the subject matter of the book by Lynn Root fascinated them. They met after the show with its producer Albert Lewis, and Freed immediately made an offer for the motion-picture rights. Lewis had had offers from other studios, and it was only after Freed offered him an associate producer's contract in his unit, along with his promise of having Vincente Minnelli direct, did he accept.

Cabin in the Sky was in the future. The problem at hand was *Panama Hattie.*

By this time Ann Sothern was already in another Maisie picture, *Get Rich Quick Maisie.* Freed went to her set and observed how well it was going under Roy Del Ruth's direction. During a break he talked to Del Ruth about his problems with *Panama Hattie,* and Del Ruth expressed interest in the possible salvaging of it. Freed went to Mayer and asked that Del Ruth take over the direction of *Hattie.* He then proceeded to make some script changes which would make the picture

Lena Horne singing "Just One of Those Things." M-G-M

Cole Porter autographed
this portrait to Freed.
ARTHUR FREED ARCHIVES

lighter. Musically, he felt, the picture would gain with the presence of Lena Horne and the inventive staging of Vincente Minnelli. Mayer appropriated an additional $300,000 to cut, fix and reshoot.

The additional writing and rewriting by McGowan, Mahoney and Joseph Schrank took four months. Edens prepared "Just One of Those Things"[18] as Lena's solo; and together with the Berry Brothers, "The Spring"; for Ann Sothern "I've Still Got My Health" (put back from the original score) as a song and dance number. The Carmen Amaya dance troupe was engaged for a specialty.[19] The finale was entirely revamped, using the Lane-Harburg song "The Son of a Gun Who Picks on Uncle Sam," bringing on the entire cast.

Shooting commenced on April 8, 1942. Del Ruth concentrated mainly on the book scenes and left Minnelli to handle the new musical numbers.

This was Minnelli's first experience behind a camera. "He didn't know anything about the technique of motion pictures, and we couldn't expect him to," Folsey continues. "In the 'Spring' number—a sort of a Greek thing—with girls posed as classical figures, Minnelli wanted a square box of light for each of them. Well, we had no equipment to do

[18] This Cole Porter song was bought by M-G-M when they acquired *Jubilee*.
[19] The Amaya troupe received $25,000 for their services and the number was later deleted from the release print.

PANAMA HATTIE

55

this. So we built a trough, put it in front of a very powerful light to give us a very sharp image. We dimmed the other stage lights down and we got the effect that Minnelli wanted. But the worst was yet to come. Then there was the Amaya group. We had twenty-seven moves of the boom in this number—up, down, in, out, dollying all around, panning and crossing over, and all this on musical cues. With all the stop and start marks taped on the floor it all looked like a bowl of spaghetti. Then he wanted yet another move. But instead we put the group on a platform just barely above the ground and pulled it by wires all across the stage."

After a month of added scenes and retakes, *Panama Hattie* finished at a cost of $1,097,907.88. Released on September 18, 1942, it grossed $4,326,000.

Freed had bet on the right horse. At the box office the film out-grossed both *Babes on Broadway* and *Lady Be Good*.

Artistically, this picture was unquestionably one of the low points in Freed's otherwise sure-fire career. He began to have second thoughts about a lot of things. He wanted to get back to Judy. In his hands was Jack McGowan's script of *Very Warm for May*.[20] This, he thought, might be a good vehicle for Judy Garland, Ray McDonald and Marta Eggerth.[21] However, even though it boasted a score by Kern and Hammerstein, the story was something else; May Graham, the singing and dancing daughter of show folk, wants to leave school and go on the stage. . . .[22] Here we go again. No more kid pictures, Freed decided.

[20] A note on the original Broadway cast: The two juvenile leads were played by Grace McDonald and Richard Quine (the roles intended for Judy Garland and Ray McDonald); in the chorus were June Allyson, Vera-Ellen and Don Loper.

[21] Marta Eggerth had just been signed to a term contract.

[22] Freed turned this property over to Jack Cummings, a fellow producer. Cummings released the film as *Broadway Rhythm*. About all that was left of *Very Warm for May* was a straw-hat theatre setting, the lovely hit melody "All the Things You Are" and a quick résumé of the other Kern-Hammerstein tunes by George Murphy at the piano.

56

3

FOR ME AND MY GAL

CABIN IN THE SKY

DU BARRY WAS A LADY

BEST FOOT FORWARD

GIRL CRAZY

The Hollywood Reporter and *Daily Variety,* two of the industry's self-serving tabloids, were "put to sleep" on Friday night, December 5, 1941. By the time they reached everybody's desk and the newsstands on Monday morning, their contents seemed ludicrous in the face of the events that had taken place the day before: Pearl Harbor.

A special meeting of the Producers Association is called for this afternoon with all members in attendance to discuss and seek ways and means of co-ordinating Hollywood's efforts with Washington's desires. . . .

REPUBLIC: War Department has requested this studio to turn over all its stock of firearms. . . .

Henry Wilcoxon, non-citizen denied admission in the Army, is with the Coast Guard in the Los Angeles Harbor. He's a British subject. . . .

It is admitted by set workers that on most of the big pictures now in work, additional ways of production will be necessary to bring them in under the wire. Actors try hard to overcome the mental confusion but the blow-ups are frequent, despite the intense effort being made to overcome them. There is general tension on the stages, with actors, directors and crew on the sets having a tough time swinging into the script's mood after they have spent in-between takes time discussing the latest headlines. Newsboys that managed to get onto sets sell out within two minutes of arrival. . . .

Use of night locations, use of arcs or other spots outside blacked-out studio sound stages are due to be vetoed for the duration. . . .

RKO: This studio's transportation department was set up on a war basis yesterday. . . .

NEW YORK: Theatre attendance was off 35 to 40 per cent in Broadway and up to 70 per cent in the neighborhoods last night as all America turned to their radios for President Roosevelt's address to the nation. . . .

Mixed in with announcements of new films, casting notes and advertisements for chorus girls, *Daily Variety* felt that one item deserved a two-column center-spread box:

SAROYAN DEVELOPS ORIGINAL FOR METRO

William Saroyan is writing an original story for Metro, which he is also scheduled to produce and direct. After a quick series of conferences with Metro top officials, including Louis B. Mayer, he started to work. It is understood that the Pulitzer prize winner (for *The Time of Your Life*) has signed no contract with Metro, but will first develop yarn. Saroyan's intention is to write an entirely new story for films. He will not attempt at this time, he says, to develop a screenplay about any of his own legiters.

The Hollywood clan of that day spent their leisure time playing golf at Hillcrest, tennis at Westside and a selected few were invited to the Lakeside County Club. Freed spent his free time at the Farmer's Market buying quantities of canned goods, Nova Scotia salmon and Jewish pastrami. From the physiological he often strayed to the philosophical. Saturdays, particularly, he could be found at bookstores like Martindale's, Hunter's and Stanley Rose's on Hollywood Boulevard.

"Hello, Mr. Freed—you know who just left a minute ago? William Saroyan," was Rose's greeting when he spotted his regular customer.

"Who?"

"You know—the guy who won the Pulitzer Prize."

"I know! I saw his play in New York." And after a slight pause: "Where's he staying?" Freed went away with Saroyan's address, phone number and a copy of his novel *My Name Is Aram*. When he arrived home he called Saroyan and invited him for breakfast at his Bel Air mansion the following day.

Saroyan was, at that time, the boy wonder of the American theatre and the *enfant terrible* of the literary world. His short stories of West Coast Armenians (of which he was one) were popular successes, and his play *The Time of Your Life,* a glittering compound of talk and tempest, had won the 1940 Pulitzer Prize.

Saroyan assumed that the conversation at breakfast was about motion pictures, noticing a copy of his book prominently placed on the breakfast table. But this was not so. "Bill, I like the things you write. I saw your play and loved it!"

"I heard your song and loved it!" replied Saroyan.

"Which one?" asked Freed.

" 'I Cried for You'—I wish I had written it!"

"Let me tell you about that song . . ." Freed went on. They ended up spending the entire day together, and a warm friendship began. Before Saroyan left, Freed asked him to come to the studio to meet Mr. Mayer.

Mayer and Saroyan hit it off right from the start.[1] With his great conversational flair Saroyan was fast to sense a great listener in the studio head. He told him colorful stories about his parents' Armenia that sounded to Mayer like writings from the Talmud. "This is a bright fellow; we should have him," Mayer later said to Freed. "He doesn't want to work in pictures though, but let me have a talk with him." Freed offered Saroyan an office at the studio and $300 weekly for his expenses. After a few weeks, the cashier called Freed's office and reported that Mr. Saroyan had never picked up his checks. Freed deduced that Saroyan must be back at his home in Fresno and called him. He urged

---

[1] After leaving Metro, Saroyan wrote a play which everybody recognized as a reflection of Mayer. It drew a devastating picture of a vicious egoist and was called *Get Away Old Man*. Considering the enthusiasm and high hopes that Mayer had for Saroyan ("another Thalberg," Mayer often remarked), this must have been extremely mortifying for him.

William Saroyan's first copy of his screenplay for *The Human Comedy* was given to Freed with Saroyan's handwritten inscription.

him to write an original story; three weeks later Saroyan delivered *The Human Comedy*.[2]

The story was read to Mayer. He cried. He was almost in tears again when he heard the asking price was $300,000. "I'll work it out," Freed consoled him. He did. Saroyan settled for $60,000 plus $1,500 per week under a producer-director contract.

Freed could not forget one particular actor's performance in *The Time of Your Life*. His name was Gene Kelly. "Arthur walked into the dressing room and tried to bait me into coming out to Hollywood," recalls Kelly. "I'd be great in pictures, he said, but I told him I wasn't ready—yet." Critics and audiences alike had finally taken notice of Kelly and he was enjoying the first real taste of success, especially since this was a new departure for him: straight acting. Naturally he wanted to stay on.

Gene Kelly was born in Pittsburgh, Pennsylvania. At the age of twenty-one he and his brother Fred hoofed in honky-tonks. At his mother's urging he became an assistant teacher at a dancing school; ultimately the school became known as the Gene Kelly School of the Dance. In the summer of 1937 he went to New York to get a job as a dance director.

But the Broadway producers were not interested in an unknown teacher from Pittsburgh. The following year he tried again, this time as a dancer, and landed in the Cole Porter musical *Leave It to Me!* Kelly along with three other boys, all dressed up like Eskimos, danced in the background while Mary Martin gave out with her "show-stopping" rendition of "My Heart Belongs to Daddy." His second show, Nancy Hamilton's revue *One for the Money,* gave him some lines in addition to dance routines. In the summer of 1939, Kelly got a chance to choreograph three shows at the summer theatre in Westport, Connecticut, run by Lawrence Langner of the Theatre Guild. One of the shows he did was a musical version of *Green Grow the Lilacs,* the play that later became the basis for the Rodgers and Hammerstein musical *Oklahoma!* Following his success in *Time of Your Life* that fall, and having decided to stay with Broadway, Kelly became dance director for Billy Rose's Diamond Horseshoe. After the show one night, he dropped into a bar, a hangout for struggling actors. There he met sixteen-year-old Betsy Blair who was appearing in a new Saroyan play, *The Beautiful People*. Then Kelly got his biggest break. He was selected by Rodgers and Hart, John O'Hara, George Abbott and Robert Alton for the title role in *Pal Joey*. Alton, the show's choreographer, was most instrumental in getting him the part since he had staged the musical

[2] A close friend of Saroyan's, Stanley Rose, had suggested he do a story about his youthful experiences as a messenger boy.

numbers in Kelly's two previous Broadway shows. *Pal Joey* opened Christmas night in 1940 at the Ethel Barrymore Theatre. On the day after Christmas Gene Kelly was a Broadway star.

While he was performing nightly and doing the usual matinees each week, his boss, George Abbott, began preparing a new musical, *Best Foot Forward*. The cast would be made up of youngsters, mostly unknowns. Furthermore, the score was being written by two vocal arrangers turned songwriters, Hugh Martin and Ralph Blane. Kelly was engaged to stage the musical numbers. In order to make it easier for his new star, Abbott scheduled rehearsals at the Barrymore Theatre on the days *Joey* was dark.

Best Foot Forward opened on October 1, 1941, at the Ethel Barrymore Theatre, and the next day Kelly accepted a second call from Hollywood and departed with his bride Betsy Blair for the Coast.

"L. B. Mayer saw me in *Pal Joey* and said, 'We'd like you to come out to M-G-M'. . . . I'm sure Arthur was behind all this," says Kelly, "but I didn't want to make a test in New York—everybody had warned me the work was inferior."

"I saw you and I'll sign you—you're fine . . . fine," Mayer insisted.

"I was elated," Kelly continues. "I thought it was time for me to make a musical. Then a call came from M-G-M, telling me that I had to make a test. I told them Mr. Mayer said I didn't have to."

What happened was a misreading of a directive from Freed by Al Altman, of the M-G-M New York office. In the telegram dated December 15, 1939:

> . . . please send me a set of stills of the Kelly boy I saw in your office whom you are going to test for the part of Willie in my picture.[3]

This brought about the following reaction from Kelly: "I wrote my first 'Hollywood' letter and said, 'I'm sorry, I won't work for you because you lied—I'd rather dance in a saloon.'" And that finished negotiations with M-G-M. But a couple of days later David Selznick, who happened to be L. B. Mayer's son-in-law at the time and headed his own studio, saw Kelly in the show and asked him to come up and see him.

"I saw you," said Selznick, "I like you—I want to sign you."

"Just like that?" asked Kelly.

"Just like that."

"That's what Mr. Mayer said—and he lied. . . ." Kelly blurted out.

Selznick burst out laughing. "Let's shake hands on the deal." They did; the contract was signed and Mr. and Mrs. Kelly arrived in Hollywood on October 2, 1941.

[3] Freed was referring to *Strike Up the Band*.

All charm and smiles Freed walked into Finklehoffe's office. Under his arm was the screenplay for his next project, *For Me and My Gal,* Judy's next picture.[4] "You know Ritzy [he was referring to Richard Sherman] has written an excellent script," Freed started to say.

"Cut the crap, Arthur, what d'ya want?" came Finklehoffe's rather brusque retort.

"I don't like the ending . . . the guy just can't end the thing."

"So?" Finklehoffe smelled a rat.

"Would you mind reading the script and see if you can think of a better ending?" Finklehoffe obliged. Two hours later he came in with a new ending. Freed loved it. And Finklehoffe resumed the work he was doing on *Girl Crazy.*[5] Two days later Freed walked in again: "Freddie, look, I love the ending . . . but it just doesn't fit in."

"But, Arthur, all you mentioned is the ending!" He took the script and rewrote the scene leading into the end. From his typewriter he walked into Freed's office and dropped it on the desk.

Without looking at the rewrite, Freed said, "Listen, about the middle part . . ."

With that Finklehoffe screamed. "Why the hell don't you ask me to start from the beginning?"

Freed smiled: "I think that's a good idea."

Now Finklehoffe began to reason. "Arthur, you know I'm working on that Cummings picture with my friend Sid Silvers."

"Would you want Sid Silvers with you?" Freed asked.

"Of course . . . but . . ."

Freed cut him short. "I'll arrange it." And with that, Finklehoffe and Silvers were assigned to rewrite the script.

After having successfully kidnaped the two writers, a neon sign kept blinking in Freed's brain: What next? (A period of inactivity was untenable for him.) *Show Boat*—a great Kern and Hammerstein musical—Universal owns it—Universal is in trouble—let's get it![6] *Meet the People*—a musical satire on the government—full of young talent—

[4] *For Me and My Gal* started out with the working title *The Big Time,* taken from a story by Howard Emmett Rogers. *For Me and My Gal* is derived from the song of the same name by George W. Mayer, Edgar Leslie and E. Ray Goetz. Freed thought of the title and recalled, "I was trying to find a title from a song and I could have picked half a dozen songs as titles, but Edgar Leslie and George Mayer were friends of mine and I liked what they wrote, so I bought the rights to *For Me and My Gal* from Mills Music Publishing Company for use of the title and song, and it became a standard."

[5] Metro had acquired the rights to the George and Ira Gershwin musical in 1939 and Jack Cummings had been assigned to produce. The studio paid RKO $35,000 for the rights to produce it and $7,500 to Rose Gershwin for the music rights (for the estate of George Gershwin) and $5,000 to Ira Gershwin.

[6] Universal had produced two films of the stage classic. In 1929, with Laura LaPlante and 1936 with Irene Dunne, Helen Morgan, Allan Jones, Paul Robeson and Hattie McDaniel. Metro bought the property for Freed from Universal for $100,000 including the negatives and all prints.

a Broadway show touring the country. Freed bought it, but felt it needed a new and original story line. He put Albert Manheimer and Devrey Freeman on to invent a new plot. *Jumbo,* the Rodgers-Hart-Billy Rose circus spectacle, was bought by Metro and Freed was assigned to produce it. *The Red Mill,* the Victor Herbert operetta, had been a Metro silent with Marion Davies. Abbott and Costello were creating quite a sensation in their first Metro picture *Rio Rita.* This would be their next for Freed.[7] After Mannheimer, McGowan and Nancy Hamilton had turned in various scripts for *Du Barry Was a Lady,* none of which Freed was happy with, he instructed Irving Brecher to do a complete rewrite returning to the Herbert Fields-Buddy De Sylva original Broadway book.

Finklehoffe was reviewing the so-far finished rewrites on the screenplay of *For Me and My Gal.* "There's a guy—just right for this picture —his name is Gene Kelly," said Finklehoffe. "But he's at Selznick."

"Do you know him?" Freed asked.

"Of course I know him. I know him from the New York stage—I already knew him in Pittsburgh."

Freed asked Mayer to get a loanout on Kelly. Ever since Kelly had come to Selznick he had not been in a single picture. And so Mayer was able to get a release and the complete contract was signed over to M-G-M.[8]

At first Selznick had great hopes for Kelly as a dramatic actor, but after several attempts he gave up this idea. Contrary to whatever has been said before, the contract was not bought; it was simply assigned over to Metro. Also contrary to other statements made in the past, Mayer had no illusions that his son-in-law, Selznick, could ever be induced to return to Metro.

During preproduction it became clearer and clearer that *For Me and My Gal* would be a departure from the rather frivolous entertainment of the prewar days. Judy was now nineteen years old; audiences too, had gotten "older" in a sense. The war was ever present in their minds, and they no longer could divorce themselves from the realities of life.

Along with Garland and Kelly was costar George Murphy. The supporting cast was made up of Marta Eggerth, Ben Blue, Horace McNally, Richard Quine, Lucille Norman and Keenan Wynn. Berkeley was set to direct.

[7] The comedy team played the roles originated by Montgomery and Stone on the Broadway stage. Costello then became seriously ill, causing the production to be canceled.

[8] Kelly's starting salary was $750. It should be noted, however, that Freed initially met with strong resistance from the studio executives concerning their signing Kelly. Eddie Mannix, studio manager, in particular, could not see any motion-picture potential in Kelly. After the preview, however, Mannix told Freed, "Remind me not to tell you how to make pictures."

Berkeley with
Judy and Gene
thinking . . .
M-G-M

In the screenplay, Judy is a naïve, young vaudeville singer, who falls in love with Kelly, an opportunist, whose only aim in life is to play the "big time," the Palace. He recognizes her talent and in order to exploit it he offers her a partnership. She accepts and in so doing must leave the act headed by her sweetheart, Murphy. On their climb to success Kelly gets a notice from his draft board. He is determined not to go to war and slams a trunk lid on his fingers to become physically disqualified for service. An altogether unsavory character.

Berkeley sensed that some counterweighting was needed: he devised a sequence in which Judy's brother, played by Richard Quine in a soldier's uniform, arrives at a get-together in a nightclub to say good-bye. Judy is stunned at the thought of losing him. At this point everybody in the scene stands up and sings their own farewell, "Till We Meet Again."

Heartwarming as this scene was, it did not prove to be enough to make the dubious character of the film's hero more palatable.

One of the memorable contributions to the picture was the impeccable selection of standard songs for individual scenes by Edens and the continuity he put together for Judy's musical montage.

Two factors slowed up the production: Judy was out sick for a total of four weeks, and Georgie Stoll, the film's musical director, could not keep up with the time schedule.

Judy and Gene in one of the classic stills from the musical sequence where they perform the film's title song. M-G-M

At the sneak preview in Westwood Village 85 per cent of the preview cards contended that Murphy should have gotten the girl (Judy). It was evident that the audience did not accept the draft dodger as the hero of the picture. "We've got to do a repair job," said Mayer. On his orders the entire cast was recalled for what turned out to be twenty-one days of retakes. Two big scenes were added to make Kelly a hero and the whole finale was reshot without Murphy.

The picture's final cost was $802,980.68. Released November 20, 1942, it grossed $4,371,000 and has remained a classic.

The fourteenth annual Academy Award banquet was held on February 26, 1942. In the best-song category the winner was "The Last Time I Saw Paris," which had been interpolated in *Lady Be Good.* Jerome Kern felt that Harold Arlen's "Blues in the Night" should have won the award, a reaction typical of this man's great generosity. The aftermath of this was that the music branch of the Academy changed its rules to the effect that only original songs composed for and used in a motion picture would be eligible.

In the spring of 1942, Edens found himself with the following workload staring him in the face: *For Me and My Gal* was not finished; coaching, vocal arranging and recording were yet to be done. *Du Barry Was a Lady:* new songs were to be added and spotted—to be done by Burton Lane, Ralph Freed, Yip Harburg and himself. *Cabin in the Sky:* Since Vernon Duke and John LaTouche, the original songwriters of the show, were both in the armed forces, Freed had engaged Harold Arlen to write additional songs with his *Wizard of Oz* collaborator Yip Harburg. Apart from co-ordinating, supervising and writing, Edens' participation became even larger. And since new plans were being welded daily, he found it necessary to call in some help.

Hugh Martin and Ralph Blane at the time were doing practically every show on Broadway as vocal arrangers. They had done *Cabin in the Sky, Du Barry Was a Lady, Very Warm for May, Pal Joey*

One can see that Judy was already having problems with Berkeley. M-G-M

At the stage door of the Capitol Theatre in New York (left to right): Ralph Blane, Jo Jean Rogers, Mickey Rooney, Judy Garland, Phyllis Rogers and Hugh Martin. Blane, the Rogers sisters and Martin were Judy and Mickey's back-up vocal group known as the Martins. RALPH BLANE COLLECTION

and *Too Many Girls,* among others. Edens' first professional contact with them came about when Judy and Mickey needed a vocal backup for their New York engagement at the Capitol Theatre. They auditioned and were hired on the spot. Since then, they had written the score to the Broadway hit *Best Foot Forward.* Edens instructed Nat Finston to put them under contract.

Coincidentally, an agent sent Freed a screen test of June Allyson, who was currently appearing in *Best Foot Forward,* which Twentieth Century-Fox had made and discarded. After Freed saw it, he ordered her signed immediately.

Martin and Blane arrived and Edens took them in to Freed's office. Edens had praised them very highly and Freed gave them a cordial greeting. They, in return, expressed enthusiasm at being at Metro. Nonetheless, there was something they were extremely unhappy about. Blane was anxious to get it off his chest: "Mr. Freed, you brought us to Metro and our first Broadway musical is being bought by Columbia Pictures and we won't get to work on our own show."

"Are you sure they bought it?" Freed asked.

"I guess so," Blane replied. "They've made a $50,000 bid which we, as authors, have not yet agreed to."

Freed cut him short. "Metro will make a counteroffer—why not?

I've already signed June Allyson," he continued, "and I'll see the show in New York. Just sit tight . . . and give Roger all the help you can!"

On May 4, 1942, the *Hollywood Reporter* once again heralded William Saroyan. But this time the headline was: WASHUP ON SAROYAN MEGGING AT M-G-M. When he signed the studio contract to do one picture, it did not mention what the story would be. He therefore took it for granted it was to be *The Human Comedy* and he was to have Mickey Rooney as its star. Rooney was already into another film so Saroyan idled away his time by writing a two-reel short, *The Good Job,* which was based on his own short story *A Number of the Poor.* It barely lived up to its title. Again, he pushed for "his picture" and Rooney, but the studio had other plans.

In June, *For Me and My Gal* was finished and Freed went to New York with Mayer, Garland and Edens. They all went to see *By Jupiter,* Rodgers and Hart's musical hit. While pit orchestras normally go unheralded, critics and audiences alike were equally extravagant in their acclaim for the exciting and refreshing sound of this one. The conductor was Johnny Green. He had been an accompanist, duopianist, composer and conductor. He had had a minor fling in motion pictures and had scored a major success with two songs, "Body and Soul"[9] and "I Cover the Waterfront."[10] Both have become classics.

After the show Freed and Edens rushed backstage looking for Green. They spotted him. "My God!" Freed exclaimed, "I've never heard anything like it . . . you are the show!"

"Well, Arthur, you are exaggerating, but I am glad," Green said.

Green seems to have total recall: "I was living at 55 East 72nd Street, with my Cadillac car and chauffeur, and my elegant wife, then Betty Furness, and eating at '21' and Toots Shor's—and so on and so forth. I then began to ponder. I didn't want to go back to Hollywood as a goddamn arranger—I don't really know what Freed wants of me—he's got Roger Edens. So I called him the next day and he said he wants me at M-G-M. . . . I had already accepted a $1,500 advance on Dick Rodgers' next musical—and I'm making $300 a week on *By Jupiter.* I'm in New York, I'm writing again and I'm pot-boiling with what a composer may have to pot-boil with, which isn't like scoring a picture. 'God knows, I love you, Arthur,' I said, 'but, frankly, unless I'm brought to Hollywood to write songs or to compose, I'm really not interested.' First they offered me $450 a week. I turned them down. Then the son of a bitch offers me $600, and I said 'no' again. When he got to $750 a week, I crumbled."

[9] Written with Edward Heyman, Robert Sour and Frank Eyton.
[10] Written with Edward Heyman.

The day after the encounter with Green, Freed went to the matinee of *Best Foot Forward*. Finklehoffe happened to be in New York and he took him along. After the performance the two men parted; Finklehoffe went to the office of his agent Leland Hayward and Freed to his hotel. When he called his office at the studio he was told that all hell had broken loose. Word had come from Thau's[11] office that Harry Cohn, head of Columbia Pictures, had called. He said, "What are you guys trying to do? Nobody wanted *Best Foot Forward*. I was all set to lock it up for $50,000—I was buying it for Rita Hayworth—I had a commitment from Shirley Temple to play the little girl and I had Glenn Miller and his orchestra. . . ." Freed went to see L.B. in his suite.

"Do you want it?" Mayer asked.

"Yes, I do—but there is something going on with Cohn."

"Well," Mayer said, "I'll take care of him."

Freed returned to his suite and there was a call from Finklehoffe. "Arthur, I'm in Leland's office and I've just finished reading a short story that is absolutely fabulous! The writer is a client of Leland's by the name of Sally Benson—it's going to appear in *The New Yorker* magazine."

"What's it called?" Freed asked.

"5135 Kensington."

"Send it over."

In less than an hour the story arrived. Freed read it and was enchanted. He got right on the phone and made a deal for the property[12] and a separate contract for Benson to come out to the studio to work for him. This was the beginning of what eventually was to become *Meet Me in St. Louis*.

That night Freed and Edens went to Café Society, a showcase for entertainers. They had been tipped off that a new and thoroughly engaging comedian by the name of Zero Mostel was appearing. They loved his act and he was hired for a featured role in Freed's next picture.

What made it possible for Freed to spread out in all these directions? To a great extent it was his utter disregard and disinterest in petty detail. The overzealous department head, the supervisor of the supervisor, the ego of the small fry, made itself felt as in any bureaucracy.

Freed had gone beyond the time-wasting memo writers. His instinct told him he needed his own production people to disencumber him from daily trivia, people who knew every facet of picturemaking,

[11] Thau's title was executive assistant to Mayer and he had his pulse on the entire studio's operation.

[12] "The Kensington Stories," a series of twelve stories by Sally Benson, eight of which were published in *The New Yorker* under the title *5135 Kensington*. The installments appeared commencing June 14, 1941, and each month thereafter through May 23, 1942. Freed bought the property for a flat $25,000.

Lucille Ball and her ladies in waiting.

from ordering a dissolve to assigning an orchestrator, from checking a wardrobe test to arranging a looping session. These would be people who could present him with facts and not eventualities. It wasn't long before he found them.

In a month's time *Du Barry,* under Roy Del Ruth's direction, was ready for rehearsal. Briefly, the script dealt with Red Skelton, playing a checkroom attendant, who falls in love with glamorous Lucille Ball, a gold-digging night-club singer. His counterpart is played by Gene Kelly, a glib, but warmhearted entertainer and songwriter. Skelton drinks a "Mickey Finn" and thinks he is Louis the XV and Du Barry (Lucille Ball)[13] is his mistress. This segment abounded with Restoration comedy shenanigans. When Skelton is about to stop an execution he snaps to. The dream is over; he accepts the cigarette girl Virginia O'Brien as his true love and Lucille Ball announces her engagement to Kelly. An added feature in the film were the Du Barry Girls[14] and Tommy Dorsey and his Orchestra.

Kelly was dissatisfied with Seymour Felix's dance direction and he asked for Robert Alton. Alton, however, was in New York and unavailable. "Well, then, where's Charlie Walters?" Gene asked. The number in question was Cole Porter's "Do I Love You?" which needed a special kind of elegance and style that Felix was totally unfamiliar with. Walters was summoned to stage the number.

[13] Lucille Ball's vocals were dubbed by Martha Mears.
[14] These were based on Varga's internationally famous pin-up calendar girls.

Walters recalls his first interview with Freed: "I think I'm the only dance director who ever read a script to find out what the characters were all about. . . . Gene just had a love scene with Lucille in her dressing room, so they were on a high note, at which point he had to leave her to go onstage. I said, 'Well, Arthur, might it not be fun to start the number inside the dressing room—and then pow— out through the door, through the audience and on to the stage to continue it.' There was a big lull. 'Chuck,' Freed said, 'I think you're going to be a director someday . . . that's the way directors think.' " Freed put him under contract and it marked the beginning of a brilliant career.

Charles Walters was born in Anaheim, California. Upon finishing high school he was obsessed with the notion of becoming a dancer. He made the rounds of the neighborhood night clubs and landed a few engagements for a dollar a night.

Leonard Sillman, a Broadway producer, was putting together a revue starring Kay Thompson, which was to feature unknown talent. It was called *Lo and Behold* and was to play Pasadena, California. He met Walters and engaged him. After the show closed Sillman told him that if he ever came to New York he had a job. But Walters was broke. He joined the Fanchon and Marco unit, toured the country

Esquire magazine's Howard Baer was engaged by M-G-M to do a series of drawings of Lucille Ball in *Du Barry Was a Lady*. M-G-M

Minnelli discusses his point of view in this scene between Lena Horne and Eddie "Rochester" Anderson. VINCENTE MINNELLI COLLECTION

and wound up in Brooklyn. His first Broadway appearance was in Leonard Sillman's *New Faces of 1933*. He then teamed up with Dorothy Fox, a Martha Graham dancer, and played a chop suey joint in Philadelphia. This led to an engagement at the Versailles night club in New York. Choreographer Bob Alton caught the show and put Walters in the Theatre Guild production of *Parade*. Walters' biggest break came in Cole Porter's musical *Jubilee,* in the role of the prince. His career began to climb rapidly: *The Show Is On,* with Bea Lillie, *Between the Devil,* with Jack Buchanan and Evelyn Laye, Richard Rodgers' *I Married an Angel* and opposite Betty Grable in *Du Barry Was a Lady.*

After his imaginative staging of "Do I Love You?" Freed asked him to redo all of Seymour Felix's work.

Cabin in the Sky went into production the same day as *Du Barry Was a Lady.*

When Metro announced that Arthur Freed would produce an all-Negro musical *Cabin in the Sky,* a Broadway show that had been an artistic but not a popular success,[15] there was almost universal disapproval. The white executives were apprehensive, the Negro press was prejudiced. The reason for their misgivings was the result of the 1936 production of *Green Pastures* (Warner Bros.). The Negro community and the Negro press contended that this film mirrored a black mentality which was ludicrous, condescending and false. It was good diplomacy on Freed's part to give extensive interviews to several Negro papers. "All of America has learned a lot from the Negro in the theatre. With

[15] The original show lost $25,000. M-G-M bought the property for $40,000, thereby putting the backers ahead $15,000.

originality and talent, he has rendered a great service to the world of entertainment and the culture of the nation. . . . The motion picture industry in its basic forms will never discriminate . . . more than ever before we are aware of the Negro problem and are daily moving toward a better understanding. One that in the end will result in a dignified presentation of a peace-loving and loyal people."

This sounds somewhat like the launching of a message picture, which *Cabin in the Sky* was not. In effect, it became a musical fantasy, depicting the humor and religious beliefs of an ethnic group. The silly plots of his recent films began to lose their appeal for Freed. *Cabin in the Sky* was a courageous undertaking and a reaching for a different dimension of filmmaking. "I will spare nothing and will put everything behind it. It will be a picture on a par with any major film under the M-G-M banner," said Freed.

On the basis of that statement one can see what enormous faith Freed had in Minnelli's talent when he gave him full reign on his first assignment as a director. This decision met with great resistance in certain quarters, inasmuch as there was a select clique of "seasoned" directors on the Metro lot. But, as usual, Freed fought the battle and

Al Hirschfeld, known for his famous New York *Times* drawings, was put under term contract by the studio to exploit their products. This is his interpretation of *Cabin in the Sky*. M-G-M

won. As a safeguard he made Albert Lewis associate producer, a man with considerable motion-picture experience, who was to assist and advise Minnelli in technical matters. Andrew Marton, a director, was delegated to guide Minnelli on his first venture through the possibilities and limitations of the camera.

The story of *Cabin in the Sky* concerns Little Joe, a good-natured gambler who is continually the center of a struggle. On one side is his devoted wife, Petunia, trying to keep him on the straight and narrow path and on the other side is the beautiful night-club singer Georgia Brown, who forever attempts to make him leave his wife for a career of gambling and high life. Little Joe is finally in a night-club fracas, and as he lies on his deathbed the struggle still goes on, this time for his immortal soul. After some complications between good and evil, Little Joe is saved by the faith of his wife and, recovering from his wounds, declares that he has realized the error of his ways.

Heading the cast was Ethel Waters as Petunia, a part she had created on Broadway. Eddie "Rochester" Anderson played Little Joe; Rex Ingram, also from the Broadway cast, played the dual role of Lucifer, Jr., and Lucius. The character of Georgia Brown, instead of being a dancing part that Katherine Dunham had played, became a singing role tailor-made for Lena Horne. As extra added attractions the film featured Louis Armstrong in a dramatic role and Duke Ellington and his Orchestra.

A most important element in the picture was the participation of the Hall Johnson Choir. Johnson, a highly educated and astute man, had a measure of anxiety about the project.[16] The following is a letter from Johnson to Lewis:

Dear Mr. Lewis:

Thanks for giving me an opportunity to read the present script of *Cabin in the Sky*. You are to be commended for your desire to include nothing which might give offense to the Negro race—a consideration too often overlooked in this business of motion-picture making. I think my nose is particularly keen in that direction but, so far, I have been unable to detect anything in this script which could possibly offend anybody. . . .

The *Cabin, as it now stands,* may be offered to the general public without reservations—needing neither explanations nor apologies. . . . To this day Negroes have never forgiven the slanderous misrepresentations of *The Green Pastures,* and when after five successful years on the stage it was finally made into a picture, they did not hesitate to express their true feelings about it. . . .

At the moment, the dialect in your script is a weird but priceless conglomeration of pre-Civil War constructions mixed with up-to-the-minute Harlem slang and heavily sprinkled with a type of verb

---

[16] He remembered the experiences in the film *Green Pastures*.

The set for "Ain't It the Truth." The number, as photographed, was later used in a "Pete Smith Specialty," one of M-G-M's shorts. M-G-M

which Amos and Andy purloined from Miller and Lyle, the Negro comedians; all adding up to a lingo which has never been heard nor spoken on land or sea by any human being, and would most certainly be "more than Greek" to the ignorant Georgia Negroes in your play. The script will be immeasurably improved when this is translated into honest-to-goodness Negro dialect.

Thanks again for the script to read. If your director is as sympathetic and intelligent as your script writer you will turn out a picture which will delight everybody and offend no one without an inferiority complex—an affliction, by the way, which has almost completely died out among modern Negroes. We love nothing better than to laugh at ourselves on the stage—when it is ourselves we are laughing at.

Very sincerely yours,
Hall Johnson

No major difficulties arose during production. But there is always an amount of tension on every film set, and in this instance the tensions, and even jealousy, emanated mostly from within the cast itself.

"I objected violently to the way religion was being treated in the screenplay," comments Ethel Waters. "All through the picture there was so much snarling and scrapping that I didn't know how in the world *Cabin in the Sky* ever stayed up there," she adds.

"Unlike Miss Waters I was enjoying myself hugely on this picture," says Lena Horne. "But the kids who were working in scenes with Ethel Waters told me she was violently prejudiced against me. Miss Waters was not notably gentle toward women and she was particularly tough on other singers."

"I was kind of a bulwark between them," says Minnelli, "because I loved Lena and I loved Ethel . . . but Ethel didn't like Lena at all. It always seemed so ridiculous to me, because Ethel was such a great artist. In New York it was her show, but now it was divided—there was the new element of the beautiful colored girl . . . but I had my own troubles."

One of the main obstacles Minnelli had to overcome was the resistance from the art department. It was Minnelli's intention at the outset to show the black race in the most beautiful terms. As an example: In the musical number "Ain't It the Truth," (Arlen-Harburg) Lena Horne was in a bubble bath. The set was a prettied-up version of a slum and what Minnelli wanted was a room in a house inhabited by poor people. He raised hell and the set was changed to his specifications. Lena looked beautiful . . . the song was a charmer, but it had to come out of the picture. The Breen Office[17] put such pressure on Freed that he had no other choice and it had to go.[18]

The film was entirely shot in sepia. The fantasy sequence was a photographic feat. A foreword, written by Elmer Rice, opened the picture.

"We made the picture for around $600,000," says Freed (in fact it was $662,141.82). "Did you ever read the reviews?" he asks with a slight grin.

Following are excerpts from reviews:

New York *Times* — May 28, 1943

Cabin in the Sky is a bountiful entertainment. The Metro picturization of the Negro fantasy, which settled down at Loew's Criterion yesterday for what should prove to be a long tenancy, is every inch as sparkling and completely satisfying as was the original stage production. . . .

Daily Variety — February 10, 1943

Cabin is a fantastic piece of American folklore, a morality fable stated in elemental, earthy terms, replete with pathos and comedy. . . .

---

[17] Refers to the Motion Picture Production Administration (Washington, D.C.) Code head, Joseph I. Breen.

[18] "Ain't It the Truth" was later used by Harold Arlen in his Broadway musical *Jamaica* (1957). The "Cabin in the Sky" number, as photographed, was used in a Pete Smith specialty (M-G-M short), and the song "I Got a Song," a number intended for Bubbles was also cut and later used in *Bloomer Girl*.

THE
DU BARRY
GIRLS
Featured in
M-G-M's
"DU BARRY
WAS A LADY"

1 . . . THEO COFFMAN
2 . . . KAY ALDRIDGE
3 . . . INEZ COOPER
4 . . . GEORGIA CARROLL
5 . . . NATALIE DRAPER
6 . . . MARILYN MAXWELL
7 . . . . EVE WHITNEY
8 . . . , AILEEN HALEY
9 . . . HAZEL BROOKS
10 . MARY JANE FRENCH
11 . . . JERRIE BULKLEY
12 . . . KAY WILLIAMS

M-G-M

January 11, 1943

Mr. Arthur Freed
Metro-Goldwyn-Mayer Studio
Culver City, California

Dear Mr. Freed:

In view of your past interest in our work and your
understanding of problems that confront us, not only as a
group but as individuals, we would like to take the liberty
of setting forth a perplexing problem for your consideration.

Due to existing conditions we, the twenty-six stock contract girls, feel the original salary of $60.00 per week
agreed upon in our contracts is not sufficiently adequate to
help us cope with the excessive increase in living expenses.

As a matter of record, due to a five week lay-off which
we suffered, and which of course is allowed under the contract, we actually received an average income of $45.00 per
week for the first six months. We feel that $75.00 per week
with an eight hour day, our overtime to be computed daily
instead of weekly, would be fair and equitable.

While we appreciate the legality of the contract, we
wish to appeal to your sense of fairness. A readjustment of
our salaries would aid us in meeting the increasing expense
of living conditions and higher taxes. We feel sure that you
will bring this matter to the attention of the proper officials
for their urgent consideration.

Sincerely yours,

Your Du Barry Girls

c/c Mr. L.B. Mayer
Mr. E.J. Mannix

M-G-M

M-G-M has a natural in its all-colored *Cabin in the Sky*. First, because it is jammed with entertainment; secondly, because, being all colored, it presents an unusual picture, a show that will get talk —box-office talk. . . . Vincente Minnelli has done a really inspired job in the direction of the picture, without which it would not be the good entertainment it is. It is his first picture effort and the job stands out.

Du Barry, on the other hand, was an out-and-out "showcase" picture. It was one of many made primarily for the sake of establishing and/or exploiting stars or would-be stars. In this instance it was "icing on the cake," and the cake was Lucille Ball. It was also tailor-made to establish Red Skelton as a great comic. The old formula of stacking a film with nothing but entertainment proved correct: It paid off at the box office ($3,496,000) in spite of an outrageous amount of money spent on it, $1,239,222.56.

Meet Me in St. Louis was to a great extent autobiographical. Sally Benson was brought out to Metro to work on a film treatment of her story in April of 1942. When dealing with autobiography, it is difficult for an author to transpose his life story, to structure it for either stage or screen. Freed felt that Benson needed the expert collaboration of playwrights Howard Lindsay and Russel Crouse, who had touched thousands of theatregoers with the warmth and sentimental appeal of their play *Life With Father*. But Kenneth MacKenna, head of the studio story department, received this letter from Crouse:

Dear Kenneth:

Thanks for your very sweet note.

I know Sally's stories and like them. In fact, they probably are a little more interesting to me than to most people because I knew the family, including Agnes, whom they largely concern.

Also I'd like to work for M-G-M which I never have.

But Howard and I are in the middle of a new play.[19] We have at least another five weeks on the play, then five weeks of rehearsal and then the tryout and then the letdown, because I punish myself pretty thoroughly in the process. So I'm afraid there is no Hollywood for me now.

But again thanks for thinking of me and love to you and Mary from Alison and me.

As ever,
Buck
(Russel Crouse)

---

[19] They were at work on *Life With Mother,* the sequel to *Life With Father.*

After two months Sally Benson was eased out of any further work on the treatment. Sarah Mason and Victor Heerman, two screenwriters, then prepared a dialogue script, which was unsatisfactory. Now writer William Ludwig and director George Cukor took Benson's story and started from scratch. After two months Cukor was drafted into the Army and work was stopped.

Freed tried to get Oscar Hammerstein. He offered him a two-year contract, both as a writer and as an associate. As appreciative as Hammerstein was, he had to decline.

A turn of events forced Freed—much to his regret—to put his project aside.

In her column in the Los Angeles *Examiner*, Louella Parsons gave a glowing report of a performance she had just seen in San Francisco. The star was Esther Williams and the show was *Billy Rose's Aquacade* at the Golden Gate International Exposition. After seeing the show, Cummings phoned Mayer to come up and see for himself.

The result was a long-term contract for Esther Williams and Mayer asked Freed to go on an immediate search for a proper vehicle. This was not an easy task since Esther Williams, then and later, never professed to be an actress. And exhibition swimming is a limited form of expression.

Freed assigned studio writer Virginia Kellogg to write an original story. In a short time she delivered *Sing or Swim*. He liked the story and disliked the title. He changed it to *Bathing Beauty*.

The finale of the film obviously was going to be a water ballet and for this John Murray Anderson was brought out from New York. He had accumulated great experience in the staging of production numbers in such shows as *Jumbo,* three editions of the *Ziegfeld Follies,* and the last edition of the *Music Box Revue*.[20] He also had directed the *Aquacade* at the Exposition in San Francisco.

As far back as 1934 Irene Sharaff had created a sensation when the Ballet Russe engaged her to design the scenery and costumes for its productions of "Union Pacific" and Stravinsky's "The Poker Game." In the years following, among the many Broadway shows that not only bore her name but had her stamp on them were *The Great Waltz, The American Way, On Your Toes, The Boys From Syracuse* and *Lady in the Dark*. Freed had known of her work for a long time. Now he brought her out and put her under contract to work exclusively for him.

At that time the head costume designer at the studio was Irene Gibbons, professionally known as Irene. (She was married to Cedric Gibbons' brother.) Before joining the studio Irene had been a famous

[20] It was his work on *Ziegfeld Follies* and *Jumbo* that made Freed aware of his talent for spectacles.

OSCAR HAMMERSTEIN, 2ND

~~~~ ,November 27, 1942

Mr. Arthur Freed
Metro Goldwyn Mayer
Culver City
California

Dear Arthur:-

      I have recently written to Frank Orsatti
telling him why I am unable to go ahead with the
proposed two-year deal at Metro. I am anxious for you
to understand the circumstances that force me to
this decision, because I am deeply appreciative of
the confidence you and L.B. have expressed in me and
I would not lightly throw aside the opportunity you offer.

      The core of the trouble is that after
moving to the Coast and working at the studio for two
years, I would wind up by making no money at all! This
is a fantastic statement but it is mathematically true.
It has nothing to do with the proposed "ceiling on
incomes". The $65,000 a year the studio offered is
just within the limit. The problem arises because I
have a fairly substantial income without working. This
consists of royalties from A.S.C.A.P., sheet music,
records and the stock and radio rights of my old plays
(I am not considering any new plays or songs I may write -
just the income of my old catalogue which goes along at
a surprisingly steady and non-fluctuating rate) These
earnings, added to whatever dividends and interest I
receive from securities, nets me, after taxes, a sum
that is only a few thousand dollars less than I get when
I add to it the income I would receive from Metro and
subtract commissions and taxes. Even this small balance
would be consumed by the expense of moving my large family
to California and maintaining them there while still
owning two homes here in the East.

      I hate to take up your time with this
lengthy recitation of my personal problems but it is
the only way I can make clear to you why I cannot
possibly go ahead on the proposed basis. The only way
I can substantially add to my normal static income is
(1) writing a successful show, against which I don't have
to incurr these extra expenses and (2) taking separate
assignments in Hollywood not involving a permanent change

in residence so that I can deduct the travelling and
living expenses involved.

      There is another not inconsiderable item
and that is the fact that while living at Pennsylvania
I have no state income tax. At any rate, this has all
been computed carefully. My lawyer, Howard Reinheimer
and I have spent many hours with pad and pencil figuring
every possible angle and this is the way it adds up.
You see, if I had no source of income here in the East
it would be profitable for me to move to the West and
work under a contract like this. But having an income
the increased earnings under the new tax situation become
so ridiculously small that it just isn't worth while.

      Again I want to thank you and L.B. and I
hope you will both understand that, much as I enjoy
working with you, I cannot afford to give up so much
time with no hope of financial reward. The tax situation
is at present full of crazy, paradoxical cases and I just
happen to be one of them. I have told Frank that if
you want me to come out there on any specific job,
either as a writer or as your associate in any particular
production, I will be very happy to come. I would
particularly like to work on the Kern "Cavalcade" or
on my grandfather's biography.

      I have just finished the adaptation of
GREEN GROW THE LILACS for the Theatre Build. (as a matter
of fact, my script has been sent out to your studio.
I would like you to read it) I am now working with
Dick Rodgers on the songs and we expect to go into
rehearsal next month, opening in New York about Feb. 1.

      I hear extravagent reports about your
production of CABIN IN THE SKY. What a great achievement
if this finally cracks the old prejudice against negro
pictures - a great thing for pictures and a great thing
for the colored people.

      My best wishes to you and L.B. Please
explain my position to him.

      As ever,

fashion designer. She represented American haute couture at its best. The professional orientation of these two women, Sharaff and Irene, pointed in totally different directions. There was no conflict in their duties; on the contrary, for years to come they were collaborators on many projects. Occasionally, Irene designed costumes for period pictures, but her main interest was contemporary clothes.

Now Freed had Esther Williams, John Murray Anderson and Irene Sharaff, but no screenplay that he was happy with and, moreover, no composer that he could think of. Suddenly he was rescued from this dilemma. His secretary announced the arrival of Johnny Green.

It dawned on Freed why he had engaged Green: Edens had been classified 1-A and therefore had become eligible for draft. Freed anxiously awaited Edens' next birthday at which time he would become exempt. But to protect himself for any eventuality, he had thought of Green as a substitute.

Now the danger was over. He picked up the phone and called Jack Cummings. "Listen, Jack, you know L.B. wants me to do *Bathing Beauty*. I feel you should do it—after all, you practically discovered Esther. If you want it I have it all set up; you get Murray Anderson[21]; you get Sharaff; and you can have Johnny Green."

Green was ushered into the office.

"Listen, boy, I just fixed it . . . you're going to work for Jack Cummings . . . he's a brilliant producer . . . it'll be good training for you."

As Green says himself: "It was like a stab in the heart. Arthur Freed was stuck with me, Roger Edens is deferred, and Arthur has sold me. Arthur Freed disrupted my whole fucking life!"

"All right, I'll agree to this," said Mayer when Freed proposed giving Cummings the *Bathing Beauty* project. But Freed went further. "Jack has been sitting on *Girl Crazy* since 1939. I don't think he'll ever make it. I can do it right now. It's perfect for Mickey and Judy." Mayer leaned back and began to contemplate this idea. "I'll use Berkeley," Freed went on. "And I can use some of the cast from *Best Foot Forward*."

Mayer straightened up. "It's yours—go ahead with it." Freed had successfully made the trade he wanted.

The Cohn dispute was resolved. The deal on *Best Foot Forward* was set. The property was purchased for $150,000. Harry Cohn, who had been the initial bidder, was bought off for $25,000 and the services of Gene Kelly.[22]

[21] A year later he worked for Freed on *Ziegfeld Follies*.
[22] Cohn needed a costar for Rita Hayworth in *Cover Girl* and Kelly delivered. But not before some further reshuffling of productions—Kelly had already started rehearsals with Eleanor Powell for *Broadway Melody of 1943* (Roy del Ruth, director, Jack Cummings, producer). When he was pulled off the picture it was canceled, but some of the musical numbers ended up in *Thousands Cheer*.

George Abbott and Richard Rodgers were going to produce *Best Foot Forward* on Broadway. Hugh Martin and Ralph Blane auditioned for it. No strangers to the two producers, they had done the vocal arrangements for several of their shows. What had they written so far? They hadn't. Blane suggested they read the script. Blane recalls: "The next day we got together. Hugh had written 'I'm Going To Be a Shady Lady Bird.'" The Martins, as their quartet was called, demonstrated the songs at the Ethel Barrymore Theatre. The producers thought it was pretty good, but told them to "come back in six months."

"We went to our respective homes," Blane recalls. "The score was only thirteen songs away. When we met again, Hugh had the opening number, mine was the second, his was the third, mine was the fourth, etc. Our ESP must have been working." They came to New York and their package was bought. Freed acquired it along with Nancy Walker, Tommy Dix, Gil Stratton, Kenny Bowers, Jack Jordan, all from the Broadway show.[23]

When *Best Foot Forward* was announced, Freed sent the following letter to Lana Turner along with a copy of the script.

Dear Lana:

You will find in the script there's very little indicated from a musical end for you, but we can discuss that and go over it with Roger and the composers at your pleasure. I believe that this venture, which is so different from anything you've done, will win you many new friends and fans, and to the multitude you already have it will show your versatility in a comedy role—and Technicolor will add glamour and beauty, if such a thing is possible. Please call me when you have finished reading the script. I will be anxious to get your thoughts.

Sincerely,
Arthur Freed

Turner had to turn down the film: She was pregnant, and the role went to Lucille Ball, with a cast supplemented by Gloria De Haven, Harry James' Orchestra and, of course, June Allyson, who had been in the Broadway production.

John Cecil Holm's book was adapted for the screen by Irving Brecher and Fred Finklehoffe. It was directed by Edward Buzzell; the dance director was Charles Walters and the musical director was Lennie Hayton. Hayton did a splendid job on this picture, even though he was a jazz composer, arranger, and pianist and just short of being "avant-garde." This was his first job on a picture produced by

[23] The film casting was somewhat a game of musical chairs. Tommy Dix took Gil Stratton's original role, Kenny Bowers took Jack Jordan's role, and Jack Jordan took Bowers'.

Gloria De Haven (left), June Allyson, Jack Jordan and Kenny Bowers performing "Buckle Down Winsocki" from *Best Foot Forward*. M-G-M

Freed, but his presence in the Freed Unit was to be felt for years to come.[24]

Freed liked the picture, and it was a success.[25] Nonetheless, for Freed, it was just another step on the way to a more important future.

It is to be noted that *Girl Crazy* went into production two weeks earlier than *Best Foot Forward*. The latter production went along smoothly; this cannot be said of the former.

Berkeley started rehearsing and shooting the "I Got Rhythm" number in *Girl Crazy*. In it were Mickey and Judy, the Tommy Dorsey Orchestra and a gigantic corps of dancers. Edens had laid out the arrangement. Edens said: "We disagreed basically about the number's presentation. I wanted it rhythmic and simply staged; but Berkeley got his big ensembles and trick cameras into it again, plus a lot of girls in Western outfits, with fringe skirts and people cracking whips, firing guns . . . and cannons going off all over my arrangement and Judy's voice. Well, we shouted at each other, and I said, 'There wasn't enough room on the lot for both of us.'" It appeared that Edens got his way. The number shot the budget an extra $97,418.99. This, together with extreme strain and hostility between Judy and Berkeley,

[24] Freed was instrumental in originally bringing Hayton to Metro in 1934. And when he returned in 1942, he was put under a long-term contract.
[25] The final cost on *Best Foot Forward* was $1,125,502 and it grossed $2,704,000.

Norman Taurog and Mickey
Rooney between scenes.
M-G-M

caused Freed to dismiss him.[26] The production was shut down for a
month. It resumed under Norman Taurog's direction.

In the picture Mickey plays a budding New York playboy, who
is sent West by his father to attend a college for men only. Judy and
Nancy Walker, the dean's granddaughters, are the only two girls
around the campus. And we know who Mickey falls for. Believing
Mickey to be a snob, Judy takes him for an automobile ride to teach
him—the hard way—the way of the West. Judy leaves him stranded in
the desert. Mickey mends his ways, stays on and pulls the college out
of debt.

The entire Gershwin score of the Broadway show was used in the
picture,[27] with the exception of "Fascinating Rhythm" (taken from
Lady Be Good).

The "Could You Use Me?" number (the automobile ride) was
to be shot on a barren strip of desert just outside Palm Springs. Why
was it not shot on the studio's back lot? Rooney wanted to go to
Palm Springs. The crew, consisting of dozens of people, including
hairdressers, make-up men, etc., left in a caravan of limousines, trucks
and buses, on a Sunday at 2 P.M. for what was to be a week's work.
Three cars were coupled together: Mickey and Judy were to be in the
first one; the camera was to be mounted in the second; the third to
carry the playback. Charles Walters, the dance director, began re-

[26] Berkeley was loaned out to Twentieth Century-Fox for *The Girl He Left
Behind* (released in the United States as *The Gang's All Here*).

[27] The 1932 RKO film had only a few songs from the Broadway show. The
Gershwins did write some new songs for that production, but Freed reverted to the
original show.

hearsing Judy and Mickey late in the day.[28] The next morning rehearsals were resumed. But at noon the cast went back to their hotel because technical difficulties had to be straightened out.

The third morning everything was ready and shooting was to begin at 8 A.M. Mickey arrived, but there was no Judy. In the blasting desert heat equipment now had to be temporarily covered up, and members of the crew sought in vain the shade of the few dressing tents. The waiting began. Suddenly, as in a movie about the Sahara, a ripple of sand rose from the ground. Within minutes, a sandstorm of dangerous intensity covered and crippled equipment, blinded and choked the personnel. The dressing tents simply flew off. For fear of being blown away, one female crew member desperately held on to the only tent pole still upright, stuffing a handkerchief into her nose. Taurog took pity and motioned her to get into one of the stand-by limousines to return to town. Duty bound, Taurog kept the crew for another ten minutes hoping for the storm to subside. Then he broke up the set.

Where was Judy? A romantic entanglement had apparently drawn her back to Los Angeles. She had left early in the morning without a word.

Everybody was idle. The crew, dispersed in various hotels, was bored and took to drink. Edens, Taurog and Walters were staying at the Desert Inn, at that time the only luxury hotel. And this idleness bred tension. One evening Edens, fully clothed, was thrown into the swimming pool.

[28] Walters also appears in the film dancing with Judy Garland in the production number "Embraceable You."

Judy Garland performing Gershwin's "Bidin' My Time." M-G-M

Days went by. Judy eventually returned and the number was photographed.

Part of the equipment had been ruined by the sandstorm and the better part of the number was reshot at the studio.

When Berkeley was replaced by Taurog and the production was suspended for a month, the schedules of Judy Garland as well as Gil Stratton, Nancy Walker and June Allyson were thrown out of kilter. During the delay Judy had to start her next picture *Presenting Lily Mars;* it could not be put off. This meant shuttling back and forth from one picture to another. The same was true of Stratton, Walker and Allyson who were simultaneously in *Best Foot Forward.*

Girl Crazy was completed on May 19, 1943. The cost was $1,410,850.85. It exceeded its budget by $322,935.30. In its release, November 26, 1943, it grossed $3,771,000.

Meet the People was unique in Freed's pictures in more than one way. For the first time in his entire career he engaged another man as producer: E. Y. Harburg. He himself became the executive producer. This already points to the fact that he had great misgivings. The picture not only turned out to be a crude and obvious film, but it also brought on the wrath of both the right and the left, in a political atmosphere already dominated by Joseph McCarthy. It also created serious difficulties during the next decade in Harburg's career.

"The hero is the people," says Harburg of his film. "The story takes the point of view that the people, after all, are running the country. . . ."

All that can be said about the cast is that June Allyson met Dick Powell. Also included were Lucille Ball, the Four King Sisters, Virginia O'Brien, Bert Lahr, Vaughn Monroe and Spike Jones and his City Slickers. The songs were mainly written by Harburg, with the assistance of Burton Lane, Harold Arlen and Sammy Fain.
So much for *Meet the People.*

So much for *Meet the People.*

Freed looked for and found the next picture for Mickey Rooney: *Honey Boy,* the life story of George "Honey Boy" Evans, one of America's great minstrel men. Gene Kelly was to appear as another great minstrel man, Evans' closest pal. Circumstances interfered with Freed's plans for Mickey.[29] But he had very concrete plans for Judy.

From his beginnings as a budding producer, Freed was responsible for the following:

[29] Rooney's induction caused a delay in making the film.

Judy takes a look at Mickey's
first-class sunburn on the
Palm Springs location.
Chuck Walters (left) and
Roger Edens (between the
two stars) look on. M-G-M

Judy, Lela Simone and Mickey along with script girl sitting atop the sound
truck on location. M-G-M

Kaprelick's drawing of *Girl Crazy* appeared on the cover of M-G-M's monthly magazine *Lion's Roar*. M-G-M

Internationally renowned artist Verté's conception for *Meet the People*'s exploitation. M-G-M

He was essential in the production of *The Wizard of Oz.* He produced *Babes in Arms, Strike Up the Band, Little Nellie Kelly, Lady Be Good, Babes on Broadway* and *Panama Hattie.* He acquired and/or put into preparation *Good News* and *Very Warm for May.* He obtained studio contracts for Judy Garland, Eleanor Powell, Ray McDonald, Lena Horne, Ben Blue, Rags Ragland, Margaret O'Brien, Harold Arlen, E. Y. Harburg, Jack McGowan, Fred Finklehoffe, John Monks, Jr., Elsie Janis, Busby Berkeley and Vincente Minnelli. He brought to the studio on special assignment Alfred Newman and Alexander Woollcott. He wrote the following songs: "Good Morning" (*Babes in Arms*), with Nacio Herb Brown and "Our Love Affair" (*Babes on Broadway*) with Roger Edens; both songs have become standards. He bought Jerome Kern-Oscar Hammerstein's "The Last Time I Saw Paris" (*Lady Be Good*), which won the Academy Award.

In the year 1942, Arthur Freed brought William Saroyan to the studio and induced him to write *The Human Comedy.* He produced *For Me and My Gal, Du Barry Was a Lady, Cabin in the Sky, Best Foot Forward* and *Meet the People.* He acquired *Show Boat, Jumbo, The Red Mill, Honey Boy* and *Meet Me in St. Louis.* He began to prepare *Meet Me in St. Louis* and *Ziegfeld Follies.* He obtained studio contracts for Gene Kelly, June Allyson, Zero Mostel, Hugh Martin, Ralph Blane, Lew Brown, Sammy Fain, Johnny Green, John Murray Anderson, Charles Walters, Irene Sharaff, Lennie Hayton and Albert Lewis. He brought designer Vertes to the studio on special assignment.

From here on, Freed's production schedule set a precedent not only for this period but for the next twenty years that has never been equaled in films. To keep up this pace would have been practically impossible on dramatic films. But musicals are another story. And what emerged was the Freed Unit: a handful of highly talented and highly efficient people.

4   *MEET ME IN ST. LOUIS*

The address of 5135 Kensington Avenue, St. Louis, Missouri, is that of the large, comfortable home of the Smith family. The time is the summer of 1903, just about eight months prior to the opening of the St. Louis World's Fair, the Louisiana Purchase Exposition.

The family consists of Mr. and Mrs. Alonzo Smith, their seventeen-year-old son Lon, Jr., their two adolescent girls Esther and Rose, and the two youngest children Agnes and Tootie, along with Grandfather Prophater and Katie, the spinster maid.

In this particular neighborhood, the Smiths have established their own little world. Each has planted his roots deep in the soil. Esther is in love with the boy next door; Rose has her eyes on a dashing young millionaire of her "set"; Lon, having just graduated from high school, is fast assuming the role of "Joe College"; the two children Agnes and Tootie are immersed in the home, the neighborhood—all the familiar faces and things they have been brought up with. Within the secure boundaries of her existence, Tootie gives her imagination free reign. Strapping old Grandpa and Katie are beloved adjuncts to the family circle.

This closely knit and loving family is looking forward to 1904 and the opening of the Fair with pride and anticipation. However, the father, an ambitious man, wants better things for his family.

90

The security and serenity of their lives are shattered when he announces his decision to accept a lucrative position in New York. After all members of the family have voiced their objections, it is the mother who finally silences them. They will have one more Christmas at home and after that they will leave for New York.

Preparations begin. But all of them are miserable at having to miss the opening of the Fair in their beloved city. The father finally realizes this and assembles the entire household and tells them that they are not moving. He has discovered that there are more opportunities in St. Louis than he ever dreamed of! This is the greatest Christmas present for the whole family. And that night, for the first time in weeks, they all go to sleep secure and at peace.

In the spring of 1904 the Smiths are among the first visitors at the Fair, glowing with pride.

Does this charming family portrait lend itself for a film script? Evidently Freed thought so.

Sally Benson, who grew up in St. Louis in a similar neighborhood, said about her "Kensington Stories": "Nothing much happens, just little incidents. The villain is New York City. It's sort of like a Valentine in the palm of your hand. . . ."

She also remarked that the St. Louis Fair opened four years before her story opens, not the previous year. But in *Meet Me in St. Louis,* this was changed and the film builds up to the opening of the Fair, with which the picture ends.

Freed is a sentimental man. He, no doubt, identified with this family, nostalgic for the security and closeness which he as a young man wanted and never found, since his family life was constantly disrupted by geographic displacements. "What I wanted to make was a simple story," says Freed, "a story that basically says, 'There's no place like home.'" It is interesting to remember that it was Freed who had said regarding *The Wizard of Oz:* "The only way to get Judy back to Kansas is by her saying, 'There's no place like home.'"

Freed had no script, no score and no cast. Mayer and the rest of the executives would have to be made familiar with the Benson stories,[1] and convinced of their merit. So far his only tangible asset was Judy Garland.

Mayer never read a script. At the time there were two women at the studio, Lillie Messinger and Harriet Frank; the former had previously been with the story department at RKO, the latter was a writer. They occasionally were called upon to read scripts, parts of books, short sto-

[1] During the time Benson was at the studio (March 30–May 9, 1942), working on a screen treatment, she assembled her stories into novel form and it was published at the end of that year by Random House under the film's title. Freed had taken it, along with the song of the same title written by Andrew Sterling and Kerry Mills.

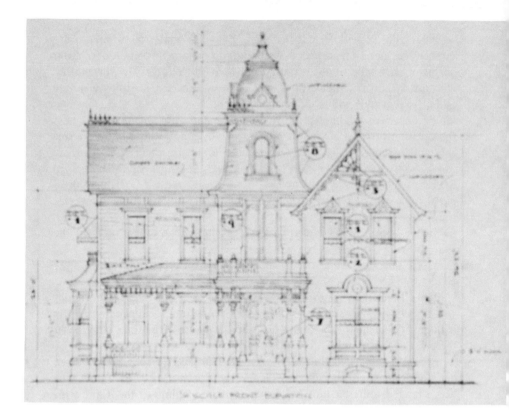

The art department's architectural blueprint for part of the "St. Louis Street." M-G-M

As the Smith and Truett houses looked after they were completed. M-G-M

ries—anything printed—to Mayer. "I was Mr. Mayer's favorite story-teller," says Lillie Messinger. "So, if Arthur wanted Mr. Mayer to like a story he asked me to tell it to him. I think I understood Mr. Mayer very well and the things he would like in a story, and that helps you in telling it." This could possibly conjure up the picture of a contemporary Sheherazade, young, seductive, spinning her tale. But Lillie Messinger was just a middle-aged, soft spoken, knowledgeable, lady. Miss Messinger told Mayer the story of *Meet Me in St. Louis:* She emphasized, she omitted, occasionally invented, and this special gift plus her intimate knowledge of Mayer's tastes brought many an author fame and fortune where otherwise his output would have wound up in a wastepaper basket.

Collectively and individually, Thau, Mannix, Katz, Cohn, L. K. Sidney, the knights around the conference table, voiced their negative opinions. There is no plot, no action, no conflict. Freed jumped right into the battle. "There is no conflict? These people are fighting for their happiness! Where is the villain? Well, the villain is New York!! What more do you want?!"

Katz was especially emphatic. "What the hell is Arthur trying to do? After all the glamour he has given us! What is in this dull family moving to New York? And this bit about 'there's no place like home?' "

"What's the matter with you guys?" Mayer asked. "I think the story is very exciting, there's a lot of action! And what about those girls who have to leave their home and their sweethearts? I tell you, it broke my heart!"

Lillie Messinger had done her job well.

Freed summoned Finklehoffe, a logical move since it was he who had called Freed's attention to the Benson stories in the first place. "Write me a screenplay, you like the Benson stories so much!" Finklehoffe was momentarily devoid of his usual self-assurance. "Gee, Arthur, I don't want to do this alone—would you mind if Irving Brecher worked with me?" Freed agreed. "Get anybody you want, but get it done."

As Finklehoffe explains: "I always worked better with another guy because I have no discipline—and I know it. Brecher is a very disciplined fellow. He'd say 'Get back in this room and sit down.' And once I get into it, I can do it!"

Brecher and Finklehoffe started working together.[2] "Nobody bothered us," continues Finklehoffe, "which was unusual, because most of the time they would pick on you and knock your brains in and say, 'I don't like it.' That was the thing I liked about Arthur. He didn't want to write the script himself, he just wanted you to do it. That's why he was always so successful—because he was immensely cognizant of creative people and treated them as such. All the rest of those alliga-

---

[2] They had to first remove themselves from their current assignment, *Anchors Aweigh.*

tors thought they were creative: they weren't. They were in the salmon business and didn't know it."

As Brecher says, *"Meet Me in St. Louis,* was a very hair-raising experience for many, many reasons, covering quite a bit of time. There were a number of scripts: a treatment by Benson, a script by Mason and Heerman, and another by a friend of mine, Bill Ludwig, all of which I read and felt were very far off. So did the studio. Anyway, I liked the characters Benson had created. So Freddie and I went to work. It was very difficult because Finklehoffe was out of town many times, on other business.[3] Freed would call Freddie to find out how things were going, because he believed whatever Freddie would tell him; he had a particular fondness for him, as compared to me. Then I would have to cover up by telling Freed that Freddie had just stepped out for a cigarette or something—and I would contact Freddie and tell him to call Freed."

In spite of all this maneuvering, they finished a draft in six weeks and handed it to Freed.

Freed's initial notion had been to make a small, intimate period picture, interspersed with musical material of the era. After reading the Finklehoffe-Brecher script, his conception of the picture began to change. What had originally appealed to him was the simplicity, sincerity and warmth of these people. To be sure, there was no plot in the true sense of the word. The emotional impact of daily life, with its laughter and its sorrow, had to be brought out. Now Freed felt that this could best be done with music.

The art department prepared a layout of sets for the production. The Smith house, for one, was to be in the existing "Andy Hardy Street," dressed up a là St. Louis of the period. The layout was practical, not very imaginative and not too costly. Freed did not look at it with much interest. His mind was going full speed in another direction and he went to see his boss.

"Is the script finished?" Mayer asked. "It's finished all right, but, it's not the picture I want to make! The boys are all harping on 'there's no plot!' Well, I'll make a plot with song and dance and music. That's the way my characters will come to life—that'll be my plot!"

"Meaning what?" Mayer asked.

"I want to make this into the most delightful piece of Americana ever. Sets, costumes . . . it'll cost a bit, but it'll be great!" Mayer sat up, just a trifle anxious. "And I'll get a great score," Freed added.

"Well, Arthur," Mayer said, "go ahead. Either you'll learn or we'll learn."

"The plans have changed," Mr. Smith will tell his family in the final

---

[3] Finklehoffe had been moonlighting by producing a legit musical revue *Show Time*. Ed Wynn was the star and Minnelli came in to doctor the show for its première in Los Angeles (April 15, 1943).

script. Freed's plans had also changed and he began to set them in motion.[4]

Assuming that his assignment was finished, Finklehoffe departed, without a word to anyone. Because of his fondness for the man, Freed decided to overlook this unorthodox behavior.

Now Minnelli enters the scene and very importantly so. Brecher was retained. He describes his collaboration with Minnelli: "I'd read a scene and act it out for him. He'd listen with his eyes closed . . . a very bright, sensitive, talented person. He would nudge me into a better line of dialogue, a better curtain line here and there. He was particularly helpful in a couple of love scenes, especially the one between Esther and John after the Christmas party, under the tree out in the snow. He made me write that scene as it is now in the picture, and I was very grateful for his help."

Minnelli saw the characters like players in a lovingly written family chronicle, alive in a setting of the period.

Judy came to see Minnelli. She took him completely by surprise when she told him she did not want to do the picture. Joseph Mankiewicz, writer-director, had intimated that her part in the picture was not the starring role, that the star was the youngest sister Tootie. Others had warned her this role would set her back twenty years. Minnelli remembers the incident. "Judy came to me. She thought—a director from New York. 'This is awful!' she said, 'isn't it?' I said, 'No, I think it's marvelous,' and I answered all her questions. But she left, still confused."

Brecher also remembers: "In a last desperate move, Freed persuaded Judy to at least listen to the script, before she decided not to do it. Happily in my reading the script, I convinced her that hers was a great part."

Two days later, *Daily Variety* announced M-G-M's forthcoming Technicolor musical production *Meet Me in St. Louis,* starring Judy Garland.

The film had now taken on a different dimension. It was to be treated with special expertise in every department. The Andy Hardy Street was *not* going to be the street the Smith family lived on in St. Louis. The art department, brilliant as it was, nonetheless, was too bound up in Hollywood clichés. The presentation of the production needed the style and imagination of Broadway at its best, transposed to the screen. And so, Lemuel Ayers, the Broadway designer, who had just made a big name for himself with the sets for *Oklahoma!* was engaged. Freed was taking every precaution against the apathy and nega-

---

[4] "The plans have been changed" became a familiar expression on many other pictures that Freed produced. It was used, however, as the opening greeting from one member of the Freed Unit to another relative to the project(s) they were working on.

Hugh Martin (seated) and Ralph Blane at the time they were in the Freed Unit and composed the score for *Meet Me in St. Louis.* RALPH BLANE COLLECTION

tivism that prevailed at the studio toward this project. He surrounded himself with the best talent he could muster.

The studio's art director on the picture, Jack Martin Smith, and Ayers went to work, made their designs and submitted them for budgeting.

At the time that the Andy Hardy Street had been considered, the set contructions and alterations on the exterior houses had been estimated at $58,275. The "St. Louis Street" would cost $208,275 to build. A decision had to be left in abeyance until the entire production was set up and a complete budget was formally submitted for approval. Landscape architects co-ordinated their designs with those of the two art directors: trees, shrubs and flower beds would have to be planted, street lights put up and the street had to be paved.

Things slowly began to take shape. But there was—as yet—no score.

Hugh Martin and Ralph Blane were coaching young studio starlet Marilyn Maxwell. She was just learning "Skip to My Lou"[5] when Freed came in to hear her. Instantly Martin froze. "He always did when Freed was around," Blane remembers. Whenever he and his partner would have any dealings with Freed, "Hugh would run to the

[5] Freed had originally intended using this traditional song in his first concept for the film.

'hang-out'[6] to have a double martini and, clutching it in the palm of his hand, would say, 'Blessed juice!' " It was Maxwell's rendition of the song that convinced Freed that he had found the songwriters for his picture. He added these two film novices to the talent he had already assembled.

The casting of the picture doesn't seem to have presented any problems—after everybody had survived the Judy Garland shock, that is—except for one crucially important part, the Smiths' youngest child, Tootie. Minnelli wanted Margaret O'Brien. "I was responsible for discovering her," recalls Minnelli. "One day I was in Arthur's office and an agent came in with Margaret. I remember she was wearing a little Scottish plaid kilt and a Scottish cap. The agent said: 'This is Mr. Freed. Would you audition for him?' She went right over to his desk and said: 'Don't send my father to the chair—don't let him fry!' Arthur's reaction was utter amazement. I went into Finklehoffe's office where he was working on an audition scene to be used in *Babes on Broadway* and said, 'I've just seen the most remarkable kid—you've just got to use her in that scene—in just the same outfit, the same costume and the same words!' And that's what we did. After that she did *Journey for Margaret,* in which she played a disturbed child from the war zone. She became celebrated as a child star who could cry, get hysterical, etc. Well, by the time I got her, George Sidney's wife, Lillian Burns, a coach at the studio, had been working with her. Well, Margaret was like a Shakespearean actress. I went out of my mind getting her to be a child again . . . to act natural and be like a kid."

The major parts in *Meet Me in St. Louis* were cast as follows: Mr. and Mrs. Smith were played by Leon Ames and Mary Astor; their four daughters, Esther, Rose, Agnes and Tootie, by Judy Garland, Lucille Bremer,[7] Joan Carroll and Margaret O'Brien; their son Lon, Jr., by Henry Daniels, Jr.; Grandpa by Harry Davenport; the maid Katie by Marjorie Main; and John Truett, the boy next door, by Van Johnson. Ultimately, Johnson did not play the part and it was recast with Tom Drake.

Meet Me in St. Louis was not going to be a musical with one number chasing the next one. When Martin and Blane read the script they realized that each of the songs had to be as good, as polished, as pertinent as any of the dialogue scenes.

---

[6] The "hang-out" was also known by its proprietor's name, Frances Edwards. It was located in an alley adjacent to the front gate of the Metro lot. Miss Edwards started the restaurant-bar, having been the hostess at the studio commissary for many years.

[7] Lucille Bremer was making her film debut in this picture. She started her professional career at the Copacabana in New York. From there she played the ingénue lead in the musical *Lady in the Dark*. After it closed, she was featured in a revue at the Versailles Club where she was spotted by Arthur Freed and signed by M-G-M.

For example, a song was needed in Scene No. 90 of the shooting script:

TROLLEY DEPOT—ST. LOUIS—LATE AFTERNOON

A trolley is there. Some youngsters on it, but a good number are still outside, chatting gaily.

Quentin (shouts)

Let her go, motorman!

The trolley starts and the crowd starts to sing.

"Hugh and I thought it was too corny to be on the nose in writing a song about a trolley," said Blane. "Instead we went home and wrote a marvelous song that would be great to sing *on* the trolley—not *about* it. We came in with one number called 'Know Where You're Goin' and You'll Get There.' It was a big rousing Negro spiritual. We loved it and so did Roger. Arthur said, 'I love it! It's great. But,' he said, 'you know what, I'll use it in *The Follies*. I know exactly where it should go. Now, about the spot where Judy sings about the trolley, I think we need a song *about* the trolley here.'" Blane continues, "We knew he was not happy with the number for that spot, so we went home and tried again. We wrote four numbers. Each time we'd feel we had a smash. They'd love it, but Arthur would say 'I'll put it in *The Follies*.' He wanted a song *about* the trolley. He was right, but we didn't think so. Anyway, in desperation, and a bit of anger too, we went home and just said, 'Oh, hell! Let's just write something about the trolley, and to hell with it!'"

Exasperated, Blane went to the Beverly Hills Public Library and found some books about old St. Louis. He found a photograph of a double-decker trolley of 1903. "Believe it or not, under the picture was written 'Clang, Clang, Clang, Went the Trolley.' Well, I dashed back—told Hugh the title and we wrote it in about ten minutes."

With Martin at the piano and Blane's rich tenor voice, they demonstrated their new version of "The Trolley Song" in Edens' office, with Freed and the whole group around them. "That's the song for Judy!" said Freed.

Their first hurdle was over. The next song needed was for a scene in which Judy and her little sister, Margaret O'Brien, are contemplating their last Christmas at home. In the script the two are in Esther's bedroom, sitting at the window looking out over the snow-covered ground, Tootie sadly realizing that they can't take the snowmen with them, which they had had such fun building.

"When we did the song for them," recalls Blane, "it went like this:

" 'Have yourself a merry little Christmas
  It may be your last
  Next year we will all be living in the past . . .'

98

"The mood of the song was negative. Roger didn't say anything, nor did Arthur; but they brought Judy in to hear it. 'I love the song,' Judy said, 'but it's too sad. If that lyric is sad and I'm sad on top of it, the audience is going to say, "Oh, my God," and they're going to be leaving the theatre.'"

Martin did not agree with Judy's criticism. But Blane changed it to begin:

> "Have yourself a merry little Christmas
> Let your heart be light
> Next year all our troubles will be out of sight
> Have yourself a merry little Christmas
> Let your heart be gay
> Next year all your troubles will be miles away."

After hearing Blane's revisions, Martin concurred. Judy loved it and that's the way it was used in the picture.

There were no problems connected with the writing of "The Boy Next Door." This song is a classic example of how to advance a story and bring the emotional state of a character to the surface without lengthy and trivial dialogue.

If they eventually wrote a splendid score for the picture, it was due to the presence of Edens. Playing an active part in designing the fabric of the picture, he made them aware of the musical incidentals which they, doubling as the film's vocal arrangers, would be responsible for. There would be, obviously, "Meet Me in St. Louis," the standard by Sterling and Mills, "You and I," a new song written by Brown and Freed, "Skip to My Lou," the traditional song which, by making major revisions in their arrangement, the songwriters received credit as having written, and another "oldie," "Under the Bamboo Tree," by Bob Cole. But when they found out that Freed had bought a song from Rodgers and Hammerstein entitled "Boys and Girls Like You and Me,"[8] they felt insulted. "Of course, with a Rodgers and Hammerstein song in the picture it would make the rest of the score sound like small potatoes," Blane remarks. "I mean, we weren't anybody at this point. This picture, we felt, would make or break us as songwriters. True, we had *Best Foot Forward* with its "Buckle Down Winsocki," but we really hadn't hit yet, and it just killed me! But not Hugh! He is a paradox. He's one of the nicest people I know—I've never heard him bitch. Anyway, they were going to put the song at the end of the picture in the World's Fair sequence." Blane made an astute prophecy: "Let them have their fun with their prodigious Rodgers and Hammerstein; the song is placed too late in the picture—people will already be reaching for their hats—it'll come out—you watch and see!"

[8] The song had been written for *Oklahoma!,* but was taken out of the show before it reached Broadway.

Dear Arthur:

Dick and I happened to look at a communication from your music department to our publisher. It contained this description:

"The trolley arrives at the place where the World's Fair is to be built and the people get off the trolley. Esther wanders by herself and John tries to find her so she won't be late for the return trolley. John sees Esther in a romantic setting—he comes up and they walk and talk. As they come to a mud puddle John picks up Esther in his arms, then she sings 'Boys and Girls Like You and Me.'"

We wouldn't presume to make any criticism three thousand miles away, but for whatever the comment is worth, we were disturbed by the incongruous feeling of going into a song which talks about girls and boys walking through the world with a girl held in the arms of a boy and the public distracted by marveling at his feat of strength, listening to the lyric and music and being enthralled thereby.

For all we know, the number may never have been shot like this or maybe it hasn't been shot at all yet. In case it hasn't been, we are hereby recording our fears for this way of going into it.

I hear you are coming to town soon. Am looking forward to seeing you.

As ever,
Oscar

Dear Oscar:

I hasten to reply to your letter about the rendition of "Boys and Girls," and also to allay your fears that the song was shot according to the notice sent to the publishers, which you quoted.

I am sure that you will be very happy when you see the rendition which we have photographed. It is done very simply, without any superhistrionics, by Judy Garland to her boy friend. The camera is on Judy's face throughout the whole rendition and all she does is sing the tender philosophy of your lyrics.

Again I repeat I am sure that you and Dick will feel very gratified at the manner in which Vincente Minnelli so simply and eloquently presented this wonderful song. I am anxious for you to see it.

As always,
Arthur

Blane was just speculating. At this point the design and the construction of the St. Louis Street took priority over everything else; the budget had been approved and its execution was handled with the care one normally applies to the casting of a star in a major role. Smith and Ayers brought in models for inspection and approval so that construction could start.

Models were also made showing the interiors of the Smith house. These models were constructed in great detail, not only for authenticity but to help Minnelli plan how he wanted to direct certain scenes in certain rooms, which in turn entailed camera moves, lighting, etc. Ayers occupied himself especially with decorative aspects of each interior. He designed grillwork and ornamentation for the exteriors; designed wall papers; suggested certain furnishings, down to such supposedly "insignificant" items as a small lamp or a piece of bric-a-brac.[9] He and Smith worked together on all visual aspects. Smith's contribution, moreover, was invaluable in respect to technical details; with his vast motion-picture experience, he translated many of Minnelli and Ayers's ideas into cinematic practicalities.

Irene Sharaff had done some costumes for *Girl Crazy* and *Bathing Beauty*. These had been merely fill-ins. Now she was confronted with the task of doing her first costume design for an entire motion picture. One of her unique qualities was her constant awareness of the decors her costumes would have to play in. In *Meet Me in St. Louis,* they would have to be authentic, yet imaginative, enhancing a curlicued, gingerbready, overstuffed period. Sharaff would have to cope with a whole new scale of color values, predicated on lighting for the camera, completely different from that of the stage. All this was a challenge, but there was no limit to the possibilities. It triggered her imagination and she went to work with enormous enthusiasm.

Some of the most exciting and rewarding hours during the making of this film were those spent on the recording stage.

Conrad Salinger, arranger and orchestrator, had been assigned to do the score. He had written brilliant arrangements for Freed pictures in the past, but he reached a new height in *Meet Me in St. Louis.*

Being a native Bostonian and always impeccably dressed by Brooks Brothers, Salinger was in looks and manner the antithesis of what musicians presumably are like. He had spent years in Paris, studying harmony and orchestration with Nadja Boulanger and had had some lessons with Ravel. He spoke perfect French and was in all respects the epitome of a "man of the world."

He had started his career on Broadway. Returning to New York after seven years in Paris, he met Adolph Deutsch, who at the time was musical director of the Paramount-Publix theatres. Deutsch engaged Salinger as his chief orchestrator. A short time later Deutsch moved over to the legitimate theatre and the two worked together on several Broadway shows.

Salinger came to Hollywood in 1938 to work for Alfred Newman at Twentieth Century-Fox. It was only a short stay however, because Salinger's first impression of Hollywood was not a pleasant one. He returned to New York and the Broadway theatre, but came back in 1939 when M-G-M offered him a long-term contract that he could not resist.

[9] Ayers brought along his assistant Lillian Braun, who at one point was dispatched to New York on a buying trip.

Edens, who was well aware of Salinger's work and had met him in New York, saw to it that he immediately joined the Freed Unit.

In musical terms, Edens and Salinger spoke the same language. Not much needed to be said. Edens would simply intimate the mood, the tempo, the texture and the setting of a prospective number to get Salinger on the right path. Even after the orchestra's first reading of his arrangement of "The Trolley Song," an excitement spread among those playing and listening. Then, when Judy came in with her dead-sure instinct of what she was to deliver, the ceiling seemed to fly off the stage. Take 1 was a print! Blane interfered. "But, Roger, Judy sang a wrong lyric!"

"She'll never do it like that again," replied Edens. "No one will ever know the few words she changed—she'll simply synchronize them!"

Salinger's arrangement was a masterpiece. It conveyed all the color, the motion, the excitement that eventually was going to be seen on the screen. With the remaining numbers and the background scoring for this film as well as all the work he was to do thereafter, Salinger always maintained sonority and texture in his writing, which made his a very special sound and style that has never been equaled in the American movie musical.

An interesting event on the recording stage: Leon Ames's voice needed to be dubbed and Minnelli didn't want a trained voice. So it was Arthur Freed who did the dubbing of "You and I," the song that he and Nacio Herb Brown had written.

There was another aspect of the Salinger sound. During those years, musical directors, vocal arrangers, orchestrators worked under the maxim: "The bigger the orchestra, the larger the vocal group—the bigger and better the sound." There was as yet no tape; sound was recorded on film. It soon became obvious—at least to the sound technicians, if not the musical directors—that the one-hundred-men orchestra and the oversized vocal group were not an asset. Film can only take a limited volume of sound, and when that point is reached, the film track becomes overloaded, the sound deteriorates and becomes distorted. Salinger's writing sounded best with thirty-six or thirty-eight men, because that was the number of players he had conceived his score for. Blane too, asked the music department not to overpower him with vocal groups resembling the Tabernacle Choir—just let him have twenty-four first-rate voices, good musicians, preferably those who could read music. Although not by design, this greatly reduced costs. Conversely, the music tracks for one of the big (non-Freed) M-G-M musicals of that period was recorded with an orchestra of 120 men. The recording stage could not accommodate that many people and the band was moved to the largest shooting stage on the lot. The sessions were complete bedlam; the results were less than adequate, to say the least, and the cost was prohibitive.

102

Meet Me in St. Louis went into production on November 11, 1943. The opening sequence of the picture was shot first. On a hot summer day in 1903 one sees a perspiring mailman approaching the Smith house at 5135 Kensington Avenue. He is whistling "Meet me in St. Louis, Looey." Lon Smith, Jr., rides up on his bicycle, loaded with groceries, picking up the tune; while the melody continues on a harmonica, one sees Mrs. Smith in her kitchen, bent over the stove, stirring ketchup in a large copper kettle. Katie the maid, enters and tastes the ketchup: "Too sweet!" Now Lon enters and tastes: "Too flat!" Agnes, dripping wet from a mishap with a garden hose, walks through the kitchen and on her way upstairs, picks up the tune for a few bars when Grandpa Prophater, almost colliding with her, joins in. Esther enters the kitchen, tastes: "Too sour!" The spirited singing of Grandpa and Agnes finishes with: "Meet Me in St. Louis, Looey, meet me at the Fair!" Then Rose enters and tells her sister Esther, "There's John Truett."

In less than five minutes, one feels as if he has known these people and the house they live in all his life. Then Minnelli introduces Tootie, the youngest member of the Smith family.

FULL SHOT—SHADY TREE-LINED STREET—A YELLOW WAGON

with a large word, ICE comes creaking down the street TOWARD CAMERA. Driving is Mr. Neely, the iceman, pipe in mouth, sleeves rolled up, leaning forward, elbows on knees. He pays no attention to the horse, who knows the route so well. As wagon PASSES CAMERA, WE MOVE UP TO rear of wagon. Inside, on a cake of ice (using a burlap pad as a cushion) sits Tootie Smith, a pixie with her hair screwed into a knot that crowns her head. Her dress is wet from the ice she is sucking. The wagon stops with a jolt. Tootie is shaken from her reverie.

Tootie

Who gets ice now, Mr. Neely?
(she gets up and goes to driver's seat)

EXT. DRIVER'S SEAT

Mr. Neely and Tootie, looking up at him from inside the wagon.

Mr. Neely

No one, Tootie.
(indicates horse)
Robin can't seem to remember that Mrs. Wilkins has moved.
Clucks to horse which resumes slow march down street. Tootie meanwhile clambers up on seat next to Mr. Neely. A scraggly white-faced rag doll lies on seat between them on a small piece of cloth.

Minnelli set to start the first day of shooting the exterior set. M-G-M

              Tootie (gently feeling doll's forehead)
Poor Margaretha . . . never seen her look so pale.

              Mr. Neely (seriously)
Sun'll do her good.

              Tootie
I expect she won't live through the night. She has four fatal diseases . . .

              Mr. Neely (shaking head)
And it only takes *one*.

              Tootie (shaking head)
But she's going to have a beautiful funeral . . .
  (nods head)
in a cigar box my poppa gave me . . . wrapped in silver paper.

              Mr. Neely (impressed)
That's the way to go . . . if you have to go.

              Tootie (definitely)
Oh—she *has* to go!
  Mr. Neely looks straight ahead, chewing his pipestem. Tootie,
  in perfect nonsequitur:

104

Tootie (indicates horse)

Mr. Neely . . . is Robin a girl horse or a boy horse?

Mr. Neely

Girl.

Tootie

How old is she?

Mr. Neely

Four.

Tootie

She's awful big for four . . . *I'm* five. Is she strong?

Mr. Neely (with pride)

She's the strongest ice horse in St. Louis.

Tootie (with a shade more politeness than heretofore, but with very definite confidence)

Excuse me, Mr. Neely, but it's pronounced St. Lewis.

Mr. Neely

Is it now? I've got a cousin . . . spells it the same way. We call him Louis.

Tootie (undaunted)

He's not a city, though, is he?

Mr. Neely (hesitantly)

Uh . . . no.

Tootie

Is he a saint?

Mr. Neely (thinks this over; then)

Mmm—no.

Tootie (shrugs, with finality)

Then there's no comparison.

Mr. Neely

Anyway, she's a great old town.

Tootie (rapidly)

It isn't a town, Mr. Neely. It's a city. It's the *only* city that has a World's Fair.
   (wagon stops. Tootie, with doll, jumps off)
My favorite. Wasn't I lucky to be born in my favorite city?

Mr. Neely (still meditating; aloud)

St. Louis—St. Lewis.
   (looks down at Tootie, smiles)
You know—I like St. Lewis better.

In spite of all the planning, Minnelli was told that there was not enough light to shoot the street set during the early morning, so the location was switched to the Trolley Depot.

The choreographer was Charles Walters. Prior to the principal photography, he rehearsed "The Trolley Song" for sixteen days. During this time, Judy was absent for six days for one reason or another, and the rest of the time she was present for an average of two hours per day.

The shooting of "The Trolley Song" was not a simple matter. There was no trolley anywhere that could accommodate the staging of the number; one had to be built. Jack Smith recalls, "I designed the trolley with the aisles wide enough so people could pass up and down. We made the ceilings high enough so that they could be lighted, and then there was the top level of the double-decker trolley. We constructed the winding staircase so that it could accommodate people and also hold the weight of all the dancers running back and forth, up and down, in their costumes, so that they could hang out the windows, which people don't do on a real streetcar. Furthermore, it was shot in process on Stage 27. We made background plates for the process on the back lot, on our existing 'New England Street.'"

Smith explains, "We started the trolley running and it had to go for several blocks. We had to have several angles; straight side, three-fourth back, one-fourth front. We took the camera around several of these blocks, including Andy Hardy Street. This was Gibbons' idea and it was a daring one. It didn't resemble St. Louis of the period, but it sufficed—and it got us over the terrible prospect of having to build St. Louis again. But we did have a small-town Midwestern depot."

Minnelli used an ingenious device for the start of the number: He kept the boy next door, John Truett (Tom Drake), out of it. The trolley leaves and the passengers begin to sing. Judy looks for him. He is nowhere. Minnelli cuts to a high camera shot and we see Drake in the distance, chasing the trolley. He catches up with it, gets on—and Judy, happily, starts the song. With that, Minnelli keeps the story going into and throughout the number.[10]

Between December 7 and January 31, the shooting schedule somewhat resembled Swiss cheese; it was full of holes. Al Jennings, assistant director on the picture, was interrupted nightly by phone calls from either Judy or Mrs. O'Brien. Judy was sick. Judy would be sick. Judy inquired about the weather reports ("It's going to rain tomorrow, won't it?"). Judy had to have a tooth pulled. Mrs. O'Brien chose a late hour to inform Jennings that her daughter needed braces on her teeth. She would have to be absent for at least ten days. Mary Astor had a sudden attack of sinusitis. Although the following memo states that she would be out for only three days, she was out for three weeks. Harry Davenport was sick with a virus infection for one week. Joan Carroll

[10] Cameraman Harold Rosson photographed "The Trolley Song" sequence; Folsey was shooting tests on the fairgrounds.

was rushed to the hospital on February 2, for an emergency appendectomy.

To: Arthur Freed
Subject: Illness in Cast — MEET ME IN ST. LOUIS
From: Dave Friedman/Al Jennings   Date: 12/18/43

Miss Garland called Al Jennings, the assistant director, at 8 A.M. today, telling him that she did not feel well but could come to work if a car could pick her up. Mr. Jennings spoke with transportation, and arrangements were made to pick Miss Garland up in the company car.

Upon arriving at the studio, she called the stage, and Jennings and I went to her dressing room. She was not well, and I called Dr. Jones, who came over and said Miss Garland should return home. She would not go without first speaking to Mr. Freed, which was accomplished, and at 10:30 A.M. I took her home in a studio car.

Date: 12/30/43

Judy Garland is still ill, and Company worked around her until 12 noon today. The balance of the day was spent in rehearsing musical number.

Date: 1/12/44

At 11:20 last night Judy Garland phoned Al Jennings, assistant director, and said she was ill, she still had her headache, her eyes were beginning to swell, and that she would be unable to come in at all today.

Mr. Jennings called me, and I notified Mr. Freed. Decision was made to let the crew come in and line, light and rehearse the difficult boom shot we planned for today, going as far as we could with it without Miss Garland.

As a result, company did not shoot today.

Date: 1/28/44

I talked with Mary Astor and found out that today, for the first time since January 10, she has no fever. However, she has developed sinusitis but believes this can be cleared up with a few days' treatment. Miss Astor is going to see her doctor this afternoon and will telephone me his opinion as to when she can come to work.

P.S. At 4:15 P.M. Dr. Kully telephoned me that he had just washed out Miss Astor's antrum and that she had a temperature of 99.8. Until her temperature becomes normal he will be unable to say before Wednesday or Thursday of next week.

2/3/44

Joan Carroll was rushed to the hospital on February 2 for an emergency appendectomy and will be unable to work for a period of two weeks. We will advise you when she is able to report. Artist is not to be paid salary during period of incapacity.

At 8:15 this morning Joan Carroll's mother, Mrs. Felt, phoned that Joan had a very sore throat and a fever of 102. They had stopped at the studio hospital last night and were given a swab for Joan's throat, which Mrs. Felt applied twice during the night. Their doctor was then on his way to their home. At 10:25 Mrs. Felt phoned that the doctor had examined Joan and she would be unable to come to work for three days. The fever had gone down a degree but Joan has strep throat. If there is enough improvement so that Joan can return to work earlier than in three days, Mrs. Felt will let us know.

Mr. Datig later verified this information with Mrs. Felt's doctor. Company completed the sequence on which we were working with the exception of shots including Joan, and moved to another set, shooting around her until 5:05 P.M. when company was dismissed because no other scenes were available.

3/1/44

At 5:05 last night, when company finished shooting, Miss Garland told Al Jennings, assistant director, that she would be indisposed and unable to come in tomorrow.

Due to Joan Carroll's illness, company is unable to shoot today and had planned to rehearse. Miss Garland being unavailable, rehearsal was canceled and company is on layoff today.

3/3/44

Joan Carroll is ill today. Being unable to shoot with her, company was on layoff, but spent the day rehearsing.

3/4/44

Joan Carroll is ill today. Company is on layoff, being unable to shoot without her.

3/9/44

Miss Judy Garland was called for 3 today. At 1:20 she phoned from home that her sinus was bothering her so badly she wondered if Mr. Minnelli could not shoot around her this afternoon, since if she could not rest her sinus might become worse and she might not be able to work tomorrow night on the exterior of the Smith House on Lot 3.

Mr. Minnelli was contacted and said that he had postponed three shots in the dining room set and moved to the living room set in order to get to the shot for which Miss Garland was called. However, rather than jeopardize tomorrow night's work, he agreed to revise again his shooting plans.

Company therefore completed work in the living room up to the shot covering Miss Garland's entrance and returned to the dining room set to pick up the three shots earlier postponed and finished shooting at 5:45 P.M.

Called Miss Garland this morning to tell her we were planning to shoot inside this afternoon rather than outside tonight, due to bad weather reports.

Miss Garland advised that she was doctoring for a cold, but would be all right to work tonight. She later called back to say that she had spoken with her doctor, who had advised her against working tonight, and therefore she would work this afternoon. Inasmuch as Mr. Davenport was not available for this afternoon due to illness, this change could not be made.

As a result company planned to work outside tonight, shooting scenes with the Halloween children only and excluding Miss Garland's scenes.

Finally, due to rain, company was not able to shoot at all.

Calls had to be canceled; scenes had to be shifted; Central Casting had to be advised not to send their extras. But mainly because of Judy's constant ailments, the company had to stumble along as best it could. The production staff used all their imagination to find ways to shoot around whoever was unavailable on a given day or days. The crowning blow came on Sunday, January 30, when once again Jennings received a call from the O'Brien household. This time it was from Marissa O'Brien, Margaret's aunt. Jennings recalls it only too well: "We were shooting the fairground sequence and had to manufacture a dust storm. Marissa O'Brien informed me that they were leaving for Arizona in the morning, because Margaret had developed a cold and a sinus condition. This was a bit of a shock, since they had a call the next day. So I called Walter Strohm, head of production. Strohm told me to call back immediately and tell them they can't go. Then I got the Swedish maid routine. Whenever Margaret's mother didn't want to talk to me, she became the Swedish maid and didn't understand English."

Date: 1/31/44

Margaret O'Brien was given a cover set call for 10 A.M. today. At approximately 4 P.M. yesterday (Sunday) Marissa O'Brien, aunt of Margaret, called Jennings at his home and advised they were leaving today for Arizona as per doctor's orders due to the fact that Margaret had had a very bad cold and sinus condition, as well as other complications.

Al Jennings contacted Dave Friedman who, in turn, contacted Fred Dantig. At approximately 5:45, when I called their home, I was told by the party who answered the phone that they had already left for Arizona. Also that Marissa had called the house from the depot sometime before, advising the party at the house that they would wire in today telling them where to send some clothes for Margaret. Up to 3 P.M. today no wire had been received and, since I am unable to find out who Margaret's doctor is, I can give you no further information at this time but will keep you posted.

Mr. L. K. Sidney will advise whether or not she is to be paid salary during period of absence.

Subject: Illness of Margaret O'Brien   1/31/44

At 5:30 P.M. on Saturday, January 29, Al Alt, acting under Al Jennings' instructions, called the O'Brien home and gave Margaret O'Brien's call for Monday, January 31. The conversation, which was carried on with Miss Marissa O'Brien (Margaret's aunt) included description of scenes and scene numbers both for the St. Louis Street exterior set and the interior of the Children's Bedroom, cover set. At this time the call was accepted by Miss O'Brien for Monday's work, and there was no mention made of Margaret being ill.

At 4:30 P.M. on Sunday, January 30, Al Jennings called me at home to advise me that Marissa O'Brien had in turn called him at 4:05 P.M. to advise him that Margaret had been suffering with a combination illness of hay fever and influenza, and was also having nervous spells. He further told me that Marissa said at this time that the doctor in charge had advised that they take Margaret away for two weeks to recuperate from her illness, that Margaret would not be able to appear for work on Monday, January 31, and that they were going to follow the physician's advise regarding the two weeks' rest.

I got in touch with Mr. Dantig and asked him to check this information, and at 5:45 P.M. (Sunday) he advised me that he had called the O'Brien home and had been told by a woman who answered the phone that the O'Briens had called her to tell her that they were at the railroad station and were leaving immediately for Arizona, and that they would advise her by wire to send necessary clothes, etc.

I in turn transmitted this information to Mr. Butcher and Mr. Freed.

Due to the inclemency of the weather on Sunday and inasmuch as it had been raining, and Margaret O'Brien's departure had left us without a cover set, it was decided to cancel Monday's call for the exterior, which in turn left us without any work at all that we could do.

On Sunday night it rained again and more rain fell Monday morning, which in itself justified the cancellation of the exterior set.

Margaret O'Brien last worked with the company on the morning of Friday, January 21, between the hours of 9:00 and 11:30 A.M., at which time her work for the day was concluded and she was dismissed. On this morning she had a slight hoarseness, which Mrs. O'Brien attributed to a hay fever allergy to dirt.

Jennings' call was to no avail: They left. Eddie Lawrence, M-G-M p.r. man, ran into them in Chicago. "Well, we were going to Arizona,"

Margaret's mother told him, "but Margaret felt so much better—we've decided to go to New York." Evidently, the cold and the sinus infection had been imaginary. But Mrs. O'Brien wrote an explanatory letter to Arthur Freed:

Dear Mr. Freed:

I want you to know how very sorry I am. I had to take Margaret out of your picture for the time being. She was in bed for a week with a very bad case of hay fever, which the doctors said came from nerves due to overwork, so I am taking her away from everything connected with work for a couple of weeks as I know a change of scenery will do her good. She has been working almost steadily for the past year and a half, going from one picture into another. *Journey for Margaret, You John Jones, Doctor Gillespie, Jane Eyre, Lost Angel, Madame Curie, Thousands Cheer, Canterville Ghost*, and now *Meet Me in St. Louis*.

Even the days she didn't work, we still had to make a trip to the studio for publicity, interviews, lessons, wardrobe fittings, etc. And I was beginning to be greatly criticized for allowing my child to work so hard. We couldn't even take a weekend off, because we were always on call, so now we are forced to take a couple of weeks off.

Sincerely,
Gladys O'Brien

In all fairness, one can say that there was some justification in Mrs. O'Brien's action.[11] Her daughter's work schedule brings to mind the grueling schedule Judy Garland was exposed to, in her early years.

During the layoff of the company, tests were being made of fabrics, color schemes and even the wallpapers Ayers had designed. These had been printed in the East at some expense, but when they were tested photographically, the Technicolor lights washed out the design, and left nothing but a blur. Ayers had to redesign it. This relatively minor item shows what meticulous attention was paid to every detail.

After two weeks, production resumed, although Joan Carroll was still recovering from her operation. The shooting began again with the scene involving only Judy and Margaret, leading into "Have Yourself a Merry Little Christmas."

It was Christmas Eve. The silence in the house is deceiving because no one is asleep. Tootie enters Esther's room, goes to the window to take a last look at the snowmen. She is very anxious; she wants to take all her possessions with her. Esther says, pointing down at the snowmen: "Wouldn't we look silly trying to get them on the train?" Tootie presses her face against the cold window pane, and tears well up and flow silently. Esther glances at John's window, her arms around Tootie, and she begins singing "Have yourself a merry little Christmas . . ."

[11] Margaret was then receiving $250 per week. Matters were straightened out, and she returned to the studio at a considerable raise in salary.

It appears that the bulldog wasn't that mean, or has Margaret O'Brien charmed the monster? VINCENTE MINNELLI COLLECTION

George Folsey recalls a lucky accident: "We had a shot looking down into the yard through the upstairs window. Since it was night, I felt it should have a sort of moonlight, softly lit snow effect. I decided to put out a big yellow light as though somebody had opened a door on the lower floor, the yellow light falling on the snow. Now we had a gray, whitish, slightly bluish snow and a shaft of yellow light. And getting all this ready, the backing, and the snow, and the lighting, fixing it and smoothing it out, and doing all the things to make it good—that consumed a lot of time. So, I got nervous about it and I said, 'Let's shoot it—let's shoot it!' I was on a platform on the set, not behind the camera. It looked good and the camera rolled. After the take was made, my head electrician came to me and told me in so many words that we were totally underexposed."

The print came back and turned out to be one of the photographic highlights of the film. "That scene is embedded in my mind," says Folsey, "that fragile, delicate image, with the gray tracy lines of the foliage that had no leaves on it. The wintery effect of that scene, with the St. Louis street in the background, could not have been achieved had it not been for George Gibson, one of the greatest painters the studio ever had."

And Minnelli puts it: "The Halloween sequence attracted me especially. In the book it happens to Agnes, because, in fact, Sally Benson was Agnes. But I changed it to express the horror of that little child . . . because she was always talking about blood."

Tootie reaches the door, manages to ring the bell, the door opens and Mr. Braukoff appears, his menacing bulldog at his side. Overcoming her almost paralyzing fear, Tootie throws the flour in his face and utters, "I hate you, Mr. Braukoff!" With that, the tension is released.

The Halloween sequence was the first of its kind Minnelli created. From here on there is hardly a picture in which he does not have a dream or a fantasy. It is his way of getting under the surface of a character, revealing the subconscious.

There is another scene in the picture which merits special mention. After having spent an evening at her house, John helps Esther to turn off all the lights because she says she is afraid of mice. Minnelli describes the way he laid out the scene: "It went into the hall, into the living room, the dining room and back into the hall—and up the staircase. Everything was in one shot because I felt intuitively it would be wrong to break it up—we rehearsed this a whole day without getting a shot."

Jack Smith says, "When Vincente described the scene to me, I realized that the outer walls had to be wild—in other words, you can take them away and show the core of the house—and photograph from the outside toward the inside. So I had to take this into account when I designed the set."

Here is Folsey's description: "You can't believe what we went

Minnelli shows Judy how he would like her to turn out the lights. M-G-M

through with that scene. Each time Judy went to turn out a light we had to make a light effect with no stop—we followed them from one place to another—going through these various rooms, sneaking through doorways. There were so many moves that my boys got themselves into impossible positions in order to get the camera track out of the way. Furthermore, the man who was pulling the camera back was now in the way of the boom—one of my guys had to be kicked in the fanny so as to get out of the path of the boom before it hit him. In addition to that, we had a tremendous amount of light changes. Since it was a continuous shot, we had neither time nor means to change our lighting equipment, consequently we ran out of dimmers, and we ran out of shutters for the lights and had to resort to venetian blinds. We got a whole bunch of venetian blinds from the property department and hung them in front of these lights, and on cue my guys would pull the blinds closed very carefully so that the light would disappear. But just for that, another light had to come up and compensate for the change in mood and a change in quality. I want to tell you that that was about as tough a job as I think I've ever had to do."

Almost a year had passed since the postman walked down Kensington Avenue. The picture was divided into four seasons. Summer, fall and winter had passed. Spring, and the big event, the World's Fair, was yet to come. Minnelli describes his visual conception of the four seasons: "Summer saw the damp, wilted white of women's dresses and men's suits, the brilliant yellow of the beer wagons, the shiny newness of early horseless carriages, the wide expanse of lawns curling under the waves of heat that rise from unpaved streets, the cool green of ice wagons and the frosty blueness of their loads; fall brings bright-colored leaves whisked from trees, the deep orange of pumpkin heads at the windows on Halloween, the crackling brilliance of a street bonfire, around which neighborhood youngsters cavort in a wild array of costumes. Our winter sequence finds the same scene blanketed in snow. In the windows are Christmas trees; holiday colors are reflected in the silver bells of horse-drawn sleighs."

Minnelli gives his vision of spring, the sequence which is to finish the picture. "The trees are covered with blossoms. The green of the lawns and shrubs gives freshness to the air. And only through color could the pageantry of the Louisiana Purchase Exposition be caught in its breathtaking brilliance."

The World's Fair sequence had its special problems—what to show and how much to do. Smith says, "Most of the Fair was shot in miniature, like the Ferris wheel. Henry Greutart sculpted two marvelous bison, which he painted white and off white with a pearlish finish on them that picked up the lights—this created quite a dazzling effect. Then, there were fireworks. As the Smith family arrives, the multicolored lights of the Fair emerge, focusing on one building at a time, the illuminated cascades and fountains, the domes of buildings, all rising to a colorful splendor."

Underscoring of the entire picture was the next order of business and this was Edens' department. Although he had worked with Georgie Stoll on the prerecording sessions of the musical numbers, he was fast realizing the conductor's inadequacy when it came to postscoring, etc. The man he wanted and got to tackle this important task was Lennie Hayton. However, he also felt he needed assistance in the control room. What he required was a highly trained musician who would be able to apply expertise in cutting and interspersing the orchestral background in order to enhance the subtleties of the dramatic situation. He summoned Lela Simone.

Lela Simone started as a recording pianist at M-G-M in 1936; in 1938 she became a member of the music department. She was born in Germany, her mother was French, her father was a German diplomat and one of the foremost publishers in Europe. She left Germany shortly after Hitler came to power and arrived in New York in August 1933. Otto Klemperer, the famous conductor, brought her to Los Angeles to appear as a soloist with the Los Angeles Philharmonic. But being dignified in both style and manner, she didn't look the part. When she entered a sound stage to work, the musicians had a hard time concentrating on their music; she was a striking beauty and easily could have passed as a double for Marlene Dietrich. In the music department she was soon requested by directors to work on the shooting stages. One film she was involved with was *The Picture of Dorian Gray*. She began absorbing and learning more about filmmaking. Finston, the music department boss, remarked at the time: "This girl won't be long in the music department—let's face it." She acquired the technique of sound cutting by observation, a great flair for machinery and by her phenomenal ear.

It was at a recording session on *Ice Follies of 1939* that Lela Simone and Roger Edens first met. He had collaborated on an ice ballet with composer-conductor Franz Waxman. In one part of the ballet, the piano had to perform an incredible feat. As Simone recalls, "I said to Waxman, if you gave this part to Rachmaninoff he would have to go home and practice it for three months. Waxman replied, 'Oh, that's ridiculous; there's a piano set up for you on Stage 2. Look at it and at one o'clock we record.' I thought I'd die! Presto! Nothing but runs. Anyway, I somehow got it going and came to the stage. It was the first piece to be recorded and Waxman started with 'Now follow me here and follow me there.' I said, 'Mr. Waxman, there is only one way to record this piece. You conduct and I play.' I got through the first take by sheer nervous energy. After we finished somebody in the back of the stage screamed. Everybody looked. Then a man came up to Waxman and said, 'Who is this girl?' Waxman said, 'This is Mr. Edens, this is Miss Simone.'"

The Smith family and company (left to right): Lucille Bremer, Leon Ames, Mary Astor, Joan Carroll, Vincente Minnelli, Judy Garland, Arthur Freed, Harry Davenport, Margaret O'Brien and Henry Daniels, Jr. ARTHUR FREED ARCHIVES

"That's exactly as it happened," recalled Edens, "I knew then and there that this incredible girl had a special talent. After we worked together on *St. Louis,* I asked her if she would like to work exclusively for me and Freed in the Freed Unit. She was delighted." For the next two decades, Simone and Edens remained close, both in their professional and personal lives.

St. Louis had been cut in preparation for the preview. And, in a way, history reversed itself: Freed decided to cut out the Halloween sequence. As though it were yesterday, Brecher reiterates the following, his voice shaking, "Minnelli came into my office on the afternoon of the preview (June 5, 1944), his face ashen. 'You know what that guy has just done? He has cut out the entire Halloween sequence.' Well, I was appalled, naturally. We all felt this was the best sequence in the film. I asked Vincente, 'What are you going to do?' He said, 'I can't do anything—you've got to go up and talk to him.' 'This guy can't stand the sight of me,' I said. 'I've had trouble with him before.' Minnelli leaned hard on me, challenged me, and knowing it would be foolhardy I went, although Freed always terrified me. 'Arthur, I hear you're dropping the Halloween sequence.' 'Yeah, what about it?' he said. 'It's out!' 'But for Christ sake, after tonight, you can always take it out—it's only a preview. It was written, you spent a fortune shooting it, why don't you let the audience see it?' He got violent verbally, and I literally ran out of his office.

"Something must have happened that day. It wasn't Minnelli. Maybe I had provoked him enough so that he had second thoughts. At the preview it was in."

The preview was an unqualified success. There was no longer any talk about cutting the Halloween sequence, but it was the consensus that the picture was too long. Blane's prophetic forecast came true: The Rodgers and Hammerstein song "Boys and Girls Like You and Me" was eliminated.

METRO-GOLDWYN-MAYER PICTURES
CULVER CITY CALIFORNIA

Dear Arthur—
I was thrilled to read the reviews on "St. Louis".
It was particularly gratifying because they vindicated a man's faith —yours— in believing in a venture, nursing it, and insisting that it emerge with the contents of its integrity and the complexion of its birth.
I think it is one of the great achievements of this industry. I'm happy its yours, and I'm grateful for the privilege of having been connected with it.
Sinc.
F³

Fred F. Finklehoffe signed his name the quick way, F³.

NO AGREEMENT OR ORDER WILL BE BINDING ON THIS CORPORATION UNLESS IN WRITING AND SIGNED BY AN OFFICER

RK NEW YORK NY JULY 10 1944 612P

ARTHUR FREED

  MGM STUDIOS

HEAR "BOYS AND GIRLS" OUT OF "ST LOUIS." PLEASE LET ME
KNOW IF TRUE. I DONT WANT JUMP OFF EAST RIVER DOCK ON
A MERE RUMOR. REGARDS

OSCAR

JULY 14, 1944

OSCAR HAMMERSTEIN
6 EAST 52ND STREET
NEW YORK CITY, N.Y.

SORRY "BOYS AND GIRLS" IS OUT OF "ST. LOUIS" BUT JUDY WILL
SING IT IN THE NEXT PICTURE. WE ALL LOVE THE SONG AND IT
WAS UNFORTUNATE THAT THE ENTIRE SEQUENCE THE SONG WAS
PART OF WAS ELIMINATED AFTER THE PREVIEW ON ACCOUNT
OF ITS LENGTH. DON'T JUMP IN THE EAST RIVER. KINDEST
REGARDS

ARTHUR

An interesting sidelight: One of M-G-M's music publishing arms, Leo Feist, Inc., thought "The Trolley Song" too long (to publish it would take thirteen pages) and asked the songwriters to cut it. The writers refused. Instead, Blane gave out a few copies to Bing Crosby, Kate Smith and the like for radio performances. In a couple of weeks, even before the picture opened, the song was a smash hit! Although the publisher had said, "I can't even get the cost of the paper back," by the time the picture opened, the song had sold well over a half a million copies.

The final cost in making *Meet Me in St. Louis* was $1,707,561.14. In spite of all the illnesses, shutdowns, etc., the picture only exceeded its budget by the normal 10 per cent. In its initial release, December 31, 1944, it grossed $7,566,000.[12]

Meet Me in St. Louis, complete with musical score, was presented as a television special on CBS, April 26, 1959, with Jane Powell, Jeanne Crain, Tab Hunter, Walter Pidgeon, Myrna Loy, Patty Duke and Ed Wynn. A stage presentation of the film, with additional songs by Hugh Martin and Ralph Blane, premièred at the St. Louis Municipal Opera on June 9, 1960.

[12] These are estimated figures as of August 31, 1957. They do not reflect income from double-bill playoff, 16 mm. rentals, the film's share when it was sold as part of a package for television showings, etc.

5

ZIEGFELD FOLLIES

THE CLOCK

THE HARVEY GIRLS

YOLANDA AND THE THIEF

After the completion of *Meet Me in St. Louis* in 1944 Freed was the most important producer on the Metro lot. He could have any property, any writer, any director, any star and any production staff. Mayer even offered him the post of head of production at the studio but he refused. What he did want, however, was his own loyal, devoted family. Or, as he so aptly put it, "My own little Camelot." During the making of *Meet Me in St. Louis* he had found what he was looking for.

Long before *St. Louis* was in the can, Freed was already in the throes of preparing *Ziegfeld Follies, The Clock, The Harvey Girls, Yolanda and the Thief, Silver Lining* (a Jerome Kern cavalcade), *Belle of New York* and *Show Boat*.

In order to make the Freed Unit autonomous he established a link between his operation and the production office on the lot. The man he chose for this position was Bill Ryan. He had been an assistant director for many years; in fact, he worked in this capacity on Freed's first "official" film, *Babes in Arms*. His knowledge of the personnel enabled him to pick the most efficient and dependable crews. He was a conservative, taciturn, well-mannered man who knew when to approach Freed and with what. Freed could safely turn over the intricacies of the

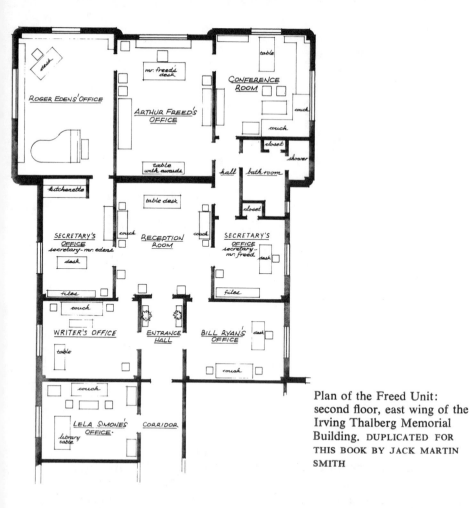

Roger Edens' Office

desk

mr. freed's desk

Arthur Freed's Office

Conference Room

table

couch

couch

closet

shower

kitchenette

table with awards

hall

bath room

table desk

closet

Secretary's Office
secretary- mr. edens

couch

Reception Room

couch

Secretary's Office
secretary- mr. freed

desk

desk

files

files

couch

Writer's Office

Entrance Hall

Bill Ryan's Office

desk

table

couch

couch

Lela Simone's Office

Corridor

library table

Plan of the Freed Unit:
second floor, east wing of the
Irving Thalberg Memorial
Building. DUPLICATED FOR
THIS BOOK BY JACK MARTIN
SMITH

physical setup of any of his productions to Ryan and dismiss them from his mind.

Lela Simone was another member of this coalition. Her specialized area was everything pertaining to sound and music, both artistically and technically. She was the unit's trouble shooter, Edens' right hand and Freed's left, and she had a talent for public relations. "Lela can do with a piece of sound track what a French chef can do with a piece of beef" was one of Freed's favorite expressions.

The cornerstone of this group was Roger Edens. His influence extended much further than his specialized musical activities—in fact, he was Freed's associate producer from the outset.[1]

This was the nucleus of the Freed Unit and there were also members in transit: Minnelli, Sharaff, Ayers, Hayton, Walters, Brecher, Finklehoffe, Bolton, Martin and Blane, and Robert Alton.

Kay Thompson, another newcomer, arrived on the scene. She was a highly successful vocal arranger and performer, a high-strung, erudite, sophisticated, elegant woman with style and ideas. Originally she was engaged by the music department as a vocal arranger. She knew Blane, Minnelli, Hayton, Walters and others, and she quickly became great friends with Edens and was a transient member of the unit. Her forte in vocal arranging was the jazz idiom and she was equally gifted in the lyric writing. She was an important addition to the musical staff; there was nobody on the lot who excelled in this field.

Ziegfeld Follies was foremost in Freed's mind. He discussed its format with Murray Anderson who had done several productions of the *Follies* in New York. Soon there was an abundance of material on Freed's desk. Over the past ten years the studio had acquired over five hundred sketches, individual musical numbers and vaudeville routines. Out of all the properties Freed felt that only a handful had any merit and the selection would be up to his unit.

Thompson and Ayers came up with an idea for a number built around a song, "Frankie and Johnnie," by Jerry Livingston and Mack David for the Broadway musical *Bright Lights of 1944.* At that time anything in any picture had to be cleared with the Breen Office.

Dear Mr. Mayer:

We have read the "Frankie and Johnnie" number for your proposed picture *Ziegfeld Follies.* We regret to report that we feel this subject matter would be unacceptable from the standpoint of the Production Code, on account of its flavor of prostitution and excessive sex suggestiveness.

Furthermore, it has been the practice of censor boards generally

[1] Edens' first on-screen credit was on *The Harvey Girls.*

to delete even the mention of this song, whenever any attempt has been made to inject it into pictures.

We strongly urge, therefore, that you steer away entirely from this extremely dangerous material and substitute something else.

Cordially yours,
Joseph I. Breen

Breen's letter shows the subjective, biased, authoritarian stick he wielded. Taste was the earmark of the Freed Unit and it goes without saying that there was nothing objectionable in the sketch.

Freed was anxious to get an official go ahead and urged Katz to set up a meeting with Mayer and his executives. Katz's misgivings disappeared and at the conclusion of the dinner meeting Freed left with an O.K.

The year 1944 was to be M-G-M's twentieth anniversary and Mayer probably gave the nod of approval, unhesitatingly, because he saw the *Ziegfeld Follies of 1944* not only as a departure from the traditional format of the musical picture but also as a showcase for his dynasty.

On January 9, 1944, M-G-M announced that *Ziegfeld Follies* would go before the cameras around March 1 with a budget of approximately $3,000,000. The studio contended this would set a precedent because the picture would be a revue, without story.

Freed's theory was that musical-revue plot action becomes a series of intermissions between the real entertainment features. Therefore, plot would be eliminated; instead, introductions and commentary would come through either sound track, description or screen title. Even animated drawings and trick photography would be utilized to keep the revue moving and essentially cinematic.

For a ballet sequence Freed had in mind a song, "You're Dreamlike," written by his friend Howard Dietz. He asked him to make some minor changes. One would expect that the vice-presidency of an organization like Loew's Inc. is a time-consuming job. But Dietz had found the time to write songs for innumerable Broadway shows and pursued his avocation with remarkable insistence.

For the realization of *Ziegfeld Follies* a voluminous array of talent had to be accumulated in all departments: Book, music, direction, chor-

Kay Thompson and Roger Edens conceived this self-portrait (the original was mural size). Purposely done in the style of a *Harper's Bazaar* cover, it was presented to Freed on the occasion of his birthday (cake in the center). The other props belong to and were identified with Thompson and Edens. "He was absolutely startled by the whole thing," remarks Thompson. "The fact that we had gone to all this trouble—left Metro, dragging all that junk up to Paul Rotha's studio, where the photograph was taken. It was certainly incredible to see how touched he was by what we had done because I never thought he was that sentimental." ARTHUR FREED ARCHIVES

Fred Astaire with his dancing ensemble shooting "If Swing Goes, I Go Too," which he wrote especially for *Ziegfeld Follies*. M-G-M

eography, art direction, costume design and camerawork. George Sidney was selected as the *deus ex machina*.

For the picture's introduction unique puppets would be used, virtually like human figures with flexibility and movement. For this feat famous puppeteer Louis Bunin was engaged. Bunin had learned his skill in Paris and had introduced his lifelike mannequins at the New York World's Fair in 1939. His animation technique was difficult to execute and time-consuming: Only seven feet of film per day could be photographed.

4/10/44

Fred Astaire and 26 male dancers rehearse "If Swing Goes, I Go Too." Alton on Rehearsal Hall A.

Bunin puppets shooting animated sequence "Leo the Lion." Lou Chek on Lot 2.

Lena Horne and Avon Long rehearse "Liza." Eugene Loring on Stage 24.

Red Skelton shooting "When Televison Comes."[2] Sidney on Stage 4.

The comedy skit "When Television Comes" was originally called "Gulper's Gin"[3] and had been written by Skelton and his sister Edna for their first radio sponsor. Originally, Sidney had used this monologue

[2] Rehearsed and shot in one day; cost; $27,502.
[3] The sketch was also known as "Guzzler's Gin."

124

for Skelton's screen test which landed him a studio contract. Folsey was the cameraman and Bobby Bronner his first assistant. "Well, Red got drunker and drunker until he was absolutely plastered," says Folsey, "and he's very funny when he's drunk. Bronner began to laugh, as all the guys did, and pretty soon he was so hysterical that he fell right off the camera boom and rolled into a corner laughing his head off. I had to grab the camera to finish the shot."

4/18/44

Fred Astaire shooting "If Swing Goes . . ." Sidney on Stage 30.[4]

"Merry-Go-Round" rehearsal: Lucille Ball, Lucille Bremer, Cyd Charisse and ensemble. Alton on Rehearsal Hall A.

Lena Horne and Avon Long rehearse "Liza" with ten colored dancers. Loring on Stage 24.

Bunin continues animation. Lou Chek on Lot 2.

4/22/44

Fred Astaire and Gene Kelly rehearse "The Babbitt and the Bromide." Alton on Rehearsal Hall B.

[4] Rehearsed eleven days; recorded one day; shot four days. Cost: $91,140.12.

Avon Long sings "Liza" to Lena Horne. M-G-M

"Merry-Go-Round" rehearsal: ensemble only. Vera Lee for Alton on Rehearsal Hall A.

Lena Horne and Avon Long shooting "Liza." Sidney on Stage 24.[5]

"Liza" was written by George Gershwin, Ira Gershwin and Gus Kahn for the Broadway musical *Show Girl,* and this was to be in its first screen presentation. Kay Thompson had composed an elaborate vocal arrangement for Avon Long and ten black singer-dancers. Lena was just there to adorn the set.

Eugene Loring had created a sensation with his performance in "Billy the Kid," choreographed by Agnes de Mille to a score by Aaron Copland, and again five years later in "Rodeo." After De Mille's success with *Oklahoma!* Freed wanted to hire her, but Alton suggested Loring, convinced of his potential as a choreographer.

Rather than do a stereotype set, Smith conceived the idea of using paper sculpture painted white. "In order to make the idea come true, I sat down with my scissors and got all kinds of cardboard and paper and started to crimp it, cut it, press it and curl it," recalls Smith. "I built palm trees, little animals and poodle dogs, all out of paper. We had paper grass, paper foliage, the house with its Spanish tile roof, stair treads leading to a veranda, all made out of paper. Naturally I reinforced the floor to support the performers." For Long's introduction Smith built a little arbor, using a series of arches in forced perspective.

Smith remembers an incident: "Irene Gibbons was doing the costumes for the number; I was in her office and Arthur Freed walked in. That was my first encounter with him. He was demanding, but he saw that I was really trying. I said, 'Well, I don't know whether I'm going to be . . .' 'You'll be on the picture, don't worry!' Freed told me. He went to the phone and called Cedric Gibbons: 'Jack Smith has got to be on this picture and I've got to own him from now on!' "

5/2/44

Edward Arnold, Jimmy Durante and Horace McNally rehearse "Death and Taxes." Minnelli for Sidney on Stage 3.

Bunin puppets animation: "Interior Theatre Lobby." Lou Chek on Lot 2.

Fred Astaire and Gene Kelly rehearse "The Babbitt and the Bromide." Alton on Rehearsal Hall B.

"Merry-Go-Round" shooting "Here's to the Girls." Fred Astaire, Lucille Ball, Cyd Charisse and ensemble. Sidney on Stage 5 and 6.[6]

---

[5] Rehearsed five days; recorded one day; shot four days. Cost $46,106.80.

[6] Rehearsed thirteen days, recorded one day; shot seven days. Cost: $129,-985.30. "Here's to the Girls" was written by Roger Edens and Arthur Freed. Astaire had to shuttle between this and "The Babbitt." Joe Niemeyer would stand in whenever he was absent from the latter rehearsal.

Fanny Brice in her "Baby
Snooks" costume chats with
Lucille Ball, during a break
in the opening number
"Here's to the Girls."
M-G-M

Helen Rose's first assignment was to design the costumes for the opening number "Here's to the Girls" (written by Edens and Freed). As a young girl she had her first success designing the costumes for the famous Shipstead and Johnson *Ice Follies.* Her first costume design for motion pictures was for three musicals at Twentieth Century-Fox in 1943.[7] Shortly afterward she decided that she didn't want to work in pictures and returned to the *Ice Follies.* Mayer saw her filmwork and decided he wanted her. At first she was reluctant to sign, but the seven-year contract she was offered provided for a six-week leave to do the *Ice Follies,* and she accepted.

The motif for the opening musical sequence was a circus. "I created lavish outfits of pink sequins, using twelve hundred ostrich feathers. With Lucille Ball's flaming red hair," says Rose, "I thought it was the best number in the picture."

Smith designed a merry-go-round using live white horses.[8] "We taught them to ride on a turntable which we built for them to rehearse on the back lot," he says. "When they came to the stage they actually stood still, with the girls seated in side-saddle manner." Sidney wanted the girls to stand up to show off their ostrich plumes. Smith ac-

[7] *Stormy Weather* for Lena Horne; *Hello, Frisco, Hello* for Alice Faye; *Coney Island* for Betty Grable.

[8] Silver, the famous horse who answered to the "Heigh-ho!" call of the Lone Ranger was used in this sequence. "Silver is a sissy!" heralded *Life* magazine when it had Lucille Ball and the horse on its cover. His tail was braided and tied with six pink satin bows, a pink ostrich feather between his ears. The studio was threatened with a lawsuit for defamation of character by Silver's trainer when the issue appeared. Matters were straightened out and Silver's reputation was saved.

commodated by running a stanchion beside the horses for the girls to hold on to.

Photographically this number presented a real problem. The entire set was bathed in pinks. "Now that was all right," says Folsey, "except that it had a flat look and there was no way for me to get highlights on the reds, blues, whites and greens of the merry-go-round. I also had to keep in mind that Fred was working down front. So I put silk gauzes up to diffuse the light and took white sheets of cloth which were sprayed pink and stretched them between the horses to blend with the rest of the set."

This was the first number Alton conceived. When he saw the dailies he was disappointed.

On May 10, Sidney looked at his first month's work and he wasn't pleased. The next day he told Freed that he wanted to be taken off the picture. "Somebody else would probably never have talked to you again for the rest of your life," says Smith, "but he respected my opinion. It's one of the things that proves the size of this man."

The same day Minnelli took over.

5/20/44

Esther Williams rehearsing "We Will Meet Again in Honolulu." Merrill Pye on Lot 1 (Swimming Pool).

Lucille Bremer and ensemble rehearsing: "Raffles"—"This Heart of Mine." Alton on Stage 30 .

James Melton and Marion Bell rehearsing "Brindisi" from "Traviata." Loring on Rehearsal Hall B.

Fred Astaire and Gene Kelly shooting "The Babbitt and the Bromide." Minnelli on Stage 21.[9]

At eight o'clock in the morning, Messrs. Astaire and Kelly sat down on a park bench, waiting to do their number. The bench stood in front of an equestrian statue on Stage 21. There were bushes around the base of the statue. There were plaster pigeons hanging down from the ceiling on invisible wires above the bronze horse. "Let's go!" cried Minnelli. "Unhuh," said Folsey, his cameraman. He pointed out that one of the wires holding one of the pigeons wasn't invisible at all; it seemed to have a piece of cotton adhering to it. The lights went out. The dancers relaxed on their bench. The grips brought in a long ladder, climbed after that bit of fluff and broke the pigeon wire. They had to crawl into the rafters and send down a new wire. This took time. Folsey noticed that the pigeon fixers seemed to have nudged the statue out of line. The experts fixed that. An hour and a half passed. Astaire and Kelly fingered their red neckties. Again they were ready.

[9] Rehearsed six days; recorded one day; shot four days. Cost, $78,725.70.

Fred Astaire and Gene Kelly in the second of three sections of "The Babbitt and the Bromide" (their only screen appearance together). M-G-M

Minnelli took a look in the lens and saw that four leaves on the left-hand bush were shiny, when they should have been dull; they were reflecting light. The property department sent the leaves to the paint shop to be sprayed. "Let's have the dancers rehearse for a bit," said Minnelli. Astaire and Kelly got up, black streaks on their white pants. It seems the bench was dirty and this was Technicolor. The wardrobe department came up to do a dry-cleaning job. Folsey looked into his lens again and said: "Joe, please powder the left side of Mr. Astaire's nose; the left side only." Someone was working on the bench with soap, grips were tearing up the camera track for reasons best known to themselves, the electricians had to put new carbons in their arcs.

"The number that I really wanted to do was 'Pass That Peace Pipe,'[10] says Kelly. "Anyhow, I thought Fred and I could have fun with it and it would be different. When I danced with Fred I was terribly uncomfortable because we don't dance alike. When it came to Fred say-

[10] The song had been written by Roger Edens, Hugh Martin and Ralph Blane expressly for the film. But it was decided not important enough to be included.

ing, 'I'd like to do this' or 'I'd like to do that,' I deferred out of great respect and admiration. I hated the third section: I thought I looked like a klotz!"

"This is a dance to a song that George and Ira Gershwin wrote for my sister, Adele, and me for the Broadway show *Funny Face* [1927]," says Astaire. "It's about two very ordinary people meeting on the street and going through very ordinary motions. They meet first as youngsters. Then they meet ten years later and have the same identical conversation. Finally they meet in heaven and go through it all again, with harps. They're old then, with white whiskers."

The statue is old too and the horse has turned gray. So have the pigeons. For that matter, so had Minnelli.

5/25/44

Fanny Brice shooting "Baby Snooks" (burglar sketch). Del Ruth on Stage 4.[11]

Fred Astaire and Lucille Bremer rehearse "Raffles—This Heart of Mine." Alton on Stage 30.

Esther Williams rehearsing "We Will Meet Again in Honolulu." Pye on Lot 1 (Swimming Pool).

Bunin puppets shooting animated sequence "Anna Held Hourglass Girls." Lou Chek on Lot 2.[12]

James Melton and Marian Bell shooting "Traviata" sequence. Minnelli on Stage 24.[13]

[11] This number rehearsed ten days; shot four days. Cost: $67,795.60.
[12] Total footage to date: 255 feet, 11 frames.
[13] Rehearsed seven days; recorded one day; shot four days. Cost: $96,950.25.

Irene Sharaff designing a costume for the "Traviata" sequence. M-G-M

"I despised Pye's set for 'Traviata,' Minnelli recalls. 'That's the set?' He thought it was wonderful." So Minnelli concentrated on Irene Sharaff's beautiful costumes. "Those costumes!" sighs Loring. "Do you know that their minimum weight was seventy-five pounds! Anytime we weren't shooting, the girls had to sit down, take off the shoulder straps, and grooves would be dug into their shoulders. That's not all . . . for that number I used the M-G-M 'Glamazons.' They were beautiful girls, six feet tall. I had to find boys that were taller than the girls . . . and here I am, me, five feet three and a half inches tall. When I'd demonstrated with the girls, my nose would come right up to their boobs!"

6/8/44

Jimmy Durante rehearsing Pied Piper sequence, "Start Off Each Day With a Song." Walters on Rehearsal Hall A.

Fred Astaire and Lucille Bremer shooting "Raffles" sequence. Minnelli on Stage 30.[14]

Esther Williams and James Melton shooting "Honolulu" sequence. Pye on Lot 1 (Swimming Pool) and (Saucer Tank).[15]

The "Honolulu" number was shot in a series of sections. There were fifty setups which would give Williams as many chances to surface and to submerge again.

The number was divided into two parts: above and below water level. The scene began with Melton singing "We Will Meet Again in Honolulu" (written by Brown and Freed) to Williams posing near the lagoon in a full-length wrap made of fourteen white fox skins. At the end of the song Williams grandly slips off the wrap, drops it to the ground and dives into the water.

The number continued in six individual sets below the water level[16]: brilliant coral caves, exotic fans, sea shells, dazzling mother of pearl. All made of rubber, linen, plastic, cork and plaster, weighted down with metal discs. The two final sets were long sea grass in fantastic shapes. Left in the water too long, the materials disintegrated or faded. After each set was photographed, the circular saucer-type tank, twenty feet deep and sixty feet in diameter, had to be completely drained before the next set could be lowered into it. The tank held roughly three thousand gallons of water.

Surrounding the tank were balconies built on different levels, with windows to shoot through. To simulate bright sunlight, the hottest arc

[14] Rehearsed thirteen days; recorded one day; shot ten days. Cost: $168,-022.64.

[15] Rehearsed nineteen days; recorded one day; shot twelve days. Cost: $84,-536.54.

[16] Four art directors were needed to create the settings: Harry McAfee, Edward Carfagno, Smith and Pye.

Lucille Bremer and Fred Astaire in front of the closed pavilion for "This Heart of Mine." M-G-M lights and shiny mirror reflectors were used. The only way to make the lighting effective was to have the actual light source in the water; therefore the entire electrical apparatus had to be handled with extreme care because of the constant danger of electrocution.

On the same day and for the next ten days Minnelli concentrated on shooting "Raffles," a musical sequence created by Alton. In it, Astaire as a jewel thief crashes an elegant party. Among the bejeweled guests he sees a ravishing girl, Lucille Bremer, in a white evening coat appliqued with two thousand ermine tails. The two are immediately attracted to each other.

In this number various musical instruments represent voices: a trumpet is the butler's voice announcing the guests; a flute and a piccolo imitate the chatter at the ball. It is a novel and fantastic dance pantomime with Astaire singing "This Heart of Mine" (written for the film by Harry Warren and Arthur Freed).

"I admired the enthusiasm in the Freed Unit and the contributions everybody made. It was like a stock company," says Warren. "I never get excited about the songs I write, isn't that funny? They must have thought I was some kind of Eskimo. . . ."

Minnelli instructed the art department to build the set in the style of Tony Duquette. Smith and Pye collaborated. For every set Smith designed for Astaire he treated the floor with a special shellac. Astaire was always very concerned about the surface of the dance floor and he liked Smith's "potion." In the number were moving treadmills and revolving sets. "The conception was Merrill's and I personally thought it was very pretentious," Smith says.

7/7/44

James Melton rehearsing section of the finale. Minnelli on Stage 30.

Judy Garland and 16 men rehearsing "The Great Lady Has an Interview—Madame Crematon." Walters on Rehearsal Hall A.

Fred Astaire, Lucille Bremer, Robert Lewis, Cyd Charisse rehearsing "Limehouse Blues" sequence. Alton on Stage 28.

Bunin puppets shooting "Interior Theatre Boxes." Lou Chek on Lot 2.

Lena Horne shooting "Love." Ayers on Stage 21.[17]

The set for "Love" was a sleazy, smoked-filled dive in Martinique, designed by Smith and Ayers. The song was expressly written for Lena Horne by Martin and Blane. Ayers directed the number. He devised a dramatic prelude to Lena's entrance: A couple gets into a violent fight, hysteria spreads through the café. Screaming, the girl runs up a flight of stairs, and disappears. In a fast move the camera pulls down and reveals Lena. The mood for the song is established.

[17] Rehearsed two days; recorded one day; shot two days. Cost: $29,725.20.

The "Dorian Gray" set repainted and redressed for "Limehouse Blues."
M-G-M

Lena disliked the number intensely. She disagreed with the director's conception, objecting to the slum atmosphere of the Negro ghetto. She even refused to record the song commercially. However, for a number of years she used the song in her night-club act but in her own style.

7/9/44

Judy Garland and the boys rehearsing "Madame Crematon." Walters on Rehearsal Hall B.

James Melton shooting "A Cowboy's Life." Pye on Stage 21.[18]

Fanny Brice, Hume Cronyn and William Frawley shooting "Sweepstake Ticket." Del Ruth on Stage 3.[19]

Backing for Bunin animation: Cyd Charisse for Marilyn Miller. Walters for Lou Chek on Lot 2.[20]

[18] Rehearsed two days; recorded one day; shot two days. Cost: $27,775.10.
[19] Rehearsed one day; shot five days. Cost: $47,940.45. Del Ruth and Walters staged the dance bit between Brice and Frawley.
[20] Total cost to complete animated sequence (twenty reels), $305,120.60.

Fred Astaire, Lucille Bremer, Robert Lewis shooting "Limehouse Blues." Minnelli on Stage 28.

The longest and most elaborate sequence in the picture was "Limehouse Blues." It took eighteen days to rehearse, two days to record, ten days to shoot and ran thirteen minutes; it cost $228,225.66. The combined talents of Minnelli, Sharaff, Alton, Robert Lewis and Salinger were responsible for this memorable piece of film.

Limehouse was a red-light district in London. The song was written by Douglas Furber and Philip Braham for Gertrude Lawrence in her Broadway debut in *Charlot's Revue* (1924). In the original libretto a bar singer becomes involved with a sailor who subsequently is stabbed to death.

Minnelli was inspired by Gertrude Lawrence's performance and D. W. Griffith's silent movie, *Broken Blossoms* (1919). He, Sharaff and Alton discussed this sequence and a form began to emerge. Alton wrote a scenario with a realistic prologue and epilogue framing a Chinese fantasy sequence. The style of the first and last would be done in English mezzo tints, very dim and foggy. The fantasy would not be

The costermongers performing in the opening section (prologue) for "Limehouse Blues"; (center with cigar), Eugene Loring; (in Chinese costume and hat), Fred Astaire; (far right), Lucille Bremer. M-G-M

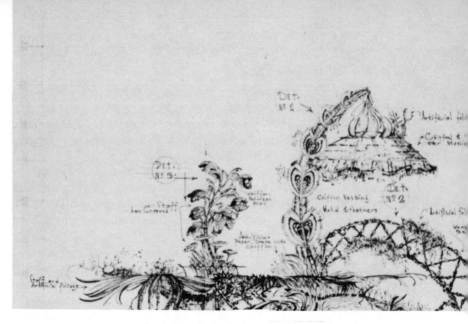

Jack Martin Smith's execution of a portion of Irene Sharaff's design for "Limehouse Blues." M-G-M

done in the conventional oriental manner but in the style of Louis XVI French chinoiserie.

"We had done *The Picture of Dorian Gray*," says Smith, "which had an English street as an exterior, still standing on a stage. I took that set for the beginning and the end of the number. I revised it and had it painted in monotones of browns, beiges, whites and yellows. And we pumped in the London fog."

"I want to tell you about that smoke," says Folsey. "The street itself was to be foggy and with spray guns we filled the set with smoke. I had a helluva time keeping it from overflowing into the café on the other side where Harriet Lee[21] was sitting on a table, singing 'Limehouse Blues.'"

Robert Lewis, well-known Broadway actor and director,[22] played a prosperous Chinese merchant and directed the dramatic portions of the prologue and the epilogue. He used a most effective piece of business in his performance: He held a cigarette in one hand and with a little wand in the other batted off the ashes.

Minnelli conjured up an atmosphere for the street: a man with a phonograph in a baby carriage, a drunken woman, and five coster-

[21] Harriet Lee was a vocal coach in the music department at the studio. She coached in the popular field.

[22] As an actor he was associated with the Group Theatre and appeared in *Golden Boy* (1937) and other Group productions. He directed the Broadway productions of *My Heart's in the Highlands* (1939) and *Heavenly Express* (1940).

136

mongers ("pearlies"), who were familiar street singers in London's Limehouse district. (Loring made a short appearance as one of the group.)

The fantasy sequence was entirely the creation of Sharaff. She not only designed the costumes but the conception of the set. She wanted it to look suspended, in limbo, against a cold backing. She used gunmetal as her principal material for both set and costumes, which served in a spectacular way to accentuate the burnt oranges, hot reds and vivid yellows. There were gunmetal palm trees, Chinese pathways and even feathers. The hats for the forty-five members in the chorus were made to look like gunmetal. They were molded in clay, cast in plaster, baked and sprayed with silver and rubbed in gold. Then they were adorned with metal scraps.

In the dream Astaire changed from his marvelously unique style of dancing to a more balletic expression. Sensitive to this change of style, Alton invented a choreography with fans which was highly original and gave Astaire props to work with. The skill and precision with which the ballet was executed was an athletic feat. Lucille Bremer, Astaire's partner and a most accomplished dancer, worked untiringly for hours on end with Alton, especially when it came to manipulating the fans. "He had fans all over the place," recalls Astaire. "When I'm doing my solos I mostly do them myself. But when I'm working with a girl I need a choreographer. Bob was good on tricks and lifts and he had ideas—and we'd work them out."

Salinger went to an Alton rehearsal. He was nervous; for him this was opening night. The prerecording of "Limehouse" was on the playback and everybody concerned would hear it for the first time. After a curt, preoccupied, businesslike "Hi! Connie," a whistle blew and Salinger jumped two feet in the air. The whistle was Alton's secret weapon: Everybody in place, everybody clear the stage—everybody knew the whistle meant something. He was not a drill sergeant, though; he was a quick-witted disciplinarian and his dancers adored him.

For hours Salinger had gone through the fan dance with Astaire and Alton bar by bar, matching music to dance, dance to music. Broken rhythms and syncopated breaks had to stay within the thematic framework of "Limehouse Blues." Salinger's tonal imagination and his theatrical flair guided him spectacularly from red-light Limehouse through a Chinese fantasy and back again.

7/22/44

"Limehouse Blues" rehearsing fantasy section. Alton on Stage 30.
Judy Garland and the boys shooting "Madame Crematon—The Great Lady Has an Interview." Minnelli on Stage 21.[23]

[23] Rehearsed ten days; recorded one day; shot three days. Cost: $57,334.85.

One of Irene Sharaff's costume designs for a member of the chorus in "Limehouse Blues." ARTHUR FREED ARCHIVES

In the lineup of suggested sequences, there was a musical number for Greer Garson, and Edens decided to write it. He was exhilarated by the idea of having Greer Garson, a great lady of the theatre, show a new facet of her talent, doing a sophisticated parody of a press interview. He says, "I went to Katie's [Thompson] office and told her about my idea. She got so hepped up about it and we both got so carried away that we decided to do it together, right then and there:

Reporters
(together upon entering)
"We are here to interview a lady known to you
Because of her ability
As the glamorous, amorous lady they call—

Fribbins (the butler)
(at the door)
"She's expecting you gentlemen,
Won't you come in.

Other Reporters
(together upon entering)
"Now we don't mean Greta
And we don't mean Betta or Loretta or The Song of Bernadetta
We mean the fabulous, dabulous lady they call—

Fribbins
(at the door)
"The other gentlemen are here,
Please come in.

All the Reporters
(in groups and individually)
"She's news,
She's front page stuff,
She's headlines,
She's tops;
And in advance the critics are all in accord—
She's gonna win the next Academy Award!
All her fans will be delighted,
Not to mention quite excited,
At her personal appearance, presently
She's stupendious, commendious,
Collossical, terrifical,
She's got it!! but DEFINITELY!!!
That glamorous, amorous lady they call . . ."

"Once we had done the introduction everything was easy, everything fell into place, it was nothing but fun," says Thompson. "Rog said, 'God, let's get Chuck [Walters] up here.' So, Chuck came up, and Ralph [Blane], and we did the whole thing for them and they just fell on the floor. 'You've got to do it just like that!' Well, I said, you both have to be the reporters. So I leaned against the desk and acted it out, Roger played it and we had a feeling we'd got it!"

Freed arranged for Edens et al. to audition the number at his house for Greer Garson. Minnelli was standing next to Freed in front of the fireplace in the living room. Seated on a sofa were Greer Garson, her husband, Richard Ney, and her mother. The conversation was uneasy and self-conscious. Edens went to the piano and overheard Minnelli saying to Garson, "I think this number will be charming for you." "Peculiar," Edens thought, "since he's never heard it."

When the group finished the audition, there was dead silence in the room. "Arthur, your house is beautifully appointed," said Ney. Freed and Minnelli just stood there with fatuous smiles on their faces. "Well, I don't think so," said Garson's mother. Ney gave the *coup de grâce:* "No, it's not for you, dear."

Stunned and totally dejected, the performers left. Getting into their car Edens exclaimed: "Goddamn it! It's great for Judy! Do you think she can do it? She can imitate you, Kay—she's a good mimic—I think it'll work!"

Walters staged the number. Judy learned it step by step and gesture by gesture imitating Thompson, with all the paraphernalia, a scarf, reading glasses, etc. When they were ready, Freed came to see Judy in the number. Thompson stood in as one of the reporters, along with Blane and Walters. "We were all on our knees," says Blane. "Freed had moved from one place to another and when Kay gave the downbeat she hit him in the crotch and Freed flew ten feet through the air. Kay murmured: 'Sorry—oh, Arthur, oh Arthur.' Writhing with pain, Freed forced out a weak 'That's all right . . .' "

"How did you like it, Arthur?" asked Judy when they'd finished. In the perfect nonsequitur of all times Freed replied: "I think Bing Crosby is going to win the Academy Award for *Going My Way* this year."[24]

To Walters' great disappointment Freed let Minnelli shoot the sequence. "Every bit of action in that number was mine. I almost cried," says Walters.

Minnelli took three days to shoot the number. He recalls, "I instinctively felt that Judy rather than simply walking in should be introduced by exposing only her arm extending across an archway with a slow, circular motion, a long chiffon scarf in her hand."

After a few preliminary meetings on the finale for the picture, Alton wrote a rough synopsis. Starting off with short vignettes of famous women in history, the finale would evolve into a colossal production number on an oversized ascending set, featuring Fred

[24] Freed was right: Crosby won the Academy Award for "Best Actor" in *Going My Way* (1944).

140

Astaire and Lucille Bremer dancing and James Melton singing "There's Beauty Everywhere" (written by Harry Warren and Arthur Freed). Instead of using the conventional device of dissolves, Alton proposed to use bubbles, which would obscure and reveal each change of image. When Alton and Minnelli discussed this they discarded the vignettes but kept the basic premise of the bubbles to make the finale an iridescent, shimmering, supernatural kaleidoscope of color.

They presented their plan to the art department, and consternation set in. But an efficient researcher found a machine making this kind of bubble; it was bought and shipped from Germany. The set was designed and built with platforms and terraced levels ascending higher and higher.

"The bubble machine, holding a volume of ten thousand gallons, was parked outside Stage 27," Smith explains. "A battery of pipelines made of galvanized iron was connected to the air vents in the ceiling. The stage is 131 feet by 236 feet to the height of 50 feet. There was more piping in there than it would take to irrigate Egypt. A group of prop men and special effect guys would feed the machine with aerosol and inject air and hot water. The bubbles then would pass through the valves cut through the air vents and clusters of bubbles would appear, 10 to 12 feet high, and many stayed airborne. The rest was satisfactory."

Freed was present when the machine was tested. "Wouldn't it be

Judy Garland in "The Great Lady Has an Interview" also known as "Madame Crematon." M-G-M

horrible if they got that soap bubble machine started and then couldn't stop it!" he said.

Astaire, Bremer, Charisse, Melton and the show girls rehearsed the number on a dry set for twelve days. Then, on the biggest boom available, Minnelli began to shoot. The bubble machine was turned on. He remembers vividly: "The camera followed the bubbles as they went off to the very top. Charlie Rosher, my cameraman, and I were on the boom. Suddenly these bubbles exploded and emitted a gas which was so overpowering that Rosher fainted. Well, if he fell off, he would have been killed—we were already forty feet up in the air. Had he fallen, by counterweight I would have gone through the ceiling. So I held on to him. He was a heavy man, you know. Finally they got us down."

The soap bubbles poured out like lava from a volcano and the fire brigade was called. Bubbles streamed down the sides, into caves, into every crevice. Armed with oversized badminton rackets several grips were detailed to keep the bubbles in place. They went around swatting unruly ones. "You've got to remember you can't direct bubbles!" says Minnelli.

Whenever the machine was stopped the crew, gasping for air,

Fred Astaire and Lucille Bremer (lower left) rehearse through the thousands of soap bubbles in the *Ziegfeld* finale. "You can't direct bubbles," said Minnelli. M-G-M

yelled "Open the doors!" and everybody ran outside. No sooner was it turned on again everybody was sneezing and coughing, and some fainted. Curious visitors entered only to make an about-face.

One day Astaire arrived with a temperature of 102. In a few days he was to leave for an overseas USO tour and had had five vaccination shots. He was feeling miserable. "With Lucille I squished through a sea of bubbles as prescribed in the number," says Astaire. Melton, in his waterproof white tie and tails, stuffed a wet handkerchief in his mouth for fear he would lose his voice.

On the seventh day of shooting Minnelli tried for the last shot of the number. After a series of hazardous arabesques, Astaire and Bremer reached the top of the ascend, ending up in a graceful pose to Melton's bel canto. Exasperated, Minnelli yelled "Cut!" Some bubbles had transformed Bremer and Astaire into two long-bearded rabbis.

From here on it was hit and miss for the rest of the day. The bubbles obscured the two figures on top; the bubbles settled on the camera lens. Finally a compromise take was printed and *Ziegfeld Follies* had come to an end. The doors were opened and everybody stumbled out in a wild exodus.

Editing had to be done in the "Bubble Finale" even before *Ziegfeld Follies of 1944* went into preview. For the first sneak at the Westwood Village Theatre on November 1, 1944, the running order was:

"Ziegfeld Days" — Bunin Puppets
"Meet the Ladies" — Astaire, Ball, Charisse, ensemble
"If Swing Goes, I Go Too" — Astaire
"The Pied Piper" — Durante
"If Television Comes" — Skelton
"A Cowboy's Life" — Melton
"Liza" — Horne, Long and chorus
"Baby Snooks" — Brice
"This Heart of Mine" — Astaire, Bremer and company
"Death and Taxes" — Durante, Arnold
"Pay the Two Dollars" — Moore, Arnold
"Love" — Horne
"Traviata" — Melton, Bell
"The Sweepstake Ticket" — Brice, Cronyn, Frawley
"Limehouse Blues" — Astaire, Bremer, Lewis
"The Great Lady Has an Interview" — Garland and reporters
"The Babbitt and the Bromide" — Astaire, Kelly
"There's Beauty Everywhere" — Astaire, Bremer, Melton, Charisse, ensemble

When "The End" title came on, two hours and fifty-three minutes had passed.

The reaction of preview audiences is taken seriously, and in this instance things did not go well. For one thing, the picture was too long. In an afterpreview panic everybody wanted to cut everything. Cool and rational as usual, Edens remarked to Simone: "If this keeps on we can always release it as a short."

Most of the comedy numbers played badly; there hadn't been a laugh in the audience. The two Durante sketches had to go, as did "Baby Snooks." The audience had not accepted Melton singing popular numbers; the cowboy number went and so did his section of "Honolulu." Esther Williams would remain under water only.[25] Fred Astaire didn't like his number "If Swing Goes . . ." So that went out. "Liza" had left the audience puzzling over a silent Lena Horne; it died on the cutting-room floor. Some comedy relief was needed in the opening number, "Meet the Ladies," and an added scene had to be devised for Virginia O'Brien for one of her usual deadpan deliveries.

How to end the picture was the big question. Even though the "rabbi" shot had been cut out for the first preview, some of the bubble shots could be salvaged, but an ending for the picture had to be conjured up.

Then somebody brought in Kathryn Grayson, who prerecorded "There's Beauty Everywhere" and Edens coached her. The last chorus of the song built up to a high B flat. Simone recalls: "One take, another take—she couldn't hit a good B flat. 'It's too high,' she said. Annoyed out of his customary politeness Roger said, 'I thought you were a singer!' We printed her last take and left the stage. We went on a search

[25] The theme song was replaced by an orchestral arrangement of "This Heart of Mine." Cutting these six sequences necessitated an over-all reshuffling of the underwater continuity to match the musical accompaniment.

Durante autographed this picture to Al Akst, the film editor on *Ziegfeld Follies*, who was Freed's brother-in-law. The inscription ironically reads "Take good care of me —don't let me find my face on the floor—your pal Jimmy Durante." RUTH FREED AKST

Astaire on his USO tour the week after *Ziegfeld* closed production; pictured in front of the Versailles Palace in France, entertaining the troops. ARTHUR FREED ARCHIVES

for a luscious B flat and found one. I cut off Grayson's anemic B flat, lined up the track on earphones and put them on the girl. I explained and told her 'Whenever we get to that point take a deep breath and hit it!' A true professional, she did it and we had our B flat."

From December to February retakes and added scenes were shot.[26] For the opening of the picture the camera panned up to heaven and moved over Shakespeare's Globe Theatre, P. T. Barnum's circus tent, David Belasco's Theatre. It finally came to a halt on the proscenium of the Ziegfeld's Theatre. In a nostalgic mood William Powell as Ziegfeld[27] brought those glorious days back to life.

In the opening number Virginia O'Brien was placed on a fake white horse, singing a take-off on "Here's to the Ladies" called "Bring on Those Wonderful Men!" (written by Edens and O'Brien's vocal coach, Earl Brent).

Grayson appeared in the final tableau standing in front of a black backdrop with *Ziegfeld Follies* spelled out in light bulbs. The tie-in from the bubbles into this scene was shot on a turntable with Grayson surrounded by girls in their bubble costumes.

[26] Directed by Norman Taurog.
[27] Powell was re-creating his role as Florenz Ziegfeld in *The Great Ziegfeld* (1936).

An additional sequence entitled "Number, Please,"[28] was shot, featuring Keenan Wynn.

After the second preview on March 12, 1945, another retake with Grayson for the finale was shot.

On August 20, 1945, with its new title, *Ziegfeld Follies of 1946* had a road-show première in Boston. The reception echoed the first Hollywood preview. Schenck ordered all M-G-M exchanges to hold their prints in their vaults until further notice. For the next seven months the studio experimented with reshuffling the continuity, restoring sequences that had been eliminated and contemplated the possibility of adding a flashy finale. Ultimately none of this came to pass.

Relieving Astaire of his anxiety, Freed informed him that the picture would indeed be released on April 8, 1946.

Although *Ziegfeld Follies* cost $3,240,816.86, in its initial release it went on to gross in excess of $5,344,000.

Even though Freed and his unit were still deeply involved with *Ziegfeld,* on June 27, 1944, the studio released the following item:

> Directional assignment on *The Clock,* the Judy Garland-Robert Walker starrer, has been handed to one of M-G-M's youngest directors, Fred Zinnemann. This comes as a result of Jack Conway's withdrawal because of illness. Conway, who was also forced to cease work in the middle of *Dragon Seed* and was replaced by Harry Bucquet, will take a long rest.
>
> Zinnemann first won recognition by his handling of *Eyes in the Night* and recently completed *The Seventh Cross,* starring Spencer Tracy.
>
> The picture will be ready to roll on August 1. Arthur Freed will produce.

In March 1943, Freed came across an unpublished short story called "The Clock" by Paul and Pauline Gallico, which he liked a great deal. It was a timely, romantic story about an American soldier on a forty-eight-hour leave in New York. He bought the property for $50,000 and assigned Margaret Green to develop a screenplay. He didn't like what she produced and in January 1944 brought in Joseph Schrank and Robert Nathan to start from scratch. Freed had known Nathan since his schooldays at Philips Exeter Academy.

On August 1, Zinnemann started shooting *The Clock.* From the very beginning the atmosphere on the set was tense and strained. There was no communication between Garland and Zinnemann. A soft-spoken, unaggressive man, Zinnemann fought an uphill battle every minute of the day, puzzling over the cause of Judy's lack of response.

---

[28] Directed by Robert Lewis. Two of the voices heard over the numerous telephone calls were Lewis as the Chinaman, and Peter Lawford as the English barrister."

Jan. 15th

PRICKLY PEAR
AIKEN
SOUTH CAROLINA

PRICKLY PEAR
AIKEN
SOUTH CAROLINA

Dear Arthur:—

This is positively and definitely the life. I feel as if I've got my head out of an olive press now that the loafing career is behind me.

I'm most curious about the "Follies" Arthur. Is it really ever going to be released? It is a most extraordinary experience for me to have performed something years before the public sees it. Dancing & entertaining in the musical line dates

so rapidly — it really worries me to think that perhaps I'll have my retirement interrupted by a stale performance five years after the actual making of the picture! As soon as that one is out of the way I'll be completely happy. I don't like to bother you about it but really feel that I'm entitled to know why things we planned so carefully seem to have gone so sour.

All best Arthur. I hear "Harvey Girls" is swell —

As ever — Fred A.

After twenty-four days the situation had become untenable and Garland went to see Freed. In effect, she had been playing for time. She had wanted Minnelli all along but he was not available since *Ziegfeld Follies* was still shooting. Now that he was free, she took the step.

"Judy came to see me," says Freed. " 'I don't know—he must be a good director, but I just get nothing. We have no compatibility.' So, I sent for Zinnemann. 'I know what you're going to talk to me about. I admire her, but things don't click between us—and if you think I should be off the picture you're right.' "

Minnelli looked over the script which was not altogether unfamiliar to him.[29] "I decided at once to make New York itself another character in the story and I introduced a number of crazy people," he recalls. "I used a lot of improvisation, not actually having a new script written, but instead I developed new ideas, new situations and dialogue as I went along."

The screenwriter voiced a formal protest to the producer:

[29] Minnelli retained three days of Zinnemann's footage. Contrary to what Minnelli reported on many occasions, Freed had no intention of shelving the property after taking Zinnemann off.

Freed in "his scene" from
The Clock, offers the star
Robert Walker a light. M-G-M

Dear Arthur:

The script to *The Clock* gives the instructions on that river scene, just as carefully as we can give them, as for instance:

They speak almost in whispers, as one with the night—

Alice (dreamily): So many stars . . .

Alice (still dreamily): I never knew their names . . . etc.

I still feel very strongly that when a director departs from the instructions in the script, he ought to (if only in politeness) discuss that departure with the writer *before* rather than *after* the scene is shot.

Bob Nathan

Minnelli defends himself: "There was a scene with a little boy at the pond in Central Park. Bob Walker made friends with him in the original script. It was all terribly 'darling.' Instead, I made him kick Walker and that made him more real, more human."

From here on the atmosphere on the set was very relaxed and everybody seemed to have fun; Judy had Vincente, Vincente had Judy.

In'the story the soldier arrives at Pennsylvania Station.[30] The main terminal was duplicated on Stage 27. Because of wartime restrictions the studio could not obtain a real escalator and had to construct a serviceable equivalent. The set cost $66,450. The expenditure for this set

[30] A la Hitchcock, Nathan, Freed and Edens appeared in the picture. In the first sequence of Pennsylvania Station, Nathan is seen silently smoking his pipe and Freed lights the soldier's (Walker's) cigarette. Edens appears later on, playing the piano in a café.

This was a tricky scene for Minnelli to shoot. Since he had to view the action, he sits on top of the set. VINCENTE MINNELLI COLLECTION

was money well spent. When Walker leaves for the war again, after a twenty-four-hour honeymoon, Judy is lost in the milling crowd; the camera rises, pulling back to reveal the giant circumference of the train terminal; a feeling of utter despair and loneliness is established that no dialogue could ever have made more intense.

George Bassman, under contract to the studio principally as an orchestrator, had been assigned to compose the score. The picture called for sensitive spotting of music, juxtaposing the crude city noises with the tenderness of the love story. Bassman delivered the sketches of his score to the music department. And Simone went to look at them to prepare the scoring sessions. She took Bassman's sketch of the main theme and went to George Schneider, head music librarian and an expert in his field. After a quick glance he said: "You're so right—this is Enesco."[31] They both realized that a change was needed to avoid a plagiarism suit. Grouchily, Bassman changed his melodic line. Under Lennie Hayton's subtle musical direction Bassman's score was recorded and effectively dubbed into the picture.

The Clock[32] was Freed's first dramatic picture. To cast Judy Garland in the role of a plain, lower middle-class girl, in a milieu of drabness, took a man of Freed's convictions. He entrusted Minnelli with the direction although he had exclusively worked in the medium of musical comedy, both on stage and screen. Freed's daring antitype casting brought to the screen an exceptionally sensitive, touching film that one could describe as the "love story" of that era.

[31] George Enesco (1881–1955), famous Rumanian composer-conductor-violinist and Yehudi Menuhin's teacher.

[32] The picture cost $1,324,207.70. In its initial release (May 25, 1945), it grossed $2,783,000.

Kaprelick's drawing.
M-G-M

Film critic James Agee said about *The Clock:* "Emotionally it is perceptive, detailed and sweet and there is more ability, life, resource and achievement in it than in any fiction film I have seen for a long time. The script by Robert Nathan and Joseph Schrank is shrewd; but the man who pours it so full of gifts is Minnelli."

Between May and October 1943 there was an exchange of letters between Hammerstein and Freed.

Freed had tentatively put *Show Boat* on his production schedule. He was interested in seeing it revived on Broadway because—if successful —it would make it easier for him to launch his picture.

OSCAR HAMMERSTEIN, 2ᴺᴰ

September 21, 1943

Mr. Athur Freed
Metro Goldwyn Mayer
Culver City
California

Dear Arthur:-

When I heard from Frank Orsatti that you wanted me to come out and work on SHOW BOAT, I was terribly sorry not to be able to accept the assignment. I understand perfectly, however, that if the studio wants to proceed with preparing this production now there is no reason in the world why it should wait for me. What I am writing to ask you is this:-

Have you any idea when the picture would be released? The reason I ask this question is that hardly a week passes that some group doesn't approach me and offer to finance a production of SHOW BOAT. The success of other revivals has made it very hot. If it is likely that Metro will release the picture within the next two years, I would have to advise these people that it is a bad financial venture to put so much money into a play and not have enought time to make back the production and turn in a profit. I realize that you can't give me a definite date. All I want is your approximate idea.

Looking foward to hearing from you, with all good wishes,

as ever,

Oscar

October 14, 1943

Dear Oscar:

Please excuse the delay in answering your letter, but it took me this long to be able to give you an intelligent answer regarding *Show Boat.* I believe that you would be perfectly safe in going ahead with the production this time, because under no circumstances could we have the picture ready for release within eighteen months. That would be a miracle. I believe it will be closer to two years. We have not started to work on the script, which would take at least four or five months, again with optimism. Preparation and shooting—six months; cutting, editing and scoring—two months; previews, etc.—another month; prints, color work, release prints, etc.—two or three months; trade showings, advertising, etc.—another three or four months; so add this up and you can see how long it takes to make a picture of this magnitude. I have very interesting ideas on *Show Boat* that I will tell you the first time we meet. I believe we can get the most important picture of its kind ever made. Let me know your plans on *Show Boat*. I would love, as you once suggested, to be associated in some way with you in this venture.

Regarding *The Belle of New York*.[33] We have a fine outline for the story and I am still counting on you and Dick Rodgers to do the score. When would you and Dick have time to go to work on this along the lines we spoke about? The way I feel about you, Oscar, "people will say we're in love."

Kindest regards,
Arthur

June 7, 1943

Dear Arthur:

. . . Regarding the Judy Garland picture you spoke to Dick and me about, we are looking forward to receiving a story layout whenever you have one. Meanwhile, we have nearly concluded a deal with 20th Century Fox which also contemplates writing a picture in the East. While this in no way affects our desire to do a Garland picture with you, it would necessarily postpone our work on it for a few months.

I saw *Cabin in the Sky* a couple of nights ago and thought it a very beautiful picture. The audience seemed to love it. Please congratulate Vincente for me on his first directorial assignment. I thought he did a fine job. The whole thing was intelligently produced and for the first time I realized the double-barreled courage that it needed because it was not only a negro picture but a fantasy as well, and both these elements have been on the taboo list for some time.

I may be in California for just two days in the early part of July and if I come, I will ring you up. Meanwhile all the best to you.

Sincerely,
Oscar

[33] The *Belle of New York* was a comic opera by Hugh Morton and Gustav Kirker. J. Robert Rubin, one of the founders of M-G-M and it's New York representative for studio affairs, purchased the property on behalf of the studio. Freed put it on his production schedule as a vehicle for Judy Garland and Fred Astaire. A story consultant at the time, Chester Erskine, prepared a treatment, Irving Brecher, a first draft screenplay.

In a period of two and one-half years—from 1943 to 1945—Freed made five pictures concurrently: *Meet Me in St. Louis, Ziegfeld Follies, The Clock, The Harvey Girls* and *Yolanda and the Thief.*

In May 1943, Edens went to New Haven to see *Oklahoma!*[34] Upon his return he gave Freed a glowing report and expressed his wish to do a Western musical.

Bernie Hyman, an M-G-M producer, had slated for production a dramatic film titled *The Harvey Girls,* to star Lana Turner, based on a book by Samuel Hopkins Adams and an unpublished story by Eleanore Griffin and William Rankin. The stories dealt with the life of the Harvey girls, employees of the Fred Harvey restaurant chain. In September 1942, upon Hyman's death, Metro began negotiating the sale of the property to another studio. When the Harvey family was informed about it they made it very clear that they would not give permission to any studio other than M-G-M to make the film. Freed dug up the material and became interested.

Rudi Monta, the studio's international copyright expert, advised Freed that although they owned all rights to the material it was essential to submit an outline of any musical screenplay to the Harvey family. He further advised that William A. Orr of the New York office's legal department would be the right person to handle the Harvey family, to secure authenticated releases, etc.

The following is Freed's skillfully worded plea, which gave Orr a valuable document to launch negotiations with the Harveys:

Night Letter

MR. WILLIAM A. ORR
BLACKSTONE HOTEL
CHICAGO, ILL.
I WOULD APPRECIATE YOUR SPEAKING WITH MR. HARVEY AND
OBTAINING HIS PERMISSION FOR ME TO MAKE AN OPERETTA
BASED UPON THE MATERIAL AT PRESENT ENTITLED "THE HARVEY
GIRLS". I HAVE BEEN PARTICULARLY ATTRACTED TO DO THIS
WITH MUSIC, AS I BELIEVE ONLY MUSIC CAN PERPETUATE IN A
DIGNIFIED MANNER THE ROMANCE AND AMERICAN FOLK
QUALITY OF THIS WONDERFUL PROJECT. BOTH EDNA FERBER'S
"SHOW BOAT" AND THE PRESENT SUCCESS "OKLAHOMA!" ·HAVE
BECOME IMPORTANT AMERICAN WORKS THROUGH GIVING THEM
THE GAIETY AND SPIRITUAL QUALITY OF MUSIC. THAT AS
STRAIGHT DRAMAS COULD NEVER HAVE REACHED THEIR
PRESENT STATUS IN THE THEATRICAL LITERATURE OF AMERICAN
FOLKLORE. THAT IS WHY I AM SO EXCITED ABOUT DOING "THE
HARVEY GIRLS", AND I WOULD APPROACH THIS MATERIAL WITH
A GREAT DEAL OF REVERENCE AND WOULD DO IT IN A MANNER
THAT I HOPE WILL PERPETUATE THE MEMORY OF THIS GREAT
INSTITUTION FOR MANY YEARS TO COME. I WOULD MAKE THIS
PICTURE IN TECHNICOLOR AND USE THE FINEST ARTISTS TO

[34] The show was then called *Away We Go!* The settings had been designed by Lemuel Ayers. It was Edens who urged Freed to bring Ayers out to work in the unit.

PORTRAY THE CHARACTERS, AND I WOULD APPRECIATE IT IF
YOU COULD OBTAIN FOR ME THE FURTHER HELP FROM THE
HARVEYS THAT WOULD HELP US ALL SO MUCH. I EARNESTLY
HOPE THAT IT WILL BE POSSIBLE TO CARRY OUT OUR PLANS AND
THAT WE CAN DO AN IMPORTANT, DIGNIFIED AMERICAN WORK.
KINDEST REGARDS.

ARTHUR FREED

During the ensuing months Freed engaged Guy Bolton, Edmund
Beloin, Nathaniel Curtis, Harry Crane, James O'Hanlon, Hagar Wilde,
Kay Van Riper and Samson Raphaelson, who worked consecutively on
the screenplay. He brought Harry Warren and Johnny Mercer together
again to write the score.[35]

Briefly, this is the history of the "Harvey system." In 1876, Fred
Harvey founded a small establishment in Topeka, Kansas, and since
then the Harvey houses had grown into an institution ranging over
three thousand miles, known to millions of travelers. In those early
years there were "loose ladies" in most public houses in the primitive
communities of the Southwest. To offset the bad influence, young
women of good character, attractive and intelligent, aged eighteen to
thirty, were brought out to serve as waitresses in Harvey's restaurants.

A stickler for authenticity, Edens researched every detail pertaining
to the Harvey family and their enterprise. "In a musical, because of
economy of footage, the music must tell a lot of the plot," Edens
explains. "A love song must also advance the story. Even without
a finished screenplay I would confer with Warren and Mercer, indicating situations which I wanted described in song. For example,
we needed an elaborate number celebrating the arrival of the train
with the Harvey girls. They delivered "On the Atchison, Topeka and the
Santa Fe."[36] I wanted to clarify the identity of each of the Harvey girls.
So, Katie [Thompson] and I wrote and interpolated a section doing
just that."

Fred Harvey had died a long time before and management had
passed on to his son and grandson, Byron and Byron, Jr. At first,
they were obstacles in Edens' way. Shrewdly he recognized that the
surest way to break down their resistance was by winning the esteem
of their right hand, Harold Belt.[37] With Raphaelson's script and most
of the score in hand, Edens went to Chicago to meet the Harveys.
Belt had already laid the groundwork. Edens, as a one-man show,
acted out story, score and action in his own inimitable fashion. At
the end of their meetings the Harveys' fears of misrepresentation were
dispelled; in fact, they realized the prestige the picture would give

[35] Warren and Mercer had collaborated on several pictures at Warner Bros.
in the late 1930s.

[36] The song went on to win the Academy Award in 1946.

[37] Edens had gone to New York and had a series of meetings with Belt at the
Barbizon-Plaza Hotel.

them. They assigned Belt as their representative and technical adviser during the production of the film.

The writing of the script had the aspects of a relay race. Bolton's suggestions could not be used; fragments of Curtis' and Beloin's script were retained; Van Riper's dialogue for the principal Harvey girl was excellent, the rest was too soft; Crane and O'Hanlon added a few laughs; Wilde made no contribution and left after a few days. Raphaelson took all the existing scripts, shortened, strengthened and tightened them, and it was his screenplay that was used. When a rewrite for a love scene was needed, George Wells accommodated.[38]

Judy Garland had expressed her preference for playing the lead in *Yolanda and the Thief,* but she was persuaded that the better part for her would be in *The Harvey Girls*. In the cast were John Hodiak, Ray Bolger, Angela Lansbury,[39] Preston Foster, Virginia O'Brien, Kenny Baker, Marjorie Main, Selena Royle, Chill Wills and Cyd Charisse, as one of the Harvey girls.[40]

Freed assigned George Sidney to direct the picture. Nothing was said about past events, the *Ziegfeld* incident was conveniently forgotten.

Midway through *Ziegfeld Follies* it became apparent that *The Harvey Girls* and *Yolanda and the Thief* would start shooting simultaneously. It followed that the productions would be split between Freed and Edens: Edens on *Harvey Girls* and Freed on *Yolanda*. Especially since Freed, in this instance, would not only be the producer but the lyric writer for the score.

The Harvey Girls went before the cameras on January 12, 1945.

When "Atchison, Topeka and the Sante Fe" was recorded, everybody, including the janitor, was on the recording stage. Judy did her choruses in one take. With the singers, solo voices and musical effects recorded on the difficult mechanics of multiple tracks, this huge musical panorama was completed in eight hours, with a one-hour luncheon break.

Ralph Blane assisted Kay Thompson on the vocal arrangement. Blane said, "I helped. Kay would write twenty ideas while I threw out nineteen. They'd just come to her like that, she was so fast! As a matter of fact, Kay could have been a great composer had she settled on one theme or one idea. She could never discipline herself to do the same thing twice. She always kept finding new ways of doing it better and better. That's all right, but it sometimes gets too good and you improve it right out the window."

Alton rehearsed "Atchison, Topeka and the Santa Fe" for twenty days. "Atchison" was an action number. It takes place on acres of open

---

[38] Total writers' payroll: $132,962.

[39] When the film was first announced for production, Ann Sothern was mentioned for the part.

[40] Total cast payroll: $443,766.67. The costumes cost $75,942.38.

Rehearsing the "Atchison, Topeka and the Santa Fe" sequence. Edens (seated on the baggage car) looks on as Cyd Charisse and two other Harvey Girls rehearse part of the scene; George Sidney (with hat on) is looking into the camera with George Folsey seated behind him; on the right of Folsey stands Robert Alton. ROGER EDENS ARCHIVES

ground[41]; a train arrives, travelers get off; there are milling crowds—a choreographer would have his hands full if he were to mount this for the theatre. But in motion pictures, stage space is limitless. Alton's conception of a number such as "Atchison" far exceeded his talents as a choreographer. His eye was more on movement than on dance steps. He had the rare gift of moving people to a musical cadence without ever making them theatrical and unreal. To be sure, this was a Judy Garland number. But in a subtle way he made Garland the focal point of the number without isolating her and yet he did not jeopardize her "stopping the show."

One of the elements which identifies a Freed picture is that the audience knows the main characters within the first five minutes, whether through dialogue or music, or both. In the very beginning of

[41] Shot on Lot 3.

this picture the audience shares Judy's daydreams as she sings "In the Valley" on the train. Moments later the "Atchison" number follows. It was not designed solely as an elaborate production number, but also to have each girl tell where she comes from and what she hopes for her future in this little town.

Sidney's aim was to give the picture a primitive look, the vitality of a pioneer town and—most of all—a lightness and gaiety. As he said: "We wanted to make a fluff."

The day came to shoot the number. Sidney was riding in his car to Lot 3. "It was the weirdest thing," Sidney says, "I turned on my radio and what did I hear? Crosby singing 'Atchison, Topeka, and the Santa Fe.' It was funny hearing the song and going out to shoot the number! That day Judy came in at one o'clock. She went through the whole thing and said, 'I'm ready!' We shot it and she did it like she had been rehearsing it for six months. It was sheer genius! Another time I was in a manhole under the camera," Sidney continues, "shooting up at the girls. Suddenly I heard a voice: 'What is this? Look what I'm mixed up with—I've got two crazy directors—one is underground and one is hanging up on a boom![42] Can't talk to my directors —they're both crazy!' It was Arthur!"

[42] He was referring to Minnelli whom he had just left shooting *Yolanda.*

One of the few scenes in which one can remember Cyd Charisse in *The Harvey Girls;* Judy to her left and Virginia O'Brien to her right. M-G-M

The company went on location in Chatsworth in the San Fernando Valley, as yet an unpopulated desert. The spot selected to shoot a scene with Judy arriving in a horse-drawn carriage to meet Hodiak was on the plateau of a mountain with a panoramic view of the entire landscape. The setting was superb. On the first day the sky was blue, the air was clear, it was hot. When Sidney and Folsey set up their camera angles, it turned out that the few clouds in the sky were in the wrong place. They had to wait. Sidney made use of the time and rehearsed. The horse-drawn carriage came around the bend and Judy panicked, being deathly afraid of horses. Unfortunately, the horse was nervous and reared. Judy retired to her trailer. By now it was twelve o'clock: lunchtime. Some members of the company had noticed a few miles away on top of a hill, what was obviously another film company at work. "Yes," said Dave Friedman, the unit manager, "that's Columbia shooting one of their Westerns." To break the monotony of the so far inactive day, some of the crew members got in a car and went to visit. "We watched and what we saw left us in utter amazement," recalls Simone. "Within thirty minutes the director shot ten setups with the cowboy hero. Someone asked, 'What are they doing?' 'They are doing a full-length quickie Western and they shoot the whole thing in six days,' came the answer from one of the technicians. When we returned to our set we were full of energy and rearing to go. But the afternoon brought no change. The clouds were still in the wrong place, the horse was still nervous . . . and the location broke up for the day."

Eventually, conditions improved and Sidney began to shoot the sequence.

Simone remembers that day well: "One of the electricians came toward me, tears streaming down his face, and said, 'Roosevelt is dead.' I was paralyzed. Many of the men were crying. I forced myself to recover and slowly climbed up toward the set, wondering what to do, when Friedman came down. I told him the news. Without a moment's hesitation he said most pointedly, 'Don't tell Sidney—we'll keep going.' I was appalled; I quickly walked away from Friedman and up to the plateau, determined to pass on the news. Fortunately, I was relieved of it; one of the crew had apparently passed me and told Sidney. Sidney turned to the assistant director George Rhein, and said, 'I want everybody up here!' By then a pall had fallen over the company. In a couple of minutes everyone was assembled around Sidney, on the top of the mountain, in complete isolation. It was like a bad dream. I do not remember Sidney's exact words. But I do remember that he made a very dignified statement which ended with 'We are going home.' Judy's reaction was pathetic: She completely fell to pieces; her hairdresser and friend walked her down the hill and drove off."

In the process of developing the story line, Freed had injected a valid point: The Harvey girls would not arrive in a pious community. "It's got to be the bad girls against the good girls," he said. Provoked by the infringement of their own private territory an out-and-out fist fight would take place between the dance-hall girls, headed by Angela Lansbury, versus Judy Garland and the Harvey girls. As a last resort, the bad girls would burn down the Harvey House.

The burning of the Harvey House was shot at night on Lot 3.[43] Although well isolated, it was nevertheless in the vicinity of other sets, structures and buildings. Most precarious of all was the closeness of a well-populated section of Culver City. Every precaution had to be taken. All available firemen and equipment were on stand-by duty. The M-G-M Police Department was there in full force to ward off intruders. But before the flames could engulf the restaurant, other preparations had to be made. A double for Judy, a husky stuntman, had to be made up, dressed and wigged, to stand in for her when she is trapped inside the house as it went up in flames. Moreover, Hodiak and Foster had to slug it out in the house, engulfed by fire and smoke.

It was ice cold, everybody shivered, while all went well during the dry runs.

Finally the time had come: Sidney and his camera crew, the actors, the stunt people, the extras,[44] were ready to shoot. "Pour it on, boys!" Sidney shouted. Crouching under the eaves, a handful of brave men poured gasoline on the roof of the house, jumped off and the flames sprang up, ignited by a torch. "Action!" shouted Sidney. Hodiak and Foster started slugging each other, fell down and in a split second the stuntmen were in their places while they ran for cover, hidden by clouds of smoke. Screams were heard. In Judy's white satin gown the bowlegged stuntman leaped out of camera range, his skirt raised above his knobby knees. "Cut!" shouted Sidney. "Fire out!" he yelled at the top of his lungs. With that, dozens of firemen jumped from their hiding places, spouting oceans of water over the burning structure.

"No good," said Sidney, calm but desperate. The fire had to be extinguished, the building had to cool off—and then it had to be built up again. Hours passed. "See you tomorrow night, George."

Folsey, the cameraman, has his own set of memories: "There was some fun too. We used to play baseball with Judy and John Hodiak on location. Judy was a southpaw. I had a very efficient crew and these capable guys went about their business and once we were established they'd go ahead and do it and it left me without apparently having anything to do. One day we were sitting at lunch and Belt said, 'George, I know what Howard does, and what Fenton does, and what Bobby does, and what Charlie does, but I don't know what you do.' And I looked at him and said, "Well, Mr. Belt, I don't do anything. I'm not supposed to do anything. I'm just here to add class and distinction to the company!' Of course, we had a big time with that joke."

[43] Sandrock Street: exterior and interior Alhambra; exterior and interior Harvey House—construction and decoration: $395,969.40.

[44] Extras' cost: $7,440 for the scene.

Hirschfeld's drawing for the studio publicity department. M-G-M

The Harvey Girls was previewed on July 12, 1945, in Inglewood. Even before the preview the picture had been tightened and some scenes had been deleted, partly because of over-all length: "Hayride" and "The March of the Doagies," two production numbers with Garland and "My Intuition" a Garland-Bolger duet did not play too well.

Thompson and Blane were packed into Edens' old Ford roadster on their way to the screening. They all were puffing nervously on their cigarettes. Edens' mind was on things to come and barely aware of his passengers, when he suddenly smelled something burning. Scrambling in panic it turned out that Blane was on fire. Totally absent-minded, Blane had put his cigarette out in the inside of his coat pocket. "Ralph—get out of the car!" yelled Edens, going sixty miles an hour. Blane tore off his jacket and threw it out the window.

Soon their anxieties were relieved: At the end of "Atchison" a cheer went up and there was continuous applause throughout the film.

Except for a few trims, no work needed to be done on the picture and it was turned in for release.

160

The following memos from Al Jennings log the absences of Judy Garland during the shooting of the picture:

At 4:30 P.M. yesterday, Thursday, the company called Miss Garland to give her Friday's shooting call. At this time Miss Garland advised the company that she could not work until possibly Monday due to having two teeth extracted and for which a bridge was being made.

At 12:45 P.M. today, Friday, I telephoned Miss Garland at her studio dressing room to enquire if the situation was the same and she advised it was.

Mr. Grady communicated with Miss Garland's dentist, Dr. Pinckus, and received the information that Miss Garland will receive the bridge on Saturday, wear it Saturday and Sunday and be in Dr. Pinckus' office on Monday morning for a checkup. Mr. Grady therefore advises Miss Garland should be ready at 1 P.M. on Monday for shooting purposes *if* the dentist reports the bridge satisfactory.

Under the above conditions it would not be wise for the company to plan a shooting day on Lot 3 for Monday, with a big crew and talent list, on the possibility of getting a couple of hours' work in the event Miss Garland is available.

Inasmuch as we have nothing to shoot at this time without Miss Garland we must also avoid a shooting call for Saturday. We therefore plan on rehearsing musical numbers Saturday and Monday.

4/19/45

Miss Garland had a 10:15 A.M. call to do loops today, 4/19/45. At 8:45 A.M. she telephoned that she was all bruised up due to fight scenes of yesterday and didn't feel well enough to work today.

4/24/45

At approximately 7:25 A.M. today, Judy Garland telephoned George Rhein, assistant director on above company, saying that she didn't feel well and didn't know whether she'd be in or not. Rhein telephoned me about it and I in turn telephoned Miss Garland, telling her that we had a crowd of people ordered for the day and would like to know definitely whether she would be in; she then said that she didn't feel well and would not be in today. Call on extras was then canceled and company had to go on layoff but utilized the day in rehearsing wedding scene, lining up shot for it and also rehearsed fight routine with stunt doubles in Harvey House.

5/15/45

At 2:30 this morning Judy Garland called Griffin, second assistant on the picture, and told him she hadn't slept all night so far because she was making Decca records until 11:45 P.M. last night. She said that after she came home she wasn't able to sleep and knew that she wouldn't look good the next day, and since the scene was an important one she felt she better stay home today, 5/15/45. She called up as she knew we had people ordered and could cancel them before it was too late.

People were canceled on quarter checks and company was forced to lay off for the day as there are no scenes we could do without her.

5/24/45

Miss Garland had a 1 P.M. call today, 5/24/45, to do loops; at 12:45 she telephoned Ted Hoffman on stage 2A that she was hoarse and would not be able to make the loops today but that the hoarseness was breaking and she'd be able to do them tomorrow. The loops then were set for 10 A.M., tomorrow, 5/25/45.

5/26/45

Judy Garland had a 10:30 A.M. call today, 5/26/45, to do loops; at 10:15 she telephoned that she was feeling ill and would not be able to do the loops.

The final cost of the picture was $2,524,315.06. Because of the overbundance of M-G-M products, the choice Loew's theatres had been prebooked, and *The Harvey Girls'* release was delayed. It opened at the Capitol (New York) Theatre on January 18, 1946. In its initial release it grossed in excess of $5,175,000.

Only a few days after Edens and Freed had discussed their plan to make a Western musical, Freed stunned him with the news that he was going to produce *Yolanda and the Thief* for Lucille Bremer. When Edens called his attention to the fact that this new project would probably have to go into production simultaneously with *The Harvey Girls,* it left Freed unperturbed.

By accident Freed had come across *Yolanda and the Thief* in a magazine. He had known the author Ludwig Bemelmans for years. "A charming writer," Freed says, "just beautiful—childlike in his way— I always liked his book—I used to call him a minor Molnar [Ferenc]."

Ludwig Bemelmans was born in the Tyrol, a province of the Austro-Hungarian monarchy. His father was Belgian and a painter, but all of his kin were in the hotel business. He came to the United States in 1914 at the age of sixteen, landed a job as a busboy at the Astor in New York, broke too many dishes and got another job as a waiter's runner at the Hotel "Splendide." When the United States entered World War One he was drafted into the American Army. His war diary is perhaps the most unconventional published in modern times.[45]

[45] *My War with the U.S.A.* (1918).

After the war Bemelmans, now a naturalized citizen, returned to his job at the Splendide.

In 1934, a visiting friend brought along May Massey, editor of children's books for Viking Press. Bemelmans had painted Tyrolean landscapes on his window shades and whenever he was homesick or lonely he pulled them down to be comforted by the familiar scenes. Massey thought that this was a man who should be writing books for children. The result of her visit was *Hansi,* a story about Bemelman's childhood in the Tyrol, which he also illustrated. This was the beginning of many articles, short stories and children's tales—*Madeline* being one of the most memorable.[46]

After the Second World War he became an habitué of the bar at the Hotel Carlyle in New York. The tabs stacked up and rather than pay he proceeded to paint the walls with beautiful fresco pictures, and it has been known as Bemelmans Bar ever since.

Bemelmans arrived at the studio on August 23, 1943. He was given an office in the Thalberg Building (the "Iron Lung"). For a couple of weeks he had absolutely nothing to do except sit. "I looked at my pristine, bare walls and decided something had to be done. So I painted the walls with a confusion of grotesque animals, quarreling waiters and bilious boulevardiers; that's the way people began to know I was there," he recalled.

Neither the executive third floor nor the maintenance department appreciated the art work. Frantic directives were given to have the paintings erased. Mayer came down to see them and turned green; they were to be scraped off until the "high-priced" estimate for repainting was submitted.

Bemelmans and his collaborator, Jacques Thiery, wrote a treatment and Joseph Schrank developed a screenplay. Freed was not satisfied and handed it over to George Wells. He was still not satisfied. He called on his old friend, Robert Nathan, to write a new screenplay. And although it turned out to be more what Freed had in mind he wanted extensive revisions. He pulled Brecher off his current assignment and asked him to work out yet another script with Bemelmans' help. Brecher openly expressed his lack of enthusiasm over writing a script for Lucille Bremer. He even went to Sam Katz and asked to be taken off the assignment. At first Katz asked Brecher to do it as a favor for Freed; finally he pleaded with Brecher and offered him a four-year contract at $2,000 a week, without options. Brecher couldn't resist and went to work.

Bemelmans and Brecher's first meeting was most congenial. To start off on the right foot Bemelmans took his paint brush and decorated the

[46] Some of his credits: *The Golden Basket* (1936); *Castle Number Nine* (1937); *Quito Express* (1938); *Life Class* (1938); *Madeline* (1939); *Small Beer* (1939); *Now I Lay Me Down to Sleep* (1943).

High Ho Silver
To Arthur
from
[signature]
Hollywood 1944

Bemelmans had a fondness for steeplechase riding.
ARTHUR FREED ARCHIVES

walls of Brecher's office. He started at one end of the room with a caricature of Brecher, holding an egg, symbolizing the basic idea for *Yolanda*. Across the wall he depicted its gestation period and ended with the birth of "the baby" on the other side of the room.

Shortly thereafter they went their separate ways. Bemelmans began work on an original story and Brecher finished the screenplay.

On January 15, 1945, three days after *The Harvey Girls, Yolanda and the Thief* began shooting. In the cast were Fred Astaire, Lucille Bremer, Mildred Natwick, Frank Morgan and Leon Ames. It was directed by Vincente Minnelli, choreographed by Eugene Loring, costumes designed by Irene Sharaff, art direction by Jack Martin Smith and musical direction by Lennie Hayton.

Bemelmans' story is a charming fairy tale. In a mythical country, Patria, a young heiress, has finished her education in a convent school and is stepping out into the world. She lives wth her eccentric duenna aunt in a magnificent palace and finds herself attracted to a charming adventurer who makes her believe he is her guardian angel. Of course, there is also a "real" angel. Complications arise, the imposter redeems himself, the two marry and live happily ever after.

Brecher broadened this little fable. What the story lacked was made up by the exquisite presentation of Astaire and Bremer's dance numbers, especially Astaire's dream ballet. But the true stars of this film were Sharaff and Minnelli: They wrapped the simple yarn in a cloak of exotic elegance and visual enchantment.

As the prelude to the picture itself, there is a group of young children in red school uniforms, seated in a lush green landscape with their lovable old schoolmaster. Here Minnelli leaned heavily on Bemelmans the painter, the illustrator and specifically on his short film *Madeline*. The scenes inside the convent, the Mother Superior and the nuns, a charming puppet show[47] and Yolanda's leave-taking to go out into the world were genuine Bemelmans.

In *Yolanda,* Irene Sharaff went far beyond costume design. She went out of her orbit, as Jack Smith says, and used her talent and imagination to put her vision on the drafting board. Sharaff, calm, decisive, organized and articulate complemented Minnelli's emotional and often nonverbal temperament. Their communication was instinctual.

"Vincente's greatest forte is his art," says Irene Sharaff. "Sometimes he gets indigestion from it. He's a visually oriented man. Have you ever seen Vincente in his office, cutting out his bits of pictures? To express himself he has to have something to look at; it is a psychic need. What his eyes perceive esthetically is Vincente's whole *raison d'être.*"

[47] Performed by the great puppeteer Remo Bufano.

Minnelli gives Judy, his fiancée, and Freed a piece of cake at the occasion announcing their forthcoming marriage. Taken on the *Yolanda* set, Judy is wearing one of her costumes for *The Harvey Girls.* ARTHUR FREED ARCHIVES

In earlier years Freed had written the lyrics for the scores of *The Broadway Melody* (1929), *Lord Byron of Broadway* and *Good News* (1930), *Stage Mother* (1933), *Student Tour* and *Sadie McKee* (1934), and *The Broadway Melody of 1936* and *1938*. His best work was done under pressure and *Yolanda* was no exception. He and Harry Warren went to Santa Barbara, locked themselves up in a hotel suite and wrote the score in three weeks.

"Bananas" was one of their songs. "I don't like it—we need a rhythm number," Astaire told Loring. Nothing more was said and Loring started working out something of his own. An idea came to him, "Jazz in Five," or, as he called it, "The Five-Four," and worked out a series of variations. "I didn't know whether it could be used, but I experimented. With my assistant I showed some of it to Warren. He was enthusiastic, sat down at the piano and played an old tune of his, 'Java Time.' We tried some of our steps to it and it worked."

Loring gave Freed a demonstration of what he had in mind and Freed loved it as much as Warren. On the following day he came in with his lyrics. "I thought of South America—coffee plantations—coffee beans . . . in my mind I saw Fred and Lucille do a dragging, slow jazz rhythm."

The number "Coffee Time" was part of the fiesta sequence, the locale a plaza, surrounded by the baroque facades of the buildings. Sharaff's principal color for the costumes was café au lait. During rehearsals Sharaff began to realize that the costumes had to be set against a

A Bemelmans painting in which the author-artist tries to give Freed and Minnelli the atmosphere the picture should have. ARTHUR FREED ARCHIVES

contrasting floor. She came up with a bizarre and most effective idea: an undulating, linear, black-and-white striped pavement. Her craftsmanship went so far as to get her down on her knees to sketch in the striped pattern for the studio painters to execute.[48]

Smith's concept for the film was based on one of his favorite painters, Tiepolo. "This was just a springboard; it gave me quite a bit of freedom," he recalls. "Yolanda's palace was pure baroque—from the ornate exterior to the interior foyer with its grand staircase and columns to Lucille's bathroom, if you can call it that."

Minnelli's emphasis on visual effects and props sometimes led him to neglect the essential—namely the actor before the camera. The bathroom scene was a case in point. Kay Thompson visited the set to watch the shooting, and recalls, "Lucille was in her elaborate bathtub, filled with soap bubbles and water, liquid soap and perfume. On the marble ledge of the tub was a telephone. It would ring, Lucille would pick up the receiver and say, 'Hello,' and that gargoyle had to show through the arch of her arm. Vince was riding the boom and had a man stationed underneath. 'We can't see the gargoyle, Mr. Minnelli.' Vince would come down and rehearse and rehearse. Meanwhile, here's Lucille sitting in the bubble water, on a vibrator. 'Fine,' said Minnelli in his soft voice, the most gentle person in the world."

The camera began to roll for takes. The phone rang, Bremer answered, trying to frame the gargoyle between the phone and her head. She squirmed out a meek "Hello." At twelve o'clock no take had yet been printed. Suddenly Freed appeared on the set. The minute Bremer spotted him she knew she held her trump card and burst into tears. Freed learned what had gone on all morning. Vengeance on his face, he shouted, "Come down here, you boom-riding son of a bitch!" The company froze and the boom came down like a shot. At this very moment Judy Garland arrived on the set, all smiles, in her Harvey-girl starched, aproned costume, and said, "Hello, darlings." With that Thompson grabbed her and they ran out.

Minnelli recalls the incident. "Arthur and I did have an enormous fight, because Lucille seemed to pass out or become weak or something. It was nonsense, because I had the water warm—body temperature— and it was just a case of nerves." Minnelli cannot remember anything about gargoyles, telephones, soap bubbles or a vibrator.

Before Astaire began to work with Loring he showed him six hours of beautifully edited film of all the dancing he had ever done. "I don't like to repeat myself—I want to do something different," he said to Loring.

As choreographers Loring and Alton differed greatly. "I always admired Bob, because he was the type of choreographer who could take

[48] The fiesta sequence cost $225,108.13 to shoot.

Bemelmans' conception for the bathtub setting. ARTHUR FREED ARCHIVES

Jack Martin Smith's drawing for the same sequence. JACK MARTIN SMITH COLLECTION

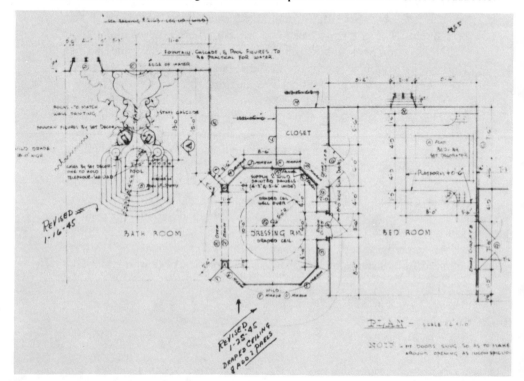

nothing—just a tune—and put steps to it and make it very good. I couldn't. I always had to have a plot."

Looking over the script Loring found a perfect spot for a ballet. Astaire is in bed, asleep. He has a nightmarish dream in which his dishonesty toward Yolanda on one hand is fighting his love for her on the other. The visual theme of the ballet was influenced by the surrealism of Salvador Dali.

The dream sequence begins and ends with a shot of a red carnation on a table in front of a window overlooking the square. Astaire throws off his bedsheets, gets dressed and, trancelike, slowly walks out of his hotel and on to the plaza. Everything is strangely quiet. Familiar characters approach him in weird and distorted shapes. At a fountain washerwomen are scrubbing their clothes to a somber, intriguing, slow musical beat. They throw out their sheets to the cadence of the rhythm and twirl Astaire into a maze. He disentangles himself and moves into a rocky landscape in an unfamiliar setting. Now the ballet actually starts and the dream unfolds.

"The idea for the sheets came out of Cocteau's *Beauty and the Beast* in which he used actual laundry so effectively," says Loring. "I tied this together with the end of the dream when Fred awakens entangled in his bedding."

Lucille Bremer sitting on the bubble machine; in one hand she holds a sponge, in the other, a brush, and the famous telephone is to the right of the gargoyle. M-G-M

In the unfamiliar landscape Astaire develops a dance pattern over a pool of water, studded with enormous gold nuggets. When Minnelli prepared to shoot this scene he had a "rock mover" in hip boots change the position of the nuggets to make what he considered a more interesting design. Loring watched this with great apprehension. "Fred is so meticulous; he knows where every part of his body is going and he is not apt to change anything. Now what are we going to do?" Astaire came on to the stage, saw what was going on and said to Loring in a very loud voice: "Gene, it's good—you're a genius. Let's start doing a new routine!" Minnelli descended from his boom; there was a discussion and the rocks were moved back.

Sharaff had designed a costume for Lucille Bremer, with an enormous scarf made out of coins and a bodice of seashells. In this costume Bremer was to emerge from and walk back into a turgid pool. To make the top form fitting, a plaster cast of Bremer's bust had to be made. The seashells were applied to the plaster cast. "You know that seashells have convolutions," says Loring, "and Lucille was very well endowed. When she finally put on the top she looked as though she had elephantiasis. Something had to be done." The scarf presented another problem. Sharaff had the coins made of light metal and stamped three dimensional. Then they were applied to the scarf and when Bremer moved she sounded like a garbage truck. Sharaff threw up her hands and said, "I just don't know. I'll tell you what, just have a very long stole with gold sequins on it and I'll drape it on her."

When Astaire approaches the pool Minnelli wanted Bremer to emerge out of the water and disappear in the water again like an apparition, with her scarves billowing in the wind.

"Running the film backwards for the turgid pool was Vincente's idea," says Loring. "But how do you make the scarves billow? The back of Lucille's stand-in had to be strapped with air jets, attached to a great, big hose. Fred had to walk into the scene backwards and end up near the rocks. And there was this air hose while he tried to walk backwards looking as though he was going forwards. But the air hose appeared in Vince's camera angle. 'Fred, please walk so the hose won't show,' said Vince. Well, I thought Fred was going to tear the place apart. Fred had had it. 'Vincente,' he said, 'I am a very slow learner. Take the goddamn camera and just shoot it!'"

Bemelmans felt that some important elements of his story had been sacrificed for the sake of adornment and ornamentation. He expressed this in the following letter:

My dear Arthur:

In the beginning of the film where the teacher comes forward (and believe me, I'm not vain about this, and if we were going to make a picture about the Munich Putsch I would say by all means use that character as the teacher), he is too military looking and from the very beginning gives the picture a wrong note. It is a Germanic note. He resembles one of those figures one used to buy outside the Hofbrau House and when you pulled its head off it turned out to be either a corkscrew or bottle opener. There is such elegance in this picture that for the teacher I would have somebody like Andre De Segurola—a Don Quixote—an intensely lonesome, wise and elegant figure. I think this is very important because as it begins now it completely surprised me. I think a little more should be made of the bell, too, as he sits down and rings the bell.

From then on I have absolutely no quarrel until we come to the train ride. I have told you this and I put it down again only for the record. There are the signposts that pass outside the windows through the entire scene—too upper Westchester and spell to me the approaches to Forest Lawn Cemetery. I don't think we need any more of that at all.

Oh, I forgot to tell you that I have now six times watched the gag with the little girl with the hat and cold cereal in the convent scene. It has never clicked with me and disturbs the beautiful mood of the rest of that scene.

The next time I became disturbed was the over-extended gag on the fake money for bribing the conductor on the train.

Then everything is wonderful. The timing of the words in the bath scene is perfect. It is curious that after seeing it so often and

The main Daliesque set for the Astaire-Bremer ballet "Will You Marry Me?" M-G-M

having written it, once in a while the creepiness of the Things in the Beyond came up through the seat into me.

As we go on, there are only two things that are difficult yet. When you cut the scene where she cries in bed there was an awful lot of good that has been cut away. For example, when the aunt says, "If you cry like that about a kiss, what will you do about—" I think the sentence was left open. Maybe when you get back we can stick some of that back into the picture again.[49]

The magic lighting of the cigar is not sufficiently miraculously evident to me, but maybe I'm overanxious and have seen it too often.

Lady Mendl, after the showing, stamped her feet so that one of her Versailles heels came off. She poked so many holes in my ribs that I now find myself on a cot in the Cedars of Lebanon Hospital, and she said, "Bemel, that is the most poifect pitcher I have ever seen and it will take me a week to get over my emotion before I can tell you what I really think of it." And the old girl is a tough audience.

I might also report to you that Liz Whitney wept through about half of it, she being a Yolanda herself.

I hope this finds you well. Kindest regards.

Your friend,
Ludwig

Yolanda was previewed on July 11, 1945, in Glendale. "At dinner we all had butterflies in our stomachs," recalls Simone, "and barely touched our food. A major studio preview had been advertised and the theatre was packed.

"So far so good, I thought, but let's get on with it. When the end titles came on the audience burst into frenetic clapping and cheers rose through the house. None of us had dared to hope for this kind of elation. The preview had been a smash!"

Yolanda and *Harvey Girls* were previewed on two consecutive days. Both met with the same exuberance of the audiences. Once again this proves that preview reactions are unreliable and misleading. They depend on a variety of factors: from the neighborhood to the quality of the popcorn; from the weather to the local PTA. To rely on them is a fallacy.

To sum it up: *Yolanda and the Thief* was a failure.[50] It took a man of Freed's courage to make the picture, different in genre and scope from any musical made heretofore. With *Yolanda* Freed opened a new horizon for the future.

[49] The duenna's line Bemelmans refers to had to be deleted by order of the Breen Office.
[50] The final cost of the picture: $2,443,322.31. In its initial release, November 20, 1945, it grossed in excess of $1,791,000. On the M-G-M financial statement the picture showed a net loss of $1,644,000.

June 26 44

My dear Arthur -

Frances , alias Hansi , the fat girl , who is our good
friend and really one of the few square jills in this life ,
has told me that you are a little disturbed about my forthcoming
book about Hollywood . I hasten to inform you that my name , even when
spelled backwards does not mead'Saroyan that I am exceedignly
fond of you my that sentiments toward Eddy mannix are almost immoral
and that nothing would bore me more than to write a book ,like
all the other books .If I shall ever write it , we will most
probably make a picture of it , and it will be amusing , I would
like to talk over the outline for it with you sometimes , Its
funny , really so .I hear that I got terribly drunk at your party
but I hope you ask me again :

Don Loper, an assistant to Freed at the time, hosted this "famous" dinner
in honor of Garland and Minnelli. The humorous menu refers to (Louis
B.) Mayer, (Don) Loper, (Arthur) Freed, (Cedric) Gibbons, (Roger) Edens
and (Lemuel) Ayers. ARTHUR FREED ARCHIVES

Betrothal Dinner

in honor of

Mr. Vincente Minnelli

and

Miss Judy Garland

❧

Host

Don Loper

Thursday, March 1, 1945

Menu

❧

Boula Boula a la Mayer

Filet of Sole a la Loper

Roast Sirloin of Beef a la Freed

Salade a la Gibbons

Baked Alaska a la Edens

Cafe Noir a la Ayers

6

TILL THE CLOUDS ROLL BY
SUMMER HOLIDAY
ST. LOUIS WOMAN
THE PIRATE
GOOD NEWS

During the winter of 1940, Jerome Kern arrived at the studio with two songs, "Contrary Mary" and "Good Girl," that he and Oscar Hammerstein II had written for Freed's forthcoming film of their Broadway musical *Very Warm for May*. Freed's admiration for Kern as a composer bordered on adulation. Besides, Kern, with his amusing, vital personality, had become a close friend. Freed was anxious to explain to him why he had to abandon *Very Warm for May*, stressing that it had nothing to do with the score; it was the contrived and unworkable book. He told Kern that he wanted to film the story of his life instead. Freed's idea was original; it was before musical film biographies such as *Rhapsody in Blue* (George Gershwin, Warner Bros., 1945); *A Song to Remember* (Frederic Chopin, Columbia, 1945); *Night and Day* (Cole Porter, Warner Bros., 1946). Kern was awed by the idea. Freed asked him to think it over.

> Mr. Kern advises me that he is agreeable to grant Metro the exclusive right to produce a picture involving a cavalcade of his music . . . for which he is to receive $161,500.

This was the opening paragraph in the deal set forth by Sam Lyons, famous Hollywood agent, for a film tentatively called *Silver Lining, A Cavalcade of Kern Songs*.

174

The terms were submitted to Mayer, who told Freed to go ahead.

Kern had written over one hundred scores, interpolated numbers, instrumentals and concert pieces between 1902 and 1941. Ownership of these scores was as widespread as one can imagine: publishers, Broadway and London theatrical producers, motion-picture companies and individual lyricists. Before they could arrive at even a vague frame for a scenario, the rights for the usage of any Kern score and/or song had to be cleared, with the exception, of course, of those already owned by M-G-M.

This was a gigantic task for the international copyright experts. Edens, working without any guidelines, considered volumes of songs, weighing their value in regard to quality, period, stageability, popularity or rediscovery. He arrived at a preselection of over one hundred songs and presented his choices to Freed, who set the complicated legal procedures in motion.

In two years the legal matters were finally out of the way and Freed had access to one of the richest song catalogues of all time: *Show Boat, Roberta, Leave It to Jane, Sunny;* songs such as "They Didn't Believe Me," "I Won't Dance," "The Song Is You," "Look for the Silver Lining" and "I've Told Ev'ry Little Star." Here was a man who spanned several decades of changing taste and remained on top throughout.

The logical man to write the story was Guy Bolton, who had been a collaborator and intimate friend of Kern's for thirty years. Bolton met Kern in 1915 when the two were teamed up to work on the Princess Theatre musicals: *Ninety in the Shade* (1915), *Nobody Home* (1915), *Very Good, Eddie* (1915), *Sally* (1920). On the opening night of their show *Very Good, Eddie,* Kern introduced Bolton to P. G. Wodehouse, with whom he had written several songs during his four years in England. For the next seven years Kern, Bolton and Wodehouse collaborated on several Broadway musicals including *Have a Heart* (1917), *Oh, Boy!* (1917), *Leave It to Jane* (1917), *Miss 1917* (1917), *Oh, Lady! Lady!* (1918). Their last show was *Sitting Pretty* (1924) for the Dolly Sisters. Kern went on to work with other lyricists, and in 1927, when he wrote the score for *Show Boat* with Oscar Hammerstein II, he reached back to a Bolton-Wodehouse-Kern show, *Oh, Lady! Lady!* and used "My Bill," one of the songs intended for that show.

"When we had our first preliminary talk about the story," Bolton recalls, "Kern asked me how on earth I expected to do it. 'If you tell the truth, it'll be the dullest picture in the world,' he said.

"I then reminded him of one or two incidents that he had seemingly forgotten. I reminded him of how he had planned to take the *Lusitania* with Charles Frohman—who so admired his talent—and only missed sailing because his alarm clock stopped in the night. I talked of his meeting the girl he married when he heard her practicing scales and

Jerome Kern. Inscribed: "To Arthur [using music notes], with every good wish from his friend Jerry." ARTHUR FREED ARCHIVES

knocked on the door and asked if he could borrow her piano to take down the number that had come to him from somewhere."

In the summer of 1943, George Wells began to develop the screenplay. It was a difficult one to write. Kern was born well off, went to school, wrote a hit song, and from there he went from one success to another. During their many talks together Kern did not come up with even one anecdote or personal experience, let alone anything dramatic.

John Lee Mahin came in to work with Wells, and Hammerstein wrote the scenes involving his relationship with the composer himself.

During a momentary lull in conversation between Freed and Kern, Freed said, "What would you say to Bob Walker playing you?"

"I don't know. Let me call Eva [his wife] and see what she thinks."

After Kern put down the phone Freed asked anxiously, "What did she say?"

"She said, 'You stay there and send Bob Walker to me!' "

The picture was now titled *Till the Clouds Roll By*. Freed chose this title for sentimental reasons: It was a song written for the Broadway show *Oh, Boy!,* in 1917, the year he first met Kern.

In the cast were Robert Walker as Kern, Dorothy Patrick as Eva

Leale Kern, Judy Garland as Marilyn Miller, Van Heflin as Hessler, Kern's arranger, and Lucille Bremer as Hessler's daughter. Guest stars included Lena Horne, Frank Sinatra, Van Johnson, the Wylde Twins, Kathryn Grayson, Tony Martin, Dinah Shore, with Cyd Charisse, Angela Lansbury and Gower Champion, making his screen debut. The book was to be directed by Busby Berkeley and the musical numbers staged and directed by Robert Alton. Production was scheduled to begin on September 17, 1945.

Judy Garland and Vincente Minnelli were married on September 17, 1945. They returned from their honeymoon and Judy was pregnant. Of course, the bridegroom was going to direct her scenes in *Clouds*.

Alton started intensive rehearsals on Judy's numbers: "Who?," "Sunny," "D' Ye Love Me" and "Look for the Silver Lining." For Judy the most strenuous was the elaborate presentation of "Who?" Even when she wasn't dancing, she had to do a lot of moving around. "Sunny" was less of a problem; in that one she was a bareback rider in a circus, but the traditional leap onto the horse's back while in full stride was to be done by a stunt rider double. "Silver Lining" would be introspective, almost static.

Judy recorded her four numbers. The first to be shot was "Look for the Silver Lining." In spite of general early morning malaise everyone was moved to tears at the first take. It took just one day to complete the number and cost $21,397.50.

Mr. and Mrs. Arthur Freed with Judy Garland and her fiance Vincente Minnelli clown around in a Los Angeles penny arcade. ARTHUR FREED ARCHIVES

The Freed Unit on the rehearsal stage with Kern (left to right): Kay Thompson, Robert Alton, Lennie Hayton, Lucille Bremer and Arthur Freed.
RALPH BLANE COLLECTION

In "Silver Lining" Judy stood behind a sink covered with dishes, hiding her condition. Things were not as easy with "Who?" The set was vast, it had elevations, and the staging was tricky. Even Judy had to rehearse this number on the set. By now she was visibly pregnant and no ingenious camera angles could conceal it. And even though she wore a large satin bow Judy was nervous. In spite of her agility she was afraid that she might stumble. In severe pain and with admirable energy she braved through the shooting. It cost $198,224.59 to shoot. "Sunny" and "D' Ye Love Me?" presented other problems. Judy's phobia about horses was well known; she had no particular fondness for elephants either. For the director, the cameraman and the editor, the problem was to fake Judy leaping on the galloping horse's back— and her stunt rider double landing on it. This needed split-second timing to make the illusion perfect, which meant a lot of rehearsing and a lot of screaming. The general confusion even got under the skin of Minnelli's gilt-painted elephants. So far they had been standing in a docile stupor, chained to the walls on the far side of the set. But suddenly they broke loose and created a panic on the set. Fortunately, the animal trainers were able to restrain them, and comparative calm was restored. In spite of everything, the number came off brilliantly. It cost $248,682.97 to shoot.

Kern attended some of the recordings and the shooting of Garland's numbers. He had no qualms about leaving his work in the hands of Freed, Edens, Alton, Salinger, et al. He spent considerably more time on the Twentieth Century-Fox lot where *Centennial Summer* was shooting, for which he had supplied an original score with lyrics by Leo Robin, Harburg, Mercer and Hammerstein.

On October 30, after an interval of six years, Kern decided to return to Broadway. A revival of *Show Boat* was scheduled to open at the Ziegfeld Theatre on January 6, 1946, the same theatre where it was originally launched in 1927. For this new production Kern and Hammerstein wrote an additional song, "Nobody Else But Me." Next, Kern was to start on a new Broadway musical with Dorothy Fields, based on Annie Oakley, with Rodgers and Hammerstein producing.

The noted composer Arthur Schwartz had many professional dealings with Kern. "He is merciless with his own work," he recalls. "He has a passion for perfection; he is a meticulous craftsman with a fetish for accuracy and detail. This drive and unselfish labor have benefited many people besides Kern. 'Composing,' he said, 'is like fishing— you get a nibble, but you don't know whether it's a minnow or a marlin until you reel it in. You write twenty tunes to get two good ones—and the wastebasket yearns for music.' Jerry writes most of his songs at the piano with pen and ink, because, he said, 'Lyric writers are too lazy to learn to read music.' He had an elaborate recording machine installed in his workshop, but never mastered it. 'Even a

Judy as Marilyn Miller, getting ready for "Look for the Silver Lining."
M-G-M

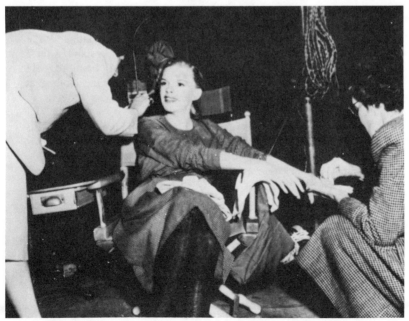

simple tool such as a screwdriver gives me cold chills,' he told me. His daughter Betty handles the recorder while he plays; records are dispatched to lyricists."

On November 5, while walking to an antique dealer, Kern suddenly fell to the ground in front of 450 Park Avenue, the victim of a massive stroke. At first he couldn't be identified and was rushed to the Bird Coler Memorial Hospital on Welfare Island. There his ASCAP membership with Oscar Hammerstein's signature was found.

Rouben Mamoulian, on his first day of a new M-G-M contract, was having lunch with Freed at the commissary to discuss a still embryonic film, *Jumbo.* For the first time since 1942 Mamoulian had come back to Hollywood to direct Freed's film of the Rodgers and Hart circus musical. Freed had already made special arrangements with Rodgers to add new numbers for the forthcoming Frank Sinatra-Jimmy Durante film. A telephone was brought to Freed's table and his secretary informed him that Kern was in a coma, having suffered a heart attack and was now in Doctors Hospital.

On November 11, 1945, Jerome Kern died. The internment was at Fern Cliff Cemetery, Hartsdale, New York. Hammerstein delivered the eulogy:

> I have promised myself not to play upon your emotions—or on your mind.
>
> We, in this chapel, are Jerry's "family." We all knew him very well. Each of us knows what the other has lost. . . .
>
> At the moment, Jerry is playing "out of character." The masque of tragedy was never intended for him. His death yesterday and this reluctant epilogue will soon be refocused into their properly remote place in the picture. This episode will soon seem to us to be nothing more than a fantastic and dreamlike intrusion on the gay reality that was Jerry's life.
>
> His gaiety is what we will remember most—the times he has made us laugh; the even greater fun of making him laugh. It's a strange objective to apply to a man, but you'll understand what I mean: Jerry was "cute." He was alert and alive. He "bounced." He stimulated everyone. He annoyed some. He never bored anyone at any time. There was a sharp edge to everything he thought or said. . . .
>
> We, in this chapel, will cherish our special knowledge of this world figure. We will remember a jaunty, happy man whose sixty years were crowded with success and fun and love. Let us think, whatever God we believe in, that we shared some part of the good, bright life Jerry led on this earth.

The minute Freed had received the tragic news of Kern's death, production on *Clouds* stopped.

Originally the screen story had started in Kern's Beverly Hills home, with friends gathered to celebrate his birthday. As a surprise,

180

an all-Kern broadcast was to be tuned in by the guests as a tribute to the composer. The script had to be rewritten and Myles Connolly and Jean Holloway were designated to make the necessary changes.

While a shooting script was being prepared, Alton was able to continue rehearsing the musical numbers. For a short period of time Busby Berkeley was the book director but was quickly replaced by Henry Koster. Coming in from left field with no shooting script on hand, he made his first and last contribution by attacking Alton's work. This produced a very audible discussion, which culminated in Koster's pale-faced exit from Freed's office.

Freed received a most gracious and generous letter from Eva Kern. Here is his deeply felt reply:

Dear Eva:

I have just read and reread your letter to me and it has touched me very deeply. There is nothing that I would want more than your help and to be able to call on you, and I am deeply grateful for this offer.

I have been making changes and working on a new opening and ending for the picture, as you anticipated. I know the terrific obligation that I have now to you and Betty and the multitudes of people who loved Jerry. Although I have not been a demonstrative person, my association with Jerry and collaborating on this venture with him is the high spot in my professional life. Jerry Kern was always an ideal of perfection to me, as an artist, as a showman and as a friend.

I am glad to hear that you are staying on for the opening of *Show Boat*. It would be and is what he wants.

Dear Eva, you have something beautiful to keep you going with the memory of the gentleness and sweetness that Jerry so thoughtfully gave to all of us who had the good fortune to know him.

I shall be anxious to see you when you return.

Sincerely,
Arthur

The major rewriting on *Clouds* had been completed and the picture was ready to resume production; total writers' fees: $166,773.34. During the hiatus Alton had shot the "Leave It to Jane" sequence, "Till the Clouds Roll By" and "How'd You Like to Spoon With Me?" To shoot these numbers cost $243,873.72. He now began rehearsals for the opening of the picture—an abridged performance of *Show Boat* costing $236,785.04. On January 22, 1946, the dramatic sequences finally got under way with Richard Whorf directing.

During the shooting of the picture Edens began contemplating the underscoring. Normally, scoring is planned when a rough cut of the entire film is in hand. But Edens selected his thematic material beforehand, in order to implant in the audience's conscious or subconscious

Lena Horne and Kay Thompson in the wardrobe department during *Till the Clouds Roll By*. The two were extremely close at this time. Lena credits Kay for helping her develop her breathing methods while delivering a song. M-G-M

ear the most typical of the Kern songs, sustaining and reiterating through the entire film four of his most beloved melodies: "They Didn't Believe Me," "You Are Love," "I Dream Too Much," "The Touch of Your Hand." By doing this, Edens felt he could make the picture and the score a cohesive unit.

For the death scene of Kern's intimate friend and arranger, Hessler, he found a relatively unknown song: "Go Little Boat." It was the subtle, delicate use of this melody that gave the scene its sadness and dignity.

The set for the finale, although structured for a grand vista, was relatively simple: a series of ascending platforms, rising high, on each of these posed a star. Musically it was a medley: "Land Where the Good Songs Go" (Lucille Bremer); "Yesterdays" (chorus); "Long Ago and Far Away" (Kathryn Grayson); "Dearly Beloved" (Johnny Johnston); "A Fine Romance" (Virginia O'Brien); "All the Things You Are" (Tony Martin); "Why Was I Born?" (Lena Horne); "The Way You Look Tonight" (Lucille Bremer); "Ol' Man River" (Frank Sinatra).

George Sidney directed this number. No boom or crane was adequate and in order to get the entire set into camera range an elevator was constructed on the opposite end of the stage. For the very last shot the camera rose in the elevator shaft to the height of approximately fifty feet. This achieved the effect of a grand crescendo. The finale cost $170,174.53 to shoot. Total cost of film: $2,841,608. *Clouds* previewed July 2, 1946. When released, January 3, 1947, it grossed in excess of $6,724,000.

At the end of 1943 Loew's Incorporated had spun off a subsidiary company: M-G-M Records. For the next three years there was not much activity. Then, in 1946, Loew's decided to exploit on a new market: the original sound-track recording. The first album chosen was *Clouds* and Jesse Kaye was engaged to co-ordinate this operation. This was no mean task, inasmuch as the sound track from the film could not simply be transferred to disks. It needed editing, bridging, manipulating to produce a commercially marketable product. Fortunately, Kaye was able to solicit the services of Simone, with the sanction of Freed.

In February of 1946, the Hollywood Bowl Association suggested that Freed produce a Kern Memorial Concert during the summer season in the style of their annual Gershwin night. Freed respectfully accepted the offer, and Edens and his assistant Simone were put in charge of co-ordinating the event.

The concert took place on July 20. It was divided into three sections: The California Junior Symphony Orchestra conducted by Peter Meremblum played a medley of Kern tunes; Johnny Green conducted the Hollywood Bowl Orchestra with all the stars from *Clouds* doing their numbers (with the exception of Dinah Shore and Lucille Bremer), an orchestra solo of "The Waltz in Swingtime," excerpts from *Show Boat,* with the cast re-creating their roles; Green and the orchestra in the "Mark Twain Suite," a Jerome Kern eulogy written by Arthur

Lena Horne singing "Why Was I Born?" which was subsequently deleted from the release print. M-G-M

Freed, and the finale of *Clouds,* ending with Frank Sinatra's rendition of "Ol' Man River." Robert Walker was the narrator for the entire program.

It was an exceedingly warm night and the Bowl was filled to capacity (eighteen thousand plus).

Twenty minutes after the concert started word came that Lena Horne was not going to show up. Since her numbers were interpolated into a continuity they could not simply be lifted out. By the time the impact of this had sunk in, the intermission had begun. In a passageway, leading to the dressing rooms backstage, Edens detected a small, broken-down baby grand. He went to Judy's dressing room, took her by the hand and told her she would have to sing "Fish gotta swim" and "Why Was I Born?" Startled at first, Judy went with him to the piano and, disregarding the traffic around them, they rehearsed the numbers.

The last part of the concert had already started and Sinatra was not yet at the Bowl. Nerves were at the breaking point. Then, during the eight-bar introduction to "Ol' Man River," a side door in the false proscenium opened, Sinatra walked on to the stage, crossed to the microphone and began to sing.

The concert was a huge success and the audience left touched and elated.

Dear Arthur!

I have never been able to express my inmost feeling audibly. But I want to make a lame attempt to thank you for the privilege of seeing "Till The Clouds Roll By." I can't begin to tell you what I think of this superb, beautiful and dignified picture. It's perfect! I want to add my simple congratulations to the many that you will receive for making "Till The Clouds Roll By." I never saw.

Kaprelick's drawing which was used in advertising and on the first M-G-M sound-track album produced by Lela Simone. M-G-M

During the summer of 1945 Lemuel Ayers brought in Edward Gross, a motion-picture executive, to meet Freed. Gross was planning to produce a Broadway musical, *St. Louis Woman,* with a score by Harold Arlen and Johnny Mercer and direction by Ayers. What he needed, though, was money to produce the show.

The gay nineties, an all-black musical, a score by Arlen and Mercer, but what attracted Freed most of all was the opportunity of starring Lena Horne on Broadway. He assured Gross of his financial backing, forming Alliance Productions, Inc., with Sam Katz as his partner. While under contract to M-G-M, neither of them could officially identify themselves with the show.

Rouben Mamoulian is part of the lives of millions of people who have never heard of him. Because of what he symbolizes both for the stage and the screen, his career warrants an outline: *Applause* (1929), an early musical, shot partly on location, mobile camera technique, first two-channel sound recording. *City Street* (1931), gangster drama, first use of voice-over to express inner thought. *Dr. Jekyll and Mr. Hyde* (1931), the camera sees via the eyes of the actor; two scenes projected simultaneously; first use of nonrealistic sounds to express and underline emotional process. *Queen Christina* (1933), a historical romance, possibly Greta Garbo's best performance (Mamoulian was able to get Garbo to rehearse for the first time). *Becky Sharp* (1935), first feature film photographed in Technicolor with colors used for their psychological and emotional values. *Blood and Sand* (1941), the colors of Spain depicted in the vein of El Greco, Goya, Velasquez and Sorolla.

Love Me Tonight (1932), with Jeanette MacDonald and Maurice Chevalier, was Mamoulian's second musical. In this film he used rhythmic dialogue and rhyme underscored with music for the first time. By now this has become an everyday technique. Even today his colleagues consider this film one of the best musicals ever made. It significantly influenced men such as Minnelli, Donen and Walters.

His impact was equally strong on the New York stage and he eventually revolutionized the American musical into an art form. In 1927, he directed *Porgy,* a play by DuBose and Dorothy Heyward; in 1928, *Marco Millions,* by Eugene O'Neill; in 1930, *Die Glückliche Hand* (The Lucky Fate), an opera by Arnold Schönberg at the Metropolitan Opera House; in 1935, *Porgy and Bess,* an American opera by George and Ira Gershwin; in 1943, *Oklahoma!,* the Rodgers and Hammerstein musical; in 1945, *Carousel,* the second Rodgers and Hammerstein musical.

It will come as no surprise that Freed engaged Mamoulian. But what, specifically, did he want him for?

Supposedly Mamoulian was to work on *Jumbo,* which Freed had planned for some time. On the studio's records, however, he was engaged to direct *The Belle of New York.* There was no screenplay, no score, nothing tangible; except, perhaps, Fred Astaire and Judy Garland in the principal roles. Freed simply wanted Mamoulian on tap when the right project came along.

In December 1945, in the hubbub of the Metro commissary, Freed tried out his lastest idea on Mamoulian: "What would you think of a musical version of *Ah, Wilderness?*" Freed often asked such loaded questions at lunch in the midst of small talk. Mamoulian reacted true to form, composed and circumspect. After a lengthy silence he said, "Let me think about it."

"I first thought—it's an excellent play, so why monkey with it?" says Mamoulian. "If you take something written for the stage and put it on the screen, you're going to lose certain values. Now, if you cannot compensate for these values, add to them, make them expand and flourish—then you shouldn't touch it. But then I went through the play

186

Roger Edens and Kay Thompson gave this picture to Freed the year after their *Harper's Bazaar* portrait. The inscription read: "To Arthur from the Lunts of Hollywood." ARTHUR FREED ARCHIVES

again and got very excited about it. And so I said, 'Yes, I want to do it!' "

The story concerns the Millers, a closely knit family living in Danville, Connecticut, in 1906. The central character is the middle son, Richard, an impressionable, dreaming adolescent. He is in love with a pretty girl from across the street but equally curious and impatient to experience the adventure of life. He is surrounded by good-natured parents, an older brother and a kid brother and sister. He is close to his uncle Sid, the lovable black sheep of the family who drinks too much. Rounding out the family is his old-maid aunt Lily, who lives in a perpetual courtship with Uncle Sid, which is ultimately consummated when he promises to give up his whiskey once and for all.

Once again *The Belle of New York* was put aside, Brecher was pulled off it and delegated to work with Mamoulian. Harry Warren and his new collaborator Ralph Blane were assigned to write the songs. They studied the earlier Metro film to get ideas for numbers.

It wasn't long before Mamoulian had a vision of how to convert O'Neill's turn-of-the-century New England comedy into a "musical play," as he termed it, *not* into a musical.

From: Rouben Mamoulian
Re: AH, WILDERNESS

It is obvious that to turn a dramatic play into a musical you have to make drastic cuts in it in order to allow time for music, songs and dancing. It is equally obvious that you cannot drastically cut a good dramatic play without spoiling it, crippling its subject and emaciating its characters. A tenuous story filled out with elaborate and overblown "musical numbers," unrelated specialties of dance and song, comedy routines, etc. has for long been the standard stuff that musicals were made of. . . . However, this is not the kind of musical we want to make. . . .

What we want to do is, for the lack of a better and newer definition, a "musical play"—meaning by that a story which will be told through the medium of integrated dialogue, songs, dance and music, with each of these elements taking an organic and vital part in the telling of that story. What happens in this case is that the dialogue scenes, which have been cut out of a good play, are not thrown overboard, but are actually translated into their musical equivalent of song and dance. As a result the story has not suffered, nor has it changed, but the *manner* of telling it has changed, and it has been enriched by added emotional values which the right kind of music brings.

The only valid reason for transforming *Ah, Wilderness* into a musical would be to tell that story in richer, more colorful and more imaginative terms, without sacrificing any of its true values, but, on the contrary, bringing to it more beauty and excitement than was there before.

188

It was evident from the beginning that this was going to be a one-man show. A man of Mamoulian's caliber and experience does not work through departments; departments are simply there to execute his plans, articulated to the most minute detail. Mamoulian's politely dictatorial *modus operandi* met with apprehension. He was equally explicit to his writer, composer and lyricist.

Here is an example:

1/9/46

To: Harry Warren, Ralph Blane, Irving Brecher
From: Rouben Mamoulian
      (copy to Arthur Freed)
Re: AH, WILDERNESS

I thought it would help us all to have in writing the tentative continuity of the opening of *Ah, Wilderness* so we can have it on hand as we progress with our work. I refer to it as tentative because if, while writing, you happen to get some new, exciting idea that departs from the enclosed, we will gladly all get together at once for discussion and modification of this outline:

THE MILLER HOME

The Miller house and family are introduced one by one . . . these introductions are to be done separately in *dialogue* by Irving, and in *music* and *lyrics* by Harry and Ralph. . . . This is a scene where we want book and lyrics to overlap, with the idea of integrating them later. . . .

We come back into the Miller house and witness the scene of Richard and the books, which should incorporate the material of pages 19, 20, 28, 29, 30, 31, 32 and 33[1]; at the end of this we *fade out* or *dissolve* into the *graduation*.

R.M.

"Since this was a color film I would work on the color scheme of the whole picture as thoroughly as I do on a script," Mamoulian says, "which means meetings with all the departments involved in the production, sets, props, wardrobe, all the details. . . . I didn't want any contrasting colors—just tints within a very narrow chromatic range—various degrees of yellow, beige and green. This I considered to be the colors of 'Americana'—like Thomas Benton, John Curry and Grant Wood."

During the first of many meetings Mamoulian had with Gibbons' art department he conveyed his color conception. "Yes," said Gibbons, "but you can't do this here. They want color on the screen." Mamoulian tried to placate the department head. "Believe me, Rouben," Gib-

[1] Referring to the script written by Frances Goodrich and Albert Hackett (1935).

bons replied, "as a friend, you're wasting your time, they won't buy it, Mayer wants to see bright colors." Mamoulian wanted this settled right then and there; he picked up the phone and called Freed: "What's this about 'the Mayer rule' about color," "I'll take care of it," said Freed. Mamoulian handed the phone to Gibbons. After Gibbons hung up he turned to Mamoulian: "You know, Rouben, I *love* the idea."

"O.K., he fixed it," recalls Mamoulian. "Freed is what a producer should be. He loves what he's doing, he loves films. If you come up with something that is tough to do he does what a producer should do; he'll fight for you—most of the time."

Warren and Blane became known as the "transportation fellas." Warren had had his success with "Chattanooga Choo-choo" and "Atchison, Topeka and the Santa Fe"; Blane had had his "Trolley Song." And now together they came up with "Stanley Steamer."

Warren stuck very close to Eugene O'Neill's style. He found it easy to set O'Neill to music, because the playwright wrote in eight-bar phrases and they come out "in cadence, like poetry," he says. "Our Home Town," on the other hand, wasn't O'Neill. More or less it came out of the Hacketts' screenplay and Warren and Blane tailored the introduction of the family to music.

He felt it important to retain the scene from the earlier film in which the father tries to explain to his teen-age son the mysteries, dangers and the puzzlement of sex. Censorship had become more rigid in the eleven years that had passed since Metro first made *Ah, Wilderness;* this time the Breen Office didn't write a directive, but instead sent an emissary to go over the script with the director.

"This man came to me and said, 'We suggest you cut the prostitute out—cut this out, cut that out—cut this word out, etc.' " says Mamoulian. "Well, I got angrier and angrier when suddenly I got this wonderful idea. 'Look,' I said, 'you want all these words out. Fine!' I took my red pencil and started cutting every phrase—I'd keep the first half, but cut the second, so that not only the censorable words would be out, but even the innocent ones. 'Now, Mr. Mamoulian,' the lowly representative began, 'after all, we don't want to destroy this, we are just trying to be helpful and constructive.' "

But Mamoulian had his own reasons; there was method to his madness. "I had a new version written in which the father finds himself embarrassed with the subject of sex to such an extent that he is never able to finish a sentence. And with that the matter would be made perfectly clear to the audience without the use of one single censorable word."

In a meeting with Warren and Blane, Mamoulian explained that music and singing would have to be interchangeable: actors, not singers, would carry the score.

Mamoulian wanted Butch Jenkins, the unforgettable freckle-faced kid from *The Human Comedy*. He was forewarned that the boy was absolute poison—this was the kid that had thrown Clarence Brown into hysterics. But the next day the boy's mother dragged Butch into Mamoulian's office by his dirty right hand (he was holding a tennis ball in his left). Butch kept staring at the ceiling and never so much as looked at Mamoulian, who asked the mother to leave him and Butch alone for a while. "Look, Butch," he said, "do you like acting?" "No," Butch answered, "I hate it." Mamoulian made a deal with him: He would let Butch off for ten minutes every time he wasn't needed but under the condition he would be back promptly. Butch extended his hand with the dirty tennis ball in it.

After several conferences between Mamoulian and Freed the cast was set: Walter Huston[2] (Nat Miller); Selena Royle (his wife, Essie); Agnes Moorehead (old-maid Aunt Lily); Frank Morgan (Uncle Sid); Mickey Rooney[3] (the Millers' son Richard); Butch Jenkins (the younger son, Tommy); Gloria De Haven (Richard's girl friend); Marilyn Maxwell (as the barroom hostess).

Mamoulian wanted to show a series of cameo scenes as a musical montage of the characters depicted by famous American painters— Benton, Curry and Wood.[4] "From them I learned what marvelous things you can do just by using different shades of the same color. One of the pictures was Grant Wood's 'Daughters of Revolution.' I told casting to get me some women who looked like them. We saw lots of elderly ladies, and finally I picked out one with dark hair who was just as if she had modeled for it. I said, 'You're marvelous! You're a true replica of that face!' She said, *'Pardonez-moi, Monsieur Mamoulian, mais je ne parle pas l'Anglais.'*"

Warren and Blane's task became easier once the picture was cast. "We wrote 'Spring Isn't Everything' for Huston," says Blane. "It was lifted out of O'Neill and set to music, it was his 'September Song.' But 'Never Again' we wrote for Morgan when he swears he will give up liquor forever."

Even at this early stage Mamoulian already knew what he wanted to do with the barroom sequence. Eager to face life in the raw, the adolescent boy visits a bar and finds himself mesmerized by a pretty, vulgar barmaid, who plies him with liquor to loosen his inhibitions. Mamoulian wanted to show visually the transformation from a cheap hussy into a beautiful dream girl as seen through the boy's eyes; even the room would change into a palace. As the illusion fades, everything would become drab and shabby. Fully realizing the problems involved,

---

[2] Huston had left Hollywood to return to the New York stage to appear in *Apple of His Eye*. Although he sang in his last professional Broadway production, *Knickerbocker Holiday* (Weill-Anderson), introducing "September Song," this would make the first time he would sing in a picture.

[3] Rooney played the Millers' younger son, Tommy, in the 1935 Metro film *Ah, Wilderness!*

[4] Legal clearances had to be obtained from the owners.

Mamoulian called a preliminary meeting with the camera department. The transformation of the girl would have to come about very slowly, involving costume and make-up changes. The set itself would also have to go through subtle, almost imperceptible changes. The technicians listened attentively and soon came to the conclusion that they could not take the responsibility for this experiment.

When Mamoulian presented this situation to Freed he was reluctant to go along with him. "This is over an audience's head—a bar is a bar and a girl is a girl." Mamoulian insisted. Voices were raised. At the height of the dispute Mamoulian's eyes were caught by a Rouault painting in Freed's office. "There is an unusual shade of blue in that thing," Mamoulian said abruptly. A collector of modern art, Freed, hot under the collar, said, "What d'ya mean!" Freed looked again. "I don't know how you ever say it, Rouben, the blue is so mixed in with blacks and grays."

Mamoulian bit off the end of his long cigar and said softly, "Now we do the scene the way I want it, yes?" Turning away from a cloud of smoke, Freed nodded.

As he was about to leave the office Freed stopped him. "I'm leaving for Boston very soon. I may as well tell you, my show *St. Louis Woman* is in trouble. You're going East, you want to see O'Neill, right? Since I've done you a favor, would you do one for me? Come up to Boston and tell me what can be done with the show." Without any hesitation Mamoulian agreed.

Eugene O'Neill. Taken at the time Rouben Mamoulian discussed the forthcoming film musical *Summer Holiday*.

To: Ralph Blane, Irving Brecher, Harry Warren

From: Rouben Mamoulian
        (copy to Arthur Freed)

Re: AH, WILDERNESS

As you know, I am leaving for New York because my little children *Oklahoma!* and *Carousel* seem to be in need of a little brushing and tuning up. I shall think of you all and miss you. I shall also hope that by the time I come back you will have a large, juicy slice of script, tied in a red ribbon, to present to me as a token of our mutual affection.

At the risk of being monotonous, may I once more remind you to keep in mind the importance of phraseology and vocabulary in any dialogue or lyrics added to O'Neill's writing. The hardest task of achieving this essential unity of style falls obviously on the young (but strong!) shoulders of Ralph Blane. They should sound as if they were O'Neill's—lyrics O'Neill could write if he would, or perhaps would if he could. Aloha!

                                                            R.M.

Mamoulian went to see O'Neill and his wife, Carlotta, at the Wentworth Hotel in New York. O'Neill was already afflicted with Parkinson's disease. When Mamoulian told him that he was about to do a musical version of *Ah, Wilderness,* O'Neill shrugged his shoulders and asked, "How can you?"[5] "Loving the play as I do, loving you as I do, and revering you as I do," Mamoulian said, "I would like to make a lot of changes. It sounds paradoxical, but I can add new values with music and color. Let me give you an example: There's that scene in the bar . . ." Mamoulian proceeded to describe his conception of the barroom sequence. At the conclusion of their meeting O'Neill was very excited by the idea. "He understood that what I was trying to do was out of admiration, and he agreed with anything I wanted to do after that," says Mamoulian.

When rehearsals for *St. Louis Woman* started, Lena Horne was not in the cast. She had flatly refused the part because she felt it didn't suit her. On February 14, 1946, the musical opened at the Shubert Theatre in New Haven.

Needless to say, Freed eagerly awaited word about the opening. After the equivocal reviews reached Freed's desk he called Mamoulian in New York, making doubly sure he would be at the Boston opening night.

There was enough enthusiasm reflected by the Boston reviews and box-office receipts to justify Mamoulian's try at saving the show. So Ayers stepped out and Mamoulian took over. The book was rewritten

---

[5] Metro acquired all visual rights when it purchased the property.

and polished, songs were reshuffled and new ones added. Freed returned to the Coast.

After the show had opened in Philadelphia, Mamoulian reported to Freed that the musical numbers needed restaging. Anthony Tudor was dismissed, and Freed dispatched Charles Walters to Philadelphia. A week after Walters had joined the company Freed sent Edens as his undercover agent to give him his assessment of the show. Edens expressed great reservations.

The show opened at the Martin Beck Theatre on Saturday, March 30, 1946, again to mixed reviews. It ran for 113 performances. Perhaps if Freed had stayed closer to the show he would have realized that six weeks on the road are not enough for a show with problems.

While Mamoulian was away Warren and Blane were hard at work. In order to get a perspective, they needed a vocal-arranger-pianist. "I knew a fabulously talented fan, Bobby Tucker, working at CBS in New York," recalls Blane. "His style of vocal arranging was quite different from Kay's. Kay is very flamboyant, showy and original. Tucker sticks right with the original material. I asked Harry to have Freed bring him out."

Tucker arrived, he transcribed all of Warren's piano parts and played at all their auditions and demonstrations.

Freed had his troubles in Philadelphia and in Hollywood. "Freed called me in," recalls Brecher, "and was very, very critical of some material of mine that Mamoulian had sent him."

"Why the hell did you do this?"

"I didn't believe in it, but this is what you told me to do, go along with what Mamoulian wants."

"Why didn't you come to me?"

"Because you told me to go to Mamoulian." Freed flew into a rage.

Brecher left Freed's office and went to see Thau to tell him that he wanted to leave the studio. Thau insisted that he talk to Mayer. Mayer called Freed in. He was shocked to find Brecher in Mayer's office and more so when he was told to apologize. Freed mumbled an apology and left. After what Brecher calls this "Pyrrhic victory," he persuaded Mayer to let him go. "Walking me to the door Mayer said, 'You won't tell anybody what I'm going to tell you now, but I wish I was going with you.'"

When Mamoulian came back to his office on the Metro lot he found the *Ah, Wilderness* score on his desk, as promised, tied with a red ribbon. But where was the screenplay? He soon learned about Brecher's dramatic departure from the studio. He found himself with a new writer, Jean Holloway, who had specialized in rewrites and still-born projects for the Freed Unit: *Red Shoes Run Faster* (for Lucille Bremer); *Forever* (Judy Garland); *Excursion; The Story of Gaby Delys.*

She submitted her first scene to Mamoulian: Mickey Rooney and Gloria De Haven meeting in an ice-cream parlor. Mamoulian read it and glowered. He puffed on his cigar. "This scene is not true to American life. The dialogue is much too sentimental and wishy-washy; kids in love don't talk like that."

A tortured look crossed Holloway's face. Being young and American born and bred, she thought she knew something about kids in ice-cream parlors. She defended her scene. The following day Mamoulian sent her a memorandum on ice-cream parlors and young love and insisted the scene be handled more flippantly. She conceded defeat and muttered that Mamoulian, the Armenian, seemed to know more about American youth than she did.

4/27/46

To: Cedric Gibbons and Jack Smith
     Irene and Walter Plunkett
     Charles Rosher
     (copy to Arthur Freed)
From: Rouben Mamoulian
Re: AH, WILDERNESS — MEMORANDUM ON SETS — #8

The following is a tentative list of sets for *Ah, Wilderness*. It is more complete and correct than the continuity of sets in the script. I am sending it to you with short, clarifying notes, and also indicating the page numbers of the script relating to each set, except those which have not been incorporated in the script.

SETS FOR AH, WILDERNESS

OPENING OF THE PICTURE IS NOT YET DEFINITELY SET

We may possibly need a couple of streets and a railroad track with a train. Discuss the use of paintings or miniatures to illustrate our little home town, and also to give the picture its correct style. (1–17)

RIDE IN THE STANLEY STEAMER

Desirable to have quite a stretch of roadway to play part of the "Steamer song" in motion. The blowout of the tire stops the trucking. Horse carriages passing by. (38)

THE OMAR KHAYYÁM SCENE

Here we need a corner of a typical American landscape where the kids are playing their scene under a tree upon a hillock. It would be nice to have a couple of long shots (Grant Wood or American primitive style) of what the kids see of the world surrounding them. This scene should be carefully discussed. Devise a way of transforming the American landscape into a Persian one, with some wild animals and gaily colored birds in evidence. Dis-

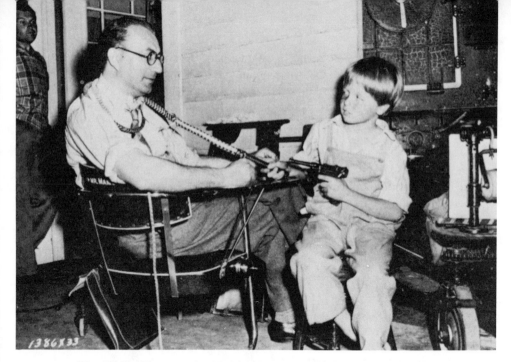

The "kid" kids around with his director: Butch Jenkins with a gun in one hand and a whip in the other. M-G-M

cuss gradual transformation of Richard and Muriel's clothes. Richard and Muriel dancing. Macomber's entrance and the swift reversal from Persia to Americana—both sets and costumes. Possibility of using transparency in this set. (40)

THE PRIVATE ROOM IN THE CAFE

The scene between Richard and Belle. Discuss this set in detail. It must be very flexible both in design and color, so it can reflect the series of moods which Richard undergoes, as the scene progresses. Possible use of transparency. Colored lights, smoke, diffusion. This is a very important set. (89)

THE MILLER HOME

The porch and exterior. The final scene and the reprise of "Spring Isn't Everything." Last shot.

A new name appears on the memo: Walter Plunkett, famous for his costume designs in *Gone With the Wind*. He was brought to the studio by Irene Gibbons to specialize in period pictures. This was his first assignment. Plunkett was full of admiration: "Mamoulian is a great example of the continental director-producer à la Max Reinhardt, having the writer, cameraman, designers and musicians working with him. He had the vision of the finished product and he knew how to achieve it. That sort of man is rare in Hollywood. For instance, for the opening scene of the film he wanted a period feeling like Currier and Ives prints. So I eliminated colors from the dresses and suits of the characters to give them a washed and faded look."

Departing from usual procedure, Mamoulian rehearsed his cast on June 3, 1946, in the opening sequence of the film for two weeks before the first shot was made. The tricky changes from music to dialogue and back again made it imperative for him to rehearse this sequence as he would in a Broadway show.

On the first day Mamoulian sensed Rooney's distrust and wondered how he could win his friendship. Overhearing Rooney amusing some actors with double talk he walked over and said severely: "I don't think we ought to frammis on the portisan between takes or even *ouvrez la fenêtre.*" They became fast friends.

Mamoulian recalls: "I was rehearsing Huston, Moorehead, Morgan, Royle, all the great acting troupers for hours, and finally I said, 'That's enough.' 'Please let's try it again,' said Huston. 'No, that's enough, Walter, now take it easy, sit down. I'm going to rehearse the love scene with Mickey and Gloria.' So they all sat down, the heavy artillery, and on came the two kids who knew from nothing, really. 'Let's go through the scene.' Suddenly it occurred to me, Oh, my God, what a long way I have to go with Gloria De Haven, I'll have to feed it to her by the teaspoonful.

" 'Now try it again and do it with one thing in mind.' "

" 'Well, you know, Mr. Mamoulian, you shouldn't rehearse me too much, because, you know, if you rehearse me too much I get stale.'

" 'Well, I'll try not to get you stale.' " During the day Mamoulian overheard Huston saying, "Gloria, are you stale?"

Mamoulian went on: "I never broke my promise to Butch. 'Butch, you can have twelve and a half minutes'; and he'd run off. And then there'd be a tug at my sleeve. 'I'm back!' I looked at my watch and it was exactly twelve and a half minutes. I didn't time him and this really puzzled me—how this guy had an inborn clock. I asked the property man to let me know what he does when I let him go. 'He goes around in the back of the stage, Mr. Mamoulian, where there's a clock and he sits and follows it. And on the dot he runs back here.' But one day I saw him cry and that broke me up, to see this tough little fellow cry. I said, 'What's the matter, Butch?' He explained he had found a little kitten on the lot and he wanted to bring it home, but neither the studio nor his mother would let him. 'I'll tell you what,' I said, 'how would you like this kitten to be with you in the picture?' 'I would love it!' 'Fine,' I told him. 'He's going to act with you and he'll be in your care throughout the film. After that you can take him home.' Butch and his kitten loved each other; the kitten was constantly kissing him. This boy has a golden heart."

On June 14, 1946, the first and, for the time being, only prerecording was made on the picture, now titled *Summer Holiday*. The song was "Our Home Town," which established all the characters in the film. In this opening song, song and dialogue were interlaced and sustained by a continuous melodic line. At the outset Mamoulian had proposed to direct-record the dialogue within any of the musical sequences. This met with opposition from all sides. Edens, for one, said, "I won't have any control over the sound if any part of the musical and dialogue sequences are direct recorded." So it was decided to prerecord these sequences and have the actors speak over a very low, just audible music track. Dialogue would have to coincide with the musical continuity.

It took two days to record this section, with the additional problem of untrained voices. It was the first sequence Mamoulian shot with his cameraman Charlie Rosher. With the exception of a few interiors, the opening was photographed outdoors, on the New England Street, adapted by Jack Smith. The family's house was the one previously occupied by the Hardys. Having just returned from his jaunt in the armed services, Mickey Rooney came back to the very spot where he had risen to fame as Andy Hardy.

Mamoulian and Plunkett had their meeting on the color conception for this scene. "Let it be summer and have the green lawns and the brick walls tell their own story," said Mamoulian. Plunkett designed costumes in various shades of whites, grays and beiges, giving them a watercolor look.

Once the opening sequence was in the can the production ran into some snags. The first was a strike in the motion-picture industry, which started on June 22, the aftermath of a seven-month strike the previous year. The issue was a conflict between the Teamsters Union and IATSE, the stagehands' union. Because of the strike there were only incomplete crews available; consequently, Mamoulian rehearsed whenever he could and prerecorded "Never Again," a song without any interpolations, with Frank Morgan and Agnes Moorehead on July 1.

Having no illusions about his vocal abilities, Frank Morgan was terribly scared. He adopted Frances Edward's refuge and downed a couple of drinks. Then he returned to the stage and the first take was recorded. "That's the worst singing I ever heard," said Edens. "We can't use it." A couple of more takes were made but the song was never used.

Edens' comment was neither cruel nor unjustified. He wisely felt that even in a stylized musical a steady diet of untrained voices might be grating on the audience's ears.

The day after the Morgan recording Mamoulian called the company to rehearse the "Stanley Steamer," but when Huston and Royle refused to cross the picket line, the company was laid off.

On July 8, the striking unions entered negotiations, and Mamoulian resumed shooting. Later that month, Charles Schoenbaum replaced

Mickey in the middle of entertaining Mamoulian and the crew at the Irvine Park location. ROUBEN MAMOULIAN COLLECTION

Rosher on the camera. Whether this was caused by personal incompatibility or because Rosher had another assignment is not clear.

"Stanley Steamer" was prerecorded, and on July 31 Mamoulian and his dance director, Charles Walters, went on location to Irvine Park. At this location the production ran into another snag. It was an exceedingly hot day, the temperature over 100 degrees, when suddenly, at 11:30 A.M., the Technicolor cameras broke down. The company sat, one hundred and fifty extras, the cast and the crew, stranded. In his diplomatic way Mamoulian turned to Rooney: "Mickey, do something for us. You know what I mean." No urging was needed and Mickey "was on." He went in front of the whole company and did the most amusing improvisations.

Another location was Busch Gardens, a public park outside Pasadena, owned and operated by the Anheuser-Busch brewery. The setting was the July Fourth picnic, and it was the only production number in the picture. The cast was divided into three groups: men, women and children. Arriving on the scene, Mamoulian set out to create a typical American picnic atmosphere. There were kegs of beer, hot dogs, pretzels, etc. He succeeded in keeping all the participants in a gay and cheerful mood, culminating in the exuberant "Independence Day" song. Taking advantage of a beautiful tree-lined lawn, Walters staged a dance for the young couples.

All this sounds very jolly. But it was extremely hot, terribly dusty and took twelve days to complete. In the beginning the production had

Gloria De Haven and
Mickey Rooney during one
of the many takes for "Omar
and the Princess." The famous
macaw that said "cut" is to
the right of Mickey. M-G-M

been hampered by events beyond anybody's control. But even dis-
counting this, Mamoulian was proceeding very slowly and was way behind schedule.

In a charming scene showing the young couple's first experience of
romantic, frustrated love, Rooney's mind wanders off into the poetry of
Omar Khayyám. The scene evolves into a song, "Omar and the Princess," the lyrics paraphrasing lines from the *Rubáiyát*.

"Mamoulian allowed me to adapt the whole number from a bro-
caded Persian print," says Plunkett. "It had a delicacy of color. I got
the idea for their costumes from a set of Persian miniatures. Smith and
I carried that over to the set with Mickey and Gloria moving across like
figurines on parchment and ivory." The set was raked; there were jade
trees, a tiny brook, arched over by a dainty inlaid bridge, and exquisite
birds. The fantasy was heightened by bathing the set in an opalescent,
greenish light.

The sequence went into rehearsal and was interrupted by a violent
flare-up of the strike. Several thousand pickets threw up human bar-
riers around the studio gates. For the many who did cross the picket
lines it was a hazardous undertaking. At the end of two days the
strikers went back into mediation.

When the Persian scene started shooting, De Haven and Rooney made take after take. "It was not easy for them to make the descent on the rather steep set, reaching certain spots on musical cues since this section was being shot in one setup," recalls Simone. "Gloria inevitably made the wrong step and the wrong turn, almost stumbling into the brook. Mickey was getting progressively more nervous. At some point I seem to have seen Mickey kicking Gloria in her behind."

The cameras started to roll again. In the midst of the take Gloria stopped.

"What's the matter?" Mamoulian recalls saying.

" 'Well, I made a mistake.'

"Gloria, whether you make a mistake or not, if you fall down on your face, get up and carry on unless I say 'cut'—you keep on going!" They started again and again she stopped.

" 'I missed a line.'

"Did I say 'cut?'

" 'No, but . . .'

"Gloria, unless I say 'cut' you keep on going. Is that clear?"

"I was standing next to Mamoulian," says Simone, "and this time everything seemed to go all right. Nobody made a wrong move, and I could hear Mamoulian quietly mumbling, 'That's it—that's it—let's keep our fingers crossed—that's it!' Suddenly a voice was heard: 'Cut,' upon which Mamoulian said, 'Production is closed—I'm leaving,' and stormed off the stage. The second assistant ran after him shouting, 'It isn't her fault! It was a macaw!' Mamoulian stopped dead in his tracks and burst into laughter. After having heard Mamoulian say 'cut' for three hours, it is not surprising that the bird finally caught on. Mamoulian broke the company for lunch."

On the way to the commissary a member of his crew came up to Mamoulian with a child's fireman's hat in his hand. "Mr. Mamoulian," he said, "Butch Jenkins came to say good-bye. He's going on a vacation and he wanted me to give you this. He said, 'You know, Sam, Mr. Mamoulian is the best man I ever worked for. Does Mr. Mamoulian have any children? Well, if he has they can play with it and if he doesn't he can play with it. I love him.' And then he ran away."

"It was enough to break your heart," says Mamoulian.

On October 5, 1946, Mamoulian began to shoot "the barroom," the last remaining sequence. It took him eight days.

For this sequence Mamoulian had put on paper eighty-nine camera and light cues, and had explicitly outlined every change of dialogue and action. It involved several costume, hair and make-up changes for Marilyn Maxwell. "At the start Marilyn was in a pale, washed-out, pink dress," says Plunkett, "that blended with the indoor complexion of the customers. As Mickey drank a little more her dress changed into a stronger shade of pink, better made and more stylish. As he continued drinking and the bar became hazy with smoke she kept changing ever so subtly until she was in a bright red dress, looking absolutely radiant."

The technicians were hesitant at first to tackle this "experiment" but eventually produced a stunning effect. Those who remember Marilyn Maxwell's performance regard it as the best in her career.

The cutting and dubbing of the film took three months. The picture was far too long and some sequences were eliminated: "Wish I Had a Braver Heart" (sung by Gloria De Haven while writing a letter to her boy friend); the first rendition of Walter Huston singing "Spring Isn't Everything" and the entire Omar Khayyám sequence. The few who have seen the Persian fantasy speak of it with delight and regret that it was never used.

Talented, creative, successful men can often be measured by the quality of their failures. *Summer Holiday* was a failure, critically and commercially. It was completed in 113 days; cost $2,258,235 ($404,-708 over budget); its initial release (April 16, 1948) grossed in excess of $1,609,000. The financial reports of M-G-M indicate a loss of $1,460,000.

But artistically it must be considered a milestone in the history of screen fare. It presented a departure from conventional patterns, and

Marilyn Maxwell rehearses lip-synching to her voice in "The Sweetest Kid I Ever Met" as Lela Simone listens. LELA SIMONE COLLECTION

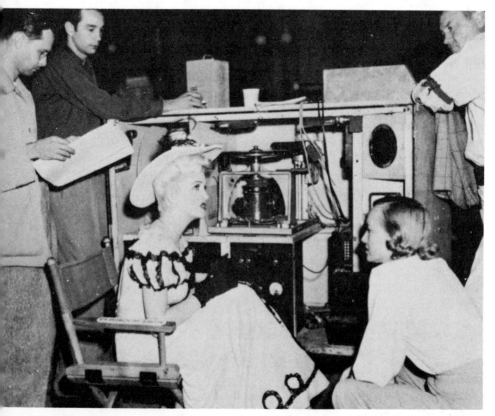

the formula soon became an accepted language in the entertainment world, on the screen as well as on the stage. On Freed's credit sheet it was a failure, but a failure of quality.

In the summer of 1946, the story department sent Freed a synopsis of a book based on the life of Vincent Van Gogh, *Lust for Life,* by Irving Stone. He sat down in the library of his suite, a pleasant disarray of memorabilia and ashtrays full of cigarette stubs, the walls hung with Rouault, Dufy, Utrillo and Leger, and read the synopsis from beginning to end. He was entranced. At least for the moment musicals were forgotten. This was the *one* dramatic film he was going to produce. He called Stone's agent at MCA: "I want to buy *Lust for Life* and I want Stone to write the screenplay."

The studio bought the property for Freed, and Stone, under contract, began adapting his book for the screen.

After *Ziegfeld Follies* Gene Kelly went into the Navy. In June 1946, awaiting his discharge, he began to contemplate his return. "I thought that M-G-M would be waiting for me with open arms, with a script, something real solid. You see, when I got into the Navy I had been nominated for the Academy Award for my performance in *Anchors Aweigh!* Then the calls started coming in: newspapers, the naval chiefs, the whole base, 'Hey! We're proud of you. You're in the Navy and you're nominated for an Academy Award!' Rumor had it that I lost by a few votes to Ray Milland for *The Lost Weekend.* So it's the last few weeks of my tenure and I'm waiting to get out. I called my agent, Roy Myers of MCA, who told me that Metro had nothing at all for me. I put in a call to Joe Pasternak, a charming man and a good friend of mine. 'I've got an idea you'll kill 'em with. You and Frank [Sinatra] will buy a used aircraft carrier and turn it into a night club.' I thought, oh, my God, another Navy picture! So I called Arthur and told him I had an idea for a picture, *Take Me Out to the Ball Game.* He said, 'Sounds good!' "

In October 1944, Lemuel Ayers had a meeting with Freed to discuss future musical projects. His first suggestion was *The Pirate,* with a score by Cole Porter. He had designed the scenery and costumes for the 1942 Broadway production of the S. N. Behrman comedy, starring Alfred Lunt and Lynn Fontanne. (The basic idea was taken from a comedy by the German playwright Ludwig Fulda, *Der Seerauber.*) When the play was in its fifteenth week Metro acquired the motion-picture rights for $225,026. Pasternak had been assigned to produce it as a straight comedy, Henry Koster was to direct and Joseph L. Mankiewicz had written a screenplay.

Ayers' second suggestion was a film of the current Broadway musical *Bloomer Girl,* which dealt with the women's revolt of 1861. Ayers had just finished designing the theatre production, conceived by Messrs. Harburg, Saidy and Herzig, while working for Freed on *Meet the People.* With a score by Arlen and Harburg, the show opened at the Shubert Theatre (New York), on October 5. Ayers tipped Freed off about the show's financial difficulties, and Freed urged Mayer to have the studio invest $65,000 in *Bloomer Girl* for the first refusal on the film rights (Metro never exercised these rights). He also asked Mayer to let him produce *The Pirate* as a musical with a Cole Porter score, starring Judy Garland.

Anita Loos and Joseph Than, both under contract, were put to work on the screenplay of *The Pirate,* to be directed by Minnelli.

Cole Porter was engaged for $100,000. As his point of departure he used the original Behrman play. When he had finished the first four songs he brought them to Freed, who was disappointed. This was Porter's third musical score with a Central American theme: *Panama Hattie* (1940) and *Mexican Hayride* (1944). *Hayride* was not a success, and his last Broadway effort, *Around the World in 80 Days,* was a dismal failure. There was talk of Porter being on the decline and Freed wanted to bring out the best in him. Very dejected, Porter went home and tried again.

After seven months Freed invited Loos and Than to his house to read their script for Porter, Minnelli, Edens and Garland. Everybody was anxious to hear it. Any inquiry about their progress had met with an exchange of knowing smiles and "We don't want to spoil it by telling you until it's finished." Loos and Than began to read. Soon it became obvious that they had totally changed the premise of the play. Instead of the leading man being an actor who impersonates a pirate, he was now a pirate impersonating an actor.

Minnelli couldn't believe his ears. While an actor could bring off the impersonation of a pirate, one would assume a pirate could only amateurishly stumble through the portrayal of an actor. The writers concluded their recital and the audience was speechless. The silence was broken when Porter, embarrassed, but with his usual politeness, said, "Uh . . . it must have been an incredible amount of work for you." "That's all that could be said," recalls Minnelli. "We walked out of there like sleepwalkers."

The following day Freed put the great husband-and-wife team Frances Goodrich and Albert Hackett on a crash schedule to bring *The Pirate* back to life.[6]

For the time being, Gene Kelly's idea for a baseball picture was laid aside, and instead he went into *The Pirate.* He was eager to play this role because in this Central American romantic farce he could show

[6] Studio records re *The Pirate* show Joseph Than on payroll November 1, 1945, to July 29, 1946, and Anita Loos on January 17, 1946, to July 27, 1946.

himself to great advantage as an actor as well as a dancer. In the role of Serafin—entertainer, clown, mystic—he saw himself as a Spanish musketeer, the heir of Douglas Fairbanks and John Barrymore.

Minnelli says that he worked closely with the Hacketts because he believes that most writers "go slumming" when they do musical comedies. Minnelli was ambivalent about his conception of the Caribbean in the 1830s. He meant to stress stylization but wanted to tell the story realistically; conversely, he decided to avoid actual locations to give the picture a deliberately artificial flavor.

Kelly wanted Porter to write a clown number and talked to him about it. He promised to try but found himself uninspired with the idea. His uncanny talent for a play on words produced a series of amusing rhymes; yet he didn't quite know what to do with them. He wrote a tune and played it for Kelly, who loved it. Responding to encouragement, Porter wrote the lyrics overnight. When Freed heard "Be a Clown" he remarked enthusiastically, "It's the best number Cole has ever written." "Tears came to my eyes," recalls Kelly, "that's wonderful—so great! But, of course, we'll need more verses; we'll have to reprise." The next day Porter had written six additional verses.

The supporting cast was Walter Slezak as Don Pedro Vargas, the corrupt mayor of the town, and, in fact, the Pirate, Mack the Black Macoco; Gladys Cooper as Aunt Inez, Manuela's (Garland's) guardian; Reginald Owen as the Advocate; George Zucco as the Viceroy; and the Nicholas Brothers, specialty dancers, who had recently closed in *St. Louis Woman*.

The choreographer, conductor, orchestrator and vocal arranger comprised the solid Freed Unit crew: Robert Alton, Lennie Hayton, Conrad Salinger and Kay Thompson.

Madame Barbara Karinska, the famous costumière, was engaged to execute the designs of artist Tom Keogh. She had done all the Picasso ballets, and one of her special talents was the use of unusual materials. "One of Judy's eight costume designs," said Keogh, "was a replica of an 1830 Worth gown. It cost $3,462.23 to make. Another was a white satin wedding dress, with handmade antique lace from France and embroidered with a thousand pearls; it cost $3,313.12. Each of the girl's costumes had five petticoats and all the embroidery was done by hand. The total wardrobe cost was $141,595.30."

Looking very frail and dispirited, Judy came in to prerecord "Love of My Life" on December 27, 1946. The songs needed the intense, exultant delivery for which she was famous. That day it simply wasn't there.

The following day Judy prerecorded "Mack the Black." She had to call on her nervous energy to do this number, which consisted of many changes of mood, tempo and rhythm, requiring her to project everything from frenzy to sentiment.

When Freed heard the playback he hit the ceiling. "It sounds like a Chinese carnival!" Simone, knowing him well, thought very hard. "Well, I've never been to one, but I'm sure it must be terribly noisy, shrill and high-pitched," she said. The number was indeed noisy and shrill; in simple words, it was totally overarranged.

For the moment, "Love of My Life" and "Mack the Black" were put aside.

Goodrich and Hackett had stayed close to the Behrman play in developing their script. To complicate matters, Cole Porter had returned to New York, and the Hacketts were working completely in the dark. Their only focal point was the Broadway play and the seven songs that Porter had already delivered: "Love of My Life," "Be a Clown," "You Can Do No Wrong," "Mack the Black," "Voodoo," "Nina" and "Manuela."

Now Minnelli wanted the story opened up to have the scene shift from the town of Calvados to the seaport of St. Sebastian. He wanted Kelly's part broadened and emphasized. Apparently he sensed that Judy was tired and not in top form. (Contrary to what has previously been written, Judy's condition was not the result of having given birth to Liza nine months earlier.)

Scenes had to be reconstructed in order to place the songs in a more logical fashion. Primarily a dancer and not a singer, Kelly wanted a chance to express himself in the language he knew best: ballet. He says, "I wanted the opportunity to do a different kind of dancing, a popular style with a lot of classic form, acrobatics and athletics." Goodrich and Hackett were able to go to work again. Half of the 108 pages they had submitted had to be either changed, juggled or entirely rewritten.

The story concerns the daughter of an aristocratic family who has been promised in marriage to the mayor of the town, an elderly, portly, gross man. Under the pretense of waiting for the ship bringing her wedding gown, she begs her aunt to take her to the nearby port. There she dreams of the sea and of the adventurous pirate Macoco, also known as Mack the Black. A dashing traveling actor falls madly in love with her, but she is infatuated with the image of the pirate. The actor pretends to be the pirate and gets himself into a pack of trouble.

Under Minnelli's guidance Jack Smith put together a conglomoration of styles: He took all of South America, the Bahamas and the West Indies and wrapped them into one package. There were the lattice blinds, the baroque sculpture, the plaza in the town of Calvados with its little pavilion in the middle, which Alton wanted. All the streets were unevenly paved with cobblestones for a realistic effect. The exteriors were built from scratch at the cost of $86,660.

After the opening scenes in St. Sebastian, Kelly and his traveling gypsies arrive in Calvados. In the plaza Kelly does a dashing number,

AA35 NL PD

WILLIAMSTOWN MASS 26

ROGER EDENS

MGM STUDIO

NINA. NINA NINA NINA. FASCINATION NINA. WHAT A LOVELY CHILD:NINA.

YOU ENCHANT ME NINA. YOUR'RE SO SWEET. I MEAN YUH. FAIRLY

DRIVE ME WILD

COLE.

807A

WU D89 PD

WILLIAMSTOWN MASS FEB 27 1947 1200P

ROGER EDENS

MGM

IN NINA. CHANGE LINE YOU BROKE MY HEART EITHER TO YOU STOPPED MY

HEART OR YOU HIT MY HEART

COLE.

1015A

WUH7 PD PERU IND MAR 8 1947 220P

ROGER EDENS

MGM

NINA/NINA NINA NINA/YOU'RE THE PRIZE GARDENIA/OF THE SPANISH

MAIN,/NINA/WHILE MY THEME SONG I SING/DON'T BE SO ENTICING/

OR I'LL GO INSANE,/NINA-TILL ALAS I GAZED IN YOUR EYES/

NINA I WAS MENTALLY FINE/BUT SINCE I'VE SEEN YUH/NINA NINA

NINA/I'LL BE HAVING SCHIZOPHRENIA/TILL I MAKE YOU MINE/STOP

ADDRESS ME WALDORF NEW YORK CITY FROM MONDAY ON UNTIL THEN

PERU INDIANA BEST

COLE.

110P

Judy Garland and Vincente Minnelli at their home on Evansview Drive in Beverly Hills just before the start of *The Pirate*. VINCENTE MINNELLI COLLECTION

"Nina," more an athletic feat à la Fairbanks than a dance. For this number Smith had to stay close to Kelly to give him the mechanical devices for his acrobatic stunts: ledges to run up the side of a building, a pillar to slide down on, and hand holds and footsteps all over the set. Smith was most inventive in constructing a wagon which converted into a stage for Kelly's traveling show. He had the side doors open up, an apron unfold, making a solid performing area.

The picture started shooting on February 17, 1947.

Minnelli had to spend a great deal of time laying out the opening scene of the picture. It was his first experience with Harry Stradling behind the camera, and he was understandably anxious. When Minnelli saw Stradling's first rushes he couldn't believe them. They were far more beautiful than he had hoped for. Due to Stradling's genius, photographically *The Pirate* was a masterpiece.

During the following two months the company, more often than not, was laid off because of Garland's illness. On some days she would come in to rehearse for a couple of hours; on others she would arrive in the morning just to leave an hour later. By April the company was demoralized and unnerved by the uncertainty of the daily schedules.

Under great stress Judy managed to record "Voodoo," and two days later she came in to shoot it. It was a night scene and she was to do the number around an open fire. On the stage floor the fires were lit, the ceiling-high doors were open and Minnelli and the company were waiting. Suddenly Judy tore onto the stage, her face emaciated, her eyes wide. Seeing the open fires she broke into hysterics, screaming: "I'm going to burn to death! They want me to burn to death!" In vain Minnelli tried to calm her. She pulled away and ran to a group of extras, pleading; "Do you have some Benzedrine?" Addressing each one individually, she kept repeating it. Sobbing, laughing, crying, completely out of control, she was led off the set. For everybody, but especially for the many crew members who had known and loved Judy since her adolescent years, it was a pathetic scene. This was the first public manifestation of Judy's rapidly deteriorating condition. But she was able to bring herself out of momentary breakdown and resume shooting the next day.

For two of the next four weeks Judy was absent. Kelly made use of this time to finish *Living in a Big Way* for Gregory La Cava, which he had started before entering the Navy.

On one of the many days without Judy, Kelly was to do his scene on the tightrope. He called the unit manager to tell him that he was not coming in because he had been out very late the night before. At another time, Kelly feigned sickness for a week to protect Judy. The entire procedure on *The Pirate* had gotten out of hand. On May 8, Freed came to the set and talked to Judy in her dressing room for two hours. He succeeded in restoring some kind of order; but not for long.

A week later Judy came in after lunch and recorded the second version of "Love of My Life." She was in better voice but unnaturally slow, obviously under the influence of drugs. Unsteady on her feet, she seemed to be in a trance. Cole Porter arrived on the recording stage a few minutes after the session started. Aside from a polite compliment, he made no comments on her rendition of "Love of My Life." Then Judy marked her way through a rehearsal of "You Can Do No Wrong" and barely could get through it. A constrained argument developed between her and Porter. The bone of contention was the pronunciation of the word "caviar" in the lyric of the song: "ca-vi-ar" versus "ca-viar," and on and on. Edens managed to alleviate Judy's unreasonableness and she went on to record the song. Judy revered Cole Porter; had she been well there would have been no argument.

"You Can Do No Wrong" is preceded by a knockabout fight. It was intended to be played in a tongue-in-cheek rage, in the mood of a farce. Instead, it became a frantic, hysterical outburst, making Judy's condition painfully apparent. In one instance, Minnelli physically restrained her. The scene had to be shot in bits and pieces. The action demanded was too strenuous for Judy, and after each take she had to rest. Stradling had problems photographing her at close range because she looked haggard and depleted. At the end of the third day of shooting Freed came to the set late in the afternoon to talk to Minnelli and Kelly. When Minnelli told him there had been enough film shot to cut the sequence together, Freed ordered him to wrap it up.

A few days later Minnelli ran a rough cut of the fight scene with his editor, Blanche Sewell, one of the best and most experienced in the business. When he saw that she had omitted a close-up of Judy in a designated spot he got so enraged that he literally jumped at her throat, which clearly shows the strain he and everybody working on the picture was under.

By June 11, after four months in production, the accumulated cost of the picture was $2,725,516, and it was only half finished.

Judy made sporadic appearances of half an hour or so for the next four weeks, and that was all.

Kelly rehearsed the first section of "Be a Clown" with the Nicholas Brothers. On July 9 the number was shot in one day but it took till 7:25 in the evening. There were a lot of extras involved and Minnelli shot take after take after take—plus camera rehearsals Kelly insisted on. Kelly kept on going, striving for perfection. By the end of the day he had danced the Nicholas Brothers into the ground.

Judy and Kelly still had to prerecord the second section of "Be a Clown." Cole Porter came to the session; he was eager to hear Judy singing what Freed had termed "the best song Cole has ever written." Judy did not agree and she made no secret of it. In fact, she did not want to sing it. "She pointed out that there were hardly any laughs, where I had attempted to provide an infinite number," said Porter. "It was very embarrassing to have it pointed out." The atmosphere on the stage became more and more tense by the minute. Her difference of opinion with Porter during the recording of "You Can Do No Wrong" had manifested itself in subdued, civil tones. But now Judy had lost her sense of humor, her self-control was gone, and she was full of bitterness and hostility. She did not win her point, though, and the recording was made as Porter had written it.

For the "Clown" number Smith had constructed a small stage in a confined space all in pinks, reds, and oranges. Stradling set up the camera to show Judy and Gene in their clown costumes in full figure. Alton had worked out their dance routine, using the old Indian-club gag, where a performer gets hit over the head each time he gets close to the wings. "But suddenly Judy showed a terrific sense of humor," says Smith. "She and Minnelli screamed and screamed with laughter— they'd look at each other and roll on the floor. It helped the whole mood of the number, but it was a bit peculiar."

After a one-day layoff Judy came in to finish the picture. She had to do six different scenes, involving four make-up and costume changes. The production department was well aware that this was their last chance. The art department was ordered to set up portions of each individual set on one sound stage. Judy went along because she herself must have realized that she was at the breaking point.

Normalcy was restored to the production. What remained to be shot was "The Pirate Ballet." Kelly and his dancers rehearsed for seventeen days to Alton's choreography. Edens worked closely with them on the rehearsal stage laying out his musical continuity, using the

Judy grimaces after throwing a vase over Gene's head during the "You Can Do No Wrong" sequence. M-G-M

thematic material of "Mack the Black." On August 7, the ballet was prerecorded; Salinger's orchestration called for two pianos, and Simone and Edens decided to play them themselves. They thought it would be fun and a relief from the strain they had been under.

"The Pirate Ballet" was an ingenious means to resolve the dramatic conflict of the story itself. Kelly, believed to be the pirate Mack the Black, is about to be executed. As his last request he asks to give a performance. His only chance is to provoke the real pirate into revealing his identity. In the ballet Kelly hypnotizes his audience, evoking fear. As the ballet reaches its climax, the real Mack the Black screams "Macoco!," jumps on the stage, is caught by Kelly's cohorts and Kelly's life is saved.

Finally on August 14, 1947, the production closed.

The diary of *The Pirate* does not present a pretty picture, and the accusing finger points to Judy Garland. But Judy was not temperamental; she was not a spoiled star, as those with only a superficial view propound with malice in their hearts. Judy was at war with herself. She was very bright and very sensitive and constantly aware of her shortcomings. Paired with her physical frailty, this produced extreme

Betty Comden and Adolph Green in their office in the "Iron Lung"—the Irving Thalberg Building—during the time they first began working in the Freed Unit on *Good News*. BETTY COMDEN COLLECTION

highs and extreme lows. The well of nervous energy on which she fed was dry. It needed replenishing.

On August 29, Freed invited Cole Porter to attend a screening of *The Pirate* in a rough cut. Present were Judy Garland, Vincente Minnelli and Irving Berlin. Porter's reaction was cautious and polite, but Berlin and Freed assured him it was a great picture. All Porter said was, "We shall see."

Between October 21 and December 19 Freed ordered Minnelli to shoot additional scenes and retakes on *The Pirate*. Porter's pessimistic comment proved to have been well justified. The production number "Voodoo" had to be eliminated and Judy had to record and reshoot still another version of "Mack the Black" to replace it. Several scenes were added, and Slezak, Cooper and Kelly were called back to work with Garland.

On June 11, 1948, the picture finally went into release, costing $3,768,496. It went over its budget by $553,888. Out of 135 days of rehearsal, shooting and layoff, Garland was absent for 99.

Box-office receipts were $2,956,000. The studio's financial report showed a net loss of $2,290,000.

Two years later, in an interview that Minnelli gave to the French

212

film magazine *Cahier du Cinema* he said, "I was very pleased the way the film turned out. Judy gave one of her best performances and the Cole Porter songs were excellent. Unfortunately, the merchandising on the film was bad, and it failed to go over when it was released."

While *The Pirate* was still in the throes of preparation, the Hacketts were frantically working on rewriting the script and Freed was confident they would turn out the screenplay he wanted. But the starting date was four months away, February 17, 1947. This was too long a period for him to remain idle.

Off and on he had toyed with the idea of reviving *Good News*. In passing he once mentioned it to Charles Walters, who recalls saying, *"Good News?* That was my high school play! I starred in it, directed and choreographed it! And I flashed back to the time I first met Arthur on the *Du Barry* set and I could hear his words: 'Chuck, that's the way a director thinks. Someday you're going to be a director.'"

Quite casually Freed announced to his inner circle that he was finally going to produce *Good News* and that Walters was going to direct. Walters was dazed but thrilled.

When word got out about this new project of Freed's, agent Sam Lyons recommended two New York writers, Betty Comden and Adolph Green.

Comden and Green began their careers as night-club performers in 1939. Their act, called "The Revuers," consisted of themselves, Alvin Hammer, John Frank and Judith Tuvim, later known as Judy

During one of the many annual joint-birthday celebrations for Roger Edens and Kay Thompson. Here Roger is surrounded by Judy, Ann Sothern and Kay.
ROGER EDENS ARCHIVES

Holliday.[7] They bagan at Max Gordon's Village Vanguard (New York) and then toured the night-club circuit: Rockefeller Center's Rainbow Room, Café Society, both Uptown and Downtown. Then they were booked into Hollywood's Trocadero, without Frank, who left the show. Twentieth Century-Fox engaged their act for *Greenwich Village,*[8] and Judy Holliday was offered a film contract. The group disbanded, and returning to New York, Comden and Green reworked the act for the two of them to go into Max Gordon's famous bistro, the Blue Angel. One night two friends, Leonard Bernstein and Jerome Robbins, stopped by. They were about to embark on a Broadway musical based on Robbins' ballet "Fancy Free," and asked Comden and Green to write the book and lyrics. This was their big break. The show was *On the Town,*[9] in which they played two principal roles, Claire and Ozzie. A year later, in 1945, they wrote the musical comedy *Billion Dollar Baby* with a score by Morton Gould.

But ultimately their goal was Hollywood. They asked their agents, A. and S. Lyons, to try for a studio contract.

"We found there weren't that many takers," says Green, "and then suddenly there was this offer from M-G-M and we took it. When we got there we first met Roger, he was terrific. He was so courtly and gallant, well, we just fell in love. Freed, too, was wonderful right away. He was very warm and very welcoming. But then we were told we were supposed to do *Good News.*"

"We were sort of taken aback," says Comden, "because we had done *On the Town* and *Billion Dollar Baby*. They probably thought we were authorities on the twenties, because *Billion Dollar Baby* was laid in the twenties just like *Good News.*"

They couldn't imagine what they were supposed to do with this college musical about a football game, since they were known for their satirical sophisticated wit. When it came to the serious business of writing they asked to see the 1930 version with Bessie Love.[10] They were informed that all the prints had been destroyed. Freed had anticipated their request and advised the film library accordingly. Edens explained, "We don't want you to become contaminated." Comden and Green got hold of the stage play and began acting out the parts. "We groaned," says Green. "Yes," says Comden. "Will Tommy Marlowe play the big game or won't he—because he is failing in astronomy?"

---

[7] Tuvim in the Hebrew language means holiday.

[8] When the picture was released in 1944, however, they were on the cutting-room floor, except for a scene in which Comden checked Don Ameche's hat while Green studied a copy of Einstein's works.

[9] It opened at the Adelphi Theatre on December 28, 1944.

[10] The legal files indicate that M-G-M acquired *Good News* (also known as *Hold 'Em Helen*) on November 29, 1929, for $50,000. The 1927 Broadway musical comedy by Laurence Schwab and B. G. De Sylva; lyrics by De Sylva and Lew Brown, music by Ray Henderson, was made into a film in 1930. Additional songs were written for the movie by Nacio Herb Brown and Arthur Freed.

214

After a meeting with Freed and Edens it was decided to have them write a completely new screenplay, retaining only the barest plot line but most of the original De Sylva-Brown-Henderson songs, including "The Varsity Drag" and "The Best Things in Life Are Free." If additional songs were needed, Edens-Comden-Green would collaborate.

Comden and Green had passed their initiation and would become an important writing team in the Freed Unit.

"We started working like beavers, day and night," they say. "But one night we took time off because it happened to be November 9 and the joint birthdays of Kay Thompson and Roger Edens—and there would be the annual birthday party."

At these annual parties a group of remarkably talented people entertained each other, giving their very best. Mostly "the cast" consisted of Edens and Thompson, of course, Lena Horne, Lennie Hayton, Ralph Blane, Judy Garland, Charles Walters, Conrad Salinger, Robert Alton, Lela Simone, and Andy Williams. This particular year Thompson had written a song for Edens, "Jubilee Time,"[11] which she performed with Williams and Blane, and Edens had written "The Passion of St. Kate," which he did with Judy, Williams and Blane. Each group rehearsed their individual blackouts with as much zest as they would have for a Broadway opening night. And each group would rehearse in strict secrecy. Spirits were high.

During the time *The Pirate* limped along its troublesome path, *Good News* was prepared, went into production and was completed between March 10 and May 27.

Since this was Walters' first stab at directing, Edens was told to stay close by, especially since he was familiar with the material.

Freed cast June Allyson, whom he had rescued from a rejected Twentieth Century-Fox test, as the lead. Sometime before, he had induced Joe Pasternak, at Allyson's request, to cast her in a part Gloria De Haven had been designated for.

June Allyson went to see Benny Thau. "I'm just getting started. I'm in a nice position now. And, you must understand, I love Chuck. I love his dance work—but I need someone with more experience. I don't wish to break in a new director. After all, this is my first big musical. . . ."

Thau called Freed and Freed called Allyson. When she sat opposite him in his office he laid it on the line. By the time she left he chose a more conciliatory tone. "I'll watch the picture—don't worry—if he's not right, we're not married to him. . . ."

Gloria De Haven was cast as the college siren. She declined and the

[11] This was to be the last of the annual parties which began when Kay Thompson and Roger Edens first found out that they had the same birth date back in 1943. After her work on the forthcoming productions of *Good News* and *The Pirate,* Kay Thompson would leave the studio along with her key backup singers, the Williams Brothers (Andy, Dick, Don and Bob) and become a sensational act on the night-club circuit.

studio put her on suspension. Patricia Marshall replaced her. Joan McCracken, who had made a name for herself in *Oklahoma!* and more recently in *Billion Dollar Baby,* was brought to Hollywood by Freed for the part. Van Johnson was cast in the role of Tommy Marlowe, the egotistical star football player of Tait College, but this did not come to pass. Then they considered Mickey Rooney, but he hadn't fared well with either critics or audiences in *Summer Holiday,* and the idea was abandoned.

Finally, Freed announced that Peter Lawford would play Marlowe. That night Lawford telephoned Comden and Green: "You've got to get me out of this picture! I'll make an absolute ass of myself. After all, I'm English, I have a British accent, I'm *not* your all-American 'Joe College.' I'm stupefied. Get me out of this!" Both of them were giggling, but they convinced him that not only did he have to do it, but that it would be good for him.

Comden and Green decided to have Marlowe fail in French rather than in astronomy, and they sat down with Edens and came up with "The French Lesson," a very effective piece of special material. (The fact that Lawford spoke flawless French was a bit disconcerting.) In addition to "The French Lesson" with Allyson and Lawford, "Pass That Peace Pipe," originally written for *Ziegfeld Follies* by Edens-Martin-Blane, was taken out of mothballs and inserted into the score. Edens and Thompson did extensive rewriting on "Good News," "Be a Ladies Man" and "The Varsity Drag," as well as writing elaborate and tasteful vocal arrangements for the entire picture.

"When I started the picture nobody realized that I hadn't even di-

"Rouge, blanc, noir . . . ," says Peter Lawford as he and June Allyson slide through "The French Lesson." M-G-M

Joan McCracken and Ray McDonald with the company in Alton's production number "Pass That Peace Pipe." M-G-M

rected a dialogue test," says Walters. "I begged Arthur to let me start with a number so that I could get acclimated. We did start with the opening number and before I knew it I had finished it. I didn't want that playback to end; it was the only thing I was familiar with. And then they fold up the playback and wheel it out—it was like my last friend was leaving. There was this awful lull. No sound or anything— Roger was there and Lela, perhaps Arthur—I don't know . . . that was the start and it was pretty frightening. But there was Bill Ryan—the most beautiful man. He trained me. He said, 'The toughest part of being a director is to get a picture to direct.' He was trying to minimize the whole thing. 'And remember this, everybody wants to do their job and you let them do it. They know a hell of a lot more about it than you do—and don't be afraid to ask, they love it.' It was just brilliant, just brilliant!"

Walters asked for Bob Alton to stage the two production numbers in the picture, "Pass That Peace Pipe," a tricky Indian affair that takes place in the drugstore, and "The Varsity Drag," the big finale. He felt more comfortable staging intimate musical numbers and shied away from big ones.

There were no snags, there was no hitch. Walters breezed through the picture and brought it in under budget. Its final cost was $1,662,718

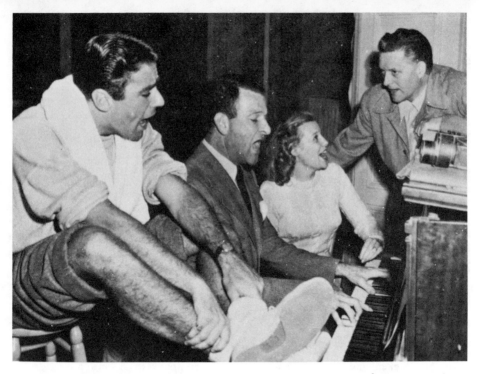

Lawford, Edens, Allyson and Alton rehearse "The Varsity Drag" from *Good News*. ROGER EDENS ARCHIVES

(under budget, $135,270). In its initial release, December 26, 1947, it grossed in excess of $2,956,000.

Comden remarks, "I always say, the three greatest pictures are *Birth of a Nation, Potemkin* and *Good News.*" And Green says, "It wasn't a thriller."

In the first half of 1947, two unrelated events came Freed's way: Irving Berlin and Gian-Carlo Menotti.

During the first week in January, Louis Shurr, the Hollywood agent, called. "Irving Berlin's in town. He'd like to have lunch with you."

"What's he got in mind, Doc?"[12]

"He'd like to borrow Lena Horne for his next show."

"Well, I've never been able to even get a song from Irving," Freed retorted, "so why should we loan out Lena?" But Shurr insisted and the three met for lunch at Romanoff's.

"What are you up to, kid?" was Berlin's opening remark, Freed said. "He always called me 'kid.' Well, Cole's done a helluva job on *The Pirate,* which goes in a month and about the same time I'm doing

---

[12] "Doc" was Shurr's nickname, short for "the doctor." He was also Lena Horne's agent.

a revival of Buddy De Sylva's *Good News*. But what I really want to do is a picture with you—*Easter Parade* with Judy and Gene Kelly."

M-G-M had acquired the motion-picture rights to the Irving Berlin-Moss Hart Broadway musical revue *As Thousands Cheer*. "Easter Parade" was in the score. And Freed had had *Easter Parade* as the title for a movie, on his mind for a long time.

"I'd love you to do it," said Berlin, "but Metro won't make the right kind of a deal, the kind I have at Paramount and RKO with percentages and so on."

"Irving, what's the difference? Figure it out on a piece of paper and I'll get you a flat sum. O.K.?" said Freed. Meanwhile, Louis Shurr sat there ignored, and Lena Horne's name was never mentioned.

Freed went to Palm Springs to spend the weekend with Berlin. He found him nervous; he was going crazy, he said, he had nothing to do—he just had to keep going. Freed couldn't understand it. Berlin had just had an enormous hit in New York with *Annie Get Your Gun*—and he had to keep going, he was nervous?

They made a gentleman's agreement on the production of *Easter Parade* and Freed had another breakfast at Mayer's house, to tell him about his weekend with Berlin. Mayer inquired about Berlin's health and wanted to know what they had been talking about. *Easter Parade,* said Freed. "Buy it," said Mayer. Freed warned Mayer: "He'll want more money than we've ever paid anybody!" Mayer just repeated, "Buy it!"

Bob Alton's ingenious piece of choreography for "The Varsity Drag." M-G-M

Benny Thau negotiated the deal with George Cohen, Berlin's West Coast lawyer. Berlin would receive $600,000 in exchange for eight songs from his catalogue plus eight new ones. When Thau asked for copywright ownership on the new compositions, Cohen turned him down. But Berlin told him, "Go ahead and let them have it. I want to do this picture."

On February 7, Berlin moved into the room reserved for very special guests in the Freed suite, along with his antique, carved oak upright piano. This was a unique instrument; on it Berlin could play everything in the key of F sharp. Pushing a lever beneath the keyboard, he could transpose whatever he played into F sharp.

Goodrich and Hackett went from *The Pirate* to writing the original screenplay for *Easter Parade*. In one week's time Berlin came up with the titles of three new songs: "Drum Crazy," "Better Luck Next Time" and "A Fella With an Umbrella."

In the span of only a few days, Freed acquired still another Berlin score, *Annie Get Your Gun,* the hottest musical then on Broadway. The producers could have had their pick of any studio at any price. But Berlin had no trouble convincing his associates, Rodgers and Hammerstein (the producers) and Herbert and Dorothy Fields (the writers), to sell *Annie* to Metro in view of Freed producing and Judy Garland starring in the picture. The price was $650,000, the highest amount the studio had ever paid for a musical property.

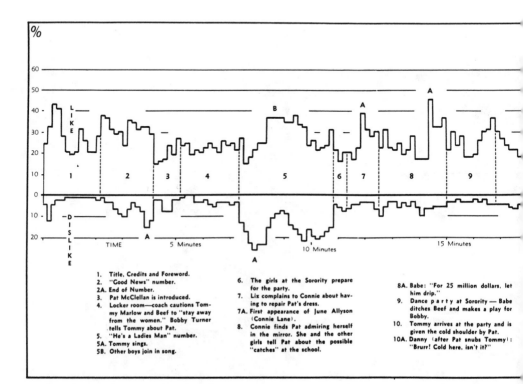

1. Title, Credits and Foreword.
2. "Good News" number.
2A. End of Number.
3. Pat McClellan is introduced.
4. Locker room—coach cautions Tommy Marlow and Beef to "stay away from the women." Bobby Turner tells Tommy about Pat.
5. "He's a Ladies Man" number.
5A. Tommy sings.
5B. Other boys join in song.

6. The girls at the Sorority prepare for the party.
7. Liz complains to Connie about having to repair Pat's dress.
7A. First appearance of June Allyson (Connie Lane).
8. Connie finds Pat admiring herself in the mirror. She and the other girls tell Pat about the possible "catches" at the school.

8A. Babe: "For 25 million dollars, let him drip."
9. Dance p a r t y at Sorority — Babe ditches Beef and makes a play for Bobby.
10. Tommy arrives at the party and is given the cold shoulder by Pat.
10A. Danny (after Pat snubs Tommy): "Brurr! Cold here, isn't it?"

"Be a Ladies Man," sings Mel Torme, Ray McDonald, Peter Lawford, Tom Dugan and Loren Tindall. The De Sylva, Brown and Henderson song had additional lyrics written by Roger Edens and Kay Thompson and was augmented offscreen by Andy Williams' high tenor voice. M-G-M

Portions of an audience reactograph chart during a preview of *Good News*.

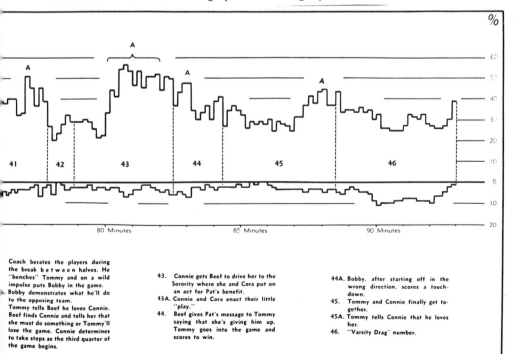

Coach berates the players during the break b e t w e e n halves. He "benches" Tommy and on a wild impulse puts Bobby in the game. Bobby demonstrates what he'll do to the opposing team. Tommy tells Beef he loves Connie. Beef finds Connie and tells her that she must do something or Tommy'll lose the game. Connie determines to take steps as the third quarter of the game begins.

43. Connie gets Beef to drive her to the Sorority where she and Cora put on an act for Pat's benefit.
43A. Connie and Cora enact their little "play."
44. Beef gives Pat's message to Tommy saying that she's giving him up. Tommy goes into the game and scores to win.

44A. Bobby, after starting off in the wrong direction, scores a touch-down.
45. Tommy and Connie finally get to-gether.
45A. Tommy tells Connie that he loves her.
46. "Varsity Drag" number.

In the Freed Unit there had been talk about an important event that had taken place on May 1 at the Ethel Barrymore Theatre in New York—Gian-Carlo Menotti's musical drama *The Medium*. Shortly thereafter it had been broadcast nationwide.

Menotti came to the United States from Italy at the age of seventeen to conclude his musical education at the Curtis Institute in Philadelphia; most American students went to Europe. His first try at chamber opera was *Amelia Goes to the Ball*. Then came *The Medium,* a more serious work, performed in conjunction with a musical farce, *The Telephone*. *The Medium* proved that he was a great theatrical talent. Freed tried to interest Mayer in putting it on the screen, with its original cast and stage set, which would have cost a pittance. This time, however, Mayer's answer was negative.

But Freed saw in Menotti a potential talent. He offered him a contract to come out to Metro, to learn the business, write and direct, as Freed had done with Minnelli. Menotti accepted and arrived in July. A talent and not a snob, he acquainted himself with studio activities, observing with an almost naïve awe. In the course of his tenure he delivered two scripts to Freed, *The Bridge* and *The Happy Ending*. The happy ending in *The Happy Ending* was a group of young children celebrating Christmas Eve in a New England cottage with their family, church bells ringing and snowflakes slowly covering the ground. They pushed their gruesome grandmother in her wheel chair onto the front lawn, leaving her in the freezing silent night. However intriguing and a foretoken of things to come, it found no buyers. At the end of his year's contract Menotti left the studio and Freed in mutual friendship and admiration.

7

EASTER PARADE

WORDS AND MUSIC

TAKE ME OUT TO THE BALL GAME

THE BARKLEYS OF BROADWAY

ANY NUMBER CAN PLAY

In a meeting with Frances Goodrich, her husband, Albert Hackett, and Freed, on June 5, 1947, the kernel of what became *Easter Parade* was discussed: A fella, who is dumped by his dancing partner, picks another girl and tries to build her into an exact duplicate of the first. The new act does badly, but when she displays her natural talent, they take off.

Freed thought this premise was wonderful. "The story must be kept simple," he said. "Keep a certain intimacy throughout . . . don't try to make it stupendous . . . remember it's 1912 . . . keep away from trite scenes." He also threw the writers a challenging plum: "The *writing* of the scenes and the way they are played will take it out of the conventional."

Helped by their rapport with Irving Berlin, the Hacketts proceeded to develop their script. Berlin says, "I worked very closely on the story with the Hacketts. Remember, this was the period of the *Ziegfeld Follies* at the New Amsterdam Roof, a period which I knew; I wrote songs for them.[1] I didn't write any of the script, but I was very much involved in how they would develop their scenes. You see, I was anxious to get my songs done in the right atmosphere; the Hacketts were wonderful!"

[1] Berlin wrote songs for *Ziegfeld Follies of 1911* and the scores for *Ziegfeld Follies of 1919, 1920* and *1927.*

In his room which Freed permanently renamed the Berlin Room, Irving Berlin is at work on his new songs for *Easter Parade*. M-G-M

This was their first assignment to write an original musical book and it helped Goodrich and Hackett to know who was going to play their backstage triangle: Judy Garland, Gene Kelly and Ann Miller, who had just signed with the studio. Also, Peter Lawford, this time as an Englishman, and Broadway comedian Jules Munshin, a newcomer to the screen, brought to the studio by Freed.

"We hadn't worked with Berlin before," says Goodrich. "Sometimes he would come in with an idea and a song to illustrate it. For example, he had a new song, 'I Love You—You Love Him,' which he had envisioned as sort of 'La Ronde,' with a Greek vase, etc. And we would say we couldn't work that out . . . and he'd answer, 'That's all right, I'll use it somewhere else.' What are trying to say is that he was very flexible."

With great zest Berlin threw himself into writing new songs for what he termed "the younger generation," Judy Garland and Gene Kelly. They included "Better Luck Next Time," "A Fella With an Umbrella," "I Love You—You Love Him," "Mister Monotony," "It Only Happens When I Dance With You," "Drum Crazy," "Steppin' Out With My Baby," and "Happy Easter." But Freed also felt the picture needed a fun number for the two stars. Berlin agreed to write it even though he had completed the eight new songs as per his contract. He returned with "Let's Take an Old-Fashioned Walk," which Freed didn't care for. Berlin replied, "You don't like it? Forget about it —I'll use it somewhere else!"[2] An hour later Berlin had written "A Couple of Swells." Freed loved it.

Edens was quick to know exactly which of the over eight hundred Berlin songs would be right for Judy, Gene and Ann. "In my opinion the one person responsible for the whole musical context of the picture was Roger Edens," says Berlin. "Look, when it came to Ann Miller, Roger dug up 'Shaking the Blues Away,' a song I had written for *Ziegfeld Follies of 1927*. He knew exactly how to present it and he made the arrangements for her. Listen, you can't say enough about Edens where I'm concerned!"

Back in 1917, Berlin had written a song called "Smile and Show Your Dimple." It didn't catch on with the public. Sixteen years later he searched for an old-fashioned number to use in the Broadway revue *As Thousands Cheer*. He took the "Dimple" melody and wrote the "Easter Parade" lyrics for it. Berlin said at the time, "A song is like a marriage. It takes a perfect blending of the two mates, the music and the words, to make a perfect match. In the case of 'Easter Parade,' it took a divorce and a second marriage to bring about the happiest of unions."

On September 15, 1947, Kelly began rehearsals on "Drum Crazy" with Alton. For personal reasons Minnelli was taken off the picture after five days and replaced by Charles Walters. Walters was slightly dazed when he heard about his *Easter Parade* assignment. He went to the rehearsal stage where Garland and Kelly were rehearsing "A Couple of Swells." "You know, Judy loved to growl, loved to pretend. She turned to me and said, 'Look, sweetie, I'm no June Allyson, you know. Don't get cute with me—none of that batting the eyelids bit or fluffing the hair routine for me, buddy! I'm Judy Garland and just you watch it.'"

Walters read the shooting script and thought it was terrible. He called Garland and Kelly and told them to stop everything; he had to talk to them. He induced them to call Freed, who was in New York, and, as he says, "I fed them the lines. 'It's no good, it's mean.'" Sidney Sheldon was brought in to exorcise the meanness out of the script.[3] "I made it a musical comedy, starting from page one, and did a total rewrite," Sheldon recalls.

[2] Berlin later used "Let's Take an Old-Fashioned Walk" in *Miss Liberty* (1949).

[3] Sheldon had been brought to the studio by Freed. An Academy Award winner for his screenplay *The Bachelor and the Bobby Soxer* he was at work preparing a musical treatment of the Jane Austen novel *Pride and Prejudice* for Freed.

Here is the counterpoint to Sheldon's statement in a studio conference memo:

> Mr. Freed wants to work into this scene a reprise of "It Only Happens When I Dance With You." Mr. Sheldon said it could be easily done by keeping the idea that Hackett and Goodrich used.

When Sheldon was brought in, the Hacketts were on vacation in Europe and when asked about Sheldon's contribution, they said, "Everything we wrote is in the picture. There was a scene in a night club, that was his. But no one ever told us that our screenplay was 'too serious.'"

Kelly had rehearsed for one month when he broke his ankle. He now admits he lied to the studio when he told them he broke his ankle during rehearsal—in fact, he broke it playing touch football in his back yard.

Whatever broke the ankle, Berlin was nervous. "What are we going to do, Arthur?"

"Don't worry, I'll handle it," was Freed's calm reply. What he kept to himself was that he was trying to get Fred Astaire for the picture. When Fred and his sister, Adele, age eight and nine respectively, were playing the Orpheum circuit, a fourteen-year-old singer was on the bill: his name was Arthur Freed. Now Astaire was in retirement—he called it a temporary leave of absence, a mental retirement, a rest from creating new steps and ideas for dance numbers. "Dancing for the screen is approximately 80 per cent brain work," says Astaire. "Only about 20 per cent of the strain is on the feet."

Freed called Astaire at his ranch in San Diego County. Would he come up and replace Kelly? Astaire had worked with Berlin five times before, the last being *Blue Skies* (Paramount, 1946). "Let me go and talk to Gene before I say yes."

Kelly told Astaire he couldn't possibly work for the next six or

Dear Arthur— These are a few ideas for Judy — #1 possibly when you first see her if all around the "Iron" happens to be an evening gown. #2 and all loaded dinner gown for going on to Mrs. Bellow (do you remember how wonderful Gertrude Lawrence looked in the orange beaded dress in "Lady in the Dark?") #3 possibly for the bedroom scene following unless you prefer her in something more feminine, like #4. And #5 for back stage dressing room. I'm off to New York — back next Saturday and will call you then.

*love,
Vincente*

Irene Gibbons during one of her typical days choosing fabrics for Arthur Freed's productions. ARTHUR FREED ARCHIVES

eight months. The prospect of doing a picture with Garland was enough to bring Astaire out of retirement.

"My experiences with Arthur have been professional bonanzas," says Astaire. "It was exciting—and most of all it was top stuff. Arthur was a very good guiding light because he was a music man. He was a songwriter of note and he couldn't be fooled. He was generous and understanding, and most of the time he knew pretty well what he wanted. If he didn't he wouldn't let you know—he'd just say 'Come on . . . do it!' Then you really get your noggin going. 'Anything you do is okay,' he'd say, but he didn't do that with everybody."

Astaire always made it a point to show Freed what he had done because he valued his opinion so highly.

Three days after Kelly's mishap, rehearsals began on the musical numbers. Edens divided his time between Walters and Alton. Alton worked mostly with Astaire and Miller while Walters concentrated on the more intimate numbers such as "The Vaudeville Montage," "Snooky Ookums," "I Love a Piano," "I Want to Go Back to Michigan," "Ragtime Violin," "When That Midnight Choo-Choo Leaves for Alabam'," and especially "Mister Monotony" with Judy.

Designing a wardrobe for the year 1914 was an interesting assignment for Irene Gibbons. "While designing these costumes," Irene said at the time, "I discovered that the fashions of today (1947–48) to a great extent have reverted back to that period and that the gowns which I designed were typical of those worn by today's women. Particularly the 'snub' waistline, the natural shoulder line, the tight skirt split to the knee and both the hobble skirt and the draped skirt . . . all very ultrastylish now."

The second and third weeks in November were taken up with prerecording sessions. Lennie Hayton was on a leave of absence from

One of Irene's costume designs for Judy
Garland and the still from *Easter Parade*
in which it was used. M-G-M

the studio and Johnny Green had been brought in to conduct. Edens
had laid out all the arrangements and handed them over to Salinger
and Leo Arnaud. In addition, at Astaire's request, Mason Van Cleave,
who had worked with Astaire on *Blue Skies,* was brought over from
Paramount to do "Steppin' Out With My Baby."

"When we had all the arrangements finished, Johnny Green came
in," Arnaud recalls. "He was not the musical director, he was the
conductor. And let me tell you, Connie and I could have recorded the
musical numbers in half the time and better, because we knew what
was in the score."

Green recalls an incident on the sound stage when Judy and Fred
were prerecording "A Couple of Swells": "Arthur always operated
under the *droit du seigneur*—red lights were for everybody else but
not for him. We were ready to go, the red light was on, I said, 'Roll
'em'—and bang the door opens and Freed and Berlin walk in. I
gestured to them, 'Shhhh,' and said, 'Slate it again, please.' Now
I've got my stick up and Judy and Fred are ready. We start. Suddenly
I hear Arthur jingling his coins in his pocket. His jingling continues,
meanwhile Irving knows he's got to be quiet, but Freed thought he was
sotto voce. Roger is in the control room with the mixer and they're both

motioning for me to cut. But I felt I wanted to continue in order to have a playback. Then I hear Arthur remarking to Berlin in one breath: 'Aren't they great, shhh!' Then he says, 'How about that—shhh!' Berlin then joins in slapping his knee. Well, it was finished and I said, 'O.K. let's hear it!' Now, if it had been a number for, say, José Greco—you understand—the flamenco dancers with their castanets, and then you hear 'Shhh!' mumble, mumble and then the slap on the knee. Well, I thought Judy and Fred were going to fall off their platform, they were laughing so hard. And, mind you, this is the great Garland and the great Astaire and an important picture, and those noises are coming from Arthur Freed and Irving Berlin. Well, you must say that's pretty funny."

Easter Parade started shooting on November 25, 1947. Everything went along smoothly, although Garland had to return to *The Pirate* seventeen times for retakes. None of this posed any problems. She loved working on *Easter Parade* and always returned to the set in high spirits.

One of Irene's costume designs for Ann Miller and a wardrobe-test still of Ann Miller with Peter Lawford. M-G-M

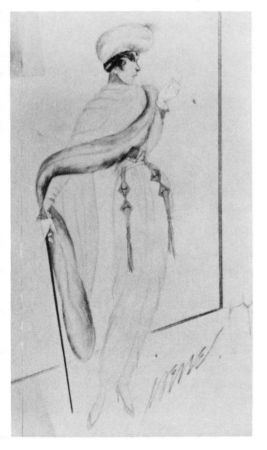

The *Delineator* sequence from Bob Alton's production number "The Girl on the Magazine Cover." M-G-M

Walters and Alton worked well together. When Alton came to the stage to shoot a musical sequence, Walters, in jest, would call to him, "I'm not ready yet for you, go away." Sometimes Freed would come down and remark at the end of a scene, "Academy! Academy!"

"We'd kind of feel good about it; it meant he was pleased with what he saw," says Astaire. Walters' reaction was less sanguine. "Well, I don't care what Academy it is; I'm going to be my own Academy. Let's make another take."

One of the big production numbers Alton devised was based on the Berlin favorite, "The Girl on the Magazine Cover." He photographed nine cover pages of magazines of the period with their familiar logos, while a male singer sang the tune.

Smith reproduced each front page and designed its background. Then these pages were blown up to giant size. Alton ingeniously posed a model in costume to fit the background. *Cosmopolitan*—a vamp; *Vanity Fair*—a bathing girl; *Delineator*—a girl in a wedding dress; *Redbook*—a girl with a dog; *Vogue*—a girl with a riding crop; *Yachting*—a girl at a ship's rail; *McCall's*—a girl after a ball; *Woman's Home*

Companion—a girl in white fox; and finally ending up with *Harper's Bazaar*—Ann Miller in a dressing room.

One of the highlights in every Astaire picture is his trick number. In *Easter Parade* it was Berlin's new song "Steppin' Out With My Baby." Astaire dances alternately with three beautiful partners in as many moods; a modified ballet, a sultry blues, and a lively jitterbug. Then he swings into his inimitable solo tap dance, the climax photographed in slow motion. This demanded four weeks of intensive study by John Nicholaus, head of the film laboratory, to arrive at the first slow motion synchron with sound, catching Astaire's split-second timing, precision and grace.

The closing scene of the picture was the famous Easter Parade on Fifth Avenue. For that day, February 9, 1948, seven hundred extra players were engaged, and over one hundred period vehicles, ancient vintage cars and horse-drawn buggies were rented. The scene was shot looking north along Fifth Avenue with the camera catching glimpses of St. Patrick's Cathedral and other famous landmarks still standing, as well as the Union Club and other buildings that have since disappeared. "That particular set was a baby of mine," recalls Smith. "On Lot 3, beside the St. Louis Street, was an empty, paved

Fred Astaire during the dress rehearsal of his first number, "Drum Crazy."
M-G-M

Peter Lawford during his portion of "A Fella With an Umbrella." M-G-M

Judy and Fred relax between takes of "A Couple of Swells." The song that Berlin wrote for *Easter Parade* has become legendary. Judy later incorporated it into her first show at the Palace Theatre, New York. M-G-M

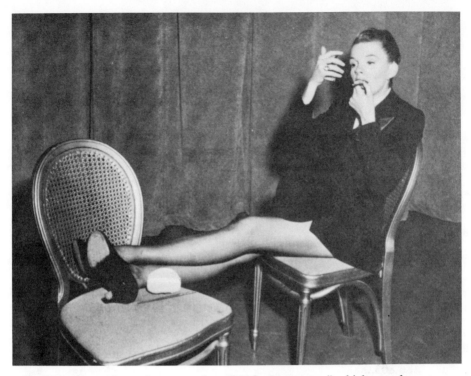

Judy adjusts her make-up between takes of "Mr. Monotony," which was deleted from the release print. Her costume was identical to the one she later wore in *Summer Stock,* in which she sang "Get Happy." M-G-M

area. I built the lower ten feet of St. Patrick's and one side of Fifth Avenue for two city blocks." The Easter Parade was staged and photographed on that side of the Avenue only. This shot was the primary film strip. The missing right side of the street was then painted into the film and by way of a complicated technical process, a so-called Newcombe[4] shot, the total view of Fifth Avenue in the New York of 1912 emerged. This had been done before with a stationary camera, but the great achievement in this particular shot was the camera rising from a low angle higher and higher, stopping to hold a bird's-eye view of two city blocks of Fifth Avenue only one side of which had been built for the film.

Before the picture was previewed, the song Berlin had written for Garland, "Mister Monotony," was eliminated. "It slowed up the picture," says Berlin, "and Arthur and I were sorry to see it go because we both liked it, a very unusual song based on a phrase. I later used it in the theatre, in *Miss Liberty* (1949) and it stopped the show and stopped everything else. Then I put it in *Call Me Madam* (1950);

[4] Named for the head of the special effects department, Warren Newcombe.

Ginger Rogers sent her congratulations to Freed. Little did she know she was also planting a seed in his mind. Rogers replaced Garland and was reunited with Astaire in *The Barkleys of Broadway*.

Ethel Merman sang it and it stopped the show again; but it didn't belong in that show and I took it out."

The *Easter Parade* preview at the Westwood Village Theatre, February 28, 1948, was one of the happiest for the Freed Unit. When the sensational last shot, showing the vast panorama of the Easter Parade, came on the screen, the audience gasped; and as the camera began to rise to the sound of a chorus of mixed voices it lifted them out of their seats. The picture cost $2,503,654 (under budget by $191,280). In its initial release, July 16, 1948, it grossed in excess of $6,803,000.

The twenty-first annual Academy Award ceremony was held on March 24, 1949, at the Academy Theatre.[5]

In the category of "Scoring of a Musical Picture," nominations were *Easter Parade,* Johnny Green and Roger Edens; *The Pirate,* Lennie Hayton; *The Emperor Waltz,* Victor Young; *When My Baby*

---

[5] The Academy had to hold the event in their own home theatre because the major Hollywood studios withdrew their financial support of the functions. The small seating capacity (950) was not adequate to accommodate guests and nominees who wanted to attend.

Smiles at Me, Alfred Newman; and *Romance on the High Seas,* Ray Heindorf. The winner was *Easter Parade.*

In spite of the fact that Green was only the conductor on the picture, Edens had generously agreed to share the credit with him. Losing sight of this fact, Green commented, "There I was slugging and struggling and I didn't need Roger Edens. I finally said 'I don't want to be on a picture with him.' I don't need Edens . . . I *am* Edens, plus Salinger, plus Hayton. I'll act as associate producer and orchestrate and conduct. After all, this is a competitive world; this is the world of the arts, and if you have that kind of versatility you ought to use it. In the whole industry there were really only three of us who did that kind of work: Edens was the king; Green, second; Saul Chaplin, third—except that neither of them could orchestrate or conduct."

My dear Arthur,

If I had written to you as many times as I have thought of you in the past six months, you would have to hire 49 secretaries to open envelopes all day and 49 new pairs of glasses with which to read all my letters.

I am writing you to thank you for being the guy you are, generous and kind, and for being so wonderful to Bob.

We are all very happy about doing the show and we feel, Arthur, that since it was you who so encouraged me when I came to your office and told you that I wanted to leave, you are in your own particular way responsible for some of the great happiness that has come our way.

We have been working like dogs and love it, and New York in the springtime is indeed lovely.

I hope that you and Renee are both well and I am looking forward to seeing you both when I get to Hollywood this summer.

Hadie Harris has asked me to a showing of *Easter Parade* and I can't wait to see it because it is filled with so much of Bob and Judy and you.

Give her my best should you see her and give my love to Roger, but save most of it for you, Arthur.

Devotedly,
Kay Thompson

Even before the Kern picture was finished, Freed's admiration for the great men of the American musical theatre made him set up the production of another biography, the story of Richard Rodgers and Lorenz Hart. He wanted to get access to another catalogue of great songs. In *Words and Music,* the story of their collaboration would merely serve as a thread to tie the musical numbers together. And, unlike *Clouds,* they would be presented as theatrical productions; the camera would be the eye of the audience.

Around the piano in Freed's suite (left to right): Ben Feiner, Jr., Richard Rodgers, Arthur Freed and Mrs. Richard (Dorothy) Rodgers, during the preliminary script conferences on *Words and Music*. ARTHUR FREED ARCHIVES

One of the conditions in the contract between Rodgers, the Hart estate and Metro was script approval. With his heavy Broadway activities, Rodgers had no intention of spending any length of time in Hollywood, so he asked Freed to do him the favor of hiring his brother-in-law Ben Feiner, Jr., as his liaison. Freed graciously agreed.

The material for the story was prepared by Jean Holloway and Guy Bolton, developed by Fred Finklehoffe and adapted by Feiner.

When Feiner sent Rodgers the script there was nothing basic that he found fault with. He made just a few marginal notes: "There were too many recurrences of Hart's disappearing act; Juilliard (in which Rodgers had great interest) referred to as 'Academy of Music' should be corrected to 'Institute of Musical Arts'; the word 'diaper' should be taken out."

Words and Music went into production on April 4, 1948. There were seven principals in the cast: Tom Drake as Rodgers, Mickey Rooney as Hart, Janet Leigh as Dorothy Feiner Rodgers, Marshall Thompson as Herbert Fields, Ann Sothern as Joyce Harmon, Betty Garrett as Peggy O'Neill and Perry Como as Eddie Anders. Guest appearances were made by June Allyson, Judy Garland, Lena Horne,

Gene Kelly, Cyd Charisse, Mel Torme and Vera-Ellen. Norman Taurog took charge of directing the dramatic scenes.

This would not be a complex picture for Freed to make. The book was of lesser importance. Alton was going to stage the musical numbers. Lennie Hayton was back after a leave of absence and ideal to handle the musical score—and with Edens on his side he felt he couldn't miss.

Of the twenty-two numbers in the film, Alton staged some in the settings of their original shows; for others he invented plot and locale. He showed Ann Sothern's dancing talent in "Where's That Rainbow?"; in "On Your Toes," he choreographed a duet for Cyd Charisse and Dee Turnell in classic ballet style to a jazz orchestration; he "moved" Lena Horne through her nightclub performances of "Where or When" and "The Lady Is a Tramp"[6]; he directed Mickey Rooney and Judy Garland in an amusing doubleplay of "I Wish I Were in Love Again," which, incidentally, was their last on-screen appearance together; in "Blue Room," he eased Perry Como out of his camera shyness and gave Charisse a solo, romantic, tender and gorgeous to look at.

"Slaughter on Tenth Avenue" was a ballet Rodgers had composed for the Rodgers and Hart musical *On Your Toes* (1936). It was originally conceived as a comic ballet for Ray Bolger and Vera Zorina. Edens changed it into a raw, exciting and sexy dramatic scenario. Alton concerned himself with the choreography of the ensemble and Vera-Ellen, while Kelly worked out his own.

[6] When "The Lady Is a Tramp" was prerecorded, a second version had to be made substituting "crap games" with "card games" to satisfy the British Board of Censors.

"Thou Swell" from *The Connecticut Yankee* as performed in *Words and Music* by June Allyson and the Blackburn Twins to Robert Alton's staging. M-G-M

"Bob Alton was a very underrated choreographer," says Kelly. "Years ago, he was the first fellow who really knew that what I was doing dancewise was different; he recognized it and said, 'Go ahead and do it.' He was a great help to me and always encouraged me very much. My form of dancing? I wouldn't know what to call it; it's certainly hybrid and, if you allow the term, it's bastardized. I've borrowed from the modern dance, from the classical, and certainly from the American folk dance—tap dancing, jitterbugging. But I have tried to develop a style which is indigenous to the environment in which I was reared—the classical ballet is completely foreign to that."

Rather than resort to cinematic techniques to show change of scenes—from street to bedroom, from bedroom to barroom—Kelly stayed within the limitations of a stage production and turned these limitations into an asset. He used a revolving stage, moving the action from scene to scene, and this was visible to the audience. For the sake of realism he went even further. After conferring with his brilliant cameraman Harry Stradling, he went to Freed. "I asked Arthur to let me use a 28 millimeter lens and place the camera into a pit on the bottom of the staircase as Vera-Ellen falls down, hit by a bullet, landing very close to the camera, which would distort her face." But Mayer had issued a mandate to the camera department: "The ladies had to look pretty at all times, no matter what." Freed told Kelly to go ahead. "If worse comes to worse we can always reshoot it."

In his presentation of this dramatic jazz ballet Kelly succeeded in giving the entire sequence the spontaneity of a live performance.

Mickey, Judy and Roger during the prerecording of "I Wish I Were in Love Again." This number from *Words and Music* marked Mickey and Judy's last screen appearance together. ROGER EDENS ARCHIVES

Hayton and Salinger molded the orchestral score into a symphonic rhapsody, achieving unity between the visual and the tonal. "Slaughter" was the *pièce de résistance* of the film. Significantly, it was placed near the end of the picture giving *Words and Music* its rousing climax. "Slaughter on Tenth Avenue" had a lasting effect on the future musicals produced by Freed.

One cannot omit mentioning Mickey Rooney's remarkable performance in the complex role of Lorenz Hart. It was Rooney's last picture under his M-G-M contract.

The picture was completed on October 1, 1948, at the cost of $2,799,970. In its initial release, December 31, 1948, it grossed in excess of $4,552,000.

The following is the opening paragraph from the *Hollywood Reporter*'s review of *Words and Music:*

> A glance at the stellar cast of *Words and Music* is enough to show that the M-G-M attraction is about the biggest musical film of the year. And it lives up fully to its promise, as magically it creates the illusion of taking the spectator right down the years to all the great Rodgers and Hart openings. It is the big, flashy, gorgeous entertainment. The tunes roll on, one hit after another, with the precision of an assembly line. . . . It is such an outstanding job in the revue department that one gladly forgives the story—which doesn't matter.

Richard Rodgers
1270 SIXTH AVENUE · NEW YORK 20, N. Y.
Telephone CI. 7-3865

November
1st
1948

Mr. Arthur Freed,
Metro-Goldwyn-Mayer Studios,
Culver City, Cal.

Rodgers gave this
letter to the Studio Publicity
Department for use
in promoting and
advertising the film. M-G-M

Dear Arthur:

It is difficult for
me to tell you how happy I am with the way the songs
are done in WORDS AND MUSIC. The orchestrations and
instrumental handling are exciting and gratifying,
but equally wonderful to me is the performance of
these songs by such an extraordinary cast of stars.
I cannot thank you enough for it.

Yours sincerely,

Dick

The foregoing letter had an aftermath: When Rodgers was approached for his personal view on the picture and Mr. Freed, his secretary told the author she would take the matter up with Mr. Rodgers. Later, the author received a letter from her in which she transmitted Mr. Rodgers' own words: "I knew Arthur Freed but not very well and did not work with him closely. I am afraid there is no interview with me on Arthur Freed."

In the summer of 1946, when Gene Kelly proposed a baseball picture to Freed, he had Stanley Donen come East to join him. As they drove cross-country on their way back to California, they conjured up a plot.

Stanley Donen started as a dancer in a chorus on Broadway. While working in *Pal Joey* Kelly befriended him and he became his protégé. When Kelly began staging the musical numbers for *Best Foot Forward,* he made Donen his assistant, in addition to getting him a role in the show. By the time Donen was nineteen years old, he had put aside enough money to come to Hollywood. He went directly to Metro where Freed was preparing the film version of *Best Foot Forward* and landed a job in the chorus and assisted Walters on the dances. When Kelly went over to Columbia to do *Cover Girl,* Donen went along to assist him (behind the camera). For the next two years he worked at Columbia as a dance director. He then returned to M-G-M (again at Kelly's request) and began collaborating with Kelly on the musical numbers for *Anchors Aweigh.* He remained working for Pasternak on *Holiday in Mexico* and *No Leave, No Love.*

When Kelly and Donen arrived back at the studio they handed Freed their seven-page synopsis.

TAKE ME OUT TO THE BALL GAME

Story synopsis for a motion picture intended for Frank Sinatra and Gene Kelly, written by Gene Kelly and Stanley Donen.

The story is laid in the period between 1905 and 1915, when baseball was really coming into its own as the national pastime.

Our general setup is this: Kelly is a short stop, Frankie, the second baseman, and Leo Durocher, the first baseman of the greatest double-play combination since "Tinker to Evers to Chance." Of course, they would be called: O'Brien, Ryan and Shaughnessy. I've worked out an Irish jig that Sinatra and Durocher will be able to dance and which will carry on the myth of Frankie's terpsichorean ability (and believe me, this will top any of our joint numbers in *Anchors Aweigh*). And, too, I guarantee not a dry seat in the house when the crooner does one of those sentimental Irish ballads.

Now, Frankie and Gene (O'Brien and Ryan) have been lifelong pals—same town, same school, same desires and ambitions—real Damon and Pythias types, but, although they're the greatest shortstop and second base combination in the major leagues,[7] *the guys don't want to play ball,* they want to be entertainers.

Then the club is willed to C. B. Higgins. When Higgins arrives it turns out to be Kathryn Grayson. . . .

Freed bought this outline for the studio. It is clear that he bought it to accommodate Kelly, not because he thought it to be inventive, original or intriguing. He put George Wells to work developing a screenplay, but he replaced Grayson with Garland. Harry Warren and Ralph Blane, directly off *Summer Holiday,* started writing the score.

It was soon evident that Judy Garland was in no condition to do the picture. Only under duress had she been able to do her two numbers in *Words and Music;* her second number for that film, "Johnny One Note," had to be shot after the picture was completed. Now came a drastic piece of recasting: Esther Williams. Wells's script had to be discarded and Harry Tugend began writing a new screenplay. Warren and Blane's score had to be abandoned. Betty Comden, Adolph Green and Roger Edens proceeded to write new songs. In Kelly's

[7] According to Kelly: "I based my idea on famous ball player Al Schacht and his partner who used to be the clowns of baseball."

"O'Brien to Ryan to Goldberg" from *Take Me Out to the Ball Game* being rehearsed on the ball field (left to right): Frank Sinatra, Stanley Donen, Jules Munshin and Gene Kelly. M-G-M

Betty Garrett performing "It's Fate, Baby, It's Fate," with Frank Sinatra in *Take Me Out to the Ball Game*. M-G-M

synopsis, Sinatra had been designated for the picture. In place of Leo Durocher, it was going to be Jules Munshin. Betty Garrett was cast in the role of a girl in love with Sinatra. Five years ago, Freed had fired Busby Berkeley off *Girl Crazy*. He had picked him up again for *Clouds,* but that didn't work out. Freed, for sentimental reasons, now gave him another chance, and assigned him to direct the book.

Of the nine songs used in *Take Me Out to the Ball Game,* five were written by Edens, Comden and Green, and one by Edens alone. The title song was a 1908 standard by Harry Van Tilzer and Jack Norworth; "The Hat My Dear Old Father Wore" was by Schwartz and Jerome, and the ninth was Rodgers and Hammerstein's "Boys and Girls Like You and Me."

The picture started shooting on July 28, 1948, and all was fun and games. Berkeley took care of the dialogue scenes, finished his job and left. Kelly and Donen went into rehearsal and resumed with shooting the musical numbers.

Adolph Deutsch was assigned as musical director. He was new to the Freed Unit and had recently signed a long-term contract with Metro. Although Edens and Salinger respected Deutsch's talent, they knew his reputation of being slow and pedantic. The first arrangement he made for the picture was "The Hat My Dear Old Father Wore

Upon St. Patrick's Day." When Edens heard it on the recording stage he exclaimed, "That man has got to work for us!"

When Deutsch began to record the underscoring, he started with the main title, arranged by Salinger and orchestrated by Robert Franklyn. He meticulously rehearsed it and the first take was made. Edens and Simone simultaneously said, "Print it!" Deutsch was dumbfounded. "It was great, Adolph," said Edens. "Let's go on to the next scene." With some difficulty Deutsch soon got used to the working speed of the Freed Unit.

When the picture was being edited for preview, "Boys and Girls Like You and Me" was taken out, although it was not only a great song but one of Sinatra's best performances. The same thing happened on *Meet Me in St. Louis.* "Well, we all thought it was a great song," says Mamoulian. "I staged it—I didn't like it—I restaged it; I restaged it seventeen times until everybody was going nuts. Finally I said to myself, 'My God, this song doesn't work.' So I told Hammerstein that it didn't belong and out it went. From then on I said, 'Look, if somebody would come in and mention, "Do you know this song, 'Boys and Girls'?"' it would land me in a lunatic asylum."

"Boys and Girls Like You and Me" was finally laid to rest.

Take Me Out to the Ball Game didn't really have a plot to speak of and it is difficult to resolve a plot that isn't there. Here is the way Kelly, Sinatra, Williams and Garrett ended the picture:

> "Keep your seats!
> Hold your hats!
> It's not the finish of the show.
> The love scene must be played out
> Before the final fade-out.
> Sinatra gets Garrett,
> Kelly gets Williams,
> For that's the plot the author wrote.
> So we'll turn this duet
> Into a quartet
> And end it on a happy note. . . ."

Ball Game was completed on October 26, 1948, at a cost of $1,725,970.54. It was well received when it previewed on December 16, 1948, in Encino, California. In its initial release, April 1, 1949, it grossed in excess of $4,344,000.[8]

In January 1948, Betty Comden and Adolph Green returned to the Freed Unit and started on their screenplay for a Garland-Astaire original. The story, delivered in March, was about a successful Broadway husband-and-wife team, their career occasionally disrupted by ex-

---

[8] It was decided that the title would be strange to British audiences, so it was retitled *Everybody's Cheering* for foreign distribution.

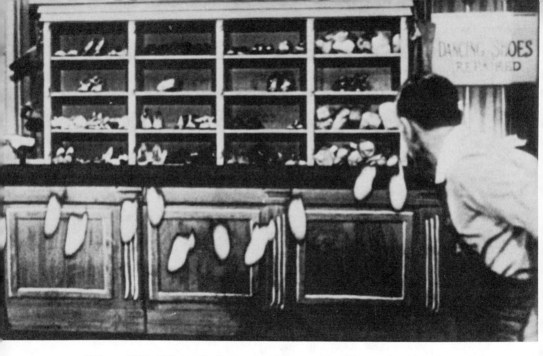

"Shoes With Wings On." Hermes Pan recalls, "I got the idea for Fred's number from 'The Sorcerer's Apprentice.' In the suite, the clerk is alone and breaks off part of a broomstick, the two come in. Then he breaks the two again and four come in . . ." M-G-M

plosions of temper. A young, intellectual English playwright comes into their lives and wants the lady to try her luck in drama. The husband's resentment and the wife's ambitions heighten their mutual professional jealously. Her excursion into drama ends in failure, and they resume their career, more in love than ever.

Comden and Green read their screenplay for Garland, Astaire and Freed. Astaire recalls: "When they read their original script to Judy and me in Arthur's office we flipped, and said we'd have a hard time living up to their performance." The usual Freed Unit personnel were assigned to the picture: Walters, Alton, Edens, Salinger, Hayton and Simone.

Oscar Levant was cast as Ezra, a composer and close friend of the leading lady and the leading man. He was to display his famous wit, sing and play the piano. In a supporting role, Billie Burke was cast as the socialite and patroness of the arts.

Freed talked to Harry Warren about writing the score, and Warren suggested Ira Gershwin as his lyricist.[9] Gershwin remembers

[9] Warren and Gershwin had collaborated in 1930 on the Broadway show *Sweet and Low,* in which they wrote "Cheerful Little Earful" and "In the Merry Month of Maybe."

the first conference on the film: "Arthur thought a Scottish number for Astaire and Garland might be interesting. Neither Harry nor I knew much about Scottish dialects, but after the conference I thought of the title for the song with its play on the word 'fling.' Harry made several attempts at a main theme, one of which we felt good about; it was the start of the song 'My One and Only Highland Fling.' For the Scottish surnames in the patter I went through all the Macs and Mcs in Who's Who; also those in the Los Angeles telephone book, careful to avoid rhyming 'McTavish' and 'lavish,' because this pairing belonged to Ogden Nash. I went for 'MacDougal' and 'frugal.' "

Astaire had a title for a song, "Swing Trot," and wanted Warren and Gershwin to write the song; he meant to use it as a promotion for his dancing schools. Gershwin's reaction was negative: "What are we going to do with that?" After they had completed their eight new songs and thought they were finished with the score, Freed told them that Astaire still wanted that song. Gershwin gave in. "All right," he said, "we'll write a song called 'Swing Trot.' "

On May 1, Astaire began rehearsing "Shoes With Wings On." He asked for choreographer Hermes Pan to help him with the creation of this number. At RKO Astaire had worked with Pan whom he considered particularly inventive for specialty numbers.

> The Barkleys have split up. Astaire continues the show with Mrs. Barkley's understudy, and this is his big new solo number. It takes place on the stage; the set is a shoe store with Astaire as the shoe-maker. The curtain opens on a number of customers of different types: a ballet dancer, a tap dancer, a child toe dancer, a Russian girl dancer, etc. are posed in a tableau during the introductory music. As the first rhythm chorus starts, the tableau breaks and Astaire waits on his customers, fitting ballet shoes, adjusting taps, etc. The customers leave one by one and he closes his store. As he is standing by the counter, a pair of shoes suddenly appear dancing on the counter to Astaire's amazement. He tries to catch the shoes but they slip away. The shoes dance all around him; Astaire falls in with their rhythm, dancing with them, until momentarily the shoes disappear. At this point we hear Astaire's voice off scene reflecting his thoughts, "I've got shoes with wings on." Astaire does a panto-mime to the lyric of the song, there is a wild tap dance with Astaire again dancing with the shoes until, in a frenzy, he grabs two guns from behind the counter and shoots the shoes. They dis-appear one after another. Astaire then throws the guns into the store window—it breaks with a terrific crash—at the same time all the shoe boxes fall out of the shelves and Astaire collapses, buried under a heap of shoes.

The multiple processes required for the execution of this number were incredibly complex. Before the number was ready to be photo-graphed, Astaire and Pan had to work out to the millimeter not only each step, each pose, each movement, but the precise area Astaire's routine would cover within the circumference of the floor. Only then could the camera and special effects people he brought in to figure out how this could be transferred to the screen.

Until now the working title of the picture was *You Made Me Love You,* but Edens suggested the title be changed to *The Barkleys of Broadway.*

Judy Garland started work on the picture on June 14. During the second week of rehearsals she began to falter and during the third the situation was very much as it had been during *The Pirate.*

Freed wanted to assure himself as to her condition and called her doctor.

Subject: JUDY GARLAND — ILLNESS
From: Arthur Freed

July 12, 1948—3:30 P.M.—memorandum of telephone conversation with Dr. Schelman, Judy Garland's personal physician.

I called Dr. Schelman to ask how Miss Garland was and he said he had given her medication to sleep. I asked him in his opinion as her physician if it would be wise to start her working in an important picture. He replied that it would be a risky procedure. He said that she possibly could work four or five days, always under medication, and possibly blow up for a period and then work again for a few days. He was of the opinion that if she didn't have to work for a while it might not be too difficult to make a complete cure but that her knowledge of having to report every morning would cause such a mental disturbance within her that the results would be in jeopardy.

I told him that I was anxious for Judy to get well, and he volunteered to come in and have a talk with me within the next few days.

He thanked me for my interest and courtesy in the matter.

Freed had no choice; he had to take Judy off the picture. He considered Ginger Rogers for the part, to bring her and Astaire together again. He talked to Astaire, who was elated about it. He said, "Gin and I had often discussed the possibility of getting together for a rematch. And here it was, out of a clear sky."

On one hand, Walters was dismayed and saddened by Judy being out of the picture, but on the other, he was thrilled with the prospect of making a film with Astaire and Rogers who, as he says, had been his dancing idols since the mid-thirties.

This would be Astaire and Rogers' tenth picture together, after a separation of nine years. Their last picture was *The Story of Irene and Vernon Castle* (1939).

Rogers and Garland as performers were dissimilar, and changes had to be made, particularly in the Warren and Gershwin score. "Natchez on the Mississip'," "The Courtship of Elmer and Ella" (a hillbilly number) and "Poetry in Motion" (a comic ballet) were dropped. It was decided to make the English playwright a Frenchman and Jacques Francois was cast in the part. To add nostalgia, Edens came up with "They Can't Take That Away From Me," a song George and Ira Gershwin had written for Astaire and Rogers in *Shall We Dance* (1937). "I would never have suggested it," says Gershwin. "After all, it meant interpolating it into a score that I had written with Warren. But I guess it was all right with Harry." (It wasn't all right with Harry.)

When Comden and Green were writing their script for Judy Garland, Edens suggested that she do an impersonation of Sarah Bernhardt. Rogers was happy to keep this scene in because she had recently been a dramatic actress.

For his piano solos Levant had chosen Khachaturian's "Sabre Dance" and excerpts from Tschaikowsky's "First Piano Concerto in B Flat Minor." In his writings Levant insists these numbers were direct recorded. This is not true. They were prerecorded on the recording stage under Lennie Hayton's direction and photographed to a playback. Hayton was also seen on camera conducting a side-line orchestra. Levant also contended that M-G-M had negotiated with Eugene Ormandy, musical director of the Philadelphia Orchestra, to conduct his numbers and to appear in the film, but that he was turned down when he asked for an enormous fee plus equal billing with Astaire and Rogers. There is no evidence to that effect. Freed, in fact, approached André Kostelanetz.

ADRESSE TELEGRAPHIQUE
RITZOTEL·PARIS 81

Hôtel Ritz
Place Vendôme
Paris

May 14th 48

Dear Arthur:

I am dissapointed beyond all words not to be able to do your picture. I am conducting the London Symphony Orchestra in London and on tour in June.

I do hope we can do something else together! Lily joins me in sending you and Mrs Freed our warmest greetings —

cordially yours Andre

Irene's costume designs for Ginger Rogers in *The Barkleys of Broadway,* with stills from the film. ARTHUR FREED ARCHIVES

"THE BARKLEYS OF BROADWAY" 1948

The Barkleys of Broadway
company (left to right):
cameraman Harry Stradling,
Ginger Rogers, Robert Alton;
(above): Saul Levitt (assistant
director) and Fred Astaire.
M-G-M

Ginger listens as Oscar philosophizes. M-G-M

The studio's still photographer took this picture on the day Judy appeared on *The Barkleys of Broadway* set after Ginger Rogers had already replaced her. Oscar Levant, as usual, doesn't appear too amused. M-G-M

The picture started shooting on August 8, 1948, and progressed without any major problems. There were a few incidents worth noting.

On the first day Freed came to the set while Walters was talking to Levant. "Freed did a terrible thing regarding Levant," says Walters. "Right in front of him, Arthur said, 'Now, Chuck, I want you to realize that Oscar is a very talented and very funny personality. And anything he wants to do, just stand back and let him get on with it.' Now you just don't do that sort of thing to a director, at least not while the actor is within earshot."

"When we finally got around to shooting our first dance," Astaire remembers, "I thought for some reason Ginger seemed taller than usual. I asked Pan, 'Am I crazy or is Ginger on stilts?' He said, 'I know—something is different.' I went to Ginger. 'Hey,' I said, 'have you grown or have I shrunk?' She laughed and confessed she had sneaked some higher heels over on me."

Less amusing was Judy Garland's appearance on the set in one of the costumes for the picture she had previously been fitted for. She was parading all over the set having great fun. She was very friendly with the crew and posed in front of the camera. Ginger Rogers put up with this charade until she couldn't stand it any longer and ran to her dressing room. No one had the courage to tell Judy to leave. When Walters finally asked her to go she refused, so he took her by the arm and escorted her out while she hurled insults at Rogers.

Edens conceived the idea of opening the picture with Astaire and Rogers doing a dance number in a Broadway show, "Swing Trot," already starting behind the titles and finishing with the curtain coming down as the titles go off and the picture begins. He felt that the immediate appearance of the most famous dancing team would accentuate the excitement of their return to the screen.

The Barkleys of Broadway was completed on October 30, 1948, at a cost of $2,325,420 (under budget by $86,953 including carrying a $23,077 charge for Garland).

When the picture was released on May 13, 1949, Bosley Crowther of the New York *Times* headed his review with "AGE CANNOT WITHER, INDEED!":

> Ginger and Fred are a couple with incorruptible style. They still have that gift of mutual timing in absolute unison, so that they're always clicking together, when dancing or trifling with the plot. Watching them work together in "My One and Only Highland Fling," a spoof of a Glocca Morra ballad, with the two of them decked out in kilts, brings a brand-new appreciation of their drive and urbane drollery. And watching them spin in rapturous rhythm to the lilt of "They Can't Take That Away

Oscar Levant after his concert in *The Barkleys of Broadway* shakes hands with the orchestra's conductor Lennie Hayton (his screen debut). M-G-M

From Me," the old Gershwin hit, renews one's fervor for the magic which they create. Age cannot wither the enchantment of Ginger and Fred."

The picture went on to gross in excess of $5,421,000.

The year was 1948. During the war and until then, enough money had been in everybody's pocket to buy whatever escapist fare was available. But now there was a drastic change in the public's taste. America had rubbed very bloody shoulders with the rest of the world; Hollywood's dream world no longer found a broad market.

Studio executives met the modest beginnings of television with the same condescending smiles they had had for the nickelodeon half a century ago. But it quickly became clear that television was here to stay. The management at M-G-M was disoriented, evaded stark facts, held on to its illusion of splendid isolation, and Mayer attempted to run the studio from his box at the race track. In this atmosphere of complacency the studio kept on making the same pictures over and over, and with the same familiar faces. In 1946, the financial statement of Loew's Incorporated showed a record net income of $18,000,000. Two years later its profits took a nose dive to the lowest level since the dark year of 1933: $4,212,000. Faced with this shocking reality, Schenck and the board of directors decided that something drastic had to be done immediately.

On the last day of 1946, the Justice Department had put an end to the monopoly of the Hollywood studios, which compounded the dire

Astaire and Rogers in their costumes for "My One and Only Highland Fling." M-G-M

One of those famous Astaire-Rogers dance steps, as they did "Swing Trot" under the main titles of *The Barkleys of Broadway*. ARTHUR FREED ARCHIVES and M-G-M

state of the company. The Southern Federal District Court ordered that the operations of production and exhibition would have to be "divorced."[10] When this "divorce" would go into effect some years later, the result would be that a picture could reach the screen solely at the discretion or taste of the theatre owner. In addition, it would mean a loss of revenue in the exhibition of a film.

In Metro-Goldwyn-Mayer's fiscal year (August 31, 1948 to August 31, 1949), Freed had in release: *Summer Holiday, Good News, The Pirate, Easter Parade, Words and Music, Take Me Out to the Ball Game, The Barkleys of Broadway* and *Any Number Can Play*. They gave the studio a combined net profit of $14,130,306. According to the financial records of Eddie Mannix, studio production executive,

[10] Loew's theatres—Metro-Goldwyn-Mayer; Fox and National theatres—Twentieth Century-Fox; Warner theatres—Warner Bros.; Paramount and Publix theatres—Paramount Pictures; Radio-Keith Orpheum theatres—RKO Radio Pictures.

M-G-M's net profit for that period was $901,000. It becomes clear that Freed carried the cost of everything from executive salaries to the bottled water in the Administration Building.

Now the Freed Unit took on a different complexion. The exponents of Tin Pan Alley had departed. A more realistic, contemporary approach and style emerged, greatly influenced by the New York stage. The exponents of this "new wave" were Betty Comden and Adolph Green. They had made their first acquaintance with the Freed Unit on *Good News;* they had returned to write the original screenplay for *The Barkleys of Broadway* and the lyrics for the score of *Take Me Out to the Ball Game.*

Comden, Green, and Kelly had known each other in New York. Kelly was most sensitive to what was in the air and was constantly searching for something new. By making twenty-four-year-old Stanley Donen his codirector he allied himself with the temperament of the young generation. In these changing times, this foursome became the new coalition in the Freed Unit.

Freed, although a specialist in musical films, never discounted the possibility of producing dramatic films. *The Clock* was his first serious attempt; *Lust for Life* was to be his second. And Menotti had written two nonmusical screenplays.

In the early spring of 1948, Edens introduced Richard Brooks to Freed. Brooks was self-assured, articulate, unflinching and he also had a great deal of charm at his command. Freed was impressed and, more than that, from this first meeting he liked the man.

Of course Freed was well aware of Brooks's reputation as a writer. He had written several novels, the most successful of which was *The Big Foxhole,* made into the movie *Crossfire* (1947). Among his screenplays were *White Savage* (1943), *Cobra Woman* (1944), *Brute Force* (1947), *To the Victor* (1948) and his recently completed *Key Largo* (1948) for John Huston.

A close relationship developed between the two men, and it wasn't long before Freed took Brooks to Mayer's house on a Sunday morning. Mayer was preparing to go to a ball game at Wrigley Field and asked them to join him. In the course of the afternoon the conversation turned to Dore Schary who had produced Brooks's *Crossfire* at RKO. Schary had worked for Mayer in 1933 as a writer and subsequently as executive producer of "the B picture unit" but in the last few years he had lost contact with him. What, in the story, was *his* idea? Why did he want the picture made?, Mayer wanted to know. Brooks answered Mayer's questions and expressed his high opinion of Schary. He was unaware of the reasons for Mayer's interest.

In view of the financial situation of the studio and the urgent need for an increase in production, Mayer was pressured by Nicholas Schenck and the board of directors to bring in a new production head.

After extensive negotiations, Schary moved into this new position on July 15, 1948.

In passing, Mayer remarked to Freed, "With all the producers I have on the lot nobody can come up with a property for Clark Gable."

As usual, Freed acted. On his instigation, the studio had already put Brooks under contract and had assigned him to the Freed Unit. Brooks found a novel, *Any Number Can Play,* written by Edward Harris Heth, owned by Twentieth Century-Fox. Freed read it, liked it, bought it and Brooks began to write the screenplay.

To produce a picture for Clark Gable would be exciting for any producer, including Freed. In addition to his most gifted writer, he sought out Mervyn LeRoy to direct the film and set out to get a brilliant cast: Alexis Smith, Audrey Totter, Wendell Corey, Barry Sullivan, Lewis Stone, Mary Astor, Frank Morgan, Edgar Buchanan, Leon Ames and Darryl Hickman.

In his screenplay Brooks explored the subject of gambling with strong psychological undertones. The plot is woven around the personal and financial crises which beset Gable, gambler and owner of a gaming establishment.

The production began on January 4, 1949, and was completed in forty-three days at a cost of $1,465,641. Fifty thousand dollars was paid to Twentieth Century-Fox for the property. Brooks received $29,167, LeRoy, $68,100, and Gable, $241,250. In its initial release, July 15, 1949, *Any Number Can Play* grossed in excess of $3,205,000.

Clark Gable, Richard Rober and William Conrad (now known to TV audiences as "Cannon") break up on the *Any Number Can Play* set. M-G-M

8   ON THE TOWN

In July 1948, when Dore Schary took over as head of production, he undoubtedly knew that he would have to deal with a small but powerful group of men who were overtly hostile toward him. Led by James K. McGinness, they were the ultraconservative, superpatriotic group around Mayer, mostly members of the Motion Picture Alliance, an organization founded for the purposes of "upholding the American ideal" and eradicating communism within the film industry. They had publicly termed Schary a "pinko." Although not a part of this group, Katz and Lichtman resigned. Schary knew that he would not be welcomed with open arms by all of M-G-M.

In spite of this pressure, Mayer at first stood firmly behind Schary, giving him a free hand to put his plans for reactivation of the studio's sagging production output into action. This so-called "free hand" in his long-term contract did, however, specify that all major decisions must have Mayer and Schenck's approval.

Schary proceeded to line up a production schedule for the coming year, with a notable absence of any musicals. He had no interest in, flair for or appreciation of musical films and felt they were a luxury the studio could do without. To assert his authority, the producers were told to inform him about all their activities, including preparation of scripts, casting, production expenditures, etc., and their daily office operation. This ruling was to include Freed.

Freed had no intention of complying. He had been offered Schary's job some years before and had turned it down, preferring to work as an autonomous producer, responsible exclusively to Mayer. Schary was informed that Freed and his unit were to be left alone.

For the year 1949–50, the following projects were on Freed's schedule: *On the Town, Annie Get Your Gun, Crisis, Pagan Love Song, How to Win Friends and Influence People, Royal Wedding, The Romberg Story, Show Boat* and *An American in Paris.* And he made a deal of far-reaching consequences.

On Lillie Messinger's suggestion the studio had bought *The Day Before Spring,* the 1945 Broadway musical, with book and lyrics by Alan Jay Lerner and music by Frederick Loewe. She and Lerner became great friends and she was unrelenting in the promotion of his career.

In 1947, she went to New York for the opening of their next musical *Brigadoon* and again in 1948 for *Love Life,* which Lerner had written with Kurt Weill. By this time she had left M-G-M to work as a story editor at Universal Pictures but stayed in close contact with Mayer. When she learned he was going to New York, she seized the opportunity and followed him at her own expense for the sole purpose of introducing Lerner. Mayer was impressed. He called Freed in Los Angeles and the next day Lerner was on a plane to California, a territory where, until then, he had found only closed doors. After a series of meetings Lerner was signed by Metro to work exclusively in the Freed Unit. He returned to New York to develop original stories.

When Comden and Green were writing their screenplay for *The Barkleys of Broadway,* George Abbott, noted Broadway producer and director, joined them for lunch in the commissary. He told them he had been brought out to direct any picture he wished to do, and his first choice was their show *On the Town,* which he had directed on Broadway. After lunch the two writers were called to Freed's office. "We're going to do *On the Town,*" Freed said. They were elated.

In the summer of 1944, when *On the Town* was in its formative stage, Lillie Messinger discussed the forthcoming Broadway show with Leonard Bernstein. He had not as yet written the score, but had ideas for song titles and played snatches of tunes for her. She was excited about the project and called Katz who did not respond positively. She called Mannix who was even less responsive. Mayer had been thrown by a horse and was in a hospital with a broken pelvis, but she decided to call him nonetheless. "Something happens to your voice, Lillie, when you feel that strongly," said Mayer. She related the story to him and mentioned the authors and the composer, "people you've never heard of, but you will in the future." The studio bought the motion-picture rights in a preproduction agreement for $250,000, one of the first to be made.

Shortly after the show opened on December 28, 1944, Mayer, Mannix and Katz went east to attend a performance. They left the Adelphi Theatre regretting that they had had anything to do with the show.

At the time Comden and Green set out for Hollywood with their newly signed M-G-M contract, they had been admonished by their agents and their lawyers never to bring up the subject of *On the Town*. They had lived up to this promise; now they were dumbfounded by Freed's pronouncement. What had taken place between the Abbott lunch and Freed's revelation? Most likely Gene Kelly had had breakfast with George Abbott and lunch with Arthur Freed.

The time was ripe for Kelly and Donen to codirect their first musical film. The problem of casting the three sailors was licked in thirty seconds: Kelly, Sinatra and Munshin, the trio from *Ball Game*. Sinatra had told Kelly after *Anchors Aweigh,* "They're not going to get me into another sailor's suit!" But Kelly assured Freed that he could persuade Sinatra.

Freed never liked the score of *On the Town* and liked it even less as screen material. At the time, Bernstein's style was considered avant-garde and it did not appeal to him. He also had reservations about the book. On the stage it had been done in a campy manner, which he felt would be offensive to movie audiences. Contractually he was not obligated to use all of Bernstein's score, but Bernstein had the right of first refusal if new songs were going to be interpolated. Freed was not keen on using Bernstein to compose the new songs and Bernstein was not keen on working on the film. To satisfy the legal department, a separate agreement was drawn up in which Bernstein also waived the right of interpolation of new material in exchange for Metro returning to him all their rights, title and interest to the song titles mentioned in the original 1945 purchase agreement.[1]

In November, Freed called Comden and Green in New York and spelled out the situation: The book had to be rewritten, only a minimal part of Bernstein's score would be retained, and they would have to write new songs with Edens. For two reasons they turned him down. For one, they were in the midst of writing a new Broadway show; and for another, they were close friends of Bernstein. Freed proposed that after a couple of weeks of studio conferences they could return to New York for the major part of their work and that Edens, Kelly and Donen would be available in the East. They agreed and signed a

---

[1] "The Nicest Time of the Year," "Ain't Got No Tears Left," "Lonely Me," "Sleep in Your Lady's Arms," "Carnegie Hall Pavanne," "Say When," "I'm Afraid It's Love," "The Intermission's Great," "Got to Be Bad to Be Good" and "Dream With Me."

Stanley Donen and Gene
Kelly, as full-fledged directors
on the set of *On the Town,*
the first day. M-G-M

contract which would pay them $85,000 for the rewrite and $25,000
for the new lyrics, in addition to their share of the 60 per cent of the
$250,000 the studio had paid for the motion-picture rights. (Any
subsidiary, motion-picture stock and amateur rights and royalties were
split: 60 per cent to the collaborators on a show and 40 per cent to
the investors.) Freed depended on their co-operation; without them
he couldn't make the picture.

The three leading characters in the show had been a trio of innocent
and simple-minded sailors, enjoying their twenty-four-hour furlough in
New York City. "With Gene as the leading character and the star of
the picture," says Comden, "the angle of the story had to be changed.
He couldn't be a helpless, naive type. The whole structure of the story
had to be changed to suit the people who were going to play the
characters." The two writers completed the first half of their work and
returned to the studio to write the new score and finish the screenplay.

Comden and Green came up with an ingenious device to show the
passing of time in the twenty-four hours during which the picture takes
place: a timestrip, running on the bottom of the screen, in the style of
the New York *Times* news billboard.

The few numbers retained from the show were "I Feel Like I'm
Not Out of Bed Yet," the opening and closing, sung by a crane op-
erator; "New York, New York," the opening section of the film, sung
by Kelly, Sinatra and Munshin; "Miss Turnstiles Ballet," danced by
Vera-Ellen; and the taxi song, "Come Up to My Place," sung by
Betty Garrett and Sinatra. The new songs were "On the Town" (all

six principals); "Prehistoric Man," featuring Ann Miller with Kelly, Munshin, Garrett and Sinatra; "Main Street," sung and danced by Vera-Ellen and Kelly; "You're Awful," sung by Garrett and Sinatra; "You Can Count on Me," a novelty number with Miller, Garrett, Pearce, Kelly, Sinatra and Munshin; "Pearl of the Persian Sea," a cooch dance performed by Kelly, Sinatra and Munshin dressed as ladies of a harem, and "That's All There Is, Folks," treated as a gag.

"*On the Town* was a very happy wedding of creative spirits," said Edens, "and Freed turned us loose on it. I began to realize my idea of making musicals without overelaborate production numbers. Intimate musical numbers are the only way to get true entertainment. People are not entertained by chorus lines any more. The whole layout of the picture, all the numbers were unforgettably exciting for all of us to put together."

Saul Chaplin came to work on the picture as the vocal arranger. He had worked with Kelly on *Cover Girl* (Columbia, 1944), after which he returned to New York where his close friends Bernstein, Comden and Green were working feverishly on their first Broadway show *On the Town*. He joined in by assisting them in an unofficial capacity. He later collaborated with Comden and Green on their aborted Broadway musical *Bonanza Bound* (1948). (This was the show that Comden and Green were working on when Freed first offered them the job of adapting *On the Town* for his production.)

Chaplin then went back to Columbia Pictures where he worked with Al Jolson and Larry Parks on Jolson's two-part biomusicals. Edens was deeply involved with the writing of the score and the entire production of the film. Chaplin was at liberty and so Kelly, Comden and Green asked Freed to bring Chaplin to Metro to help organize and arrange the musical material under Edens' guidance.

When the shooting script and the songs were submitted to the Breen Office for approval the following directives were given:

Regarding the songs:
1. "New York, New York": "It's a helluva town" is unacceptable.
2. "Prehistoric Man": "Lots of guys are *hot* for me" is unacceptable. "Libido—I love that libido" is unacceptable. "They sat all the day just beating their tom-toms" is unacceptable.

Regarding the script:
1. ". . . we direct your particular attention to the need for the greatest possible care in the selection and photographing of the dresses and costumes of your women. The Production Code makes it mandatory that the intimate parts of the body—specifically, the breasts of women—be fully covered at all times. Any compromise with this regulation will compel us to withhold approval of your picture.

2. Page 20: The kissing here and elsewhere throughout this production should not be unduly passionate, prolonged or open-mouth.
3. Page 75: The costumes of the girls in the cooch show should be adequate to cover them and there should be no offensive motions in the dance routines; specifically, there should be no grinds or bumps.

The production went into rehearsal on February 21, 1949, with the following cast: Gene Kelly as Gabey, Frank Sinatra as Chip, Jules Munshin as Ozzie, Betty Garrett as Hildy, Ann Miller as Claire, Vera-Ellen as Ivy Smith, Alice Pearce as Lucy Schmeeler and Florence Bates as Mme. Dilyovska; musical direction and orchestration by Lennie Hayton and Conrad Salinger; vocal arrangements by Saul Chaplin; director of photography, Harold Rosson; art direction by Jack Martin Smith.

Kelly and Donen wanted to shoot the entire film in New York. This was a practical and financial impossibility. However, a compromise was reached: the first unit would go to New York for most of the exterior scenes involving the six principals.

Kelly succeeded in making Sinatra and Munshin really dance. "I took Frank's hands off the mike, so to speak," as Kelly says. He taught them the simple steps and they learned them with great good will and gusto. But it seems that while Sinatra and Munshin at first were not too happy with the casting of their partners, they grew to love Garrett and Miller. "Those girls could move—and they gave us a lot of oomph," Sinatra says.

Kelly and Donen rehearsed on two adjacent rehearsal halls. They would bounce forth and back from one to the other, showing each other what they were doing. Comden and Green would drop in and watch; sometimes Edens came down and for a while would sub for the rehearsal pianist; Chaplin would bring in his vocal arrangements; Freed would visit. One day the whole group had to move to a stage to rehearse on a set. The piano was loaded on a truck, they all jumped on and with Chaplin crouching behind the keyboard, they drove through the studio streets singing at the top of their lungs, "We're going on the town . . ."

The picture started shooting on March 28, 1949.

As soon as the production schedule was set up, permissions for filming had to be obtained from the City of New York for the shooting at diverse sites in New York and the Navy Department for filming at the Brooklyn Navy Yard. The studio also had to solicit the co-operation of the Department of Commerce and the Police Department for the clearing of traffic, etc., and the protection of the company.

Jack Smith had a conference with Kelly and Donen about the set for the Museum of Anthropological History, and he didn't lose any time seeing Gaylord and Greutart, head of special effect props and head of the sculpture department, respectively. "I know you are busy, but this won't take too much of your time," he began. "We need a dinosaur resembling the *Tyrannosaurus rex,* 15 feet high, 40 feet long and 25 feet wide. You never heard of it? . . . Well, of course, it must be collapsible, and make it so that it can be put together again," Smith said and he told Greutart to make a life-size sculpture of a *Pithecanthropus erectis* in the image of Jules Munshin. "No problem," Greutart replied cynically. "Just send Munshin down here for a few minutes and you'll have your apeman."

When the scene was shot in the exhibition room of the museum, there stood the two specimens from 6000 B.C. In constructing the skeleton and inventing the mechanism for its collapse, Gaylord used corrugated paper in big cubes, and with a buzz saw carved each vertebra. He then inserted wire, connecting all 283 pieces, which acted as a ripcord for the collapse and the restoration of the structure. However, the precaution of being able to restore the skeleton proved unnecessary. The scene was shot, Munshin kicked the dinosaur, it collapsed, and the first take was a print.

Scenically, the replica of the roof of the Empire State Building at night was the most challenging for the art department. Smith placed the mock-up of the observation roof in the center of Esther Williams' swimming pool on Stage 30. By putting it into the 10-foot-deep pool, he made it an island which rose 45 feet into the air. Surrounding the edifice on three sides was a 250-foot-wide by 60-foot-high backing, with the skyline of New York (facing north) painted on it, showing both sides of Manhattan with the East River, Central Park, the Hudson River and the George Washington Bridge. He cut out tiny windows with lights behind them and miniature neon signs flashing in the streets. Putting the observation roof into the pool enabled the camera to shoot upward when Jules Munshin is hanging over the ledge of the roof, 102 stories in the air.

This was another instance where Jack Smith manufactured reality by artificial means.

Dear Gene & Stanley:

I just ran the cut numbers of *On the Town* and they were the greatest and most inspiring works I have seen since I have been making moving pictures.

Pressburger and Powell can't shine your shoes—red, white or blue.

Much love from your proud producer.

Arthur

In April, while the shooting of the picture went along smoothly at the studio, a second unit, under director Andrew Marton and cameraman Charles Schoenbaum, went to New York to photograph process plates needed for the picture.[2]

On May 5, when the principal photography, with the exception of the ballet, was completed, the first unit with all six principals and crew left for the New York location.

From the time Kelly, Sinatra and Munshin come off their destroyer in the Brooklyn Navy Yard for their twenty-four-hour shore leave, they covered New York from the Battery to the George Washington Bridge; from the top of the RCA Building down to the Prometheus statue in Rockefeller Center, from the Brooklyn Bridge to the Italian section of Lower Manhattan; from a tour through Central Park to Grant's Tomb; from Wall Street to the roof of the Loew's Building; from the Statue of Liberty to the top of the Empire State Building; from Washington Square in Greenwich Village to Times Square; in and out of subway entrances to the top of a Fifth Avenue double-decker bus; from the Third Avenue "el" and back to their boat at the Navy Yard.

This was the first time any major studio sent a company to shoot

[2] Marton also shot footage for *Annie Get Your Gun*, which was in production at the same time.

Jack Martin Smith and Henry Greutart's reproduction of the *Tyrannosaurus rex* dinosaur, 15 feet by 40 feet by 25 feet. In the right rear: a *Pithecanthropus erectis* in the image of Jules Munshin. M-G-M

musical sequences on public sites in New York. It is one thing to shoot dialogue scenes outside, even in the brouhaha of New York City streets. (If one does not get a clear dialogue track one postrecords it, —"loop it," as the process is called.) But synchronizing action, lip-sync and dancing, or all of these, is another story. There must be a playback machine always in earshot of the director and the performers. This is not much of a problem in stationary shots; but in moving shots, in confined spaces or in long shots, it becomes quite a problem. To hear the record for synchronization, the performer has to be relatively close by, but if the loudspeaker is in earshot it often gets within camera range. In each individual shot the trio not only had to synchronize to their prerecorded voices, but had to walk in strict tempo to the music, even in the instrumental portions of the number.

An experienced, well-respected unit manager had been in New York for a couple of weeks to lay the groundwork for the location. By the time the company arrived he was unfortunately "out of commission," and it was difficult to depend on an inexperienced assistant director. For the first days Kelly and Donen scouted locations and laid out their camera shots with their cameraman Harold Rosson.

Kelly and Donen had planned the continuity of the scenes for the opening like mosaic pieces which would have to fit together perfectly. This was imperative because each shot had to fit a certain portion of the prerecorded music track, some sections as short as fifteen to twenty feet or ten to fourteen seconds. This needed mathematical planning and for many reasons it was not possible to shoot the opening sequence in continuity. This meant jumping from one part of New York to the other, depending on traffic conditions, but more importantly on the position of the sun. A shot in a narrow street in Chinatown, for instance, could only be made during an hour or so in the forenoon; the rest of the day the street would be dim and shadowy.

The first scenes to be shot were the opening and the closing of the picture at the Brooklyn Navy Yard. In both of these a crane worker is slowly walking up the empty pier at sunrise singing, "I feel like I'm not out of bed yet." A Navy destroyer is moored at the pier.

The Navy had been most co-operative. They had brought the destroyer in and agreed to have it pull away and out to sea for the last shot of the film, hopefully on its own steam, and only *once*.

Donen was set up to shoot this in an extremely high shot with the camera up on a crane. Everything was ready at six o'clock in the morning. But the skyline of Manhattan was barely visible; it was foggy and drizzling and shooting that day at the Navy Yard had to be abandoned.

There were more days at the Yard and at the Brooklyn Bridge when the weather was unfavorable, and this meant hours of waiting for a change. After a couple of futile early calls, Sinatra asked to be called

Sinatra, Donen and Kelly rehearsing part of "New York, New York" atop the Loew's Building in New York. M-G-M and STANLEY DONEN COLLECTION

only if and when the camera was ready to roll. But clouds move in unpredictable and often rapid ways. Sometimes the cameraman can foretell a break in a cloud formation minutes ahead and by the time the sun breaks through he is ready to shoot; in the few minutes between clouds, so to speak, a scene can be photographed. But this possibility offered small chance of success with Sinatra resting in his hotel suite on Central Park South.

The setting of the last shot was an exact duplicate of the opening. But now the three sailors are returning to their ship, their twenty-four-hour leave is over; their girl friends arrive to bid them good-bye, and another three are coming off the ship, singing, "New York, New York—It's a Wonderful Town."

An important and rather lengthy section, taking place on the roof of the RCA Building, needed special preparation. In order to make the spectacular 180-degree shot, which Kelly and Donen had planned, it was necessary to build a monorail around the entire circumference on which the camera was attached. "I hung upside down, strapped to the camera, to get a shot of the six principals looking down at the city," recalls Rosson.

Other problems arose. The Police Department cleared a street in the Italian section, and as a precaution Sinatra was kept hidden when the company arrived. The very short scene was rehearsed without him. But word had gotten out somehow and the very minute he stepped out of a building to do the scene thousands of people poured out of doorways, stores, and hung out of windows, screaming and yelling. The police managed to keep them away for as long as it took to shoot the scene and then whizzed him off in a patrol car.

The roof of the Loew's Building presented another set of hazards. The square footage of the surface was so minimal that it could hardly accommodate the three principals, Donen, the cameraman and his assistant. The equipment had to be hooked up half a floor below; the roof itself was only bordered by a two-foot-high scalloped ledge. Munshin, afflicted by a fear of heights, at first could not be induced to even set foot on it. He began to stammer incoherently until he crawled on his knees onto the roof. While Kelly was rehearsing, practically bending over the roof's edge, Donen had a rope tied around Munshin's waist under his sailor suit. Out of camera range, a member of the crew held fast to the rope and after much coercing, in agony, Munshin managed to go through the action of the shot.

Going from one locale to another meant moving all the necessary equipment completely across town and back again, following the favor-

One of the sequences from "A Day in New York" ballet (deleted from the release print) with Gene Kelly and Vera-Ellen. M-G-M

able light and other conditions. In spite of a hectic schedule, anxiety about the weather, mobs impairing activities, etc., everyone, principals as well as crew, worked without complaints of any kind.

They sang on the Brooklyn Bridge; they walked through the Jewish district; they sang at the Statue of Liberty; they rode on horseback through Central Park; they sang on Wall Street; they walked under the Third Avenue el, and they rode a double-decker bus on Fifth Avenue.

The shot on the upper deck of the bus was made in the early afternoon in the height of the day's traffic. A square block, between 60th and 61st Streets from Fifth Avenue to Madison Avenue, was cleared of traffic and, the playback machine was blaring on the bus circling the block to get on to Fifth Avenue at the right speed. The three male voices, backed by an orchestral accompaniment, pierced the air, cut through the street noises and awakened the old gentlemen at the Metropolitan Club from their behind-their-newspaper snoozes. By the time the bus passed their building the second time they had tottered to the windows and stared in utter amazement and disbelief at the passing parade. After half a dozen tries the scene was in the can.

The company returned to the studio on May 23 to resume shooting and to resolve the pending problems concerning Kelly's ballet. According to his contract, a scenario for the ballet was to be sent to Bernstein in New York, along with requirements for music. He then was to send his sketches back to the studio to be orchestrated; after that he was to come out to the studio for five working days. When Bernstein had not received a scenario at the given time he wired Freed, expressing anxiety about the situation, "as time was growing short." Kelly called Bernstein and it was agreed that they would work together on the ballet during the week he was to be at the studio.

Bernstein arrived on June 3 and had meetings with Kelly and Saul Chaplin. "It wasn't so much writing a new piece, it was reorganizing old material that he had," recalls Chaplin. An important part of the ballet was based on a Bernstein song which was lifted from the stage show when it was out of town, titled "Ain't Got No Tears Left." It eventually became one of the main themes of "Age of Anxiety."

"Leonard Bernstein talked about the ballet and I thought it should be like what Agnes de Mille did in *Oklahoma!* So I substituted Frank and Julie with dancers and did the same with the girls, except for Vera-Ellen. One of the girls was Carol Haney," Kelly says. The ballet, now titled "A Day in New York," is a reflection of Kelly's experience of that day. It shows his love for Vera-Ellen, and in essence is a repeat of the over-all story of the film.

The picture was completed on July 2, 1949. The entire venture, including the New York location, took all of forty-seven days. The final cost was $2,111,250.

On the Town was previewed at the Bay Theatre in Pacific Pali-

Garden of Allah Hotel
8152 SUNSET BOULEVARD   HOLLYWOOD 46, CALIFORNIA

Dear Mr. Freed:

I am returning to new york today. I am very sorry not to have seen you before leaving. I want to thank you for giving me a chance to be in *On the Town*, and for taking such good care of me. I enjoyed working in my first picture so very much. It was so painless, really such fun —. Thank you for being good me —.

sincerely,
Alice Pearce

May 10th, 1949.

sades on September 9. It was a roaring success. Kelly, Donen, Edens and Simone were standing at the back of the theatre when Freed came running up the aisle, shouting, "If it were a show it would run a year!" It had already run 463 performances on Broadway!

There was another preview at the Loew's 72nd Street Theatre in New York on November 22, 1949. This time the response was overwhelming.

The picture went into release on December 30, 1949, and grossed in excess of $4,440,000. Mayer, Mannix, Katz et al. had hated the

At the Hollywood première of *On the Town* (left to right): Mrs. Arthur Freed, Louis B. Mayer, Mrs. Louis Mayer and Arthur Freed. M-G-M

show when they went to see it on Broadway. Now they could not help but say, "Freed did it again!"

Much has been written about *On the Town,* more than about most musicals made during the past twenty years. Therefore it seems appropriate to report in this space some comments from the creators of the film:

Stanley Donen: "Arthur just had some sort of instinct to change the musical movie from the backstage world into something else. His impulse was to do something different; he really had a basic understanding of the musical film that no other film producer had—with the exception of Roger Edens.

"In this film we tried a great many new things, aided as we were by the theme which was very cinematic. There was no stage, no theatre, simply the street. We never told ourselves, 'Now we're going to do something no one has ever done before.' We simply thought that this was the way one should deal with, one should conceive, a musical comedy. This is the way we felt—we didn't realize we were making any innovations. . . ."

Gene Kelly: "It was only in *On the Town* that we tried something entirely new in the musical film. Live people get off a real ship in the Brooklyn Navy Yard and sing and dance down New York City. We did a lot of quick cutting—we'd be on the top of Radio City and then on the bottom—we'd cut from Mulberry Street to Third Avenue— and so the dissolve went out of style. This was one of the things that changed the history of musicals more than anything."

The interoffice memo from Kenneth MacKenna to Arthur Freed is an example of the relations between the Freed Unit and Dore Schary.

Dear Arthur:

For the record, I think it is only right that you should know that, contrary to what you told me Adolph Green reported of his talk with Milton Beecher yesterday afternoon, this was not a casual word in the hall. Milton went looking for him at my request, called his office several times and eventually found him.

Milton explained to him that Dore and I felt that it was not only necessary, but only common courtesy to Dore that they do not go back to New York until Dore had read the final script and approved it. Milton went so far as to discuss with him whether the lyrics were finished and told him that either he or I would get in touch with them and give them word on Dore's approval of the script as soon as possible.

I think you will agree that this is not just "a casual word in the hall."

In addition to this, Milton tried to reach you—came to your office at 11:00 this morning and left word and failed again to reach you at noon. I am sure you will realize from this that there was no attempt or intention to leave you out of this conversation or to treat the conversation with Green in a casual manner.

Kenneth MacKenna.

Arthur Freed: "'Why adaptation?' somebody invariably asks. 'I thought the play was perfect. Why did you change it all around in the movie?' Undoubtedly the producer saw the stage show himself, and the chances are he also thought it was practically perfect—as a play. But if he has learned anything at all about his own business, he knows that a play and a motion picture are two separate and widely different things. A movie is a story told by a camera, an entertainment medium much more realistic than those from which it often borrows its basic material. It's harder work and takes a little more courage to reject an obvious, literal translation—and not to have too much reverence for the story's original form—although the producer must also be careful that he doesn't 'improve' it into a failure."

New York *Herald Tribune*   Friday, December 30, 1949

10,000 WAIT TO SEE
MUSIC HALL SHOW

7-Block 2-File Line Is Called
All-Time Record

A crowd estimated at close to 10,000 persons stretched the seasonally long lines of persons waiting to see the three-hour holiday show at Radio City Music Hall to a record length of seven blocks at 11:30 A.M. yesterday.

The day this issue was distributed on the desks of the upper echelon, Freed, Edens and Simone entered the commissary for lunch. A prominent rival producer was overheard saying, *"Here comes the royal family."*

The twenty-second annual Academy Awards were handed out at the RKO Pantages Theatre on March 23, 1950. *The Barkleys of Broadway* was nominated for "Best Cinematography," and two Oscars went to Roger Edens and Lennie Hayton for the "Best Scoring of a Musical Film" for *On the Town*. A special award was given to Fred Astaire for his unique artistry and his contributions to the technique of musical pictures. Ginger Rogers, his long-time partner who recently costarred with him in *Barkleys,* presented the miniature statuette— "For raising the standard of musical films." It was a particularly important event because the Academy had not yet found it necessary to give a yearly award for the best dancing or dance direction—a reflection on the general attitude prevalent in the film industry toward the importance of dancing and dancers.

The Academy no doubt well remembered Astaire's recent pictures: *Ziegfeld Follies, Yolanda and the Thief, Easter Parade* and *The Barkleys of Broadway.*

270

9

ANNIE GET YOUR GUN

CRISIS

PAGAN LOVE SONG

ROYAL WEDDING

After Jerome Kern's death the new producing team of Rodgers and Hammerstein approached Irving Berlin to write the score for their new Broadway musical *Annie Oakley*. At first Berlin resisted; he felt insecure and doubted that he could do the property justice. But Hammerstein had no doubts whatsoever; Berlin was the only one who could write *Annie*. The producers were persistent and finally Berlin went to Atlantic City for a week to think about it. He came back with two songs: "Doin' What Comes Natur'lly" and "They Say It's Wonderful." With these songs Berlin felt he could audition for Rodgers and Hammerstein. What followed is public knowledge. Most of Berlin's shows and most of his films have some "hangovers"—tunes previously performed or published. There were none of these in *Annie Get Your Gun*. He wrote eighteen new songs.[1]

Sidney Sheldon was assigned to adapt Herbert and Dorothy Fields's book. He began work in October 1948, and it took him five months to finish. Once again it was a question of skillfully translating a stage show to the screen. Having definite ideas about this kind of trans-

---

[1] The show opened at the Imperial Theatre (New York) on May 16, 1946, with Ethel Merman as Annie Oakley and Ray Middleton as Frank Butler. It ran for 1,147 performances.

formation, Freed guided Sheldon through the process. In this instance Freed stayed very close to the original book. He opened it up—broadening its physical layout, taking advantage of the potential of the camera.

An important piece of casting had to be done, namely, the role of Frank Butler. Freed searched for a new face, a new voice and a dynamic tall young actor. John Raitt, who had starred in the Broadway production of *Oklahoma!,* was brought to the studio and tested. Although he delivered the songs beautifully, he was not photogenic and neither his personality nor his physical presence projected strongly enough. Then an agent brought in Howard Keel, an American who was currently scoring a great success in the London production of *Oklahoma!* Not only did Keel have a marvelous baritone voice; he was 6 feet 4 inches and looked like the ideal leading man for Judy Garland's Annie. Freed advised the studio to put him under a long-term contract.

Once again the Breen Office demanded certain changes in the script and the score:

To: Arthur Freed
Subject: ANNIE GET YOUR GUN
From: Robert Vogel   Date: 3/23/49

Dear Arthur:

The Breen Office reiterates to me that the Secretary of the Interior has gotten very Indian-minded and will raise hell about our showing the Indians lousing up the train in *Annie Get Your Gun.*

It doesn't come within the Production Code scope, but they are trying to protect us in a matter which they feel sure is going to get us into trouble.

I asked them how the stage play could keep running for three years, and they replied that these outfits frequently let plays go by and raise the devil about pictures, because the former reaches a smaller audience than the latter.

I don't know exactly what one is supposed to do about this kind of thing, frankly, but I felt I owed it to you to relay the warning.

RV

In the number "Doin' What Comes Natur'lly," the stage lyrics were not acceptable. Edens found a solution without having Berlin do any rewriting. He dug up a modified "radio lyric" version which had been used by the Columbia Broadcasting System. But as a matter of interest, here are some of the examples of lyrics the Breen Office objected to:

Still they raised a family
Doin' what comes natur'lly

Knows one sex from the other
All he had to do was look

272

There he is at ninety-three
Doin' what comes natur'lly

She gets all her stockings free
Doin' what comes natur'lly.

In the song "You Can't Get a Man With a Gun," they ordered the words "nightie" and "pajamas" deleted to "something else not associated with the bedroom." In the song "My Defenses Are Down," "I've had my way with so many girls" had to be changed "to get away from the objectionable sex-suggestive interference."

The next step, and an important one, was to assign a director. Once more Freed rescued Busby Berkeley from oblivion. Alton, of course, was to stage the more elaborate musical numbers. Nonetheless, the book of *Annie* had to be handled with emphasis on the characters so strongly established in Berlin's lyrics and music. One has to pose the question: Why Berkeley? It remains a puzzle.

Garland had been anxious to do *Annie*. When Berkeley was assigned she did not voice any objections, in spite of the fact that as far back as *For Me and My Gal* and *Girl Crazy* the two had never been compatible. No doubt, the director of her choice would have been Charles Walters.

For Freed's screen version the creative department consisted of the unit: Edens, Simone, Ryan, Salinger, Deutsch and Tucker. The supporting cast included Frank Morgan, J. Carroll Naish, Edward Arnold, Keenan Wynn, Geraldine Wall, Benny Baker and Clinton Sundberg. Production was scheduled to begin the first week of April 1949.

In the last week of March and the first week in April, Judy recorded the following songs: "I've Got the Sun in the Morning," "I'm an Indian Too," "You Can't Get a Man With a Gun," "Doin' What Comes Natur'lly," "Let's Go West Again," "The Girl That I Marry" (reprise). With Keel she recorded "Anything You Can Do" and "They Say It's Wonderful." With Morgan, Wynn and Keel she recorded "There's No Business Like Show Business."

On the recording stage everything went smoothly but the whole atmosphere was barren of the excitement that Judy created whenever she sang. "In the monitor booth, for the first time Roger and I smiled each other into a more or less artificial enthusiasm," recalls Simone. " 'That was very nice, wasn't it?' " we said. " 'Nice' was a term we had never used for Judy before."

Judy was unsure about what to do with the part. It was the first time in her career that she was not doing a "Judy Garland picture." Here she had to portray a character independent of her own personality. Perhaps during the recording sessions Judy was only vaguely aware of this, just aware enough to make her insecure. But as she got into actually playing the part she became more sure of it.

Judy, holding her daughter Liza, came out to the back lot with Freed to watch Berkeley working with the extras on *Annie Get Your Gun*. ARTHUR FREED ARCHIVES

To: MacArthur-Datig-Craig-Hendrickson-Butcher-Freed-Cohn-Spencer

Subject: ILLNESS — JUDY GARLAND

From: Ed Woehler   Date: 3/17/49

Miss Judy Garland was given a call to be ready at 10 A.M.—today—Thursday, March 17, to shoot wardrobe, wig and make-up tests for *Annie Get Your Gun*.

At 9:45 P.M.—Wednesday—Miss Garland called the assistant director and said she would be unable to be ready at 10 A.M., but that she would be able to be ready at 2 P.M. She further stated that the doctor was with her at the present time and advised her to sleep as late as possible, and she was suffering from an attack of "intestinal flu."

At 3:45 A.M.—today—Miss Garland called the assistant director and said that she would be unable to come in at all today.

Tests were canceled.

The production started on April 4. Judy was not in the first scenes Berkeley shot. In setting up the shooting schedule the production office apparently aimed at keeping Judy away from Berkeley as long and as often as possible and having her work with Alton instead. Much different from the usual energy that accompanied the beginning of any Freed picture, *Annie Get Your Gun* started with an undercurrent of tension. When on the second day of shooting Keel fell off his horse and broke his ankle, the consensus was that it was a bad omen. The first diagnosis was that Keel would not be able to walk normally

Busby Berkeley (center), the Freed unit's montage and second unit director Peter Ballbusch (right center), and John Arnold (left), head of the camera department, during the "Wild, Wild West" second-unit footage.
PETER BALLBUSCH COLLECTION

for at least three months. The shooting schedule had to be revamped immediately to work around him.

At the end of the first week and a half Judy did her first scenes with Berkeley. One was a simple scene taking place in the interior of a Pullman car and the other, the exterior of the Wilson Hotel where she would sing "Doin' What Comes Natur'lly." The first day Judy arrived on the set Berkeley began to shout at the crew. Very possibly this triggered off a whole set of memories, going back into her adolescence. It wasn't long before she walked off the set, complaining that she was severely ill.

A couple of days later Judy went to look at dailies. During the running of the film she slid down lower and lower in her club chair and, while the room was still dark, got up, walked over to a water container, threw a handful of Benzedrines in her mouth and washed them down.

In all her years Judy never fell for the "ahs" and "ohs" of her entourage—nor of anybody's, for that matter. She always knew. She was the first one to see that not only was the direction dreadful, but that she was totally wrong for the part.

When she went back to the set the next day she resumed rehearsing the rather elaborate production number "I'm an Indian Too" with Alton. While Alton was shooting the number, his assistant Alex Romero, who was also performing, had to hold Judy up; she was not able to stand on her feet. She was completely intoxicated with drugs and unable to work without them. During these days she would come in at odd times, at eleven or one o'clock in the afternoon. Alton was trying to set up a take with her when Freed came to the set. The camera started rolling and after a few feet Judy's knees buckled and she fell down. At this point Freed jumped up and, totally out of control, started shouting at Judy to the embarrassment of the cast and crew. Tactfully, people moved away.

On May 3, Freed looked at only twelve days of shooting and fired Berkeley. He said, "Buzz had no conception of what the picture was all about. He was shooting the whole thing like a stage play. Everyone would come out of the wings, say their lines and back away upstage for their exits."

The next day Walters got an urgent call from Freed. "Arthur asked me to come in and look at the *Annie* footage. So in I went—and my God—it was horrible! Judy was at her worst. She couldn't decide whether she was Ethel Merman, Mary Martin, Martha Raye or herself. 'I want you to take over the picture,' Arthur said. 'Okay,' 'but first I must have a long talk with Judy.'"

Walters met Judy in his office and they talked for three hours. Judy broke down: "It's too late, Chuck, I haven't got the energy or the nerve any more." But he was able to convince her to try again.

TO: Mr. J. J. Cohn, cc Messrs: Mannix and Freed

Subject: JUDY GARLAND—REQUEST FOR SALARY DE-
DUCTION

From: Walter C. Strohm   Date: 5/4/49

Mr. Cohn:

Miss Garland called me at 2:15 P.M. today and was very upset that she was unable to continue working for the day and had caused us so much inconvenience and said that she would personally feel better if we would not pay her for today.

Miss Garland had a 9 A.M. call with the Ballbusch unit to shoot montage scenes in the "Int. Royal Box." She arrived on the stage at 8:45 A.M. and worked until 11:45 A.M., at which time she notified the assistant director that she was feeling ill and could not continue working the balance of the day.

For your information, the scenes we were shooting this morning required $1,240 worth of "bits" and "extras." When Miss Garland returns to work it will be necessary to call back eighteen people at $15.56 each and one bit at $100 and will require approximately two hours to complete this sequence in the "Int. Royal Box."

"I'm an Indian Too" was completed; it took six days to shoot. Now Walters took over from Alton, overlapping from the end of the number into Judy's dialogue scene with J. Carroll Naish. The interior Indian village set was crowded with all of Alton's dancers and extras. They had worked in the morning without accomplishing much; Judy had only arrived at 11:15. They broke for lunch.

When the company returned a stern-faced gentleman made his way through the crowd, looking for the assistant director Al Jennings, who watched his approach with apprehension. This is no tourist, he thought, this is trouble. "Where is Miss Garland?" He was led to her dressing room. After a few minutes he walked out and Walter Strohm, the studio's production manager, rushed in. "My God, he shouldn't have delivered the letter!" Before Jennings could explain, Strohm told him to get Judy and resume shooting. She was sent for but did not answer the call. She sent a message instead: "I shall never come back—now or ever."

The lights were turned off, Walters and Alton were visibly shaken, and a pall settled over the company. Strohm called Mayer, who said, "Dismiss the company. The production is closed."

The gentleman, an attorney for the studio, had delivered a letter, putting Judy legally on suspension.

Only a few technicians were still wrapping up their equipment when Judy's hairdresser emerged from her dressing room. "Where is everybody?" she asked Jennings. "Get them all back: Judy is on her way." When Judy came out everybody had gone.

To: Messrs. Strickling, Witbeck, Wheelwright, Datig, Grady, Kress, Strohm, Craig, Arthur Freed

Subject: JUDY GARLAND (Actress)

From: F. L. Hendrickson   Date: 5/11/49

For your information, Judy Garland's contract has been suspended commencing as of May 10, 1949. She is not to be called or requested to render services of any kind whatsoever unless the matter is cleared with Mr. Mannix or Mr. Schary.

A few days later Judy Garland was taken by her doctor to the Brigham Hospital in Boston for a complete rest. In spite of her suspension the studio carried the cost for both her doctor and her hospitalization. Still very much concerned about her, not only professionally but personally, Freed sent her a warm letter, accompanied by a bouquet of flowers. She answered him promptly:

Arthur, dear—

I can't thank you enough for the beautiful flowers nor for the wonderful, wonderful note on Monday—Glad you miss me—but I'll be back—

"Annie"

Freed's other activities helped him to shake the shattering experience. *On the Town* was shooting on location in New York. Richard Brooks had just returned from a research trip to Bogota, Colombia, in preparation for his first directorial assignment, *Crisis*. Alan Lerner was working on *Royal Wedding* and Robert Nathan had just turned in his script to *Pagan Love Song,* a musical based on William S. Stone's *Tahiti Landfall.*

But the immediate problem was *Annie.* For a brief moment Betty Garrett was considered to replace Judy. Her contract with the studio had expired and her agent offered her for a sum so outrageous that it was not even negotiable. Then Betty Hutton's name came up. Freed screened *The Perils of Pauline,* a picture made by Paramount (her home studio). Freed thought she was right for the part and asked Walters for his opinion. "It's a nice challenge,—trying to make Betty Hutton legit for once. You know, cutting down that chewing-up-the-scenery and tearing-down-the-curtain routine of hers."

Ever since Hutton had seen Merman on Broadway in *Annie Get Your Gun,* it had been her dream to play this part. On June 21, 1949, a contract was drawn up between M-G-M and Paramount Studios for the loan-out of Hutton for the sum of $150,000, contingent on her availability no later than September 30.

Walters had been waiting in the wings until he picked up the Los Angeles *Times* one morning in mid-August. He turned to Hedda Hopper's column and a line jumped out at him: "When shooting resumes on *Annie Get Your Gun,* George Sidney will be megging." Walters immediately called Freed who said, "Oh, you know Hedda . . ." So Walters called Hedda. "Oh my God," she said, "you didn't know! I'm sorry! It's true. I got it from L.B." "So, there you are. And that's how I didn't direct *Annie,*" says Walters.

Walters had been working under his old contract as a chore-

Frank Morgan in his wardrobe and make-up test.
ARTHUR FREED ARCHIVES

During prerecordings: Howard Keel, Betty Hutton, Roger Edens and Adolph Deutsch. M-G-M

ographer and it had expired. His manager was negotiating a new deal and Walters claims that the studio offered too little money. Sidney, idle for some time, had his eye on the picture. And he had the power of his father, L. K. Sidney, a studio executive, behind him. Mayer asked Freed to put him on the picture. Sidney and Sheldon got together to make appropriate changes in the script, stressing comedy instead of dance numbers, changes that Hutton had asked for. Some recasting had to be done, which also necessitated modifications in the screenplay. Frank Morgan had died and was replaced by Louis Calhern; Benay Venuta replaced Geraldine Wall; and Annie's siblings had grown too old.

Betty Hutton reported to the studio on September 26 and started working with Edens in preparation for the new prerecordings, which, of course, also included ensemble numbers with the new cast. Deutsch

Howard Keel sings "The
Girl That I Marry" to
Betty Hutton. M-G-M

Betty Hutton. Photo taken
by George Sidney.
ARTHUR FREED ARCHIVES

Betty Hutton in Helen
Rose's wardrobe change.
ARTHUR FREED ARCHIVES

and Salinger had to transpose the orchestrations in order to accommodate her range. Sidney and Alton resumed production on October 10. By then the picture had already cost $1,877,528. The budget was now increased to $3,707,481.

Walter Plunkett had designed all the costumes for the picture and most of Garland's costumes had been fitted and made. When Hutton was cast, Helen Rose assigned herself to design her costumes. When Sidney came on the picture he threw out most of Plunkett's original and stylized concepts for the "Indian number."

On one hand, Hutton was dying to play Annie; on the other, she felt very uneasy. She was an outsider on the lot and well aware of what it meant to be the replacement for one of Metro's biggest stars. When she met Sidney she said, "Frankly, I know a lot of people don't want me to play this." He didn't deny it. And he was equally open with her. "You have to be directed in this picture; you are playing a character. You are not playing the girl from Vincent Lopez's band. You understand that?"

"I must admit that I, too, had reservations toward her," says Simone. "I worked very closely with her and soon we became friends.

She is a very vulnerable human being and most aware of her short-comings. It was admirable to watch how she constantly labored to overcome them." In the shortest time Hutton gained the respect of everyone working with her.

Sidney, an expert marksman, proceeded to teach Hutton and Keel how to handle a gun. "With her knack of rhythm she quickly managed to handle a gun so that you believed it."

One of the sets designed by Paul Groesse, art director on the picture, was Buffalo Bill's Wild West Circus. He had a 250-foot-long backdrop painted, simulating Monument Valley, desert, mountains, rugged terrain and all. The circus, which was shot merely for a few minutes of "atmosphere effect," also included such live props as 1,000 spectators in the front row of a tremendous grandstand (several thousand others were painted in), 175 cowboys and Indians, 135 riding horses, 25 wagon horses and hundreds of trick riders, gunmen and other rugged types.

A camera truck with six photographers and Technicolor equipment would race across the field at fifty miles an hour, keeping barely ahead of a troupe of Hollywood Indians and a double for Hutton.

Some minor items included 7,000 square feet of canvas for the backdrop; 25,000 feet of lumber and 14,000 feet of canvas for the circus set; 1,940 feet of backing for the bleachers; a maypole with 25,000 feathers; 550 painted arrows, 280 bows and 190 spears. All in all, the set took two months to construct and was put up in less than a week.

According to Groesse, except for the dirt in the arena, which was tinted a deep yellow, and the bleachers, which had to be built high enough so that the camera would not photograph the oil wells, "the scene did not present any problems." This "brief effect" cost $200,000.

The finale of the picture was a colorful spectacle showing the combined shows of Buffalo Bill and Pawnee Bill, based on "There's No Business Like Show Business."

Sidney aimed at getting a feeling of excitement, glamour and magic of the greatest business in the world—show business. For this sequence he built two towers, one 500 feet high on which two cameras were perched,[2] and another 200 feet high, with one camera. From this vantage point the cameras, using a variety of lenses, rolled simultaneously, focusing on 800 horsemen riding in closely knit circle formation clockwise and counterclockwise around the central figures of Hutton and Keel. In addition, Sidney used over 1,040 extras and two mounted bands, consisting of 224 musicians. It took only one day to shoot. Jack Smith evaluates the finale: "This shot was the first of its kind in all the history of motion-picture color photography."

[2] The 500-foot tower required an airplane beacon to prevent planes from hitting the structure as they landed at the Culver City and adjacent airports.

Annie closed production on December 16, 1949, after forty-six days of shooting, four and one-half days ahead of schedule, at a total cost of $3,768,785 (over budget of $61,304).

The picture was previewed at the United Artists Theatre in Long Beach, on January 29, 1950. The reaction of the audience was gratifying, with unanimous raves for Betty Hutton.

The usual after-preview meeting was set up in Schary's office early the next morning. Simone was the last one to arrive. "I'll make this brief: Judy out, Betty in, picture finished; preview. We knew it was long. Schary tells Freed how great the picture is. 'However, Arthur,' he says, 'the shooting match has to be cut.' A slight snicker was heard from someone at the table, ha-ha-ha; naturally everybody thought it was a joke. But he was serious." After the meeting the consensus of opinion was that Schary perhaps didn't realize that the central point of the story *was* the shooting match; or that, he just didn't understand musicals.

Annie Get Your Gun went into release on May 23, 1950, and grossed in excess of $8,010,000.[3]

When Richard Brooks signed his contract with M-G-M, instigated by Freed, his aim was not only to write but to direct. Freed had promised him "If it isn't the first one, it will be the second." With his

[3] Including re-release in 1956–57.

Louis Calhern (in white costume), who replaced Frank Morgan as Buffalo Bill in this scene from *Annie Get Your Gun,* with (from left) Keenan Wynn, Edward Arnold (Pawnee Bill) and J. Carrol Naish. M-G-M

ARTHUR FREED

MGM

DEAR ARTHUR: DELIGHTED ABOUT "ANNIE" PREVIEW. TOLD GOOD NEWS TO

NICK SCHENCK. SORRY ABOUT "WEST" NUMBER BUT UNDERSTAND PERFECTLY.

WILL NOTIFY RECORDING COMPANIES AND SALVAGE WHAT WE CAN. PLEASE SEND

SOUNDTRACT OF "DEFENSES ARE DOWN" THIS NUMBER HAS NEVER BEEN EXPLOITED

AND IF I COULD GET ONE OR TWO GOOD RECORDING WOULD GO AFTER IT.

CONGRATULATIONS AND BEST REGARDS TO ALL

IRVING

1022A

first screenplay, *Any Number Can Play,* behind him, Freed now kept his promise. Brooks was to write his own script and direct it. He selected a story by George Tabori, "Barsa," which dealt with the political turmoil of a dictatorship in South America that had strong echoes of Juan Perón and his wife, Eva. In order to absorb the socio-political atmosphere he would have to dramatize, he set out for Bogota, Colombia, in March of 1949, armed with a 16-millimeter camera.

HOTEL CONTINENTAL
Bogota, Colombia

Bogota, April 19, 1949

Dear Arthur,

The saga of this odyssey I shall save for some quiet interlude between pool shots. Cables cost too much and the phone service here works on those occasions when its Latin temperament permits it.

I believe one of the most important things about this trip is the proof that our story is sound. Every major point works. However, I never would have been satisfied until I had seen it myself. We had the skeleton before—I think we have the meat to put on it.

Please forward, at an odd moment during a lull in conversation, my best and fondest regards to Ira and Lee, Oscar, Renee, etc. If I seem overly sentimental, it is because I never realized before how much I liked all of you and how much I miss you.

Richard

He then visited several Central American countries, and as soon as he returned to the studio he began mapping out his scenario.

Dr. Eugene Ferguson, a famous American brain surgeon and his wife, Helen, decide to make a vacation trip to an exotic South American country, unaware of its political turmoil. Their first outing is to a jai alai game where they witness an assassination attempt on the brother of the country's dictator. They immediately decide to return to the U.S.A. On their way they are arrested, their passports are taken away, and they are forcibly taken to the palace of the dictator, Raoul Farrago.

The dictator's wife, Isabel, informs Ferguson that her husband is suffering from a brain tumor, a fact that has been kept a closely guarded secret. The medical personnel of the country is neither equipped nor willing to operate. Therefore, they request him to perform the operation.

Ferguson is confronted with an ethical problem: Under the Hippocratic oath he has to administer to any human being, regardless of personal beliefs and attitudes. He makes his decision. He will operate, but under the condition that he can come and go as he pleases.

The revolutionaries send a message to Ferguson: His wife has been kidnaped and if he performs the operation she will die. The messenger, however, turns traitor to the cause and instead delivers the letter to Señora Farrago.

The operation is successful and the doctor is allowed to leave. It is only then that he finds out that his wife has been kidnaped. He fights his way through the crowds who have been told the dictator is dead. He bursts into the dictator's room and demands to know why the letter had not been delivered to him. The dictator threatens to murder the doctor. The mob storms the palace, kills Isabel, and as they reach Farrago's room, still weakened by the aftereffects of the operation, he drops dead.

Brooks didn't want any romantic elements in the film. In his original draft the doctor was a widower, hopefully Spencer Tracy, traveling with his ten-year-old daughter, who would become the kidnap victim.

When the picture was in the casting stages Tracy was working on a film. As an outside chance, Cary Grant's name was mentioned for the part of the doctor. By accident Brooks was introduced to Grant at Santa Anita race track. During their conversation the picture came up. Grant was curious and asked to read the script. "I have never directed a picture; would you object?" Brooks asked. "No," replied Grant. "If you can write them I guess you can direct them."

The studio made a deal with Grant for $200,000. And with his playing the doctor the consensus of opinion was that the script needed an element of romance. Another point of disagreement between Freed and Brooks was the question of shooting the picture on location. Understandably, Freed did not want to take the responsibility of sending a novice director to a country far away from the studio. On that point, too, Brooks had to give in. "There were endless battles and a barrage of outrages between myself and Cedric Gibbons. I had tremendous respect for his talent, but I guess politically and socially we were the exact opposites. He knew so much and I knew so little that all my demands or ideas were argued against.

Brooks told Gibbons he wanted to go to South America. "We have South America on the back lot," Gibbons said.

So Brooks took his bicycle and spent the next two weeks investigating every foot of existing structures on Lot 2 and Lot 3. He finally compromised.

José Ferrer was set for the part of the dictator, but his wife, an important character, was yet to be cast. The choice narrowed down to Sylvia Sidney or Signe Hasso. Both were tested; Signe Hasso looked more like Eva Perón.

Along with contract players Leon Ames and Paula Raymond, four old-timers were cast in secondary parts: Ramon Navarro, Gilbert Roland, Pedro DeCordova and Antonio Moreno.

Freed and Brooks both felt that the film did not warrant a lush, sensuous sound track. They wanted to score the picture with a solo guitar—they had been influenced by the very effective zither score in *The Third Man.*

In the past, Johnny Green had functioned at the studio sporadically. In August 1949, his old friend Dore Schary made him the general music director, and from then on he made his presence felt. "I don't think that Arthur's idea was a felicitous one, "says Green. "I thought *Crisis* would be infinitely more effective with an orchestral score." The prodigiously knowledgeable Dr. Miklos Rosza, under contract to the studio, was handed the chore of writing a score for solo guitar. Vincente Gomez was engaged as the solo guitarist and was also given a part in the picture.

Helen Rose, now the head of the wardrobe department, submitted her first sketches for the dictator's wife's costumes. Since every department had to calculate the studio overhead into every cost sheet, the price quotes on these sketches were rather steep. Even Freed, certainly not a penny pincher, balked. He saw things in their proper perspective; this was not a fashion show musical. He deviated from usual studio procedure and told Simone to go out and buy the necessary wardrobe for Signe Hasso. "This was not too difficult a task," says Simone, "although at that time haute couture was as yet nonexistent in Los Angeles. There was one gown I had difficulty finding because it had to serve a definite purpose. The dictator's wife goes from an elegant dinner party to pray in a church, a Catholic church, meaning that she had to cover her head. I wanted the head covering to be part of a super-chic evening dress and set out to find it. I found it at Adrian's. The long, black matte jersey gown had a long panel which Signe just could drape over her head when she entered the church." Understandably, Helen Rose did not like this procedure. But she accepted it with good grace and held no resentment toward anybody concerned. The entire wardrobe cost on the picture was $5,040.

To familiarize himself with brain surgery in particular and the

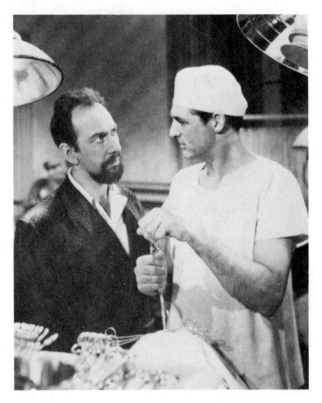

José Ferrer and Cary Grant in a scene from *Crisis* prior to the operation. M-G-M

atmosphere of an operating room in general, Brooks asked a famous Los Angeles surgeon if he could watch him perform a brain operation at the Cedars of Lebanon Hospital. He watched the procedure for two and a half hours and, as he says, "I learned a lot." He asked the doctor to recommend a technical adviser for the picture, and the doctor suggested one of his chief surgical nurses. Brooks engaged her and she spent weeks with Grant before the picture started, teaching him to handle the instruments properly, in order to look professionally correct. By the time Grant had gone through her "course" the two of them taught the other people cast for parts in the operating room.

Crisis started shooting on January 4, 1950. Brooks ventured into his first directorial job with all his antennae out, noticing, observing, learning every minuscule detail. The crew, always snobbish and clannish toward a first-timer, did not react well to his personality.

"Preston Ames, for instance," says Brooks, "the art director on the picture, I never argued with him. But with others I *would* argue and no one would listen. Let me give you an example: I would say to Ray June, the cameraman, 'I don't want this kind of lens.' June would say, 'What do you know about lenses? Can you tell me from here to here what distance we are now or what lens I'm using?' I would say, 'No, I can't.' And he'd say, 'Well, before you talk to me you find out.' But that forced me to learn about lenses!"

Brooks recalls an interesting incident. For a scene with Grant he used a crane with an arm formed like a question mark, with the camera hanging suspended from its nose and the whole apparatus running on large wheels on tracks. It weighed about a ton and a half. Brooks, always anxious to see the action exactly at camera angle, walked on the boards ahead of the camera until the arm of the crane veered slightly to the left and the crane stopped on the chalk mark on the boards. Irritated, Ray June said to Brooks, "Sit in a chair and just say action." But Brooks battled it out. When the camera rolled for a take, Brooks walked alongside as he had done throughout rehearsals and stopped well ahead of the chalk mark. But for some reason the crane did not stop; it kept on rolling and over his right foot. Brooks didn't want to stop the scene and said nothing. With the one and a half ton crane resting on his foot he finally said, "Cut." "No good for me," said the camera operator, "there was a bump, somebody hit the camera." But the assistant director, Howard Koch, saw what had happened. "For Christ sakes," he called out, "the crane went right over his foot!" Grant became as white as a sheet. A nurse from the studio emergency hospital was called to the set and urged that Brooks be taken to a hospital

Cary Grant clowns with director Richard Brooks on the *Crisis* set upon his return from the hospital. M-G-M

immediately. But Brooks didn't want to go. "If they get me off this set they'll never let me back on." Grant was too shaken to continue and implored Brooks to go to the hospital. "Cary, I'm not leaving, because once they get me out of here there's going to be another guy here, this afternoon, thirteen minutes from now." "Nonsense," said Grant, "you're my director on this picture—and that's that!"

Brooks was taken to a hospital in Culver City. The crane had squeezed all the blood out of his foot, but no bones had been broken.

Production closed on February 23, 1950. It took forty-four days to shoot, six and one-half days behind schedule, at a cost of $1,616,455 (over budget $93,777).

It was previewed on April 11, 1950, and released on July 7, 1950. In its first run it lost $713,000.

Crisis must be remembered as the beginning of the brilliant directorial career of Richard Brooks. It was regarded as a good picture by the few who saw it; it could have been an important one. Brooks was badly stymied by the opposition of the conservatives at Metro and, paradoxically, the liberals as well. Controversial subjects of any kind, let alone stories making any social comment, were severely frowned upon, in some instances made and eventually disfigured beyond recognition. Even Freed, with all of his power and influence, could not change the viewpoint of the opposition.

The advertising campaign on *Crisis* was launched under the heading "CAREFREE CARY ON A VACATION!"

Freed summoned Robert Nathan, his old friend and the author of "all those pictures Arthur never made,"[4] to his office. He had bought a book, actually a travelogue, *Tahiti Landfall,* by William S. Stone who lived in Tahiti but at the moment was working at Metro. "Make up a story," Freed told Nathan, "because there is none." Nathan agreed. "Fine . . . but are you sure you'll make it in Tahiti?" "Yes, absolutely." Nathan says, "I went next door to Bill's house and he told me all he could about Tahiti, of which I knew absolutely nothing."

What Freed had in mind was to make a picture titled *Pagan Love Song,* using his song (music by Nacio Herb Brown) and writing the score for the picture.

Nathan wrote a very nice script, as he says, a story of Tahiti, in which the only singing would be done by Lotte Lehmann, the middle-aged German lieder singer, with Cyd Charisse and Van Johnson in the starring parts. He completed his screenplay and again Freed termed it "the greatest script you've ever written," like all his other stories that were never produced. Nathan's seven-year contract had run out, and he left the studio.

Without as much as a fragment of a possible story in his hand,

[4] See Filmography for complete list of Freed's unproduced films.

Freed assigned Stanley Donen to direct the picture, his first solo. He asked Jerry Davis, a young writer, to write a script for Esther Williams and Howard Keel as the leads.

The studio's location and travel departments were set in motion to arrange the expedition to Tahiti, with a tentative starting date of February 1950. The M-G-M offices in Sydney, Australia, and Auckland, New Zealand, were alerted to co-ordinate the travel plans. The first thing that came to light was that Tahiti had no airport. And alternatives proved impractical, until an air charter company offered its services.

Technicolor advised the studio that the film would have to be kept in specially built containers at 50 degrees Fahrenheit and the Monopack at zero Fahrenheit temperature and would have to be loaded in the dark.

While cablegrams were sent and long-distance calls were made from one continent to another, Edens, Ryan and Simone went about their work as usual. Ryan, stoic as always, carried out instructions and tried to cheer up the personnel of the Metro travel office. Edens was busy in coaching Betty Hutton in *Annie* for the prerecordings. In addition, he was working very closely with Alan Lerner and Burton Lane who were in the process of writing the score for *Royal Wedding* and also stayed close to Lerner on the preparation of the script. Simone was engaged in assisting Edens on the sound stage for *Annie,* predubbing the completed playbacks and doing the final dubbing for the release print of *On the Town.*

Davis had devised a script in which Keel is a schoolteacher from the States who comes to Tahiti to take over a run-down plantation willed him by an uncle. Esther Williams is English born but raised on Tahiti, where she lives with her wealthy family but also indulges in the idyllic native life. They meet, fall in love, quarrel and are finally reconciled. On the basis of this story Harry Warren and Freed wrote the score.

Shortly after Donen had been officially assigned to direct, he was called to Schary's office, where he found Freed and Williams. "I will not do this picture if Stanley is going to direct it," she said. "It's as simple as that." Schary and Freed proceeded to praise Donen's talent but in vain. "I couldn't face him every day, because I know he thinks I have no talent whatsoever." On *Take Me Out to the Ball Game,* she felt Donen and Kelly had treated her with disdain, and understandably she was not willing to go through this again. Donen was taken off the picture.

A few days later Freed decided to give Robert Alton a second chance at directing. A few years back Freed had promoted him to his first directorial assignment, *Merton of the Movies,* after which Alton laid aside his aspirations to become a director. With *Pagan Love Song* he would have another go at it, but under the unfavorable aspect of making a picture far away from home.

When Warren and Freed had completed their score, among their songs were "House of Singing Bamboo," "Singing in the Sun," "Etiquette" (for children), "Tahiti" and, of course, "Pagan Love Song," Freed's smash hit and by now a standard. These titles lead one to think that perhaps Freed was striving to make *Pagan Love Song* a film leaning on the Broadway show *South Pacific,* which everybody was talking about since it had opened that year.

Travel to Tahiti proved to be so complicated that it was decided to use Kauai, one of the Hawaiian Islands. Before the company left for the location, the prerecordings were made during the second and third weeks of March 1950, including "Why Is Love So Crazy," "Here in Tahiti We Make Love," "Sea of the Moon" and "Music on the Water." Deutsch and Salinger had provided luscious orchestrations and Tucker the vocal arrangements.

Between March 3 and March 28, the company and crew, totaling about sixty-five, left for Honolulu. Alton, Ben Feiner, Al Jennings, the assistant director, and Simone remained in Honolulu while the rest flew by interisland plane to Kauai.

The screenplay for *Pagan Love Song* was handed in on the evening before Alton left for location. Alton was petrified of flying and the flight on the stratocruiser was a long one. When he arrived in Honolulu a tropical storm was blowing, which set him even more on edge. But there was business to take care of before going on to Kauai. Auditions were held for non-Polynesian expert swimmers for Williams' water ballet. Everybody who could hold himself above water came to audition: Eventually a dozen or so first-class swimmers were recruited. A prerecording had to be made of Tahitian music by Tahitian natives. None could be found and Simone gathered together a trio of Polynesian night-club entertainers familiar with the steel drums and rhythms of Tahitian folk music. At that time the only recording facility available was a small room with some sound equipment in a shack behind a music store. The recordings were made with nervous energy, if nothing else, but they turned out to be usable. Feiner, the associate producer on the picture, who had flown across with Alton, Simone and Rosher, the cameraman, tried his best to help as much as he could. After a week in Honolulu the group boarded an interisland plane for Kauai. Simone gives a vivid description of the flight: "This was the most disastrous flight I have ever been on. To begin with, the plane was crammed full of natives with bird cages, dogs, packages, and smothered under leis of flowers. Alton was sitting next to me, frozen with fear. At a certain juncture between the two islands the plane shook, dropped, rose and dropped again, like a roller coaster. The passengers were screaming hysterically, I was petrified, and I thought Alton was not going to arrive in one piece, if we ever got there. Suddenly the plane made its descent and we flew right up to a steep hillside; at the last moment the plane veered around and quite suddenly we were on the ground. I staggered out of the plane and recognized our unit manager, Eddie Woehler. Forgoing any polite greeting, I asked, 'Is there a boat from here to Honolulu?' Yes, there was, a mailboat every four weeks. It was a reassuring thought."

In 1950, Kauai was the closest thing to paradise one can imagine. But finding accommodations for some eighty-five people presented difficulties. In the island's only village, Lihue, was one dilapidated hotel, the Kauai Inn. The studio rented a modern house for Williams and her infant son, Benjy, and furnished it from top to bottom. The crew had to be put up in two separate little used country inns, about ten miles from Lihue.

Alton at once began to explore the island and its beaches in search of the most colorful background for his scenes. The "House of Singing Bamboo" was built in a coconut grove near a lagoon, blooming with lush tropical growth. A small secluded bay on the extreme end of the island was designated for the shooting of Williams' water ballet and, sooner or later, the other necessary sites were found.

For the first week of shooting, from April 3 on, it either rained or was so cloudy that next to no footage could be shot.

Bunny Dull, a studio representative specializing in locations, had been on Kauai a month to familiarize himself with weather conditions, housing facilities, native casting, etc. When Simone, exasperated by the constant rain, asked some of the natives whether this kind of weather was unusual, they smiled broadly and said, "But, lady, this is the rainy season!"

Alton did not have the temperament of a man who could take upheavals in his stride. The authority he had always exercised as a choreographer vanished altogether when he found himself with the responsibility of directing. His indecisiveness and his anxiety were transmitted to the crew and even more so to his stars. The fact that he could not view the footage he had shot was disastrous, especially in view of his lack of experience. He was dominated by fear of Freed, of the studio and of jeopardizing his chances in his new capacity. As a case in point, here are excerpts from his almost daily letters to Freed: "You cannot possibly realize the difficulties we have had. We have rain every day and grab shots whenever we can. The generator has broken down twice—many times I okayed takes even though we had no light and rain for five or six hours. Numbers are not sufficiently rehearsed, and of course no time has been allowed for me to stage anything." And then comes the pathetic postscript: "These are not alibis as I

Esther Williams' water ballet from *Pagan Love Song*. M-G-M

292

Esther talks to her husband, Ben Gage, on the mainland, with the help of a Kauaiian schoolteacher. M-G-M

know everything can be fixed at the studio or here before we leave. I would like to try the bicycle number again, but if you prefer not to, please let me know."

The number Alton refers to is Keel riding down a country lane on a bicycle singing, "Singing in the Sun." Keel had broken his arm. But even without that complication an extra large bicycle had to be made to accommodate his long legs. Even so, Keel looked awkward, and his broken arm had to be camouflaged by a towel, but Alton shot it anyway.

Alton's main concern was not to fall behind schedule. He shot a love scene with Williams and Keel on a site he had selected for its panoramic view across the island and the ocean. There was a bend in the road, high up on a hillside, and one of the few spots on the island that was never without a considerable breeze. When he set up his camera for a close two shot, Simone mentioned as tactfully as she could, hoping to ease the tension, "Bob, we will have to nail down Esther's hair." Anxious to make a take, any take, he proceeded to shoot the scene. In a break Simone took Williams aside. "Esther, where are your contact lenses?" "Why?" Williams asked good-humoredly. "You keep looking past Howard's face—you don't seem to see him." "Frankly," she said, "I don't." Alton was too preoccupied to notice any of this.

For Williams' water ballet a dozen or so boys and girls had been imported from Tahiti as extras. They were neither very attractive nor were they proficient swimmers. They spoke an almost incomprehensible mixture of Polynesian and French. But they had a great time. Their romantic impulses were aroused at all times, even when standing waist-high in the water. Alton was a puritan, appalled by this behavior and anxious to keep this immorality from the then seventeen-year-old Rita Moreno, in her first movie role. This group was put up in the main house of the hotel. One night the traffic from room to room was stopped by Al Jennings. "From here on, all doors will be open all night long!" It didn't help much.

In this atmosphere a humorous situation surfaced—humorous, at least, in retrospect. It began when Williams' sarong became visibly snugger. "I think I'm pregnant," Williams confessed to Simone with a smile, "but don't tell anybody." After Simone recovered from the shock the two decided a doctor had to be found on Kauai to make the necessary tests. The doctor was located, but now things became complicated. "Do me a favor, Lela, you sign your name." Williams overlooked the fact that everybody including the old island doctor recognized her at sight. Moreover, Simone was married, and even her loyalty to her friend and to the studio had to have certain limitations. The situation developed into a farce. In order to communicate with her husband, Ben Gage, on the mainland, the Japanese schoolteacher in the village had been charmed into letting Williams use his elaborate ham radio system to talk freely with Los Angeles. She spoke to her husband via the relay of a Los Angeles ham operator. Simone listened to the rest of the dialogue while collapsing into a chair. "I'm fine— but Lela is in trouble—it seems she's pregnant." In vain Simone tried to stop Williams. "Ben will understand what I mean—I simply cannot announce over the air waves that I'm pregnant." "But what about *my* husband," said Simone, "what about *his* finding out?" Then it turned out that the relay man in Los Angeles happened to be a sound mixer at M-G-M. The next morning the news was all over the studio. When Simone called Freed via transoceanic telephone, Freed opened the conversation with "When is the big event?" and roared with laughter. He knew her well enough to be sure that she would never make a situation like this public. This was about the only amusing highlight on the location.

The company returned to the studio on May 26. A few interiors remained to be shot: the bicycle number in process and the native fête.

Pagan Love Song was completed on July 8, 1950 at a final cost of $1,906,265 (over budget $399,749).

On the long list of Arthur Freed productions *Pagan Love Song* has a singular distinction: It is the only mediocre picture he ever made. An over-all evaluation of his output indicates the scale tipping up and down, from outstanding to excellent, from fair to just plain good. *Pagan Love Song* was Freed's nadir.

It is impossible to find any artistic merit in the film and its enter-tainment values are modest, at best. How did it slip through Freed's fingers? He had taken chances with directors before, Williams had her faithful audiences, Keel sang beautifully and looked handsome. Freed's and Warren's score, if not the greatest, would be carried by the endur-ing popular appeal of the title song. The exotic beauty of a tropical island would do the rest. The screenplay was written while Freed was already heavily committed to preparing films of incomparably grander and weightier dimensions.

The picture went into release on December 29, 1950, and grossed in excess of $3,205,000.

After his initial meetings with Freed in November of 1948, Alan Lerner had returned to New York to think about an original story for a musical. Shortly thereafter Freed arrived to see *Love Life* and *Brigadoon*. He expressed great interest in *Brigadoon* and asked Lerner to find out how he could acquire it. Back at the studio Freed received a letter from him containing the following excerpts:

> I had a meeting a few days ago with my comrades in charge of the destiny of *Brigadoon* and I passed on to them the gist of our chats about it. I advised them in view of the not too savory con-ditions in Hollywood now not to be too unrealistic about selling our little golden goose. As you know, we've never been in a great hurry about it because the show shows promise of still another two seasons of solid business. I did acquaint them, though, with the very plain fact that there are precious few men in Hollywood who have the setup, the taste and the stars to film it, and that after being out there for a few weeks I have more confidence in your unit at M-G-M than any other. The result of the conclave was that if it were bought by you the price would be two hundred and fifty thousand. You can toss it around in your spare time and let me know what you think some time in the future while I'm out there. As a personal favor, however, please don't bruit this figure around because in the talks there have been with other studios the asking price was either higher or a percentage arrangement was discussed. . . .

> As a matter of fact, I'm looking forward to the whole venture

with much more eagerness and anticipation than, frankly, I thought I would. Maybe that is because I feel at ease in the surroundings for which I'm very grateful to you.

Alan Jay Lerner was born in 1917, the son of department store magnate Joseph J. Lerner (Lerner Shops). He received an exemplary education; as an undergraduate at Harvard he wrote the lyrics and music for the Hasty Pudding show *Fair Enough.* At that time Lorenz Hart gave him encouragement and some advice, which Lerner took very seriously. Lorenz said, "If you're going to write for the theatre you must be brutal with yourself and brutal with your time."

During his summer vacations Lerner studied music at Juilliard. In the course of a boxing match at Harvard he received an injury which cost him the sight of one eye.

After graduating in 1940, he took a job writing radio material for a New York advertising agency. It was during that time that he met composer Frederick Loewe. Together they wrote a musical, *Life of the Party,* which had a small success in Detroit, and in 1943 they wrote their first Broadway show, *What's Up,* which turned out to be a flop. Their first success came in 1945, with *The Day Before Spring.* While it had only a moderate eight-month run on Broadway, Metro bought the screen rights for $250,000. *Brigadoon,* in 1947, was their first big hit. Lerner and Loewe's association was as yet not consolidated and the following year Lerner collaborated with Kurt Weill on *Love Life.*

Alan Lerner's recollection of his beginnings with Freed and Metro differ from Lillie Messinger's account. Lerner says, "Fritz went on a sabbatical and I came to California with the intention to write a film. It was more of a vacation. Both Warner Brothers and Paramount offered me pictures but I didn't want to do them. And finally I was with Arthur Freed who said, 'Why don't you come here for ten weeks without anything to do and if you find something we both like we'll do it. If you don't—no harm done, go home.' So I came for ten weeks and ended up staying six months."

Lerner came up with an original idea, as he called it, inspired by Fred and Adele Astaire's personal life, specifically Adele's marriage to Lord Cavendish. The advent of the marriage of Princess Elizabeth of England to the Duke of Edinburgh added color to the story.

Lerner discussed, or tried to discuss, the first draft of his screenplay *Royal Wedding* with Freed. "I'd walk in and he'd inevitably say, 'Hi, kid, I just spoke to Oscar,' or 'I just spoke to Cole,' which naturally makes you feel great! 'Arthur, did you read my script?' 'Oh yeah, just a couple of points. . . . Well, should we have lunch?' And there would be a sentence on Monday, a grunt on Tuesday and another sentence on Wednesday. And by putting it all together you found out that he was just about always right."

But even with only such fragmentary comments Lerner finished a screenplay they both liked. He was ready to start on the score with Burton Lane, who had been brought back to the studio for this assignment.

Here is a short synopsis of Lerner's story: A brother-and-sister team take their hit show to London and arrive at the time of the royal wedding. The brother meets and falls in love with an English dancer; the sister, with a member of British nobility. The story ends with a double wedding of the two couples.

Astaire was, of course, to star in the film, and June Allyson was cast as his sister. For the part of the English dancer Freed thought Moira Shearer would be ideal. She had moved into the limelight by way of the film *The Red Shoes*. There was an urgent exchange of messages between M-G-M and Sadler's Wells about her availability, which came to an abrupt halt when Astaire remarked, "I know she's wonderful, but what the hell could I do with her?"

Concurrently, a road company of *The Philadelphia Story* was playing Los Angeles with Sarah Churchill in the lead. Freed saw her performance, liked her (besides, she was the daughter of Britain's Prime Minister Sir Winston Churchill), and she was screen tested and signed. Peter Lawford fitted right into the part of the aristocrat. An interesting piece of casting was Keenan Wynn playing a pair of twin brothers, the American and English agents of Astaire and Allyson. Charles Walters was assigned to direct, Nick Castle to handle the choreography, Saul Chaplin, the vocal arrangements, and Johnny Green, as musical director.

It was imperative for M-G-M to acquire color footage of the royal wedding. The only Technicolor footage available was a documentary produced by the Rank Organization; permission had to be granted by the British Board of Censors and Buckingham Palace. The screenplay had no problems passing the Board, but the Board made a long list of "Americanisms," foreign to British audiences. It was decided not to change Lerner's dialogue but to re-record certain sentences for the Commonwealth's release prints. To secure the approval of the royal family the studio called on Vice-Admiral the Earl Mountbatten of Burma to intercede. Through his influence a letter of approval finally arrived from Gaumont-British Distributors Limited.[5]

Lerner and Lane had finished their score: "Every Night at Seven" (Astaire and Allyson); "The Sunday Jumps" (Astaire); "Open Your Eyes" (Astaire and Allyson); "Happiest Day of My Life" (Sarah Churchill); "I Left My Hat in Haiti" (Astaire); "I Got Me a Baby" (Astaire) and "What a Lovely Day for a Wedding" (ensemble).

Astaire had mentioned a vaudeville number to Lerner; one day when Lerner and Lane were driving to the studio the title suddenly hit Lerner: "How Could You Believe Me When I Said I Love You When You

[5] Gaumont-British charged M-G-M $190 per foot for the rights of usage of their film.

Judy Garland and Fred Astaire in wardrobe and make-up test for "How Could You Believe Me When I Said I Loved You When You Know I've Been a Liar All My Life!" ARTHUR FREED ARCHIVES

Know I've Been a Liar All My Life?" "I thought it was very, very funny," says Lane. "By the time we got to the studio I had the tune. We played it for Astaire." He liked it: "It is authoritatively acknowledged as the longest song title in history," Astaire states in his autobiography.

On May 1, 1950, Astaire began rehearsing "The Sunday Jumps." Lane laid out a "jazz figure" for him, with hesitations and developments. As Astaire got further into the choreography he dispensed with Lerner's lyrics and worked out his routine to a straight instrumental.

Allyson started rehearsing "Every Night at Seven" with Astaire. After eight days she announced that she could not do the movie after all, she was pregnant. "That settled that," says Astaire. "I said bye bye to June, much to my chagrin. Now, we had a problem. Who do we get?"

After six weeks at Brigham Hospital Judy Garland had returned in a much better state of health. But she did not return to the Freed Unit. Instead she went into a Pasternak picture, *Summer Stock,* directed by Charles Walters. Freed brought her back—to replace June Allyson. Upon hearing the news Walters said to Freed, "I'm terribly sorry, but I cannot go through it again. I've just spent a year and a half of my life with her, and I'm ready for a mental institution. Take me off!" Freed assigned Stanley Donen.

Some musical shifting needed to be done. One of the last songs Lerner and Lane had written, "You're All the World to Me," had not yet been placed in the story. Edens gave it to Garland and also asked Lane and Lerner to write a special song for her. "I had already gone

Old friends Jane Powell and
Johnny Green go over songs
for *Royal Wedding.* M-G-M

back to New York," says Lerner, "and Burton played his melody for
me over the long-distance phone. I took it down and worked out the
lyrics in three days and phoned them back to him." The song was
"Too Late Now."

For the first week everything went well. The second was a short
week, and for a few days Judy worked with Chaplin on her vocals.
At the end of the third week, on June 9, the Freed Unit gave a birthday
party for her on the rehearsal stage. But beginning the fourth, she
told Donen that she would not be able to rehearse both mornings
and afternoons and still be in condition to start the picture. Donen told
her that these were the last days of rehearsals before the shooting date
and implored her to take this into consideration. "Take your choice,"
she said. Freed intervened and made the change to afternoons. On
Saturday, June 17, at 11:25 A.M., Judy called to say that she would not
be in to rehearse. Donen again pointed out to her that this was the
last day before prerecording. No matter, she was not coming in.

Freed was apprised of the situation, and with much pain in his
heart he had to give Judy up. In good conscience he could no longer
afford to indulge an emotional attachment. No other producer in the
business would have stood behind a star of even Judy's caliber with
Freed's generosity, patience and loyalty.

And with that, Judy Garland's association with Metro-Goldwyn-
Mayer came to an end.

Wasting no time, the following Monday Freed asked Astaire what
he thought of Jane Powell. "Grab her—please!"

Needless to say, Powell was elated and began rehearsing two days
later. Bobby Tucker replaced Chaplin as vocal coach-arranger.

Freed did not think that the song "You're All the World to Me,"
the song intended for Judy, was suitable for Jane Powell. For the past
three pictures Astaire had been after Freed to let him do a number
in which he would be dancing on the walls and the ceiling. Freed found
the right spot for the number and turned the song over to Astaire.

In view of Jane Powell starting the picture so late, only some of
the prerecordings were made before the picture went into shooting.
The remaining numbers would be recorded during filming.

Johnny Green had worked with Jane Powell many times before and
he had known Astaire all his life. There were no problems on the sound
stage and everything came off to everybody's satisfaction.

Green comes forth with an elaborate analysis of his status: "I was
now general music director and executive in charge of music. The
reason I'm stressing that point is that when I came back in '49 with
those two jobs, and the enormous administrative work that I had, the
opportunity for me to be part of anything as inbred and as constantly
together, not only together physically, but together in terms of mental
preoccupation as that Freed Unit was impossible. You know, it was
like something from the Ozarks—like the father who sleeps with the
daughter and the sister who sleeps with the brother. I mean it was
not to be believed—I didn't have time for that kind of *Schweinerei*.
You see, I had powers that nobody had ever had before or after.
The only two who came close to the autonomy and the authority that
I had were Newman at Twentieth, and Heindorf at Warner Brothers.
Where assignments were concerned there were contretemps that developed into impasses and when these got to Schary's desk, four out
of five times I won. But when I suggested a musical director and
Freed didn't want him and said, "No," then Freed won." Obviously,
the Freed Unit was the object of enormous jealousy and envy.

In most producers' offices much time was spent writing interoffice memoranda. Freed always considered this a waste of time and so did his unit. The writing matter in the Freed Unit consisted of needed documentation and paper work expediting its efficiency. Most of the time Freed was shooting two pictures simultaneously, was in postproduction stages on another and preparing two, three or four forthcoming projects. With such relentless schedules the unit carried out its multiple daily tasks with what must have been inexhaustible energies.

The Freed Unit had no time for the procedures Green had set up in his department. Green was a prolific memo writer and holder of meetings. Edens and Simone were not excluded from his interoffice communications. For weeks they were urged to attend the Wednesday morning meetings. One Wednesday they dashed down to Green's bungalow. They were late, the meeting had started, and they squeezed into the back of the overcrowded room. Green stopped in the middle of a sentence and said, "We now have the pleasure of the presence of the Freed Unit!" "Roger and I had to stand up against the back wall," recalls Simone. "The entire room was set up with school desks. And there sat, with pad and pencil, an imposing group of music men: Dr. Miklos Rosza, Bronislau Kaper, David Raksin, Georgie Stoll, Adolph Deutsch, David Rose, André Previn, Al Sendry, Bob Franklyn, Sandy Courage, Bobby Tucker, Saul Chaplin, George Schneider, and diverse office personnel and Lennie Hayton. He sat at his little desk, in the last row, with a handkerchief over his face, fast asleep. "Now this concerns all of you," Green said pointedly. "I have devised a new way of identifying our playback discs" . . . or words to this effect. This, of course, didn't concern us in the least. Roger and I looked at each other and sneaked out."

In the course of a conversation with Minnelli, Simone mentioned Green's schoolroom. "I don't believe it!" he exclaimed. On a Wednesday morning she took him to see for himself. As they approached Green's bungalow a truck was unloading children's school desks. "How utterly embarrassing," muttered Minnelli, "and they're so small, as if for midgets!"

Royal Wedding started shooting on July 6.

Astaire and Powell give a performance of their number "Open Your Eyes" on an ocean liner, crossing to Europe. Halfway across, the ship runs into a storm. Furniture begins to slide across the floor, people can barely hold on. And as the ship rocks more and more violently Astaire incorporates the listing into the routine. This effect was worked out by Donen and Jack Smith, the art director on the picture. "We went to the back lot and got on our boat-rocking device," recalls Smith. "We could rock a whole ship on that. So I built a dance floor and the salon of the ship back on that set." When the number was photographed, the special effects man operated the hydraulic lifts under the dance floor on cue with Astaire's routine.

302

When Astaire had set his routine for the number "You're All the World to Me," dancing on the walls and ceiling, Donen and Smith again worked out the mechanics. "It was executed simply by putting the room inside a barrel," explains Donen, "as in a fun fair. Everything in the room had to be tied down hard and the room turned inside this barrel and the camera turned with it. So that you weren't aware that the room is upside down and that Fred is actually dancing on the walls and the ceiling."

Smith designed a cube-shaped room and had Bethlehem Steel construct what he calls "a squirrel cage," which revolved 360 degrees. A giant commutator was put up in the rear of the stage to transform the power to the lamps and lights in the revolving set. As with everything else, the lights and lamps had to be fastened to the floor, and the light source had to go with it. The camera operator was strapped onto an ironing board, the camera tied onto him and this whole package turned around with the set. As the set turns, Astaire moves from the floor to the wall, to the ceiling, to the other wall and back again, without ever being anything but upright. Donen had laid out the number so methodically that it took him only half a day to shoot it. It was the first time that a technical device such as this was ever used. Only recently was a similar device used in *2001: A Space Odyssey.*

Royal Wedding finished on October 5, 1950, after thirty-three days of shooting, six and one-half days ahead of schedule, at a cost of $1,590,920 including carrying charges on Garland of $20,604 and Allyson of $3,334.

Astaire makes some comments on the film: "While Janie was not primarily a dancer, I knew she could do what was required. She surprised everybody. As to Stanley, I always felt he would be ideal and I was happy to be a part of his first solo effort."

And Lerner expresses his opinion: "I'm not proud of the script that I did on *Royal Wedding*. There was so much trouble on the picture, and then it finally ends up with poor Jane Powell."

Royal Wedding[6] was released on March 23, 1951, and grossed in excess of $3,925,000.

The twenty-third annual Academy Awards were held on March 29, 1951, at the RKO Pantages Theatre. During the 1950 qualifying year Freed had in release *Annie Get Your Gun, Crisis* and *Pagan Love Song. Annie* was nominated in four categories: "Best Scoring of a Musical Picture"—Roger Edens and Adolph Deutsch; "Best Color Photography" —Charles Rosher; "Best Art and Set Decoration"—Paul Groesse and Richard Pefferle (with their department heads Cedric Gibbons and Edwin B. Willis); and "Best Editing"—James E. Newcomb. The Oscars went to Edens and Deutsch.

[6] For Great Britain and the Commonwealth it was released as *Wedding Bells.*

Astaire performs "You're All the World to Me." The sketch, in numerical order, shows how it was photographed. M-G-M

10

AN AMERICAN IN PARIS

SHOW BOAT

Every Saturday night Freed challenged Ira Gershwin to a game of pool. And so it was on November 21, 1949. He loved these evenings because he never failed to beat Gershwin. But even when away from it all, his mind ran on a single track. Offering Gershwin a cigar, he asked, "How about selling me "An American in Paris"—the title?" Gershwin, saying nothing, proceeded to light his cigar. "And I want to take George's 'An American in Paris' and use it for a ballet, uncut, to finish the picture," Freed continued.

"Of course, you'll use *all* Gershwin music," Gershwin said, while settling comfortably into a chair.

Once Kelly had mentioned to Freed the idea for a story about an ex-GI, an aspiring painter who decides to remain in Paris after the war. Now Kelly was elated, and he and Freed agreed that there was only one man to direct the picture: Minnelli.

Freed was equally convinced that Lerner was the man to invent the story. Although Lerner had not yet finished his score for *Royal Wedding,* Freed had no difficulty persuading him.

In order to isolate himself, Lerner spent some time in Palm Springs. He handed Freed the first forty pages at the beginning of December 1949. "Now it was March," says Lerner, "I was getting married and I still hadn't a clue about how the story would end. The night before the wedding I was still on page 40." Frederick Loewe was staying at Lerner's house and challenged him to finish the script. Lerner sat down at eight o'clock that night, and by eight o'clock the next morning he sent it in. It began:

> This is Paris . . . and I'm an American who lives here . . . My name is Jerry Mulligan . . . And I'm an ex-GI . . . In 1945, when the Army told me to find my own job, I stayed on . . . and I'll tell you why . . . I'm a painter. All my life that's all I've wanted to do. . . . And for a painter, the mecca of the world for study, for inspiration and for living is here on this star Paris. . . .

"To make a character live," says Minnelli, "you try to know how he reacts in everyday life. You want to know what he lacks, what his dreams are, his desires and his failures." Lerner drew his characters accordingly. In his story Jerry Mulligan pursues both career and romance. On one hand, he is entangled with a rich American woman, Milo Roberts, who supports him, and on the other, he is in love with a pretty French orphan, Lise Bouvier, who on her part is supported by a seasoned entertainer, Henri Baurel. These characters, as Lerner invented them, became real people by their weaknesses as much as by their virtues.

When Lerner returned from his honeymoon he reviewed the script with Freed. Before they started, Freed suggested an amusing bit for the picture: "I just had a great idea. Kelly walks down the street in the morning with his canvases under his arm, and there he passes a man sitting on a stool, a canvas on an easel in front of him—he's painting. Now listen to this, he's dressed in a white suit, he wears a Panama hat and he has a cigar in his mouth. D'ya like it? Then Kelly stops, turns around and does a double take. And who d'ya think the man is? Of course, Winston Churchill!"

"You must have had lunch with Sarah! No, Arthur, it's very funny! We'll put it in."

When they came to a montage in which Kelly is seen painting a progression of canvases for his impending exhibition, Freed said, "There's only one way to do a montage: as a chorus of a song, so that the montage becomes part of a musical number. It mustn't be scored like an isolated piece of film."

"He was right of course," says Lerner. "I never forgot it. After that, every time I used a montage I could hear Arthur's words."

For the musical director the logical choice was Johnny Green, in whose career George Gershwin had played a prominent part. As the head of the music department his duties and responsibilities were time consuming and he called on Saul Chaplin to assist him. By that time Edens was already very much occupied wih the preparation for *Show*

Boat, and Freed and he decided to divide their attention between the two pictures, as they had done with *Yolanda and the Thief* and *The Harvey Girls.*

Freed, Minnelli, Kelly, Green and Chaplin spent many an evening at Ira Gershwin's house, going through the entire Gershwin catalogue of published and unpublished songs to arrive at a selection appropriate for the film. Finally, a tentative list was turned over to the legal department to obtain the necessary clearances.[1]

A great deal of thought was given to the final choice of numbers: "I Got Rhythm," "Love Walked In," "Our Love Is Here to Stay," "I'll Build a Stairway to Paradise," "I've Got a Crush on You," "Embraceable You," "But Not for Me," "Nice Work If You Can Get It," "That Certain Feeling," "Liza," "Tra-la-la," and "By Strauss." And, of course, Gershwin's tone poem, "An American in Paris."

"By Strauss" was a parody of Viennese waltzes that the Gershwins had improvised one evening in 1936 while Minnelli was visiting them. They had only noted down about half when they dropped the whole thing. A few months later they received an urgent wire from Minnelli

---

[1] Music publishers and the Gershwin estate received $158,750. Ira Gershwin received $56,250, as consultant and to write new and/or additional lyrics (both English and French) for the songs selected.

The original title page of George Gershwin's "An American in Paris" written in ink by the composer. IRA GERSHWIN COLLECTION

asking them to finish it for his Broadway revue *The Show Is On.* They did and airmailed it to him. Using it in the picture required legal releases. Although this would not have presented any problems, Gershwin thought it would be just as easy to write an entirely new verse. With the exception of one line, Gershwin wrote new lyrics for the number "Tra-la-la," placing the emphasis on love.

"Our Love Is Here to Stay" has a more significant history. It was the last song George Gershwin wrote before his death in 1937. At that time George and Ira Gershwin were working on the score for *The Goldwyn Follies.* In his book *Passport to Paris,* Vernon Duke claims that there was no more than a twenty-bar lead sheet when he was called in to complete the song. He further states that Levant played some Gershwin phrases for him, some "motives,"—airs, as Duke calls them—to help him arrive at an authentic Gershwin composition. Ira Gershwin, however, disputes this, and claims that George had finished the chorus and that he, Ira, worked with Duke solely on the incomplete verse.

From the very beginning Kelly had been anxious to do the picture in Paris, although for obvious practical reasons Freed had misgivings.

When it came to casting the picture it was a *fait accompli* that Oscar Levant would be in it. He was cast as Adam Cook, a part tailor-made for him, based on the character of Dave Diamond, a concert pianist and a protégé of Levant's. However, when it came to casting Lise Bouvier, the French orphan, the executives insisted that Minnelli make a test of Sally Forrest, recently signed to the studio. They also suggested the Danish baritone Carl Brisson for the part of Henri Baurel. Both emerged as unsuitable. Then Cyd Charisse and Vera-Ellen were proposed for Lise, but Freed insisted on a bona fide French girl. Lerner was very anxious to get Maurice Chevalier to play the music hall entertainer. "But at that time he was *persona non grata,"* says Lerner. Then he spotted Georges Guetary in the Broadway musical *Arms and the Girl.* Lerner called Freed on the coast and Freed, relying on Lerner's judgment, signed Guetary. When Billy Grady, head of the casting department, submitted a list of names for the part of Milo Roberts, Freed, without a moment's hesitation, selected Nina Foch, a superb actress endowed with the natural elegance the part required.

But the casting of Lise was still up in the air. By sheer accident Freed noticed a photograph of an unusual girl on the cover of the magazine *Paris Match.* He called Kelly in New York and asked him to fly to Paris to test two girls: the girl on the magazine cover, Leslie Caron, and Odile Versois, an established English-speaking French actress. Kelly was impressed with Caron, having seen her two and a half years earlier in the Ballet des Champs-Elysées' production of "Le Rencontre (Oedipus and the Sphinx), but he made both tests anyway, and air expressed them to the studio. Minnelli and Freed ran them and their decision was unanimous.

The *American* set as it was reconstructed and redressed. The buildings are numbered by the art department for reference to the architectural blueprints on file. M-G-M

Leslie Caron arrived in Hollywood accompanied by her mother, who once had been in a Gershwin musical. When she presented herself to Freed, Simone and Edens looked at each other and remarked, "They've sent the wrong girl!" She looked awkward, was untidily dressed and spoke hardly any English. She was initially very shy, but soon began to feel comfortable.

In order for Freed to make Kelly appear to be a talented painter in the picture, he brought out Saul Steinberg, the creator of the legendary cartoons for *The New Yorker* magazine and equally well known for his most imaginative *trompe l'oeil* art. A studio was set up for him at the back of a sound stage where he happily painted all day long, frequently interrupted by visits from his admirers. But he developed serious doubts about the script, about the picture as a whole and about his own role. He expressed his misgivings to Freed and demanded to be consulted in the final editing of the film. This was out of the question,

310

and Freed was annoyed. Steinberg went back to New York. He was replaced by a virtually unknown painter named Gene Grant, whom Minnelli describes as "Utrillo-like," and who in art circles, was known as a specialist of the Left Bank.

At this time a new talent joined the Freed Unit: Carol Haney. She was born in New Bedford, Massachusetts, and all her life had been obsessed with the desire to become a great dancer. When she was in high school she realized how mediocre her training had been and began to develop a technique by herself. As soon as she was graduated from high school she went to New York and, to support herself, worked as a hash slinger. When and wherever dancers were needed she auditioned and at one of these auditions Jack Cole spotted her and immediately took her under his·wing. With his unerring eye he detected her potential as a dancer and her remarkable individuality. She soon became a member of his famous dance group and ultimately wound up in Hollywood. Auditioning at M-G-M with dozens of others, she attracted Kelly's attention and was signed to a stock dancer's contract. In *On the Town,* Kelly gave her a small but important bit and from here on she was his side-kick—in effect, his assistant choreographer.

Ever since the musical layout of *An American in Paris* had been formulated, Levant was depressed, which was not unusual, but this time he had good reason. Freed had declared categorically that there would be no "concert music" in the picture. "There will be no lulls in this film," he had said very pointedly. Since the term "concert music" could only be identified with Levant, he fell into a kind of sulking melancholia. But his vanity and his exhibitionism didn't let him rest. In his mind he mulled over possibilities for insinuating himself into the picture, concert music and all. But for the moment he had to bide his time.

Rehearsals began on June 5, 1950. Kelly worked out the choreography for the musical numbers while, in an adjacent hall, Haney concentrated on Caron. Most of the time Chaplin was at hand and at the end of each day he reported his activities to Green. When rehearsals were further along, Salinger was often called in to watch for the purpose of getting the "feel" for the texture of his orchestrations.

Mr. Green reminisces: "We had a very important teammate working with us all the time in the person of Conrad Salinger. Due credit should be given to him." Coming from Johnny Green, this testimonial is most interesting in view of the fact that Salinger was part of the "incestuous Ozark" group in the Freed Unit he so violently criticized.

The prerecordings started on July 20 and were finished by the time production started. These sessions were sparked with a special kind of electricity and all involved felt as if they were on the threshold of something extraordinary. Particular attention was paid to the phrasing and timing to correspond precisely with Kelly's choreography. He, or he and Caron, performed their numbers to the playbacks while the orchestra et al. watched in silence. The atmosphere was that of a first night.

Minnelli was faced with the task of fabricating Paris on the Metro lot. He submerged himself in mountains of clippings with his art director Preston Ames, a man who had been an art student in Paris for five years. "I must have spent a month on 'Waterfront Street' alone," says Ames. "I tried to figure out what I could do and what angles I should use to make all this look like Paris. But when I thought I had come up with a solution I had not taken into consideration choreography, movement and music." Ultimately Ames dressed up "Waterfront Street," "French Street" and part of the tunnel extending into "Quality Street." He cut out the Sacre Coeur Church in profile and placed it at the top of a hill. When Ames brought Minnelli his design for the Café Flodair, Minnelli had found a photograph of the frescoes in the caves at Lascaux in central France and, with his mania for authenticity, instructed Ames to have them reproduced on the walls of the café.

One of the exteriors necessary was a quai on the Seine. Nobody in Ames's department believed it could be done; nor did Kelly. "For this," they argued, "you've got to go to Paris." Ames stopped them by asking Kelly a simple question: "Have you ever danced on cobblestones?" Kelly was convinced he could, but his colleagues were skeptical. The set was built on Stage 30 with a practical construction in the foreground. The bridge of the Archeveché and the view of Notre Dame in the background were painted on a 100-foot cyclorama merging with the construction in the foreground. The tank was filled to simulate the Seine and the water was agitated by a motor.

Ames was still not satisfied. The "river," moved, but it didn't flow anywhere; and the Quai, the Seine and Notre Dame in the background had no perspective, no depth. "What can we do?," he asked George Gibson. "I brooded over this," recalls Gibson. "We hung some

Nina Foch and Gene Kelly seated in the Café Flodair. The primitive frescoes are seen on the restaurant walls.
M-G-M

Georges Guetary and Minnelli's human candelabras in "I'll Build a Stairway to Paradise." M-G-M

lights, twenty-five feet high, to get a reflection of the water in the foreground. Then we took small lighting fixtures, painted the glass black, and submerged them in the water, so that the two sources of light would give effect of a long perspective to the river bank." The ultimate solution was to leave either side of the tank in darkness.

Featuring Georges Guetary, "I'll Build a Stairway to Paradise" was the only production number in the picture. Minnelli wanted a typical Folies-Bergère set, with an elaborate staircase, plumed show girls and odd chandeliers. Ames designed it with the staircase illuminated from below and Minnelli had show girls carrying candelabras. Guetary would ascend the staircase singing and Kelly had the steps electrically wired so that each step would light up in the rhythm of the music under Guetary's feet. Levant remembers Guetary rehearsing the number, "He was pure Carol Haney: he imitated her to a 't.'"

Kelly looks down from his third-floor pension, but the photograph picks up the sound stage floor. What you see on the screen is effected via a Newcombe shot. M-G-M

Walter Plunkett designed all the costumes with the exception of the modern clothes for Nina Foch, Caron and the costumes for the Guetary number, which Orry-Kelly created.

Keogh Gleason, the set decorator on the picture, had worked with Minnelli on *Father of the Bride.* When his boss, Ed Willis, assigned him he was warned: "It's your turn for the kiss of death." Minnelli had been known to fire most set decorators and many vowed never to work for him. But Gleason had weathered the storm. He attributes his rapport with Minnelli to being able to understand exactly what Minnelli wanted. "He would ask wardrobe, for example, for a change and they'd always bring him the opposite, because they completely misunderstood him."

Headed by Peter Ballbusch, the second unit was dispatched to Paris to shoot establishing shots, among them the opening aerial view and Kelly and Foch arriving at the Ritz Hotel. "We had to find an exact duplicate of Foch's car back at the studio," says Ballbusch. "That car was of an unusual color, and once we had found the car we took gallons of paint to make it the right color." The wife of Geoffrey Unsworth, the British cameraman on the unit, looked like an image of Nina Foch and to find a double for Kelly didn't prove too difficult.

On August 1, 1950, the picture went into production.

The opening scene depicts a Paris street in the morning hours, lively

314

with neighborhood characters: a man examining the display in a shop window, a bookseller opening his store, an old woman selling flowers from a pushcart, and a nun setting out milk for the cats. With that came the hitch. Many times in the past Minnelli had obstinately expected animals and birds to respond to his demands and was unyielding when they didn't. After confusion, impatience and much delay, a starved cat was sent for. She drank the milk while the camera rolled.

Two weeks into the picture Levant came out of his depression with a brilliant idea which he typically called the "Ego Fantasy." The piece was the third movement of the Gershwin "Concerto in F." He would play the piano solo; he would play diverse orchestral instruments; he would be the conductor; and, as a spectator sitting in a box, he would be applauding his own performance.

But even he did not have the temerity to spring this on Freed. Instead he went to Minnelli. After Levant had described the number, Minnelli was ecstatic. He immediately relayed the idea to Freed who again showed his flexibility. "It's great. Go ahead," was his terse reply. And, as an afterthought, "How's Oscar? Still depressed?"

When Levant came in for the recording he was exceedingly nervous. As his intimate friend, Freed was very aware of his sudden changes of mood and very protective of him. "We made a take," recalls Green, "in which Oscar's playing—over-all—was brilliant. Everybody was listening to the playback and quite properly falling over, because the tempo he played that movement in was insane. Everybody in the control room was applauding, Oscar was pulling on the poor, benighted cigarette, pacing up and down.

The "Ego Fantasy" was a spectacularly executed stunt. The number was shot on Stage 5-6, set as a legitimate concert hall. At the beginning Levant is seen at the piano and as the conductor, from the back, lifting his baton for the downbeat. A double was needed for the conductor. Writer and most erudite amateur musician Adolph Green, all his life, had wanted to conduct a symphony orchestra. This was his chance. He was about comparable in height to Levant, he knew the score inside out, and he had seen enough famous conductors to imitate their gestures to perfection. It was imperative for the audience never to see his face nor the faces of any of the players. "Levant's dream concert called for an unusual lighting treatment," says cameraman Gilks. "Everybody on the stage appeared in silhouette. Whatever instrument Levant played, he was a dark figure, preliminary to a close shot. Then, on a musical cue, he leaned in a closely controlled key light and thus disclosed himself to the audience." At the conclusion of the performance the camera cuts to Levant in a box applauding and shouting "Bravo!" then cuts back to the stage when Levant, the soloist, shakes hands with Levant, the conductor. This tricky effect was achieved by Ries's optical department. Shot for shot, the number was laid out beforehand, so that, in spite of the intricate lighting, Minnelli was able to shoot the sequence in one day.

When Oscar came to do his first picture for Freed, Simone recalls "being afraid to even meet him." But it didn't take long for them to become friends. He showed enormous warmth and great respect for her as a musician. His gift for stripping away pretensions was phenomenal, because in many ways he felt himself to be somewhat of a fake. His phobias were sometimes amusing and always interesting. When Levant came back for *American,* Simone had a large bouquet of red roses sent to his room. Meeting her later that day he was almost in tears. "No flowers, please, no flowers—no funerals!" "I know how he appreciated the gesture," she says, "but he always gave his phobias free reign."

Levant found a short cut to Metro via Twentieth Century-Fox. "I would drive over to the Fox Studio, enter the back gate and the guards would check me in. Then I would leave by the South Gate, a minute later, where the guard would check me out. This went on for two weeks. The gate people assumed I was working in a picture at Fox, but I was only there for one minute every day. It was like an Alec Guinness picture. Two weeks later when I entered the back gate six L.A. policemen were waiting for me on motorcycles. I had to explain my 'short cut' to M-G-M. It would have been the kind of job I liked, working for just one minute a day."

It took Chaplin only ten minutes to get home from the studio, except when Levant drove him; then it was more like half an hour. Levant could not bear to drive through any street that harbored a bad memory: a ticket he got, an incident at a party, a house whose owner he didn't like. There were many such streets and he made many detours. Chaplin was a good sport about it all.

The *raison d'être* for making the picture in the first place was to do a ballet to Gershwin's tone poem. So far this plan was unrealized. Kelly thought of dancing his way through the streets of Paris, as he had done through the streets of New York. Freed promptly dissuaded him. "Let's not repeat ourselves," Freed contended, "do it here, at the studio, in the Paris of the impressionists."

In Lerner's script a masked ball was to precede the big ballet. As could be expected, Minnelli had created a picture with great emphasis on visual appeal. And the ballet, at the end of the film, would surely be drenched in impressionist color. The notion of the masked ball worried him, but, he says, "All of a sudden I thought of doing the ball in black and white. I called Arthur and he not only agreed but was delighted. Black and white would rest the eyes so that, when the ballet comes on, color again would be fresh and more immediate."

Ames was overworked, and Jack Smith, although immersed in the production of *Show Boat,* came to the rescue. He recalls, "It was a huge set. I got all the poplar trees and grape vines, all in white, put them on the walls and made baroque architecture out of greens. In *The Great Ziegfeld* we outdid baroque and I knew how to concoct these things."

"It was a balcony set, done over," Gleason comments. "There were 193 extras, three acrobats and three stuntmen. We had branches brought in and I threw them in the crowd. Then Preston threw some; then Vincente got in the act. He arranged each of them and kept adding more. With all the people in the set—and with that black and white —it wasn't very successful."[2]

So far the only reality for the ballet was the decor: Paris, seen through the eyes of Dufy, Renoir, Utrillo, Rousseau, Van Gogh and Toulouse-Lautrec. As to the designer, the choice was unanimous: Irene Sharaff.

Freed phoned Sharaff's New York agent, Gloria Safier, who was able to pry her client out of a Broadway musical, which she hated doing anyway, and Sharaff came back to Metro.

"I had seen in the papers that *An American in Paris* was being made, but I didn't know what it was all about when the call came in. I hadn't seen Arthur for a long, long time," Sharaff says.

In her first meeting with Freed she was told that the ballet is "all about impressionist painters." "That's lovely, what's the story?" "Well —it's about impressionist painters," Freed repeated.

"Don't you have a libretto?"

There was none.

"Who's designing the sets?"

"You are!"

When Sharaff ran the picture it was finished, except for some very small scenes and Caron's introduction. Taking advantage of Sharaff's presence, Kelly discussed this with her. He was reaching for something similar to Vera-Ellen's "Miss Turnstiles" sequence in *On the Town*. As a gift, as Sharaff says, she came up with an inventive solution.

When Levant asks Guetary about Caron, "What's she like?" the camera would pan to the mirror on the wall of the Café Hugette and in its frame Caron would appear in six vignettes. Orchestrated in a collage of "Embraceable You" rhythms by Salinger, each of them would embody a specific aspect of her personality in a monochromatic setting for each mood: beautiful—baroque; sexy—Victorian; old-fashioned—Louis XVI; jazzy—the twenties; studious—Jacobean; gay and happy—Biedermeier. At the conclusion the screen would split into the six images, effected by Ries.

At the end of the so-called retrospect, Levant, in his inimitable way, ad libs: "Tell me, Henri, what's she *really* like?" In the beginning of

---

[2] Plunkett's costumes were as bizarre as the occasion. So-called artists were adorned in hats simulating a pair of dice, a teapot, spiraled cornucopias, etc.

the picture he improvised another line. He describes himself as "the world's oldest child protégé." In a later scene, intent on interrupting a conversation between Kelly and Guetary, the rivals, he is his normal, nervous self: Puffing feverishly on his cigarette, he lifts his coffee cup to his lips, the cigarette falls in it, he puts down the cup and blurts out, "Did I ever tell you about my command performance in front of Hitler?"

Even before the shooting of the picture was completed, Minnelli, Kelly and Sharaff spent every free minute and many evenings together, turning their combined energies toward laying out the ballet. A transition from reality into fantasy had to be found. Minnelli called Lerner in New York and asked him to rewrite the scene leading from the black and white ball into the ballet, with Kelly, in a state of confusion and despair, almost delirious for fear of having lost his girl.

Lerner's new scene put Kelly on a terrace of the Beaux Arts Building where one would find him again at the end.

Sharaff locked herself in her office with a phonograph and a recording of "An American in Paris." "I played it over and over," she recalls. "It's very curious; in listening, certain characters came out of

Leslie Caron in one of the six vignettes to Salinger's arrangement of the Gershwin classic "Embraceable You."
M-G-M

my unconscious, suggested by motives and themes of Gershwin's music. I can't say that the painters I selected are all favorites of mine—some of them are. I did actually work out the sequence and the Pompiers and the continuity of the ballet. I think I did it from the point of view of color. But the painters themselves dictated the continuity."

Then each painter was given a proper locale, adhering to the style of each: Dufy for the Place de la Concorde; Manet for the flower market; Utrillo for a Paris street; Rousseau for the fair; Van Gogh for the Place de l'Opéra; Toulouse-Lautrec for the Moulin Rouge. The leitmotiv, symbolizing the girl, would be a rose, as the carnation had been in the *Yolanda* ballet.

Sharaff made sketches for the backdrops in the manner of each painter and conjured up individual characters, especially for the opening Dufy scene: "There was a tall, black chap, dressed as an African chief, with a white burnoose and a turban; and the boy on the bicycle. . . ."

Then she invented the Pompiers, the soldiers, and the Furies, their feminine counterpoint. Ames detailed and scaled her sketches, to serve as models, and with these Minnelli, Sharaff and Ames went to confer with George Gibson, whose task was to find the proper technique for enlarging the sketches to size.

"For instance: the Place de la Concorde. It had to look like a Dufy watercolor," says Gibson. "So you can imagine what it meant trying to run a wash 40 feet high by 150 feet long. We thought the nearest would be clouds—we'll paint it like a cloud. Then, there was Utrillo. As you know, there the brush strokes are small. But we had to make them big and heavy—Utrillo's technique had to be interpreted. We really ran the gamut: from pastel to watercolor to oil. For the Van Gogh, the Opéra, we used Textone, a thick, plastery substance. It was painted flat, because the damned stuff would drop off, that's how heavy it was. We resorted to a simulation of an impasto brush stroke. We'd paint the stroke and then put a little shadow in it. . . ."

It would take six weeks to complete the backgrounds, with thirty painters working around the clock.

A vital part of the whole scheme was the fountain on the Place de la Concorde. Using Sharaff's sketch, Henry Greutart, head of the sculpture department, made a 24-inch by 30-inch miniature, which was conceptually different than what Ames had proposed. "It should have the feeling a painter made it, not an architect," said Greutart. "I'm sure Preston won't mind. . . ."

"Greutart had made a wonderful fountain," says Minnelli, "but then came an awful interlude with Preston. He had the fountain made with solid statues and broken lines painted on them. And he insisted that this was the right way to do it. I couldn't make him understand how I was going to use light and darkness. . . ."

The fluidity of Greutart's final version came about by racking and twisting heated plastic. "I gambled on this material; fiberglass and plastic were just coming in vogue. We certainly couldn't have made it out of plaster."

Slowly each element, every detail came into focus, a conglomeration of ideas, suggestions and inspirations, selected and interpreted by Minnelli, Kelly and Sharaff. Freed backed them up all the way and his enthusiasm stretched their imaginative talents even further.

Freed and Minnelli had lunch with Irving Berlin in the commissary. They showed Berlin Sharaff's drawings for sets and costumes.

"Am I to understand that you fellas are going to end this picture with a seventeen-minute ballet and that's it? No dialogue? No singing? Nothing?"

"Yes," answered Freed and Minnelli jointly.

"I hope you boys know what you're doing."

"This depressed us terribly," says Minnelli.

The company shut down on November 1. Even though the ballet had not yet been shot, a screening of a rough cut was set up for Lee and Ira Gershwin and Renee and Arthur Freed. Lee Gershwin gushed: "Arthur, you are the greatest producer that ever lived!" Renee Freed avoided giving a direct answer.

Architectural sketch for Paris street scene.

Lenore Gershwin, Oscar Levant, Ira Gershwin and Arthur Freed at the first screening of the film (not shown in the photograph is Mrs. Arthur Freed). IRA GERSHWIN COLLECTION

Before rehearsals started, an estimated budget for the ballet was prepared and forwarded to the New York office. When it reached Nicholas Schenck's desk a storm broke loose. Without having seen the film, as far as New York was concerned, the picture was complete and could be released as is. So far the picture had cost $1,948,848, and the first budget for the ballet was estimated at $419,664 (exclusive of costumes). The initial uproar was followed by countless verbal exchanges between Schenck, Mayer and Schary. But Freed never wavered. His stand was as adamant as the one he had taken when "Over the Rainbow" was to be eliminated from *The Wizard of Oz*. It was Mayer who backed Freed and influenced Schary to come over to his side.

"I said, 'Go,'" Schary recalls. "There was quite a bit of hell being raised about spending that kind of money for one number. But I remained firm on my approval. You can only operate in that kind of job if you're willing to back up the people you trust. And *then* you have some problems. But I felt so strongly about Gene, a brilliant talent, and Minnelli, so gifted, and Irene, there's nobody quite like that, and Freed had impeccable taste."

Schary continues: "I told Schenck this picture is going to be great because of the ballet—or it'll be nothing. Without the ballet it's just a cute and nice musical. So that's what we're gambling on."

Kelly started rehearsing on November 2, assisted by Haney. He was allotted six weeks during which Minnelli took a leave of absence to direct *Father's Little Dividend*, which would allow him to return in time for the shooting of the ballet.

Irene Sharaff's rendering
for Caron's costume for
the "Utrillo" sequence.
ARTHUR FREED ARCHIVES

When Kelly was formulating the choreography for the six sections, he found a problem he was unable to solve. He went to see Sharaff and said, "There has to be some bridge to take me and Leslie from one section of Paris to the other and wind up in a different style." "Use the four Pompiers and the four Furies," she said. "They can take either of you from one place to another." And with that, the stumbling block was removed.

Kelly was anxious to stay away from a strictly classic form of ballet, except for the Renoir section, because there it fitted, as he says. He kept Caron romantic and moderately classic in order to provide a contrast with his own, individual American style.

"Our chief trouble was with the Rousseau set; being primitive it seemed to go against the score. So, we made the groups tap dance their way through a fourteenth of July celebration in the Cohan manner."

On many occasions Kelly consulted with Minnelli, busy on the *Dividend* set. All the while Sharaff fed Kelly her costume sketches, one at a time. "One can't do 210 costumes at one sitting, you know," she says. "Gene had them photostated and hung them up on a laundry

322

Kelly as Du Chocolat
at the Moulin Rouge
(Toulouse-Lautrec).
M-G-M

line so that he could tell. This also helped him in putting groups together."

In the Toulouse-Lautrec section the style of dancing was dictated by the pose of the American jockey on Lautrec's poster "Du Chocolat." Kelly refers to this particular section as "strong dancing," a form of expression very kindred to Haney, who was instrumental in helping him perfect every movement.

In the opening and closing sections on the Place de la Concorde Kelly wanted to interpret the spirit of Dufy rather than use a choreographed form of dancing. What Kelly was after was to translate the feeling each painter evoked with a minimum of dance and a maximum of emotion.

Throughout the planning stages and rehearsals Chaplin stayed at Kelly's side. He did the adaptation for the seventeen-minute ballet and arranged it for two pianos for rehearsal purposes. Salinger embellished and adjusted sections of the entire Gershwin piece. "Now it's true, it was based on George Gershwin's arrangements," says Chaplin, "but if you play a recording and then play ours from the movie, they're

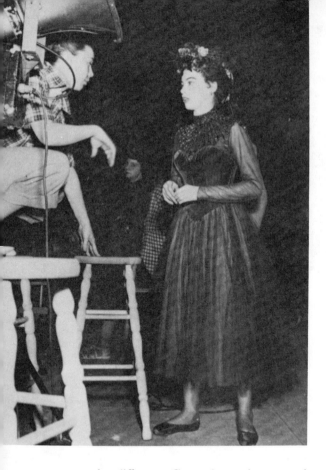

Carol Haney (left) gives Leslie Caron some last-minute direction before the "Van Gogh" sequence is ready for a take. M-G-M

quite different. George's music was written as a straight concert piece and it's fine. But ours had to fit the ballet movements devised by Kelly, an added problem."

Ira Gershwin was consulted on whatever alterations needed to be made in the original score.

On December 1 and 2, the ballet was prerecorded. So far much has been said about the visual aspects. An enormously important part of the whole was the sound of the Gershwin score.

When Johnny Green was appointed the general music director at the studio, he began to make changes. The first thing he did was to replace the mixer on the recording stage with a man equipped with a trained ear and musical knowledge. Next he reseated the orchestra, backing it against the long wall of the rectangular stage and ordered vitally necessary acoustic adjustments. Green also restructured the orchestra by getting new talent to unseat old-time, second-rate players. With this general rejuvenation Green brought about a new M-G-M sound, of which the track for the *American in Paris* ballet is a prime example. As a conductor's performance, this recording is regarded as one of the finest ever made.

324

Scene 2 of the *An American in Paris* ballet, Place de la Concorde (Dufy). Kelly, the Pompiers, the Furies and the African chief (upper left). M-G-M

Scene 3, Flower Market (Manet). Kelly and Caron in a *pas de deux*. M-G-M

Scene 4, Montmartre Street (Utrillo). Kelly does routine with four GIs: Alex Romero, Ernie Flatt, Dick Humphries, Bill Chatham (all choreographers today). M-G-M

Scene 5, Carnival Square (Rousseau). Kelly and Caron dance in the style of George M. Cohan. M-G-M

On December 6, when Minnelli came back to shoot the ballet, he brought with him John Alton, his cameraman on *Father's Little Dividend*. "I regretted that I hadn't had him for the whole film," says Minnelli. "I think he is one of the greatest cameramen that I have ever worked with. Alton is very flexible; he doesn't have a set mind like Gilks had, and he is capable of modifying his way according to the director's indications."

This was Alton's first Technicolor assignment. But even so, he had very definite ideas as to how to bring about certain color effects. "The secret of the ballet's photography," he says, "was the *fumata* (smoky) quality, which changed all the colors to pastel. In the ballet we used English color quality for the first time. I was inspired, like everybody else on the picture, by the electrical force Gershwin's music generated. In my case this showed itself in the way I used light. . . . We all worked like a team. Every morning we would rush to the studio, eager to do something, even ahead of time. We were just like kids going to the candy store. That's how excited we were. . . ."

Many of Alton's colleagues believed that no one could have shot the ballet the way he did: shooting directly into a light, or using less than the minimum of light deemed necessary for a good negative. And others considered him to be "a very arrogant man."

There was a row with the electricians' union. "They tried everything to stop his cutting down on lights," says Gleason. "Alton could light properly and quickly. But the laboratories would say 'It's no good,' because it was cutting down on the procedures. John also said he didn't need any catwalks. That really blew the top off. Of some sixty lights, Alton would use three or four, which cut down tremendously on labor. It's a wonder he didn't have a light dropped on him . . ."

To: Arthur Freed
Subject: AN AMERICAN IN PARIS BALLET NUMBER
From: Joe Finn   Date: 12/13/50

The ballet number for *An American in Paris* as of Saturday, December 9, has cost

$366,000

On the basis in which they are now photographing the number, it is estimated that it will require, in addition to the above, 8 shooting days and 4 rehearsal days to complete the number. This would complete the number on December 23. Therefore, this would add to the above, 8 additional shooting days which at the present time are averaging approximately $19,000 a day.   152,000

and 4 rehearsal days which are averaging $6,000 a day.   24,000

This would make the final cost of the number $542,000

The ballet was completed on January 2, 1951. What remained to be shot was the finishing scene of the picture. In that scene Gene sees a car pull up at the bottom of a long flight of stairs. Caron gets out and runs up toward him. He runs down toward her and as they embrace the camera tilts up to reveal Paris by night.

"I knew how Vincente loved stairs," says Ames, "and the Montmartre stairs go on for blocks. I used those originally built for Ronald Colman's *Kismet*. I laid out a series of shots, all kinds of tricky things, to indicate three different levels."

The scene on these stairs eventually became a Newcombe shot. "I used the duplicating machine invented by Douglas Shearer," says Newcombe. "The camera is placed on the machine and manually tilted. Later we photographed a painting of the background in exact perspective to the actual set, and matching precisely the speed of the first tilt, it gave us the result we were after."

Production closed on *An American in Paris* on January 8, 1951, at a cost of $2,723,903 (which included $542,000 for the ballet and $12,500 as a bonus to Kelly).

On January 9 Freed asked Simone to take the rough cut of the picture to New York to run it for a reluctant board of directors, who were appalled at the cost. Simone arrived in New York early one morning and as soon as the Loew's office opened she called in. "I'm here and the print is in the building. Please call me as soon as you know when Mr. Schenck wants to see the film."

Weeks later she was still waiting for the call. "I thought I would go stark raving mad. I called the office three times a day. In a theatre at night I was in constant fear that there might be a message at the

Scene 7, Place de l'Ópera (Van Gogh). Kelly and Caron meet sandwich man displaying Toulouse-Lautrec exhibition. M-G-M

Scene 10, Place de la Concorde (Dufy). Kelly, Caron and the *American in Paris* corps de ballet in the grand finale of the seventeen-minute ballet.
M-G-M and GENE KELLY COLLECTION

Plaza. Mr. Schenck was out of town. Mr. Schenck was in Florida. Mr. Schenck wasn't well. . . ."

Then came the day when Schenck and his board decided that they were ready to see the film. Simone got to the projection room early. Then she waited for the two o'clock screening. "It was quite a hot day. The iron door in the back opened and in came, one after the other, some ancient gentlemen, tottering and looking like wilted flowers. All in all there were about ten; they seated themselves separate from one another, sort of strewn all over the room. Nobody spoke—it was funereal. After another few minutes Mr. Schenck entered, clad in impeccable white, accompanied by Mr. Vogel. With some effort the old gentlemen lifted themselves out of their seats, turning toward Mr. Schenck, who quite slowly and carefully walked to the center of the room. 'Hello, General . . .' I was absolutely flustered by this. It was like an oriental court ceremony. . . ."

There was no reaction during the screening. When the lights came on at the end of the picture nobody said a word. Schenck turned and left and so did the tottering gentlemen, with the exception of Mr. Vogel, who came over to Simone and said, "Please come to my office. I would like to call Arthur." In his office Vogel got Freed on the tie line to the studio and expressed very subdued praise. After all, it was after the fact. Putting down the phone he turned to Simone, "Am I wrong? It seems to me that I once saw some paintings on 57th Street that looked like certain sets in the ballet."

Schary remembers a call from Schenck after the screening: "Well, Dore, it's pretty good. I'm not so sure about it, though. It's very special. Does the ballet have to run eighteen minutes? Can't you cut it?"

In other words, none of these people understood what the ballet was all about. One must question whether the interoffice communications, especially crucial in this instance, were ever read. Apparently only the dollar quotations had jumped off the pages.

When the production closed, Chaplin's job was done. Now Green prepared the underscoring for the picture. "I know Johnny very well," says Simone. "We always got along, because he knew that I was probably the only person at the studio who never gave him a line. But he is an impossible man to work with. On the scoring stage he would make take after take just because he was aggravated with a flute player . . . or because the orchestra hadn't laughed at his jokes."

Simone worked with mixer Bill Steinkamp on the dubbing and for three days on nothing but the ballet. The night before the preview, at 2 A.M., they made the perfect take. "I'm sorry, Bill," came the voice from the recording room in the basement, "we ran out of film."

March 21, the Freed Unit went to the very secret sneak preview at the Crown Theatre in Pasadena. Everybody was nervous. They went for dinner at the Stuft Shirt near the theatre. Minnelli and Simone were the first to arrive and went right to the bar. It was six o'clock, the place was empty with the exception of the bartender, who was polishing glasses.

"Two double martinis," said Minnelli.

The bartender looked up and casually said, "Sorry—Election Day!"

"We were ready to commit suicide," says Simone. "We struggled through dinner, with Arthur jingling coins in his pockets. At the preview, as usual I was sitting next to Steinkamp to help him with the uneven sound volume." During the newsreel the projectionist switched the sound controls over to Steinkamp and when the main titles came on, the sound was much too low.

"Up, Bill. Up, up, up," Simone urged. No luck. Two of the three sound horns in the theatre had suddenly gone out of commission.

The entire picture ran off in a very soft pianissimo. The effect was disastrous; people began to wander out. "Everything was like under water," says Minnelli. "For some reason nobody stopped the film. So, we went back to Ira's house feeling suicidal."

A second preview was held on April 8 at the Bay Theatre in Pacific Palisades. It was an overwhelming success.

When the film was being edited for release, some musical numbers were deleted and minor cuts were made to tighten the picture. Kelly was sorry to see his favorite number eliminated. "I've Got a Crush on You" was a solo number to which he had given particular thought and attention. "Love Walked In" and "But Not for Me," both Guetary solos, were also taken out of the film. The former held up the tempo in the early part of the picture and the latter didn't play in the surrounding whirl of the Beaux Arts ball. At the ball some trims were made, especially in view of the long ballet that followed.

An American in Paris was released on November 9, 1951, and grossed in excess of $8,005,000.

According to Freed, "Limehouse Blues," "Slaughter on Tenth Avenue" and the *Yolanda* ballet were the stepping stones that gave him the inspiration for the *American in Paris* ballet.

Sharaff comments: "All the people in the unit loved making movies, which is a terribly exciting and wonderful adventure. I probably helped to spark their enthusiasm, because I was a fresh person coming in. Freed lacked manners, but he had this tremendous longing to create something beautiful."

Lerner compares the "continual generation of excitement and creativity in the Freed Unit" with Malarmé's Paris café days, when the poet would come down, read his poems to his friends and then go upstairs to rework them some more.

Kelly says: "If the camera is to make any contribution to dance, the focal point must be the pure background, giving the spectator an undistorted and all-encompassing view of dancer and background. To accomplish this end, the camera must be made to move with the dancer, so that the lens becomes the eye of the spectator, *your* eye. Minnelli, Sharaff, Chaplin and I worked in close harmony; none of us made a move without the other. In short, we really tried to make a *ballet,* not just merely a dance, not a series of beautiful, moving tableaux, but an emotional whole, consisting of the combined arts which spell ballet, whether on the screen or the stage."

Four months after *American* went into release Freed was in Paris and ordered a screening of the picture. One night, in the small projection room underneath the offices of M-G-M, the picture was to be run for Raoul Dufy. Freed, Simone and a handful of guests were waiting for the great painter to arrive. Understandably, Freed felt anxious. "My stomach was in my throat," says Simone. "I was as nervous as though I had composed the score, written the screenplay and played all the parts." The door to the projection room was at the end of a stairway.

IRA GERSHWIN
1021 NORTH ROXBURY DRIVE
BEVERLY HILLS, CALIFORNIA

Dear Arthur —
In the package is my getting even with you for your having beaten the hell out of me at pool all year.
I hope you like it. If you don't — I know two potential purchasers who will pay a handsome price for it — myself being one of them.
Ira

Ira Gershwin's oil painting of Arthur Freed. This was his token of appreciation for the extraordinary production of *An American in Paris* as well as his admission that he had been beaten at pool the whole year. Entitled "The Smug Winner," the painting was Gershwin's Christmas gift to Freed. It also recalled that pool match on the night the film *An American in Paris* was born. Freed loaned the painting to the Museum of the City of New York as part of the George and Ira Gershwin exhibition held on May 6, 1968. ARTHUR FREED ARCHIVES

Through this door Dufy was being carried in on a wooden chair; a small, very slight man with a friendly, charming smile. He watched the picture with apparent interest and from the time the ballet came on the screen he made some muffled, yet audible comments to his companion. He was enormously impressed with the ballet and it was obvious that he was not just being polite. For Freed and all those who created it, this was a triumph.

Once again, Freed relished having two trains running on parallel tracks; in this case, *An American in Paris* and *Show Boat*. In addition, he found pleasure in pursuing other plans. Betty Comden and Adolph Green were at the studio writing an original story and screenplay for

Ira Gershwin inscribed the poster for Freed and, as he had done many times, affixed the signature from a canceled check of his late brother.
ARTHUR FREED ARCHIVES

Singin' in the Rain, with the Brown-Freed catalogue, having just signed a three-picture contract; Alan Lerner was at work on a new draft of *Huckleberry Finn*[3] and would soon collaborate with Burton Lane on the musical score; Freed had acquired Lerner and Loewe's Broadway show *Brigadoon*[4]: Sigmund Romberg had signed a contract with Freed to star in his life story; Joseph Fields was writing a new screenplay of *Jumbo;* Oscar Hammerstein II continued discussions on a musical biography of his grandfather, which he titled *Romance With Music.*

By 1950, *Show Boat* had become a household word. In the theatre, the show had had its original première on December 27, 1927; it had been made into a silent picture, with some songs thrown in with the advent of talkies in 1929; in 1936, the stage production was transferred

[3] Previous attempts were made by Sally Benson in 1945, with a score by Hugh Martin and Ralph Blane; and Donald Ogden Stewart in January 1950 (Lane and E. Y. Harburg had begun to write some songs).

[4] The studio paid $180,000 to Lerner and Loewe directly.

to the screen, this time as a sound film with the entire Kern score; when Metro bought the rights the studio had financed a revival on Broadway (January 5, 1946) as a trial balloon for yet another screen production. Freed and Edens went to New York to see it. Returning to the studio, they ran the 1936 Universal film.

After years of analyzing what was in Freed's opinion the essential flaw in the original libretto and in two unsatisfactory screenplays by George Wells and Jack McGowan, respectively, he and Edens ran the film again, this time with John Lee Mahin, a nonmusical, exclusively dramatic writer. They presented him with suggestions in order to make the story tighter, more dramatic and more plausible. To begin with, in Hammerstein's treatment of Edna Ferber's novel, Gaylord and Magnolia are separated for twenty years, which makes for an absence of action and drama, and when they reunite they are elderly people. Secondly, as the story ends, Kim, their child, has grown up and the story finishes with an ending which actually should be a beginning.

Mahin concurred. "Let them separate," he said, "but keep them comparatively young. Don't drop Julie out of the story, because she's the most vital character, and have her, in some way, be the means of bringing them together again."

Even before Mahin set out to reconstruct the story and formulate it into a screenplay, the Breen Office raised its ugly head again:

> Dear Mr. Mayer:
>
> We understand that you are planning a production of *Show Boat.*
> We call your attention to the Production Code:
>> Section II—Sex
>>> Article 6—Miscegenation (sex relationship between the white and black races) is forbidden.
>
> Cordially yours,
> Joseph I. Breen

However, the 1936 production had set a precedent and the Breen Office was powerless.

Now Mahin could go to work, visualizing Howard Keel and Kathryn Grayson whom Freed had cast in the leading roles. George Sidney was assigned to direct; Bob Alton to direct the musical numbers; Adolph Deutsch as musical director; Conrad Salinger as orchestrator; Bobby Tucker as vocal arranger; Jack Martin Smith as art director; Walter Plunkett as costume designer; Charles Rosher as director of photography, and Roger Edens, supervisor of the entire production.[5]

Originally Freed wanted Judy Garland to play Julie. Since Julie had become even more of an integral part of the story, it was imperative to find the right actress. But there was intervention. "Dore Schary was friendly with Dinah Shore," says Freed. "He talked to her about doing

---

[5] Screen credit of Ben Feiner, Jr., as associate producer was "in name only."

334

the part and actually promised it to her, which he had no right to do. *I* was making the picture. All of a sudden I got a lot of flowers from Dinah. 'Dore,' I said, 'she's all wrong for the part.' 'But Arthur,' Dore said, 'how am I going to get out of it?' 'I'll get you out of it,' I told him. I sent for Dinah. 'Dinah,' I said, 'I'd love to do something with you— but you're not a whore, and that's what the part is.'" In the meantime Plunkett had already started to sketch Dinah Shore's costumes.

Freed wanted Ava Gardner for the part. Sidney made a test with Gardner, mouthing to a recording of Lena Horne. "I must say, there wasn't much enthusiasm about Ava, even making a test," says Sidney. The test was very good, but Plunkett reports that she didn't like her clothes, she didn't like anything. In fact, she wanted to be kicked off the picture.

Sidney looked on John Lee Mahin as a straight writer, the man who wrote *Test Pilot* and *Boom Town* for Gable, among others. "Now, you put him on a musical and he has to adjust himself," he says.

"I had no script conferences with Sidney," says Mahin, "none at all. Edens worked with me on the film from beginning to end."

To cast Joe, the Negro deckhand, was just a matter of a call to the casting department. But Edens was determined to find a Joe who— after hundreds of others—would not just sing the song adequately or even well. He had to be sensational, a term that normally was not in his vocabulary. One morning he stormed into Simone's office, where the latest issue of *Time* magazine was on her desk, with the music section face up. "Read it!" he said.

William Warfield, a young Negro baritone, had made a sensational debut in a Town Hall recital in New York, *Time* reported. His program had been strictly classical, from Handel, Brahms and Schubert to Debussy and Strauss. A student of the Eastman School of Music, nightclub appearances to earn a living, and then Warfield sang in Handel's "Messiah." After that a sponsor and the Town Hall recital.

She beamed, he beamed and took the review to Freed.

Edens was able to locate Warfield and asked him to come to California to audition. Some weeks later he arrived, a tall, massive young man, with a pleasant and easy manner. His audition consisted of some German and French songs. Edens asked, "Would you like to play Joe in *Show Boat* and sing 'Ol' Man River'?" Warfield answered with a bright smile, and what he said was unexpected: "I would love it, Mr. Edens, but I've never really sung a popular song before. I guess it won't be too difficult." And with that Warfield was signed.

Freed remembers that Sidney came to him with great reservations about Warfield's lack of experience as an actor. What Sidney did not know was that Warfield had toured in *Call Me Mister,* had done a straight role in Dorothy Heyward's *Set My People Free* and had played and sung the role of Cal in the Theatre Guild's production of *Regina*.

When Edna Ferber wrote *Show Boat,* Joe E. Brown had been the man who gave her the inspiration for Captain Andy. Now, twenty-five years later, Freed cast him in the part.

In Hammerstein's version, Ellie and Frank were hicks. Freed disagreed. He made them more sophisticated and gave the two roles to Marge and Gower Champion. Agnes Moorehead was cast as Parthy Hawks, the proverbial female with a heart of gold. Rounding out the cast were Robert Sterling, Leif Erickson and Adele Jergens.

So far, everyone had put off the question of where to find the show boat, but now the search was on. It was decided to shoot the picture on location, on the Mississippi River. On the eve of Sidney, Rosher and Smith's departure to explore the situation, Smith had a brainstorm. He recalls, "I had done a few pictures on the Mississippi and knew that we would be shooting at the wrong season of the year. The ice would be coming, the wharfs would have to be built and the architecture of the towns might have to be changed. I foresaw four billion problems. So the night before we left I sketched out a scheme; I laid out the boat and proved to everybody that we could do it on the back lot, on the Tarzan Jungle Lake, where we would have a full city block to tow the show boat. In the morning I rushed with the plan to Gibbons, and together we went to see Joe Cohn, supervising executive of production. Cohn hit his bald head, saying, "God, if you could do it here it would save us a fortune!" So the three men left for Natchez and Vicksburg to shoot exteriors and atmosphere shots for the opening of the picture, using local townspeople. For one of the last scenes in the picture they photographed the *Sprague,* the riverboat which was at one time known as "The Big Mama of the Mississippi." Sidney remembers vividly the problems he ran into. "We almost got killed because the *Sprague* had no power. We got permission to use it and had it pulled out in midstream by two little tugs. The Mississippi is a miserable river, full of eddies and swirls. We got this damn thing out there, having already spent five days putting in the lights. And then we wanted some smoke coming out and had to make phony smoke, and the thing caught fire, the tugs lost the boat and the boat started to turn around. . . ."

After returning to the studio, Smith went back to his drawing board to figure out how to construct the *Cotton Blossom* and how to overcome the almost insurmountable technical problems.

When Adolph Deutsch was assigned as musical director, he accepted with one stipulation. "At the first production meeting I said that I would only do *Show Boat* if I could approach Kern's music simply, as he intended it to be heard and played." Deutsch's statement was obviously directed at Salinger, who was not only an intimate friend but a disciple of Jerome Kern's. His reaction to *Till the Clouds Roll By* is revealing: "I was a little uncomfortable because the arrangements, vocal as well as instrumental, were, I thought, a little overembellished and

336

Scouting locations and a suitable riverboat along the Mississippi River (left to right): George Sidney, director, Charles Rosher, director of photography, and Jack Martin Smith, art director. M-G-M and JACK MARTIN SMITH COLLECTION

overarranged for a man who was as simple as Jerome Kern. In other words, to me the purity of Kern's music was like the purity of a Grecian column, a Grecian temple. I felt that it didn't need as much arranging as it got. I mentioned it to Connie and he was crestfallen and quite hurt about it."

When Deutsch and Salinger went to work on the prerecordings, their close relationship, their talent and their intelligence made them meet on middle ground. Since the picture was going into production on November 17, Deutsch started twelve days before for a full week of prerecordings. "Salinger knew more about Kern music than Kern himself," remarks Deutsch. "That's why he was so crestfallen when I said he had overdone *Clouds*. If Connie had had a free reign he would have done a splendid job. But when you have to conform to dance and vocal arrangements you are not your own master."

Deutsch speaks as a pure musician. On *Show Boat* the same constellation existed as on *Clouds*. There were numbers, intimate ones as well as production numbers, and again there were Alton with his choreography and vocal arrangements by Bobby Tucker—in Deutsch's view perhaps an improvement over those by Kay Thompson in *Clouds*. In both instances Edens was the catalyst—he was a musician as well as a showman.

From the time Ava Gardner had reconciled herself to playing Julie

The completed *Cotton Blossom.* M-G-M and JACK MARTIN SMITH COLLEC-
TION

whether she liked it or not, she had made up her mind to sing her two
numbers herself: no dubbing. Both songs, "Can't Help Lovin' That
Man" and "Bill," not only require a voice but vocal skill of a high degree. Coaching her, Edens knew from the very start that his efforts
were in vain. Accompanying her at the piano, he recorded a test which
turned out to be pale, thin and tentative. He decided to audition voice
doubles: Marni Nixon, Anita Ellis, Carole Richards and Annette Warren. He found Warren's singing voice best suited as a match for Gardner's speaking voice.

When it came to the prerecordings Gardner still insisted on singing
the songs herself. As a precaution a set of tracks was also made by
Warren.

Before making any takes Warfield went through his whole number
once with the orchestra for the benefit of the sound engineer. Edens
picked up the phone in the monitor room and called Freed, who was in
the commissary having lunch with Mayer. "Arthur, you *must* come to
Stage 1 right now and bring Mr. Mayer!"

The commissary, almost adjacent to the recording stage, frequently
was a stopover for employees with a few minutes to spare before returning to their offices. And so it was that day. By the time Freed and
Mayer arrived, everybody on the crowded stage felt something special

338

was going on. Warfield made his first take of "Ol' Man River," the first and also the last. When the recording was played back on the big horns for everyone to hear, there was uproarious applause. Mayer had tears in his eyes and Freed even stopped playing with his coins. Edens had succeeded in what he had set out to do: This performance was truly sensational.

Five weeks after the keel was laid, the *Cotton Blossom,* complete, was resting proudly in the water, her 19½-foot paddle wheel ready to spin, her stack smoking, her boilers set and ready to provide sufficient steam to operate an ear-splitting whistle and a calliope.

"We drained the lake," says Smith, "and constructed the boat as you would a house on top of steel pontoons." The boat measured 171 feet in length over-all. It had a 34-foot beam and was 57 feet to the tip of her stacks. The 19½-foot paddle wheel, with its nineteen buckets or paddles, was powered by two modern aircraft engines of 225 horse-power each. This power was transferred to a belt drive which went to a three-speed transmission.

The show boat had three decks: the Texas (top), the second and the main. Behind the walls of the lower deck was a veritable jungle of machinery. Two oil-burning asbestos tanks generated smoke for the main stacks. Two boilers provided steam for the whistle, for escape at the sides of the boat and for the main stacks on the rear to simulate steam piston exhaust, and for the calliope.

"It was impossible to have the boat navigate itself, because the lake was only ten feet deep on one end and four on the other," Smith says. "Therefore, we laid out the course of the boat and put two retard-ing cables on the stern so we could steer it, and three touring winches on the bow so we could aim it in any direction for a given number of feet. Thirty seven men were needed to operate the boat, using a walky-talky ship-to-shore intercommunication. I said, 'Let's try the boat. Start the paddle, make it go faster, it's now showing enough white wa-ter,' which it didn't; it looked almost insipid. So I got some expanded metal laths and put them on each paddle and that churned the water deliciously and made kind of whipped cream in the back."[6]

Sidney recalls looking at Smith's designs for the boat. "Jack," I said, "I'd love to have a double staircase." And he said, 'On boats?— I've never built one.' "Is there any problem?" I asked. 'No, if you want it you've got it.' "

Smith, on the other hand, contends that he had the idea from the outset. "I thought, you know, stairways in musicals are A B C types (left, center and right). So I said, 'Why don't we put a show business front end on the boat?' " What Smith is referring to is a staircase on either side and the gangplank in the middle.

[6] The total cost of constructing the *Cotton Blossom* was $126,468. It was probably the most expensive prop ever built.

A little baseball game between scenes: Robert Sterling is at bat and the catcher is Joe E. Brown. M-G-M

"The boat's got to be bigger," Sidney remembers saying. "You've got the boat, but I've got no room for the camera! So we had to lengthen it, which caused a lot of riot." Eddie Stones, head of construction, recalls that they did not modify the boat but constructed a separate outrigger which was placed in the middle of the lake to make it possible to shoot from the sides and the back.

"After the boat was built," recalls Sidney, "came the moment they were going to flood the lake and see if the damn thing would float or fall over. That was a tense moment." Sidney's anxiety seems to have been unwarranted since the boat was resting on steel pontoons.

To give the boat extra buoyancy however, Smith had frogmen go under water nightly to add lead weights to the sides of the boat in accordance with the daily variance of the load. Along the side of the boat Smith built a little shore of Natchez with all the architecture, the buildings, the station and the bales of cotton, with a lane leading up to the little village on the hill.

Alton had to improvise the performers' arrival on the *Cotton Blossom.* He did it in blitzkrieg fashion: giving directions, grouping his dancers, shouting for props. "Eight of you on the right, eight of you on the left, sixteen across the boat, the rest of you come in underneath on both sides! Girls, get some tambourines." To achieve his total visual effect Alton was greatly helped by Plunkett's imaginative costumes.

Plunkett worked very differently than, for instance, Irene Sharaff. While she would make a sketch and have the fabric manufactured, Plunkett used a more realistic, much less costly approach. "I learned very early in my career never to sit down and make a sketch with a fabric I hoped to find, because it doesn't work that way. Get the fabric and feel it and know what kind of a costume it would make—and then design the costume. For example, a salesman showed me a French fabric which was fuchsia and green satin stripes. It was a stunning piece of silk. So I designed a costume in that fabric for Kathryn Grayson."[7]

In a number of scenes fog played a dominant role. Shooting in late November–December, natural fog would often flow in from the Pacific. However, no two days were alike in light quality. It was Rosher's uncanny ability to remember all the camera and lighting details of the original setup that enabled the company to resume shooting as though there had been no interruption.

One day the *Cotton Blossom* nearly burned down. One of the tanks generating the smoke for the stacks by oil injection caught fire. With the exception of a few actors and some special effects men, the entire crew was ashore. The flames hit the Texas deck first and spread rapidly. The access road leading to the embankment was a narrow coun-

[7] The cost of the costumes for the production totaled $98,725.

Kathryn Grayson and Ava Gardner relax on the top deck of the *Cotton Blossom,* while Sydney Guilaroff's assistant, Jane Gorton, arranges Grayson's hair. M-G-M

try lane, which made it extremely hazardous for the fire brigade to get their equipment in position. "It pretty near cost us the whole ship," says Smith. "We had to refurbish and repaint the boat and provide better safety measures,"[8]

John Lee Mahin visited the set one day. "I remember Margaret Booth coming to me and saying, 'Well, he's shooting this all wrong. I don't know how it's going to be cut.' Well, she was only the supervising cutter for the studio, really, and I saw some of it and I didn't see anything wrong."

When Sidney became ill Edens replaced him. In the scene he directed, Gardner and Sterling leave the *Cotton Blossom* for the last time, which leads into Warfield's performance of "Ol' Man River." Although Edens had never directed before, he knew exactly what he wanted and went about it with his usual practical, unaffected attitude. "Roger directed this scene very well and most efficiently," says Simone, "because he was so totally adverse to advertising himself. The crew had known him for years and realized his enormous knowledge in every phase of picturemaking and responded accordingly. There were no problems whatsoever."

When the sequence was assembled in a rough cut, Edens invited Ira Gershwin to come to see it. "Now we can do *Porgy and Bess*," he said as soon as Warfield's last note had faded. Little did Gershwin know at that moment he not only had his Porgy but also had his Bess. Warfield was married to Leontyne Price.[9]

Sidney had shot "Can't Help Lovin' That Man" and "Bill" during the early part of production. After a couple of weeks of screening the two scenes for a number of in- and outsiders, Warren was called back to rerecord the songs, now to Gardner's lip-synch. What ensued until after the production had closed was a kind of a parlor game: Warren's tracks were in; Warren's tracks were out. Gardner's tracks were in, and then they were out; and so on and so forth, depending on the comment of whoever had seen the sequences last.

The closing shot of the picture shows Gardner watching the *Cotton Blossom* winding her way down the Mississippi. "I painted the opposite side of the river," says Smith, "and had it hung right into the water. It gave the effect of the boat moving many miles downstream."

The picture closed production on January 9, 1951. Freed, Edens and Sidney took a look at a rough cut. They were not thrilled. The picture was slow and draggy; it had no momentum. A solution had to be found.

Edens studied the film in detail. This was his picture and he was not going to let it founder. He came to the conclusion: Gaylord and Mag-

[8] Restoration cost: $66,955.

[9] The Warfield and Price revival of *Porgy and Bess* began its European tour on September 7, 1952.

342

Ava Gardner hears
Kathryn Grayson audi-
tioning for a job in a
Chicago night club.
M-G-M

nolia stay rich too long and remain poor too long, delaying Gaylord abandoning her; in the final scene, Gaylord comes to the dock, sees his child Kim[10] for the first time; does a reprise of "Make Believe"; Magnolia approaches them and suddenly a little old lady appears who does a three-minute monologue reminiscing about their past.

Then Edens began to cut the picture. The rich and the poor scenes were tightened to the bone. He took out the little old lady altogether. He then took shots of Gaylord and Magnolia's reactions to the old lady's ramblings and wound up with the couple embracing—with no dialogue—which he ultimately would emphasize in the scoring of the entire scene.

In his underscoring of the picture, Edens—in the main—used "Make Believe" and "You Are Love." This effected the same kind of emotional continuity that he had brought about in *Till the Clouds Roll By*.

Before starting the dubbing of the picture Simone asked Edens, "And who is singing?" The answer was a not very enthusiastic: "Ava."

[10] Kim explains in that scene the origin of her name: "The stork dropped me plunk in the middle of Kentucky, Illinois and Missouri."

The picture was previewed at the Bay Theatre, Pacific Palisades, March 22, 1951. The one change that was made afterward was that Gardner's voice was out and Warren's voice was in. At the second preview on April 3, 1951, at the Picwood Theatre, West Los Angeles, this change had a very noticeable and positive effect on the audience. The New York preview was held at Loew's 72nd Street Theatre on May 21, 1951. As with previous New York sneak previews the studio engaged an outside organization to conduct a "preview survey." Film Research Surveys usually handed out 358 cards: splitting them in half between men and women. Two thirds were given to those under thirty and the remainder, to those over thirty years of age. The report indicated 51 per cent considered it excellent; 39 per cent, very good and 10 per cent, good. Gardner was rated highest, with 78 per cent male and 80 per cent female. When asked whether they would recommend *Show Boat* to a friend: 100 per cent remarked: "See it!"

When Simone and Jesse Kaye discussed the forthcoming soundtrack album he felt that for reasons of exploitation and sale Ava Gardner's name on the cover would be an added plus. Simone took great pains in the dubbing of Gardner's tracks, backing up her voice with the accompaniments to make her sound more palatable.

Show Boat was completed at a cost of $2,295,429. It went into release on July 13, 1951, and grossed in excess of $8,650,000.

ARTHUR FREED
  MGM
DEAR ARTHUR I THINK SHOW BOAT WILL BE A DAZZLING SUCCESS
I AM GOING TO PHONE YOU SOON AND TALK TO YOU ABOUT IT
CONGRATULATIONS
  OSCAR

Freed was called upon to produce[11] the twenty-fourth annual Academy Awards on March 28, 1952, held at the RKO Pantages Theatre. During the preceding year he had three pictures that would qualify: *Royal Wedding, Show Boat* and *An American in Paris*. Early in the proceedings, Charles Brackett, president of the Academy, came out to present an Honorary Award: "The Board of Governors unanimously voted the following—'In appreciation for his contribution to the creation and improvement of the motion picture musical film; not only because of his extreme versatility as an actor-singer, director and dancer, but because of his specific and brilliant achievements in the art of choreography on film . . . the Academy is pleased to present an Honorary Award to . . . Mr. Gene Kelly.' Mr. Kelly is in Germany. Stanley Donen will accept the award for him."

Brackett then introduced Darryl F. Zanuck, three-time Thalberg Award winner, who said, "Last night the Board of Governors of the Academy voted the Irving G. Thalberg Memorial Award to Mr. Arthur

[11] Referred to that year as general director.

Freed, for his extraordinary accomplishment in the making of musical pictures. Turning out musicals can be a routine job. It isn't with Mr. Freed. In his hands the film musical has taken on a new scale. He has replaced mere prettiness of production with extraordinary beauty. He has brought a thorough knowledge of music and dancing to his job and learned to mix the elements of charm, humor and melody in a production which makes an Arthur Freed musical completely distinctive. His *Show Boat* and *An American in Paris* are perfect examples of creative art. It is no accident that the producer of *An American in Paris* is a connoisseur and collector of modern art. In that picture he did more to bring the French impressionists into the delighted consciousness of this country than ten thousand solemn lectures could have done. By his achievements he has added stature to the whole industry. Arthur, will you come up, please? I am running out of superlatives."

Freed, visibly moved, fondled the coveted bust of the late Metro production chief as he expressed his gratitude.

"Twice," he told the audience, "the name Irving G. Thalberg has been the most important name in my professional life. First when I came to Metro—and tonight. I am deeply grateful."

When the individual awards for outstanding contribution in the major categories were handed out, the first Oscar to *American* went to Orry-Kelly, Walter Plunkett and Irene Sharaff for "Color Costume Design," followed by five Oscars for Keogh Gleason; Preston Ames;

Hirschfeld's drawing of the *Show Boat* cast when the picture went into release. M-G-M

Johnny Green and Saul Chaplin; Alfred Gilks and John Alton; and Alan Jay Lerner.

The tenseness usually felt during the final twenty minutes of the Academy ceremonies seemed to be missing. Winners Karl Malden, Kim Hunter, Humphrey Bogart and Vivien Leigh had been generally expected. When George Stevens took his award for "Best Direction" on *A Place in the Sun,* it was taken for granted that it would also receive the "Best Picture" Award.

"The retreating crowd was stunned into momentary silence when Jesse Lasky read *'An American in Paris,'*" said *Daily Variety.* "The audible gasp from every section of the house was quickly replaced by applause as Arthur Freed trotted up the stairs."

Clutching his two statuettes, Freed beamed, saying, "It's a doubleheader."

This was the first time a musical had won the award for the best picture of the year since 1936, when *The Great Ziegfeld* was so honored, and only the third time in the history of the Academy that a musical has had its way, the only other having been *The Broadway Melody* (1929), with a score by Arthur Freed and Nacio Herb Brown.

Out of ten nominations that went to the Freed Unit, *American* took six Oscars. The four remaining nominations were to Vincente Minnelli, "Best Director" (*An American in Paris*); Alan Jay Lerner and Burton Lane, "Best Song," "Too Late Now" (*Royal Wedding*); Adolph Deutsch and Conrad Salinger, "Best Scoring of a Musical Picture" (*Show Boat*); and Adrienne Fazan, "Film Editing" (*An American in Paris*).

On March 24, 1953, a group of about fifty guests were assembled at Freed's house. The occasion was the ceremony during which the French consul general would bestow on Freed the coveted Légion d'honneur. The award read: "To Arthur Freed for the many contributions to making French culture better to the American and International public."

11

SINGIN' IN THE RAIN
THE BELLE OF NEW YORK

The New Yorker magazine film critic Pauline Kael wrote about *Singin' in the Rain:* "This exuberant and malicious satire of Hollywood in the late twenties is perhaps the most enjoyable of all movie musicals —just about the best Hollywood musical of all time." Several years after the film was released Betty Comden and Adolph Green were in Paris and reported: "Suddenly a small lithe figure came sliding across at us like a hockey player zooming over the ice. It was Truffaut himself [the famous French director] and he was breathless and awestruck at meeting the authors of *'Chantons sous la Pluie.'* In total disbelief we heard him go on to say, through his interpreter, that he has seen the film many, many times, knew every frame of it, felt it was a classic, and that he and Alain Renais, among others, went to see it regularly at a little theatre called the Pagode, where it was even at that moment in the middle of a several-month run."

The picture's title song was written by Nacio Herb Brown and Arthur Freed and the score of the film consisted mainly of songs written by these two men.

In 1921, Freed met Brown. Together they wrote a song titled "When Buddha Smiles," Brown collaborating musically with King Zany. Freed and Brown took their song to New York and began to peddle it. Harms,

Arthur Freed during his early days as an assistant director at Famous Players-Lasky (later Paramount) Pictures.
RUTH FREED AKST

Inc., agreed to publish it. Now the two young men approached Paul Whiteman, at that time the king of Jazz. He liked it and recorded it; it sold over a million copies. Even though this was their first hit together, the two separately had had a modicum of success; Brown with an instrumental "Doll Dance" and Freed with "I Cried for You" ("Now it's your turn to cry over me") with Abe Lyman and Gus Arnheim.

The quick success on Tin Pan Alley did not tie Freed to New York. The movies, silent as they were in 1928, lured him back to California. He started working at Famous Players-Lasky as an assistant director to Alfred Green and played mood music, on the piano, on the shooting stages.

Brown and Freed collaborated on writing songs for Carter De Haven's *Hollywood's Music Box Revue*. Shortly thereafter Freed opened his own theatre in Los Angeles, the Orange Grove, where he produced such plays as *White Cargo, Rain, Desire Under the Elms* and *The Pickings;* for the latter he wrote a number of songs with Harry Barris and to entertain the audience during the intermission he engaged an unknown singer, Bing Crosby.[1]

Suddenly motion pictures began to talk—and sing. And Irving Thalberg, head of production at M-G-M, decided to make a musical. He discussed the idea with Ralph Spence, his most successful writer of

[1] Crosby later introduced Brown-Freed's "Temptation" in *Going Hollywood* (1933) and "Beautiful Girl" in *Stage Mother* (1933).

348

screen titles for silent pictures. Spence happened to be a friend of Freed and Brown's and with what seems to have been a prophetic instinct, he advised them to be prepared. By the time they met Thalberg they came fortified with what they considered the best from their trunk. "Actually we wrote 'The Broadway Melody,' 'The Wedding of the Painted Doll' and 'You Were Meant for Me' before we met Thalberg," says Freed. "Thalberg spoke to us about a musical he wanted to make for which Eddie Goulding had a story he called *Whoopee*," recalled Brown, "but he couldn't use the title because Ziegfeld did a show called *Whoopee* with [Eddie] Cantor. Goulding's was a backstage story, patterned after the two Duncan sisters."

Billy Rose was on the Metro lot at the time and wanted the song-writing assignment for himself. He proceeded to write a song with Freed's title "Broadway Melody" and hired an orchestra to demonstrate it for the studio head. When Thalberg heard it he said, "I want to hear Brown and Freed's songs with that orchestra before I decide." With his wife, Norma Shearer, his brother-in-law, Douglas Shearer, and Freed and Brown, they went to KFI radio station. With the sixteen-piece orchestra, Brown at the piano and Freed singing "The Wedding of

When M-G-M released this photograph the caption read: "Leo, the World's greatest living trade-mark, now becomes the World's only talking trade-mark. Here we see him getting his voice registered for use in Metro-Goldwyn-Mayer pictures." M-G-M

the Painted Doll," "You Were Meant for Me" and "The Broadway Melody," it wasn't too difficult for Thalberg to decide.

Adopting Freed's song title for the picture title *The Broadway Melody* would be Hollywood's *first* "all talking, all singing, all dancing" musical. With Charles King, Anita Page and Bessie Love in the leading roles, the picture went into production with Harry Beaumont directing. The film was being shot in black and white, but Thalberg felt "The Wedding of the Painted Doll" needed color and would make a perfect finale for the picture. This, the first color musical number ever photographed, was shot when Thalberg was in New York. When he returned to the studio he didn't like it and said, 'Let's do it again,' a pronouncement he often made on many of his pictures.

The Broadway Melody took twenty-six days to complete at a cost of $379,000. The world première took place at Grauman's Chinese Theatre on Friday evening, February 1, 1929. The picture went on to gross a record $4,366,000 ($2,808,000 domestic and $1,558,000 foreign). When the Oscars were being handed out on April 3, 1930, *The Broadway Melody* was named the "Best Picture of the Year."

This, their first screen effort, landed Brown and Freed a studio contract. During that year they received $250 a week from M-G-M and made $500,000 from royalties. It also put them into the A-A classification in ASCAP, having five of the ten best-selling songs in America.

In the wake of the startling birth of the talkies, total confusion reigned within the Hollywood studios: Elocution teachers and vocal coaches had a field day; sultry vamps labored to sound as sexy as they looked; male stars were frantic to get rid of their southern or midwestern accents; others simply had to learn to speak English. The sound de-

The opening night program: February 1, 1929

Adolph Green, Betty Comden
and Arthur Freed in the
Freed Unit's conference room
discussing the screenplay for
Singin' in the Rain. ARTHUR
FREED ARCHIVES

partments worked overtime to develop a method for the synchronization
of sound and picture.

Brown and Freed's next assignment was a dramatic picture, *The
Pagan,* for Ramon Navarro. One morning, at eleven o'clock, they were
asked to write a title song for the film; at one o'clock that same day
they delivered "Pagan Love Song." Freed recalls the publisher Jack
Robbins asking him, "What the hell is a page-an? How the hell am I
going to plug that song?" "That song" sold over 1,600,000 copies.
(This, it may be remembered, is the same Mr. Robbins who thought
"Over the Rainbow" was unsingable and opted for taking it out of *The
Wizard of Oz.*)

Hot on *Broadway Melody*'s success, M-G-M conjured up *Hollywood Revue of 1929,* bringing together practically all of the studio's
stars (with the exception of Garbo). Brown and Freed contributed "You
Were Meant for Me," "Tommy Atkins on Parade" and "Singin' in the
Rain." "I'll never forget how Herb and I got around to writing 'Singin'
in the Rain,'" says Freed. "He came to me one afternoon with the
news that he'd just written a great tune for a coloratura soprano. He
sat down and played it with all the classic trills. All I could think of
was that a vamp in the bass and a few minor changes would give it
the zip for some lyrics I'd written." Brown played it again Freed's
way. "Singin' in the Rain" was the show-stopping color finale of
Hollywood Revue of 1929. It grossed $2,421,000.

On May 29, 1950, Comden and Green came back to the studio,
claiming they had just signed a new contract under which they would
write both screenplay and lyrics, with a clause stating that if existing
songs were to be used, these could only be from the catalogue of Irving

Berlin, Cole Porter or Rodgers and Hammerstein. But actually they were still under the contract they had signed in November 1948.

Freed was not exactly happy when the two writers abruptly called his attention to their "new contract." "Kids, I never heard of any such clause," he said. "Now, about *Singin' in the Rain*. With *my* songs . . ." Comden and Green say, "We sneered imperiously, skulked out of the office and went on strike." After two war-torn weeks during which they repeatedly accused Freed of reneging on an official document, something told them to look at the contract. What they found was: "M-G-M is not obligated to have Betty Comden and Adolph Green write the lyrics of the compositions for the screenplay on which they are working." With that they had to buckle down and go to work.

They sat for hours listening to Edens playing Freed and Brown songs, ranging all the way from "Should I?" to "Would You?" This threw them back in time. "Many of these songs had been written for the earliest musical pictures made," they say, "between 1929 and 1931, during the painful transition from silents to sound. And it occurred to us that, rather than try to use them in a sophisticated, contemporary story or a gay-nineties extravaganza, they would bloom at their happiest in something that took place in the very period in which they had been written. With this decision made, we began to feel the ground beneath our feet at last."

Through the studio grapevine the two writers heard that Howard Keel had been penciled in for the lead and they made a few dispirited stabs at a yarn about a minor Western actor in silents who makes it big with the advent of sound as a singing cowboy. But their thoughts kept coming back to the dramatic upheavals of that period, when great careers were wrecked because the public's image of a favorite would be instantly destroyed by a voice that did not match the fabled face. "We remembered particularly the downfall of John Gilbert, the reigning king of the silent screen in 1928, whose career was finished off by one single talking picture, in which, with his director's encouragement, he improvised his own love scene, insisting on the phrase 'I love you,' repeated many times with growing intensity, exactly as he had done it the year before in front of the silent camera."

All of this inspired Comden and Green to build their story on just that period, transposing their hero from an actor to a song-and-dance man. In their view this would be a part more suitable for Gene Kelly rather than Howard Keel. "But it was impossible for us to approach Kelly, because he was deeply involved, head and feet, starring in and choreographing *An American in Paris*."

Set to direct the picture, Donen was in on all of this from the very beginning. He recalls, "I can remember it as though it was yesterday. When they came to write the picture we talked about 'We're going to make this movie of silent to sound' and 'It's going to be with the

Freed catalogue.' So we ran a series of old Metro movies, such as *Platinum Blonde* and *Bombshell,* to see if one could be made into a musical. After Comden and Green crapped around, saying 'Shall we do this— shall we do that?' they started writing the picture for Gene and me— with Gene in the lead, and *not* Howard Keel."

After what the two writers considered "an agonizing month," trying to get a grip on themselves and their screenplay, it all began to fall into place and their work "gushed in a relatively exuberant flow." "To our gratified surprise," they say, "not only did Roger seem delighted with it all, but Arthur, to whom we read each section as we completed it, gave it his happy approval."

Comden and Green maintain that Dore Schary, having replaced L. B. Mayer, gave his go-ahead to the production. However, Mayer was still at the studio and it was he who said "O.K."[2]

"At Arthur's suggestion," recalls Comden, "Gene, who was by now finished shooting *An American in Paris,* was given the script to read, and we geared ourselves for a friendly refusal. Instead he and Stanley, who also read it, came rushing over to us in the commissary the next day, bursting with enthusiasm and filled with ideas."

Before Kelly went on a much-needed holiday, without any premonition of the impact *An American in Paris* would make on the audiences of the world, he took the time to talk to Comden and Green. "So much of it was based on early material they had written for themselves when they were the Revuers," says Kelly, "that I knew the material backwards." Although he liked the idea of doing a big ballet he didn't want to end *this* picture with it, as was indicated in the script.

By present-day standards the following Breen Office memo reads like fictional farce:

Dear Mr. Mayer:

We have read the complete script, dated April 11, 1951, for your forthcoming production *Singin' in the Rain,* and wish to report that, with the exceptions noted below, this material seems to meet the requirements of the Production Code.

At the outset, we direct your particular attention to the need for the greatest possible care in the selection and photographing of the costumes and dresses for your women. The Production Code makes it mandatory that the intimate parts of the body—specifically, the breasts of women—be fully covered at all times. Any compromise with this regulation will compel us to withhold approval of your picture.

Page 5: We assume that the girl in the safari outfit will be adequately clothed.

[2] Mayer resigned June 22, 1951, three days after *Singin' in the Rain* went before the camera.

Page 6: Care will be needed in the burlesque house scene, both in the selection of women's costumes, and the routine performed by Don and Cosmo.

Pages 24 and 25: None of the show girls in the process of changing their clothes should be shown in their underwear. Also, their dancing costumes must be selected with great care.

Pages 27 and 28: This dialogue between Cosmo and the girl must be delivered without any offensive sex suggestion flavor:

Girl: Oh, Mr. Brown—could you really get me into the movies?

Cosmo: I should think so—

Girl: Really?

Cosmo: There are ways—

Girl: Oh, what would I have to do?

Page 31: The same applies to this dressing scene.

Page 33: The following line by Cosmo is somewhat pointed and we suggest that it be altered: "She's the first dame who's said no since you were four."

Page 36: Lina's costume in this scene should also be selected carefully.

Page 53: Good taste will be essential in handling this scene where Lina is "wired for sound."

Page 65: Don's line "What are you doing later?" approaches the element of sex perversion and we ask that it be eliminated.

We wish to remind you that we cannot approve photographing women in their underwear. Please bear this in mind when Don runs through the dressing room.

You understand, of course, that our final judgment will be based upon the finished picture.

Cordially yours,
Joseph I. Breen

When it came to casting, Freed wanted Oscar Levant to play Cosmo, Kelly's partner and a piano player. "Betty, Adolph, Gene and myself," says Donen, "were just frantic. We wanted a dancer for the part." They got their way and Donald O'Connor was cast.

For the part of the silent movie star Lina Lamont, Nina Foch was screen tested but was found not true to type. Jean Hagen, under contract to the studio, got the role.

Once again Freed did a provocative piece of casting. Debbie Reynolds, a girl who had done a small part in a Metro picture, was set to play the girl Gene falls in love with. The cast was completed with Millard Mitchell, Douglas Fowley, Rita Moreno and guest star Cyd Charisse. Lennie Hayton was in charge of musical direction; orchestration by Conrad Salinger and Skip Martin; Walter Plunkett for costume design; Randall Duell for art direction; John Alton on camera; and Roger Edens, associate producer.

354

Plunkett had the task of creating more than five hundred costumes for principals and bit players. "I entered the business at the height of the flapper's reign," he recalls. "Many of Jean Hagen's costumes are, as nearly as I can remember, duplicates of some I did in all seriousness for Lilyan Tashman. And she was the epitome of chic at that time."

When Plunkett brought in his first sketches to Freed he objected, "Oh, my God, skirts were never this short at that time, Walter, they can't be." Plunkett thought that for the satirical effect this kind of exaggeration was essential and he went to Edens. "I said, 'Help, for God sakes, we've got to keep this and fight Arthur on this thing.'" In the course of conversation with Freed, Edens tactfully introduced his view on the costumes and Plunkett got his way.

For a plush party given by the head of "Monumental Pictures," Plunkett allowed his reminiscences free reign, remembering such familiar figures of the day as the flapper in beaded chiffon, the vamp in black velvet and jet and the heroine with wide eyes and baby face in short, bouffant net. "For that sequence we used more than one thousand yards of ostrich feather fringe and fifty pounds of beads."

The design and execution of Plunkett's costumes cost the production $157,250.

Turning the clock back on Hollywood was not as simple as it might look to the casual observer. Randall Duell and set decorator Jacques Mapes spent months unearthing designs for the actual cubicle to house the cameras. Those early microphones had to be re-created from originals long since relegated to museums. Old Cooper-Hewitt stage lights were built to specifications and early recording and dubbing equipment was reproduced. Twenty-five-year-old still photos of the M-G-M studio played an important role in duplicating the studio of Monumental Pictures. Even an old glass sound stage, last remaining relic of the early days, was pressed into service. The stage, for many years used as a building for the construction of equipment, was emptied, and once again those glass walls heard the grinding of an old silent camera and the inevitable "Hearts and Flowers," played as mood music by musicians on the set. For the mansion occupied by Kelly as an early-day movie star, Duell-Mapes used the same tables, chairs, rugs and chandeliers that graced the rooms in which Gilbert and Garbo romanced in *Flesh and the Devil*. Debbie Reynolds even used Andy Hardy's jalopy.

The songs selected for the picture were "Broadway Melody," "Should I?," "Beautiful Girl," "All I Do Is Dream of You," "You Are My Lucky Star," "I Got a Feeling You're Foolin'," "Broadway Rhythm," "Would You?," "Good Morning," "Singin' in the Rain," "You Were Meant for Me" and "Make 'Em Laugh," Freed and Brown's new song, which also was their last collaboration.

"Fit As a Fiddle" (1933) had music by Al Hoffman and Al

Randall Duell's drawing for Kelly's "Singin' in the Rain" number, as a take was being made of the location; and the famous photograph from the sequence. M-G-M and GENE KELLY COLLECTION

Goodhart and lyrics by Freed; "Moses" had music by Roger Edens, lyrics by Comden and Green, and both were incorporated into the score.

Rehearsals started on April 12, 1951. Debbie Reynolds worked with Ernie Flatt, concentrating on tap dancing, while Kelly, Donen and Haney worked on the staging of all the musical numbers.

When production started on June 18, Donen and Kelly did not get along with cameraman John Alton, and he was replaced by Hal Rosson with whom they had worked in *On the Town*.

Kelly had a problem working out the "Singin' in the Rain" number. "Here I found myself with a classic and I always hated the Jeanette MacDonald-Nelson Eddy way of going into a song," he says. "Roger came up with the solution: 'Start off with doodedoo do—doodedoo do,' he said."

During the dress rehearsal of the number, at around 5 P.M., the technicians noticed their man-made storm losing intensity. Instead of the desired downpour, all they got was a tired drizzle, and this no matter how high they turned the control valves. All of the studio's water tanks were checked. Finally, a survey was made of the local water situation. It was late summer and at five o'clock each day local residents of Culver City turned on their sprinkler systems in their gardens.

"They thought I was crazy," says Kelly, "because I went to the set and had them dig holes in the ground to accumulate the rain water, to give me puddles which I would use for certain steps in my dance routine."

The scene with its famous lamppost was shot on "East Side Street." When Kelly was laying out the number, Duell came down to the set and made chalk marks for the spots on the street that were to be hollowed out. "Of course they had to be exact," he says, "because it was essential to Kelly's dance rhythm."

It took just a day and a half to complete the number.

In several scenes Debbie Reynolds is lip-synching and rerecording Jean Hagen's speaking voice. "We used Jean Hagen dubbing Debbie dubbing Jean," Donen explains. "Jean's voice is quite remarkable, and it was supposed to be cultured speech—and Debbie had that terrible western noise." When Reynolds is supposedly singing for Hagen her voice was dubbed by Betty Royce.

Kelly and Donen split up their work; Kelly would be shooting on one sound stage and Donen on another. "By this time," says Kelly, "I'd tell Stanley to go over there and direct that scene and I'd see that *my* number gets done. That was a marvelous kind of interdependence and independence we had with each other."

When the selection of songs was made it became apparent that

'Wiring Lina Up for Sound.' (Left to right): Douglas Fowley, Gene Kelly, Jean Hagen and Kathleen Freeman. M-G-M and GENE KELLY COLLECTION

there was nothing in the Brown-Freed catalogue suitable for Donald O'Connor. Donen went to see Freed. "We need another song, Arthur."

"What kind of a song do you want?" Freed asked.

"Well, it should be kind of 'Be a Clown' type number from *The Pirate,* because he's trying to cheer Gene up. Arthur came back with 'Make 'Em Laugh,' which, in my opinion, is 100 per cent plagiarism, and partly we are to blame. None of us had the courage to say to him, 'For Christ sake, it obviously works for the number, but it's a stolen song, Arthur.'"

"Make 'Em Laugh" was rehearsed and recorded. While it was being shot Irving Berlin was visiting Freed and the two went to the set. Freed asked Donen to have the new song put on the playback machine for Berlin to hear.

"So we all walked over to the machine and Arthur started jingling his coins. Berlin is a tiny little man—his head started to move in the direction of the sound. 'Why, why, why—that's "Be a Clown,"' he said, 'I have never heard anything like that in my life!' He then began to sputter and turned to Arthur. 'Who wrote that song?' 'Well, the kids and I—we all got together and . . . come on, Irving, that's enough now.'" Donen concludes: "'The kids and I!' He wasn't going to take the rap alone on that. And Irving Berlin, of all people—one of Cole Porter's closest friends."

Only a man of Cole Porter's tact and distinction would have chosen to ignore the existence of that song.

During the early part of the production Donen and Edens went to look at the first batch of Plunkett's costumes. They were so delighted that they decided to do a separate fashion number. "We all got together on that," says Plunkett. "We tossed around different ideas; what are camp things of the period? like pearls with tweed, and I said, 'Monkey fur as trimming, for instance.' I then began to list the things I would do in silly fashion." The number entitled "Beautiful Girl," sung by Jimmy Thompson, had a spoken narrative, written by Edens, describing a costume for each month of the year. All those who saw the number in the process of being shot and in the rushes roared with laughter.

Kelly had laid out "The Broadway Ballet," depicting himself as a young hoofer of New York's roaring twenties, from burlesque shows and cheap night clubs to stardom on the Great White Way. Duell made renderings of sets, varying from the night club, the speakeasies, theatre interiors, Fifth Avenue on a crowded afternoon and an imaginative depiction of Times Square at night, with the familiar signs of Broadway suspended in midair against an impressionistic background. Originally this number was to cost $80,000, but now it was estimated at approximately $600,000. Without a moment's hesitation Schary and Schenck told them to go ahead.

For the fifteen-minute ballet sequence Lennie Hayton translated

One of the sequences from "The Broadway Ballet" featuring Gene Kelly and Cyd Charisse. M-G-M and GENE KELLY COLLECTION

thirty-two bars constituting the melodies of "Broadway Melody" and "Broadway Rhythm" into a complete choreographic movement, capturing the spirit of the era. Hayton worked with Kelly, Donen and Haney in creating this ballet form from the popular songs, turning them into a symphonic arrangement as a background for the intricate choreography.

In a section of the ballet Cyd Charisse appears in a pink, dreamy wasteland, wrapped in a twenty-five-foot-long piece of white China silk, which at times billows up in the air. Haney worked with Charisse on the choreography, experimenting with the wind machines. By the time it was shot the white panel complemented every movement of Kelly and Charisse's *pas de deux*.

The ballet had rehearsed for one month and took two weeks to shoot.

"The biggest single joke of the entire picture," says Donen, "takes place after the ballet is over. Kelly and O'Connor are in a projection

360

The closing shot with Debbie Reynolds and Gene Kelly. M-G-M

room describing this fifteen-minute ballet to the head of the studio, Millard Mitchell. Then one sees the entire ballet—$600,000 worth. And now we're back in the projection room. Kelly says to Mitchell, 'Well, what do you think of it?' And the producer replies, 'I can't really visualize it until I see it on the screen.' "

Singin' in the Rain closed production on November 21, 1951. As on all of Freed's pictures the closing day was celebrated with a set party, which Duell arranged on Stage 28 in the standing set of the producer's house. "We brought the guests into the stage door and in order to get in I rigged up several pipes of rain. So, the only way you could get to the party was by taking an umbrella, which we handed out at the door and everybody walked through the rain."

The following is an interoffice memorandum from Freed to Ralph Wheelright, studio executive in charge of advertising display:

To: Mr. Ralph Wheelwright
Subject: SINGIN' IN THE RAIN
From: Arthur Freed   Date: 7/30/51

Dear Ralph:

Just received the copy of the advertising billing for *Singin' in the Rain,* and I notice that you omitted the most important credit of the last ten years in not giving credit to those famous writers and composers of screen musicals, Nacio Herb Brown and Arthur Freed.

I do not care how much you reduce my credit as the producer, but as an artist I rebel against not receiving proper credit as a lyricist. I know you will plead you have been so tied up with *Quo Vadis* and learning how to spell Mervyn LeRoy, and your new duties on the Executive Board of this great studio have made you a little ruthless in giving anybody else credit.

However, remember the old days when you were just a fella like one of us—plugging along, and try to incorporate this credit, which after all, is the only thing that can sell the picture.

Thank you.

When the picture was being edited for the preview, several scenes were taken out of it such as Debbie Reynolds singing "You Are My Lucky Star" to a billboard of Kelly, and Kelly's song-and-dance rendition of "All I Do Is Dream of You," which he had done in an almost identical fashion as "I Got a Crush on You" in *An American in Paris*. Some tightening was done.

Singin' in the Rain was previewed at the De Anza Theatre, Riverside, on December 21 and again on March 11, 1952, at the Loew's 72nd Street Theatre in New York.

The picture cost $2,540,800 (over budget $620,996). It was released on April 10, 1952, and grossed $7,665,000.

On June 18, 1951, *The Belle of New York* began shooting. Promptly at 9 A.M. a horseshoe made of hundreds of flowers arrived with "Good Luck" wishes from the Kelly-Donen (*Singin' in the Rain*) company, which also went into production that same day.

Scanning the blackboard in the production department for daily activities, one unit manager muttered, "The Freed Unit is at it again."

Fred Astaire sits under horseshoe of flowers sent from the *Singin' in the Rain* company to *The Belle of New York* company, as Chuck Walters, director, and Arthur Freed cross their fingers for good luck. M-G-M

Ever since 1945, when Freed put *The Belle of New York* on his production schedule, Fred Astaire had expressed his keen interest in doing the picture. At one time the project had to be aborted during rehearsals because Judy Garland, Astaire's costar, dropped out.

Favorable circumstances now prompted Freed to put it on his active list. Charles Walters, Bob Alton, Harry Warren and Johnny Mercer were all available. Astaire had starred in a Jack Cummings picture and Freed wanted him back in his unit. As usual, Freed's eyes were on the future. Alan Lerner had planted a seed in Freed's mind: a fashion picture, with two leading couturiers in France, Mainbocher and Givenchy, as leading characters. Astaire would be ideal for the part of Mainbocher.

The Belle of New York revolves around a playboy, dependent on his puritanical aunt for his income, who has left five girls waiting at the altar. He discovers a young Salvation Army worker and becomes so in love that he is even talked into going to work. Convinced that he is not good enough for her, he breaks off the engagement, but she pursues him by pretending to be a vamp. In an effort to save her from the advances of a shady character in a night club, a brawl ensues, and the two are reconciled.

The only similarity between the comic opera of the same title (1898) and the screenplay of *The Belle of New York* is the character of the young welfare worker.

In order to give this slight thread of a story an added flavor, Freed decided to set it at the turn of the century, split in four seasons, in the style of the Currier and Ives paintings.

Warren and Mercer wrote eight new songs: "Seeing's Believing," "Oops," "Naughty But Nice," "Baby Doll," "Who Wants to Kiss the Bridegroom?," "Thank You, Mr. Currier, Thank You, Mr. Ives," "I Wanna Be a Dancin' Man" and the title song. Edens wrote one additional song: "Let a Little Love Come In."

Vera-Ellen would be costarring with Astaire.[3] Edens suggested Fifi D'Orsay for the role of the aunt, Walters wanted Mae West (but she wanted too much money), and finally Marjorie Main was cast. Alice Pearce and Clinton Sundberg were given the roles of Vera-Ellen's fellow mission workers. Keenan Wynn and Gale Robbins completed the cast.

With Walters at the helm, Alton staging the numbers, Adolph Deutsch as musical director, Conrad Salinger and Maurice de Packh orchestrating, Bobby Tucker as vocal arranger and Jack Smith as art director, the picture went before the camera.

Astaire's trick number "Seeing's Believing" had him dancing over Washington Square Arch and the rooftops of New York. "In order to

[3] Her voice double would be Anita Ellis.

Astaire has a brief go at being a Sanitation Department worker in *The Belle of New York*. M-G-M

The art director's still cameraman caught Freed on the set. From his expression, it doesn't look like things are going too smoothly (the disarray has nothing to do with it). M-G-M

have Fred float through the air," says Smith, "we did it against a blue backing. We also painted the floor and the sides of the building blue as well. And to have him jump from cornice to cornice, I used springboards, landing mats and trampolines." The film then went to the Ries department where Astaire was superimposed on the actual set.

Smith designed and constructed a horse-drawn trolley car for Astaire's specialty number "Oops." Astaire and Alton had to figure out how he would dance through the trolley, as it started and stopped. Ultimately his routine carried him onto the back of the horse. When Astaire rehearsed this precarious section he jumped off and twisted his ankle, and shooting of the number had to be delayed.

Al Jennings, the assistant director, observed; "Marjorie Main was always afraid of Alice Pearce, of what she might be doing behind her back; Main was scared to death that Pearce would steal a scene from her. Nobody could steal a scene from Marjorie Main!"

Each change of season was introduced by a still picture of the incoming scene, bordered by an ornate frame, in the Currier and Ives style. The frame then opened up and the picture unfroze as the action continued. The winter sequence opened on Vera-Ellen and Fred Astaire ice skating. Jack Smith comments: "Currier and Ives' prints are very hard to reproduce in cube form, because of their perspective. To make it

Judy Garland had Richard Avedon take this picture of her, which she autographed to Roger (Edens) "for life, forever—love, Judy." At the same sitting he took the very popular photograph in which she holds hundreds of
roses. ROGER EDENS ARCHIVES

come true we used a dry brush effect on the set pieces and the backdrop,
to make it look like a lithograph."

The Belle of New York closed production on October 3, 1951, at
a cost of $2,606,644. It was released February 2, 1952, and grossed
$1,993,000.

Variety and *The Hollywood Reporter* judged the picture as "light."
The New York papers found it even lighter. Astaire sees it differently:
"Arthur had this idea—and we all had this feeling—'Let's do the impossible': an old New York show with fantasy. As my partner I had a
girl who was a good dancer, Vera-Ellen. And some of the best dance
numbers you could ever get. It was just a musical show that did not
make it; and it makes me so mad, because *The Belle of New York*
was one of my favorite films." When Astaire read the reviews mentioning the "thin plot," it reminded him of the following incident: "When

the English critics lambasted a play by Noel Coward several years ago for being 'thin,' Coward retorted with: 'Very well—from now on I will write nothing but very fat plays for very fat critics.'"

Following the close of production of *The Belle of New York,* Edens and Walters, with Freed's permission, went to New York to prepare and stage Judy Garland's first appearance at the Palace. During the previous months Edens had squeezed time out of his busy schedule to put together Garland's show at the Paladium in London, a one-night affair. But the Palace was to be a four-week run and Garland's first appearance on Broadway. With his usual skill, he selected her material, arranged song medleys and wrote for her the by now notoriously famous opening:

> ". . . And so with deep humility
> I stand in front of you
> I'm proud to play the Palace
> It's like a dream come true.
> That is why I want to shout it up and down
> Just to tell Broadway that the two-a-day
>   is back in town!"

Edens had sent Judy Garland off to fame with his "Dear Mr. Gable." And now, at the most crucial time of her life, with these lines he put her on her feet once again.

To relax the terrified Judy, Walters went on with her opening night in the "tramp" number: "We're a Couple of Swells."[4]

Freed was proud of "his boys," and happy for Judy.

In January 1951, Freed had a meeting with Alan Lerner concerning his next assignment, *Huckleberry Finn.*

Quite a few years back, in 1944, Freed first thought of doing the Mark Twain classic as a musical. He had Sally Benson develop a screenplay, and Hugh Martin and Ralph Blane went to work on writing a score. In 1946, after their work was completed, Freed announced that Claude Jarman, Jr., would play the lead, a ten-year-old boy who had just become an M-G-M star in *The Yearling.* Suddenly Freed was faced with a problem: Although the completion of *Till the Clouds Roll By* had to be delayed because of Kern's death, on his active schedule, in various stages of production, were *Good News, Summer Holiday* and *The Pirate.* This proved too much for Freed, and he shelved *Huckleberry Finn* for the time being.

In 1950, Freed picked up where he had left off and engaged Donald Ogden Stewart to write an entirely new screenplay. He aban-

---

[4] To put her in a completely familiar atmosphere, Hugh Martin accompanied Judy at the piano onstage.

Irene Sharaff's costume designs for the Duke and some of Huck's friends. ARTHUR FREED ARCHIVES

ALAN JAY LERNER

Dear Chief:

       Yes, I'm really enclosing a lyric. And there isn't one line missing! I hope the shock won't be too great.

       "I'm From Missouri" is in the works and I'll have it in a few days at the latest. "I'll Wait For You By The River" has two lines missing. Gene's number I'll get to next week-end.

       I now weigh twenty-two pounds and have the color of the pages of a first edition of Dante's Inferno. Other than that I'm fine.

       Glad everything is going well. Keep me posted.

               Love, love, love,

               Alan Jay Lerner
               Fourth Assistant
               To The Second Secretary
               Of the First Ass-Kisser
               Of The Head of Music
               Department.

doned the Martin-Blane score and assigned Burton Lane and E. Y. Harburg to write a new one. Stewart had finished a first draft and the songwriters had written three songs when the McCarthy witch hunt began. Stewart and Harburg were among its first victims: they had to go.

Freed came to a logical conclusion: Alan Lerner had worked with Lane on *Royal Wedding;* Freed asked him to write a new screenplay and work with Lane on the score. While Lerner was at work, the question of casting came up. "I want to make *Huckleberry Finn* the kind of picture that Mark Twain would love," Freed remarked. "I consider it the best book ever written in America." Needless to say, Freed was after an impeccable cast and Danny Kaye was discussed. It was an intriguing idea, especially in view of Lerner's approach to the characters of the Duke and the Dauphin.

Plans took on a concrete form when Kaye agreed to play the Dauphin. The number-one contingent was called in: Vincente Minnelli, Irene Sharaff and Gene Kelly, who would not only play the Duke but also choreograph. Freed did not waste any time in assembling the rest of the cast: Dean Stockwell as Huck; William Warfield as the runaway slave Jim; Louis Calhern, Frieda Inescort and Margaret O'Brien as the Grangerford family.

Lane hated everything he had done with Harburg and had told Freed about it. "When Arthur put Alan on the project, everything started to happen. I became very excited and the songs came fast."

"That screenplay and those songs I consider some of the best stuff I've ever written," says Lerner.

On August 28, 1951, *Huckleberry Finn* went into rehearsal, in spite of the fact that Kelly was still in the midst of shooting *Singin' in the Rain.* Since Carol Haney had to be at his side, Ernie Flatt was brought in as assistant dance director.

For the next month Sharaff was busy designing costumes for the principals. Minnelli worked with Kaye, Warfield and Stockwell.

Then, on September 21, Freed called Minnelli into his office and informed him that production would be closed. Kelly had made up his mind that *Huckleberry Finn* would not be his next picture.

What was behind this sudden switch? Kelly's Metro contract had just come up for renewal. The United States Government had recently passed a bill, making it possible for American citizens to spend no less than eighteen months tax free in a foreign country, and Kelly was determined to take advantage of it. He instructed his agent Lew Wasserman of MCA to negotiate a new contract on that basis.

It is remarkable indeed that Freed did not make the slightest effort to block these negotiations. It seems to indicate Freed's irrevocable loyalty to a man of Kelly's talent, who, for many years, had done brilliant work under his banner.

On the last day of the year Schary called a meeting with the Freed Unit to announce that Kelly would immediately leave the States to make a "ballet picture" in Europe. This came as no surprise to the Freed Unit, because Kelly had batted around his notion for the last couple of months. But, to *everybody's* surprise, including Schary's, Freed spoke up. "I want to go on record here and now that I am *not* for making this film!" he said. He went on to say, however, that because of his admiration for Kelly he was willing to go along with it.

12 *INVITATION TO THE DANCE*

On New Year's Eve 1951, Gene Kelly arrived in Paris. During his short stay he had several meetings with Henry Henigson, M-G-M's European location manager, who was familiar with the facilities of film studios in London, Paris, Munich, Rome and Stockholm as well as with general working conditions in Europe. Before embarking on his ballet picture, Kelly had to fulfill a commitment to star in *The Devil Makes Three,* a Metro picture to be made at the Bavaria Film Studios in Munich. But while in Paris he fell ill and had to have an appendectomy. He spent ten days recuperating in Klosters, Switzerland, before starting work in Germany.

Meanwhile, Freed and the unit were preparing various projects, the most immediate being an original musical, using the song catalogue of Arthur Schwartz and Howard Dietz. Comden and Green seemed to have become experts at this kind of screenplay and were assigned. Since Schwartz and Dietz had worked exclusively for the theatre, a backstage story seemed indicated, with Fred Astaire in the leading role. Once again Freed mined Broadway and brought the brilliantly talented set designer Oliver Smith into the unit. It didn't faze him that Smith had never worked in films. He even remarked at the time that

Smith was "the most underestimated genius of the American theatre and ballet."[1]

Alan Lerner was at work on two screenplays: *Green Mansions* (a nonmusical) and the adaptation of his *Brigadoon* for Gene Kelly.

Another project hit a snag: Sigmund Romberg had died on November 28, 1951, and Joe Fields's biographical script had to be rewritten. Oscar Hammerstein, a collaborator and close friend of the late composer, offered Freed any assistance he might need. Fields had also completed his work on *Jumbo,* and Freed assigned Stanley Donen to direct and was considering Debbie Reynolds and Donald O'Connor as stars.[2]

With this schedule Freed felt that he would neither have the time nor the concentration to produce *Lust for Life* and, reluctantly, he turned it over to John Houseman.[3]

From the day *Huckleberry Finn* closed, intensive research went on for any remotely feasible musical material for the picture Freed had now titled *Invitation to the Dance*—from Monteverdi to Stravinsky to Duke Ellington; from "Coppélia" to "Der Rosenkavalier" to "The Whiffenpoof Song." Literally hundreds of recordings were bought, listened to, eliminated and reconsidered. This musical safari continued long after Kelly's departure. For Simone and Edens it was a miserable undertaking inasmuch as they didn't have the faintest clue as to what they were looking for. All they had to go on was that Kelly wanted to divide *Invitation* into four separate sections: a circus, a modern ballet, a popular song sequence and a children's ballet.

Before leaving for Munich, Kelly had lunch with Gian-Carlo Menotti in Paris, where he discussed a vague outline of a *commedia dell'arte* circus ballet. Kelly reported to Freed that Menotti was enthusiastic, but Kelly was indecisive and nothing ever materialized.

From the time Kelly started his picture in Munich, Freed sensed that not even one of the sequences for the film was clear in Kelly's mind. There were no synopses, no composers, no designers—in other words, after two months the ballet picture was still in embryonic state.

To protect Kelly and for very valid practical reasons, Freed suggested the possibility of doing *Brigadoon* before *Invitation,* or doing part of *Invitation,* then skipping to *Brigadoon* and back. In a letter to Freed, Kelly expressed his reaction:

> I personally am dead set against doing *Brigadoon* first for the
> following reasons: Number one is that I feel I am "hot" on the

---

[1] Aside from Smith's great achievements on the Broadway stage, he was one of the founders and managing directors of the American Ballet Theatre.

[2] Freed had previously considered Judy Garland, Frank Sinatra and Red Skelton for the leads.

[3] It is interesting to note that Houseman chose Minnelli to direct the film, whereas Freed's choice had been Richard Brooks.

dance picture. Would like to get at it and get it out of my system. . . . Since we can only get the ballet people in the summertime, that means we would have to wait a whole year and not do the picture until 1953.

The above shows Kelly's unawareness of the reality of the situation. Those people, bound by yearly contracts and only available during the summer, have to make commitments at least a year ahead.

In the same letter Kelly tried to convey to Freed his faith in the project. He goes on to say that the music, especially in regard to the "Popular Song" sequence, is his major concern and suggests Freed send Edens over for four weeks to set it up, possibly record it in Culver City and send the playbacks to him. He even mentions a tentative schedule.

Another idea he passed on to Freed was for a modern ballet based on Arthur Schnitzler's *Reigen* (Rondelay). "It's the best one I've had since I left Pittsburgh. We can use a dozen dancers in it and really run the gamut, in other words, it will have lots of sex and glamour and romance and humor, with the accent on the women."

At the outset Kelly had been confident that he could take on the staggering task of producer, director, choreographer, star, performer, in addition to engaging and supervising musicians and designers—all of this without the creative personnel and the facilities of a major studio. Now some doubts crept in and he told Freed, "I recall a very sage observation you made one day about Oliver Smith—that he was not only a designer but a producer as well, and knew the value of the dough spent on things. With that in mind, I am again wondering whether we would not be better off in having him over here to do the whole production."

At the time Kelly did not know that Smith had been approached about this and had turned Freed down.

One of Kelly's favorite dance numbers had always been the animated cartoon sequence in *Anchors Aweigh,* and he wrote Freed that he had made up his mind to make the children's ballet an animated cartoon.

The panorama Kelly unfolded for Freed shows how eager he was for his moral support and approval, approval of things Freed had no firsthand knowledge of.

Freed's first decision was that *Invitation* would be made at M-G-M's British studios in Boreham Wood, Elstree, fifteen miles from London. This was a safety valve, so to speak, against what is known as "a runaway production."[4] Ben Goetz, Mayer's son-in-law and an old friend of Freed's, was chairman of the studio. It was a postwar, modern, branch of the home studio; the fact that it was subject to the

---

[4] A production operating entirely on its own momentum, without any directives from the home lot.

INVITATION TO THE DANCE

edicts of the Home Office in regard to the importation of foreigners was regarded a minor handicap.

Freed agreed on Igor Youskevitch and Nora Kaye, and the studio negotiated contracts for both, with a starting date of July 7. Now the unit knew that there would definitely be a circus ballet.

But what contemporary composer would be the right choice? It had to be one with a definite flair for the theatre and with an unerring sense of period and style. Taking these attributes as a point of departure, Simone played a recording of Jacques Ibert's "Divertissement" for Freed. He listened attentively and after he had heard one third of the recording, he said, "That's the man!" He ordered Johnny Green to locate Ibert. At the time Ibert was not in his sumptuous apartment in Paris or in his palace in Versailles, but in Rome, fulfilling his duties as the president of the famous French Music Academy at the Villa Borghese. Negotiations with Ibert via his Paris representative were not too simple in respect to rights, etc. But he was interested and ultimately a contract was signed.

To clear the rights for Schnitzler's *Reigen* was not easy in itself; during the previous year the French motion picture *La Ronde,* directed by Max Ophuls, had gone into release. Rudi Monta was in the midst of trying to clear up the legal muddle. But Freed, ever optimistic, saw no reason to delay contractual obligations for this sequence.

Literally hundreds of American popular songs were submitted to Kelly. Finally these were narrowed down to twenty-five songs for which clearances were obtained. Rights were acquired in all categories: vocal-visual; vocal-nonvisual; instrumental-visual; instrumental only; partial vocal-visual.

On March 29, on the Munich set, a trans-Atlantic call for Kelly was announced. Freed's voice came over the wire, informing him of the results of the Academy Awards ceremony. It took a few minutes for Freed to count off the six awards *An American in Paris* had received. After Kelly had caught his breath, Freed added, "There are two more little items I want to mention: You won a Special Award—Stanley accepted the Oscar for you—we'll keep it on ice!" For a moment Kelly was speechless, until he asked, "What's the second 'little' item?" "Oh, it's a mere nothing," came the reply. "I won the Thalberg Award. That's all for now, see you in May."

At the beginning of April Kelly was through with *The Devil Makes Three.* Physically, as well as mentally, exhausted and badly in need of some time off, he went back to Klosters, intending to be in top shape by the time Freed would meet him.

Being the kind of employer Freed was, he asked Simone—he did not *tell* her—whether she would go to London for the duration of *Invitation to the Dance.* She agreed and Metro's London office was instructed to secure a work permit for her. After several postpone-ments, on May 7, Freed and Simone left for Paris via New York. Green, accompanied by his wife, came along for the purpose of exploring the European music market and to take at least a brief look at the recording facilities at the Boreham Wood studios. Their departure and their travels would not be without incident.

On May 7, Freed had made a dinner date at the Copacabana night club with Lee and Ira Gershwin, who happened to be in New York, and also invited Simone. Before long a lady came to their table and, smiling timidly, asked if she could join them. She was known to all of them, but Freed was in one of his absent-minded moods, and it was obvious that he didn't know who she was. Lillian Ross was a person that one doesn't easily remember by sight but rather by the printed word. Ross had recently written a series of articles for *The New Yorker* on the behind-the-scenes events during the making of *The Red Badge of Courage,* the picture which ultimately provoked Schenck to dismiss Mayer. Vividly remembering her comments on Freed, and on Freed and Mayer, and keenly aware of her ever-ready scalpel, Simone tried to whisper who she was into Freed's ear, helped along by the noise of a very brassy band. Still he didn't get it. The Gershwins, aware of Ross and her usual motives, made no attempt at conversation. Ross sensed there was no gain in staying and took her leave.

One of the first contacts Green made in London was with Malcolm Arnold, who was well known in musicians' circles. He had played first trumpet with one of London's major orchestras and was beginning to make a name for himself as a serious composer. At the time he was interested in doing something substantial in motion pictures and when Green offered him the assignment of writing the score for *Reigen,* now titled *Ring Around the Rosy,* he accepted eagerly.

John Hollingsworth, the famous young ballet conductor of Sadler's Wells and Covent Garden, was engaged as the conductor and musical director for the picture. Green also engaged Robert Farnon, for the "Popular Song" sequence. He also made an agreement with the Royal Philharmonic to record the picture.

Green had pressed as many professional and social activities into his brief stay as he could and returned to his desk in Culver City.

Kelly now turned his attention to visual matters. For the decors of "Ring Around the Rosy" Simone brought up Rolf Gerard's name to Freed and Kelly. Gerard, residing both in Paris and New York, had made his name as a scenic and costume designer at the Metropolitan Opera and with an impressive list of ballet productions. When Freed and Kelly met with Gerard they were impressed with his artistic flexibility. He was engaged for the sequence. Shortly thereafter Freed took the opportunity to attend to some private business interspersed with excursions to satisfy his incurable urge for collecting. By June 1 he was back at the studio.

Kelly held a press conference in Paris announcing his projected ballet picture. ARTHUR FREED ARCHIVES

Within a few days of Freed's departure, Carol Haney arrived with Jeanne Coyne, dancer, stand-in and Kelly's valued helper for a number of years. Logically, this would have been the time to go to London but this had to be delayed because of English tax laws. The Home Office permits a non-British subject to remain and/or work in Great Britain for 186 days within a year without having to pay income tax; the 186 days need not be consecutive. To safeguard the longest possible stay in London, Kelly decided to remain in France until the last moment. To concentrate and to be undisturbed by any outside interference, he rented a country estate. It was a beautiful, serene place, about ten kilometers outside of Chartres and only forty-five minutes by fast car from Paris. Here Kelly went into a kind of gestation period. As yet he had no vision of what he wanted to project on the screen. He seemed disturbed, distracted and unsure of himself. He was about to make an experimental picture, and he found himself without the security blanket of Freed's presence and minus any kind of creative major studio personnel. He had isolated himself; he was far away from home.

Simone was genuinely concerned. After evaluating the situation, she tried to bring Kelly back to his earlier suggestion: to get Edens to come over for the "Popular Song" sequence. After some moments of reflection, Kelly came up with quite a paradoxical reply, "That would be bad for your career, wouldn't it?" At first she honestly didn't understand what he was talking about. When the complexity of his reply became clear to her she answered bluntly, "My career? I am doing a job."

Days passed and his anxiety grew in facing starting dates, some contractual commitments, an incomplete cast and, most of all, the absence of any libretti. He began to realize that he had underestimated the time it would take to co-ordinate all these elements.

One night Haney and Simone attended a gala performance of "Les Indes Galantes," the big ballet spectacle at the Paris Opéra, and reported in glowing terms the extraordinary performance of the young prima ballerina, Claude Bessy. Kelly, of course, knew of her, and, after meeting her, concluded that she would be perfect for "Ring Around the Rosy."

Maurice Lehmann, then head of the Paris Opéra, was very reluctant to allow Bessy to accept the offer. She would have to make several trips to London; she might miss performances in Paris; he couldn't rearrange her schedule, etc. In addition to this, the Home Office in London rebelled; with Covent Garden and Sadler's Wells there was no need to import dancers from France. But they finally gave in.

Kelly had been intrigued with the performance of another French dancer, Claire Sombert, in a production of the Roland Petit Ballet. He engaged her for the part of the ballerina in "The Circus," which he originally had intended for Nora Kaye.

As an advance guard, Simone left for London at the end of June. After recovering from the shock of powdered eggs for breakfast, she went to Boreham Wood to familiarize herself with the personnel and the facilities. She prepared for Kelly's arrival by selecting several spacious dressing rooms in a separate building and had them converted to working space. She asked the assistant director to get a piano, a spinet, into one of the rooms. After several days she inquired as to its whereabouts. With some embarrassment she was told it had not yet arrived. Another two days passed when she received a call announcing its arrival. What she found was an early eighteenth-century heavily ornamented clavichord. The very obliging assistant director, not familiar with the American term "spinet," had searched all over London to find this antiquity at the cost of £300. Until she heard the price Simone was amused, but she ordered it to be returned, and a regular piano was brought in.

One of Simone's main concerns was the setup on the recording stage. Ibert had shown her some of his sketches, which gave her an idea about instrumentation and size of orchestra. It would require the full complement of the Royal Philharmonic, the skillful handling of the recording engineer plus the proper acoustics and sound equipment. What she found was a shooting stage which occasionally was used to record some background music, a microphone setup unsuitable for the elaborate and intricate sound of an Ibert score, and a terribly nice and accommodating recording engineer, who told her in all honesty that he was an experienced hand at recording dialogue, but totally unfamiliar with the technique of recording music.

One redeeming feature was the excellent food in the studio commissary. When she asked Irene Howard, the casting director and the late Leslie Howard's sister, how it was possible to dine better there than in the best of London's hotels and restaurants, she was told that Goetz fortunately owned a big ranch which supplied the commissary.

Kelly finally arrived in London on July 2 to actually begin preparation for *Invitation*. He brought with him a synopsis of "The Circus": A clown (Kelly) in a Pierrot costume à la Marcel Marceau is in love with the prima ballerina (Sombert), who in turn has eyes only for the tightrope walker (Youskevitch). In an effort to prove his worth, the clown climbs the high wire and falls to his death, but not before bringing the two lovers together.

After all his searching for an art director for "The Circus," it was not through compromise that Kelly began to work with M-G-M's Alfred Junge. A soft-spoken man of German origin, Junge was an eminently talented artist who, among many achievements, had won international acclaim for his design for the motion picture *Black Narcissus* (1948). Because of his great flair for theatrical design and color effect, he and Kelly understood each other well, and after only a couple of meetings Junge went ahead with the designs for the first sequence.

Elizabeth Heffenden, also under contract to the studio, in collaboration with Junge started designing the costumes and worked closely with the property department on the many props Kelly wanted for a dance routine.

Youskevitch was in London a week before Kelly and was making the best of his free time. When Nora Kaye arrived, Kelly informed her that she would not be in "The Circus" but would play the role of the prostitute in his second sequence, "Rosy." When she realized that her part was small, she backed out. "That was quite a blow to me," Kelly wrote Freed, "and will necessitate a lot of mental reshuffling on my part. Prestige-wise, I feel it very necessary we get a ballet 'name' to take her place. If we can't get Renee Jeanmaire, then we should snag Tamara Toumanova." Freed cabled him that it was impossible to get Jeanmaire and advised him to sign Toumanova.

The atmosphere in Boreham Wood was very different—in size and activity—from Culver City. With its neat, well-kept buildings and stages, its beautifully landscaped grounds and its quiet, dreamy streets, it had the aura of a country club. The staff was friendly, willing, but confused by the energy and insistence on speed of the American arrivals.

Simone had located two excellent young pianists in London and engaged them for the duration of the picture. Using Ibert's piano sketches, Kelly, assisted by Haney, began rehearsing Sombert and Youskevitch's *pas de deux*.

A month and a half after rehearsal for the twenty-nine-minute "Circus" sequence had started, the first prerecording sessions were set for August 11 and 12. Not having the faintest notion what the acoustics on the sound stage—which was not a sound stage—were going to be, Simone arranged for the first three hours of rehearsal with Hollingsworth and the ninety men of the Royal Philharmonic to evaluate the sound quality and to check the recording equipment. The session produced deplorable results. The carpentry department was ordered to construct sound bafflers on the spot, to modify acoustic defects, and to replace the antiquated microphones. The orchestra was reseated and, after another test, Hollingsworth and Simone were ready to record. Ibert too, shocked at first, was now satisfied and after lunch, the first take was made.

Invitation to the Dance began principal photography on August 19, 1952.

Kelly had choreographed what he called the "Parade of the Clowns" for which he needed jugglers and tumblers. He also urgently needed a tightrope walker to double for Youskevitch. A theatrical agency in London advised that a traveling circus was currently performing in Brighton and Simone was dispatched to check it out. There she found a remarkable tightrope walker and a fine troupe of acrobats.

LELA SIMONE
METROBIT
BOREHAMWOOD (ENG)
    LOOK AT GOETZ REPORT AUGUST TWENTY-SIX WHICH INCLUDES SHOOTING FOR FIRST FOUR DAYS. IS THIS REPORT CORRECT THAT ON THE TWENTY-FIRST THERE WAS ONLY THIRTY SECONDS NET, ALSO ON TWENTY-SECOND ONLY FORTY-FIVE SECONDS NET WITH EIGHT SETUPS? CABLE ME AND KEEP CONFIDENTIAL EXCEPT FROM BEN GOETZ. REGARDS.
                                        ARTHUR FREED

Before answering Freed's cable Simone decided to communicate with him clandestinely from here on, thus evading the controlled studio channels.

FREED
MGM
    ON AUGUST TWENTY-FIRST GENE SHOT MOST DIFFICULT PART OF CLOWNS DANCE PHOTOGRAPHICALLY AND ALSO FOR PERFORMANCE AND PHYSICAL STRAIN STOP ON AUGUST TWENTY-SECOND GENE SHOT EIGHT SETUPS WITH TROUPE OF ACROBATS DOUBLING FOR CLOWN STOP THE ACROBATS HAD NOT BEEN

AVAILABLE FOR REHEARSALS PREVIOUS TO SHOOTING STOP FILM
SHOT IN THESE EIGHT SETUPS TO BE USED FOR INTERCUTTING
CLOWNS PARADE STOP SCREEN TIME IN PROGRESS REPORT
INACCURATE DUE TO HAVING BEEN SHOT TO TEMPOTRACKS AND
NOT TO FINAL PLAYBACK STOP FROM NOW ON YOU WILL FIND
ATTACHED TO DAILY PROGRESS REPORT EXPLANATORY NOTE
FROM MYSELF PERTAINING TO THE DAYS ACTIVITIES

LELA

After three weeks of shooting, Kelly had eleven minutes and twenty seconds on film. During that time two days had gone by without a printed take.

The most comprehensive description of the circumstances under which Kelly had to work can be found in the following exchange of communications between Simone and Freed:

Dear Mr. Freed:

The reasons for Gene's slow progress during the first four days of shooting are many. I will try to give you a comprehensive picture of the conditions under which he works. But I want to preface my report by saying that any of the existing handicaps of a production nature are caused by this studio not being equipped to make a picture like *Invitation* at such speed as we are used to in Culver City, let alone to make two pictures at the same time. (The Gable picture,[5] being behind schedule, is still shooting.)

The evening before the first day of shooting Gene tried on his costume and—after he had had innumerable fittings—found out that it was all wrong. It looked homemade. It didn't fit anywhere. The costume designer had been told in detail how it should be cut etc., but the workshop was (and still is) incapable of making a professional job on the costume.

The costume had to be completely remade overnight. When we started shooting the next morning, it was by no means perfect, but passable. But it had to be fixed between takes—and so we lost time.

Next: Gene's shoes didn't fit, due to being made very badly. His hat was too big and he lost it the moment he started to dance.

The camera crew was totally unfamiliar with moving a boom into certain marks at definite speeds and to musical counts.

In addition to all this, the general working tempo of the crews over here is much, much slower than anything we are used to in America. Assuming one is ready to shoot a scene at ten o'clock, there is nothing to do, but let the crew break for tea. After half an hour it is necessary to rehearse the shot once more and so more time is gone.

Should one want to work an extra fifteen minutes at the end of the day to finish a setup, the crew must be informed and the workers decide themselves, whether they want to work or not.

All this, as you can tell, doesn't make for great speed. And the Gable picture still shooting didn't and doesn't help Gene either. To

[5] *Mogambo*.

380

give you an example: There are only two playback machines available on this lot. I knew that one of these machines would be needed for the Gable picture. So, weeks ahead of time, I asked the production department to be sure to get an extra playback machine for us, in case our dates conflicted with the Gable picture. During our first week's shooting the playback machine on our set burned out. I immediately sent for another one. I was told it had been sent to London for the Gable picture, at that time shooting in a London theatre. The third stand-by machine I had asked for had never been ordered.

Very fortunately this happened around the time of the first tea break. The sound people, by now all friends of mine, worked through their tea break (which is unheard of) in order to repair the motor of the playback as best they could. By the time the machine was returned to the stage, we actually had lost only twenty minutes. This was very lucky indeed. It just as well could have been a delay of many hours. . . .

There are so many things I could tell you which slowed us up; most of them too stupid to be believed. But it all adds up to the one thing: Each and every department here is actually not geared to do the simplest things efficiently and fast. Least of all for a picture without a script, which consequently requires the constant attention and alertness of *everyone* involved.

As far as Gene, Carol, Jeannie and—may I immodestly say— myself are concerned, we have been doing everything, watching everything and anticipating everything under the sun. No matter how exhausted, Gene has been working every night at his house, planning the shots and the work for the next day. We all know that Gene sometimes goes overboard, trying to get the "perfect" scene on the screen. Here, though, he has been more reasonable than I have ever seen him. He is at all times aware of cost and has been most inventive in doing things the most practical and economical way.

With my very best regards,

Yours,

Lela

Simone's letter was written at the start of the day. That same day, September 4, would not go by without some most disturbing events.

INVITATION TO THE DANCE

DAILY REPORT FOR MR. ARTHUR FREED
FROM
LELA SIMONE

September 4

At nine o'clock rehearsal of Youskevitch and Claire Sombert's reprise—in order to determine the finishing position for Youskevitch's solo, preceding the reprise.

After tea break, shooting of the last eight bars of Youskevitch's solo. In this scene Youskevitch is doing the most difficult double turns. During the first take Youskevitch's knee went bad. In spite of this he kept trying again and again. He finally had no control any more. By lunchtime it was evident that—at least—he had to rest for a while.

During lunch the doctor came. He ordered rest. The nurse massaged the knee.

After lunch Youskevitch was able to dance, but couldn't do the difficult ending of his solo.

Just before teatime there was a fire on the set. A fireman was injured and taken to the hospital. There was a slight delay, caused by this accident.

After tea Gene rehearsed Youskevitch and Sombert's reprise again: this time with the camera. This scene runs over 300 feet. Around five o'clock we started shooting the reprise. By six o'clock there was no O.K. take yet.

At six-fifteen there was another break for the crew, because we had arranged to shoot till nine o'clock.

We had an O.K. take of the long scene by nine o'clock. After that we shot a c.u. of Youskevitch. Screentime: about 360 feet.

L.S.

Dear Lela:

Your report of September 4 and also your letter of the same date carefully perused and after reading them I immediately stopped to have some tea. Tell Gene that if we do a fifth ballet it seems we should call it "Tea Party."

Now, Lela, specifically in answer to your letter, you unnecessarily seem to defend Gene. I have the most complete confidence in Gene and, incidentally, also in you, so from here on let's forget about any necessity for personal defenses.

I am naturally asked so many questions by the management here that your reports are very important, and since I have received them I have a clearer picture of the problems. As a suggestion, couldn't Madame Karinska or somebody else responsible in England execute the costumes after designing, because I am sure the expense of this item would be money well spent in saving mistakes and annoyances such as you evidently had at the start of shooting.

I spoke to Gene on Sunday and told him how delighted I was with the first rushes. I think they were brilliant. Roger and Vincente who saw them with me shared the same feelings. I expect to see another batch sometime today.

Now as for the local situation, we record the first of the week on the Astaire picture which is now called *The Band Wagon*. Betty and Adolph wrote a wonderful script and the numbers in rehearsal are really exciting. Fred Astaire and Cyd Charisse are magnificent together and I have Gene to thank for bringing Cyd to life. We all miss you here and it seems strange starting a picture without you. Thank you for the good job you are doing. I am very grateful for your help.

My warmest regards,

Sincerely,
Arthur Freed

When the circus troupe arrived, the tightrope walker's apparatus was set up on a separate stage for him to rehearse on. Under his supervision this equipment had to be anchored deep into the cement floor by the construction department. A few days later an earth-shaking noise rocked the adjoining buildings. The immediate reaction was that a bomb had gone off. Scurrying around, the company found the high-wire man in the net, the anchors broken out of the cement floor and the supporting poles caved in.

The troupe of acrobats consisted of an Arabian family: the father, gray hair and gray bearded; his four young sons and two daughters. Simone arrived on the set while they were demonstrating their act for Kelly. "In the background I noticed a tall, heavy-set, blond, blue-eyed woman. To my amazement, I heard the following exchange in German with a Berlin accent: 'Up—Otto—up! *Mach schnell.* Papa —hold on!' 'Ach, I'm falling over.' 'Good. *Ach du lieber* . . . they want to see it again. Are you tired, Papa?' *'Nein.* Up again . . . hold on to me.'

"It turned out that the blond Brünhilde was the wife of the Arab and manager of the troupe. She said, 'I tell you Papa, he is the best husband there ever was. *Ja,* we are a happy family. No, we don't live in Germany, we only go there for engagements. We don't have much in mind with the Germans.' Now a little Negro boy appeared, about five years old, takes Brünhilde's hand and says, 'Mama, can I have some chocolate,' 'Nah, sure, my Shrimple,' and turning to me, 'This is our Ali. Yeah, we adopted him—all legal—with the lawyer. The mother was one of those German girls, you know *Kraft durch Freude,* flouncing around with all the soldiers. And then she had a surprise when little Ali was black!! Such a sweet little boy! Well, the girl, all she wanted was to get rid of him. In court the judge says to me: "Frau Abdullah! After all, aren't you a German woman?!" 'No,' I said, 'your honor, that I am not! I only look like one. I am Egyptian, even though I look like Germania. Looks are deceptive, your honor.' "

With "The Circus" not yet completed, Kelly had to begin shooting "Ring Around the Rosy" on Saturday and Sunday September 13 and 14, because of Claude Bessy's commitments at the Paris Opéra. She had to fly back Sunday night.

This, the second sequence in the picture, was the story of a bracelet, given by a loving husband to his wife, and its stopovers from one love object to the next, until it comes back to rest on the arm of the wife: from husband to wife (David Paltenghi—Daphne Dale); from her to artist (Youskevitch); from him to model (Bessy); from her to gangster (Tommy Rall); from him to debutante (Belita); from her to crooner (Irving Davies); from him to the hat-check girl (Diana Adams); from her to the soldier (Kelly); from him to the prostitute (Toumanova); from her to the husband; and from the husband back to the wife.

One month earlier, Gerard had arrived with his ballet sketches in the manner of an opaque film negative. Kelly asked him to change his conception into a much more conventional design. Gerard's wife, Kyra, an exceptionally elegant and fashion-conscious woman, involved herself in the proceedings. Her costume suggestions were executed by the famous London couturier Stiebel.

Some minor problems had to be solved in some haste. Silk tights were needed for the dancers, but there was an embargo on silk in Great Britain and none could be found in London. A few days before all establishments in Paris closed for their long summer vacation, Simone bought a batch of flesh and black leotards and smuggled them in her personal luggage on one of her trips across the channel. It was also time to find the bracelet for "Ring Around the Rosy," almost the principal character. It not only had to be a pretty piece of jewelry, but its design and profile had to be adaptable for the superimposure in the opening shot, with all the performers circling around it. After a search through Portobello Road, Islington, Chelsea and New Bond Street, the bracelet was found at some expense: £300.

In the middle of September Simone told Goetz: "I want to make you aware of the fact that I can only work here for 186 days. Otherwise I'll have to pay taxes here *and* pay taxes in America."

Goetz ignored Simone's warning.

Soon the day came when Raymond had to advise Goetz of Simone's predicament and Goetz called for her. "You'll just have to leave the country as often as you can to gain time; you'd better start this weekend." From here on, Simone commuted to Paris, leaving London by Friday midnight and not returning before Monday morning. For the same reason Kelly went with her on some of these exhausting trips. One Monday morning they arrived at Le Bourget Airport; at 6 P.M. they were still there. No planes had taken off; the fog was as thick as a wall. At Boreham Wood the company was assembled with dozens of extras, and the entire day was wasted. Finally Kelly and Simone were loaded into an overcrowded plane, which slowly taxied to the runway, attendants running alongside with blazing torches. A couple of minutes later the plane came to a halt and it was announced that it couldn't take off. Simone dashed to a phone and alerted the studio's Paris office to get them on the boat train to London no matter what. Somehow, somewhere there are two people who lost their accommodations that night on the sold-out train.

For the next five weeks Kelly juggled between "The Circus" and "Ring Around the Rosy." The day came when the tightrope walker had to do his stunt. He was extremely nervous, although he worked with a net during camera rehearsals. Then came the crucial moment. There he was, twenty feet up over the cement floor, and the net was taken away. Dead silence. After the first take was completed, whoever was not absolutely needed on the set left the premises. Power of concentration (and prayers) made this come off without a fatality.

One night at 3 A.M. Simone was awakened by a call from Ibert in the suite above her, asking her to come to his suite. When she got there, Ibert informed her that he had to return to Paris immediately because he had received news that his daughter, a well-known musician, had disappeared. Madame Ibert was sitting in an alcove, a pendulum in her hand, repeating over and over: *"Elle est morte, elle est morte."* The Iberts left on the earliest boat train for Paris. Even before they had arrived Simone contacted their son who told her that after a lengthy search, the police had found his sister dead, at the bottom of the stairs in their boarded-up chateau in Versailles.

At the time this tragedy occurred Ibert was to write and record

Kelly rehearses with Igor Youskevitch and Claire Sombert who costar with him in "The Circus" sequence. M-G-M

the incidental music for "The Circus." After six days Ibert phoned Simone: "There is only one thing for me to do and that is to work. Furthermore, I have a contract I must fulfill." Simone said to herself, "I am not going to bring this man back on the same boat train, to the same hotel." She ordered a black and white work print of the sequence; she would take it to Paris and would work with him in the projection room at the Paris office.

A couple of days later she took her detailed timing charts and related to Ibert what Kelly had in mind in regard to the score.

The first session for "Rosy" was set up for October 24. Before going to the recording stage Simone looked at the score and became somewhat alarmed. However, she started the session without any comment. After taking the orchestra through the reading of the first scene, Hollingsworth, a man with a biting sense of humor, said into the microphone, *"Götterdämmerung!?"* It soon became apparent to them that Arnold's score was not in tune with what Kelly had photographed. Not only out of respect to Arnold, but also for legal reasons, Simone decided to record the score anyway, advising Hollingsworth not to waste time by going for the perfect take.

Even though Kelly was now ostensibly finished with "The Circus," he couldn't just concentrate on "Rosy." He had less than thirty working days left in England to finish three sequences, he therefore had to put the "Popular Song" sequence into rehearsal, which meant casting, designing, costuming and recording.

Dear Mr. Freed:

We had to completely revamp our previous schedule on "Ring Around the Rosy" and the "Popular Song" sequence for several different reasons. The first and most important one is Gene, having been ill and even now not feeling too well. He was in bed for a few days, as you know, and only through his tremendous will power did he somehow manage to get back on his feet again. He is now working at the studio only in the afternoons. But we all are getting briefed the night before, so that when we come in in the mornings we can carry on without him.

The next difficulty which arose is the loss of weekends for work. There is a sort of a sit-down strike on in *all* the studios here and we are advised that we absolutely must not work, even rehearse on Saturdays, unless there is a real emergency.

Then we ran into difficulties with Malcom Arnold. Until last week we were under the impression that he would do the "Popular Song" sequence. At the very moment we needed to start working with him, he had a nervous crisis and his doctor advised him not to take on another assignment. Now we quickly had to find another man and decided on Robert Faron. He had to be brought in for conferences, his contract had to be set up—in other words, there were unavoidable delays.

By the way, Malcolm Arnold is perfectly well again and will continue to do the same good job on "Ring Around the Rosy" he has done so far, I am sure.

Farnon apparently is a very nice man and full of enthusiasm for the job, which always helps. I am sticking with him very closely so that we get an American song sequence and not polite, English jazz. I have played a lot of tracks from our pictures for him; this will give him an idea as to what we want to hear.

Gene also was slowed down to some extent by lack of equipment and the general slowness of the departments. You are well aware of this, but Gene nevertheless wanted me to mention this to you again.

Yours,
Lela

Correspondence had been going back and forth between Kelly, Freed and Green about the selection of songs and clearances. Green had selected eleven songs and some of the quotations for their usage were quite high.[6]

On November 7, the first prerecordings for the "Popular Song" sequence, now titled "Dance Me a Song," were made, interspersed with the remaining shooting of the footage needed for "Rosy." Kelly recorded "The Whiffenpoof Song," "Sunny Side of the Street" and "Wedding Bells Are Breaking Up That Old Gang of Mine." The other songs were recorded by adequate English band vocalists without any particular distinction and some legitimate singers from various West End productions.

By November 17, Kelly was still not finished with "Rosy," but he had to begin shooting the third sequence, i.e., A.M.: "Rosy," P.M.: "Dance Me a Song," and vice versa.

One month later Simone wrote a lengthy report to Freed:

Please forgive me for my long silence. But there was nothing special I had to tell you and I knew that you saw the rushes coming in comparatively rapid succession.

You have by now seen most of the "Popular Song" rushes, including "St. Louis Blues." We can't wait to hear from you about it. The fact that the photography in some of the songs is not really good depressed Gene no end. I, for one, was very upset about "Sunny Side." This, being Gene's solo, should have been bright rather than bleak. I also thought that we were altogether too far away from him throughout the number. I wished Gene could have done it over.

During the last week Gene shot "I Feel a Song Coming On." It is a wonderful opening for the "Popular Song" sequence—the

[6] Rights and usage totaled $27,145.

Gene Kelly with Alan Carter and the chorus shooting "They Go Wild, Simply Wild, Over Me" from the "Dance Me a Song" sequence. M-G-M

girls and boys in rehearsal clothes, your idea you told Gene in Paris. Gene also finished "Whiffenpoof" last Friday. Gene started rehearsing with Toumanova on Saturday. He will rehearse Sunday and Monday and start shooting on Tuesday. We hope he can finish it by Friday the 19th. I think he has a good chance—if Tamara "gives," which in high heels and a completely foreign style of dancing is difficult for her. By the way, we are all crazy about her: She is a wonderful woman.

If Gene is finished with Toumanova next Friday he will see the rushes and leave for Klosters, probably Saturday or Sunday. After the Christmas holiday the following things will be left to do: Post-score the prologue and the Toumanova sequence. Finish up a few leftovers on the "Circus Ballet" scoring. Record a few bridges for the "Popular Song" sequence. Also, the cutting of the picture will have to be finished, dissolves checked for length, the Toumanova scene will have to be cut, the final composite of the prologue shot to be checked, etc. For all this I have made a most detailed work chart. According to our instructions, work will be done in every department while we are away.

By the time we arrive in Klosters we will probably know what the situation is about the cartoon sequence or rather the fourth

388

sequence of the film, whatever it may be. We are prepared to do a lot of work during the holiday. I am taking material with me (records, scores etc., but *not* as many as we had in Paris!), so that in Klosters Gene can "think" out ideas for the next ballet.

Enough for today. Take my warmest regards and give my best to everyone in the unit.

Always yours,
Lela

On December 17, Goetz advised Freed "that Kelly had finished photography on three of the sequences, with the exception of "I'm Always Chasing Rainbows," which Kelly intends using in the animated cartoon "Children's Ballet." Included in the last shipment of film were the cost sheets *so far*. "The Circus" cost $180,264 (screentime, thirty-one minutes); "Ring Around the Rosy," $158,370 (screentime, thirty-four minutes); and "Dance Me a Song," $137,812 (screentime, twenty-eight minutes); for twenty-seven days of rehearsal and fifty-six days of shooting.

Two days later, Kelly, his two assistants and Simone arrived in Klosters, Switzerland. Everybody was exhausted and drained, coughing profusely and overcome by the clean Alpine air after months in London's yellow fog.

Offhand one might get the impression the Klosters holiday was a glamorous excursion, with skiing, fun and frolic. There was *some* skiing and *some* fun, but not without the cloud of unsolved future problems, anxieties and disappointments about the past hanging overhead.

For months Kelly had been in contact with cartoonists in Paris and London. Although the French animators were of high caliber compared to the English, they could not assure him of any completion dates.

Simone notified Freed: "Because of Gene's limited time in England he will shoot the 'Children's Ballet' in Ireland.[7] In order to shoot the live portion of this ballet properly, Gene will have to work with [Joseph] *Barbera*—not [Fred] *Quimby*—over here. Barbera did the cartooning in *Anchors Aweigh* and Gene has complete confidence in him, while he feels very negative about Quimby."

Starting out as a novice, within three weeks Kelly was a top skier and the talk of the country. One afternoon, making his descent into the village, his ski hit a sandy spot, he fell and one of his poles went through his upper thigh. His companion rushed him to a doctor in nearby Davos who stitched up the wound.

It was getting dark and Kelly had not yet returned to the hotel, the Chesa Grischuna. Simone kept a vigil at her window. "Suddenly

---

[7] Ireland entered into the plan because of the English law forbidding the use of child actors. Although the law was broken on pictures like *Oliver Twist* and *Fallen Idol,* Goetz advised that "the studio should not put itself on the spot by breaking the English law."

I saw the skiing partner carry Gene into the hotel. I thought this was the end! I rushed to his room and all he could tell me was 'We must wait.'" The doctor couldn't determine yet whether the pole had gone through the muscle or the bone until he would examine the X rays. Kelly and Simone agreed that not a word of this must get out. It was 3:45 P.M. At 5, a call came from Los Angeles asking for Simone; Edens was on the line. Instead of the expected New Year's wishes, Edens shot a question: "What happened to Gene?" Simone was dumbfounded. How could this news have traveled so fast? Among the few natives who witnessed the accident there must have been an alert informer who knew how to make a quick buck.

After an agonizing three days' waiting period, it turned out the pole had miraculously missed the muscle and the bone. Three weeks later Kelly was on his feet as before.

The group returned to Paris awaiting a pronouncement from Culver City.

Dear Gene:

We have at last run the assembled picture as best we could minus color and minus music. There is no question as to your contention that the picture needs another brilliant sequence for variety and to round out the complete picture such as you first visualized.

Now let me run briefly through the picture with you; the pros and cons as I see them. First, I think "The Circus" ballet will go down in cinema history. It is imaginative, beautiful, eloquent and reaches balletic magnificence in conception and execution that has never been seen on the screen. In simpler language, the dancing is great; the music of Ibert which I have heard so far is first-rate; the set and costumes and photography complement everything you have done in this sequence.

Now let me speak about "Ring Around the Rosy." So we can have something to argue about, I don't believe that this measures up to all you had hoped for. The music, or at least most of what I have heard in this ballet, is not distinguished. The sets and costumes are not the best, just adequate, and, I believe, in many states, especially New York, we may bump into censor trouble. I am not saying this in the form of criticism but making an honest appraisal as I see it, and as long as I share responsibility in this project I want to serve you so that when this picture is released you will not have any regrets.

I know what you have been up against. I know the difficulty you have had in getting cast; I know the resourcefulness you have had to use in doing as much as you have already done. But, Gene, I honestly believe that there is a good deal of work to be done on this sequence and it doesn't matter how much, it has to be right. I'm afraid that in its present state it is not right.

There is a lack of dancing and too little Kelly. On this point I know you have felt that you didn't want to project yourself too much as a star through this picture, but you are a star, and audiences, I'm sure, will feel disappointed and cheated in not getting more dancing from you, that you have given them so brilliantly before. As a choreographer and creator you have presented Youskevitch and Sombert brilliantly. You can't do less with yourself. No one in the past has hit higher spots than you; don't abdicate.

Now let me ramble a little about the "Popular Songs." Here, I have to start with saying that musically and vocally you have had to compromise too much. A good many of the performers are uninteresting. The title "Dance Me a Song" promises more. I'm not saying that all the people should be stars any more than Leslie Caron or Claire Sombert were stars till you put that Kelly touch on them. Tommy Rall is excellent and his dancing is exciting, but with some of the others, again you've had to compromise too far. The sets and costumes also are not as good as I know you would have wished.

I have said all these things as we have always done, and I certainly want you to argue and I certainly want you to express yourself as to just how you feel about all of this. I have discussed the procedure with Dore and Eddie and their advice is that we should complete the scoring of "The Circus" ballet and "Ring Around the Rosy" and see the full color prints; then you should take a real rest and after we finish *Brigadoon* complete *Invitation to the Dance* here in the studio. I concur with this advice because then you can get the balletic stars you need, the costumes, the scenery, the music and everything that will help you to complete this picture and make it the distinguished enterprise you conceived.

Here again as to the cartoon, if it's the right thing to do it can be accomplished here without risk. At the present time we can announce that you have completed your work in Europe and that you will do a sequence on your return to Hollywood. Incidentally, several stories have appeared during the last few months that you were going to do a sequence of the picture here. When I join you in Paris in the next few weeks we can sit down and make a concrete plan. . . .

Let me close with this: We want this to be a great picture. There is already greatness in it. We want to do the popular songs with the great stars singing them as we first talked about it. We want you as a creative artist to have everything that can help you accomplish your work.

Everyone sends their warmest regards and respect and I send you my love.

Affectionately,
Arthur

At the time of writing, Freed put in a call to Kelly. Kelly sat down and wrote a six-page, single-spaced letter to Freed in answer to his criticisms and comments. Following are excerpts:

Dear Arthur:

After our conversation last night on the telephone, I thought it would be a good idea if I went ahead and gave you a breakdown on the whole picture, how we see it from over here, and how it stands up to date from this point of view. . . .

To take the "Popular Song" sequence as an example. Admittedly, there are a few weak personalities in there but that's where we're faced with a dilemma. Take the two weakest numbers, "Just One of Those Things" and "They Go Wild Over Me." It would be sensational if I could get Astaire and Rogers to do "Just One of Those Things" and Donald O'Connor to do "They Go Wild Over Me" but—and it's a big "but"—we couldn't have personalities like this just do a chorus of a song and not do a piece. That would throw the whole movie out of kilter; their particular following would want to see them do more. They would feel cheated. On the other hand, the numbers we do have in there like "Orange Colored Sky," "Whiffenpoof Song," "Old Gang of Mine" and "St. Louis Blues" are as exciting as any I've done and I'm convinced the public will agree. I think we can take a few letdowns in between as a breather. Even in a great show like the *Ziegfeld Follies* we couldn't hit and keep the same peak standard throughout. . . .

The "Popular Song" sequence must rest on a firm foundation of wonderful singing with voices that will thrill the public. Here's my thoughts on how they'll hit the audience: "Sophisticated Lady"— this piece is pure nostalgia. It is no world shaker visually. It is just charades, stated that way. The tempo track we have now is nothing, but we couldn't find anybody over here and, brother, we tried! Get Nat "King" Cole or somebody like him and they'll scream. "Wedding Bells Are Breaking Up That Old Gang of Mine"—all us bums know this one. Not a guy who ever drank beer didn't cry into it with this tune. This is a cinch the way it is. "They Go Wild Simply Wild Over Me"—another weak sister. Just a breather.

As you know, Arthur, I'm not defending my treatment of these songs, but anent our conversation on the phone, I wanted to give you my point of view on them. If anything is your racket, kiddo, this is—and just because I've been away a year I hope you're not going to forget that I'm nothing but most grateful for any criticism you have to offer. I have never yet found it anything but construc- tive and that's still the way I feel, so let's keep pitching at each other. . . .

I have always felt in our primary discussions about the film that we were not to make this an artistic flop, but an artistic and com- mercial success, and that we could best do that by trying to offer the widest *variety* in our piece. . . . I have always felt we should sandwich in between the "Songs" and "Ring Around the Rosy" a "Children's Ballet," and the thing that would make this visually the most different was the use of the cartoon medium. For my dough, this still holds good. Unless we're forced by economic reasons to abandon it, I think it would be a shame to do so. It would complete

André Previn, in this studio publicity still, age nineteen, was already orchestrating and conducting. But *Invitation to the Dance* was his first official job for Arthur Freed . . . and by no means his last. M-G-M

the circle of variety: "Ring Around the Rosy," "Cartoon" ballet with two little children, "Popular Songs" and "The Circus" ballet. That's a more varied assortment than any old Palace vaudeville bill we could find. . . .

Now the consensus of the feeling in Culver City, as you stated to me on the phone, seems to be that I should do another number, some stock dance, let's say like the one in *Singin' in the Rain*. Let's assume for the present there's not enough of me in the picture. Where and how then do we cure this and get me another number without glutting the public with the sight of Kelly slowing it up like a dancing Orson Welles. At any rate, up until I get your letter this week, this will give you something to mull about. . . .

All your little unit sends love and joins me in saying we miss you. It's good to know it will only be a few months before we can work at close range again.[8]

Regards from the old team.

Love,
Gene

Simone returned to London to pull together the odds and ends: scoring of "The Circus" and "Ring Around the Rosy"; recording crowd tracks and sound effects; temporary dubbing of the two sequences which Freed was urgently awaiting at the studio. She finished just under the wire as far as her work permit was concerned and returned to Paris.

[8] Kelly is referring to *Brigadoon,* which was to be photographed in Scotland and at the Boreham Wood studios.

While Freed and Edens, almost daily, were occupied with evaluating the entire footage, Schary, Mannix and Thau gazed into their crystal ball. Now came a period of no work and no play; everyone was tense and unable to relax, waiting for a decision to be made.

The zeal with which Kelly had entered into *Invitation* and which sustained him throughout the pressures and tribulations during production, was now gone. Because of his self-imposed exile he had to remain in Europe for another six months! It was a time of frustration and anxiety.

After many months of deliberation, it was decided that Arnold's score would be abandoned and a composer was brought in to fit a new score to the film. This sounds easy, but is almost impossible to do. Freed's choice was André Previn, the noted composer, conductor and pianist under contract to the studio.

To be in no way influenced, if only subconsciously, Previn refused to hear Arnold's score.

"When 'Ring Around the Rosy' was turned over to me," he says, "I was faced with the problem of writing a balletic score, entirely dictated by the already existing and unchangeable film. Every nuance of tempo, every phrase, every meter change had to be fitted exactly to the picture; a normal procedure for the scoring of a film, but certainly the hard way to compose a ballet. When the final timing sheets and click-track charts were put in a bundle they looked like the Manhattan Telephone Directory. No end of credit must be given to Lela

Kelly works with Carol Haney, who appears as the exotic Scheherazade in the "Sinbad the Sailor" sequence. M-G-M

394

Kelly shooting the live portion of the animated sequence in "Sinbad the Sailor." When the film is developed he will be superimposed onto the animated portion. M-G-M

Simone. She practically lived in the projection and cutting rooms with me, and it is due to her musicianship and technical skill that not one frame was wrong by the time we got to the scoring stage."[9]

Kelly returned home the first week of August, very anxious to start work on the cartoon sequence, the final ballet in the film. When he met with Edens to discuss adapting a work of one of the acknowledged great composers, Edens had already made up his mind: Rimsky-Korsakov. Kelly went straight into rehearsal.

After two days he was requested to write a synopsis. He called it "Sinbad the Sailor." This got the whole project off the ground with Edens adapting the music; William Hanna, Joseph Barbera and Fred Quimby cartooning; the live portion designed by Randall Duell; David Kasday as the Genie and Carol Haney as Scheherazade. In front of the blue backing Kelly demonstrated his choreography for the animators, with Haney and Coyne doubling for the characters to be drawn in.

[9] Aside from conducting the postrecording, Previn played the piano solos.

Edens spent many hours on the rehearsal stage, bringing with him Salinger, who had the task of adapting Rimsky-Korsakov.

At the end of two months the sequence was prerecorded under the baton of Johnny Green. It took Green three full days to record this twenty-one-and-a-half-minute section, with the live portion still having to be postscored. "Sinbad," with Joseph Ruttenberg at the camera, began shooting on October 3. "Gene is an ardent professional," says Ruttenberg. "He figured out mathematically all the different angles for the animation. Everything has to be on counts and he did his dancing with little animated images, which weren't there yet, and then Barbera and Ries had to match everything. It was very interesting and very tedious work."

The sequence was shot in ten days at a cost of $947,659 (animated portion: $323,025).

For the next three and one-half years the picture was intermittently tampered with: cut and recut, dubbed and redubbed. In October 1954, Tammy Rall was called in to redub his taps. In 1955, Kelly and Coyne redubbed Kelly's taps. And there it sat until 1957.

One might pose the question why it took M-G-M so long to release *Invitation to the Dance*. Most likely the answer can be found in a number of adverse circumstances.

What was the sales potential of the picture? As an art film it would play—at best—to limited audiences. Even though the divorcement between theatre ownership and motion-picture studios had not yet been put into effect by Loew's, Inc., as distributors of M-G-M products, their major outlets were theatres seating two thousand plus. These houses were not feasible for a ballet picture with Gene Kelly as the only big name on the marquee. There was the opportunity of booking into independent chains and theatres, but the distribution division was confronted with a lack of interest.

Another negative aspect was the rapidly declining motion-picture attendance, which shook the industry and with it the management of M-G-M. At the end of 1956, Dore Schary was dismissed[10] by Joseph Vogel, recently elected president of Loew's, Inc. Vogel assigned Ben Thau to administer the operation.

It was under Thau's new regime that *Invitation to the Dance* was taken off the shelf and premièred at the Plaza, an art theatre, in New York, on March 1, 1957. By this time the accumulated cost was $1,419,105. It grossed $615,000 ($200,000, domestic, $415,000, foreign).

[10] The studio had shown an operating deficit of $3,000,000. This was the heaviest operating loss since the critical $6,500,000 deficit in 1947–48.

13   *THE BAND WAGON*

METRO'S "THE BAND WAGON" IS A MAJOR ACHIEVE-
MENT IN A SCREEN GENRE (*Bosley Crowther, New York*
Times, *July 19, 1953*)

"BAND WAGON" A RARITY: LITERATE MOVIE MUSICAL
(*Otis L. Guernsey, Jr., New York* Herald Tribune, *July 19, 1953*)

No mistake about it, a review of *The Band Wagon* at the Music
Hall boils down to a collection of superlatives. It is the best musical of the month, the year, the decade, or, for all I know, of all
time. For my money it's better than *An American in Paris* which
was good enough. . . . (*Archer Winsten, New York* Post, *July 19,
1953*)

His recent successes with *An American in Paris* and *Singin' in the
Rain* gave Freed the idea to acquire another song catalogue as the basis
for a new musical film. He found it next door, so to speak: Howard
Dietz, lyric writer and vice-president of Loew's, Inc., and his principal
collaborator, composer Arthur Schwartz. "Dietz was our head publicity
man, a great friend of mine and a helluva lyric writer," says Freed. "I
always said to Howard, 'One day I want to do a picture with your
songs!'"

At the age of twenty-eight Dietz wrote his first lyrics for Jerome Kern's Broadway show *Dear Sir* (1924). A couple of years later he received a letter from a young lawyer by the name of Arthur Schwartz: "This is what's on my chest: I'd love to work with you on songs. Don't be too amused at the fact that I speak of tune writing under a lawyer's letterhead. I'm giving up the law in a few months to spend all my time at music." Two weeks later Dietz replied, "As I have written a first show in collaboration with a well-established composer, I don't think that our collaboration is such a good idea."

After Dietz had written the lyrics for two flop shows, the producer of a forthcoming Broadway revue entitled *The Little Show* felt that Dietz and Schwartz would make a good team and introduced them. Since then they have written over four hundred songs together.

Freed took "I Love Louisa," one of Schwartz and Dietz's hit songs, as the title for his new musical. With his genius for mixing a mélange of talents, he handed an expanded team free reign to come up with something new for a "terrific picture." Not a small order. The team was Vincente Minnelli, Betty Comden and Adolph Green, Roger Edens, Fred Astaire, Michael Kidd and Oliver Smith, and as a witty raisin in the pie, Oscar Levant.

The appearance of Oliver Smith in the Freed Unit was a propitious event. His first scenic design was for the Ballet Russe de Monte Carlo's "Saratoga," followed by settings for "Rodeo" and *Rosalinda.* In 1944, Smith formed a creative triumvirate with Jerome Robbins and Leonard Bernstein to present "Fancy Free" for the Ballet Theatre. Out of this, two things developed. He became codirector of the Ballet Theatre with Lucia Chase and decided to turn "Fancy Free" into a full-length musical comedy, *On the Town.* With its success, Oliver Smith, designer, was launched as Oliver Smith, producer. He went on to co-produce and design *Billion Dollar Baby, No Exit* and *Gentlemen Prefer Blondes.* This was interspersed with the decors for shows such as: *Brigadoon,* and *High Button Shoes.*

For Smith, as well as Michael Kidd, this would be his first experience in motion pictures. From 1942–47, Kidd was solo dancer with the Ballet Theatre, appearing in "Helen of Troy," "Petrushka," "Billy the Kid" and the world première of "Fancy Free." He was scenarist, choreographer and dancer for *On Stage.* He choreographed and directed the musical numbers for *Finian's Rainbow;* choreographed *Love Life* and *Arms and the Girl;* staged dances and musical numbers for *Guys and Dolls.* Kidd received the Antoinette Perry (Tony) Awards for his work on *Finian's Rainbow* and *Guys and Dolls.*

Astaire and his sister, Adele, had starred in Schwartz and Dietz's Broadway revue *The Band Wagon* (1931); Minnelli had staged the musical numbers for their show *At Home Abroad* (1935); Comden and Green's first two Broadway shows were produced by Smith; Kidd had worked for Smith in the Ballet Theatre. Over the years each of them had developed and polished his talents and skills. Now this group's paths crossed again in the Freed Unit.

Freed originally brought Smith out to be the designer and coproducer on *Invitation to the Dance*. "Kelly wanted me because of my association with ballet in the theatre," Smith says. "But the more I thought of it and heard about it, the less I liked it. I sort of felt a *Mata Hari* at work."[1] He urged Freed to let him participate in a "block-buster musical," in order to learn all the tricks of the trade. Freed indulged him, as he says, and assigned him as the production designer on *I Love Louisa*.

It was some time before Smith got his wish. He made good use of it; he sat in a projection room and ran all of Freed's pictures. Especially interested in the visual elements, decors and the use of color, he often visited the art department, the head of which was an idol of his youth. "He's one of the reasons I went into scenic design," recalls Smith, "going to movies and seeing Gibbons' scenery and productions, which were enormously stylish." Smith established an immediate rapport with Gibbons, in contrast to the hostility he met with in the art department in general.

The first week in February 1952, Comden and Green checked in at the studio to begin work on their original story and screenplay. Smith had already been there for a couple of months. Schwartz and Dietz arrived shortly after, as did Kidd. There were many meetings, discussions and get-togethers. Although these were temperamentally dissimilar people, their common denominator was talent, taste and craftsmanship. Here again Freed acted wisely. Disregarding studio rules, his people worked wherever and whenever at their discretion, which evoked jealousy and criticism. But this lack of regimentation did in no way impair the efficiency in Freed's Unit; on the contrary, it furthered it.

Now came the process of reviewing the catalogue of songs, even though there was no story or even an outline yet. All of the songs were written for lavish productions and Broadway revues, with no story point or character situation. Intermittently Astaire and Minnelli would join the group, everybody reminiscing about their theatrical careers.

Comden and Green were having labor pains over inventing a plot. But Freed had total confidence in the inventiveness of "his people," and with no qualms he left with Simone to meet Gene Kelly in Europe for the preliminaries on *Invitation*.

The basic idea Comden and Green came up with was so much a part of their lives that it took them a while to recognize it. Only after zigzagging through feasible subjects and contrived plots did the logical

---

[1] Smith and the author were associated on *Mata Hari,* David Merrick's ill-fated million-dollar Broadway musical, which closed during its Washington, D.C., tryout in 1968.

Cyd Charisse listens as Schwartz (left) and Dietz go through the songs that had been selected for *The Band Wagon*. M-G-M and HOWARD DIETZ COLLECTION

premise emerge—the making of a Broadway musical, a show within a show.

An aging star, feeling he is washed up, leaves Hollywood, returns to Broadway and gets a part in a show. "We were very nervous in the beginning about Fred's [Astaire] character," says Comden, "because it was based in so many ways on his actual position in life. It was not a man down, out and broke, but a man midway in his career, a man thinking of possibly retiring, or continuing to look for fresh fields." When they timidly presented the character they had drawn to Astaire, he loved it immediately.

Out of everybody's past experiences grew a story line: the two stars of the show; the writers; the actor-director-impresario; the frantic excitement of getting the show on its feet; the agony of out-of-town openings; the isolation of this life to the rest of the world.

Out of the mass of songs Edens extricated "By Myself," a little-known song from *Between the Devil*. This triggered off the springboard for Comden and Green's story and served to introduce Astaire's character. Incidents from their personal lives carried them further. When Astaire would arrive in Grand Central Station, he would be met by his fan club. That was exactly what had happened years ago to Green when he had returned to New York, their act washed up. "I entered the lobby of the station and saw Betty carrying a placard reading 'The Adolph Green Fan Club.'"

The writers in their story would be a married couple. Otherwise

400

they would pretty much resemble themselves, although Minnelli thought they were modeling them after Garson Kanin and Ruth Gordon; while Smith was sure they were the epitome of Oscar and June Levant. As their plot developed, the character of the actor-director-impresario was written with José Ferrer in mind, who had just staged and produced concurrently several Broadway shows and starred in one of them.

As it finally evolved, the screenplay for *I Love Louisa* was the result of many lengthy, arduous and animated conferences between Freed, Edens, Comden and Green, Minnelli, Kidd, Astaire and Smith.

Smith has some lively recollections of his apprenticeship in his new environment: "Once we had a five-hour conference and I got such a migraine I had to be carried out feet first from the Thalberg Building; it took four hours to pull me together. I think it's because of the concentration of power and tremendous personalities. You see, you'd be sitting there, listening, and suddenly jump up and go very fast. It took me a while to be able to adjust to that rhythm and learn to relax."

Each of these highly talented, perceptive people voiced their own opinions and often conflicted on artistic issues. "This is where Arthur, I think, is such a genius—that he would select all these people. And somehow out of this bouillabaisse comes something that really works," Smith remarks with insight.

In the screenplay, the main character Tony Hunter is quickly established as he arrives back in New York to try for a comeback. Lily and Lester Marton, his cheering fan club, entice him on the spot with a script for a Broadway show they have written. Moreover, they know the man who should put it on, Jeffrey Cordova. They meet him backstage during one of his performances in *Oedipus Rex,* no less. Being a great ham, he is flattered at the prospect of doing something frivolous: a musical comedy. He sees himself in a new light. The Martons describe their show: A writer and illustrator of children's books makes big money on the side by writing lurid murder mysteries, full of violence. This makes him feel he has sold his soul to the devil. With this Cordova springs to life: "Kids, you're geniuses! It's brilliant, contemporary, perceptive—this show is a modern version of *Faust!* We will not only have Tony Hunter but the great prima ballerina, Gabrielle Gerard, in our show." When Cordova opens his show in New Haven it is a hopeless catastrophe.

At first Hunter and Gerard start out hating each other. He is too old and a hoofer, she is too tall and a square, but later they are in love. Hunter is determined to save their show, takes over and reverts back to the Martons' original script. Cordova accepts defeat, joins the company as their costar and, under Hunter's direction, the show eventually opens in New York and is a smash hit.

It was almost banal to suggest Clifton Webb for the role of Cordova. He was approached; he wouldn't think of playing a secondary part;

even declining he asked a mint of money; generously, he suggested England's answer to Fred Astaire, Jack Buchanan. Oddly enough, both had starred in Schwartz and Dietz's revues. Before arrangements could be made for Buchanan to come over for a screen test, Freed considered Vincent Price and Edward G. Robinson. Buchanan arrived and got the part.

Freed cast Nanette Fabray and Oscar Levant to play Lily and Lester Marton. Fabray had appeared in the Broadway musicals *Love Life* and *Arms and the Girl,* but this was her first musical film. When Levant looked in on what Comden and Green were writing, he found his role intriguing. "I had always played a bachelor before, but here I was married! And I'd treat her atrociously—just as though she were my real wife!"

After Cyd Charisse's great performance in *Singin' in the Rain,* Freed felt she was ready to star opposite Astaire as Gabrielle Gerard. James Mitchell was cast as Gerard's mentor and fiance, and Thurston Hall as the principal backer of the show.

There was a lack of rapport between Smith and Edens; one could even call it animosity, which they hid behind their excellent manners. Edens had little reverence for Leonard Bernstein's score for *On the Town,* while Smith, who admired Bernstein, was negative about Edens' musical contributions to the picture version. But these two gifted men were able to breach the gap with mutual respect.

Edens made the final selection of the songs to be used in the picture from six of Schwartz and Dietz's Broadway shows: "Something to Remember You By" (ensemble) from *Three's a Crowd* (1923); "I Guess I'll Have to Change My Plans" (Astaire and Buchanan) from *The Little Show* (1929); "I Love Louisa" (Astaire, Fabray, Levant and ensemble), "New Sun in the Sky" (Charisse and boys), "The Beggar's Waltz" (Charisse in ballet), "Sweet Music" (Fabray and Levant), "High and Low" (ensemble) and "Dancing in the Dark" (Astaire and Charisse dance) from *The Band Wagon* (1931); "Shine on Your Shoes" (Astaire), "Two-faced Woman" (Charisse, Mitchell and ensemble), "Louisiana Hayride" (Fabray and ensemble) and "Alone Together" (Astaire and Charisse dance) from *Flying Colors* (1932); "You and the Night and the Music" (Astaire and Charisse dance) and "Never Marry a Dancer" (Fabray, Levant and Astaire) from *Revenge with Music* (1934); "Got a Bran' New Suit" (Fabray, Levant and Astaire) from *At Home Abroad* (1935); and "By Myself" (Astaire), "Triplets" (Astaire, Levant and Buchanan) and "You Have Everything" (Charisse and Astaire dance) from *Between the Devil* (1937).

"When we wrote 'Dancing in the Dark,'" recalls Schwartz, "I played it for Max Dreyfus, the dean of music publishers [head of Chappell and Co.], who was a man of small praise about anything. As a matter of fact, I would imagine if God, after his six days of creation,

402

had asked Dreyfus' opinion, Max would have looked down and he would have said, 'Nice.' And that's what he said about our new song for *The Band Wagon,* 'Nice.'" At the time "Dancing in the Dark" was written it was the consensus of opinion that the song would not be a success.

For the record Schwartz reports, "The whole placing of the songs— Roger Edens! Well, he was a giant in this field of choosing and arranging and rearranging things. He was a wonderful talent. And Arthur, being a songwriter, being the best producer of musicals who ever lived —they knew their way around."

Dietz and Schwartz were going over the songs with Freed. "Boys, we need another song!" a pronouncement Freed made on almost all his pictures. "In the script this director, Buchanan, is saying that practically anything you can do will work if it's entertaining. I want a "There's No Business Like Show Business.'" The two left, went into the "Berlin Room" and within half an hour came out with "That's Entertainment!"

Several months before, an MCA agent had tipped Freed off to a young, talented costume designer and client of his, Mary Ann Nyberg. She had worked for Jean Louis at Columbia Pictures and was now at liberty. When Freed met Nyberg he not only found her most attractive but recognized her great fashion sense, aside from the exuberance. He signed her to a studio contract, and her first important assignment was designing the costumes for *I Love Louisa.*

Freed was never really satisfied with *I Love Louisa* as the title and changed it to *The Band Wagon.* But it belonged to Twentieth Century-Fox.[2] He met with Lou Schreiber, vice-president of that studio, and bought it for $10,000.

The rehearsal period for *The Band Wagon* was long; it started on August 11, 1952, and lasted six weeks. Sets were being sketched, designed and constructed. It started with a clash. "Oliver took a look at me and I took a look at him," says Preston Ames, "and I thought, 'How are we going to get along?'" Ames contends that he was the art director on the picture and that Smith was only responsible for the musical numbers. According to Oliver Smith, this is not true. "We were doing interiors. We would use whatever we could from the warehouse and revamp it. And then, on top of that, the colors and the whole thing went against the rather traditional Metro setup, which was totally realistic. When everything was assembled, Preston and I would look at it and then *I* would decide what would be used."

Keogh Gleason gives credence to Smith's assertion. Gibbons, for instance, had an aversion to greens and reds, which he considered only fit for Christmas tree decorations. "But Smith and Minnelli wanted a dark bottle-green background, with a brilliant red sofa in front of it.

[2] Fox had acquired the Broadway revue but only retained the songs for their film *Dancing in the Dark* (1949).

There was a tremendous argument, but Smith got his way," says Gleason.

Gleason is referring to Cordova's library set. He was set decorator, and Minnelli told him he wanted miniature stage sets as part of the bric-a-brac of that room, forty of them. These miniatures were known as Pollock's Little Theatres, made in London. Gleason scouted every

The art department's blueprint of Oliver Smith's special penny arcade game. M-G-M

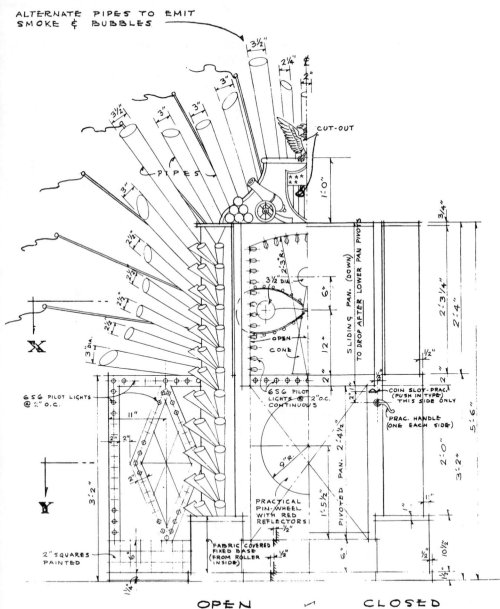

OPEN   CLOSED

An art department still of how the machine looked after it suddenly opened up. M-G-M

available source, to no avail. Minnelli urged cabling England, but Gleason resorted to having some made in the art department.

Astaire was rehearsing his specialty number "Shine on Your Shoes" in a penny arcade, assisted by LeRoy Daniels, a bootblack. Daniels had been found in downtown Los Angeles, at the corner of Sixth and Main. Minnelli told Smith he wanted a "button" for the number. Smith invented a fun machine, which sounded like a calliope, shot out flags, rockets and a kaleidoscope of colors. It took fifteen draftsmen working night and day to get it ready at the cost of $8,800.

As on any other picture, Minnelli presented Smith with his overstuffed clipping file, to which he paid no attention. Only in one instance did Minnelli use one of his photographs, "The Isle of the Dead," by the German painter Arnold Boecklin, for a back projection, to symbolize the disaster of Cordova's opening night.

The wardrobe department, a special conclave in the hierarchy of the studio, viewed the appearance of "that girl," Mary Ann Nyberg, with green eyes; no one ever seemed to remember her name. With every sketch she turned in, the cost of execution rose. She cites an ex-

Fred Astaire and LeRoy
Daniels going through
"Shine on Your Shoes."
M-G-M

ample: "I designed a green net coat with big polka dots for Nanette
Fabray. The cutter did the sleeves seven different ways and that on
seven different days. I would come in and she'd say, 'I know exactly
what you mean.' Then she would recut. I would come in the next day
and there'd be a different sleeve. This went on and on."

Each and every costume Nyberg designed came out wrong. She not
only didn't have any assistance from the wardrobe department; she was
sabotaged at every corner. She was desperate and went to Sam Kress,
head of the wardrobe department. She confronted him with facts and
figures: delays, mistakes, exorbitant, unjustified charges for time and
labor. Cornered, Kress had to come around, and he engaged two young
cutters to work under her supervision.

One day Nyberg came to Freed's office in a white dress with a
pleated skirt; very simple and very elegant. "This is exactly the dress
I want Cyd to wear for the 'Dancing in the Dark' sequence!" Freed told

her. She had gotten this "broomstick" dress from a supplier in Arizona for $25. By now it was no longer being manufactured, and she ordered the wardrobe department to copy her dress. "Those women fooled with that dress, how to put it on a broomstick and how to pleat it, until I was absolutely enraged! Would you believe it, that simple little dress cost $1,000!"

One of the misfortunes the production had to face was the long, extremely painful and complicated dental surgery Buchanan had to undergo from the time he arrived. Rehearsals, prerecordings and shooting schedules had to be adjusted to his dentist's appointments.

Much different from any other Freed picture, *The Band Wagon* started production on September 17 and alternated for one month between rehearsals, prerecordings and shooting. Daily shooting began on October 20.

A singing double was needed for Charisse, and Edens chose Pat Michaels, a perfect match for her speaking voice. She prerecorded four songs. Almost immediately afterward she became seriously ill and was out of the running. As an alternative he tried to get Carol Richards, but she was not available. Finally, although she was not ideal, India Adams was engaged.

Weeks before Fabray was to prerecord "Louisiana Hayride," Edens began to coach her. The rapport he had had with Ethel Merman, Judy Garland, Ann Sothern and countless others was there once again. Fabray talks in glowing terms about this experience: "Roger developed my voice note for note and vowel by vowel. He found that my best note was a high B flat and my best sound was an open A: 'Hay—ride.' Hour by hour he worked with me to develop my lung strength."

Deutsch was the musical director with, of course, Salinger on or-

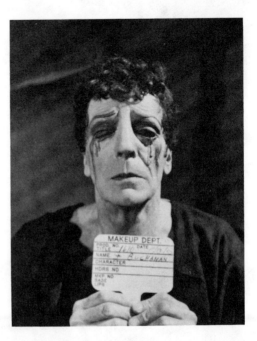

Jack Buchanan's make-up test as Oedipus Rex in *The Band Wagon.* M-G-M

THE BAND WAGON

chestrations, joined by Skip Martin, and at times by Alexander "Sandy"
Courage. Martin, a master in jazz arrangements, orchestrated "Shine
on Your Shoes" and "Louisiana Hayride." And an attentive listener
can recognize "Dancing in the Dark" and "That's Entertainment!" as
pure Salinger (that is not to say that his other numbers were of lesser
quality).

Comden and Green's script called for a cameo appearance of a
movie star. Schary noticed that Freed had penciled in Ava Gardner,
to whose sex appeal he was not very susceptible. He instructed Howard
Strickling to give out a press release, announcing Esther Williams for
the spot. But once again, this was Freed's picture and Gardner made
the appearance.

From the time the picture started production, tensions set in.
Astaire worked, carrying the heavy burden of his wife's terminal illness. He and Kidd, with all their mutual admiration, were not yet secure with one another. Buchanan, irritable because of constant physical
pain, was petrified about working with Astaire. Smith and Nyberg had
their daily struggles within their respective departments. Levant, recovering from a heart attack, was more of an *enfant terrible* than ever.

Astaire lays out the chor-
eography and rehearses
"Never Marry a Dancer."
The number was cut from the
release print. ARTHUR
FREED ARCHIVES

Nanette Fabray having
her false legs adjusted.
Minnelli talking to
Astaire, is as usual,
oblivious. M-G-M

Astaire, Fabray and
Buchanan at the start of
"Triplets." M-G-M

Choreographer Michael
Kidd added his own
comic touch in staging
the number. M-G-M

Sensitive to the mood on the set, Charisse, with her extremely shy and retiring personality, stayed aloof. Fabray's warmth and exuberance were rebuked as a false note; she was ignored by everybody and remembers it well: "I would say, 'Good morning, Cyd'—'Good morning, Fred'—nobody would say hello to me. I thought it was me, I became paranoid. But nobody talked to anybody; it was the coldest, unfriendliest, the most terrible experience I can ever remember." In such situations the captain of the ship, in this case the director, should be the conciliatory factor. But Minnelli is a man blessed with blinders.

George Folsey, cameraman on the picture, had worked many times with Minnelli before and had adjusted himself to his pedantry. The production department had repeatedly sent warnings: The picture was going too slow. Minnelli, intolerant of delays, blamed Folsey, and he was taken off the picture. Harry Jackson, a cameraman from Twentieth Century-Fox, was brought over to replace Folsey.

Production was now accelerated because *Band Wagon* faced an ominous predicament: It was November 15, and Buchanan had less than one month remaining to his contract with only one third of the picture completed. In view of that, a new procedure was put into effect: For one solid week Minnelli concentrated on shooting nothing but dialogue scenes. Then, from November 21 through 28, the production closed down and Kidd staged two versions of "That's Entertainment!" and "Triplets"; Astaire staged his and Buchanan's number, "I Guess I'll Have to Change My Plans."

In that number Smith's sensitivity to theatrical values led him to design a set which would in no way distract but rather emphasize the elegance and performance of two great stars. "That was very Paul Klee; I thought it was time to broaden the perspective and not just take from Dufy," recalls Smith. "You see, the art department was obsessed with Raoul Dufy. I thought, we'll expand that vocabulary just slightly. That's one of my favorite sets in the picture, actually."

Rehearsals on "Guess I'll Have to Change My Plans" were finished; prerecordings done. But when Buchanan came to the set to shoot his dance *a deux* with Astaire, in top hat, white tie and tails, he was absolutely terrified.

"Triplets," as Schwartz describes, was first used in *Flying Colors* with people who looked so dissimilar that it was ridiculous. Clifton Webb was 6 feet 2 inches, Imogene Coca was 5 feet and Philip Loeb was 5 feet 8 inches—and the number flopped.

Originally this number was intended for Astaire, Buchanan and Levant. Not for the first time Levant feigned illness and Fabray was put in his place. Kidd made the triplets infants, sitting in high chairs, jumping off, dancing and *all* of the same height.

To achieve this effect, specially made boots of saddle leather were molded and made to fit over the knees. Baby shoes were then added to

Cyd Charisse and the dancing ensemble in the lengthy production number "Two-faced Woman," which was deleted from the release print. M-G-M and ARTHUR FREED ARCHIVES.

the bottom of the boots, and the boots were strapped to the knees of the performers. Their real feet and legs were covered with specially made black velvet stockings. The dance was performed on a black floor. Consequently, in the finished picture, the black legs and feet were not visible, and the audience is given the impression that the actors are dancing on baby legs. Since the entire dance was executed while standing upon the knees, it was, of course, very strenuous, and the actors could not remain in the boots for more than twenty minutes at a time.

Astaire, Fabray and Buchanan begin the refrain:

> "We do everything alike,
> We look alike, we dress alike,
> We walk alike, we talk alike . . ."

To make up for his "moonlighting" as a lyric writer, Dietz changed a line:

> "M-G-M has got a Leo but Mama has got a trio . . ."

412

On the day before shooting "Triplets" another misfortune hit the production. While rehearsing "Louisiana Hayride" Fabray had jumped onto a barrel which had not been reinforced and tore open her leg. Stitches were required and before she could be placed back into her contraption novocaine had to be administered. Buchanan, still in extreme pain, had novocaine injected into his gums (the doctor was careful not to paralyze his face). Furthermore, standing on one's knees the tendency is to bend forward, and a great deal of time was spent rehearsing in the apparatus in order to stand up straight. Says Astaire, who prefers using his toes, "As a knee dancer I'm a good singer. This could ruin me!" Says Fabray, "It was just a long day of pain, terror and anxiety."

Dietz wrote a revised lyric of "That's Entertainment!" to wind up the picture. When the original song was submitted to the Breen Office, Freed received the following interoffice memo:

> Production Code Administration has *n.g.'d* the line "simply teeming with sex" in the song "That's Entertainment!"

But Freed contested the Code's ruling and won out.

The finale of the picture came into being through adverse circumstances and not by design. At first it was planned as a production number but it became more of a sign-off. Buchanan was in his last few days before returning to England; Levant was unapproachable about rehearsing anything. Looming in the background was still the big production number "The Girl Hunt" ballet, for which Kidd had been rehearsing disjointed sections, with his two assistants standing in for Astaire and Charisse.

Unperturbed by the prosaic realities of life, Minnelli called Nyberg: "I want Cyd's dress to be sumptuous, just breathe romance; I want it to be terribly romantic!" Exploiting Charisse's sensational figure and tiny waist, Nyberg designed an extremely simple gown with a fitted waist and a flared skirt, ideally suited for a dance number. Then the plans were changed. "There will be no dancing," said Minnelli, "but I want some flowers on her shoulder." "Well, all right," replied Nyberg, "but it's not exactly my idea of what I had in mind." "Yes, I know, but couldn't you put like—some gardenias on her shoulder?" "O.K., Vincente, and I'll add a little microphone in each one saying, 'I love you—I love you.'"

Want it or not, Levant had to rehearse the end of the number. "The physical effort involved worried me," he recalls. "And I told my doctor that I would have to walk down a long ramp, taking large strides at great speed. He told me not to do it. And I *refused* to do it. Astaire said in disgust, 'All right, I'll carry you down!' And so I did it."

Minnelli shot take after take of this strenuous ending. Nerves were wearing thin. "Oscar was trying to pick a fight with Fred," recalls Fa-

Fred Astaire and Oscar Levant in a scene from *The Band Wagon*.
Astaire sits in front of one of Pollock's miniature theatres. M-G-M

bray, "but he wouldn't talk to him. Then he tried to pick a fight with
Vincente, and he wouldn't pay attention. And as a last resort, he began
picking on me. He was witty, quick, had a sharp tongue and he had
been hollering at the grips and everybody. He spent two hours chop-
ping at me viciously. Finally I let him have it—I could by this time—I
couldn't take it any more. I told him off for the grips, and I told him
off for me to such a point that he went staggering off, clutching his
heart. Everybody burst into applause—they were so grateful. But Vincente and Fred had disappeared, and here I was left alone facing this
poor, sick man."

When the storm had subsided and Minnelli returned to the set, he
said to Levant: "There's nothing the matter with you, it's all in your
mind!" Levant, horrified, replied, "In my mind? What a horrible place
to be!"

In Comden and Green's script they had placed a murder mystery
ballet for which they expected to develop a plot. This did not materialize because Edens told them it was not in their province but in Dietz
and Schwartz's. They wrote a song called "The Private Eye" and between staging all his other numbers Kidd played around with it, with-

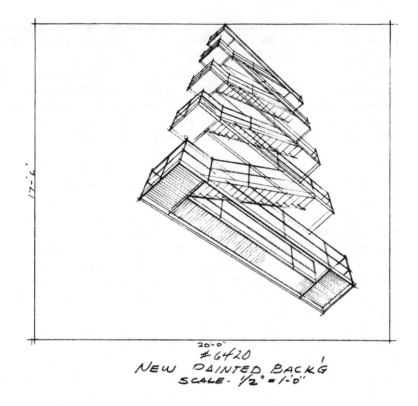

17'-6"

20'-0"
#6420
NEW PAINTED BACKG'
SCALE - ½" = 1'-0"

Smith's drawing for the staircase section of "The Girl Hunt" ballet.
M-G-M

On the sound stage as
Astaire used the set. M-G-M

out much enthusiasm. Then, inspired by a spread in *Life* magazine, Edens came up with the idea of doing a Mickey Spillane ballet. This was discussed by Freed, Smith, Kidd and Minnelli—everybody was elated. Edens asked Schwartz to submit some suitable themes, which he recorded on tape in New York and sent back to him at the studio.

Edens had a big job on his hands. Unlike "An American in Paris," a tone poem, what he had to work with was a disparate ray of themes and motives which he actually had to compose into a musical continuity.

He worked closely with Kidd, who was a native New Yorker who knew the backgrounds Spillane had drawn in his famous detective mysteries: the empty, deserted city streets, the eery, terrifying experience of the lonely subway platform late at night, and the popular bop joints with their joyless, menacing tension. He visualized a new Astaire: the tough detective, a character dancer with athletic overtones. All this being totally alien to the traditional Astaire style, Kidd was scared to death to show it to him. His two assistants, Pat Denise and Alex Romero, had to practically force him to demonstrate it. To Kidd's utter amazement, Astaire loved it.

Alan Lerner was at the studio working on *Brigadoon*. He had lunch with Freed, and Minnelli joined them. Looking very pointedly at Lerner, Minnelli said, "We need a narration in *Band Wagon*." For ethical reasons Lerner, at first, was very reluctant; after all, this was Comden and Green's picture; but Freed and Minnelli gently pressured him. "No conditions, no money—I'll do it for fun," Lerner said. Minnelli even promised he would claim to have written it himself.

Cyd Charisse as she first appeared in the "Bee Bop" sequence from the ballet. One of the most extraordinary shots from the number.
M-G-M

The narration for what was now titled "The Girl Hunt" ballet was a satire on the proverbial detective story. Astaire, as the detective-narrator, in slouch hat and street suit, brilliantly portrayed the antithesis of Astaire in top hat, white tie and tails. Charisse, in the dual role of the blond and brunet seductress, exuded sex appeal rarely equaled on the screen.

On December 17, production shut down; rehearsals for the ballet started, tensions subsided and an altogether fresh wind began to blow. Edens, Smith, Nyberg, Minnelli and Kidd, plus a new group of dancers, found themselves in a very congenial atmosphere.

"It was probably one of the happiest collaborations I've ever had," says Smith, "and it certainly included some of my very best work in my own estimation. I would consider it sort of a high point and it is something I certainly am very proud of."

Deutsch, Salinger and Martin prerecorded sections of "The Girl Hunt" on January 9, 1953, under Edens' guidance. Most scenes without actual dancing were left for postscoring, others were shot to temporary piano tracks and some simply to counts. The narration and sound effects such as machine-gun fire, gun shots, fist fights, screams and the solo trumpet's mournful tune over the deserted streets were postsynchronized.

The prerecording session over, Minnelli was ready to shoot the ballet on January 12. "Always at the end of the film they are worried about budget. So I promised Arthur faithfully that I would shoot the whole thing in three days. We had rehearsed it very well and I made a point of honor to get it done. But it seemed so complicated . . ."

Minnelli shows Astaire how he would like him to hold Cyd during a close-up.
M-G-M

Two classic photographs of Fred Astaire and Cyd Charisse during the ballet. Astaire today considers "The Girl Hunt" ballet his favorite number. M-G-M

According to the daily report of assistant director Jerry Thorpe, it took seven days to photograph "The Girl Hunt" ballet.

The Band Wagon finally closed production on January 28, 1953.

For the scoring of the picture and the ballet, Edens eagerly awaited Simone's return from Europe and *Invitation to the Dance*. "How did it go?" she asked. "Be glad you weren't here," came Edens' cryptic reply.

When all the pieces, bridges and sections, the narration and the sound effects were put together and dubbed, the thirteen-minute track of "The Girl Hunt" ballet, even without the benefit of the screen image, emerged as what one might call a musical rhapsody with a voice over. Salinger, especially, achieved a sonority and texture comparable to the best in the legitimate field.

The final cost of producing the picture was $2,169,120 ("The Girl Hunt" ballet cost $314,475).

When the main titles were being prepared, there was an enormous problem about Oliver Smith's credit. At that time no production designer was allowed to join the art directors' union, but Freed railroaded his membership through. Freed's edict was over the head of Gibbons and the whole hierarchy of Metro. "This is another reason that people like myself are so loyal to him," Smith emphatically comments, "and with all his strange individual qualities, really, he's the best musical producer I've ever worked with, and I've worked for every one of them, practically."

The picture went into general release on August 7, 1953. On the Sunday following its New York opening, Bosley Crowther in the New York *Times* took his whole column to make some additional comments:

> There was some instinctive hesitation in the mind of this reviewer the other day when he came out and said *The Band Wagon* might be one of the best musical films ever made. Lofty comments of that nature sometimes have a way of popping up a few weeks or months later and causing the maker's face to turn bright red. But another inspection of the picture, which is now on the Music Hall's screen, and a hasty review of the record emboldens us to let the comment stand. As a matter of fact, we'll make it stronger: It *is* one of the best musicals ever made.

So much for the critical acclaim. What did it do at the box office? In its initial release *The Band Wagon* grossed in excess of $5,655,505.

14

BRIGADOON

IT'S ALWAYS FAIR WEATHER

KISMET

SILK STOCKINGS

The year 1953 was Freed's twenty-fifth year at M-G-M and fifteenth anniversary as a producer. He had written songs for over thirty films and had produced thirty-eight pictures. He had won every desirable award including the Légion d'honneur. Now another award came his way, and from a most unexpected source: A unanimous First-class Certificate for the Orchid Phalaenopsis Grace Palm Easter Parade from the Royal Horticulturist Society of Great Britain. This is the highest award that can be given in the field; the only other recipients so far had been the King and Queen of England and the British branch of the Rothschilds.

A key to Freed's personality can be found in the way he acquired his first orchid plant. Early in 1948, he went to a little town near Santa Barbara, California, where an important orchid auction was to be held the following day. Since he knew practically nothing about orchids, his astute business sense told him he could be stung badly if he didn't handle this cautiously. In a carefully conceived plan he introduced himself to the auctioneer for the purpose of meeting the prominent commercial orchid growers attending the sale. The next day, when the sale got underway, Freed sat back and watched the proceedings until he noticed two of the top men bidding against each other. He knew that the plants involved had to be the best of the lot, so he entered the bidding and kept raising until the other men dropped out.

420

Freed became an avid and earnest student on the subject of orchids. He read every available book and quickly learned all about the intricacies involved in breeding prize orchids. After a search for the best available men in the field, he hired two experts to take charge.

Situated on his eleven and a half acres in Malibu, the greenhouses, managed by his brother Hugo became a show place. His hybrids were exhibited at important flower shows at home and abroad, all tastefully arranged and displayed with the help of fellow orchid grower Walter Plunkett.

In years to come, "Arthur Freed's Orchids" would be known and sold all over the world; receiving over three hundred awards and culminating in May 1971 with the Westonbirt Orchid Gold Medal, the most prestigious international award bestowed on a perfect specimen.

But Freed's main concern was still Culver City. In 1953, several properties were active, although the unit had gradually slowed down. These properties were being analyzed with greater circumspection and evaluated from the vantage point of changing times. Television had become the entertainment of the masses, in most instances a low-level diversion, but good enough to keep the dollars away from the box-office till. Freed had a keen sense of what was in the wind; he also was a master in manipulating circumstances without even knowing it.

Jumbo was on the agenda, and Edens, Donen and art director Paul Groesse went east to scout small circuses. When they returned, discussions were held concerning the restrictive clauses in Billy Rose's original contract; Ben Hecht and Charles MacArthur's book along with Rodgers and Hart's score could not be tampered with. On that condition Freed dropped the project. Instead he asked Edens to continue work on the Romberg biomusical even though a satisfactory screenplay had not been completed.

Helen Deutsch, a prominent M-G-M screenwriter, had been developing the adaptation of the Arlen-Harburg musical *St. Louis Woman*. Freed intended it for Ava Gardner, Frank Sinatra and Gene Kelly, with George Sidney directing. But before long, Sinatra and Gardner separated and the whole project fell apart.

Always looking into the future, Freed screentested the following people: Valerie Bettis, Broadway dancer-actress; Harold Lang and Helen Gallagher, both from the recent Broadway revival of *Pal Joey;* Jose Greco; Anne Jeffreys of *Kiss Me, Kate;* Cesare Siepi of the Metropolitan Opera and Dolores Gray, star of the London production of *Annie Get Your Gun.*

Lerner had delivered a first draft for *Brigadoon,* continued his work in *Green Mansions,* and with a new collaborator, Arthur Schwartz, took on Freed's latest plan *Kismet.*

Later in the year Comden and Green were expected to write an original musical for Kelly under a new three-picture contract.

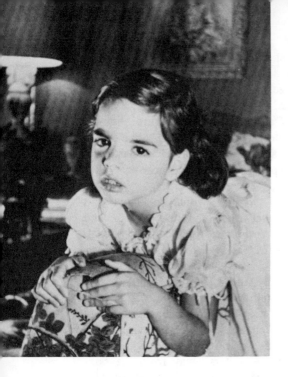

Freed took this picture of
Liza. When she came by with
her father to pick it up she
left the following note:

GOOD WISHES
FROM MGM
TO ARTHUR
LIZA

The 1953–54 schedule of the Freed Unit shows that "slowing down"
is a relative term.

In May 1953, Freed took Lerner's draft of *Brigadoon* to discuss
with Kelly in Paris. But before leaving he inquired about Irene
Sharaff's availability. Irving Lazar, her agent, advised that she had a
firm offer from Twentieth Century-Fox for a picture she was not very
keen on doing. Freed told him to set up a deal.

Shortly after Freed departed, Schary called Simone and asked her
whether she would have the time to work with Charles Vidor on
Rhapsody. Vidor's picture, an important one with Elizabeth Taylor,
was about a concert pianist, a concert violinist and an extravagant
amount of music. Simone was available because of a lull in the Freed
Unit production. Schary confirmed this arrangement with Freed in Paris.

Edens also took advantage of this pause by working with Judy
Garland in preparation for her Warner Brothers musical *A Star Is
Born*.

Freed and Kelly discussed the production plans: rehearsals in Paris,
exterior locations in Scotland, interior scenes photographed at the
Boreham Wood studios and the musical numbers in Culver City. He
went on to London with the intention of signing Moira Shearer in the
leading role opposite Kelly, as well as engaging the Sadler's Wells
Ballet Company for the ensemble. Unable to give the respective agents
a definite starting date, all the negotiations ended with polite regrets.
Before returning home, Freed had a serious talk with Kelly. He was

extremely concerned about the precarious weather conditions in Scotland; in fact, he decided to produce the entire film in Culver City when Kelly returned in late October.

Back at his office Freed succeeded in getting Frederick Loewe and Alan Lerner together again, to collaborate on some new songs. However, this would have to wait awhile since Lerner was recovering from a serious illness.

The collaboration between Lerner and Schwartz had been of short duration. Their breakup coincided with Freed's disillusionment about Schwartz. All Lerner wanted—and wants—is to write, as he has often stated. After working with Schwartz for a period of time, writing some new songs for *Kismet,* he found himself fighting Schwartz's legal battles, which were, in some instances, very petty. He had to operate like an agent. He wrote Freed that he was quite fed up with the "aura" of the partnership, pointing out that it had nothing to do with the recuperation period he was going through. He expressed feeling sorry for a man of Schwartz's talent, so concerned with credits and such.

In Freed's reply, his main concern was Lerner's health and, secondly, *Brigadoon.* In his letter he included some comments on Schwartz:

Dear Alan:

I hope that you'll take it easy now and get back your strength and not worry about anything.

Naturally, I've been giving a lot of thought to *Brigadoon* because at long last the starting date is getting closer and closer. In going over the music I realize more than ever what a great score it is.[1]

Confidentially, I've been a little put out about Arthur Schwartz's conduct, and while I would be the last person in the world not to fight for the proper credit of any creator, I certainly resented the ultimatums and, it seems to me, pettiness of the whole affair. Frankly, I've lost my desire and enthusiasm for working with him. It seems to me the desire to work with you and, incidentally, myself should have made anything else secondary. I'm a funny guy; I just don't like one-sided love affairs.

Vincente and I will come to New York soon. I will only stay three or four days, but Vincente will remain with you to go through the script which should be a very simple task. I want you to know that Vincente is bubbling over with enthusiasm about doing *Brigadoon* and I can see Liza in kilts next Christmas.

In the meantime, take care of yourself and give my love to Nancy. I'll be talking to you soon.

Love,
Arthur

[1] *Brigadoon* won the New York Drama Critics' Circle Award for a musical in 1947, citing Frederick Loewe and Alan Jay Lerner for "having made a real contribution to the lyric theatre. It is an altogether original and inventive piece of work."

Freed might have stressed his disenchantment with Schwartz because he always felt that Fritz Loewe was the man for Lerner.

After meek beginnings Lerner and Loewe had written a number of successful shows, covering a wide range of historic times and places, from the highlands of Scotland to the great plains of the wild West. Whatever libretto Lerner wrote, Loewe had the rare gift of inventing his tunes, his melodies, in the specific emotional and stylistic language of whatever country or landscape he found himself in. This man was born and raised in Germany, the son of an operatic tenor father and an actress mother. His musical education was solid; his instrument was the piano. He went to the Stern Conservatory in Berlin and studied piano with Ferruccio Busoni and Eugène d'Albert; composition and orchestration with Nikolaus von Reznicek. He came to the United States with his father in 1924, at the age of twenty-three. For the next seven years he pawned his career for miscellaneous jobs such as prize fighting, knocking out Tony Canzoneri (later featherweight champion of the world); he played "tingle-tangle" piano in Greenwich Village, Third Avenue bars and beer halls in Manhattan's Yorkville section. In the late thirties he started writing songs for Broadway shows, but these amounted to nothing. In 1942, he went to Detroit with a friend to do a show for a new theatre; and here is where destiny stepped in: He met Lerner.

As a precautionary measure, the legal department submitted the book and lyrics of *Brigadoon* to the Breen Office, which replied that the songs "The Love of My Life" and "My Mother's Wedding Day" could not be used.

In his first draft Lerner had modified the leading character; originally a singer, he would now be a dancer, Gene Kelly. And when Freed found himself without Moira Shearer, he replaced her with Cyd Charisse.

The first week in October, Lerner turned in his final screenplay for which no new songs were needed. It concerned two New Yorkers who get lost while hunting in Scotland. They happen on Brigadoon the one day it is visible every hundred years, and the villagers are in a joyous mood. A wedding is to take place and the two outsiders join in the fun. Particularly Kelly, who falls for Charisse hard enough to want to join her in the past and leave the present world.

Kelly was back at the studio, and Edens began to work with him on the songs. Three songs, "Heather on the Hill," "Almost Like Being in Love" and "There But for You Go I," were written for a legitimate voice and did not come easily to Kelly; he needed special coaching. This time Edens was able to get Carol Richards for Charisse's singing double.

Freed had offered the part of Kelly's friend to Donald O'Connor, but his contract with the studio had expired and Van Johnson was given the role. The parts of the young Scottish couple about to be married were handed to Virginia Bosler (from the Broadway cast)

Two of Irene Sharaff's costume designs for *Brigadoon*. ARTHUR FREED ARCHIVES and ROGER EDENS ARCHIVES

and Michael Maule, whose numbers would be dubbed by John Gustafson. Maule's rival was cast with Hugh Laing, and Elaine Stewart, a Metro starlet, was Kelly's American fianceé. As the old sage of Brigadoon, Freed brought over the famous British actor Barry Jones.

Assigned to the production were Joseph Ruttenberg, director of photography; Irene Sharaff, costume designer; Preston Ames, art director; Keogh Gleason, set decorator; Johnny Green, musical director; Conrad Salinger, orchestrator; Robert Tucker, vocal arrangements; Carol Haney, assistant choreographer; Commander Ian Murray, dialogue and technical adviser; Roger Edens, associate producer.

It was the time of innovations: "3-D," VistaVision, CinemaScope and Stereophonic Sound and Metro did not want to fall behind the times. They decided to shoot *Brigadoon* in two ways simultaneously: CinemaScope and Wide Screen. A special boom was built to carry the heavy cameras with their two operators. It would also be recorded in stereophonic sound.

On this picture the art department, the artists, the painters and the landscape architects had to overcome a colossal handicap: an exterior motion picture shot on a sound stage. Preston Ames did extensive research on Scotland.

According to the script the story would take place on two main sites: the hills of Scotland and the village of Brigadoon. These were to be constructed on three separate sound stages, until Ames came up with the ingenious idea of combining everything on one stage, creating a vast panorama. He presented his idea to Minnelli. "I think you're crazy," said Minnelli, "but do it! But remember, I want lots of heather!"

To execute this enormous undertaking, the construction department built hillsides and valleys, a village with many cottages and a bridge spanning a brook; there were livestock and all the trappings of the outdoors. One man was responsible for creating the visual illusion of the Scottish countryside: George Gibson, the same man who so masterfully executed the backdrops for the *American in Paris* ballet. His backing for the *Brigadoon* set was 600 feet wide and 60 feet high. Gibson's painting was so realistic that even the birds were attracted by "their natural habitat" and flew through the open stage doors straight into the backdrop. "Our biggest problem was the heather," recalls Gibson. You see, the texture of heather is small and we couldn't get enough to satisfy Minnelli. So we wound up painting sumac purple to represent purple heather, which we placed against the backing. I realized it was way out of character, but painting it you had texture and you had the quality of color—and it felt like heather." Even to the naked eye, the highlands of Scotland, covering forty thousand square feet on Stage 15, gave the illusion of reality—at a cost of $382,280.

The set was up and on the Saturday before the first recording session Minnelli shot a test for the opening of the picture: the Scottish highlands in a dense fog. As the fog slowly lifts the village of Brigadoon comes into view in the distance. It is, of course, impossible to regulate and control fog "slowly lifting." Therefore, Minnelli and Ruttenberg came to the conclusion that the scene had to be shot in reverse. As the camera started rolling and moving on long dolly tracks, the air would be clear and the village visible. On cue the special effects crew would pump quantities of chemical fog into the set, ultimately obscuring the entire landscape and the village. Then, by reversing the film, the desired effect would be obtained.

Another problem was that the entire footage of this opening had to be synchronized with the musical prologue, sung by male voices, telling the story that was to follow. This made it necessary to shoot the test to a music track, a track of a given and unchangeable length. With the last note of the prologue the village had to be in the clear, not before and not after. Simone mathematically figured out the over-all length of the music track in relation to the distance the camera would cover, and calculated at what speed the camera had to move and come to a halt precisely. When the test was shot, stop watch in hand, she guided the camera crew. The fog had rolled in in enormous, black, erratic puffs. The doors were opened, the ventilating system was turned on and it took fifty-four minutes to blow out the fog. Then came two more takes, both of which were good. For this test only one camera was in operation. The first three takes were shot in CinemaScope. The next take was to be shot in Wide Screen, but when Ruttenberg wanted to change his lens he found that it didn't fit and another camera had to be ,sent for. After two completed Wide Screen takes, the fog was too heavy and the company was dismissed at 6:55 P.M.

When the test was viewed it was exactly what everybody had hoped for. The test would be used in the picture.

Preparing for prerecording, Edens laid out all the musical arrangements before turning them over to Salinger, giving special consideration to Kelly's numbers. Green came in just to conduct the score, making it possible for him to carry on with his burdensome tasks in the music department. With his beautifully voiced arrangements of "Once in the Highlands" and "Brigadoon," Tucker added to the opening shot a magic of his own.

Brigadoon was progressing smoothly when Schary issued an urgent request. He asked Edens to put a musical short, in stereophonic sound, into production in order to beat Twentieth Century-Fox to the punch. With George Sidney directing and Green conducting, in one week's time Schary had his short: Tschaikowsky's "Caprice Italien," a composition eminently suited to show the virtues of the new sound.

On December 2, the week before *Brigadoon* started shooting, Michael Maule was abruptly dismissed and recast with Jimmy Thompson. Thompson's only solo appearance so far had been as the singer-narrator in the "Beautiful Girl" sequence in *Singin' in the Rain*. He was now thrown into a principal acting assignment for which he had had very little training. John Gustafson, a young chorus singer, had already prerecorded Maule's songs and Thompson was to lip-synch to the tracks.

In many instances on this production Minnelli and Kelly did not see eye to eye. "Vincente and I were never in synch, I must confess," recalls Kelly. "I remember him telling me that he hadn't liked the Broadway show at all, and I loved it. I think he only took on this assignment because we all asked him to, because we felt we needed him badly." Kelly envisioned *Brigadoon* as an outdoor picture, a Scottish Western, while Minnelli saw it as a theatrical artifice. In staging the numbers he had another problem with regard to CinemaScope: to fill the screen with people. However, in two of the major numbers he exploited the new directional sound by bringing on the principals and crowds from the extreme ends of the screen to justify the width of the image.

A few weeks into shooting Lerner got word that Minnelli and Kelly were changing the script as they went along. He went to Freed in protest and was told to go right down to the stage. "I really only ought

Cyd and Gene on the interior highland hillside shooting "The Heather on the Hill." M-G-M

to say one thing about all this," Lerner said pointedly, "I know I can write better than anybody on this set. So, if you want anything changed, ask me." From that day on, the two stuck to Lerner's script.

In the wedding sequence the script called for the gathering of the clans and a frantic search went on for bagpipe players. Calls were made to all known Scottish societies and fraternal organizations. Finally, twenty-five players were rounded up. To get a true outdoor sound and to circumvent the acoustical limitations of a sound stage the bagpipes were recorded in an empty field on Lot 2.

The block sequence, "The Gathering of the Clans," "The Wedding and "The Chase," is a prime example of Sharaff's genius. Her use of color in designing elaborate tartans and primitive garments gave the picture, but especially this sequence, an added dimension.

One of the highlights of the Broadway show was "The Sword Dance." A Scottish ritual, the dance was executed within the circumference of two crossed sabers. Kelly tried to get Matt Maddox, a great dancer and an expert at this, but he was not available. Instead, he engaged George Chakiris.

After the wedding ceremony a riot breaks out when the rejected

428

lover proclaims he is running away and then Brigadoon will vanish forever. This leads to "The Chase."

Minnelli and Ruttenberg shot the entire chase, with its dispersed group of hunters, in one setup, without a cut. It was a highly complex affair; the whole sequence was shot to a prerecorded music track; deer were running through the landscape; the hunters were thrashing around carrying torches. "It was marvelous," says Minnelli, "because it was all so nervous and wild."

It took seventeen days to shoot this sequence at the expense of $442,898.

Brigadoon closed production on March 18, 1954, at a cost of $2,352,625.

When the picture was being prepared for preview (June 10, 1954), Kelly and Charisse's number "There But for You Go I" was deleted.

Brigadoon was released in CinemaScope on September 8, 1954, and grossed $3,385,000.

Without its being said in so many words, Edens' time as Freed's associate producer had to come to an end. In many instances he had gone far beyond his ability as an associate during his years with Freed, and Freed realized the time had come to launch Edens as a producer, yet keep him close by.

Edens was anxious to produce on his own and when Freed got cold feet on the Romberg story he handed it to him. He put his unit at his disposal, he generously relinquished his title as executive producer and, by gentleman's agreement, assured himself of a mutually beneficial future relationship.

With his secretary Belva Lannan, Edens moved into a suite on the other side of the Freed wing, which he furnished and decorated in his conservative taste.

To get his production going, he abandoned Joe Fields's script and assigned Leonard Spigelgass to write a screenplay, based on the book *Deep in My Heart,* by Elliott Arnold.

The life story of Sigmund Romberg would not exactly have been Edens' choice for his first vehicle. But he, like Freed and the extraordinary Unit, went into any project with total enthusiasm.

Spigelgass completed the script and the Unit began to function. Edens shared Ryan and Simone with Freed and assigned Donen to direct, Deutsch as musical director, Tucker as vocal arranger, George Folsey on camera, Eugene Loring as choreographer, Adrienne Fazan as film editor and Walter Plunkett as costume designer.

In this, his first picture, Edens did a most unconventional piece of casting. He gave Helen Traubel, the famous Metropolitan Opera star, the role of Romberg's mature lady friend and sponsor. Not only her vocal qualities and her interpretation of Romberg's songs, but her

Minnelli in the jungles of Venezuela scouting for *Green Mansions'* location.
VINCENTE MINNELLI COLLECTION

vibrant, endearing personality brought to life what otherwise would have been a tedious, heavy, saccharine operetta.[2]

After Traubel's appearance in *Deep in My Heart,* Edens took on the precarious task of launching the Wagnerian singer into her famous night club career, beginning with an engagement in Las Vegas. She came onstage to the applause of a polite, but opera-allergic audience. With a few apologetic words for the arias she was going to sing, she stepped to the microphone. With the downbeat of the conductor she sailed into a bawdy, sonorous "St. Louis Blues," which brought the house down. After a well-tempered selection of songs she left the stage, and when she was called back again and again she stayed far up-stage and in almost a whisper sang Brahms's "Lullaby," in German.

That was showmanship.

On June 15, 1954, Minnelli, armed with Lerner's draft of *Green Mansions,* set out for Cuba, British Guiana, Panama, Peru and Venezuela. Preston Ames had left two weeks earlier. The object of the expedition was to find jungle locations for the film. "I was in this one motor plane" says Minnelli, "with Indians and their babies who vomited in the aisles, goats and hound dogs, I never thought we'd get there in one piece." After one solid week of rain in the heat-infested Venezuelan jungle, sleeping in tents with leaking roofs, they began to shoot rolls of still photographs and 16 mm film.

[2] *Deep in My Heart* started production on May 3, 1954, and was completed on August 3, 1954. It cost $2,104,025.23 and grossed $4,075,000.

Finally relaxing in a DC-6 on the way to Los Angeles, Minnelli came across an article in *Life* magazine. "Think we have the answer to Pier Angeli's troubles," it began. "She is terribly anxious to play the elfin part of Rima, the bird girl of the forest, in Alan Jay Lerner's adaptation of the W. H. Hudson fantasy *Green Mansions,* which Arthur Freed will produce and Vincente Minnelli will direct this summer. She is a strong contender but hasn't been promised anything."

The *Life* release was planted by Howard Strickling's publicity department and Freed had okayed it. Upon Minnelli's return to the studio he walked into Freed's office and almost in unison they said, "Why not test Pier Angeli?!"

The test became a minor production. Minnelli was less interested to probe Pier Angeli's acting talent than to shoot an elaborate sample scene, illustrating the manner in which he felt this innately difficult story could be told on the screen. He asked Lerner to select an appropriate scene for this purpose.

Lerner had many trying times during this period. His father died, he and Loewe were searching for the answer to the as yet unanswered question of how to convert George Bernard Shaw's *Pygmalion* into a Broadway musical, and he had to fulfill his commitment to Freed on *Green Mansions.*

In his covering letter, attached to the test scene, Lerner said, "It goes without saying that at this point in the writing, the script is my lover. I don't know whether she's bad or good—I only know I love her." Lerner wanted the character of Rima to actually speak like a bird. Minnelli, conversely, believed that long sections should have no dialogue at all. "That is where the bird sounds will come in. The music will grow out of the birds' voices."

At great expense a set was designed and built: a smoldering jungle, with all its flora and fauna and a man-made lagoon. Minnelli tried

Pier Angeli's screen test for *Green Mansions*. Out of focus is Minnelli. VINCENTE MINNELLI COLLECTION

to convey to Helen Rose the garment he envisioned for Pier Angeli. "It should be like a transparent cobweb." As he turned to leave she threw a "Dear God, help me" look up at the heavens.

Minnelli started this twelve-day production on October 11, with Edmund Purdom, a young English actor, as Angeli's partner. Simone was ready with a playback of the "Bird Symphony" and Ruttenberg was on the camera.

When Freed and the others saw the test the uppermost question was: Who was the actress to make Rima believable? It didn't take Freed long to realize that there was no such person. As a filmmaker he had never been quite convinced of the property and he dropped the project.

Green Mansions as film fare already had an ill-fated past. In 1928, RKO commissioned Walter Plunkett to create a cobweb gown for Dolores Del Rio. Neither gown nor film ever materialized. In 1947, Pandro Berman announced production at M-G-M with a screenplay by Ted Reeves and Elizabeth Taylor in the leading role. This too came to naught. Then, in 1957, Berman reactivated the property with Audrey Hepburn starring and Mel Ferrer directing. He didn't like Lerner's script. "It needs a little more *Tarzan*," he said at the time, "and *King Solomon's Mines*."

Comden and Green had had their crack at the motion-picture industry, the legitimate theatre and now they chose to satirize television, the one-eyed monster in the living room. Kelly was anxious to direct again, with his codirector Donen, and it had to be a starring vehicle for himself. Kelly purports that *It's Always Fair Weather* "was

Dan Dailey, Gene Kelly and Michael Kidd in one of their first scenes from *It's Always Fair Weather*. M-G-M and BETTY COMDEN COLLECTION

born here in my home." Remembering Alexander Dumas' *Twenty Years After,* namely, *The Three Musketeers* twenty years after, he suggested they model this story after the format of *On the Town* ten years later, using the same cast.

Before getting together with Kelly in Los Angeles the two writers had plotted out in their minds a show for Broadway on the idea of *On the Town,* with the three service buddies meeting again some years later. "While we were trying to think of another idea for Gene," Comden reports, "by chance we told him this story. Gene liked it." Forgetting Broadway, they came in to outline their story for Freed who asked Edens to sit in on the meeting. Edens as well as Freed liked what they heard, and Comden and Green started their screenplay.

In their story, a trio of former GI chums meet ten years after World War II. Somehow the warm friendship that existed during the war years has deteriorated; different interests have driven them apart. Ted is a cynical fight manager and bitter about a busted romance; Doug, an ulcer-ridden television executive; and Angie's dream of becoming a famous chef ends at a hamburger stand. Through Doug, his two pals meet Jackie Leighton, co-ordinator for Doug's show "Midnight With Madeline," a popular video program take-off on "This Is Your Life," femceed by Madeline Brandville. To boost the TV ratings Jackie hits on the idea of commercializing the "sentiment" of the reunion. She tricks the three into coming on the program and the deception is accomplished amid pandemonium, a spectacular free-for-all brawl follows, and a romance between Jackie and Ted starts.

In addition to their writing assignment, Comden and Green were finally given the opportunity to write the lyrics for an entire film musical. But who was to write the music? Edens, who had collaborated with them before, was not available because he was preparing his production of *Deep in My Heart.* After his brilliant accomplishment on *Invitation to the Dance,* Freed gave André Previn his first chance at composing songs.

"Betty and Adolph initiated me into the mysteries of how to construct a musical," says Previn. "They pointed out the fact that the songs must be inevitable instead of the way they were inserted in other producers' films. As an example: I'll never forget one movie where Mario Lanza came into an agent's office and said, 'Is Mr. So-and-So in?' 'No, he'll be back in five minutes,' replied the secretary. 'Oh, I see,' and Lanza began to sing. After the song was over the poor bastard came through the door. That's exactly what Arthur, Roger, Betty and Adolph didn't allow."

As a medium, television was already so strongly established that it invited satirization. In certain quarters, however, this hadn't sunk in. "There was a classic, huge luncheon," recalls Comden, "and tele-

Michael Kidd in his solo
"Jack and the Space Giants"
from *It's Always Fair
Weather*. The number was
deleted from the release
print. M-G-M

vision had reared its head with full force. Everybody was summoned and there we were. There was ice cream served in the form of small chocolate 'Leos', the M-G-M lion. We watched them melt before our eyes and it seemed so symbolic. But no one caught on. One of the chief executives made a tremendous speech about the divorcement ruining the movie business. Now we all knew about that. But television was never mentioned—these people weren't on this planet at all. They just didn't know."

For *Fair Weather,* the *On the Town* cast did not come to pass. Neither Sinatra nor Munshin was available. Kelly wanted at least one other dancer for the trio. Michael Kidd was still under contract to the studio and Donen, for one, was very eager to have him do an acting-dancing part. Dan Dailey, one of Louis "Doc" Shurr's clients, was sold to Freed as the third buddy. Now Kelly had two dancers to work with. Dolores Gray was cast as the brash hostess of Dailey's television show and Cyd Charisse as the program's co-ordinator.

One of Donen's ideas was to divide the CinemaScope screen into three parts for the first time to introduce the careers of the trio simultaneously to the song "March, March."[3] "I Like Myself" was another elaborate number written for Kelly which he would perform on roller skates.[4] "Situation-wise and Saturation-wise" was a satirical song-and-dance routine for Dailey on the methods of Madison Avenue.

[3] Four days of rehearsal, one and one-half days of shooting, cost: $73,161. Clark Burroughs, a member of The Hi Los, was Kidd's singing double.
[4] Twelve days of rehearsal, four days of shooting, cost: $174,836.

434

Previn, Comden and Green had also written a song called "Love Is Nothing but a Racket," which they envisioned as a very slow seductive beguine for Charisse and Kelly. "We can't have a ballad of that kind in this picture," Kelly said to Previn. "Because nobody wants to stand still for a ballad." They were crestfallen. Finally Kelly compromised: "If you want to keep the song in you'll have to let me do it my way." Kelly recorded the song at quadruple the tempo of the original. "Thank God that number was cut from the film," Previn remarks.

There were a lot of things that didn't wind up in the movie, among them a quite remarkable "Jack and the Space Giants," a long number that Kidd had choreographed and for which Previn had written a very complex ten-minute score. It was recorded and shot but not previewed. In this ballet Kidd was the solo dancer with a group of children, and Previn speculates that it might have been deleted for what he calls "intramovie jealousy," or possibly there was simply no room for a ten-minute ballet. Kelly throws some light on this: "We also did one to order for Michael Kidd, really out of courtesy, because the public didn't know Michael, and he was the other third of the trilogy which seemed to look lopsided. But that number was cut; it didn't come across —it didn't work out. And I think it was cut rightly so."[5] On the other hand, Donen says, "It was good enough to stay in the picture. It wasn't terrible. It could have been in."

After Comden and Green had returned to New York another song was needed for Dolores Gray. They couldn't come back and Previn couldn't go to New York.

"Roger wasn't on the film except as kind of a 'gray eminence,'" Previn recalls, "which he was on all of Freed's pictures. And so Roger said he'd write the lyrics." The song was "Music Is Better Than Words."[6]

On this film Previn was the musical director, conductor, composer and arranger. "If I'm not mistaken," says Previn, "I think that was the first time that somebody did the whole thing. In a way it was a great luxury. It meant that Michael and Gene, for instance, could talk to me in terms of balletic material without having the songwriter say 'Yes, but that's not exactly my tune.' On the other hand, to be honest, I don't think that too many of the songs were very good and that's because I was too intent on having them sound clever or well arranged and all that. I just wasn't a good enough songwriter to divorce those two things. Throughout the prerecordings and even the scoring, there was no back-seat driving. Arthur would come on the stage and wander around, filled with pride and excitement, but he would *never,* like so many other producers, make his weight felt with some minutiae that

[5] Four days of rehearsal, two days of shooting, cost: $50,527.
[6] Shot during retakes, costing $34,900. The song was also used in *Designing Woman* (M-G-M 1955).

he wanted changed. That was just one of the aspects that made him exceptional."

Throughout the making of *It's Always Fair Weather* the excitement that prevailed in *On the Town* was missing. What started out to be satirical fluff became a rather self-conscious, weighty commentary. The lack of empathy between the participants existed both off and on the screen.

Carol Haney, Kelly's assistant choreographer, was absent from the production. She went to New York to play a principal part in the Broadway musical *The Pajama Game,* which made her a star. When George Abbott offered her the part she seriously considered turning it down out of loyalty to the Freed Unit, but Freed encouraged her to accept it and arranged a release from her contract.

It's Always Fair Weather started production on October 13, 1954, and closed on March 15, 1955. The final cost was $2,062,256. It was released on September 1, 1955, and grossed $2,485,000.

Contrary to the critics who liked the picture, the two directors did not. "We wanted to make an experiment by treating a serious subject within the context of a musical comedy," says Kelly. "It was a good story for which we needed a little bit of realism, but we missed our goal, because we didn't succeed in giving it a feeling of nostalgia. At any rate, *It's Always Fair Weather* was a failure."

Donen is even harsher. "I didn't really want to codirect another picture with Kelly at that point. We didn't get on very well and, for that matter, Gene didn't get on well with anybody. It was the only picture during which the atmosphere was really horrendous. We had to struggle from beginning to end. I can only say it was an absolute one hundred per cent nightmare."

Comden and Green were thrilled when they read the reviews. But, when they saw that the picture went into release in eleven drive-in theatres, double-billed with *Bad Day at Black Rock,* they were indignant. "We stormed into Dore Schary's office and said, 'What is this all about, Dore? This needs careful and delicate handling. It's a musical picture and people think they all sound the same: same sounds, same faces. As soon as they pass the theatre and see Kelly, Charisse, Dailey, they will think they might have seen it last year. You've got to pick the special qualities to sell it.' "

"Look," said Schary, "I personally produced *Bad Day at Black Rock,* a picture that won several prizes, and I was preparing a campaign for it. One day I drove by a second-run theatre called the Hawaiian on Sunset and Vine, and saw it playing there. That answers the question."

When Comden and Green were about finished with their screenplay, Freed was elected president of the Screen Producers Guild (later known as Producers Guild of America). In this position he took his responsibilities seriously. He arranged meetings, introduced innovations and received recognition for his many accomplishments. As a matter of fact, he took his job so seriously that it occupied most of his time, and during the making of *Fair Weather* his guiding hand was frequently absent. And then, there were always the orchids.

Freed came to produce *Kismet* in a roundabout way. Reading the minutes of an executive meeting, he learned that Edwin Lester, head of the Los Angeles Civic Light Opera Association, had acquired the stage rights for a musical adaptation of *Kismet,* which Metro owned and had produced as a dramatic film with Marlene Dietrich and Ronald Colman. Freed proceeded to assign Lerner to write a screenplay and to compose the score with Schwartz. This was the time Lerner was in deep personal difficulties and had severed his collaboration with Schwartz. *Kismet,* the Lester production, with a score by George Forrest and Robert Wright, adapted from themes by Alexander Borodin, had opened on Broadway and was a smash hit.

Forrest and Wright, two mildly successful songwriters, had put their names in indelible ink in the annals of the Broadway stage with their Edvard Grieg adaptation of *Song of Norway.*

Freed was at the première of *Kismet* in Los Angeles on August 17, 1953, saw a good thing and grabbed it. He negotiated a deal and acquired the motion-picture rights to the production for $125,000. He paid Boosey and Hawkes the trifling sum of $16,500 for copyright and Chappell (music publishing house) even less, $7,500. The property was his.

Charles Lederer and Luther Davis, who had written the book for the show, were engaged to write the screenplay. Freed summoned his favorite director, but Minnelli didn't beat around the bush: "I hated the show, I don't want to do it!" In all the years with Minnelli Freed had never heard him express his opinion so harshly and bluntly. For the moment he made a quick retreat and let matters rest.

A few days later Minnelli was called to Schary's office. Evidently Schary had heard about his negative response concerning *Kismet.* When Minnelli left his office he had lost the battle on *Kismet,* but had won a crucial point: He would have to do *Kismet,* but following it he could do *Lust for Life,* and that's what he wanted.

Founded on Edward Knoblock's *Kismet,* the Baghdad fable tells of how the supposedly magical powers of Hajj, the street poet, are commandeered by the scheming Wazir to advance his own power. The poet is an opportunist who fixes things so that his daughter can wed the Caliph and he can be sent to some far-off romantic oasis, spending the rest of his life comforting Lalume for the loss of her Wazir husband.

The casting of the picture was a matter of convenience: Howard Keel as Hajj, Ann Blyth as his daughter Marsinah, Vic Damone as the Caliph and Dolores Gray as Lalume. Leaving the home grounds,

Freed reached far out and cast Sebastian Cabot, a British stage actor but unknown to American film audiences, in the role of the Wazir. He added Monty Woolley in a small part for his charm and his beard.

Living by the principle "Forgive and forget," he engaged a top man, Jack Cole, to choreograph and stage the musical numbers.

Cole, choreographer, performer, head of a famous dance group and authority on East Indian and Latin American dance, had magnificently staged the musical numbers for the West Coast, Broadway and London productions of *Kismet*. But he and Freed had met a long time before.

When Freed did *Ziegfeld Follies* he wanted Cole to stage and direct "Limehouse Blues." Cole was already at M-G-M about to stage Marlene Dietrich's numbers in the dramatic version of *Kismet* (1944). "Well, how do you like it out here?" Freed had asked Cole jovially. "He was being very charming," recalled Cole. "And I suddenly became socially difficult; it was always one of my problems. I gave him my capsule version of what I felt about Metro: It was a politically oriented studio, with a lot of queen bees like Cedric Gibbons and his sister-in-law, Irene. I denounced all the heads of departments who tried to direct pictures." Cole went right down the line about the nepotism that existed. Freed became angrier by the minute. But then Cole started making derogatory remarks about Edens and about "the immediate group." Cole admitted that was "smart-ass." "I was out in the hall and nothing more was said about my working on *Ziegfeld Follies*."

When Cole was called to Freed's office to discuss *Kismet* in February 1954, he was taken aback. "Perhaps he has forgotten," he thought. When the two faced each other it was all smiles and pleasantries and the disagreement of ten years past was forgotten and forgiven.

Minnelli and Cole knew each other well; in their younger years, they had worked together at the Radio City Music Hall. They began discussing *Kismet* to consolidate their individual tastes and temperaments. Once they had agreed on the main concepts they went to talk to Freed. As always Minnelli had done his research; it was all going to be monochromatic; even at this early stage he talked at great length about color; it was going to be "like Olsen and Johnson in Baghdad, but very beautiful and chic." The decor was going to be like a Persian painting with an unreal sky and gold clouds. It was going to be a fairy tale, all done tongue in cheek.

While Minnelli started working with Preston Ames on the sets and Tony Duquette, erstwhile California interior decorator, who was brought in to design the costumes,[7] Cole began rehearsing with a hand-picked group of dancers and beautiful girls.

Previn was the musical director on the picture. Most of the songs from the Broadway show were retained: "Stranger in Paradise,"

[7] Minnelli had used Duquette's statues in the "This Heart of Mine" sequence of *Ziegfeld Follies* and he made special props for *Yolanda and the Thief*.

Freed on one of the exterior
sets for *Kismet*. ARTHUR
FREED ARCHIVES

"Baubles, Bangles and Beads," "The Olive Tree" and "This Is My Beloved." There were no musical problems with any of these and they
were being prepared for prerecording. On the other hand, "Nineveh,"
the first dance number that Cole was choreographing was as exciting
as it was complex and intricate, and it caused an altercation between
Green and Cole, which Freed solved in Green's favor.

Kismet started production on May 23, 1955.

The momentary enthusiasm Minnelli had displayed before the picture went into production was a low ebb by now. What was to have been
a farcical fairy tale became heavy-footed and grim. Minnelli, bored, restless and totally preoccupied with *Lust for Life,* concentrated almost exclusively on the decor at the expense of everything else. There simply
was no fun in the whole enterprise. Ten days before the picture was
completed, Minnelli had to leave for France to start shooting *Lust for
Life*. Donen was brought in to finish *Kismet*.

Cole, vital and intense, tried his utmost to inject his sophisticated
humor, but only fragments of it reached the screen.

Production closed on July 22, 1955, at a cost of $2,692,960. It went
into general release on October 8, 1955, and grossed $2,920,000.

Unlike most people, Freed did not spend the New Year's holiday
of 1956 making resolutions in order to break them; instead he took
inventory and made assessments. The day after, he sat at his desk
when his secretary, Helen Wendt, brought in his usual morning coffee.
He turned in his swivel chair and looked out the window. And there it
was, as it always had been and still is: "Smith and Salsbury Mortuary,"
the dismal Charles Addams house. "You know, Helen, I have a feeling
they're doing better business than Leo the Lion." During her eight years

Howard Keel, Dolores Gray, Mike Muzurki and Vincente Minnelli go over a scene from *Kismet*. M-G-M

with Freed, Helen Wendt had become his most trusted friend; she knew him well. As she walked out of his room she said to herself, 'We're at some sort of a cross road." A minute later Freed buzzed her: "Where is my *Wonderland* script?"

As the last of the major studios, Metro was falling apart. Producers were no longer under contract and only a handful, including Freed, were in the process of legally setting up their own independent companies. The famous M-G-M roster of stars no longer existed. Less than a dozen stars were retained for one picture a year, among them Charisse, Astaire and Kelly. If at all, audiences by now were only attracted to musicals with the marquee value of a hit Broadway show. Most of the old-timers had spoken for years of the changing times without truly believing it, let alone doing something about it. Freed, however, had seen it coming for quite some time and began to route his plans according to the new scene.

The studio had acquired the Cole Porter catalogue in 1954 and once more Freed had commissioned Comden and Green to write an original screenplay. On this new day of a new year he took another look at that *Wonderland* script: two young screenwriters—a small-town girl coming to Hollywood to break into movies— With a decisive move-

440

Between takes, one of the street merchants looks at the day's *Hollywood Reporter*.
ARTHUR FREED ARCHIVES

ment Freed put it aside. *"Déjà vu,"* he said aloud. Not again, he thought, no more of this.

"If I hear another word about Alan and his *Pygmalion,*" Simone said to Edens, "I'll jump out the window and Adolph can join me!" For over a year there hadn't been one day without Lerner and his *Pygmalion* coming up during every conversation. At last Lerner and Loewe had completed book and score, satisfied at having done well by Shaw. But still they were in a quandary about a title and Lerner talked to Freed, who spontaneously said, "London Bridge is falling down—*My Fair Lady!*"

Freed went to Philadelphia to see *My Fair Lady.* On the morning after the opening he and Lerner had breakfast together. Freed had shared Lerner's glory as if he had written the show himself. Lerner asked him what he was going to do next. "I'm buying *Gigi* and I want you and Fritz to do it for me." "I'd love to write it," Lerner told Freed, "but there would have to be a wait of at least six months." And there was the question of Loewe who had never done a picture and had no intention of doing one. It would take a great deal of convincing. "I'll wait six months," Freed said, "and you take care of Fritz."

From Philadelphia, Freed went to New York. One of the first shows he went to see was Cole Porter's *Silk Stockings* in which he had a financial investment. It was a musical adaptation of *Ninotchka,* and M-G-M had first refusal on the screen rights. He decided to buy it and make it as his first independent film for M-G-M release.[8] While in New York he saw Porter frequently. Needless to say, Porter was delighted with the prospect of having his latest Broadway success brought to the screen by Freed, a man he considered "the top Hollywood musical producer of all time." He promised Freed that he would be available to work as he wanted him during his yearly sojourn in California.

Freed took his time returning to the Coast. The first thing he did was sign into effect Arthur Freed Productions, Inc., the independent producer's contract his lawyers had worked out with Loew's, Inc. Among the benefits he was given a 25 per cent interest in all the motion pictures he would produce with the studio providing the financing. Over the years he had received thousands of shares of Loew's, Inc., stock as a bonus, but this was the first time a participation deal was extended to him.

At the moment he was between pictures. He did assign Leonard Spigelgass to start on a draft of *Silk Stockings,* which would star Fred Astaire and Cyd Charisse. He also started the complicated negotiations for the rights to *Gigi* by appointing Irving Lazar as his representative. For any producer this would be a normal schedule of activities; for Freed it was like an unsolicited holiday. And all the familiar faces were going on a different trip.

Since the beginning of the year Edens was no longer down the hall. For the time being, his field of operation was at Paramount Pictures where he was preparing production of his film *Funny Face.* And Freed kept his promise; he let him have most of the Freed Unit.

After an urgent call from Sid Luft at Warner Brothers in July 1954, Edens had written the key sequence, "Born in a Trunk," for Judy Garland in *A Star Is Born,* collaborating with Leonard Gershe, a young and promising writer.[9] Shortly thereafter, Gershe asked Edens to read his unproduced stage play *Wedding Day.* Examining it, Edens was convinced of its potential as a musical film using George and Ira Gershwin's score for *Funny Face.* M-G-M bought the property for Edens and acquired the score from Warners. The script as adapted by Gershe and Edens was sent to Audrey Hepburn. Her reply came quickly: She loved it and wanted to do it. Edens naturally wanted to do the picture at Metro with Hepburn and Fred Astaire on loanout from Paramount. Their answer was no. Metro then turned around and sold Paramount the entire package: Edens, Gershe, Donen, Deutsch,

---

[8] Acquiring the property and score amounted to $300,000.

[9] Edens could not receive credit as composer because of his exclusive contract with M-G-M.

The Freed Unit at Paramount: Roger Edens, Fred Astaire, Kay Thompson and Audrey Hepburn during the prerecording sessions on *Funny Face*.
ROGER EDENS ARCHIVES

Salinger, Simone, plus Kay Thompson, Ray June, Gene Loring and the Gershwin score.[10]

Cut off from parental guidance, Edens, with a good deal of daring, went to produce *Funny Face* on alien grounds, but secure with familiar faces of the Unit around him.

The first draft for the *Silk Stockings* screenplay was not yet finished when Freed fired an explosive opening shot at the executives: Mamoulian was going to direct the picture. The reaction was unanimous and boiled down to "Arthur, not again!" On the third floor no one cared even to remember Mamoulian's last picture of ten years ago, *Summer Holiday*. Freed stood firm; it was going to be Mamoulian or no *Silk Stockings!* Finally, with ill grace, they gave in and he was engaged.

Astaire had finished *Funny Face* and was back at his ranch in San Diego County. He met with Freed and expressed his reservations about doing *Silk Stockings,* mainly because of his age. Furthermore, he had never met Mamoulian and was somewhat apprehensive about

[10] With additional songs Edens would write.

working with him. Freed relayed this quite candidly to Mamoulian and with his usual self-confidence Mamoulian asked Freed to arrange a luncheon with Astaire. "Just let me talk to him," he said.

During the luncheon the ice was broken. To begin with Mamoulian told Astaire that the only reason he had accepted the assignment was because of him and Cyd Charisse. Astaire was flattered but not satisfied; he again spoke of his age. "What kind of nonsense is that? I see all the young actors today on the screen and none of them can match you in charm or romantic appeal. So, for heaven's sakes, get off that peg—you're not too old!" said Mamoulian. He then went on to describe what he meant to do in general terms. "With you a dancer playing the film producer and Cyd, a dancer playing the Russian girl, I think we can introduce a new element—pantomime—in place of extended dialogue. We'll have high comedy with the three Russian commissars and a love story that is believable and touching." Completely charmed, Astaire agreed to do the film.

Freed was less than happy with Spigelgass' first draft and consequently had not shown it to Astaire or Cole Porter. So far he and Astaire had only decided that two new songs needed to be added by Porter. Astaire went to see Porter but to his great disappointment he found him disinterested, even bored, whenever the subject of *Silk Stockings* came up. In his letter to Freed, Astaire tells about it.

> Dear Arthur,
>
> I was delighted to meet with Rouben M. yesterday. He is of course a wonderful man and I'm so pleased with his viewpoints on the picture. I think when Cole hears about this new approach, he will have renewed interest in the project. Frankly, I could get *no place* with him about the picture. He did nothing but play me songs for *Les Girls*. He would change the subject and simply couldn't talk about *Silk Stockings*. Cole is funny like that, I know, but I'm sure he'll be inspired anew when he hears in detail what I heard yesterday. Cole has a way of losing interest in the revival of the vehicles he has *already done on the stage*.
>
> All the best, Arthur, and I was delighted to be back with you at Metro yesterday, talking business.
>
> See you soon,
Yours,
Fred
>
> P.S. Incidentally—are you using VistaVision or CinemaScope? Not that it matters probably, but CinemaScope "sends" me more than VV.[11]

As soon as Mamoulian had settled in his office he began to work. As always, he was an avid, succinct memo writer. He had no intention

---

[11] CinemaScope with recently perfected Eastman color film would be used.

of drastically changing the plot and the characters of Spigelgass' script. What he was aiming at was to cut the dialogue down to a minimum and relate the love story through music, song and dance. What dismayed and irritated him in the script was the overemphasis on exterior values such as props, jewelry and decor. The memos started going out. Here are some excerpts:

To: Leonard Spigelgass
From: Rouben Mamoulian
       cc: Arthur Freed

We should be concerned at this time only with the essence of our theme and story and, most importantly, with the characters involved in it. In other words, we should work from the inside out. Create the soul and the body first, then adorn it with clothes and jewels (if any)!

I don't like Ninotchka's [Charisse's] character background as it stands both in the film and the stage play. Her experience in killing with a bayonet during the war should be eliminated. . . . I would like to see in her character an element through which she would find an immediate and sympathetic communion with Canfield [Astaire]. I suggest that as a child she started in the Russian ballet . . . to emphasize again the point of dancing and music. She is cold and even antagonistic to them [the three commissars] because she loves them passionately and considers them to be the devil's temptation.

The love story between Canfield and Ninotchka is the main theme of our picture. If we fail with it, all the shooting is for nothing. This is, now, the weakest point in the script. It is abrupt, unprepared for and unbelievable. It also greatly lacks charm.

In spite of his very critical assessment of Spigelgass' script Mamoulian took the trouble to write a couple of sample scenes to convey his ideas to the writer. But evidently his efforts were in vain, and Spigelgass was taken off the assignment.

Harry Kurnitz had been known as one of the most gifted comedy writers until he became a victim of the McCarthy witch hunt and was blackballed in Hollywood. Freed offered Kurnitz the rewrite assignment and paid him the same four-digit weekly salary he had received before the Washington cabal.

Kurnitz started writing diligently and turned in yellow pages at the end of every day. Oscar Levant was back in the Unit as a "special idea" man. At the end of the first week, yellow pages in hand, Kurnitz turned to Simone: "Let me ask you something. Is this funny?" It wasn't, but after all it was only the beginning. By the time Kurnitz's second week was over the yellow pages filled everybody's wastebasket. Mamoulian went to Freed: "Arthur, those scenes, is this Kurnitz? It's impossible!" Out of sentiment and with remarkable generosity Freed in-

Astaire and Charisse re-
hearse one of their numbers
in *Silk Stockings*. M-G-M

sisted on letting Kurnitz finish the job while everyone sat around and
waited. It was only after he had turned in his last page that Freed dismissed him.

Already Freed had signed Gene Loring to re-create his Broadway
choreography; Hermes Pan to work with Astaire on his numbers; Janis
Paige as Peggy Dayton; and the three commissars, Peter Lorre, Jules
Munshin and Joseph Buloff. Russian dialect coach Zoya Karabanva
was working with Charisse; Randall Duell had begun designing the
sets; Helen Rose, the costumes. He had also assigned Previn as musical
director, Salinger on orchestrations and Tucker on vocal arrangements.
It was October 1, 1956; the starting date for the picture was only a
little more than a month away and he didn't have a shooting script.

Porter came to see Freed and presented him with a new song, "Fated
to Be Mated." In addition, Astaire asked him to write a rock-and-roll
number which he wanted to do in his proverbial top hat, white tie and
tails. Porter had never attempted to write in this idiom, but promised
that he would try. He called a musician friend and told him he knew
nothing about rock and roll; would he bring him some recordings? He
listened to them and then added the Porter touch by writing "The Ritz
Roll and Rock."

Levant was curious to hear Porter's two new songs and sat down to

Rouben Mamoulian shows
Cyd Charisse how he would
like her to move during the
Silk Stockings transformation
sequence. M-G-M and ROUBEN
MAMOULIAN COLLECTION

play them. After he finished, Simone awaited an appraisal. "You know Cole is the only person who sent a glass of water back at Le Pavillon," came the reply. The two laughed; but suddenly they realized the present situation was not a laughing matter: no shooting script.

Freed and Levant came back from lunch.

"Were you nice to him or terrible, Oscar?" Simone asked.

"I'm always my most demented charming self."

"In that case, why don't you go in and suggest Leonard Gershe?"

After one short interview with Gershe, Freed assigned him to salvage the script. Gershe listened attentively to Mamoulian, and a shooting script was finished in two weeks, and he made further adjustments and changes for a month into production.

Prerecording began a week before shooting with "Without Love," "Chemical Reaction" and "All of You." Tucker coached Carol Richards, Charisse's voice double.

Astaire asked Freed and Mamoulian to come down to the set to show them his number with Charisse, the first number in the picture, "Paris Loves Lovers." They had barely finished when Freed jumped up: "Fred, you're the king! You're it! Most marvelous thing I've ever seen!" Everybody was raving except Mamoulian; he didn't like it and just sat there. Astaire was concerned and went over to him. "How about it?" Mamoulian didn't beat around the bush. "Well, Fred, you know everything you do is very good, but this isn't right. It's a good dance but it's not dramatic enough." Astaire, highly sensitive to criticism, got quite upset. All the while Freed was poking his elbows into Mamoulian. Mamoulian took Astaire and Pan aside and it wasn't long before Astaire agreed with his suggestions.

Silk Stockings began principal photography on November 7, 1956.

Loring had worked very hard with Charisse on her numbers. "She's not strong—she's not a powerhouse, she just looks that way," he says. "In the 'Red Blues,' for instance, she looks like a dynamo. She has bursts of energy, not for long, and then she gives up. I had planned the shooting so that the tough stuff came in the morning when she was energetic and I'd do the easy scenes in the afternoon. So we had to shoot out of sequence."

On the Broadway stage a hat was used as the first step in the transformation of the girl commissar into a glamorous female of the Western world. In the picture Loring very appropriately replaced the hat with a pair of silk stockings. He staged a very ingenious pantomime dance which shows Charisse discarding her military garments including her proletarian underwear, stepping behind a chiffon curtain, simulating nudity in a flesh-colored body suit. Loring was rehearsing that part of the dance when the film censor board caught wind of it. Some gentlemen arrived on the set to be sure that nothing lewd was in the making. When they convinced themselves that Charisse was wearing a body suit they made their ruling: She must at no time be shown in full front or profile to the camera. They seemed to enjoy themselves and remained until the number was completed.

Joseph Buloff, Jules Munshin and Peter Lorre performing for Mamoulian, which cost the studio $5,000. M-G-M

At the time an economy wave was in full force, coupled with the musical chairs being played in the top two positions of the parent company. Nicholas Schenck was board chairman and Arthur Loew, president. After less than a year Loew handed the responsibilities over to Joseph Vogel; Schenck retired and Loew became board chairman. Vogel fired Schary immediately and put Benny Thau, long-time associate of Mayer and a close friend of Freed, in charge of running the studio.

With all these maneuvers, many were fearful of losing their jobs and much of the ease and fun of former days had disappeared. Only the three Russian commissars, Lorre, Munshin and Buloff, clowned their way through the day's work. Mamoulian loved them, even though they frequently behaved like naughty children. One morning he came to the set to begin shooting their number "When We Get to Sweet Siberia." After a camera rehearsal he was ready to shoot, but discovered the set full of people: Astaire, Charisse, Paige, Freed, Simone, Loring, Pan, Ryan, some executives and half a dozen producers. Mamoulian said to

Janis Paige as Josephine.
M-G-M

his assistant director, "What on earth is going on? Why are they here?"
"They just want to see the three comedians do their number," he was
told, "and have a little laugh." Well, Mamoulian thought, this beats all.
But he went ahead for the shooting of the first take. After a few lines of
dialogue the trio went right into their song: "When you work for sweet
Mamoulian—It's like working for Napoleon." Mamoulian couldn't believe his ears. He recalls, "The whole lyric had been rewritten about me.
I sat there and I thought that I'm going crazy. Then I looked around
and everybody was watching me instead of the comedians—they were all
in on the gag." This gag took three weeks to prepare, to write the lyrics,
to rehearse and prerecord it. They went to Freed to ask permission. "Of
course," he said, "go ahead." In turn, he advised the executives of the
proposed joke on Mamoulian and told them it would cost about $5,000.
Miraculously, they all said, "Go ahead—why not?" And here they were,
on the stage, to have a little laugh.

Loring staged "Josephine," a vaudeville number, for Janis Paige,
which was a take-off on Napoleon's wife. It was a brash and bawdy
production number consisting of several choruses. It was shot toward
the end of production, disregarding the already assembled rough cut,
and photographed with two endings to cover the possibility of present-

450

ing it in a short version. As it turned out, even the shorter version was later abridged.

During the making of *Silk Stockings* there were frequent disputes between Mamoulian and Freed. Exceedingly nervous in face of the negative attitude of the third floor and not completely convinced that Mamoulian would bring the picture in on time, Freed often displayed great irritability. His mood was also aggravated by the presence of a team of efficiency experts sent out by the new regime in New York. They were to make a detailed report on the efficiency—or inefficiency —of every department in every phase of picturemaking. They looked into the operation of technical departments, of which they knew nothing. They interested themselves especially in the performance of the creative personnel, which they could evaluate even less. Ultimately, they based their survey on the end figure of the cost sheets.

When Mamoulian came back to M-G-M for *Silk Stockings,* he was very well aware of his past reputation and was determined to do away with it, once and for all. Making his point very openly he got Bill Ryan in his corner. And Simone, his friend and admirer, set her mind to help. As soon as the footage for a block sequence was in the cans, a rough cut was made and it was presented to Mamoulian and Freed. Whatever changes or polishing were needed were done immediately, and the picture was mounted on completed reels. Without waiting for the end of production, Simone dubbed the existing footage. By the time Astaire went to the stage to shoot his last sequence, "The Ritz Roll and Rock," the entire picture was dubbed, including

Fred Astaire and his dancing ensemble doing "The Ritz Roll and Rock." M-G-M

dialogue loops, sound effects and taps. In the last reel of the picture *leader* was intercut for the exact length of "The Ritz" number so that on completion it could be just spliced into the reel. Even some underscoring had been done while the picture was still shooting and what remained to be done would be recorded a couple days after production closed.

Silk Stockings was completed on January 31, 1957, at a cost of $1,853,463.21.

For once there were no delays, which sometimes ran into months, accruing not only costly overhead charges but interest payments on the capital invested in the film. The picture was previewed nine days after the last shot was made.

After having finished their survey, the team of experts assessed *Silk Stockings* as the most efficiently produced of *all* M-G-M musicals.

The picture was released on July 18, 1957, and grossed $4,417,753.

Bosley Crowther's New York *Times* review began:

> There should be legislation requiring that Fred Astaire and Cyd Charisse appear together in a musical picture at least once every two years. Previously they were together in *The Band Wagon,* and the world was brightened. That was way back in 1953. Now they are together in *Silk Stockings,* and somebody should declare a holiday. . . . Under the direction of Rouben Mamoulian the whole thing moves with a suave and graceful flow. And Arthur Freed's beautiful production is no less than the subject deserves.

15

To: Dore Schary (cc: Arthur Freed)
Subject: GIGI by Colette and Jacques DeVal
From: Kenneth MacKenna   Date: 12/10/51

Dear Dore:

Are you familiar with the French film *Gigi* based on the novel by Colette? It was a completely delightful film but much too censorable in its present form for our purposes. Since then, Anita Loos has made a stage play of it, but I'm told that she and Gilbert Miller, the Broadway producer, have no share in the motion-picture rights. The picture rights are controlled by the Hackims (Robert and Raymond) and Joe Fields has an interest.

Fields has discussed this with Arthur Freed as a vehicle for Caron and he feels very strongly that a charming musical, sophisticated and French in flavor but censorship proof, could be made from this, the idea being that the young girl is being trained "to please men and get a husband" rather than in the original, merely to please men!

If you have not seen the film, I suggest that we get a print for you and that then you discuss it with Arthur Freed.

GIGI   453

Schary ignored MacKenna's suggestion and could not be persuaded to see the film. Freed liked it. "Nice little film," he said, and that's where the matter rested. But from here on, *Gigi* hovered in the atmosphere. In 1953, the Broadway production with Audrey Hepburn played Los Angeles and Freed went to see it. In 1954, Colette died. Freed read Colette's novella again with renewed interest when he received the following telegram:

ARTHUR FREED
MGM
DEAR ARTHUR I AM ABOUT TO BEGIN WORK ON OUR BROADWAY MUSICAL OF GIGI AND WOULD GREATLY APPRECIATE IF YOU WOULD SEND ME A COPY OF THE CENSORSHIP REPORT ON THE PROPERTY AS IT WOULD GREATLY HELP ME IN TRYING TO CLEAR AWAY THEIR OBJECTIONS RIGHT NOW KINDEST PERSONAL RE-GARDS

ANITA LOOS

Freed asked Robert Vogel for the report of the Code Office, now being headed by Geoffrey Shurlock. He sent a copy on to Loos and kept the original for himself.

To: Mr. Arthur Freed
Subject: GIGI
From: Robert Vogel   Date: 3/25/55
Dear Arthur:

I understand you would like a memo listing the elements in *Gigi* which are objectionable under the Code. Here they are:

1. *All* the characters in this story participate, or did participate, or intended to participate, in a man-mistress relationship.
2. The heroine is deliberately trained to enter such a relationship. This is shown in detail and with much sympathy.
3. From all the above the story indicates very definitely that such low relationships are commonly accepted practices.
4. Most important, never is there the slightest indication that such relationships are sinful. On the contrary, there is the very deliberate weighing of whether the young girl should get married or become a mistress.
   This is high point of the objection—the fact that people will put an illegal relationship in the same class as marriage.
5. The boy is shown to have a number of illicit relationships before he falls in love with the heroine. (This may be considered incidental if you can tone down the affairs so there is no direct indication of him living with these girls and if you infer the girls, the incidental characters, keep chasing him. He's not the aggressor. He's the handsome devil whom all the girls are after.)

454

What, actually, is immoral in this story, Freed asked himself—is it immoral to depict human relationships as they really are?

Not for the first time he analyzed the changed market. A few years after the war the European film began to make its impact: realistic, life in the raw, crude at times, to be sure, but divested of the glossy coating of Hollywood's dreamland formula. Without approval from the Production Code or the Motion Picture Producers Association Seal of Approval (MPAA), these European films had found their audiences in the art houses and ran to an ever-growing number of customers. The traditional Hollywood film was suffering from a terminal disease. And Freed knew it.

At the end of 1955, Freed requested MacKenna's office to set up a meeting with the Code Office to find out under what conditions it would pass Colette's *Gigi*. Here is, in part, the outcome of the meeting as reported by Marjorie Thorson, MacKenna's associate:

To: Mr. Arthur Freed   cc: Kenneth MacKenna
Subject: GIGI by Colette
From: Marjorie Thorson   Date: 12/10/55

After several meetings with the Code Office, a method of treating *Gigi* in a manner satisfactory to them was finally evolved. As you requested, I am setting down briefly the gist of our approach to the story. The chief objection which the Code Office has made through the years is that the story condones if not glorifies what they call the "system of mistresses." We don't agree with this point of view but find that their objections will be overcome if there is less emphasis on this institution in certain specific ways.

We maintain that *Gigi* is a highly moral story, although told lightly and with warm comedy overtones; basically, it is the triumph of an apparently naive little girl who simply wants no part of this shabby way of life, and in her own completely straightforward way manages to win her point.

Nothing need be said in the film about the fact that Madame Alvarez, the grandmother, or Gigi's own mother were not married. Both the grandmother and the great-aunt are seriously, even desperately concerned with the fact that Gigi should make a "good match." They are directing her education hopefully in the direction of a match with a rich man. The women dote on Gigi, but each has a somewhat different point of view on what is best for her.

Great-aunt Alicia's big and moving scene would come when, believing that Gigi has taken her advice and has gone to Gaston on his own terms, she strips herself of all her pride and pretensions to tell the girl the truth. Gigi is perhaps not even surprised.

Madame Alvarez, torn between the worldly wisdom of Great-aunt Alicia and the impractical romanticism of Gigi's mother, doesn't quite know where she stands. But, again, she wants the best for Gigi. Not quite sure what the best is, she vacillates.

Gaston, the would-be protector, also adores the child, but without ever realizing that he is falling deeply in love with her. He brings her gifts, but they are completely proper ones.

It is Gigi who first realizes that she loves Gaston. She is horrified at his suggestion that she come to him without marriage; but finally, when it appears to be a question of losing him or having him on his terms, it is her love which is important—*not* the riches which Great-aunt Alicia is urging as the reason for the match. But Gaston himself is suddenly horrified at what he is doing to this innocent child, and cannot go through with it; subsequently offering her marriage.

With this background, the Code Office agrees that there's nothing wrong with Gaston's playing around with several girls, and nothing untoward in the fact that he is marriage shy and doesn't want to be trapped. Moreover, the story itself proves that in one way or another, because one girl is greedy and grasping, and another unstable, they really are not satisfactory wives for a man with a great family tradition to continue. But Gigi is everything he would want in a wife.

The grandmother has her own little romantic fiction, which is that Honoré Lachaille, the rakish uncle of Gaston, was once her lover or in some way romantically involved. Actually, they were nothing more than good friends, and that in itself would be an excellent reason why Grandmother and Gigi flee from Trouville when the older Lachaille and Grandmother meet there.

Within this framework, the incident, provided it is treated with taste, can be preserved just about intact.

Await your thoughts,
Marjorie

After reading the report Freed paid Shurlock a visit. It resulted in the Production Code administrator stating: "Arthur, I know you're not going to do anything wrong. You've got our approval—go ahead the way you want to do it."

Freed sent Irving Lazar to Paris to meet with Colette's widower, Maurice Gaudeket, to secure the screen rights for a musical adaptation. Meanwhile, he asked for a print of the 1950 French film; he wanted to study the dialogue Colette had collaborated on. By this time, though, the distributing company had gone out of business and it took a couple of weeks to locate a print. When it finally arrived, he asked Simone to translate it and put it into script form.

Lazar returned with a signed contract for $125,000 in his pocket. With this official document in hand, Freed instructed Howard Strickling to send out a publicity release announcing his forthcoming musical production of *Gigi* with Alan Lerner assigned to handle the adaptation and to supply the lyrics for the songs. In view of an already an-

456

nounced Broadway musical, this produced an onslaught of protests from Gilbert Miller and his associates, including Anita Loos. It seems that Gaudeket had given them the rights as well. Freed paid them $87,000 to kill their project. To protect his property totally he bought all rights to the film for a mere $6,000. And, last but not least, for services rendered, he paid Lazar $10,000.

In June 1956, MacKenna advised Freed that Lerner was to report to the studio on or about July 23 to begin work on *Gigi,* and that Lazar had told him that "while Lerner is willing to do the screenplay, he is unwilling to write lyrics for *Gigi.*"

Lerner checked in at the end of July. He asked Freed to excuse him from having to work in the writers' cubicles at the studio and to let him write the script in Europe. Freed readily agreed. Nothing was said about the lyrics. They discussed briefly the casting of the girl. Lerner was strongly in favor of Audrey Hepburn, the original Gigi on Broadway; Freed was still thinking of Leslie Caron. He asked Lerner to go to Paris to approach Maurice Chevalier about the part of Honoré. For years it had been Lerner's dream to write something for him and he promised Freed that he would do everything in his power to get a commitment. More or less, as a gesture, he also promised to see Caron who had recently received outstanding notices for her performance in *Gigi* on the London stage. Armed with a copy of Simone's transcript of the French film he departed.

During the first week in Paris, Lerner went to dinner at Maxim's. Inspired by the ambiance of the city he had just begun writing when he received a disturbing cable from his agent: As per his contract he would have to write the lyrics for the film. Desperate, he called Loewe in New York and begged him to write the score with him. But all Loewe would promise was to read his script. Lerner called Audrey Hepburn in Switzerland and received an equally negative response.

However, all this was offset by his visit with Chevalier. He had no difficulty getting him to accept the part; Chevalier had known Colette, was familiar with the story and liked the French film, and he was impressed with the reviews of *My Fair Lady.*

Once the rights were settled, Freed assured himself that Minnelli would direct the picture. If there ever was a property suited to his talents *Gigi* was it!

Back from abroad, just before the Christmas holidays, Lerner turned in his first draft. Caron was set to play Gigi; negotiations were in progress for Chevalier, but still unsettled was the casting of Gaston. The role required more than a good actor: He had to be suave, elegant, sophisticated yet sympathetic, and European. Lerner suggested Dirk Bogarde, but he proved to be unavailable. And what of the problem of the composer to collaborate with Lerner? In his first draft Lerner had indicated and suggested ideas for songs. He mailed his script to

Loewe who was spending the holidays in Bermuda, reminding him of his promise to at least read it.

In January 1957, a mini-crisis arose. Freed received a letter from Caron telling him that in spite of her admiration for Minnelli she had great difficulty expressing herself under his direction and suggested David Lean or George Cukor. After a momentary pang of annoyance Freed dismissed her letter of protest; the little girl he had brought over from Paris was going to do the picture with Minnelli whether she liked it or not!

Cukor sent Freed an interoffice memo, in which he quoted part of a letter he had received from a close friend, Isabel Jeans, the English actress. She told him that she had twice been asked to play the part of Gigi's Aunt Alicia, both in New York and London. Each time she had had to turn it down because of other commitments. But now she was very anxious to do it in the film. Cukor added that she would bring humor and enormous style to the part. For the moment Freed put the suggestion on file. He was considering Gladys Cooper, but he wanted to give the matter more thought.

A few days later Lerner called Freed. Loewe had returned from Bermuda ecstatic over the adaptation and eager to be a part of what he believed would be a great picture. Freed smiled. "I knew all the time he would come around."

Dear Fritz:

I just want to tell you how delighted and grateful I am that you are going to do the score of *Gigi* with Alan. I am sure now we will have a unique and wonderful picture and am looking forward to working with you.

You can rest assured that I will do everything to follow your advice and suggestions and make this a happy association.

Thank you very much.

Sincerely yours,
Arthur

Dear Arthur:

Thank you so much for your nice letter. I am delighted to work with you on *Gigi*—especially as I just read the script and found it enchanting.

Alan and I are raring to go, and I have the feeling that we will come across with a lulu of a score.

My best wishes to you and Madame—and au revoir à bientôt.

Fritz

Slowly and carefully Freed tied the elements together. Inspired by the marvelous contribution Cecil Beaton had made to *My Fair Lady,* Freed believed him to be the one man with the knowledge and taste to create the Paris of 1900. He called his New York attorney, Arnold

Weissberger, and told him that he would like to engage Beaton not only to design the costumes and sets, but to be in charge of all visual aspects of the film.

Freed was dead set against manufacturing France at the studio and decided to shoot all of the exteriors and some of the interiors in Paris and the surrounding area.

A great deal of thought was given to the casting of Gigi's grandmother, finally resulting in Hermione Gingold for the role. Gingold had been most successful on the London and New York stage, had appeared in several musicals, and had projected her engaging personality during her frequent appearances on Jack Paar's late-night program.

"Why does Arthur want to make a picture about a whore?" This question had been asked when project *Gigi* had come to the attention of the executives. And when Lerner's first draft reached their desks the question was *still* being asked. But Freed was unperturbed. Lerner himself was not entirely satisfied with his first version. "I did a first draft of the screenplay which the studio didn't like," he recalls. "But Arthur was ahead anyway because he knew *that* screenplay was just a loose frame until the score was developed."

Lerner and Loewe were at work in Paris on the songs. After a month Freed and Minnelli joined them. Minnelli was anxious to familiarize himself with possible locations while Freed was eagerly awaiting the final script and to hear the score.

Lerner showed Freed some further script revisions. He made some significant points, such as making Honoré (Chevalier), the aging *bon vivant,* a more detached character, a sort of master of ceremonies, a philosopher. Freed followed these suggestions. Lerner also suggested the proper interpolation of songs within the development of the story. Out of this evolved the opening song "Thank Heaven for Little Girls," in which Chevalier is a narrator. Gaston, a man with too much wealth and too many women, is clearly established in the duet with his uncle Honoré, "It's a Bore!"

Some of the key scenes in the picture were to take place at Maxim's. Over a number of years Freed had become a frequent guest there and was a friend of the owners, Maggie and Louis Vaudable. He knew only too well that to shoot the scenes at the restaurant would present a problem inasmuch as it would have to be closed to the public for a number of days. The Maxim's sequences were to be shot in August, but the Vaudables, although anxious to accommodate Freed, informed him that during July and August they were at their busiest because of the enormous influx of tourists. Nonetheless, a contract was drawn up: Maxim's would be closed for four days without any possibility of an extension—even if only for an hour. The price would be $12,000 per day and the restaurant staff used in the scenes would be paid individually.

Cecil Beaton's costume design for Gigi's first scene.
ARTHUR FREED ARCHIVES

From the moment Freed and Minnelli arrived in Paris and the inevitable notices appeared in the newspapers their phones didn't stop ringing. Everybody offered their services: from location experts to talent agents, from technical advisers to wigmakers, and there were also some shady proposals. All these calls were ignored. Instead, a production apparatus was slowly being set up. Sasha Kamenka, a well-known and highly recommended French unit manager, was engaged. The sixth floor of the Hotel Raphael was leased and production offices were organized. James Fasbender, a young studio accountant, was sent over from Culver City to function in what was now Arthur Freed Productions, Inc., France.

Back at the Freed Unit in Culver City, Bill Ryan was co-ordinating departures for the Paris location. Bill McGarry, assistant director, along with Preston Ames, studio art director, had already left, followed by

460

Lela Simone at the end of May. Joseph Ruttenberg, director of photography, and André Previn, the picture's musical director, had their tickets for the first week in July.

From morning to night Minnelli went from one end of Paris to the other, searching for exactly those interior and exterior locations that he envisioned: a façade of a house in the style of art nouveau, the perfect spot in the Bois de Boulogne, the exterior of Gaston's house. To find the interiors was more difficult because of the technical equipment, cameras, lights and cables, that were needed to be brought into buildings. As an example, the Musée Jacquemart-André was ideal for the interior of Gaston's house; beautifully furnished rooms, marvelously polished parquet floors, damask hangings, with tasteful accessories in place. But when the very first approach was made to the lady curator, she fell into a state of shock at the mere suggestion of filming in the rooms. It took weeks of diplomacy to get a signed agreement on the condition that only the most necessary machinery could be brought in, with a minimum number of lights, plus a demand for the highest possible insurance policies.

To obtain permissions from private citizens for all this was one thing; from the City of Paris and its diverse departments—including

Beaton's costume design for Gigi's evening at Maxim's.
ARTHUR FREED ARCHIVES

Beaton's costume design for Gigi's last scene. ARTHUR FREED ARCHIVES

the police—was another. These officials had had bad experiences before with unauthorized film companies devastating the Tuileries Gardens with their heavy equipment, creating traffic jams in public squares, etc. They wanted none of it. Eventually it was Freed's Légion d'honneur and his connections with high government dignitaries that brought permissions. In every instance the City of Paris charged for each piece of equipment or material that was brought to the locations. A major crisis arose when Minnelli conveyed to the Department of the Seine that he wished to shoot a skating scene in the Palais de Glace (the Ice Palace), an enormous rotund building, roofed with a huge glass dome, that was only open during the winter months. "Ice in August?" was the outcry. "Ice in August," said Minnelli. But more than that, some repainting and reconstruction on the main floor was necessary to bring it into the period.

"When Arthur Freed, the impresario of so many brilliant musical films asked me to design *Gigi* for him," recalls Cecil Beaton, "I was somewhat abashed. My first reaction being that I had in recent years been associated with so many designs evolving around 1900. How could I not repeat myself? How could I see this epoch with a fresh approach?" Beaton started to reread *Gigi* for the seventh time and, by degrees, was seeing its scenes through the eyes of Colette, as he says. "The colors I should employ, the atmosphere to create must not be mine, but hers." It was with a new stimulus and a fresh palette that he started on his preliminary research. Looking through old bound volumes of *Les Modes, Le Théâtre, Femina* and *Cahiers d'Arts,* he spotted details that seemed to belong to Colette's world. Soon a large sketchbook was entirely filled with atmospheric impressions: "of little girls in tartan dresses; in *broderie anglaise* with black boots and stockings; of great jeweled ladies supping at Maxim's or in a display of feathers airing themselves in all manner of equipages in the Bois."

Beaton arrived during one of the worst heat waves Paris had ever seen. Even the best hotel suites were without air conditioning and to walk in the streets during the day was practically impossible. Nonetheless, he and Minnelli, with unfaltering energy, surveyed the locations that by now had been settled. Beaton then began to make the rounds of all the specialists and draftsmen he had to muster for the prospective execution of his designs: Karinska, dresses; Paulette, millinery; Repetto, gloves and hose; Jacques Fath, accessories; Guillaume, hair styling; Breslave, men's suits; Gilot, men's hats. One major obstacle faced him: All these people, all these firms irrevocably closed down promptly on August 1 for their summer vacations. He had to assure himself that, should the need arise, they would stay on the job past that date.

Meetings were usually held in Freed's suite at the George V, with the help of buckets filled with ice cubes to rub wrists and necks to survive the heat of the day. Beaton brought his sketchbook and displayed his designs for Freed's delighted approval. The casting of the aunt was discussed. "Vincente wanted Adrienne Allen," Beaton remembers. "I was terribly against that. Although she and I are close friends I nevertheless thought she was out of style and not photogenic. I wanted Isabel Jeans." Freed suddenly remembered Cukor's memo and Isabel Jeans's plea. That, paired with his faith in Beaton's judgment, swayed him to engage her for the part.

"But, Arthur," Lerner asked rather desperately, "what about Gaston?"

"I told you—you shouldn't worry. I've engaged Louis Jourdan!" Freed said very offhand. Actually, Jourdan at first had declined because he didn't want to do a singing part. It took a lot of convincing to get him to accept.

The big day arrived when Lerner and Loewe were going to audition their score. Howard Dietz and his wife were in Paris and Freed invited them to Lerner's suite on the top floor of the George V.

Assembled were Freed and his wife, the Dietzes, Beaton, Minnelli and Simone. While demonstrating the songs Lerner was sitting next to Loewe on the piano bench, occasionally playing along with him. Starting with "Thank Heaven for Little Girls," they went through "It's a Bore!" "The Parisians," "She's Not Thinking of Me," "I Remember It Well," "Gaston's Soliloquy—Gigi," "I'm Glad I'm Not Young Anymore" and "Say a Prayer for Me Tonight." "After Alan and Fritz had finished, all of us were elated," recalls Simone. "We didn't even feel the heat any longer." When Dietz was ready to leave he shook Freed's hand and said, "Arthur, this will be the most charming flop you've ever made!"

Beaton returned to England with a sheaf of notes on Minnelli's requirements: *"The Bois:* 150 people, dogs, carriages, respectable family, two or three aristocratic men on horseback, two women in habits, twelve children, smart Gigi for finale. *Maxim's:* Twenty characters after "Sem" caricatures, nobility, actresses, Indian, Polaire, Lady de Grey, Gigi—simple elegance. *Gaston's montage:* Princely extravagance and audacity. *Trouville:* Bathing machines, tennis, diabolo, alpaca swimming costumes, etc." Spending his weekdays in London feverishly at work, not on depicting the trees and flowers of high summer around him, Beaton says, but the pinchback life of Paris and Trouville of half a century ago. And almost before the paint was dry he would fly off again to Paris to present his designs to Freed and Minnelli before

One of Honoré's costumes by Beaton. ARTHUR FREED ARCHIVES

Beaton's costume design for Grandmama. ARTHUR FREED ARCHIVES

handing them to the costumers. There were many other things he had to do. The beauties who were to portray the ladies of the demimonde had to be selected with great care. But most of these beauties, models by profession, had gone off in all directions for their summer vacations. It was a job in itself to contact them and to bring them back to Paris. Other items had to be found: "Six swans to attack Gaston; one white horse to tread delicately among the diners at the Pré Catalan[1] and subsequently to eat a diamond bracelet." Even if the

[1] The Pré Catalan was closed for the summer. Le Grand Cascade Restaurant was used as its substitute.

horse could be found, where, in Paris, in August would a confectioner make (out of silver sugar) a bracelet for a horse to eat?

Minnelli added more and more people to dress up his sets. To find the physiognomies, the types suggested by Sem drawings, he auditioned hundreds of actors. He selected each one as though he or she would play an important part in the picture. With Karinska already overloaded, Beaton rented some clothes from Costumes de Paris and had other costumes executed by M. Berman of London. There was a cocktail party at Maxim's, arranged by the publicity department of M-G-M. Members of all communications media were invited to meet those involved with *Gigi:* Freed, Minnelli, Lerner and Loewe, Caron, Jourdan, Chevalier, etc. What made things slightly uncomfortable at first was the fact that Jourdan knew no one, and Caron had never met Jourdan nor Chevalier. Even Previn was introduced to Lerner and Loewe, with much anxiety on both sides. But the party served as a meeting ground and the somewhat awkward get-together was carried off with great aplomb under the eagle eye of the press et al.

Out of necessity, the prerecordings for *Gigi* were made in a completely unorthodox and lopsided manner. At the Radio Diffusion Française, Chevalier, Caron and Jourdan recorded their numbers to Previn's piano accompaniment. Voice and piano were recorded on separate bands and Simone made sure that the voices didn't leak into the piano track and vice versa because ultimately the full orchestra

The press party at Maxim's. Leslie Caron meets Maurice Chevalier as Louis Jourdan, Alan Lerner and Frederick Loewe look on. ARTHUR FREED ARCHIVES

would be added to the voice tracks at the studio in Culver City. At the time the French studios were not as technically proficient as they are today and the procedure was precarious. Previn had worked with Jourdan on his "Soliloquy—Gigi." To record it Jourdan came to the studio one evening, very tense and very nervous. He rehearsed for a while and then began a series of takes with Previn at the piano and Simone in the monitor booth. Jourdan was less than pleased with what he heard on the playbacks. But Previn and Simone were most reluctant to intensify his anxiety by advice or criticism. When Simone felt that he had made a quite remarkably good take of the song, she called Freed and asked him to come over. A few minutes later he arrived with Minnelli and the good take was played for them. Freed listened while pacing up and down the recording studio. With the last note, still pacing, he remarked to Simone, "It sounds just like Harrison in *My Fair Lady*." "That's just what it is, Mr. Freed," said Simone, referring to the material and not to Jourdan. Suddenly Jourdan left the studio without any exchange between him or Minnelli or Freed. Instinctively, Simone felt that he was not going to return. Catching up with him outside she asked him to have a drink with her at a nearby café. Simone tried her best to explain Freed's occasionally crude manner and his unawareness of the effect it might have on its recipients. When they parted, Jourdan agreed to talk to Minnelli the following morning. It had been a long and painful conversation because, in effect, Jourdan was going to walk off the picture. At 8 A.M. that morning Simone called Minnelli. "Look, Vincente, you must see Jourdan as soon as possible, otherwise there will be no Jourdan!"

By the time Freed joined Minnelli and Jourdan that morning the cloud had passed. After a lengthy confrontation they had come to an understanding.

Before production actually started, tests for costumes, make-up, hair styles and general color schemes were made. In addition to the three principal characters, tests were also made of Eva Gabor, cast as Gaston's mistress, Liane d'Exelmans, and Richard Winckler, a promising young French stage actor, engaged to play the skating instructor Sandomir.

In toto, sixty-five tests were photographed at the Palais de Glace on July 25. This being a roving company there were no facilities of any kind. A makeshift wardrobe-make-up-hairdressing department was set up in a long corridor, off the main floor. There was a shortage of tables, mirrors, electric outlets and lighting fixtures. With these improvised accommodations everybody had to fend for themselves. The tests were developed and screened at the L.T.C. Film Laboratory near St. Cloud, a short drive from Paris, which was contracted for the entire Paris location. Beaton was most disappointed with what he saw. "The colors came out far from the same as those seen by the eye," he

At the Bois location: Lela Simone (profile), Bill McGarry, assistant director (center), and Joseph Ruttenberg (with white cap). Behind him are two of the French crew. LELA SIMONE COLLECTION

recalls. "Leslie's mouth was dark red, her silken hair had become like an old beet root. Louis, recently arrived with a crew cut from a sun-bathing holiday on the Riviera and in spite of the application of a lighter make-up, looked like Harry Belafonte—hardly the ideal for the pampered, oversophisticated Gaston." These tests taught Beaton to avoid certain colors in the future. Some bright reds would become claret color, grays were apt to become Prussian blue, chartreuse yellow would be like a Jaffa orange and turquoise blue would predominate with such force that it had to be treated with caution. In fact, the greater restraint used in color the more pleasing the result on the screen is likely to be.

With at least a dozen companies shooting or preparing to shoot in Paris during the summer, Kamenka, weeks ago, wisely had hand-picked the crew. Ruttenberg had ordered all the technical equipment for the picture as early as June. Cameras, lights, generators, reflectors and a small boom arrived from the Boreham Wood studios in England by blimp!

Location photography was scheduled to begin on Monday, August 5, for a period of approximately one month. The sites selected were the Bois de Boulogne, Palais de Glace, Montfort-l'Amaury, Musée Jacquemart-André, Cour de Rohan, Avenue Rapp, Jardin des Tuileries, Place Furstenberg, Place du Palais Bourbon, Jardin du Luxembourg, Jardin de Bagatelle, Pont Alexandre, Trouville, La Grande Cascade Restaurant and Maxim's.

BOIS DE BOULOGNE: "Thank Heaven for Little Girls"

The police had cordoned off a large section of the Bois, alleys and crossroads, and were rerouting the heavy traffic to and from Paris. The camera was on the tracks laid parallel to the road on a foot path which was far from smooth and had to be planed. Arc lights were lit, reflectors were up, the sound truck was ready and Chevalier's record was on the playback. A lily horn mounted on wheels was in position to move along with the camera for Chevalier to lip-synch.

"With a pioneering spirit, determined to overcome all difficulties, we met in the Bois that summer morning," recalls Beaton. Freed, Minnelli, Ruttenberg, Simone and the huge technical crew, together with a vast crowd of extras, were gathered. *Calèches* of every sort, men and women on horseback, crowds of passers-by, all in 1900 costumes; tremendous activity of watering carts, the camera moving on its crane, megaphoned instructions. The preparations for organizing an elaborate first shot took all morning. Detail upon unexpected detail had to be contended with. "Cecil," Minnelli said, "look around, these rented costumes are disasters!" "Yes, they are, aren't they?"

Beaton was calm and prepared for anything. With two girls following him with boxes of ribbons, plumes and flowers, by a sort of legerdemain he made each costume look stylish and elegant. Carriages, dog carts, equestrians and pedestrians all had to move past a certain point at a given time, while the camera on its boom paused to reveal Chevalier, in top hat, under an artificial acacia tree, greeting the passing world of fashion.

Minnelli rehearsed and rehearsed; he wanted to get the quality of a Constantin Guys painting. However, the technicians on the camera were not ready, so the army was dismissed for the serious business of a French midday meal. Beaton joined Freed for lunch at the nearby Swiss Chalet which could only be reached by rowboat. "Arthur did not seem worried that the morning had produced no result," recalls Beaton. "'What's the difference—Vincente's done a lot of planning—it'll work out!' I marveled that the man could behave so philosophically knowing that a day's shooting cost him $40,000."

When the company reassembled, heavy clouds had come over the tree tops and the Meteorological Department advised that the brilliant weather of the last month was about to break. Toward midday the sun reappeared and a take was grabbed and retaken four times. The carriages rolled by with clockwork precision, the *grandes cocottes* looked liked empresses in their elegant carriages. Chevalier continued to greet the passers-by with the same grinning spontaneity, yet Minnelli had not achieved the perfect shot.

Again he rehearsed. It was already late afternoon and Ruttenberg didn't want to make another take. "I'm getting back light instead of nice sunlight—I don't want to lose it and not see any faces." Freed induced him to shoot it anyway. The take was unusable.

Watching the parade go by for the last time Minnelli said to Simone, "I want some grooms to sit on the back of this carriage." It was almost evening and hardly possible to produce two youngsters out of thin air. Luckily the head doctor of the American Hospital, Dr. Robert Kernan, was a visitor on the set and Simone's doctor as well as her friend. His two children, a boy of ten and a girl of twelve, became the grooms—the girl simply wore a boy's costume.

On the second day Ruttenberg met his crew at 8:30 A.M. As predicted, the weather had changed and he was walking around with his light meter trying to find the sun. Everything and everybody were put in place as on the day before. But at Minnelli's request more false trees were anchored into the ground. That wasn't enough; he wanted more branches. The extra call had gone up from 165 of the previous day to 179.

Speaking in staccato Americanese Minnelli eventually managed to get everyone to understand his orders. McGarry, the assistant director, was shouting at the top of his lungs. Some of his instructions were comic: "Get that extra man who lost his mustache by the Serpentine to change places with the man with a beard over here." Every time he alluded to the Bois he used the word "Bras," and the beauties, the *grandes cocottes,* were called the "stock girls." "Send for the stock girls, we need 'em quickly," or "Send a dozen cocottes up here at once!" Grand ladies in huge hats would drive by in great style, but McGarry would still be upset. "There's one cocotte missing! Anybody seen another cocotte?"

And so the day wore on. A wind had come up. The artificial trees fell. Horses reared. Not only the parade but the entire area was engulfed in clouds of dust. The horse manure had to be picked up. Water tanks had to wet down the road. The exhilaration of the first day was wearing thin. Another rehearsal. The playback blared Chevalier's ode to the little girls and the whole procedure was once again repeated. As the last carriage disappeared from view, the lead carriage turned around and returned once more to the starting position. Wardrobe and make-up people rushed to the carriages fixing, brushing down and fluffing up. One girl, too tightly corseted, passed out. Madame Karinska, with her artistic ardor, restrung the corset to her satisfac-

Maurice Chevalier, Leslie Caron and Louis Jourdan pose for the closing
scene. ARTHUR FREED ARCHIVES and M-G-M

tion but again the actress swooned. A tumbler of water and light
taps on her face did not succeed in bringing around the lady in the
neighboring fitting room before a heavy thud proclaimed another victim: *"Encore une autre est tombée"* (Again another has fallen).

Minnelli had made eight takes of one setup when he had to stop
because of the fading light. It was not until four in the afternoon that he
was able to get his next shot. With the sequence still incomplete, the
company was dismissed at five-thirty.

Before leaving the set Minnelli took Ruttenberg aside. "I think I'd
like the tracks moved over three inches to the right." Ruttenberg, feeling dusty, grimy and exhausted, was too weary to argue. What he had to
do, though, was to change all his marks, his angles and his lights.

For the third day's shooting the sun behaved beautifully; the required shots were "in the can" after only minimal delays, and the day's
yield was considerable.

On the fourth day the company was in good luck: The weather
was beautiful, the trees were standing and the scene was ready to
shoot. But there was a different Gigi—a metamorphosis had taken
place: She was dressed in a billowing mass of Parma violet lace and
ostrich feathers. Out of necessity, motion pictures have to be photo-

Minnelli in the tree and Beaton with his ever-present still camera during the "Battle of Flowers." VINCENTE MINNELLI COLLECTION

graphed out of continuity and so the very last scene in the picture was now ready to go before the camera: She passes by greeting her friends and drives off with her husband in their carriage. Later that afternoon Caron changed back to a little girl, in tartan, playing ball with her school friends.

The following day was to be a change of scene. Another part of the Bois was decorated with bunting and flags. A dozen carriages were covered with orchids, roses and lilies for the Battle of Flowers.

The weather was uncertain; a strong wind blew hats off in every direction. But the weather was ignored while Minnelli and his crew continued their elaborate and intricate preparations to follow the procession of carriages from above on the moving crane on which the camera was perched.

The cocottes were fitted out in new clothes and Paulette hats. But they were tired and angry that day. The first freshness had worn off and they were cold. At first they had been placid and willing to please. Only a few remained so. One red-haired Juno, who spent most of her time asleep, caused a little trouble. After she had thrown a fit of hysterics about having to wear a tight corset for eight hours on end, she calmed down enough to go to sleep in the open air with her hat thrown back and mouth open. "It was unfortunate that a bee should fly in her direction," recalls Beaton, "that it should make for the open mouth and sting Juno's tongue. But most spectacular of all our girls was Monique Van Vooren, a tall blonde with a Mae West figure and a personality of equal proportions. Today at the Battle of Flowers, the big moment was upon her when as Queen of the Carnival she was to ride in the lily-covered carriage with Jourdan.

"Dressed in a tall muslin bonnet, covered with field flowers, Van Vooren had to acknowledge the plaudits of the crowds. Flowers were thrown at her; then in homage, someone heaved a huge bouquet of roses onto her lap. She buried her head rapturously in the flowers, and immediately suffered an acute attack of hay fever, sneezing all the rest of the processional way.

"Van Vooren sneezed as Bernhardt never could have sneezed. She sneezed in rehearsal and then for ten takes, again finally when the microphone was tuned in for a special sound track, she sneezed, putting her whole soul into her 'hatch-oos.'"

It amazed Beaton to see how serious everyone had to be in order to get this gag shot. Suddenly he noticed the skies becoming gray. "A large warm raindrop spluttered down ominously onto Mlle. Cortiz, who," he remembers, "looked like an alabaster figure on a Victorian tomb, as she sat in her carriage of carnations. Another drop followed; it awoke our sleeping Juno, now recovered from her bee sting, in her phaeton of roses and marguerites. Then suddenly there was a deluge. The crowds of extras hid beneath newspapers under the streaming trees. The most Spartan horsemen were still standing in position. Van Vooren, a cat that swallows canaries all day and night long, refused to allow her spirits to be dampened, but her muslin bonnet soon looked a bit limp."

The Battle of Flowers ended in a waterspout. The entire company, soused and cold, but undaunted, moved to the welcome rays of arc lights in the ice-skating rink off the Champs-Elysées. Here the stock girls dried out, and, wearing new clothes, came to life again.

PALAIS DE GLACE: Intrigue on Ice

The Palais de Glace presented many problems. But more than that, there was intrigue on camera; Gaston's mistress carrying on with the skating instructor, and off camera, intrigue against a young, talented actor who was to play the gigolo skater. Minnelli had rehearsed with Richard Winckler, who was to make his first appearance in an American film. Just a few days before the sequence was to be shot, Eva Gabor told Freed that she wanted Jacques Bergerac to play the part. Rather than jeopardize the shooting schedule, Freed most reluctantly agreed to her whim. But where was Bergerac? After some phone calls by Simone and McGarry he was discovered at the Hotel du Palais in Biarritz. Bergerac called very late that night and was told to get to Paris immediately to play a role in the picture. That morning, at the start of business, his agent was contacted and a deal was made: $5,000 for what turned out to be three days' work.

Minnelli was less than pleased at this turn of events, having to dismiss a talented French actor for no reason at all. Simone was elected to handle the situation and to save embarrassment for all concerned, to keep Winckler away from the set the following day. She had his address in an outlying district of Paris, but there was no phone. His call was for seven that morning and she was there waiting to explain why he was no longer needed. What at first he considered to be an insult was softened by her concern for him. But he could not be dissuaded from staying on, to wait for the arrival of his successor.

The summer exodus from Paris had taken along a good portion of proficient ice skaters. The few left were rounded up and engaged not only to appear but to function as instructors. The sun beating through the glass roof made beautiful patterns on the rink, but it also melted the ice. The generators kept breaking down under the load they had to carry. The echo of Lerner and Loewe's "A Toujours," was bouncing off the walls while the instructors put the amateur skaters through their paces. Ruttenberg was figuring out how to catch the marvelous rainbow effect of the sun's rays falling through the dome of the building. Simone put on skates and tore back and forth across the ice relaying Minnelli's orders. While this hectic mêlée was in progress Bergerac ar-

Eva Gabor with her amour Jacques Bergerac, faking the ice skating at the Palais de Glace location. You can notice the apparatus that was rigged up to give the impression they are actually skating. ARTHUR FREED ARCHIVES and M-G-M

rived. The wardrobe department was faced with a problem: He was one foot taller and twice as broad as his predecessor. A rented costume had to be provided and fitted on the spot. Then, furnished with skates, he was summoned onto the ice to rehearse his scene. He was dumbfounded. "I can't skate," he stammered. In the scene Sandomir, the skating instructor, was to flirtatiously waltz with Gaston's mistress, Liane d'Exelmans. Assisted by two professional skaters, Bergerac bravely ventured onto the rink—and immediately fell, head first, on the ice. A small wooden sled was constructed for Gabor and Bergerac to stand on which would be pulled across the rink at an angle, cutting off their lower extremities. And they would have to sway to and fro, simulating a swift skating glissando. This exhibition was being rehearsed when McGarry came running up to Minnelli: "Madame Dumer just fell—she broke her arm!" Minnelli looked at him blankly and advised Gabor and Bergerac to sway a little more.

In spite of all the commotion Minnelli shot the sequence in two days and Ruttenberg achieved his rainbow shot.

MONTFORT-L'AMAURY: Intrigue at the Inn

The Auberge de la Moutière in Montfort-l'Amaury, about an hour's drive from Paris, is a charming old country inn surrounded by an exquisite garden and shaded by old trees. In the scene to be shot, Liane is having a clandestine rendezvous with Sandomir. Uncle Honoré, the old roué, prevails upon his nephew Gaston to live up to his gentlemanly honor by following Liane to the inn, bribing Sandomir into removing himself and thus leaving Liane alone and humiliated.

Simone picked Minnelli up at six o'clock in the morning to drive to Montfort. When he stepped into the car she noticed that he looked ill. "Don't laugh—I had the doctor last night—I have whooping cough!" Simone cautiously moved as far away from him as possible. They arrived at the location before Ruttenberg and his crew. Enchanted by its interior Minnelli took out his finder and laid out the scene he wanted to shoot. When Ruttenberg arrived he showed him what he planned to do. Since this was the first time Minnelli had mentioned anything about shooting indoors, Ruttenberg had not ordered any lights. There was only one entrance to the very small, low-ceiling dining room and some French doors leading into the garden. The front door barely allowed the cameras to be brought in. Meanwhile, Ruttenberg called Paris for some lights. This naturally meant a delay of a couple of hours.

The interior scene was shot with great difficulty, after which the camera was set up outdoors. After extensively rehearsing the scene with Gabor and Bergerac, the first take was made when a soft slow rain began to fall. Urged on by Freed, Ruttenberg photographed the scene again with artificial light and wrote on the slate: shot under protest. And with that the company broke and returned to Paris to come back the following morning to finish the sequence.

MUSÉE JACQUEMART-ANDRÉ: Gaston's Humble Abode

In addition to its own fragile elegance, a collection of Second Empire treasures was on exhibition at the museum. This made shooting in one of its *grand salons* like walking on eggs. Permission had been granted for one day only and, as agreed, all heavy equipment remained outside, cables were sent in through the windows.

The sequence was shot with the natural light coming from the outdoors. But by nightfall the scenes were still not finished. The arc lights Ruttenberg now needed had to be put on platforms erected in the building's courtyard and he had to match the texture of his daylight shots. When the doors of the museum were closed that night not only had nothing been damaged, but the crew had left the premises exactly as it had found it.

JARDIN DES TUILERIES: Gigi Goes to the Park

Angry and frustrated, Gigi leaves her aunt's house and runs to the park. She finds herself surrounded by lovers, in the flesh and in marble, and expresses herself in song: "I Don't Understand the Parisians."

The spots Minnelli had designated for the shooting were nowhere close to the power source. Hundreds of feet of cable were needed to reach from the street up to the camera, the sound truck, the lights, etc. Through some negligence in the production end, insufficient cable had been ordered to cover the distance. Phone calls went out to every local studio, but all companies were shooting and there was no cable available. Simone calmed the crew and advised them to start shooting without sound in order to gain enough cable footage, and a couple of dialogue lines interpolated in the song would be postrecorded.

After a few hours the news of shooting had spread, and thousands of sightseers were cordoned off by policemen. During the usual hubbub preparing for the next setup, Dr. Kernan, the American doctor, arrived. He took Minnelli and Simone by the arm, and they stepped behind a sparsely branched tree. There in full view of the large audience he pulled up their sleeves and poised his hypodermic needles into their arms. This had been a daily procedure to sustain them through the extraordinary exertions of every work day. But what did the people think? "Good God, Vincente," said Simone. "We'll be arrested! I'm sure they're thinking he's shooting us full of dope!"

For once Minnelli was without his boom. He had a high parapet erected and put the camera on top of it to shoot down on Caron in front of a statue. Time was running out and so was the sunlight. It was a difficult shot to make and nerves were getting raw. When Freed arrived he watched the hectic goings-on for a couple of minutes. He got increasingly more irritable. "What is Minnelli doing? Why isn't he shooting the scene?" he said. No explanation of certain technical difficulties made any impression on him. He got angrier by the minute until he finally gave vent to a flow of invectives and left. The last setup of Gigi feeding the swans was abandoned, and it was decided to shoot that section in Culver City.

AVENUE RAPP: In the Rain

Isabel Jeans arrived in Paris to be photographed as Aunt Alicia leaving her house. Beaton had ordered Berman's to ship her costumes from London. She got dressed, made up and waited while the rain came down in buckets. It rained for three solid days. There were no cover shots, the only location interior remaining was Maxim's and that was designated for set days during the following week.

COUR DE ROHAN: Gaston in Love

Gigi's modest living quarters were in a compound that once, a long time ago, was the residence of one of France's oldest and richest aristocratic families. In time, the district had gone to seed. Now small apart-

Joseph Ruttenberg behind his camera at the Cour de Rohan location.
JOSEPH RUTTENBERG, ARTHUR FREED ARCHIVES and M-G-M

ments had replaced the suites of rooms and were mostly inhabited by those who preferred to live in dilapidated grandeur.

That night Gaston would storm out of Gigi's house, furious at having been rejected and begin his "Soliloquy." The number was novel in its conception and realization. Alternating between rage and puzzled contemplation, he would walk through streets, cross squares and bridges, pass fountains and, stunned at realizing he has fallen in love, sing the title song of the film. A changed man, he would return to Gigi's apartment.

In the cobblestone courtyard, space was limited for the company and all the machinery. Surrounded by buildings, Ruttenberg had to take his time lighting the set. In the midst of electricians and other crew members scurrying about, Minnelli had an idea. "Preston—I want some potted geraniums." Ames swallowed once, turned on his heels and went out to the boulevard to find them.

Freed arrived as the camera was rolling. The scene didn't particularly interest him and he turned to leave when an old electrician stepped in his way. His reflex was unfortunate. He kicked the man, swore once and was gone. A fuse had been lit. In a matter of minutes ugly words were on the lips of many in the crew. The situation exploded when the foreman told his people to "wrap up." And turning to Simone, he said, *"Madame, on s'en va!"*

Half an hour later she met him and three of his group in a bar on the Boulevard Montparnasse. They sat down over a drink, had a talk and work was resumed the next morning.

MAXIM'S: She Is Not Thinking of Me!

The daily time sheet for the Maxim's sequence called for all principals, the cocottes, groups A and B of men and women, an orchestra of eleven, a barman, chasseur, two waiters and boys to arrive at six in the morning; ready to shoot at nine.

The property men had to supply the following accessories: the agreed quantity of comestibles, drinks and glasses, coffee service, one box of Havana cigars, matches of the period, a basket for wine, menus, banknotes of the period, a circulating table of hors d'oeuvres, an emerald bracelet (and five copies, all handmade).

On Wednesday night Maxim's closed for the week. It took the restaurant staff a couple of hours to clear everything out of the way before turning it over to the company. At 3 A.M. Minnelli, Ruttenberg, Simone and the electricians arrived to the sound of the hammering of carpenters restoring the restaurant to its original 1900 decor. Minnelli explained to Ruttenberg how he wished to make his opening shot. They would enter the restaurant, go through the tiny foyer, continue through the small, narrow barroom, move through the adjoining passageway, turn a sharp corner and wind up in the main dining room, disclosing it in full view. Of course, the bar would be crowded, and the passageway, banquettes and tables on both sides would be fully occupied. Ruttenberg realized that he would barely have enough room to squeeze his camera along this path. And turning the corner would be practically impossible. He persuaded Minnelli to cover the shot in two setups. The mirrors on the walls were another problem. Ruttenberg had to think of some way to move his camera and lights through the room without reflecting in the mirrors. However, he would have to improvise this once all the actors were seated and grouped by Minnelli.

Maxim's has an art nouveau ceiling of painted glass panes which let the light through. Ruttenberg suggested an effective shot up to the ceiling and told his men what lights he would need. By this time costumes were being brought in and property men arrived with their goods. There was no use staying around any longer and the group went home for a couple of hours sleep.

At 6 A.M. sharp the entire company, including actors, models, the restaurant employees and the band, converged on the location. Minnelli began to place his people, composed groupings, arranged table settings, surveyed and resurveyed everything to the smallest detail. The Maxim's sequence was on its way: a gigantic improvisation.

Ruttenberg looked up at the ceiling, where a pane had been broken. It had to be replaced with one in the corner. A stepladder was brought in at the very moment Freed showed up. People were bumping into one another. Wardrobe mistresses were tripping over the camera tracks as they rushed in to assist Beaton. Heels ripped long skirts. Noticing the man going up the ladder Freed blurted out, "For God sakes, Joe. Look what you've done! It's going to cost us a fortune!" The maître d' alleviated Freed's anxieties. "Oh, monsieur, that is nothing. Every night we break many with the corks popping off the champagne bottles —we have much glass in the basement."

Caron arrived and asked for her dressing room. She was taken up rickety stairs to a small room, cut in half by a screen. Wrinkling her nose she expressed her discontent. On the other side of the screen some models were dressing. There was barely enough room for her to be helped into the magnificent white satin gown that Beaton had designed for her. The black satin pigeons extending on either shoulder poked people in the face as she squeezed by on her way downstairs. Jourdan stood pressed into a corner, as elegant as ever, in white tie and tails, a pained expression on his face. "My feet hurt. The shoes don't fit!" "Take them off," said Simone dashing by. "We'll never see your feet in the sequence."

Neither would one see the feet and the skirts of most of the actresses seated on banquettes in the overcrowded room. Beaton's experience had taught him that designing for film presents different problems than for stage productions. "To generalize," he says, "it is safe to say that very seldom is a costume seen full length in the average motion picture. Hence, the interest of each design must rest almost entirely above the waistline. Only disappointment will follow if the costume depends upon the skirt for its interest, and elaborate ornamentation on the hem is apt to be of wasted effort." At Maxim's, an ornamented hem would only have served to sweep up the cigarette stubs.

The scene would be photographed in low-keyed lighting. Ruttenberg felt that the limited space precluded a large amount of equipment and that low-keyed lighting was most appropriate for naturalness and authenticity. No colored lights would be projected at all. He had many extensive camera rehearsals with his eyes glued to the finder. For fear of the mirror reflections he had black scrolls painted on some of them; he changed the positioning of his lights. In addition, Minnelli posed the cocottes with the largest hats in half-standing, half-leaning positions to block out part of the mirrors.

Beaton wondered if all the scenes could possibly be completed in four days: the crowd whispering their "gossip song"; Gaston arriving with Liane, singing "She's Not Thinking of Me," while she waltzes with Honoré; Gaston arriving with Gigi and the love scene between them. In the prevailing bedlam, to stage two scenes separated by a long time span and involving the two women in Gaston's life, was almost insuperable for the director.

After a few chaotic hours, Minnelli normally so gentle and soft-spoken, let out a scream: "Everybody out who is not in this scene!"

"The two French assistant directors were very hurt," Minnelli recalls. "But I said, 'Lela, you stay with me and that's all.'"

The first day carried everybody on a wave of novel if not grueling excitement. Getting down to brass tacks was the order of the second day. On the third, the cast was demoralized. The temperature had risen to a point where even the wood paneling in the room shed oily drops of perspiration. The corseted cocottes were swooning like punctured balloons. Others were draped over any unoccupied surface. For hours many of the actors on their banquettes were pinned behind tables without as much as a glass of water—to preserve the authentic table settings. Beaton, undaunted, did not let up: No hat must be askew, no egret out of place. "In the arc lights the roses at each supper table wilted, the extras wilted also and during the intervals between takes fell into sprawling attitudes of sleep. The confusion, noise and heat in this inferno continued until all participants were prostrate from exhaustion," recalled Beaton.

Minnelli was about to roll for a take when Simone noticed a stranger sitting at a back table, out of camera range. "Who is that woman?" she asked irritatedly. "That *woman*," said Minnelli, "is Janet Flanner! And if we're lucky she may do an article on the picture." As *The New*

At Maxim's: Louis Jourdan, Eva Gabor and Maurice Chevalier with the cocottes and their escorts. ARTHUR FREED ARCHIVES and M-G-M

Yorker magazine's prodigious observer-correspondent for over thirty years, Janet Flanner's column "Letter from Paris" appears regularly under the pseudonym Genêt. Her visit was quite an honor. For over an hour she watched the vortex of activities around her. "She wants to meet you," Minnelli said to Simone who was replacing a melted disc on the playback. For a few minutes her responsibilities were forgotten and she went over to introduce herself. Miss Flanner expressed her amazement at the flood of detailed orders she had seen Simone follow through without a moment's rest. Her comments were very flattering, and Simone's day was made.

This is an excerpt from Genêt in *The New Yorker* (dateline, August 28):

As part of the worry and responsibility of closing Maxim's to the public for a few days, so as to work authenticity between its historically sentimental walls and beneath its fragile, colored glass ceiling, there was reinstalled in the front room that old red velvet bar where, over the decades, cocottes and rich gentlemen met each other by intention or organized surprise. The film's subsequent hothouse scenes of flirtations, champagne drinking, and waltzes in the supper room have been peopled by Vincente Minnelli, the director, with some of the most extraordinary-looking young and old women that Paris has seen in a long while. There are dark beauties with white skins and ripe shoulders, such as the Impressionist artists painted; girls by the dozens with hourglass shapes and hats the size of tea trays, loaded with roses found only in Renoir's gardens, or heavy with black ostrich plumes; and one straw-haired comedienne, dressed in canary yellow, with a face as blank and deadpan as a *Puvis de Chavannes* fresco. Along with the entrancing period costumes, Cecil Beaton has re-created period faces and heads by discovering elderly actresses who still resemble Sem's famous cartoons of years ago—those eccentric, beak-nosed old grisettes, like macaws with pompadours. . . .

To judge by the parts of the picture that have been photographed here and shown to some of Colette's old admirers, *Gigi* may well be the most authoritative Parisian movie so far filmed, as well as the most sensuous, effective, and respectful one yet made from any of Colette's writings.

During the morning of the fourth and final day an increasing sense of urgency came over Minnelli, Ruttenberg and Simone. When the company broke for the two-hour French lunch, sighing with relief, Minnelli and Simone collapsed on two uncomfortable banquettes. Over yet another cup of black coffee they kept asking each other: Can we make it?

When everyone was back in his place again, stern and determined, they sailed into the race against the clock. As Minnelli called, "Print it!" for the last time—at 8 P.M.—Maxim's looked like the aftermath of an orgy. But the battle had been won.

For the next few days things didn't turn out too favorably. Minnelli was bitten by a swan in the Jardin de Bagatelle, the unsteady weather in Trouville canceled that location altogether, and there was a call from Benny Thau at the studio. The picture by then was already close to half a million dollars over budget, and he urged Freed to close the location and return to Metro to finish production as soon as possible. Neither Freed nor Minnelli was pleased by this request, but the wrath they might incur by staying on prompted their return to Culver City.

Before the company resumed shooting at the studio, Lerner had rewritten, tightened and polished most of the dialogue scenes, and with Loewe had written an additional number, "The Night They Invented Champagne." Beaton was one of the first to arrive at the studio, and in collaboration with Preston Ames he supervised the execution of his designs for the interiors.

There was a welcome respite of a week for everybody because Min-

Beaton's design for Honoré's bedroom. ARTHUR FREED ARCHIVES

nelli was ill. Hampers of costumes and properties plus endless cans of sound film had arrived from Paris. As soon as she could get her hands on the film, Adrienne Fazan, the film editor, assembled a rough cut. "The film came back with a choice of two or three takes, or four or five, for one scene," she recalls. When Minnelli looked at the footage he told Fazan that she had not used the takes of his choice. He wanted to see all the others—"and that made it very difficult," she says.

The personnel of the camera department and the laboratory noticed a definite difference in the processing of the footage. They reasoned that the technicians at L.T.C. in St. Cloud had not followed the instructions of Eastman Kodak and had experimented. The results were extraordinary, and Ruttenberg and Minnelli asked the studio lab to imitate the French methods.

Beaton's favorite design for the picture was Honoré Lachaille's bedroom. The art department turned in an exorbitant estimate on this set. Freed queried Beaton who told him that there had never been an

Caron pulls Jourdan, who in turn pulls a donkey, on the beach in Venice, California. ARTHUR FREED ARCHIVES and M-G-M

art nouveau set like it on the stage and "it would make all the difference in the world." With the exception of the bed, he said, the furniture would not have to be made. "You're the doctor," Freed said, "anything you prescribe I will do!"

As production resumed on September 13, Simone concerned herself with unraveling the maze of the location film, getting Previn and Salinger started on the orchestrations, replacing the temporary piano accompaniment, and engaging Betty Wand to dub Caron's singing voice.

After ten days of shuttling between Gigi's apartment and Aunt Alicia's house, the company moved to Venice Beach in nearby Santa Monica, to shoot what was to have been Trouville.

By means of photographs of paintings by the French artist Boudin, Minnelli had conveyed to Beaton the "look" he was after at the beach. "That was very helpful to me, to know what was in back of his mind," says Beaton. "But when Minnelli arrived he was very upset and annoyed with me because I had done all the costumes in black or very dark colors." Beaton had followed Boudin's color scheme implicitly. But Minnelli insisted he wanted all the costumes in bright colors, with beach chairs and umbrellas in washed-out pastels. This was not Boudin but Renoir and Manet. Too much of a craftsman to argue, Beaton jumped into a studio truck, dashed to the wardrobe department, grabbing costumes right and left as he walked down the many aisles. Adding a scarlet shawl here and bright-colored ribbons there he was able to save the situation. Keogh Gleason, the set decorator, helped Beaton out. With a painter and his spray gun he provided the colored chairs and umbrellas.

Minnelli wanted to photograph Gaston and Gigi riding donkeys down the beach at sunset. "I had my camera all ready," says Ruttenberg, "and the time was right. Suddenly, I noticed off in the distance a big fog cloud coming in and I said: 'Vincente, you've got to get the scene now or it's no good!'" But Minnelli wasn't ready yet. He was down with Jourdan and Caron, rehearsing. Ruttenberg alerted his crew to stand by. At the top of his voice he shouted, "Vincente! We're shooting!" Minnelli ran out of camera range and the scene was finished just before the cloud covered the setting sun.

Rather than chance the ever present hazard of outdoor shooting, the second half of the location, "I Remember It Well," with Chevalier and Gingold, was shot on Stage 11. In the scene they sit at a table on the casino terrace overlooking the beach, reminiscing about their love affair many years before. (One wonders why the scene was shot in front of a painted backdrop, simulating pink clouds hanging in the sky as the sun sets.)

Before shooting, Freed and the company surprised Chevalier with a seventy-fifth birthday party on the set. The press covered the occasion not only as a birthday party but as a "Welcome back" for Chevalier after many years of ostracism. There was a lot of pink champagne, an oversized birthday cake, and Chevalier was not ashamed to show how touched he was.

Gingold's performance of the song was incredibly moving. When Chevalier asks, "Am I getting old?" and she replies, "Oh no, not you—" she not only answered for herself but seemingly for millions of his fans.

"I Remember It Well" as it was photographed on the sound stage. ARTHUR FREED ARCHIVES and M-G-M

"Oh I'm So Glad That I'm
Not Young Anymore!" sings
Chevalier. ARTHUR FREED
ARCHIVES and M-G-M

Freed wanted Chevalier to do one number re-creating his famous
Paris music-hall days, and Lerner and Loewe had written "I'm Glad
That I'm Not Young Anymore." To get his point across to the audience,
Freed had him don his trademark: the straw hat.

Sem drawings were to be used when Gigi reads about Gaston's latest extravaganzas in the illustrated pages of *La Vie Parisienne*. But
Freed changed his mind and hired David Stone Martin, the American
artist, to paint four gouaches depicting the montage that follows. It

One of David Stone Martin's watercolors for *La Vie Parisienne* inserts.
ARTHUR FREED ARCHIVES

Caron's retake of "I Don't Understand the Parisiennes." ARTHUR FREED ARCHIVES and M-G-M

shows Gaston amusing himself by opening the Opéra House and the Pré Catelon, both closed for the season, staging a Battle of Flowers and giving a masked ball. For Pré Catelon the white horse had to be cast. Beaton recalls the audition: "We were out on Lot 2 watching a succession of performing white horses. At last the search ended happily; here was a Lippizzaner horse that was delighted to dance all sorts of intricate steps and then eat a diamond bracelet."

The new number, "The Night They Invented Champagne," takes place in Gigi's small living room, with Gaston and her grandmother. Minnelli felt it had to have movement and choreography. He asked Charles Walters to stage it. In a matter of hours Walters gave the number the right mood and Minnelli shot the same day.

Before the picture closed down one scene had to be reshot with

Isabel Jeans in her bathtub with Hermione Gingold (before the retake). Notice that there doesn't seem to be any water in the tub; hence, the retake. ARTHUR FREED ARCHIVES and M-G-M

Before leaving, Beaton presented Freed with this watercolor painting of Leslie Caron, inscribed: "To Arthur, from Cecil, '57. With all good wishes & thanks."
ARTHUR FREED ARCHIVES

Isabel Jeans, and close-ups had to be made with Louis Jourdan and Eva Gabor. The retake was Aunt Alicia in her bathroom, sitting in a Victorian tub, talking to her sister. Patiently she had sat in the lukewarm water all morning. But when the film came back the tub had leaked, the water could not be seen and the effect was lost.

After running the Maxim's sequence Lerner was incensed by the absence of any close-ups of Jourdan. In Minnelli's conception a close-up was out of place. But Lerner insisted. A corner of Maxim's had to be duplicated; the paneling had to be dyed and matched; long-stemmed tulip glasses had to be flown over from the Paris restaurant; the lighting had to be meticulously adjusted to the original scene. The shot of Gabor dancing with Chevalier was deleted and replaced with a closer shot of her, sitting with Jourdan at the table, waving at her friends.

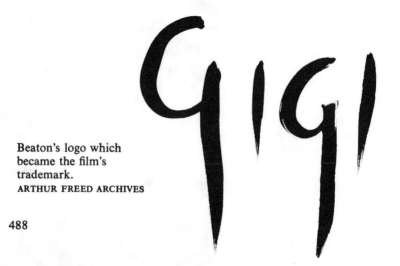

Beaton's logo which became the film's trademark.
ARTHUR FREED ARCHIVES

Gigi closed production on October 30, 1957, and now the major work of postproduction started.

Minnelli hurried back to Europe with Ruttenberg to film *The Reluctant Debutante*. Beaton, too, was about to leave and brought Freed a list of complaints on the color balance, a factor the laboratory would have to concern itself with. Before going through his list Freed crossed out the word "complaints" and substituted it with "suggestions." All the scenes he cited were too yellow, a color which he feels is too pronounced in motion-picture photography. Before bidding Beaton "bon voyage" Freed asked him for one more favor: Would he do the logo for the *Gigi* title as well as the art work for the advertising campaign? Beaton was happy to oblige.

The musical numbers were run repeatedly by Freed and Lerner. The latter commented that his lyrics were not given enough importance and, in particular, complained about Caron's rendition of "The Parisians." If Lerner had been at the Paris recording sessions he could have voiced his opinion then, but now it was too late. Or was it? The number was run again with Simone and Previn. When the lights went on, the comment was, "Too fast." Freed and Lerner sauntered out. At the door Freed turned to Simone, "Try to slow it down somewhat." And to Lerner, "She'll do it."

Simone addressed Previn. "For once, André, it's yours! You slow it down!"

She went to lunch with Salinger. This episode had triggered something off. The many years of strenuous work and the countless incidents where the impossible had been achieved began to close in on her. Not to speak of the frustration in not being able to explain the technical absurdity of this last request; it would have been like speaking Hindustani to a Chinese man. Getting up from the table she said, "Connie, I'm going home." That was the last Freed ever saw of her.

After getting over the shock of losing Simone, Freed faced the preparation for the preview without anyone around able to pull all the strings together.

"Then Margaret Booth came on the scene, which was my fault," says Fazan. "I asked for her to do the looping, but she came in on the cutting and started tearing the picture apart. She cut all the warmth out of it—with Chevalier, Caron, Gingold, everybody!"

The preview of *Gigi* took place at the Granada Theatre in Santa Barbara on January 20, 1958. "It was a total disaster," says Lerner. "It was twenty minutes too long—there were just too many things wrong with it." Fazan remembers that event vividly. "Lerner and Loewe were there and they were just dumbfounded. 'That's not the film we wrote,' they said."

Freed was disturbed, in spite of the fact that out of 252 cards 223 rated the picture from "outstanding" to "good."

On his desk was a list of cutting suggestions from Kenneth Mac-Kenna. Here are some of them:

To: Mr. Arthur Freed
Subject: GIGI
From: Kenneth MacKenna   Date: 1/21/58

Dear Arthur:

This is going to be a memorable film and one that will be classed with some of your greatest—this goes without saying. However, I am sure you have already come to many of the same conclusions that I would like to suggest to you. For what it is worth, here are my reactions:

I would suggest eliminating the scene where Gaston is dressing and buying an automobile while Chevalier waits downstairs. It really develops nothing and is just opulent and time killing.

I think the "Parisians" song would benefit greatly by being cut in half.

I am sorry to say that in spite of its visual beauty, I found the whole first Maxim's sequence lacking in dramatic quality and in some ways disappointing musically. Certainly Gaston, by this time, has found out that he has been cheated, and dramatically to eliminate Maxim's and dissolve straight to Honoré shaving brings us to a very good scene, one that is storytelling and entertainment at the same time. If you feel that to eliminate the entire Maxim's is too drastic, I would certainly eliminate the recitation in unison with its gossip. This to me did not get over and is too intellectual in its stylized conception. I would think it could be eliminated and still keep the song "She's Not Thinking of Me."

I am sure when this picture is given more pace and fifteen or twenty minutes taken out of it, the heightened dramatic impact will give you a surprisingly and satisfactorily new audience reaction.

Then came a meeting in Thau's office at which Lerner was the spokesman. A great deal of money would be needed to reshoot roughly one quarter of the picture, not to mention re-recording, redubbing and editing charges. Thau informed them that if the picture was not in the lab and an answer print out of the state by March 1 the studio would have to pay $63,000 in state tax. This, however, was a minor consideration in view of the fact that $2.5 million was at stake. He did agree that the picture needed a good deal of work and that it lacked warmth. He promised to talk to New York.

In the meantime, a second preview was in the making. "Arthur and I sat there and recut," says Lerner. At the Fox Theatre in Pomona, one week later, 248 out of 263 cards considered the picture "outstanding" to "good," and Lerner and Loewe still were not satisfied. "I understand they told Vogel that they would buy the picture and pay for everything that needed to be done," Fazan recalls. "The executives

490

Jourdan and Caron rehearse
their retake in the next-to-last
scene. ARTHUR FREED
ARCHIVES and M-G-M

saw that they were serious and said 'All right, go ahead and do what you want—cut and reshoot it the way you want to.' " Thau denies this and contends that Lerner and Loewe wanted to "buy into" the picture, not "buy" the picture. At any rate, the money was approved.

But Jourdan was in Paris, Caron and Gabor were in London, Gingold was in New York. Availabilities had to be cleared and contracts had to be negotiated. And who was going to direct? And what about a cameraman in the class of Ruttenberg? Walters was called to the rescue and Ray June was assigned to photograph. Lerner made cuts in the script, added additional dialogue scenes, wrote new lyrics and then left the studio once more. With the pink sheets in hand, Bill Shanks, who had replaced McGarry as assistant director, drew up a shooting schedule.

On February 10, the day before the retakes were to begin, Freed received some depressing news. It was a memo indicating what had already been spent so far on postproduction: editorial (picture, sound, music): $50,292; music: $213,989; dubbing: $18,182; sound department music recording charge: $14,705; miscellaneous: the cost of the California personal property tax, $63,000.

Walters began by redoing major parts of Jourdan's "Soliloquy." That day thirty takes were printed of different setups. The next day was spent on some rewritten dialogue scenes with Gingold, Caron and Jourdan; Gingold redid her last line in the picture: "Thank heaven," at Lerner's request, more softly. Next came another day of Jourdan and his "Soliloquy"; after that an insert shot of him and Gabor at Maxim's with a new lyric to "She's Not Thinking of Me!"

This Sem drawing was used under 'The End' title.

The following week began with Caron lip-synching to Betty Wand in a slower version of "The Parisians." Then came a pickup shot of her sitting on a Victorian bench in a park on Lot 2 and an added scene with Jourdan coming by in a carriage. Three days later (February 20) the retakes were finished.

The final figures on *Gigi:* After twenty-four days of shooting in France, thirty-five days at the studio, twelve days behind schedule, eleven days of retakes and added scenes, the picture cost $3,319,335 (over budget $442,159).

On the afternoon of March 3, the day before the fourth preview scheduled for Encino, a meeting was held in Freed's office. Fazan walked in as Lerner and Booth were going over the cuts which were to be made. The list was endless. "How can I possibly do all that before tomorrow?" Fazan asked. "Don't worry," said Booth, "you'll do it—I'll be there!" It's a wonder Fazan didn't explode. After all, as Fazan reported, Booth was the person who originally had harmed the picture "by snapping it up" for the first preview. "That was a night I will never forget—how Margaret conducted herself and treated me," Fazan recalls. "I didn't get home until five in the morning. In one instance, though, I got my way—Minnelli's version of Jourdan's 'Soliloquy' went back in and that is as it should be."

Previn, too, will never forget the "Soliloquy." "Alan kept after Louis to redo it every week. And by the time you made twenty takes no one could remember what it was about on Take 1 that was any different or less good than on Take 19. Bill Saracino, the music editor, and I worked many nights. At about 2 A.M. one morning, I went into his cubicle and noticed cans of film clear up to the ceiling. "Is this all the music from *Gigi?*"

"No! Those are just Louis' voice tracks of the 'Soliloquy.'"

"Well," Previn concludes, "we probably used a mélange of one hundred takes in the end."

Finally, *Gigi* was ready to be released. Freed was obstinately opposed to open in one of the big New York houses, to make a "killing" for a few weeks, and then let the distributors take over. He wanted to give the film the prestige and the impact of a Broadway stage production—in short, a world première in one of the Shubert's smaller theatres. Easier said than done.

These small houses are usually reserved for a handful of important theatrical producers in anticipation of a long run. Freed stubbornly pursued his goal; he contacted the Shuberts and asked for a lease on the Royale Theatre in West 45th Street. The Shuberts hesitated to gamble on the success or failure of a movie. Furthermore, none of their choice theatres in the forties, west of Broadway, had ever been booked for motion-picture presentations. They finally agreed under one condition: a four-wall lease, meaning the house and nothing more.

And so the film had a gala opening on May 15, 1958. Everybody who prided himself in being a first nighter was there and afterward filled the tables at Sardi's, eagerly awaiting the notices as with a Broadway show. Freed grabbed Crowther's review in the New York *Times.* Crowther began:

> There won't be much point in anybody trying to produce a film of *My Fair Lady* for a while, because Arthur Freed has virtually done it with *Gigi,* which had a grand première at the Royale last night. . . .

At the Cannes Film Festival, the following week, *Gigi* was invited as the gala closing feature. Lerner was aghast at the French subtitles and decided then and there to do something about them. He went to Paris and searched out the top French, Italian and German translators. Under his supervision the French and Italian writers proceeded to translate the dialogue and lyrics, while Loewe worked with the German. With the exception of Chevalier who did his own, the entire film was dubbed by a group of talented multilingual actors. It was the first time that an American musical film had been transferred into foreign languages, musicals being the lowest on the totem pole in the European entertainment market.

By instigating this, Lerner played an important part in the subsequent success of the picture abroad. Moreover, he set up a company for the purpose of producing a commercial album in French. It was recorded by Phillips with Chevalier, Sasha Distel and Marie-France to the original orchestra tracks of the picture. It became a great success and was later released in the United States by Columbia Records.

Even before the inevitable Academy Awards ceremony the medals began rolling in: the Costumers Award to Arthur Freed (why not to Beaton?); the Golden Scissors of the American Cinema Editors to Adrienne Fazan; the Screen Directors Guild Award to Vincente Minnelli; the Screen Producers Guild Award to Arthur Freed; Four *Downbeat* magazine awards: "The Best Musical Motion Picture of 1958," "Title Song" and "Best Original Song," and a special citation to Maurice Chevalier; the Screen Writers Guild Award to Alan Jay Lerner; the Hollywood Foreign Press Association Golden Globe Award as "The Best Musical of 1958"; Photoplay Award for "The Most Popular Picture of the Year" and from Italy, the David Di Donatello Award.

The thirty-first annual Academy Award ceremony was held on April 6, 1959, at the RKO Pantages Theatre and was seen nationwide on NBC Television. *"Gigi* swept the boards and set a new, all-time Academy record to date, with nine Oscars, and a special award to Maurice Chevalier," said *Daily Variety* the following day. "NINE (COUNT THEM!) NINE 'OSCARS' GO TO 'GIGI,' " was the bannerline of the *Film Daily*.

Best Picture of the Year: *Gigi*
Best Director: Vincente Minnelli
Best Writing (based on material from another
     medium): Alan Jay Lerner
Best Color Cinematography: Joseph Ruttenberg
Best Art and Set Decoration: Preston Ames and Keogh Gleason[2]
Best Song: "Gigi"
Best Scoring of a Motion Picture: André Previn
Best Costume Design: Cecil Beaton
Best Film Editing: Adrienne Fazan

In the history of the Academy to the present date no musical has garnered greater acclaim.[3]

---

[2] As is the case of all M-G-M pictures, the heads of the respective departments also received an Oscar.

[3] Including Chevalier's Special Award for his performance in *Gigi, Gigi* tied *West Side Story*'s ten awards in 1962. *Gigi* was an original Hollywood musical whereas *West Side Story* was an adaptation of the already established Broadway hit.

In its initial release and subsequent re-release in 1966, *Gigi* went on to gross $13,208,725. In 1970, the picture was sold to NBC Television for a two-time showing at a record price of $2,000,000.

All the accolades, all the laurels even the most ambitious of men could have hoped for had come Freed's way. But from its inception to the final result, he was far less authoritative, far more ambivalent in his mode of operation than on any of his films. He often faltered when previously he would have stood firm. One might speculate about the reasons for Freed's attitude during the production, which brings to mind significant changes around him.

There no longer was a Roger Edens to construct the continuity of a musical and its balance between music and dialogue. Trapped by his contract, Minelli had to leave the picture and was unable to protect his intention of making of a truly French story rather than letting an element of Hollywood imitation imagery seep in. Cecil Beaton has a word to say about this: "All the scenes that were taken in Hollywood were very damaging. To me the whole success of the film was the Parisian flavor and that was created by making it in France. As soon as we had a swan on the back lot—it looked like the back lot. Then they made Caron sit on a horrible iron chair, which you can see in all interior decorator shops. And suddenly it looked like Hollywood instead of France."

These are harsh words, to be sure. Perhaps *Gigi* was not the ideally perfect picture Freed had hoped for. But it was the zenith of his life.

A stage production of the motion picture musical *Gigi* (with a revised book by Lerner and additional songs by Lerner and Loewe) was presented as part of the San Francisco-Los Angeles Civic Light Opera Association series in May 1973, prior to its opening on Broadway November 16, 1973, at the Uris Theatre. In the cast were Alfred Drake (Chevalier role), Daniel Massey (Jourdan role), Agnes Moorehead (Jeans role), Maria Karnilova (Gingold role) and Karen Wolfe (Caron role). The notices were disastrous and it closed on February 10, 1974. All that remains is an original cast recording.

The chapter ends as it began—.

ARTHUR FREED=
      634 STONE CANYON DR BELAIR CALIF=   1959 APR **7** PM 4 08

DEAR ARTHUR CONGRATULATIONS YOU CERTAINLY DESERVE IT REMEMBER THIS IS THE PICTURE WE COULD NEVER GET DORE SCHARY TO LOOK AT WHEN I BROUGHT THE FRENCH FILM TO THE STUDIO LOVE=
      JOE FIELDS=

16

THE SUBTERRANEANS

BELLS ARE RINGING

LIGHT IN THE PIAZZA

In the opening-night program of *Gigi* the back page announced the current Broadway hit musical *Bells Are Ringing,* starring Judy Holliday, as a future presentation by M-G-M. With the combination of Comden, Green, Jule Styne and Judy Holliday, Freed was swift to grab it for the sizable sum of $400,000. But the show was still playing to standing room only and he would have to wait until the expiration of Holliday's contract, as well as for her approval of a screenplay.

On January 21, 1958, the day after the frustrating first preview of *Gigi,* Freed announced to the long faces around him his latest acquisition, Jack Kerouac's current best seller *The Subterraneans.* Kerouac had established himself with his first successful novel *On the Road* as one of the leading representatives of the "beat" movement. The Subterraneans, a new breed of young people, detached from the standard mores of society, creating a new life style, filled with madness and zeal, confusion and courage, find each other in the North Beach area of San Francisco.

There was enough of the old guard left in the executive offices at the studio to talk up a storm of protest. The core of Kerouac's story is the relationship between a white boy and a black girl; the studio executives were adamant about eliminating the black girl. The youth of

496

America was losing itself in the sounds of progressive jazz; totally ignorant of the germinating rebellion of the young and the rapidly growing integration between the races, the reigning Metro powers still danced to the tune of a Viennese waltz.

Freed's intention was to make this a low-budget,[1] black-and-white avant-garde picture, without the Metro gloss, a prophecy of things to come. But in order to get any support from the studio he had to make the major concession about the girl. He fully realized that this meant losing a big slice of the meaning in Kerouac's story.

Robert Thom, novelist and playwright, recently signed by the studio, was handed the challenging task of developing a screenplay out of the disjointed original story. He kept only three of Kerouac's key figures: Leo, the paranoid young writer, Mardou, the manic-depressive girl, and Yuri, the poet saint. All the other characters were his own invention.

Mardou is a highly disturbed promiscuous girl, who intermittently plays with the idea of returning to a mental institution. A young man, the author of a mediocre first novel, leaves his mother, to join the "beats." He meets Mardou in a café and eventually moves into her miserable, grimy "pad." In the course of their relationship he decides to live life fully—to become a great writer. Mardou becomes excessively jealous, an unfamiliar emotion for her. To forestall being left by her lover, she leaves him at the very moment she discovers that she is pregnant. After a long search he finds her again and they admit to each other that they are in love. He wishes to be the father of the child legally and proposes to marry her.

Around the two leading characters is an embroidery of colorful personages: the poet saint, a half-witted, wide-eyed young man who sleeps standing up; a young artist, Roxanne, who paints only her own portraits and hates men; a best-selling, rich author, overdressed and displaying a long cigarette holder.

Roxanne was the first role to be cast. Freed wanted an eminently talented young actress, Janice Rule, who happened to be Thom's wife.

The Thoms invited Freed to a screening of *Crime and Punishment U.S.A.*, starring George Hamilton in his first screen appearance, directed by Denis Sanders and produced by his brother Terry. This was the Sanders' first feature film. They had produced and directed a twenty-three-minute 35 millimeter dramatic two-reel short, *A Time Out of War,* at UCLA, which won an Academy Award in 1954. Their only other credit was as screenwriters for *The Naked and the Dead.* Freed engaged Denis Sanders to direct *The Subterraneans* and Terry to co-produce, another manifestation of his daring and generosity.

The milieu depicted in the film demanded on-screen as well as off-screen contemporary jazz. André Previn was the obvious choice as

[1] Freed acquired the property for the astonishing low sum of $15,000.

musical director, composer and performer. He assembled a group of great fellow musicians including Gerry Mulligan, Shelly Manne, Art Farmer and Red Mitchell.

Kerouac's black girl underwent a transformation: She became white and French, played by Leslie Caron. George Peppard, a relative new-comer to the screen, was cast as the writer. After an eight-year hiatus Roddy McDowall returned to Metro, the scene of his childhood debut, for the part of Yuri. Gerry Mulligan made his first acting appearance in the role of a humanitarian minister, in addition to playing saxophone to Previn's piano. And Carmen McRae was signed for a solo singing spot.

Freed lost out on another point: The studio insisted that the picture be made in CinemaScope and Technicolor. Bobby Brunner, erstwhile camera operator to George Folsey who had gotten his wings on *It's Always Fair Weather,* was assigned as director of photography. The picture went into production on August 24.

Thau was not surprised at the negative reports he received daily on the Sanders' work. Toward the end of the second week he had a conference with Sol Siegel, recently appointed production head, and they decided to dismiss them. Ranald MacDougall, who had just finished *The World, The Flesh and the Devil* for Siegel, would be the new director.

After forty-two pictures Freed was no longer inclined to fight it out. In this instance he would have had to battle men he had always worked with. His irrevocable loyalty stood in the way. He could have made *The Subterraneans* anywhere, independent of any influences. But few men would pack up, after almost thirty years, and leave their "home." His environment at the studio, his rooms, spelled it out very clearly. In a building where names on office doors were mostly transient, there was no need to put a signpost to identify his wing. This is where he had lived most of his life, in his library, overflowing with books, paintings and memorabilia; in his living room, behind his disorderly, productive desk; in the music room with its piano and the stacks of recordings and sheet music. It was too late to put up new tents.

On Wednesday, September 9, the studio released a statement to the trade papers announcing MacDougall's take-over of *The Subterra-neans* "following differences of opinion among producer Arthur Freed, studio executives, director Denis Sanders and associate producer Terry Sanders." *The Hollywood Reporter* chose to print what it considered the reason for the blow-up "according to an informed source," while *Daily Variety* used the Sanders brothers' formal statement and Freed's comments on their remarks:

The Sanders: "We are shocked and angry at Mr. Freed for being summarily fired by telephone. Our first indication that the com-

Roddy McDowall and George Peppard in a game of chess, on *The Subterraneans* set, as Leslie Caron looks on. M-G-M

plete area of agreement between Mr. Freed and us was deteriorating was his unexplained breaking his promise to give us two weeks' rehearsal."

Freed: "I have only the kindest regards for 'the boys,' but I had to relieve them of their jobs after consultation with Sol Siegel and Benjamin Thau. I did not fire them by telephone. We discussed the situation at the studio last Thursday and Friday, and at my home on Sunday."

The Sanders: "Mr. Freed also wanted to know where the tender moments in our love story were. We told him we were telling a story about people who didn't know how to love, and that this was the greatness of the film. . . . We feel that if it had been understood at the outset that we would have to adopt a Victorian morality in order to make this film, we never would have accepted the assignment."

Freed: "Nobody established any kind of morality. They had two weeks to rehearse, which was more than enough time.[2] But the boys are hurt and I understand that. I tried to help them as I have other young directors, Vincente Minnelli, Charles Walters, Richard Brooks, Stanley Donen. I wish them the best of luck."

MacDougall read Thom's screenplay. After a few hours of intense concentration he developed a concept which necessitated some rewriting. He did think the script was marvelous but that Thom had gotten a little carried away with "free wheeling imagery." But Thom had had it. He was not going to do any further revisions. MacDougall, a highly

[2] According to Bill Shanks's assistant director's report, rehearsals began on August 14, two weeks prior to commencement of principal photography.

talented and experienced writer, began making the changes. He clarified and remolded most of the characters and added some important scenes, including an entirely new first scene for the sake of a stronger continuity.

Before going any further he talked to Thau. "This will not be a commercial venture," he told him, "the poetry has to be expressed and that's not going to be comprehensible to an ordinary audience. They won't even understand many things in the film that are part of the individual mystique of these people." He left a somewhat concerned Thau: Are we going from the frying pan into the fire?

With some trepidation MacDougall went to see Freed. He explained in detail the changes he wanted to make. To begin with, Urie McCleary's sets were too clean and too orderly; they had to reflect the life style of the subculture. No Helen Rose costumes. No Sydney Guilaroff hair styles and no William Tuttle make-up à la Norma Shearer. As to the characters: Evidently Yuri (Roddy McDowall) had to be a "pot head." To emphasize Roxanne's narcissism there would be a mirror over her mantel, lined with red jars and votive candles, her reflection becoming

The Subterraneans gather in Artie Johnson's living-room set. André Previn, lower right, at the piano, Janice Rule and George Peppard, center, dancing, and, between their two arms, sits Nanette Fabray, Ranald MacDougall's wife, who did a bit in the scene. M-G-M

a self-contained icon. He would also present a poetry reading, using the writings of Allen Ginsberg, Kenneth Patchen and quotations from Rimbaud.

Freed went along with MacDougall on all points.

Production resumed on September 11. As luck would have it, Ruttenberg suddenly became available and replaced Brunner as director of photography. The first scene MacDougall completed was Carmen McRae in the Black Hawk Café singing "Coffee Time," with new lyrics by Freed. The number had been prerecorded by Previn and his combo. It took one day to get this out of the way. The only change he made was to replace June Walker with Anne Seymour as Peppard's mother.

"Leslie was most uncertain and unsure of herself," recalls Mac-Dougall "and she had the most uncertainty about me. But we had a talk and I quite frankly told her that certain things she was doing were quite bad. Perhaps she was shopping around for something." It was obvious that Caron was not satisfied with their talk. MacDougall offered her a gentleman's agreement: "If after one week we haven't achieved some kind of rapport that means something to you—I'll bow off the picture." He told Freed about this pact. He felt it vitally important for the picture that Caron and he understood each other and that she trusted him. He had seen her in the Sanders' footage and felt she had no idea what she was doing.

During his first encounter MacDougall ran into similar problems with other members of the cast. "Peppard was a very unsettled human being. And he and Leslie weren't even speaking to one another." The tension on the set was heavy. Rule, McDowall and Peppard were a tight little clique, as MacDougall soon noticed. The fact that Janice Rule went home at night to her brother-in-law, Denis Sanders, to report the events of the day, didn't help matters.

"The performers were a cage of apes, but after a while, as we started working together and with the changes I was making, they began to feel secure with me and we were a team."

The production department allotted three days for location shooting in San Francisco, covering eleven locations and twenty-eight setups. Freed was incredulous. But MacDougall had chosen his sites on a previous trip, planned all his setups in advance and finished on schedule. Not that it was easy.

MacDougall was relentless with some of the departments. The sets, of course, had been toned down and looked more real. He was constantly after the make-up people: "No one looks like that waking up in bed," he told the hairdressers. And he occasionally even whispered into Ruttenberg's ear: "It's too Metro."

MacDougall also ran into difficulties in a violent fight scene between Caron and Peppard which, in a different sense, he also found "too

Gerry Mulligan, who played a principal role and also jazz saxophone in *The Subterraneans,* autographed this picture to Freed: "To my good friend Arthur, Gerry."

pretty." He tried and tried again. At 5:30 P.M., exhausted and resigned, he okayed a take. The following morning the crew expected him to go to another scene. But he decided to reshoot the previous afternoon's work. "I was able to break down the barrier between Caron and Peppard. I rehearsed them and, rather deliberately in order to intensify the physical action I'd get between them, would stare into their faces. I was breaking down any sense of privacy they had—and it worked."

The Subterraneans closed production on October 23, 1959, at a final cost of $931,724.93. After twenty-nine days of production MacDougall began to prepare the preview cut with his editor, Ben Lewis.

Much of the music in the picture was on scene and direct recorded brilliantly by Previn and his group. His postscoring was equally extraordinary: progressive jazz of the highest quality. "Jazz should never be used strictly as background music," he says. "Jazz, as an art form, was never designed to accompany anything, just as you can't expect visual action in a visual medium to be subservient to background music."

The picture was previewed at the Encino Theatre on January 20, 1960. When the lights went on there was stunned and bitter silence among the studio people. Nobody knew what to do.

The film showed the confusion, the disorientation, and the frustration of the new breed of young people. Anyone with an open mind would understand what motivated them, what made them so alienated, rather than condemn them for what, in essence, was their vulnerable naivety. But *The Subterraneans* was slashed to pieces and made totally incomprehensible. Although there were no problems with the censors, Margaret Booth proceeded to mutilate the film beyond recognition, in an effort to protect the healthy roar of Leo the Lion and to uphold the "American image."

Here are some examples:

MacDougall had opened the picture with a canvas in the style of Jackson Pollock behind the main titles, with deliberately flung colors à la Rothko; underneath, sounds of jazz. He dissolved to a beatnik mission house, the Reverend (Gerry Mulligan) lovingly playing his saxophone, the cross on his breast gleaming in the night. The camera moved across the faces of the assemblage and introduced the protagonists. Over this a title read:

> These are Subterraneans. The Beat.
> They are hip without being slick.
> They are wise without being corny.
> Most of them are lost.
> They exist. They are everywhere now.
> On the Left Bank in Paris. In Soho, London.
> In Greenwich Village, Venice West.
> and
> North Beach, San Francisco

This opening was eliminated and with it went the foundation for what was to follow.

Instead, the picture opened with a pedestrian, cliché scene between the aspiring writer and his mother, supposedly establishing the generation gap. MacDougall had introduced him as a would-be Thomas Wolfe, sitting at a table, piles of notebooks around him, talking to the typewriter. This scene was robbed of all its significance. When Leo (George Peppard) leaves his home and his nagging mother (Anne Seymour) once and for all, she consoles herself with her martini and her television set. This, too, was cut out, most likely because it marred the mother image.

Julian (Scott Marlowe), most recent lover of Mardou (Leslie Caron), addressing the narcissistic man-hating Roxanne (Janice Rule) remarks, "Women become more like men and men become more like women. One day we'll meet in the center—on neuter territory." Preposterous—unthinkable! It landed on the cutting-room floor.

When dawn breaks and a party comes to an end, the young people pair up to overcome their desperate loneliness. Offensive! Out it went.

And so—all through the film.

Contractually the director has no right to touch his picture after the first preview cut. MacDougall comments on what happened: "They cut the poetry out completely and, I must say, ruthlessly. There is a way of cutting—but they hadn't a clue of what was happening up there —or for that matter in Greenwich Village, or in Soho or the Left Bank. But the Subterraneans were doing it. And they were the predecessors of what afterward became the beatniks, Haight-Ashbury and the drug scene."

Freed and MacDougall never expected the picture to become a commercial success. But neither of them could foresee that the bone and marrow would be cut out of it.

One of the more glamour-oriented reviewers (*Variety*) wrote:

> Those who have suspected all along that beatniks are dull have proof in Metro's *The Subterraneans*. How the Arthur Freed production will fare financially depends to a great extent on whether beatnikism has sustained enough of its initial attention.

In its initial release, on June 23, 1960, it lost $200,000.

The proverbial backstage story about the star getting sick and the understudy going on in her place came true for Judy Holliday. During the out-of-town tryout of *Born Yesterday* Jean Arthur feigned illness, Judy Holliday went on and brought the house down with "Harry, do me a favor. Drop dead!" Jean Arthur never returned and Judy Holliday became a Broadway star. When she re-created the role of Billie Dawn, the dumb blonde, in the motion picture, she walked off with the Academy Award. From there it was on to *The Marrying Kind, It Should Happen to You* and *The Solid Gold Cadillac,* among others.

In 1956, Comden and Green decided to write a musical for the ex-partner from their days as The Revuers. They were determined to use Judy's singing voice, which had been ingloriously mute since they were together (she also doubled on drums). The two writers made up an original story for her about a shy little phone operator in a New York answering service who does good deeds for her customers and finally wins a glamorous husband for herself. Judy Holliday kept *Bells Are Ringing* incandescent on Broadway for over two years.

The composer of the show was Jule Styne who had first worked with Comden and Green on the revue *Two on the Aisle*. He was also the composer of *High Button Shoes, Gentlemen Prefer Blondes* and *Hazel Flagg*.

When it came to the adaptation of Freed's screen version of *Bells,* Lazar negotiated Comden and Green's contract for the astronomical sum of $100,000. In it was a stipulation that they would provide an unlimited number of new songs with Styne, as well as revising any existing lyrics. At the time the contract was signed they were appearing on Broadway in a collection of their songs and sketches, *A Party With Betty Comden and Adolph Green.* Freed permitted them to write their first draft in the East, with the clear understanding that it would be delivered to him by December 31, 1958, containing no more than 110 pages.

The screenplay did arrive on time, but the book alone without any lyrics was 153 pages long (a little under two hours). There were no new songs accompanying the script; instead a request for additional time to stay with their hit show.

Freed called Comden and Green and informed them that he was not accepting their first draft because it was much too long. They agreed to revise and cut and were given to understand that only their next script would be considered as the first draft, provided it was within the contractural limits as to length. Freed also granted them an extra two weeks to continue their Broadway show and they agreed to report to the studio on January 26.

Dean Martin had been signed as Judy Holliday's costar and Minnelli was handed his twelfth directorial assignment for Freed. *Bells* had been scheduled to go into production during February, but under the circumstances this was out of the question since there was no satisfactory script, and so the starting date was postponed until June.

On January 6, Lazar called MacKenna to tell him that Comden and Green would agree to report on February 16 with two or possibly three songs. "Where did the date February 16 come from, Irving?" Lazar said that Freed had okayed it. A short while later Freed came into MacKenna's office to tell him that he hadn't approved any such thing. They got Lazar on the phone. A further extension to February 9 was granted.

February 9, 1959

Dear Irving:

Confirming our telephone conversation of this morning, I want you to know that both Freed and I are very disappointed that in spite of the many promises made to us that we'd have two and possibly three songs by the time Comden and Green reported for the eight weeks of exclusive work, they were unable to show Freed and Minnelli so much as one line of lyrics as of last Friday. According to Arthur, the only thing they had to show was a title for a song which they submitted for Arthur's approval.

I don't have to remind you that in the many talks you and I have had over the telephone since January 5th on the subject of our reluctant extension of our permission to let them appear on the New York stage, in every instance you promised us that this additional work of theirs on the stage would in no way interfere with their working on the additional three songs requested nor delay their delivery.

In our conversation of January 7th, you said if we'd extend their New York time, they would surely bring two songs with them and might bring three.

Again in our conversation of January 13th, you repeated that they still were hoping to bring two songs and possibly three.

Neither Arthur, you nor I want to complicate the working conditions for Comden and Green, but as I said to you this morning, it's always a question of our being forced to live up to the letter of the contract and they wanting their convenience to take precedence.

Sincerely,
Kenneth

Through her agent, Abe Lastfogel of the William Morris Agency, Judy Holliday requested a discussion of the screenplay with Freed and Minnelli before any revisions were made. She also asked for and received permission from Metro to appear in the Los Angeles and San Francisco stage productions of the show with a terminating date of July 4. This meant another postponement.

Freed received Comden and Green's next draft and four new songs: "To Love and to Lose," "Do It Yourself," "Better Than a Dream" and "My Guiding Star." He returned the screenplay to them: It ran two hours and twenty-two minutes.

Dear Betty,

I am enclosing a footage breakdown of the picture.

You can see that without figuring any footage for music that we run over 9,600 ft., added to this I am sure we will have thirty minutes of music.

With 90 ft. to a minute, we have the problem of cutting about 2,000 ft. of the book. This has to be done to make any sense; so, forgetting everything else for the moment, we have a simple problem of arithmetic.

As far as Judy is concerned, there is nothing monumental and I wouldn't worry too much about that. She had a few good suggestions and one or two things, I believe, I convinced her wouldn't work.

As you know, cutting is a real professional job but I know you agree there is no alternative. The success of this picture depends in not getting long and stagy. By that I mean, overdialogued, regardless of the brilliance of the dialogue.

This picture should be no longer than *Gigi,* which was under two hours. I'm sure I don't have to emphasize that fact. We don't want to make the mistakes that were made in *Pajama Game* and *Damn Yankees,* which did not feel like motion pictures. We never did before, let's not do it this time.

Betty, I think I've always understood your problems as well as Adolph's and you must know the respect that I have for your talents and also how much I value your friendship. Also rest assured that as far as Judy is concerned, that we will be grateful for any good ideas, but I'm sure we will have no problem in eliminating any unpractical ones.

A script conference on *Bells Are Ringing* (left to right): Dean Martin, Vincente Minnelli, Betty Comden, Arthur Freed, Jule Styne and Adolph Green. ARTHUR FREED ARCHIVES

Let's all pitch in as we always have—Vincente and I are both looking forward to making a wonderful picture.

I'll call you next week. Meanwhile, regards to the family.

Love,
Arthur

Keeping in touch with the writers by telephone, Freed decided *Bells* would start on August 15, with shooting to commence on October 6. The following actors from the Broadway show were signed: Jean Stapleton, Bernie West, Dort Clark and Hal Linden. New to the cast were Fred Clark, Frank Gorshin and Eddie Foy, Jr.; costumes were to be designed by Walter Plunkett; art direction by Preston Ames; music conducted and adapted by André Previn; Milton Krasner on camera and Adrienne Fazan as film editor.

The problem with the script was simply that the stage show did not lend itself to a screen adaptation. Comden and Green opened it up and added scenes, but their screenplay not only became overlong but lost the qualities it had before the footlights. It was neither fish nor fowl. The alternative was to transfer the original to the screen, a procedure which Freed had always rejected in the past.

Now it was already August and contractual obligations had to be met. Freed had no recourse but to send the production on its way. Minnelli, Krasner, Ames and a second unit went to New York to shoot exteriors and backgrounds. Meanwhile, Freed tried to establish some kind of communication with Judy Holliday, which was not too easy. She was exceedingly unsure of herself and of what she was to do in the picture and stayed that way throughout the shooting. Freed tried to make her more comfortable by casting the man in her life, Gerry Mulligan, currently in production in *The Subterraneans*. Even that didn't ease the situation.

From the start of principal photography on October 8 until the day it closed, December 24, 1959, it was one constant struggle. Holliday came to Plunkett, dissolved in tears; she thought she looked terrible, she was gaining weight from day to day, she was all wrong for the part. "She wanted to pay Metro for all expenses on the film up to that day," says Plunkett, "and let them recast it with someone else . . . she just couldn't do it." Minnelli constantly tried reassuring her. "And then," he says, "she had a fight with—of all people—Comden and Green, because she felt they hadn't changed the script enough to make it cinematic. Well, that caused a situation between them and Arthur, since they were always joined at the hip."

There were more than the normal mishaps and absences with Judy: laryngitis, a kidney infection, a suitcase fell on her leg, then came a bladder infection. As part of the action in a scene she was required to walk across the room with the back of her dress on fire. The igniting apparatus became overheated and her skin was burned. With all this, coupled with her feeling of insecurity, she was miserably unhappy throughout production.

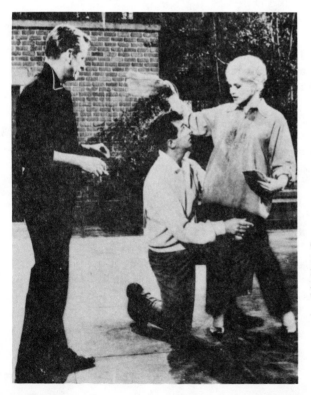

Charles O'Curran, choreographer on *Bells Are Ringing*, rehearses Dean Martin and Judy Holliday in "Just in Time." ARTHUR FREED ARCHIVES and M-G-M

Minnelli and Martin clowning on the set.
M-G-M and VINCENTE MINNELLI COLLECTION

When Rudi Monta received the lyrics to the song "Drop That Name" he saw no point in attempting to approach any of the people whose names were mentioned for their specific written consents. He got as far as Brigitte Bardot, Jean Cocteau, Marilyn Monroe, Vincente Minnelli, Fred Astaire, René Clair, Jose Ferrer, the former Grace Kelly . . . and gave up.

For Freed this was not a happy experience. He was dissatisfied—he felt he had missed his mark. Neck to neck with *Bells Are Ringing* he had to stand up under the pressure *The Subterraneans* had put on him. At last, temporarily it seems, his energies were depleted. But soon his vigor was restored when he read the reviews and got the box-office reports.

Bells Are Ringing cost $2,203,123. It was released on June 23, 1960, and grossed $3,985,950.

This was Judy Holliday's last screen appearance. Much of her unhappiness might be attributed to her obviously fragile physical condition, which culminated in her tragic death on June 7, 1965.

Freed had produced the 1951 Academy Award ceremony. Now the Board of Governors approached him to return as the permanent producer starting with the thirty-second show. He was honored to accept. By his side were some of the old guard: Edens, Walters, Minnelli, Previn and Green.

Freed's first independent producer's contract was for three years, which called for his producing four motion pictures. He had completed *Silk Stocking, Gigi, The Subterraneans* and *Bells Are Ringing*. A new deal was negotiated under the same terms. In addition, he would produce a television spectacular for the studio.

Light in the Piazza was his first motion picture under the new agreement. From the time he read Elizabeth Spencer's novella (*The Light in the Piazza*) in *The New Yorker* to the release of the movie, there were no problems, no frictions, no personality conflicts, no hold-ups, and even the weather on the Continental locations was clement—it was sunshine all the way.

Spencer was the first to win the newly initiated McGraw-Hill Fiction Award for her sensitive story. It deals with a wealthy American woman who takes her young, mildly retarded daughter on a holiday to Italy where the girl falls in love with a dashing young Italian. The mother does not regard her daughter's handicap as an obstacle and does everything humanly possible to help her child get what she wants.

It goes without saying that the studio wanted the girl's affliction toned down, which, in effect was more a charming infantilism than a sickness. This time Freed didn't even discuss it. He went ahead and engaged the writer of his choice, Julius J. Epstein, to adapt Spencer's book.

1960

15000 CORONA DEL MAR,
PACIFIC PALISADES, CALIFORNIA.

THURS —

Dear ARTH —
I Had to go to Texas the day
after I saw "Bells" at the Pantages.
So haven't had a chance to tell you
what a great job it is.
It certainly is far superior to the
stage piece. Judy is simply superb
and Dean Better than he's ever Been.
It Bears all the great Freed
trademarks — and that makes me
just a Bit homesick —
            All my Love —
                    Roger

According to Arthur Freed's Archives, this is the last known letter written by Roger Edens to Arthur Freed.

Rather than be encumbered with Culver City, Freed decided to make the picture abroad, with locations in Italy, and interiors at Boreham Wood, England.

He sent Epstein's first draft to Guy Green, an Academy Award winner for his photography on *Great Expectations,* who had recently become a successful director (*The Mark* and *The Angry Silence*). Green, a very selective Englishman, was intrigued with the story and let Freed know that he would be interested in directing the picture. A deal was made and Green came to the studio to meet with Freed and Epstein. Before arriving he read a trade-paper release that Yvette Mimieux had been signed for the role of the girl; he was not too pleased about it.

The changes Green suggested were the most minor Epstein had ever made in his many years in the business. Freed, Green and Epstein saw eye to eye on every point. The casting of the production was not difficult with the exception of the young Italian. For the time being, however, the other principals were set: Olivia de Havilland as the mother, Barry Sullivan as the father and Rossano Brazzi as the father of the Italian boy.

Then a telegram arrived from George Hamilton. An overzealous publicist apparently had intimated that Hamilton was not available and he informed Freed that he *was* eager to test for the boy in his picture. Green shot test scenes with Mimieux and Hamilton. "I was very disappointed with what she did alone, but when she played with Hamilton he kind of inspired her and she sparked."

On May 3, 1961, everyone assembled in Florence, Italy. Freed, Mimieux and Hamilton came from Los Angeles, De Havilland with her Dior wardrobe from Paris and Brazzi from Rome. Green, production manager Aida Young, cameraman Otto Heller and some of the crew arrived from England. All the necessary cameras and equipment came from Metro's warehouses at Cinecitta Studios in Rome.

"Film Troupe Invades Florence Gallery" was the headline of a syndicated column, which appeared in American newspapers. This sounds like another ugly Hollywood story but it was nothing of the kind. For the first time in the history of Florence's Uffizi Art Gallery, Freed was given permission for his company to photograph within its ancient walls. The Medici family collection represents much of the world's finest works of art. Its corridors, lined with Greek and Roman sculptures and hung with priceless tapestries, provided a setting that could not have been purchased with the combined fortunes of the world. The Italian Government was exceedingly co-operative and gave the production full use of the gallery without charge.

Then Green wanted to shoot a scene with Mimieux and Hamilton standing on one of the Excelsior Hotel balconies. But the manager was "an awkward customer," Green says. He wouldn't allow the company

On the Florence location for *Light in the Piazza* (right to left): Olivia de Havilland, Arthur Freed, Yvette Mimieux and Aida Young, Freed's assistant. The inscription from Miss de Havilland reads "Dear Arthur—Remember? A photographer from Milan recently sent me this. Love—Olivia." ARTHUR FREED ARCHIVES

to disturb the guests. By a strange coincidence Green ran into a man who had the room off that balcony: Would he mind their using it?

"Which company is this?"

"Metro-Goldwyn-Mayer," Green replied.

"Fine, I'm a stockholder!"

Under the daily and very generously extended tutelage of Brazzi, Hamilton became more and more Italian.

Before going on to Rome locations the company took advantage and photographed a local celebration: the Feast of St. John the Baptist, patron saint of Florence. Every June, fireworks and football games in sixteenth-century costumes are held in the Piazza della Signoria.

In Rome the Italian Government was again very helpful in accommodating the production in working on the Via Veneto, one of the city's most congested thoroughfares. The police detoured traffic for three days while Green shot scenes with his principals.

Freed also got permission to use the Ostiense Railroad Station which was the VIP terminal, reserved for the arrival of world-famous dignitaries. Three first-class trains, two second-class, two electric engines—fourteen cars in all—were transported six hundred miles from Sicily and Torino areas into Rome for this particular sequence. It was also the one hundredth anniversary of the unification of Italy, and its crack trains had been sent to Torino to be ready for the liberation day celebration, when troops are transported into Rome for the gala fiesta. Italian officials insisted that no ordinary trains would do: Only the best was good enough for the American filmmaker.

Sand was sprinkled across the tracks to safeguard Hamilton as he rushed across the railway ties to catch Mimieux before she departed. Green had his second train racing in the opposite direction for the hazardous scene in which the actor disregards the oncoming train, dashes across the tracks, slips and comes within inches of being caught under the grinding wheels.

While on the Continent, each day's film was air freighted to the British studios for processing and promptly returned. It was screened in one of the local theatres.

The company went to Boreham Wood to shoot the interiors, the last week of June. Green recalls Freed being everywhere, including on the set at the studio. "Like all directors I am kind of nervous about producers being around. Arthur would arrive about ten, pick himself a spot, sit there and probably stay till four. He didn't say a word but be interested and observe. I began to feel uncomfortable if he *wasn't* around."

When production closed on July 12, Freed left Green and Aida Young to handle the postproduction and returned to Los Angeles. Mario Nascimbene, well-known Italian composer, had been engaged

Director Guy Green with Olivia de Havilland and Yvette Mimieux. M-G-M

In Freed's handwriting, the introduction he wrote for his film.
ARTHUR FREED ARCHIVES

to write the score, including a title song, with lyrics by Freed. It was recorded at the studio under the baton of Dock Mathieson.

By mid-August a rough cut was sent to Culver City.

After it was screened Freed called Green at the London studio to tell him how impressed he and everybody else was with the picture. He suggested some minor cuts, mainly the shortening of the football game and deleting some of De Havilland's close-ups, with which Green readily concurred.

Light in the Piazza opens with establishing shots of Italy, and Freed wrote a prologue to be superimposed.

In Young's capable hands, postproduction work in London went smoothly and she wrote her last report to Freed. Nascimbene had recorded the score, which she felt did a great deal for the picture. Dubbing was to start within days and the finished print would be shipped to him as arranged. She also called his attention to the fact that the picture had come in under budget: $553,280.75. The estimated cost had been $1.1 million.

The preview of *Piazza* was a rousing success and so were the usually prosaic trade reviews:

'LIGHT IN THE PIAZZA' IS A
MEMORABLE LOVE STORY

Freed-Green Film Has Wide Appeal

Truly an uncommon love story, and one told with rare delicacy and force, Arthur Freed's *Light in the Piazza* is mature in the correct sense of that term, dealing with adult problems only adults are equipped to solve. . . ."

Friday, Jan. 5, 1962 *The Hollywood Reporter*

With *Light in the Piazza* first item out of its 1962 hopper, Metro has hit that elusive bull's-eye at which picturemakers inevitably aim —the film that achieves the rare and delicate balance of artistic beauty, romantic substance, dramatic novelty and commercial appeal, the latter being the natural end product of the first three. . . ."

Hollywood, Jan. 3, 1962 *Variety*

514

The picture was released on February 9, 1961, and grossed $2,345,000.

Olin Clark, M-G-M's eastern story editor, who had originally secured the property for Freed, enclosed with his letter one from Elizabeth Spencer.

Dear Olin Clark:

I have seen *Light in the Piazza* twice now, and I want to express my thanks through you to everyone responsible for making the picture. An author approaches this experience fearfully. So much has been seen to happen when books are transferred to film. The range is a wide one, but would seem often to include murder in every degree along with lots of plain bad taste. Still, one has to go and see: no power on earth could keep us away; so imagine my relief to find the movie Messrs. Freed, Epstein, Green, etc. have actually done—sincere, sweet, moving, and as kindly attentive to the pages as I wrote them as one's own friends might be.

It's easy to go on into details. There were people I might have cast differently, some scenes I might quarrel with. On the other hand, there were a good many touches of quite brilliant interpolation; for instance, in the scene where they return to the hotel from the fiasco over the passports and the girl looks for a long time at herself in one of those wavy old Venetian mirrors as though trying to discover herself and says, Did I do something wrong? Your Miss Mimieux will go far, I think.

Well, enough of this. Do tell them all. The little book sort of wrote itself in a way and seems to have a lucky existence.

I do hope we meet again, perhaps on account of some other story.

Very sincerely yours,
Elizabeth Spencer (Rusher)

Dear Arthur:

Never, but never, has a letter like this one from Elizabeth Spencer crossed my desk during the twenty years I've been in this job.

It was completely unsolicited and not even did the author's literary agent know that she was going to write it.

So it's a case of "the perfect tribute" with no strings.

I've sent a suitable acknowledgment to Miss Spencer, but I assume that you will want to write to her personally.

Best, as always,
Olin

17   *THE FALL OF THE EMPIRE*

Freed left Metro-Goldwyn-Mayer in January of 1970. He had not produced a motion picture since *Light in the Piazza*. The M-G-M empire had fallen and with it Freed's autonomy. Managements came and went, and with them, new and unfamiliar faces.

Freed was keenly aware of the radical change on the contemporary scene. The Beatles had conquered the world and the young flocked to the cinema veritée. A musical to make an impression on this new audience would have to be the exception to the rule.

In 1960, Freed asked the studio to buy *Camelot* and *Paint Your Wagon*, both Lerner and Loewe shows. He reactivated one of their earlier Broadway shows, *The Day Before Spring*, and also discussed the possibility of developing an original musical, based on Gershwin's "A Foggy Day in London Town." Joseph Vogel, then still president, refused to allow him to buy any properties and, in principle, was against any period musicals. But he did agree on *The Day Before Spring* because the studio owned it. In 1946, Jack Cummings had taken the property, had discarded the entire show including Lerner and Loewe's songs and had only retained the title. Johnny Green and Frank Loesser had written a new score. The project was shelved. Now Freed assigned Joseph Stein, prominent Broadway playwright, to adapt the original book with its original score. Stein worked on the script for eight months and turned it in in November. Sol Siegel didn't like anything about it and again Freed was turned down. During that year the only Arthur Freed production was the Academy Awards presentation.

Freed had not given up on *Camelot*. He was more than eager to make the picture with the original Broadway cast: Richard Burton, Julie Andrews and Robert Goulet, Minnelli directing. But Vogel still wouldn't budge. In February 1961, *Camelot* was sold to Warner Brothers for $2 million. In July, Freed became first vice-president of the Academy of Motion Pictures Arts and Sciences and again produced the "Oscar" show. By the end of the year Siegel left the studio.

At the start of 1962, Freed was able to persuade Vogel to buy *My Fair Lady*. As the studio's emissary, Lazar was sent to New York to see W. Spencer Harrison of the Columbia Broadcasting System,[1] which controlled the motion-picture rights. Lazar made a bid of $4.5 million. Unbeknown to Freed, Lazar and Vogel, Jack Warner had advised Harrison that he would outbid any offer by a million dollars. This, of course, collapsed the deal, and Warner Brothers bought *My Fair Lady* for $5.5. million.

Shortly thereafter Freed bought an English comedy that had played on Broadway, *Odd Man In,* by Robin Maugham (an adaptation of Claude Magnier's French play *Monsieur Masure* with the approval of Vogel and Robert Weitman,[2] who had replaced Siegel as production chief at the studio. Julius Epstein did the screen adaptation, with the title *A Likely Story,* to star Gina Lollobrigida and Tony Curtis, with Charles Walters directing. The film would be an English production.

Freed again produced the Academy show while making preparations for his next picture. Epstein turned in his final draft, and Freed put him on the adaptation of the recently acquired Broadway musical *Carnival,* based on the M-G-M picture *Lili.*

Before the year was out, Freed started developing three television spectaculars: the Gershwins' *Lady Be Good,* Vincent Youmans' *Great Day* and Harold Arlen's *Blues Opera—Free and Easy* (based on *St. Louis Woman*).

In 1963, Vogel resigned his position as president and was replaced by Robert O'Brien, who, since 1957, had been executive vice-president of Loew's, Inc. This was O'Brien's first contact with the complexities of motion-picture production.

Early in the year, Walters backed out of *A Likely Story* for reasons of health. None of the highly qualified directors Freed proposed were accepted by the stars, and with that the project was dead. Undaunted,

[1] The company had completely underwritten cost of the Broadway production.
[2] Weitman had previously headed M-G-M television production arm.

Freed went ahead with his plans for *Carnival*. He received a commitment from Gower Champion to direct and sent Epstein with his final draft to New York for script conferences. He also put a binder on James Mitchell and Pierre Olaf, both from the Broadway cast, and a highly satisfactory screen test was made of Yvette Mimieux for the role of Lili. Then came a brief, to-the-point telephone call from Weitman, informing Freed that *Carnival* would have to be abandoned. The new management was establishing studio policy without being very communicative about it.

As past president of the Screen Producers Guild, Freed was asked to chair its annual Milestone Award dinner. He was instrumental in designating Irving Berlin as the recipient of the organization's coveted Laurel Award. But he had a difficult time persuading him to come out for the dinner. For the program Freed selected Frank Sinatra to sing a medley of Berlin songs. Publicly announced as "The Greatest Milestone Award Ever," it was held at the Beverly Hilton Hotel on March 3. Mayor Sam Yorty declared it "Irving Berlin Day" and Los Angeles radio stations played nothing but Berlin songs for twenty-four hours. Saluting Berlin, speakers at the dinner included toastmaster George Jessel and former Milestone Award winners Adolph Zukor, Samuel Goldwyn, Jack Warner and Stanley Adams, president of ASCAP.

"After accepting I worried because it was the first dinner that I had been given—or rather accepted—since 1913, which was a dinner the Friar's Club gave me," recalls Berlin. He went on to describe the evening: "Arthur produced the tribute affair beautifully. It was a very emotional night."

In the course of the evening Freed steered the conversation on to a subject which he had been carrying in his mind for quite some time. His dream was—and had been—to make a picture about Irving Berlin, the man, but he knew that was impossible. Failing that, he wished to make a movie about his career. Berlin was enthusiastic at the prospect of doing a picture, and he promptly came up with the title of one of his songs, "Say It With Music."

George Cohen, Berlin's West Coast lawyer, informed Freed that a deal could be made for $1 million. Freed went to see O'Brien. "I walked in and met a stranger," he recalled. "I'll let you know," was the answer.

The studio lawyers began negotiating with Cohen. They proposed giving Berlin 25 per cent of the film's net profits. That was turned down. Cohen told them that his client would be willing to take 10 per cent of the gross, from the first dollar, without receiving any cash up front; that he would write six new songs and put his entire catalogue at Freed's disposal for use in the projected musical. "I wanted them to budget this picture at $6 million—that's why I told them I wouldn't take any cash," says Berlin. "It had to be an important

Irving Berlin at the Milestone Award dinner in his honor, hosted by the Screen Producers Guild of America, flanked by Freed and Frank Sinatra. ARTHUR FREED ARCHIVES

picture." Finally an agreement was reached whereby Berlin would receive $1 million, payable over a ten-year period, against 12½ per cent of the profits.

In his next Academy Awards production Freed promoted his forthcoming picture. He had Edens devise a medley of Berlin songs to be sung by Ethel Merman, who had made many of them famous. Walters staged her act, which started with "Alexander's Ragtime Band" and ended with her walking off the stage and up the center aisle of the auditorium belting out "There's No Business Like Show Business," as she shook hands with the nominees.

In May, Arthur Freed became president of the Academy of Motion Pictures Arts and Sciences, a position he held four terms, the maximum for that office.

By then, Berlin had completed his new songs and the day came when he, Freed and Minnelli played them for O'Brien and Weitman. One was called "The Ten Best Undressed Women."

Weitman's only comment was "I don't think we can use it—we'll have trouble with the censors." (This was 1963!)

Arthur Laurents, playwright and screenwriter, was engaged to invent an original story for *Say It With Music*. Lazar negotiated his deal for $250,000. At the end of June he was at the studio conferring with Freed, Berlin and Minnelli, who was set to direct. Laurents' contract permitted him to write wherever he chose and allowed for a skiing holiday in Switzerland. The screenplay he delivered at the end of the year dealt with a man, i.e., Robert Goulet, and his romances with girls from four different countries: United States (Ann-Margret), England (Julie Andrews), France (Brigitte Bardot) and Italy (Sophia Loren)[3]. The entire conception was thought bad, and the project was left in abeyance until a suitable writer could be found.

With no picture going into production, Freed took his duties as Academy president quite seriously. The organization was in dire need of adequate and permanent quarters and one of his first endeavors was to bring this to fruition. His frequent contact with members of the Academy brought him some tentative and some very concrete offers. On a number of occasions he was asked by Jack Warner (Warner Brothers), Howard Koch (Paramount) and Mike Frankovich (Columbia) to come to their studio to produce on his own terms. He was flattered by their overtures but chose to remain at Metro.

The Milestone Award Dinner of 1964 was given in honor of Arthur Freed. In terms of recognition from the industry, this was the only award he had as yet not received. Before the award was presented, a thirty-minute film was screened showing highlights from the many motion pictures he had produced. After thunderous applause from his colleagues he received the trophy, which was inscribed: "This wreath of honor for his historic contribution to the American Motion Picture." Freed was deeply touched.

As soon as his new contract for three years and four pictures was signed, Freed brought in Leonard Gershe to work on a new story for *Say It With Music*.

Freed was interested in *Hello, Dolly!* On inquiring, he found out that Paramount still held the right of first refusal to produce it but the legal department assured him that he would be informed if and when it would lapse. However, he was *not* advised when Paramount did not exercise its option and *Hello, Dolly!* was grabbed by Twentieth Century-Fox.

Gershe had worked on his script for nine months when Freed brought Edens back as his associate producer.

Berlin was enthusiastic over Gershe's draft and voluntarily added another new song, "I Used to Play It by Ear." Edens worked closely with Gershe and devised an ingenius stream-of-consciousness ballet, incorporating twenty-eight songs from the composer's catalogue. After a year's work, Freed, Edens, Minnelli and Gershe went to New York to confer with O'Brien. "We had to wait in his outer office for two hours," says Gershe. "I was furious—not for myself, but that they had the incredible gall to keep Arthur Freed waiting!" When their meeting was finally concluded, O'Brien told Freed personally that he'd better get

[3] In November 1963, Ann-Margret and Sophia Loren were officially announced to star in the film.

another writer on the script and do an entire rewrite. No comment was made about Edens' musical continuity.

From August 1963 to February 17, 1966, Comden and Green worked on another treatment, illustrative material and a first and second draft. "We got these excited phone calls from Irving Berlin who was really star-struck with happiness and he said, 'This is it.' We were very gratified and pleased—I think we felt justified at his pleasure." The writers thought they had solved the problem, which was making the Berlin catalogue work, a catalogue that stretches over two thirds of a century. Their story was a panorama embracing several periods of the twentieth century. Three stories were told simultaneously, jumping back and forth from one to the other, 1911, 1925 and 1965, carrying out the thesis that no matter how times change, human relationships and the need for love remain the same.

In September 1966, Edens left Freed and went over to Twentieth Century-Fox as associate producer on *Hello, Dolly!*

A short time later, Metro-Goldwyn-Mayer experienced the third in what was to become a series of company shake-ups. When Vogel was still president, Louis B. Mayer tried to reclaim his throne, but he died, unsuccessful. Then the board of directors put O'Brien in as president and Vogel left. Now, Philip J. Levin, a New Jersey real estate magnate, a major stockholder in the company and a board member, attempted to gain control via a proxy fight. But Levin and the dissident group lost out to O'Brien and the ruling managment.

"Say It With Music will be the greatest physical musical ever made," said Freed in an interview with *The Hollywood Reporter.* "It will cover all of Irving Berlin's career with his songs to be used in medley, ballet (by Jerome Robbins and Bob Fosse), vocal and imaginative forms." Starring Fred Astaire, the ten-million-dollar film would start production at the end of 1967.

Then Freed came up with yet another project, *The Boy Friend.* The studio had acquired the Broadway hit musical in 1957 with the intention of starring Debbie Reynolds. Screenplays had been written by Dorothy Kingsley and George Wells. Now Freed decided to make it exactly as it had been done on Broadway, but with a cast of new faces. He hired George Kirgo, a writer under contract to the studio, to handle the adaptation. In April 1967, his screenplay was finished and subsequently turned down by Weitman.

At the time the 1967 Academy Awards ceremony was to go on, AFTRA was on strike. As the Academy's president Freed could not produce the show; he could, however, publicly declare that the show would go on, no matter what. At the last minute the union differences were ironed out, and millions of people were able to see the event on television and hear it on radio.

During the summer of the same year a tribute to Arthur Freed

was presented by the Gallery of Modern Art in New York (now the New York Cultural Center), with a retrospective film series detailing his extensive career. Beginning on June 20 and continuing for nine weeks through August 20, it was extended through September 7 by public demand.

On January 22, 1968, the Los Angeles *Times* reported:

> One of the biggest and most important musicals in the history of M-G-M, Irving Berlin's *Say it With Music* will star Julie Andrews under the direction of Blake Edwards . . . to be presented in 70 mm. and Super Panavision, as a reserved-seat attraction. The spectacular musical will be coproduced by Arthur Freed and Blake Edwards. The announcement was made yesterday by M-G-M president Robert H. O'Brien. *Say It With Music* will go before the cameras at M-G-M's Culver City studios in early 1969 with an all-star cast—one of the largest arrays of musical talents assembled for one motion picture.

Freed's last term as Academy president had expired, which made it possible for him to again produce the Awards scheduled for April 8, 1968. On April 4, Dr. Martin Luther King was assassinated and the

Academy Board of Governors considered canceling their annual event. Freed convinced them to postpone the show for two days and he canceled their annual Governor's Ball.

Bob Hope, as usual, was the master of ceremonies for the fortieth Oscar presentation. Late that night he came out and, rather than introducing the next presenters, he said, "A Hollywood figure already heavy with honors is about to put on more weight. Four times president of the Academy, six times producer of these annual attempts to beguile you into your neighborhood theatre, former Thalberg winner, whose personal productions have garnered twenty-one Oscars over the years, and a friend to movie audiences and picturemakers throughout the world, our Board of Governors tonight salutes with a special Oscar the lyrical Mr. Arthur Freed."

At the beginning of 1969, Edgar M. Bronfman, heir to Seagrams Distilleries of Canada, acquired control of M-G-M. O'Brien moved up to chairman of the board and Lewis F. Polk, a former executive with General Mills in Minneapolis, was appointed president.[4] Weitman resigned to become a producer at Columbia Pictures and Clark Ramsay, another home-office executive, moved out to Culver City to head the studio.

However, by midyear the studio was once again on shaky ground. The financial report showed a net loss of $35,366,000. Entered Kirk Kerkorian, millionaire head of Tracy Investments (controllers of several large Las Vegas hotels), who began acquiring large blocks of M-G-M stock with the sole intention of overthrowing the Bronfman regime. He succeeded in obtaining the necessary majority by fall. That fight cost Bronfman $51 million (holding 1 million shares) as against Kerkorian's 2.2 million shares.

Polk was swiftly ousted and James T. Aubrey, Jr., once head of CBS Television production, was named Metro's new president. Within a few days *Say It With Music* was canceled. Aubrey then began to dispose of all that had made M-G-M the greatest and most valuable studio.

First, he decided that all the costumes and props (i.e., furniture, autos, trolleys, even the show boat) that accumulated over thirty-five years should be sold. Rather than have the studio handle the sale, he made a flat deal of $1.4 million with David Weisz, a California auctioneer. That famous auction began on May 3, 1970, lasted three weeks and netted the Weisz company over $10 million.

Second, he sold the sixty-eight acres of Lot 3 to Levitt & Sons, Inc., ITT (builders of Levittown, New York). All the famous streets were leveled and in their place stands a modern housing development named Raintree County. Lot 2 also went and Aubrey even tried to dispose of

[4] Bronfman had persuaded board member General Omar Bradley to resign in order to get Polk a seat as a director of the company.

the main lot to an automobile assembly company, but the Culver City zoning board put a stop to that. Then he ordered the music department's library burned, with the exception of one score for every film retained; out-takes, prerecordings, music tracks and the enormous stock-footage library also went. The vast script library was about to go up in flames, but was stopped by someone who cared and they were sent to the USC library. Aubrey also sold M-G-M Records to Polygram, a foreign entertainment conglomerate. Ironically, Polygram has begun to re-release most of the musical soundtrack albums that have been collector's items for many years.

The ax finally fell on September 17, 1973, almost four years from the day Aubrey took over, when he announced that Metro-Goldwyn-Mayer would no longer be a film-producing company (with the exception, perhaps, of one or two films a year), that its film exchanges would be closed, and it no longer would distribute motion pictures. Foreign theatre holdings would be sold off as would its library of previously produced films.[5] "There is no way that a movie company can survive today if the production and distribution of motion pictures is its only business," he said. "Television was one of the markets that the studio would concentrate on—producing television series." "Diversification" was another word he used in making his formal statement to the press. By that he was referring to M-G-M's Grand Hotel in Las Vegas, which was about to open. And so, the curtain slowly fell on the end of what was once the most powerful empire in the motion-picture industry.

Arthur Freed decided to leave the studio in December 1970. It was three months after his seventy-fifth birthday and he was tired. He left without having met Aubrey.

Berlin's contract was paid off. "That's right," he recalls. "These figures—it's fine to be able to do it to get a million dollars. You don't keep a helluva lot of it. It's much more important to me if they had made the picture. And they could have. It was to be Arthur's and my swan song in motion pictures. But those 'civilians' as I call them—the guys in New York—making decisions that should have been made by Arthur Freed. They were stupid! And they lost all rights to my new songs."

One of the last deliveries a studio mailboy made to the Freed suite was a registered parcel from Germany. It contained the International Union of Film Critics Gold Medal Award for the Arthur Freed Film Retrospective which had been entered in the nineteenth Berlin International Film Festival. The inscription read: "To Honour Arthur Freed, Master Musical Maker, Berlin Festival 1969."

---

[5] The Justice Department's descent decree, a decade earlier, did not apply to foreign operations.

524

POSTSCRIPT

It is my hope that the reader who has followed me as I probed Arthur Freed's life might understand the obsessive interest which prompted me to seek out all those whose lives he touched.

For the research of this book my interviews took me to New York, London, Paris and Rome, among other places. But when I began writing I always set aside a couple of hours each day to spend with Freed at his house. Although our conversations centered mostly around matters pertaining to his work, in the course of time, rarely exposed traits of his personality rounded out my knowledge of the man as a whole.

He took me into his confidence and became my fatherly friend. It is for this reason that I wish to forgo a summing up; I do not wish to take the risk of appearing biased. I therefore decided to let one of Freed's oldest and most objective friends, Irving Berlin, have the last word:

> My evaluation of Arthur Freed as a producer is this: His greatest talent was to know talent, to recognize talent and to surround himself with it. To talk to him or to hear him sometimes, in one sense, he's a very ignorant guy. If you just talk to him without knowing his record, you'd say "How the hell did he come to do it?" But he

did it. I don't remember Arthur saying, "Don't you think this would be better, Irving?" Never. Never a word. He let people alone. He was pretty smart that way and he was a good politician. He knew how to handle men; he knew when to say "yes" and when to say "no." But he never bothered people if he had confidence in them. You don't think he'd dictate to Alan Lerner and Frederick Loewe? And he certainly couldn't dictate to me. I would welcome it if I agreed with him, but I could tell by his face whether it was good or bad and what he thought, and then I'd have to sit by myself and say, "What do *I* think?"

He was never considered one of the top songwriters. Nevertheless, there are songs that he wrote which are played much more than those of a lot of guys who are supposed to be better songwriters. You take "Singin' in the Rain," for God's sake! When it first came out, no so-called professional songwriter would say, "This is something—this is a great blockbuster," but it is now. As a songwriter, *knowing* songwriters gave him the talent for producing.

And he had very good taste which ordinarily you wouldn't expect from a songwriter, Tin Pan Alley type.

He discovered a lot of people and he would take much more pride in that than in writing "Singin' in the Rain." But again, I must say his greatest talent was his recognition of talent. You take Roger Edens and all the other talented people he had in his unit—he didn't tell them what to do, but they did it. He was smart enough to know that they could do the job. After all, all you have to do is look at the record—

And he knew style—he didn't do it, but he had an eye for it. He had to decide what to do—he put his stamp on it—like the President of a country.

(Editor's Note. Arthur Freed died suddenly on April 12, 1973.)

**THE PRODUCER OF THE MOST OUTSTANDING
SERIES OF MUSICALS IN MOTION PICTURE HISTORY**

ARTHUR FREED

The above appeared on a single card in the end credits for *That's Entertainment!* (M-G-M, 1974).

FILMOGRAPHY

OF ARTHUR FREED PRODUCTIONS

The following credits were obtained from the "Main Title Billing" sheets that were prepared by the legal department of Metro-Goldwyn-Mayer. The credits also include the music that was used in the film, as furnished by the music department's cue sheets. After each title the following form is used: In parenthesis, the production number, as assigned by the studio; also in parenthesis, the start of production; the close of production; retakes; and the release date of the film. Other parentheses within the body of the credits indicate names of persons who worked on the film at any time, but did not receive on-screen credit. The term "music" is followed by "visual," referring to on-screen songs and/or instrumentals; "nonvisual," referring to music that was used in the underscoring of the film; "deleted" refers to songs that were cut from the release print; "not used" refers to songs that were acquired but not used in principal photography of the motion picture. Also indicated is the running time of the release print.

AMERICAN IN PARIS, AN (1501) (August 1, 1950–January 8, 1951; April 2, 1951) November 9, 1951. Story and screenplay by Alan Jay Lerner; lyrics by Ira Gershwin; music by George Gershwin; musical direction, Johnny Green and Saul Chaplin; choreography, Gene Kelly (assistant, Carol Haney); color by Technicolor; director of photography, Alfred Gilks; ballet photographed by John Alton; color consultants, Henri Jaffa and James Gooch; art directors, Cedric Gibbons and Preston Ames (Jack Martin Smith, Irene Sharaff); film editor, Adri-

528

enne Fazan; Gene Kelly's paintings by Gene Grant; recording supervisor, Douglas Shearer; set decorations, Edwin B. Willis and Keogh Gleason; special effects, Warren Newcombe, Irving Ries; orchestrations, Conrad Salinger; montage sequences by Peter Ballbusch; costumes designed by Orry-Kelly (Walter Plunkett); Beaux Arts Ball costumes designed by Walter Plunkett; ballet costumes designed by Irene Sharaff; hair styles designed by Sydney Guilaroff; make-up created by William Tuttle; technical adviser, Alan Antik; assistant to the director, Jane Loring; directed by Vincente Minnelli.

CAST: *Jerry Mulligan,* Gene Kelly; *Lise Bouvier,* Leslie Caron; *Adam Cook,* Oscar Levant; *Henri Baurel,* Georges Guetary; *Milo Roberts,* Nina Foch; *Georges Mattieu,* Eugene Borden; *Mathilde Mattieu,* Martha Bamattre; *Old Woman Flower Vendor,* Mary Young; *Therese,* Ann Codee; *Francois,* George Davis; *Tommy Baldwin,* Hayden Rorke; *John McDowd,* Paul Maxey; *Ben Macrow,* Dick Wessel; *Honeymoon Couple,* Don Quinn, Adele Coray; *Boys with bubble gum,* Lucian Planzoles, Christian Pasques, Anthony Mazola; *Nuns,* Jeanne Lafayette, Louise Laureau; *Postman,* Alfred Paix; *American Girl,* Noel Neill; *Maid,* Nan Boardman; *Jack and Kay Jansen,* John Eldredge and Anna Q. Nilsson. MINOR BITS: *Customer,* Madge Blake; *Winston Churchill,* Dudley Field Malone; *Dancing Partner,* André Charisse. *"Stairway" Girls:* Jean Romaine, Mary Jane French, Pat Dean Smith, Joan Barton, Ann Robin, Mary Ellen Gleason, Judy Landon, Beverly Thompson, Beverly Baldy, Angela Wilson, Sue Casey, Ann Brendon, Marietta Elliott, Lorraine Crawford, Lola Kenricks, Meredith Leeds, Marily Rogers, Pat Hall, Madge Journery, Marlene Todd. *An American in Paris Ballet Company: Furies,* Mary Menzies, Svetlana McLee, Florence Brundage, Dee Turnell; *Place de la Concorde ensemble:* Harriet Scott, Janet Lavis, Sheila Meyers, Lila Zali, Betty Scott, Eileen Locklin, Pat Sims, Linda Scott, Shirley Lopez, Shirley Glickman, Phyllis Sutter; *Fireman:* Dick Lener, Don Hulbert, John Stanley, Ray Weamer, Harvey Karels, Bert Madrid, Dick Landry, Rudy Silva, Rodney Beiber, Manuel Petroff, Robert Ames, Betty Hannon, Linda Heller, David Kasday, Marion Horosko, Pamela Wells, Dorothy Tuttle, Tommy Ladd, Albert Ruiz, Alex Goudovitch, Eric Freeman, Dick Humphries, Alan Cooke, John Gardner, Ricky Gonzales, Bill Chatham, Ernie Flatt, Ricky Riccardi; Graham Johnson, Eugene Fuccati; *Four Servicemen in Rousseau Place:* Ernie Flatt, Alex Romero, Dick Humphries, Bill Chatham; *Lautrec: Cancan Dancers:* Betty Scott, Shirley Lopez, Pat Sims, Dee Turnell, Sheila Meyers, Janet Lavis; *Gaulou,* Eleaner Vindever; *Toulouse-Lautrec,* Dick Lenner; *Oscar Wilde,* Gino Corrado; *Aristide Briand,* Alba No Valero.

MUSIC. VISUAL: "How Long Has This Been Going On?," "Nice Work If You Can Get It," "Fascinating Rhythm," "By Strauss," "I Got Rhythm," "But Not for Me," "Do Do Do," "Bidin' My Time," "Love Is Here to Stay," "Someone to Watch Over Me," "Tra-La-La," "I Don't Think I'll Fall in Love Today," " 'S Wonderful," "Liza," (George and Ira Gershwin); "I'll Build a Stairway to Paradise" (the Gershwins-B. G. DeSylva); "Concerto in F"—Third Movement and "An American in Paris" (George Gershwin); last piece includes seven "La Sorella" based on excerpts from "Los Inocentes" (Estelles, Belgado, Silva, Gillini) four bars each in length. Ballet running time: 17 minutes, 10 seconds. NONVISUAL: "Embraceable You," "Strike Up the Band," "Oh Lady Be Good," "That Certain Feeling," "Clap Yo' Hands," "Love Walked In" (Gershwin). SONGS DELETED: "I've Got a Crush on You," "But Not for Me," "Liza" (Gershwin), "Somebody Loves Me" Ballet (Gershwin-De Sylva).

Running time: 113 minutes.

ANNIE GET YOUR GUN (1450) (Garland-Berkeley, March 7–May 21, 1949; Hutton, October 10–December 16, 1949; February 6, 1950.) May 23, 1950. Screenplay by Sidney Sheldon;

music and lyrics by Irving Berlin; book by Herbert and Dorothy Fields; based on the musical play produced on the stage by Richard Rodgers and Oscar Hammerstein II; musical numbers staged by Robert Alton; musical direction, Adolph Deutsch; color by Technicolor; director of photography, Charles Rosher; color consultants, Henri Jaffa and James Gooch; art directors, Cedric Gibbons and Paul Groesse; film editor, James E. Newcom; recording supervisor, Douglas Shearer; set decorations, Edwin B. Willis and Richard A. Pefferle; special effects, A. Arnold Gillespie, Warren Newcombe; montage sequence by Peter Ballbusch; women's costumes by Helen Rose (Walter Plunkett); men's costumes by Walter Plunkett; hair styles designed by Sydney Guilaroff; make-up created by Jack Dawn; directed by George Sidney.

CAST: *Annie Oakley*, Betty Hutton; *Frank Butler*, Howard Keel; *Buffalo Bill*, Louis Calhern; *Chief Sitting Bull*, J. Carrol Naish; *Pawnee Bill*, Edward Arnold; *Charlie Davenport*, Keenan Wynn; *Dolly Tate*, Benay Venuta; *Foster Wilson*, Clinton Sundberg; *Mac*, James H. Harrison; *Little Jake*, Bradley Mora; *Nellie*, Diana Dick; *Jessie*, Susan Odin; *Minnie*, Eleanor Brown.

MUSIC. VISUAL: "Colonel Buffalo Bill," "Doin' What Comes Natur'lly," "The Girl That I Marry," "You Can't Get a Man With a Gun," "There's No Business Like Show Business," "They Say It's Wonderful," "My Defenses Are Down," "I'm an Indian Too," "Anything You Can Do" (Berlin). NONVISUAL: "I'm a Bad Bad Man" (Berlin). DELETED: "Let's Go West Again" (Berlin).

Running time: 107 minutes.

ANY NUMBER CAN PLAY (1444) (January 4–April 26, 1949; May 5, 1949) July 15, 1949. Screenplay by Richard Brooks, from the book by Edward Harris Heth; director of photography, Harold Rosson; art directors, Cedric Gibbons and Urie McCleary; film editor, Ralph E. Winters; music score,

Lennie Hayton; recording supervisor, Douglas Shearer; set decorations, Edwin B. Willis and Henry W. Grace; make-up created by Jack Dawn; hair styles designed by Sydney Guilaroff; technical advisers, S. A. Landy, Louis W. Bianco; dialogue director, W. R. Anderson; directed by Mervyn LeRoy.

CAST: *Charley Enley Kyng*, Clark Gable; *Lon Kyng*, Alexis Smith; *Robbin Elcott*, Wendell Corey; *Jim Kurstyn*, Frank Morgan; *Ada*, Mary Astor; *Ben Gavery Snelerr*, Lewis Stone; *Tycoon*, Barry Sullivan; *Sarah Calhern*, Marjorie Rambeau; *Ed*, Edgar Buchanan; *Dr. Palmer*, Leon Ames; *Pete Smith*, Mickey Knox; *Lew "Angie" Debretti*, Richard Rober; *Frank Sistina*, William Conrad; *Paul Enley Kyng*, Darryl Hickman; *Sleigh*, Caleb Peterson; *Mrs. Purcell*, Dorothy Comingore; *Mr. Reardon*, Art Baker.

MUSIC. VISUAL: M-G-M Anniversary Fanfare #2 (Rozsa); Main Title, End Title and Cast (Hayton); "You Are My Lucky Star," "Should I" (Brown-Freed).

Running time: 112 minutes.

BABES IN ARMS (1088) (April 12–July 18, 1939; August 1, 1939) October 13, 1939. Screenplay by Jack McGowan and Kay Van Riper (Florence Ryerson, Edgar Allan Woolf, Joe Laurie, John Meehan, Walter DeLeon, Irving Brecher, Ben Freedman, Anita Loos); based on the musical by Richard Rodgers and Lorenz Hart; musical adaptation, Roger Edens; musical director, George Stoll; orchestrations, Conrad Salinger (Leo Arnaud); art director, Merrill Pye; set decorator, Edwin B. Willis; wardrobe, Dolly Tree; director of photography, Ray June; film editor, Frank Sullivan; directed by Busby Berkeley.

CAST: *Mickey Moran*, Mickey Rooney; *Patsy Barton*, Judy Garland; *Joe Moran*, Charles Winninger; *Judge Black*, Guy Kibbee; *Rosalie Essex*, June Preisser; *Florrie Moran*, Grace Hayes; *Molly Moran*, Betty Jaynes; *Don Brice*, Douglas McPhail; *Jeff Steele*, Rand Brooks; *Dody Martini*, Leni Lynn; *Bobs*, John Sheffield; *Madox*, Henry Hull; *William*, Barnett

530

Parker; *Mrs. Barton,* Ann Shoemaker; *Margaret Steele,* Margaret Hamilton; *Mr. Essex,* Joseph Crehan; *Brice,* George McKay; *Shaw,* Henry Roquemore; *Mrs. Brice,* Lelay Tyler. MINOR BITS: Charles Brown, Irene Franklin, Kay Deslys, Patsy Moran, Rube Demarest, Sidney Miller.

MUSIC. VISUAL: Main title (Edens-Arnaud); "Babes in Arms," "Where or When," (Rodgers-Hart); "Ja Da" (Carlton); "Rockabye Baby" (Danning); "Silent Night" (Gruber, arranger, Edens); Montage $\#1$ and $\#2$ (Edens); "Good Morning" (Brown-Freed); "Darktown Strutters Ball" (Brooks); "Opera vs. Jazz" (arranger, Edens); "Broadway Rhythm" (Brown-Freed); Sextette from "Lucia di Lammermoor" (Donizetti); "You Are My Lucky Star" (Brown-Freed); "Bob White" (Hanighen-Mercer); "Indignation March," "Nursery March" (Edens); "I Cried for You" (Brown-Freed); minstrel show (arranger, Edens); "My Daddy Was a Minstrel Man" (Edens); "Ida, Sweet As Apple Cider" (Leonard); "Moonlight Bay" (Wenrich-Madden); "I'm Just Wild About Harry" (Sissle-Blake); "Lindy" (Edens); Finale (arranger, Edens); "God's Country" (Arlen-Harburg); "Stars and Stripes Forever" (Sousa). NONVISUAL: "Give My Regards to Broadway" (Cohan); "Toot Toot Tootsie" (Kahn, et al.); "Broadway Melody," "Singin' in the Rain" (Brown-Freed); "The Lady Is a Tramp" (Rodgers-Hart); NOT USED: "Let's Take a Walk Around the Block" (Arlen-Harburg); "I Wish I Were in Love Again" (Rodgers-Hart).

Running time: 97 minutes.

BABES ON BROADWAY (1204) (July 14–October 14, 1941; November 7, 1941) January 2, 1942. Screenplay by Fred Finklehoffe and Elaine Ryan; original story by Fred Finklehoffe; (unpublished story by Joseph Santley; "Convict's Return" by Harry Kaufman): (Robert Tree West, John Monks, Ralph Spence, Gertrude Purcell and Edmund Hartman, Charles Reisner, Vincente Minnelli, Elsie Janis); musical adaptation, Roger Edens;

musical director, George Stoll; vocals and orchestrations, Leo Arnaud, George Bassman, Conrad Salinger; director of photography, Lester White; recording director, Douglas Shearer; art directors, Cedric Gibbons, Malcolm Brown; set decorator, Edwin B. Willis; musical presentation, Merrill Pye; gowns by Kalloch; men's wardrobe, Gile Steele; make-up created by Jack Dawn; film editor, Frederick Y. Smith; directed by Busby Berkeley (George Sidney).

CAST: *Tommy Williams,* Mickey Rooney; *Penny Morris,* Judy Garland; *Miss Jones,* Fay Bainter; *Mary Ann,* Virginia Weidler; *Ray Lambert,* Ray McDonald; *Morton Hammond,* Richard Quine; *Mr. Stone,* Donald Meek; *Thornton Reed,* James Gleason; *Mrs. Williams,* Emma Dunn; *Mr. Morris,* Frederick Burton; *Inspector Moriarity,* Cliff Clark; *Alexander Woollcott,* himself; *Announcer,* William A. Post, Jr. MINOR BITS: *Secretary,* Donna Reed; *Mason,* Joe Yule; Ava Gardner, Sue Garland, Roger Moore.

MUSIC. VISUAL: "Babes on Broadway," "How About You," "Blackout Over Broadway" (Burton Lane-Ralph Freed); "Hoe Down" (Edens-Ralph Freed); "Chin Up! Cheerio! Carry on!" (Ralph Freed); "Anything Can Happen in New York" (Lane-Harburg); "Mary Is a Grand Old Name" (Cohan); "She Is Ma Daisy" (Lauder-Harper); "I've Got Rings on My Fingers" (Scott-Weston-Barnes); "Yankee Doodle Boy" (Cohan); "Bombshell from Brazil" (Edens); "Mama Yo Quiero" (Jararaca-Paiva); minstrel show (arranger, Edens); "By the Light of the Silvery Moon" (Edwards-Smith); "Franklin D. Roosevelt Jones" (Rome); "Alabamy Bound" (Henderson); "Waiting for the Robert E. Lee" (Muir-Abrams). DELETED: "Ballad for Americans" (LaTouche-Robinson). Out-take used entirely in *Born To Sing* (1943).

Running time: 118 minutes.

BAND WAGON, THE (1610) (September 3, 1952–January 28, 1953; February 9, 1953) August 7, 1953. Story and screenplay by Betty Comden and Adolph Green; songs by Howard Dietz and

Arthur Schwartz; dances and musical numbers staged by Michael Kidd; musical direction, Adolph Deutsch; musical numbers designed by Oliver Smith; associate producer, Roger Edens; color by Technicolor; director of photography, Harry Jackson (George Folsey); color consultants, Henri Jaffa, Robert Brower; art directors, Cedric Gibbons and Preston Ames; film editor, Albert Akst; orchestrations, Conrad Salinger, Skip Martin and Alexander Courage; assistant director, Jerry Thorpe; recording supervisor, Douglas Shearer; set decorations, Edwin B. Willis and Keogh Gleason; special effects, Warren Newcombe; costumes by Mary Ann Nyberg; hair styles by Sydney Guilaroff; make-up created by William Tuttle; directed by Vincente Minnelli.

CAST: *Tony Hunter,* Fred Astaire, *Gaby,* Cyd Charisse; *Lester Marton,* Oscar Levant; *Lily Marton,* Nanette Fabray; *Jeffrey Cordova,* Jack Buchanan; *Paul Byrd,* James Mitchell; *Hal Benton,* Robert Gist; *Col. Tripp,* Thurston Hall; *Guest star,* Ava Gardner. MINOR BITS: *Shoe Shine Boy,* LeRoy Daniels; *Troupe members:* Dee Trunell and Himmie Thompson; *Girls* in "Private Eye" number: Dee and Eden Hartford, Julie Newmar; *Man,* Steve Forrest; *Gushy Woman,* Madge Blake; *Tall Woman in Penny Arcade,* Sue Casey; *Specialty dancer,* Matt Mattox.

MUSIC. VISUAL: "By Myself," "Dancing in the Dark," "I Love Louisa," "Shine on Your Shoes," "That's Entertainment!" "I Guess I'll Have to Change My Plan," "Triplets," "New Sun in the Sky," "Louisiana Hayride," "Beggar's Waltz," "High and Low," "You and the Night and the Music," "Something to Remember You By" (Schwartz-Dietz); Girl Hunt Ballet (Schwartz), narration by Alan Jay Lerner. NONVISUAL: "Right At the Start of It," "Is It All a Dream?," "Sweet Music" (Schwartz-Dietz); Main title, opening night, "The Egg" (Salinger); "Carriage in the Park" (Edens and Salinger); "Off-Scene Noodles" (Deutsch); "Oedipus Rex Bridge" (Edens and Courage). DELETED: "Never Marry a Dancer,"

"Gotta Brand New Suit," "Alone Together," "Two-faced Woman," "Sweet Music," "You Have Everything" (Schwartz-Dietz). NOT USED: "The Private Eye," "Alone Together" (Schwartz-Dietz). "Two-faced Woman" used with India Adams prerecording in *Torch Song* (1953).

Running time: 112 minutes.

BARKLEYS OF BROADWAY, THE[1] (1433) (August 8–October 30, 1948; December 28, 1948) May 13, 1949. Original screenplay by Betty Comden and Adolph Green (Sidney Sheldon); associate producer, Roger Edens; music by Harry Warren; lyrics by Ira Gershwin; musical direction, Lennie Hayton; orchestrations, Conrad Salinger; vocal arrangements, Robert Tucker; musical numbers staged and directed by Robert Alton; color by Technicolor; director of photography, Harry Stradling; color director, Natalie Kalmus, associate, Henri Jaffa; art directors, Cedric Gibbons and Edward Carfagno; film editor, Albert Akst; recording director, Douglas Shearer; set decorations, Edwin B. Willis and Arthur Krams; special effects, Warren Newcombe; dance number, "Shoes With Wings On," directed by Hermes Pan; dancing shoes effects, Irving Ries; Miss Rogers' costumes by Irene; men's costumes by Valles; hair styles designed by Sydney Guilaroff; make-up created by Jack Dawn; directed by Charles Walters.

CAST: *Josh Barkley,* Fred Astaire; *Dinah Barkley,* Ginger Rogers; *Ezra Millar,* Oscar Levant; *Mrs. Livingston Belney,* Billie Burke; *Shirlene May,* Gale Robbins; *Jacques Pierre Barredout,* Jacques Francois; *The Judge,* George Zucco; *Bert Felsher,* Clinton Sundberg; *Pamela Driscoll,* Inez Cooper; *Gloria Amboy,* Carol Brewster; *Larry,* Wilson Wood. MINOR BITS: *Blonde,* Dee Turnell; *Ladislaus Ladi,* Hans Conried; *Genevieve,* Joyce Mathews; *First Man,* Roger Moore; *Guest in theatre lobby,* Bess Flowers.

MUSIC. VISUAL: "Swing Trot," "You'd Be Hard to Replace," "Bouncin' the Blues,"

[1] Released in England as *The Gay Barkleys.*

532

"My One and Only Highland Fling," "Weekend in the Country," Shoes With Wings On," "Manhattan Downbeat" (Warren-Gershwin); "Sabre Dance" (Khachaturian); "Piano Concerto No. 1 in B Flat Minor" (Tschaikowsky); "They Can't Take That Away From Me" (George and Ira Gershwin). NONVISUAL: "Angel," "This Heart of Mine" (Warren-Freed); "Ginger Comes Home" (Hayton). NOT USED: "These Days," "There Is No Music," "The Poetry of Motion," "Call on Us Again," "Natchez on the Mississip'," "The Courtin' of Elma and Ella," "Taking No Chances With You," "Second Fiddle to a Harp," "Minstrels on Parade" (Warren-Gershwin).

Running time: 109 minutes.

BELLE OF NEW YORK, THE (1545) (June 18–October 13, 1951; October 17, 1951) February 22, 1952. Screenplay by Robert O'Brien and Irving Elinson; adapted for the screen by Chester Erskine, from the play by Hugh Morton; (Irving Brecher, Fred Finklehoffe, Sally Benson, Jerry Davis and Joseph Fields); lyrics by Johnny Mercer; music by Harry Warren; musical direction, Adolph Deutsch; vocal arrangements, Robert Tucker; musical numbers staged and directed by Robert Alton; color by Technicolor; director of photography, Robert Planck; color consultants, Henri Jaffa, James Gooch; art directors, Cedric Gibbons and Jack Martin Smith; film editor, Albert Akst; recording supervisor, Douglas Shearer; orchestrations, Conrad Salinger and Maurice de Packh; set decorations, Edwin B. Willis and Richard Pefferle; special effects, Warren Newcombe, Irving G. Ries; women's costumes designed by Helen Rose; men's costumes designed by Gile Steele; hair styles by Sydney Guilaroff; make-up created by William Tuttle; associate producer, Roger Edens; directed by Charles Walters.

CAST: *Charlie Hill,* Fred Astaire; *Angela Collins,* Vera-Ellen; *Mrs. Phineas Hill,* Marjorie Main; *Max Ferris,* Keenan Wynn; *Elsie Wilkins,* Alice Pearce; *Gilfred Spivak,* Clinton Sundberg; *Dixie McCoy,* Gale Robbins; *Clancy,* Henry

Slate; *Bowery Bums:* Tom Duggan, Percy Helton, Dick Wessel; *French,* Lisa Ferraday; *Judkins,* Roger Davis; *Frenchie's Girls:* Lyn Wilde, Carol Brewster, Meredith Leeds. MINOR BIT: *Herman,* Benny Rubin.

MUSIC. VISUAL: "When I'm Out With the Belle of New York," "Bachelor Dinner Song," "Seeing's Believing," "Baby Doll," "Oops!" "Thank You Mr. Currier, Thank You Mr. Ives," "Naughty But Nice,"[2] "I Wanna Be a Dancin' Man" (Warren-Mercer); "Let a Little Love Come In" (Edens). NONVISUAL: "Fred Toasts the Girls" (Deutsch); "Fred Drinks to the Bride" (Edens).

Running time: 82 minutes.

BELLS ARE RINGING (1760) October 7–December 24, 1959) June 23, 1960. Screenplay and lyrics by Betty Comden and Adolph Green; music by Jule Styne; based on the musical *Bells Are Ringing,* book and lyrics by Betty Comden and Adolph Green, music by Jule Styne, as presented on the stage by the Theatre Guild; music adapted and conducted by André Previn; orchestrations by Alexander Courage and Pete King; choreography. Charles O'Curran; director of photography, Milton Krasner; in CinemaScope and Metrocolor; art directors, George W. Davis and Preston Ames; set decorations, Henry Grace and Keogh Gleason; color consultant, Charles K. Hagedon; film editor, Adrienne Fazan; special effects, A. Arnold Gillespie, Lee LeBlanc; assistant director, William McGarry; hair styles by Sydney Guilaroff; make-up created by William Tuttle; costumes designed by Walter Plunkett; recording supervisor, Franklin Milton; photographic lenses by Panavision; directed by Vincente Minnelli.

CAST: *Ella Peterson,* Judy Holliday; *Jeffrey Moss,* Dean Martin; *Larry Hastings,* Fred Clark; *J. Otto Prantz,* Eddie Foy, Jr.; *Sue,* Jean Stapleton; *Gwynne,* Ruth Storey; *Inspector Barnes,* Dort Clark; *Blake Carton,* Frank Gorshin; *Francis,*

[2] Title song of Warner Brothers film (1939).

Ralph Roberts; *Olga,* Valerie Allen; *Dr. Joe Kitchell,* Bernie West; *First Gangster,* Steven Peck; *Ella's Blind Date,* Gerry Mulligan. MINOR BITS: *M.C.,* Hal Linden; *Woman,* Madge Blake; *Nervous Man,* Olan Soulé.

MUSIC. VISUAL: "Bells Are Ringing," "The Party's Over," "Just in Time," "Long Before I Knew You," "It's a Perfect Relationship," "Do It Yourself," "It's a Simple Little System," "Better Than a Dream," "Hello, Hello There," "I Met a Girl," "I Love Your Sunny Teeth," "Oh How It Hurts," "Hot and Cold," "The Midas Touch," "Mississippi Steamboat," "Mu Cha Cha," "Drop That Name," "I'm Going Back" (Styne-Comden-Green). NONVISUAL: "Is It a Crime," "My Guiding Star" (Styne). DELETED: "Is It a Crime" (Styne-Comden-Green). NOT USED: "To Love and to Lose," "My Guiding Star" (Styne-Comden-Green).

Running time: 126 minutes.

BEST FOOT FORWARD (1284) (January 18–March 23, 1943; April 5, 1943) October 8, 1943. Screenplay by Irving Brecher and Fred Finklehoffe (Dorothy Kingsley, Virginia Kellogg); book by John Cecil Holm; music and lyrics by Hugh Martin and Ralph Blane; produced on the stage by George Abbott; musical direction, Lennie Hayton; orchestrations, Conrad Salinger, Jack Matthias, LeRoy Holmes, George Bassman and Leo Arnaud; new songs and vocal arrangements by Hugh Martin and Ralph Blane; dance direction, Charles Walters (Jack Donahue); photographed in Technicolor; director of photography, Leonard Smith; color consultant: Natalie Kalmus, associate, Henri Jaffa; recording director, Douglas Shearer; art directors, Cedric Gibbons and Edward Carfagno; set decorations, Edwin B. Willis and Mildred Griffiths; costumes supervised by Irene; men's costumes by Gile Steele; make-up created by Jack Dawn; film editor, Blanche Sewell; directed by Edward Buzzell.

CAST: *Lucille Ball,* herself; *Jack O' Riley,* William Gaxton; *Helen Schlessenger,*

Virginia Weidler; *Bud and Elwood C. Hooper,* Tommy Dix; *Blind Date (Nancy),* Nancy Walker; *Minerva,* June Allyson; *Dutch,* Kenny Bowers; *Ethel,* Gloria De Haven; *Hunk,* Jack Jordan; *Miss Delaware Water Gap,* Beverly Tyler; *Chester Short,* Chill Wills; *Major Reeber,* Henry O'Neill; *Miss Talbert,* Sara Haden; *Captain Bradd,* Donald MacBride; *Greenie,* Bobby Stebbins; *Killer,* Darwood Kaye; *Colonel Harkrider,* Morris Ankrum; *Mrs. Dalyrimple,* Nana Bryant; Harry James and his Music Makers. MINOR BIT: *Mrs. Bradd,* Bess Flowers.

MUSIC. VISUAL: "Wish I May," "Three Men on a Date," "Ev'ry Time," "The Three B's," "I Know You by Heart," "Shady Lady Bird," "Buckle Down Winsocki," "My First Promise," "Alive and Kickin'," "You're Lucky" (Martin-Blane); "Flight of the Bumblebee" (Rimsky-Korsakov). DELETED: "That's How I Love the Blues," "What Do You Think I Am"[3] (Martin and Blane); "I Cried For You" (Brown-Freed).

Running time: 95 minutes.

BRIGADOON (1645) (December 9, 1953–March 17, 1954; March 20, 1954) September 8, 1954. Screenplay by Alan Jay Lerner; music by Frederick Loewe; lyrics by Alan Jay Lerner; based on the musical with book and lyrics by Alan Jay Lerner and music by Frederick Loewe; presented on the stage by Cheryl Crawford; technical adviser, Commander T. A. Murray; musical direction, Johnny Ereen; choreography, Gene Kelly; orchestrations, Conrad Salinger; costumes designed by Irene Sharaff; choral arrangements by Robert Tucker; in CinemaScope and Ansco (Wide Screen and Technicolor); director of photography, Joseph Ruttenberg; art directors, Cedric Gibbons and Preston Ames; film editor, Albert Akst; color consultant, Alvord Eiseman; recording supervisor, Wesley C. Miller; set decorations, Edwin B. Willis and Keogh Gleason; special effects,

[3] Used in (same prerecording) *Broadway Rhythm.*

Warren Newcombe; assistant director, Frank Baur; hair styled by Sydney Guilaroff; make-up created by William Tuttle; associate producer, Roger Edens; directed by Vincente Minnelli.

CAST: *Tommy Albright*, Gene Kelly; *Jeff Douglas*, Van Johnson; *Fiona Campbell*, Cyd Charisse; *Jane Ashton*, Elaine Stewart; *Mr. Lundie*, Barry Jones; *Harry Beaton*, Hugh Laing (courtesy New York City Ballet Company); *Andrew Campbell*, Albert Sharpe; *Jean Campbell*, Virginia Bosler; *Charlie Chisholm Dalrymple*, Jimmy Thompson; *Archie Beaton*, Tudor Owen; *Angus*, Owen McGiveney; *Ann*, Dee Turnell; *Meg Brockie*, Dody Heath; *Sandy*, Eddie Quillan. MINOR BITS: *Mrs. McIntosh*, Madge Blake; *Man at Bar*, Stuart Whitman; *Specialty dancer*, George Chakiris; *Townsman*, Pat O'Malley.

MUSIC. VISUAL: "Down on MacConnachy Square," "Waitin' for My Dearie," "I'll Go Home With Bonnie Jean," "The Heather on the Hill," "Almost Like Being in Love," "Entrance of the Clans," "Wedding Dance," "The Chase" (Lerner-Loewe). NONVISUAL: "Brigadoon," "Prologue," "Vendor's Calls," Bible Scene (Lerner-Loewe). DELETED: "There But for You Go I" (Lerner-Loewe).

Running time: 108 minutes.

CABIN IN THE SKY (1267) (August 31–October 24, 1942; October 28, 1942) April 9, 1943. Screenplay by Joseph Schrank (Eustace Cocrell, Marc Connelly); based on the musical with book by Lynn Root, lyrics by John LaTouche and music by Vernon Duke, produced on the stage by Albert Lewis in association with Vinton Freedley; additional songs by Harold Arlen and E. Y. Harburg; Duke Ellington; associate producer, Albert Lewis (Roger Edens); musical adaptation, Roger Edens; musical direction, George Stoll; orchestrations by George Bassman, Conrad Salinger; choral arrangements, Hall Johnson; director of photography, Sidney Wagner; recording director, Douglas Shearer; art directors, Cedric Gibbons and Leonid Vasian; set decorations, Edwin B. Willis and Hugh Hunt; costume supervision, Irene, associate, Shoup; men's costumes, Gile Steele; film editor, Harold F. Kress; directed by Vincente Minnelli (one musical number staged by Busby Berkeley).

CAST: *Petunia Jackson*, Ethel Waters; *Little Joe Jackson*, Eddie "Rochester" Anderson; *Georgia Brown*, Lena Horne; *The Trumpeter*, Louis Armstrong; *Lucius* and *Lucifer, Jr.*, Rex Ingram; *Rev. Green* and *the General*, Kenneth Spencer; *Domino Johnson*, "Bubbles" (John W. Sublett); *The Deacon*, and *Fleetfoot*, Oscar Polk; *First Idea Man*, Mantan Moreland; *Second Idea Man*, Willie Best; *Third Idea Man, Moke* (Fletcher Rivers); *Fourth Idea Man, Poke* (Leon James); *Bill*, Bill Bailey; *Messenger Boy*, "Buck" (Ford L. Washington); *Lily*, Butterfly McQueen; *Mrs. Kelso*, Ruby Dandridge; *Dude*, Nicodemus; *Jim Henry*, Ernest Whitman; Duke Ellington and his Orchestra; The Hall Johnson Choir.

MUSIC. VISUAL: "Cabin in the Sky," "Honey in the Honeycomb," "Love Me Tomorrow," "In My Old Virginia Home" (Duke-LaTouche); "Taking a Chance on Love" (Duke-LaTouche-Fetter); "Happiness Is Just a Thing Called Joe," "Li'l Black Sheep," "That Ole Debbil Consequence," "Some Folk Work" (Arlen-Harburg); "Going Up" (Ellington); "Forward," "The Prayer," "Dusky Jezebel," "Sweet Petunia," "But the Flesh Is Weak" (Edens); "Old Ship of Zion" (arranger, Hall Johnson); "Shine" (Mack-Dabney); "Things Ain't What They Used to Be" (M. Ellington). NONVISUAL: "Ain't It the Truth" (Arlen-Harburg); "Revelations" and "Jezebell Jones" (Edens). DELETED: "Ain't It the Truth" (vocal), "I Got a Song" (Arlen-Harburg).

Running time: 99 minutes.

CLOCK, THE[4] (1331) (Zinnemann—August 1, 1944; Minnelli—September 1–November 21, 1944) May 25, 1945. Screenplay by Robert Nathan and Joseph

[4] Released in England as *Under the Clock*.

Schrank (Margaret Gruen); based on a story by Paul and Pauline Gallico; director of photography, George Folsey; musical score, George Bassman; recording director, Douglas Shearer; art directors, Cedric Gibbons and William Ferrari; set decorations by Edwin B. Willis and Mac Alper; special effects, A. Arnold Gillespie and Warren Newcombe; costume supervision, Irene, associate, Marion Herwood Keyes; film editor, George White; directed by Vincente Minnelli (Jack Conway, Fred Zinnemann).

CAST: *Alice Maybery,* Judy Garland; *Corporal Joe Allen,* Robert Walker; *Al Henry,* James Gleason; *The Drunk,* Keenan Wynn; *Bill,* Marshall Thompson; *Mrs. Al Henry,* Lucille Gleason; *Helen,* Ruth Brady. MINOR BITS: Roger Edens, Arthur Freed, Robert Nathan, Ruby Dandridge, Moyna Macgill (Angela Lansbury's mother) in scene with Keenan Wynn.

MUSIC. VISUAL: "Parting Is Such Sweet Sorrow," "Judy's Dilemma," "Four O'Clock Deadline," "The Walk Before Breakfast," "Bob's Fruitless Search," "The Race Against Time," "Song of the City" (Bassman); "Twentieth-century Wonder" (Bassman-Sid Cutner); "Lobby at the Astor" (Mario Castelnuovo-Tedesco-Bassman); "Church Wedding," "Milk Delivery Montage" (Tedesco); "If I Had You" (Ted Shapiro et al.); "How Am I to Know" (King); "Our Love Affair" (Edens-Freed); "Stompin' at the Savoy" (Benny Goodman et al.); End title and cast, "Two-faced Woman" (Kaper).

Running time: 90 minutes.

CRISIS (1486) (January 4–February 23, 1950) July 7, 1950. Screenplay by Richard Brooks; based on a story by George Tabori; music by Miklos Rozsa; played by Vincente Gomez (guitar soloist); director of photography, Ray June; art directors, Cedric Gibbons and Preston Ames; film editor, Robert J. Kern; recording supervisor, Douglas Shearer; set decorations by Edwin B. Willis and Hugh Hunt; special effects, A. Arnold Gillespie and Warren Newcombe; hair styles by Sydney Guilaroff; make-up created by Jack Dawn; directed by Richard Brooks.

CAST: *Dr. Eugene Norland Ferguson,* Cary Grant; *Raoul Farrago,* Jose Ferrer; *Helen Ferguson,* Paula Raymond; *Senora Isabel Farrago,* Signe Hasso; *Colonel Adragon,* Ramon Navarro; *Gonzales,* Gilbert Roland; *Sam Proctor,* Leon Ames; *Dr. Emilio Nierra,* Antonio Morena; *Rosa,* Teresa Celli; *General Valdini,* Mario Siletti; *Guillermo Cariago,* Vincente Gomez; *Senor Magano,* Martin Garralaga; *Father Del Puento,* Pedro de Cordoba; *Senora Farrago,* Soledad Jimenez.

MUSIC. VISUAL and NONVISUAL: original music composed by Miklos Rozsa.

Running time: 96 minutes.

DU BARRY WAS A LADY (1266) (September 1–November 6, 1942) August 13, 1943. Screenplay by Irving Brecher; adaptation by Nancy Hamilton; additional dialogue by Wilkie Mahoney (Albert Mannheimer, Jack McGowan, Harry McCall, Jr., Charles Sherman); based on the play produced by B. G. De Sylva and written by Herbert Fields and B. G. De Sylva with lyrics by Cole Porter; words and music by Cole Porter; additional songs by Lew Brown, Ralph Freed, Burton Lane, Roger Edens, E. Y. Harburg (Hugh Martin and Ralph Blane); musical adaptation, Roger Edens; musical direction, George Stoll; orchestrations, George Bassman, Leo Arnaud, Alex Stordahl, Sy Oliver; musical presentation, Merrill Pye; dance direction, Charles Walters; photographed in Technicolor; director of photography, Karl Freund; color director, Natalie Kalmus, associate, Henri Jaffa; recording director, Douglas Shearer; art directors, Cedric Gibbons, Edwin B. Willis and Henry Grace; costume supervision, Irené, associate, Shoup; men's costumes, Gile Steele; make-up created by Jack Dawn; special effects, Warren Newcombe; film editor, Blanche Sewell; directed by Roy Del Ruth.

CAST: *May Daly/Mme. Du Barry,* Lucille Ball; *Louie Blore/King Louis XV,* Red Skelton; *Alec Howe/Black Arrow,*

Gene Kelly; *Willie/Duc de Rigor,* Douglass Dumbrille; *Charlie/The Dauphin,* Rags Ragland; *Mr. Jones/Duc De Choiseul,* Donald Meek; *Cheezy/Count De Roquefort,* George Givot; *Rami, the Swami/Taliostro,* Zero Mostel; *Tommy Dorsey and His Band,* themselves; *Ginny/Lady of the Court/Nurse,* Virginia O'Brien; *Niagra,* Louise Beavers; *Doorman/Du Barry's Gatekeeper,* Charles Coleman. MINOR BITS: *Announcer's Voice,* Don Wilson; *Nick,* Sig Arno; *Dorsey Vocalists:* Jo Stafford, John Huddelston, Chuck Lowry, Clark Yocum, Dick Haymes; *Oxford Boys:* Nelson Knoop, Don Moreland, Wayne Dickerson; *Drummer,* Buddy Rich; *The Du Barry Girls: January,* Georgia Carroll; *February,* Marilyn Maxwell; *March,* Natalie Draper; *April,* Kay Aldridge; *May,* Kay Williams; *June,* Hazel Brooks; *July,* Aileen Haley; *August,* Eve Whitney; *September,* Ruth Ownboy; *October,* Theo Coffman; *November,* Mary Jane French; *December,* Inez Cooper.

MUSIC. VISUAL: "Well, Did You Evah," "Do I Love You," "Katie Went to Haiti," "Friendship," "Taliostro's Dance" (Porter); "Du Barry Was a Lady" (Lane-Ralph Freed); "I Love an Esquire Girl" (Edens, Ralph Freed and Lew Brown); "Madame, I Love Your Crepes Suzettes" (Lane-Brown-Ralph Freed); "Thinking of You" (Donaldson-Ash); "A Cigarette, Sweet Music and You" (Ringwald); "Sleepy Lagoon" (Coates); "You Are My Sunshine" (Davis-Mitchell); "I'm Getting Sentimental Over You" (Bassman); "Salome," "Ladies of the Bath" (Edens); "King Louis," "Get Me a Taxi," "On to Combat" (Amfitheatrof); "The Chase" and "The Duel" (Tedesco). NONVISUAL: "But in the Morning, No," "When Love Beckoned (In 52nd Street)" (Porter); "Bird in a Gilded Cage" (Von Tilzer). DELETED: "A Petty Girl is Like a Melody" (Martin-Blane).

Running time: 101 minutes.

EASTER PARADE (1418) (November 25, 1947–February 7, 1948; March 12, 1948) July 16, 1948. Screenplay by Sidney Sheldon, Frances Goodrich and Albert Hackett (Guy Bolton); original story by Frances Goodrich and Albert Hackett; lyrics and music by Irving Berlin; musical numbers staged and directed by Robert Alton; musical direction, Johnny Green; orchestrations, Conrad Salinger, Mason Van Cleave and Leo Arnaud; vocal arrangements, Robert Tucker; color by Technicolor; director of photography, Harry Stradling; color director, Natalie Kalmus, associate, Henri Jaffa; art directors, Cedric Gibbons and Jack Martin Smith; film editor, Albert Akst; recording director, Douglas Shearer; set decorations, Edwin B. Willis and Arthur Krams; special effects, Warren Newcombe; women's costumes by Irene; men's costumes by Valles; hair styles by Sydney Guilaroff; make-up created by Jack Dawn; associate producer, Roger Edens; directed by Charles Walters.

CAST: *Hannah Brown,* Judy Garland; *Don Hewes,* Fred Astaire; *Jonathan Harrow III,* Peter Lawford; *Nadime Gale,* Ann Miller; *Mike (Bartender),* Clinton Sundberg; *Francois (Headwaiter),* Jules Munshin; *Essie,* Jeni LeGon; *Boy with Astaire,* Jimmy Bates; *Leading Man,* Richard Beavers; *Al (Stage Manager),* Dick Simmons. MINOR BITS: *Specialty Dancer,* Dee Turnell; *Showgirls:* Joi Lansing, Lola Albright.

MUSIC. VISUAL: "Happy Easter," "Drum Crazy," "It Only Happens When I Dance With You," "Everybody's Doin' It Now," "I Want to Go Back to Michigan," "Beautiful Faces," "A Fella With an Umbrella," "I Love a Piano," "Snookey Ookums," "Ragtime Violin," "When the Midnight Choo-Choo Leaves for Alabam'," "Shaking the Blues Away," "Steppin' Out With My Baby," "A Couple of Swells," "The Girl on the Magazine Cover," "Better Luck Next Time," "Easter Parade" (Berlin). NONVISUAL: "When I Lost You," "At the Devil's Ball," "This Is the Life," "Along Came Ruth," "Call Me Up Some Rainy Afternoon," "That International Rag" (Berlin). DELETED: "Mister Monotony," "I Love You—You Love Him," "Let's Take an Old-Fashioned Walk," "A Pretty Girl Is Like a Melody" (Berlin).

Running time: 103 minutes.

FOR ME AND MY GAL (1244) (April 3–May 23, 1942; July 29, 1942) November 20, 1942. Screenplay by Richard Sherman, Fred Finklehoffe and Sid Silvers (Jack McGowan, Irving Brecher) (Elsie Janis, technical adviser); original story ("The Big Time") by Howard Emmett Rogers; musical adaptation, Roger Edens; musical direction, George Stoll; dance direction, Bobby Connolly (Gene Kelly); vocals and orchestrations, Conrad Salinger, George Bassman, Leo Arnaud (Roger Edens); director of photography, William Daniels; montage, Peter Ballbusch; recording director, Douglas Shearer; art directors, Cedric Gibbons and Gabriel Scognamillo; set decorations; Edwin B. Willis and Keogh Gleason; musical presentation, Merrill Pye; gowns by Kalloch; men's costumes by Gile Steele; make-up created by Jack Dawn; film editor, Ben Lewis; directed by Busby Berkeley.

CAST: *Jo Hayden*, Judy Garland; *Jimmy Metcalf*, George Murphy; *Harry Palmer*, Gene Kelly; *Eve Minard*, Marta Eggerth; *Sid Simms*, Ben Blue; *Danny Hayden*, Richard Quine; *Eddie Milton*, Keenan Wynn; *Mr. Waring*, Horace McNally; *Lily*, Lucille Norman; *Members of Jimmy's Company*, Betty Welles and Anne Rooney.

MUSIC. VISUAL: "For Me and My Gal" (Meyer-Leslie-Goetz); "The Doll Shop," "The Confession," "Vaudeville Montage," "Love Song," "The Small Time" (Edens); "Oh Johnny Oh" (Olman); "They Go Wild Simply Wild Over Me" (Fisher); "Oh You Beautiful Doll" (Ayer-Brown); "Don't Leave Me, Daddy" (Verges); "By the Beautiful Sea" (Carroll-Atteridge); "When You Wore a Tulip" (Wenrich-Mahoney); "Do I Love You?" (Christine-Goetz); "After You've Gone" (Creamer-Layton); "Tell Me" (Kortlander-Callahan); "Till We Meet Again" (Whiting-Egan); "We Don't Want the Bacon" (Carr-Russell-Havens); "Ballin' the Jack" (Smith-Burris); "What Are You Going to Do to Help the Boys" (Van Alstyne-Kahn); "How 'Ya Gonna Keep 'Em Down on the Farm?" (Donaldson-Lewis-Young);

"Where Do We Go From Here" (Johnson-Wenrich); "It's a Long Way to Tipperary" (Judge-Williams); "Goodbye, Broadway, Hello, France" (Baskette-Reisner-Davis); "Smiles" (Roberts-Callahan); "Oh Frenchy" (Conrad); "Pack Up Your Troubles" (Powell-Asaf); "When Johnny Comes Marching Home" (Lambert-Edens). NONVISUAL: "Chicago" (Fisher); "Do You Ever Think of Me" (Burtnett); "Darktown Strutters Ball" (Brooks); "Sidewalks of New York" (Lawlor-Blake); "Some of These Days" (Brooke); "What Do You Want to Make Those Eyes at Me for" (McCarthy-Johnson-Monaco); "We'll Knock the Keligo Out of Heligoland" (Morse); "Anchors Aweigh" (Zimmerman); "Marine Hymn" (Phillips); "K-K-K-Katy" (O'Hara); "There's a Long Long Trail" (Elliott-King); "Over There" (Cohan). DELETED: "I Never Knew" (Edens); "Three Cheers for the Yanks" (Martin-Blane).

Running time: 104 minutes.

GIGI, an Arthur Freed production (1723) (August 5–October 30, 1957; February 20, 1958) May 15, 1958. Screenplay and lyrics by Alan Jay Lerner; music by Frederick Loewe; based on the novel by Colette; music supervised and conducted by André Previn; orchestrations by Conrad Salinger; in CinemaScope and Metrocolor; costumes, scenery and production designed by Cecil Beaton; art directors, William A. Horning and Preston Ames; director of photography, Joseph Ruttenberg (Ray June); set decorations, Henry Grace and Keogh Gleason; color consultant, Charles K. Hagedon; assistant directors, William McGarry and William Shanks; make-up by William Tuttle and Charles Parker; film editor, Adrienne Fazan; recording supervisor, Dr. Wesley C. Miller; hair styles by Guillaume and Sydney Guilaroff; vocal supervision, Robert Tucker. (French unit: directeur de la photographie, Georges Barsky; chef décorateur, Maurice Petri; Iᵉ assistant metteur en scène, Michel Wyn; systeme sonore en France, Poste Parisien; laboratoires en France, Laboratoires Franay, L.T.C. St.

Cloud); directed by Vincente Minnelli (Charles Walters).

CAST: *Gigi*, Leslie Caron; *Honoré Lachaille*, Maurice Chevalier; *Gaston Lachaille*, Louis Jourdan; *Mme. Alvarez*, Hermione Gingold; *Liane d'Exelmans*, Eva Gabor; *Sandomir*, Jacques Bergerac; *Aunt Alicia*, Isabel Jeans; *Manuel*, John Abbott. MINOR BITS: *Show Girl*, Monique Van Vooren; *Mannequin*, Mauja Ploss; *Charles (Butler)*, Edwin Jerome.

MUSIC. VISUAL: "Thank Heaven for Little Girls," "It's a Bore!," "The Parisians," "Gossip," "She's Not Thinking of Me," "The Night They Invented Champagne," "I Remember It Well," "Gaston's Soliloquy," "Gigi," "I'm Glad I'm Not Young Anymore," "Say a Prayer for Me Tonight" (Lerner-Loewe). NONVISUAL: "Ice Skating Sequence—à Toujours" (Lerner-Loewe).

Running time: 116 minutes.

GIRL CRAZY (1285) (January 4–May 19, 1943) November 26, 1943. Screenplay by Fred F. Finklehoffe (William Ludwig, Dorothy Kingsley, Sid Silvers); music by George Gershwin; lyrics by Ira Gershwin; based on the musical *Girl Crazy*, music by George Gershwin, lyrics by Ira Gershwin, book by Guy Bolton and John McGowan; musical adaptation, Roger Edens; musical direction, George Stoll; orchestrations, Conrad Salinger, Axel Stordahl, Sy Oliver; vocal arrangements, Hugh Martin and Ralph Blane; dance direction and solo dance with Miss Garland by Charles Walters; "I Got Rhythm" number directed by Busby Berkeley; director of photography, William Daniels, Robert Planck; recording director, Douglas Shearer; art director, Cedric Gibbons; set decorations, Edwin B. Willis and Mac Alper; musical presentation, Merrill Pye; costume supervision, Irene, associate, Irene Sharaff; film editor, Albert Akst; directed by Norman Taurog (Busby Berkeley).

CAST: *Danny Churchill, Jr.*, Mickey Rooney; *Ginger Gray*, Judy Garland; *Bud Livermore*, Gil Stratton; *Henry Lathrop*, Robert E. Strickland; *Rags*, Rags

Ragland; *Specialty*, June Allyson, Polly Williams, Nancy Walker, Dean Phineas Armour, Guy Kibbee, Marjorie Tait, Frances Rafferty; *Mr. Churchill, Sr.*, Henry O'Neill; *Governor Tait*, Howard Freeman; Tommy Dorsey and his Orchestra. MINOR BITS: *Cameraman*, Roger Moore; *Fat Man*, Henry Roquemore; *Boy*, Don Taylor; *Committee Woman*, Bess Flowers; *Boy*, Peter Lawford.

MUSIC. VISUAL: "Sam and Delilah," "Treat Me Rough," "Broncho Busters," "Bidin' My Time," "Embraceable You," "Do," "Barbary Coast," "Fascinating Rhythm," "But Not for Me," "I Got Rhythm" (Gershwin); "Happy Birthday, Ginger" (Edens). NONVISUAL: "When It's Cactus Time in Arizona," "Boy, What Love Has Done to Me" (Gershwin).

Running time: 99 minutes.

GOOD NEWS (1404) (March 10–May 23, 1947; May 27, 1947) December 26, 1947. Screenplay by Betty Comden and Adolph Green; based on the musical comedy by Lawrence Schwab, Lew Brown, Frank Mandel, B. G. De Sylva and Ray Henderson; associate producer, Roger Edens; color by Technicolor; director of photography, Charles Schoenbaum; color director, Natalie Kalmus, associate, Henri Jaffa; songs by B. G. De Sylva, Lew Brown, Ray Henderson, Betty Comden, Adolph Green, Roger Edens, Hugh Martin and Ralph Blane; musical direction, Lennie Hayton; vocal arrangements, Kay Thompson; art directors, Cedric Gibbons and Edward Carfagno; film editor, Albert Akst; recording director, Douglas Shearer; set decorations, Edwin B. Willis and Paul G. Chamberlain; women's costumes by Helen Rose; men's costumes by Valles; hair styles by Sydney Guilaroff; make-up created by Jack Dawn; (production numbers staged by Robert Alton); directed by Charles Walters.

CAST: *Connie Lane*, June Allyson; *Tommy Marlowe*, Peter Lawford; *Pat McClellan*, Patricia Marshall; *Babe Doolittle*, Joan McCracken; *Danny*, Mel Torme; *Peter Van Dyne III*, Robert

Strickland; *Bobby,* Ray McDonald; *Coach Johnson,* Donald MacBride; *Pooch,* Tom Dugan; *Professor Burton Kennyon,* Clinton Sundberg; *Beef,* Lon Tindall; *Cora, the Cook,* Connie Gilchrist; *Dean Griswold,* Morris Ankrum; *Flo,* Georgia Lane; *Mrs. Drexel,* Jame Green. MINOR BITS: Richard Tripper, Bill Harbach. (Off-screen vocal back-up by the Williams Brothers.)

MUSIC. VISUAL: "Tait Song,"[5] "He's a Ladies' Man,"[6] "Lucky in Love," "Best Things in Life Are Free," "Good News," "Just Imagine," "The Varsity Drag" (De Sylva-Brown-Henderson); "The French Lesson" (Edens, Comden, Green); "Pass That Peace Pipe" (Edens-Martin-Blane); "My Blue Heaven" (Donaldson). NON-VISUAL: "Wedding of the Painted Doll" (Brown-Freed). DELETED: "An Easier Way" (Edens-Comden-Green).

Running time: 83 minutes.

HARVEY GIRLS, THE (1348) (January, 12–June 4, 1945) January 18, 1946. Screenplay by Edmund Beloin, Nathaniel Curtis, Harry Crane, James O'Hanlon and Samson Raphaelson, additional dialogue by Kay Van Riper (Guy Bolton, Hagar Wilde); based on the book by Samuel Hopkins Adams and the original story by Eleanore Griffin and William Rankin; associate producer, Roger Edens; words and music by Johnny Mercer and Harry Warren; musical direction, Lennie Hayton; orchestrations, Conrad Salinger; vocal arrangements, Kay Thompson; musical numbers staged by Robert Alton; color by Technicolor; director of photography, George Folsey; color director, Natalie Kalmus, associate, Henri Jaffa; film editor, Albert Akst; recording director, Douglas Shearer; art direction, Cedric Gibbons and William Ferrari; set decorations, Edwin B. Willis and Mildred Griffiths; special effects, Warren Newcombe; costume supervision by Irene; costumes designed by Helen Rose; men's costumes by Valles; make-

up created by Jack Dawn; directed by George Sidney.

CAST: *Susan Bradley,* Judy Garland; *New Trent,* John Hodiak; *Chris Maule,* Ray Bolger; *Em,* Angela Lansbury; *Judge Sam Purvis,* Preston Foster; *Alma,* Virginia O'Brien; *Terry O'Halloran,* Kenny Baker; *Sonora Cassidy,* Marjorie Main; *H. H. Hartsey,* Chill Wills; *Miss Bliss,* Selena Royle; *Deborah,* Cyd Charisse; *Ethel,* Ruth Brady; *Marty Peters,* Jack Lambert; *Jed Adams,* Edward Earle; *Rev. Claggert,* Morris Ankrum; *First Cowboy,* William "Bill" Phillips; *John Henry,* Ben Carter; *Second Cowboy,* Norman Leavitt; *"Goldust" McClean,* Horace McNally. MINOR BITS: Byron Harvey, Jr.; *Harvey Girls:* Ruth Brady, Dorothy Gilmore, Lucille Casey, Mary Jo Ellis, Mary Jean French, Joan Thorson, Jacqueline White, Daphne Moore. Dorothy Tuttle, Gloria Hope; *Dance Hall Girls:* Vera Lee, Dorothy Van Nuys, Eve Whitney, Jane Hall, Bunny Waters, Hazel Brooks, Erin O'Kelly, Peggy Maley, Kay English, Dallas Worth.

MUSIC. VISUAL: "In the Valley (Where the Evening Sun Goes Down)," "Wait and See," "On the Atchison, Topeka and Santa Fe," "Oh, You Kid," "It's a Great Big World," "Swing Your Partner Round and Round" (Warren-Mercer); "Training Sequence" (Edens); "Judy's Rage" (Salinger); "Honky Tonk" (Duncan). DELETED: "March of the Doagies," "Hayride," "My Intuition" (Warren-Mercer).

Running time: 104 minutes.

INVITATION TO THE DANCE (1605) (United Kingdom, August 19–December 19, 1952; United States, October 3–October 13, 1952) March 1, 1957. U.S. credits: color by Technicolor; directors of photography: "Circus" and "Ring Around the Rosy," F. A. Young; "Sinbad the Sailor," Joseph Ruttenberg; color consultants, Alvord Eiseman and Joan Bridge; art directors: "Circus" and "Ring Around the Rosy," Alfred Junge; "Sinbad the Sailor," Cedric Gibbons and Randall Duell; film editors: Raymond Poulton, Robert Watts and Adrienne

---

[5] Additional lyrics by Edens and Thompson.
[6] Title changed to "Be a Ladies Man."

540

Fazan; assistant director, John Street; photographic effects, Tom Howard; special cartoon effects, Irving G. Ries; make-up by Charles Parker; (production co-ordinator, Lela Simone); "Circus" music by Jacques Ibert; conducted by John Hollingsworth; played by the Royal Philharmonic Orchestra; direction and choreography by Gene Kelly (assistant, Carol Haney). Additional credits in United Kingdom countries: sets and costumes of "Ring Around the Rosy" designed by Rolf Gerard; costumes of "Circus" designed by Elizabeth Haffenden; production manager, Dora Wright; continuity, Ann Forsyth; hairdressing supervisor, Joan Johnstone; camera operator, Cecil Cooney; recording supervisor, A. W. Watkins; Technicolor consultant, Joan Bridge; make-up supervisor, Charles Parker; assistant to Mr. Kelly, Carol Haney; music co-ordinator, Lela Simone; cartoon sequence ("Sinbad the Sailor") by Fred Quimby, William Hanna and Joseph Barbera.

CAST: *The Lover,* Igor Youskevitch (by arrangement with Ballet Theatre); *The Loved,* Claire Sombert; *The Clown,* Gene Kelly; "Ring Around the Rosy," Gene Kelly, Igor Youskevitch, Tommy Rall, David Paltenghi, Claude Bessy, Tamara Toumanova, Diana Adams, Belita, Daphne Dale, Irving Davies; music composed and conducted by André Previn (composer at the piano); "Sinbad the Sailor," based on music by Nikolai Rimsky-Korsakov; adapted by Roger Edens; conducted by Johnny Green; orchestration by Conrad Salinger; *Sheherazade,* Carol Haney; *The Genie,* David Kasday; *Sinbad,* Gene Kelly.

MUSIC. NONVISUAL: "The Circus" (Ibert); "Ring Around the Rosy" (Previn); "Sinbad," and "Sheherazade" (excerpts); "Nightingale and the Rose," "Danse Des Bouffons" from "The Snow Maiden" (Rimsky-Korsakov, arranged by Edens). DELETED: "Dance Me a Song"—popular song section. NOT USED: Summer Sequence by Ralph Burns; Malcolm Arnold's score for "Ring Around the Rosy."

Running time: 92 minutes.

IT'S ALWAYS FAIR WEATHER

(1663) (October 13, 1954–March 15, 1955; April 6, 1955) September 1, 1955. Story and screenplay by Betty Comden and Adolph Green; Songs: music by André Previn; lyrics by Betty Comden and Adolph Green; music arranged and conducted by André Previn; vocal supervision by Robert Tucker and Jeff Alexander; dances and musical numbers by Gene Kelly and Stanley Donen; photographed in Eastman color; director of photography, Robert Bronner; art directors, Cedric Gibbons and Arthur Lonergan; set decorations, Edwin B. Willis and Hugh Hunt; color consultant, Alvord Eiseman; assistant director, Al Jennings; costumes designed by Helen Rose; film editor, Adrienne Fazan; recording supervisor, Wesley C. Miller; special effects, Warren Newcombe and Irving G. Ries; hair styles by Sydney Guilaroff; make-up created by William Tuttle; directed by Gene Kelly and Stanley Donen.

CAST: *Ted Riley,* Gene Kelly; *Doug Hallerton,* Dan Dailey; *Jackie Leighton,* Cyd Charisse; *Madeline Bradbille,* Dolores Gray; *Angie Valentine,* Michael Kidd; *Tim,* David Burns; *Charles Z. Culloran,* Jay C. Flippen; *Kid Mariacchi,* Steve Mitchell; *Rocky Heldon,* Hal March; *Mr. Fielding,* Paul Maxey; *Mr. Trasker,* Peter Leeds; *Mr. Stamper,* Alex Gerry; *Mrs. Stamper,* Madge Blake; *Roy TV director,* Wilson Wood; *Mr. Grigman,* Richard Simmons. MINOR BITS: *Lady,* Almira Sessions; *Chef,* Eugene Borden.

MUSIC. VISUAL: "March, March," "Time for Parting," "Blue Danube," "Stillman's Gym," "Baby, You Knock Me Out," "Situation Wise," "Once upon a Time," "I Like Myself," "Thanks a Lot but No Thanks" (Previn-Comden-Green); "Music Is Better Than Words" Words" (Previn-Edens-Comden-Green); "Sleeper Phones" (Previn). NONVISUAL: "The Binge," "Ten Year Montage" (Previn). DELETED: "Jack and the Space Giants" (ballet). NOT USED: "I Thought They'd Never Leave," "Love Is Nothing but a Racket" (Previn-Comden-Green).

Running time: 101 minutes.

KISMET (1676) (May 23–July 22, 1955) December 8, 1955. Screenplay by Charles Lederer and Luther Davis; adapted from the musical *Kismet,* book by Charles Lederer and Luther Davis; founded on *Kismet* by Edward Knoblock; music and lyrics by Robert Wright and George Forrest; music adapted from themes of Alexander Borodin; music supervised and conducted by André Previn and Jeff Alexander; orchestral arrangements by Conrad Salinger, Alexander Courage and Arthur Morton; musical numbers and dances staged by Jack Cole; photographed in Eastman color; director of photography, Joseph Ruttenberg; art directors: Cedric Gibbons and Preston Ames; set decorations, Edwin B. Willis and Keogh Gleason; special effects, Warren Newcombe; color consultant, Charles K. Hagedon; costumes by Tony Duquette; film editor, Adrienne Fazan; recording supervisor, Dr. Wesley C. Miller; vocal supervision, Robert Tucker; assistant director, William Shanks; hair styles by Sydney Guilaroff; make-up created by William Tuttle; directed by Vincente Minnelli. (Stanley Donen).

CAST: *Poet Hajj,* Howard Keel; *Marsinah,* Ann Blyth; *Lalume,* Dolores Gray; *Caliph,* Vic Damone; *Omar,* Monty Woolley; *Wazir,* Sebastian Cabot; *Jawan,* Jay C. Flippen; *Chief Policeman,* Mike Mazurki; *Hassan-Ben,* Jack Elan; *Police Subaltern,* Ted DeCorsia. MINOR BITS: *Princesses,* Patricia Dunn, Reiko Sato, Wonci Lui Julie Robinson (Mrs. Harry Belafonte); *Brave Shopkeeper,* Ray Aghayan; *Beggar,* Aaron Spelling.

MUSIC. VISUAL: "Rhymes Have I," "Fate," "Bazaar of the Caravans," "Baubles, Bangles and Beads," "Stranger in Paradise," "Gesticulate," "Bored," "Night of My Nights," "The Olive Tree," "Rahadlakum," "And This Is My Beloved," "Sands of Time," "Not Since Nineveh" (Wright-Forrest).

Running time: 113 minutes.

LADY BE GOOD (1182) (February 24–May 1, 1941) September 12, 1941. Screenplay by Jack McGowan, Kay Van Riper and John McClain (Ralph Spence, Arnold Auerbach, Herman Wouk, Robert McGunigle, Vincente Minnelli); based on an original story by Jack McGowan; music by George Gershwin; lyrics by Ira Gershwin; additional songs by Jerome Kern and Oscar Hammerstein II, Roger Edens and Arthur Freed; musical direction, George Stoll; musical continuity (for Eleanor Powell), Walter Ruick; vocals and orchestrations, Conrad Salinger, Leo Arnaud and George Bassman; musical numbers staged by Busby Berkeley; directors of photography: George Folsey, Oliver T. Marsh; recording director, Douglas Shearer; art director, Cedric Gibbons, associate, John S. Detlie; set decorations, Edwin B. Willis; musical presentation, Merrill Pye; gowns by Adrian; hair styles by Sydney Guilaroff; film editor, Frederick Y. Smith; directed by Norman Z. McLeod.

CAST: *Marilyn Marsh,* Eleanor Powell; *Dixie Donegan,* Ann Sothern; *Eddie Crane,* Robert Young; *Judge Murdock,* Lionel Barrymore; *Buddy Crawford,* John Carroll; *Joe "Red" Willet,* Red Skelton; *Lull,* Virginia O'Brien; *Mr. Blanton,* Tom Conway; *Bill Pattison,* Dan Dailey, Jr.; *Max Milton,* Reginald Owen; *Mrs. Carter Wardley,* Rose Hobart; *M.C.,* Phil Silvers; *The Berry Brothers,* themselves; *The Singer,* Connie Russell.

MUSIC. VISUAL: "So Am I," "Oh Lady Be Good," "Fascinating Rhythm" (George and Ira Gershwin); "You'll Never Know" (Edens); "Your Words and My Music" (Edens-Freed); "The Last Time I Saw Paris" (Kern-Hammerstein); "Saudades" (Edens). NONVISUAL: "Alone" (Brown-Freed); "Hang on to Me" (George and Ira Gershwin). NOT USED: "I'd Rather Dance" (Brown-Ralph Freed).

Running time: 111 minutes.

LIGHT IN THE PIAZZA, an Arthur Freed production (United Kingdom, 648) (May 7–July 12, 1961) February 9, 1962. Screenplay by Julius J. Epstein; based on a story by Elizabeth Spencer; music composed by Mario Nascimbene;

542

conducted by Dock Mathieson; director of photography, Otto Heller; in Cinema-Scope and Metrocolor; art director, Frank White; special effects, Tom Howard; recording supervisor, A. W. Watkins; sound recordist, Cyril Swer; sound editor, Robert Carrick; dubbing mixer, J. B. Smith; production manager, Dennis Johnson; assistant director, Basil Rayburn; camera operator, Jack Lowin; continuity, Kay Mander; stills cameraman, David Boulton; wardrobe mistress, Dolly Smith; hairdresser, Joan Johnstone; make-up, Tom Smith, assistant make-up, Basil Newall; photographic lenses by Panavision; associate producer, Aida Young; edited by Frank Clark; Miss de Havilland's costumes by Christian Dior; directed by Guy Green. Made at M-G-M Studios, Boreham Wood, England.

CAST: *Margaret Johnson,* Olivia de Havilland; *Noel Johnson,* Barry Sullivan; *Clara Johnson,* Yvette Mimieux; *Signor Naccarelli,* Rossano Brazzi; *Signora Naccarelli,* Nancy Nevinson; *Fabrizio Naccarelli,* George Hamilton; *Guiseppi Naccarelli,* Rosella Spinelli; *Miss Hawtree,* Isabel Dean; *The Minister,* Moultrie Kelsall; *The Consular Agent,* William Greene; *The Priest,* Robert Rietty; *Concierge,* Steve Plytas; *Marchese,* Luciano Barontino; *Policeman,* Bonas Eugevio; *Train Conductor,* Peppino Demartino.

MUSIC. VISUAL: None. NONVISUAL: composed by Nascimbene; NOT USED: lyrics to main title theme by Arthur Freed.

Running time: 101 minutes.

LITTLE NELLIE KELLY (1153) (July 29–September 19, 1940; September 27, 1940) November 22, 1940. Screenplay by Jack McGowan (Marvin Barowsky, Jack Mintz); based upon the musical comedy written, composed and produced by George M. Cohan; musical adaptation, Roger Edens; musical direction, George Stoll; director of photography, Ray June; recording director, Douglas Shearer; art director, Cedric Gibbons, associate, Harry McAfee; set decorations, Edwin B. Willis; women's costumes by Dolly Tree; men's costumes by Gile Steele;

make-up created by Jack Dawn; film editor, Frederick Y. Smith; directed by Norman Taurog.

CAST: *Nellie Kelly/Little Nellie Kelly,* Judy Garland; *Jerry Kelly,* George Murphy; *Michael Noonan,* Charles Winninger; *Timothy Fogarty,* Arthur Shields; *Dennis Fogarty,* Douglas McPhail; *Mary Fogarty,* Rita Page; *Moriarity,* Forrester Harvey; *Sergeant McGowan,* James Burke; *Keevan,* George Watts. MINOR BITS: *Intern,* John Raitt; *Mounted Cop,* Pat O'Malley.

MUSIC. VISUAL: "Nellie Kelly, I Love You" (Cohan); "Nellie Is a Darlin'," "Death Scene," "Nellie Montage" "It's a Great Day for the Irish" (Edens); "A Pretty Girl Milking Her Cow" (adapted, Edens); "Singin' in the Rain" (introduction) (Edens); "Singin' in the Rain" (Brown-Freed). NONVISUAL: "Everybody Works but Father" (Havez). DELETED: "You Remind Me of My Mother" (Cohan).

Running time: 98 minutes.

MEET ME IN ST. LOUIS (1317) (December 7, 1943–April 7, 1944) December 31, 1944. Screenplay by Irving Brecher and Fred F. Finklehoffe (Sally Benson, Doris Gilbert, Sarah Y. Mason, Victor Heerman, William Ludwig); based on the book by Sally Benson; lyrics and music, Hugh Martin and Ralph Blane; photographed in Technicolor; director of photography, George Folsey; color director, Natalie Kalmus, associate, Henri Jaffa; musical adaptation, Roger Edens; musical direction, George Stoll (Lennie Hayton); orchestrations, Conrad Salinger; dance director, Charles Walters; recording director, Douglas Shearer; art direction, Cedric Gibbons, Lemuel Ayers, Jack Martin Smith; set decorations, Edwin B. Willis and Paul Huldschinsky; costume supervision, Irene; costumes designed by Irene Sharaff; make-up created by Jack Dawn; film editor, Albert Akst; directed by Vincente Minnelli.

CAST: *Esther Smith,* Judy Garland; *"Tootie" Smith,* Margaret O'Brien; *Mrs.*

Anna Smith, Mary Astor; *Rose Smith,* Lucille Bremer; *Mr. Alonzo Smith,* Leon Ames; *John Truett,* Tom Drake; *Katie (Maid),* Marjorie Main; *Grandpa,* Henry Davenport; *Lucille Ballard,* June Lockhart; *Lon Smith, Jr.,* Henry H. Daniels, Jr.; *Agnes Smith,* Joan Carroll; *Colonel Darly,* Hugh Marlowe; *Warren Sheffield,* Robert Sully; *Mr. Neeley,* Chill Wills. MINOR BITS: Johnny Tevis, Darryl Hickman.

MUSIC. VISUAL: "The Boy Next Door," "The Trolley Song" and "Have Yourself a Merry Little Christmas" (Martin-Blane); "Skip to My Lou" (arranger, Martin-Blane); "You and I" (Brown-Freed); "Meet Me in St. Louis" (Mills-Sterling); "Brighten the Corner" (Gabriel); "Under the Bamboo Tree" (Cole); "Summer in St. Louis," "The Invitation" (Edens); "All Hallow's Eve," "The Horrible One," "Ah, Love!" (Salinger); "Over the Banister" (arranger, Salinger); "Good-bye My Lady Love" (Howard); "Under the Anheuser Bush" (Von Tilzer); "Little Brown Jug" (Eastburn, arranger, Hayton); "The Fair" (Hayton). DELETED: "Boys and Girls Like You and Me" (Rodgers-Hammmerstein).

Running time: 113 minutes.

ON THE TOWN (1453) (March 28–July 2, 1949) December 30, 1949. Screen play by Betty Comden and Adolph Green; based upon the musical, book by Adolph Green and Betty Comden, from an idea by Jerome Robbins, with music by Leonard Bernstein, lyrics by Adolph Green, Betty Comden and Leonard Bernstein, directed on the stage by George Abbott and produced by Oliver Smith and Paul Feigay; music by Leonard Bernstein and Roger Edens; lyrics by Betty Comden and Adolph Green; musical director, Lennie Hayton; orchestrations, Conrad Salinger; vocal arrangements, Saul Chaplin; associate producer, Roger Edens; color by Technicolor; director of photography, Harold Rosson; color consultants, Henri Jaffa, James Gooch; art directors, Cedric Gibbons and Jack Martin Smith; film editor, Ralph E.

Winters, recording supervisor, Douglas Shearer; set decorations, Edwin B. Willis, associate, Jack D. Moore; special effects, Warren Newcombe; costumes by Helen Rose; hair styles designed by Sydney Guilaroff; make-up created by Jack Dawn; directed by Gene Kelly and Stanley Donen.

CAST: *Gabey,* Gene Kelly; *Chip,* Frank Sinatra; *Brunhilde Esterhazy,* Betty Garrett; *Claire Huddesen,* Ann Miller; *Ozzie,* Jules Munshin; *Ivy Smith,* Vera-Ellen; *Mme. Dilyovska,* Florence Bates; *Lucy Shmeeler,* Alice Pearce; *Professor,* George Meader. MINOR BITS: *Brooklyn Girl,* Bea Benaderet; *Waiter,* Eugene Borden; *Francois,* Hans Conried; (Judy Holliday dubbed the voice of a sailor's date).

MUSIC. VISUAL: "Anniversary Fanfare ⚹2 (Rozsa); "New York, New York," "Taxi Number" (Bernstein-Comden-Green); "Turnstiles Ballet," "A Day in New York Ballet" (Bernstein); "On the Town," "Main Street," "Prehistoric Man," "You're Awful," Night Club Songs— " 'That's All There Is, Folks,' " "Count on Me," "Pearl of the Persian Sea" (Edens-Comden-Green).

Running time: 98 minutes.

PAGAN LOVE SONG (1489) (April 3 –July 8, 1950; July 31, 1950) December 29, 1950. Screenplay by Robert Nathan and Jerry Davis (Ivan Tors); technical adviser, William Stone; based on the book *Tahiti Landfall* by William S. Stone; music by Harry Warren; lyrics by Arthur Freed; associate producer, Ben Feiner, Jr. (Roger Edens, Lela Simone); musical direction, Adolph Deutsch; vocal arrangements, Robert Tucker; orchestrations, Conrad Salinger; color by Technicolor; director of photography, Charles Rosher; color consultants, Henri Jaffa, James Gooch; art directors, Cedric Gibbons and Randall Duell; film editor, Adrienne Fazan; recording supervisor, Douglas Shearer; set decorations, Edwin B. Willis, associate, Jack D. Moore; special effects, A. Arnold Gillespie, Warren Newcombe; costumes by Helen Rose;

hair styles designed by Sydney Guilaroff; make-up created by William J. Tuttle; directed by Robert Alton.

CAST: *Mimi Bennett*, Esther Williams; *Hazard Endicott*, Howard Keel; *Kate Bennett*, Minna Gombell; *Tavae*, Charles Mauu; *Teuru*, Rita Moreno; *Manu*, Philip Costa; *Tani*, Dione Leilani; *Papera*, Charles Freund; *Countess Mariani*, Marcella Corday; *Tua*, Sam Maikai; *Angele*, Helen Rapoza; *Mama Ruau*, Birdie De-Bolt; *Mata*, Bill Kaliloa; *Monsieur Bouchet*, Carlo Cook.

MUSIC. VISUAL: "The House of Singing Bamboo,"[7] "Singing in the Sun," "Etiquette," "Why Is Love So Crazy," "Tahiti" "The Sea of the Moon" (Warren Freed); "Pagan Love Song" (Brown-Freed). NONVISUAL: "Cocoanut Milk" (Edens). DELETED: "Music on the Water," "Here in Tahiti We Make Love (Warren-Freed).

Running time: 76 minutes.

PANAMA HATTIE (1205) (July 15–October 3, 1941; November 11, 1941; April 6–May 25, 1942) September 18, 1942. Screenplay by Jack McGowan and Wilkie Mahoney (Lillie Messinger, Mary McCall, Joseph Schrank; technical adviser, Sergio R. Orta; sketches by Fred Finklehoff and Vincente Minnelli); based on the musical book by Herbert Fields and B. G. De Sylva; produced by B. G. De Sylva, music and lyrics by Cole Porter; musical adaptation, Roger Edens; musical direction, George Stoll; Musical numbers staged by Vincente Minnelli; dance director, Danny Dare; additional songs by Roger Edens, Burton Lane, E. Y. Harburg and Walter Donaldson; vocals and orchestrations, Conrad Salinger, George Bassman, Leo Arnaud; director of photography, George Folsey; recording director, Douglas Shearer; art director, Cedric Gibbons, associate, John S. Detile; set decorations, Edwin B. Willis, Hugh Hunt; musical presentation, Merrill Pye; gowns by Kalloch; hair styles by Sydney Guilaroff; film editor, Blanche

Sewell; directed by Norman Z. McLeod (Roy del Ruth).

CAST: *Hattie Maloney*, Ann Sothern; *Dick Bulliet*, Dan Dailey, Jr.; *Red*, Red Skelton; *Leila Tree*, Marsha Hunt; *Flo Foster*, Virginia O'Brien; *Rags*, Rags Ragland; *Jay Jerkins*, Alan Mowbray; *Rowdy*, Ben Blue; *Geraldine Bulliet*, Jackie Horner; *Lucas Kefler*, Carl Esmond; *Admiral Tree*, Pierre Watkin; *Colonel John Briggs*, Stanley Andrews; Lena Horne and The Berry Brothers; (Carmen Amaya Dancers). MINOR BITS: *Waiter*, Joe Yule; *Spy*, Roger Moore; *Shore Patrol*, Grant Withers.

MUSIC. VISUAL: "I've Still Got My Health," "Just One of Those Things," "Make It Another Old-Fashioned, Please," "Fresh as a Daisy," "Let's Be Buddies" (Porter); "Hattie From Panama," "Good Neighbors," "I'll Do Anything for You" (Edens); "The Son of a Gun Who Picks on Uncle Sam" (Lane-Harburg); "Did I Get Stinkin' at the Club Savoy" (Donaldson); "The Spring" (Moore-J. Le Gon); "La Bumba Rhumba" (Hyde); "Berry Me Not" (Phil Moore); "Hail Hail, the· Gang's All Here" (Sullivan). NONVISUAL: "My Mother Would Love You," "They Ain't Done Right by Our Nell" (Porter). DELETED: "Salome," "Stop Off in Panama" (Edens); "Cookin' With Gas" (Hayton-Edens).[8]

Running time: 79 minutes.

PIRATE, THE (1400) (February 17–August 14, 1947; August 27–October 21, 1947; November 18, 1947) June 11, 1948. Screenplay by Albert Hackett and Frances Goodrich (Joseph Mankiewicz, Joseph Than, Lillian Braun, Anita Loos, Wilkie Mahoney); based on the play by S. N. Behrman as produced by the Playwrights Company and the Theatre Guild; songs by Cole Porter; musical direction, Lennie Hayton; instrumental arrangements, Conrad Salinger; (vocal arrangements, Kay Thompson, Robert Tucker, Roger Edens); dance direction by Robert Alton and Gene Kelly; color by Techni-

[7] Original music of "Hayride" written for *The Harvey Girls*.

[8] Used in *Maisie Gets Her Man* (1942).

color; director of photography, Harry Stradling; color director, Natalie Kalmus, associate, Henri Jaffa; art directors, Cedric Gibbons and Jack Martin Smith; film editor, Blanche Sewell; recording director, Douglas Shearer; set decorations, Edwin B. Willis and Arthur Krams; costume supervision, Irene; costumes designed by Tom Keogh, executed by Karinska; hair styles designed by Sydney Guilaroff; make-up created by Jack Dawn; main title paintings by Doris Lee; directed by Vincente Minnelli.

CAST: *Manuela,* Judy Garland; *Serafin,* Gene Kelly; *Don Pedro Vargas,* Walter Slezak; *Aunt Inez,* Gladys Cooper; *The Advocate,* Reginald Owen; *The Viceroy,* George Zucco; *Specialty Dance,* the Nicholas Brothers; *Uncle Capucho,* Lester Allen; *Isabella,* Lola Deem; *Mercedes,* Ellen Ross; *Lizarda,* Mary Jo Ellis; *Casilda,* Jean Dean; *Eloise,* Marion Murray; *Gumbo,* Ben Lessy; *Bolo,* Jerry Bergen; *Juggler,* Val Setz; *Gaudsmith Brothers,* themselves; *Trillo,* Cully Richards.

MUSIC. VISUAL: "Nina," "Love of My Life," "Mack the Black," "You Can Do No Wrong," "Be a Clown" (Porter); "Sweet Ices, Papayas, Berry Man," "Sea Wall," "Serafin" (Edens); "The Ring," "Judy Awakens" "The Tight Rope," "Not Again" (Hayton); "Gene Meets Mack the Black," "The Mast," (Salinger); DELETED: "Voodoo" (Porter). NOT USED: "Manuela" (Porter).

Running time: 102 minutes.

ROYAL WEDDING[9] (1502) (July 6–October 5, 1950; October 17, 1950) March 23, 1951. Story and screenplay by Alan Jay Lerner; music by Burton Lane; lyrics by Alan Jay Lerner; musical direction, Johnny Green; dances by Nick Castle; orchestrations, Conrad Salinger and Skip Martin; color by Technicolor; director of photography, Robert Planck; color consultants, Henri Jaffa, James Gooch; art directors, Cedric Gibbons and

[9] Released in United Kingdom and all Commonwealth countries as *Wedding Bells.*

Jack Martin Smith; film editor, Albert Akst; recording supervisor, Douglas Shearer; set decorations, Edwin B. Willis and Alfred E. Spencer; special effects, Warren Newcombe; hair styles designed by Sydney Guilaroff; make-up created by William J. Tuttle; directed by Stanley Donen.

CAST: *Tom Bowen,* Fred Astaire; *Ellen Bowen,* Jane Powell; *Lord John Brindale,* Peter Lawford; *Anne Ashmond,* Sarah Churchill; *Irving Klinger/Edgar Klinger,* Keenan Wynn; *James Ashmond,* Albert Sharpe; *Sarah Ashmond,* Viola Roache; *Furser,* Henri Letondal; *Cabby,* James Finlayson; *Chester,* Alex Frazer; *Pete Cumberly,* Jack Reilly; *Dick,* William Cabanne; *Billy,* John Hedloe; *Charles Gordon,* Francis Bethancourt. "Haiti" number: Dee Turnell, Judy Lenson, Doreen Hayward, Shirley Rickert, Marian Horosko, Carmes Clifford, Italia De Nubelo, Betty Hannon, Charlotte Hunter, Janet Lavis, Sheila Meyers, Pat Simms, Dorothea Ward, Joan Vohs, Marietta Elliott, Svetlana McLe, Doris Wolcott, Bee Allen, Joane Dale, Shirley Glickman, Jean Harrison, Lucille Lamarr, Virginia Lee, Jetsy Parker, Dorothy Tuttle. MINOR BITS: *Steward,* Andre Charisse; *Woman Guest,* Bess Flowers.

MUSIC. VISUAL: "Ev'ry Night At Seven," "Sunday Jumps" (instrumental), "Open Your Eyes," "The Happiest Day of My Life," "How Could You Believe Me When I Said I Love You When You Know I've Been a Liar All My Life," "Too Late Now," "You're All the World to Me," "I Left My Hat in Haiti," "What a Lovely Day for a Wedding" (Lane-Lerner). NONVISUAL: "How About You" (Lane-Freed), "The Devonshire Regiment" (arranger, Paul Marquardt). NOT USED: "Sunday Jumps," "I Got Me a Baby" (Lane-Lerner).

Running time: 93 minutes.

SHOW BOAT (1520) (November 17, 1950–January 9, 1951; February 5, March 1, 1951) July 13, 1951. Screenplay by John Lee Mahin (George Wells, Jack McGowan); based on the musical

Show Boat by Jerome Kern and Oscar Hammerstein II; from novel by Edna Ferber; musical direction, Adolph Deutsch; musical numbers staged and directed by Robert Alton; orchestrations, Conrad Salinger; vocal arrangements, Robert Tucker; color by Technicolor; director of photography, Charles Rosher; color consultants, Henri Jaffa, James Gooch; film editor, Albert Akst; art directors, Cedric Gibbons and Jack Martin Smith; set decorations, Edwin B. Willis and Alfred Spencer; special montage director, Peter Ballbusch; special effects, Warren Newcombe; hair styles designed by Sydney Guilaroff; make-up created by William J. Tuttle; costumes designed by Walter Plunkett; associate producer, Ben Feiner, Jr. (Roger Edens); directed by George Sidney.

CAST: *Magnolia Hawks,* Kathryn Grayson; *Julie Laverne,* Ava Gardner; *Gaylord Ravenal,* Howard Keel; *Captain Andy Hawks,* Joe E. Brown; *Ellie May Shipley,* Marge Champion; *Frank Schultz,* Gower Champion; *Stephen Baker,* Robert Sterling; *Parthy Hawks,* Agnes Moorehead; *Cameo McQueen,* Adele Jurgens; *Joe,* William Warfield; *Pete,* Leif Ericson; *Windy McClain,* Owen McGiveney; *Queenie,* Frances Williams; *Sheriff (Ike Vallon),* Regis Toomey; *Mark Hallson,* Frank Wilcox; *Herman,* Chick Chandler; *Jake Green,* Emory Parnell; *Kim,* Sheila Clark; *Drunk Sport,* Ian MacDonald; *Troc Piano Player,* Fuzzy Knight; *George (Caliope Player),* Norman Leavitt; *Show Boat Cast Girls:* Anne Marie Dore, Christina Lind, Lyn Wilde, Marietta Elliott, Joyce Jameson, Betty Arlen, Helen Kimbell, Tao Porchon, Mitzie Uehlein, Judy Landon, Nova Dale, Mary Jane French, Marilyn Kinsley, Alice Markham. *Show Boat Cast Boys:* Michael Dugan, Robert Fortier, George Ford, Cass Jaeger, Boyd Ackerman, Roy Damron, James Roach.

MUSIC. VISUAL: "Captain Andy's Entrance," "Cotton Blossom," "Captain Andy's Bally-hoo," "Where's the Mate for Me," "Make Believe," "Can't Help Lovin' That Man," "I Might Fall Back on You," "Buck and Wing-Finale Act 1," "Hey, Fellah," "You Are Love," "Why Do I Love You?" "Happy the Day-Finale Act 1," "Queenie's Bally-hoo," "Life Upon the Wicked Stage" (Kern-Hammerstein); "Bill" (Kern-Bolton-Wodehouse); "After the Ball" (Harris); "Auld Lang Syne" (arranger, Deutsch). NOT USED: "Nobody Else but Me," "Ah Still Suits Me," "I Have the Room Above" (Kern-Hammerstein).

Running time: 108 minutes.

SILK STOCKINGS, an Arthur Freed production (1709) (November 7, 1956–January 31, 1957) July 18, 1957. Screenplay by Leonard Gershe and Leonard Spigelgass (Harry Kurnitz); suggested by *Ninotchka* by Melchior Lengyel; music and lyrics by Cole Porter; book of original musical by George S. Kaufman, Leueen McGrath and Abe Burrows, produced on the stage by Cy Feuer and Ernest H. Martin; music supervised and conducted by André Previn; orchestral arrangements by Conrad Salinger; all dances in which Fred Astaire appears choreographed by Hermes Pan; all other dances choreographed by Eugene Loring; in CinemaScope and Metrocolor; director of photography, Robert Bronner; art directors, Cedric Gibbons and Randall Duell; set decorations, Edwin B. Willis and Hugh Hunt; color consultant, Charles K. Hagedon; assistant director, Al Jennings; make-up by William Tuttle; hair styles by Sydney Guilaroff; costumes by Helen Rose; film editor, Harold F. Kress; recording supervisor, Dr. Wesley C. Miller; vocal supervision, Robert Tucker; additional orchestrations, Skip Martin, Al Woodbury; music co-ordinator, Lela Simone; directed by Rouben Mamoulian.

CAST: *Steve Canfield,* Fred Astaire; *Ninotchka,* Cyd Charisse; *Peggy Dayton,* Janis Paige; *Brankov,* Peter Lorre; *Vassili Markovitch,* George Tobias; *Bibinski,* Jules Munshin; *Ivanov,* Joseph Buloff; *Peter Ilyitch Boroff,* Wim Sonneveld. MINOR BITS: *Vera,* Belita; *Gabrielle,* Barrie Chase.

MUSIC. VISUAL: "Josephine," "Too Bad," "Paris Loves Lovers," "Sterophonic

Sound," "It's a Chemical Reaction, That's All," "All of You," "Satin and Silk," "Without Love," "Fated to Be Mated," "Siberia," "Red Blues," "The Ritz Roll and Rock" (Porter). NONVISUAL: "I've Got You Under My Skin," "Easy to Love," "I Concentrate on You" (Porter). NOT USED: "Hail Bibinski," "As on Through the Seasons We Sail" (Porter).

Running time: 118 minutes.

SINGIN' IN THE RAIN (1546) (June 18–November 21, 1951; December 26, 1951) April 10, 1952. Story and screenplay by Adolph Green and Betty Comden; suggested by the song "Singin' in the Rain," lyrics by Arthur Freed; music by Nacio Herb Brown; musical direction, Lennie Hayton; musical numbers staged and directed by Gene Kelly and Stanley Donen (assistants, Carol Haney and Jeanne Coyne); color by Technicolor; director of photography, Harold Rosson (John Alton); color consultants, Henri Jaffa, James Gooch; art directions, Cedric Gibbons and Randall Duell; film editor, Adrienne Fazan; recording supervisor, Douglas Shearer; orchestrations by Conrad Salinger, Wally Heglin and Skip Martin; vocal arrangements by Jeff Alexander (Roger Edens); set decorations, Edwin B. Willis and Jacques Mapes; special effects, Warren Newcombe, Irving G. Ries; costumes designed by Walter Plunkett; hair styles designed by Sydney Guilaroff; make-up created by William Tuttle; associate producer, Roger Edens; directed by Gene Kelly and Stanley Donen.

CAST: Don Lockwood, Gene Kelly; Cosmo Brown, Donald O'Connor; Kathy Selden, Debbie Reynolds; Lina Lamont, Jean Hagen; R. F. Simpson, Millard Mitchell; Zelda Zanders, Rita Moreno; Roscoe Dexter, Douglas Fowley; and Cyd Charisse. MINOR BITS: Dora Bailey, Madge Blake; Rod, King Donovan; Phoebe Dinsmore, Kathleen Freeman; "Beautiful Girl" singer, Jimmie Thompson; Girl Dancers: Patricia Denise, Jeanne Coyne; Male Dancing Quartet, Bill Chatham, Ernest Flatt, Don Hulbert, Robert Dayo; Kid, David Kasday; Man in Talking Motion Picture, Julius Tannen.

MUSIC. VISUAL: "Singin' in the Rain," "Temptation," "All I Do Is Dream of You," "Make 'Em Laugh," "I've Got a Feelin' You're Foolin'," "Wedding of the Painted Doll," "Should I," "Beautiful Girl," "You Were Meant for Me," "Good Morning," "Broadway Melody," "Broadway Rhythm," "You Are My Lucky Star" (Brown-Freed); "Fit as a Fiddle and Ready for Love," (Hoffman-Goodhart-Freed); "Moses" (Edens-Comden-Green).

Running time: 103 minutes.

STRIKE UP THE BAND (1141) (April 19–July 16, 1940; August 13, 1940) September 30, 1940. Original screenplay by John Monks, Jr., and Fred F. Finklehoffe (Herbert Fields, Kay Van Riper); lyrics and music by George and Ira Gershwin, Arthur Freed and Roger Edens; chorals and orchestrations, Conrad Salinger and Leo Arnaud; musical director, George Stoll; director of photography, Ray June; recording director, Douglas Shearer; art directors, Cedric Gibbons and John S. Detlie; set decoration, Edwin B. Willis; musical presentation by Merrill Pye; women's costumes by Dolly Tree; men's wardrobe by Gile Steele; make-up created by Jack Dawn; fruit models created by Henry Rox; film editor, Ben Lewis; directed by Busby Berkeley.

CAST: Jimmy Connors, Mickey Rooney; Mary Holden, Judy Garland; Paul Whiteman, himself; Barbara Frances Morgan, June Preisser; Phillip Turner, William Tracy; Willie Brewster, Larry Nunn; Annie, Margaret Early; Mrs. Connors, Ann Shoemaker; Mr. Judd, Francis Pierlot; Mrs. May Holden, Virginia Brissac; Mr. Morgan, George Lessey; Mrs. Morgan, Enid Bennett; Doctor, Howard Hickman; Miss Hodges, Sarah Edwards; Mr. Holden, Milton Kibbee; Mrs. Brewster, Helen Jerome Eddy.

MUSIC. VISUAL: "Strike Up the Band" (George and Ira Gershwin); "Our Love Affair" (Edens-Freed); "Do the La

Conga," "Nobody," "Drummer Boy," "Nell of New Rochelle (Edens); "Sidewalks of New York" (Lawlor-Blake); "Walking Down Broadway" (arranger, Edens); "Light Cavalry Overture" (Von Suppe); "Over the Waves" (Rosas); "Heaven Protect the Working Girl" (Sloane-Smith). NONVISUAL: "Five Foot Two, Eyes of Blue" (Henderson); "After the Ball" (Harris).

Running time: 120 minutes.

SUBTERRANEANS, THE, an Arthur Freed production, (1757) August 24–October 23, 1959) June 23, 1960. Screenplay by Robert Thom (Ranald MacDougall); based on the novel by Jack Kerouac; music by André Previn; director of photography, Joseph Ruttenberg (Robert Bronner); in CinemaScope and Metrocolor; art directors, George W. Davis and Urie McCleary; set decorations, Henry Grace and Hugh Hunt; special effects, Lee LeBlanc; costume designer, Moss Mabry; color consultant, Charles K. Hagedon; film editor, Ben Lewis; recording supervisor, Franklin Milton; assistant director, William Shanks; make-up created by William Tuttle; photographic lenses by Panavision; (associate producer, Terry Sanders; director, Denis Sanders); directed by Ranald MacDougall.

CAST: *Mardou Fox*, Leslie Caron; *Leo Percepied*, George Peppard; *Roxanne*, Janice Rule; *Yuri Gligoric*, Roddy McDowall; *Charlotte Percepied*, Anne Seymour; *Adam Moorad*, Jim Hutton; *Julien Alexander*, Scott Marlowe; *Arial Lavalerra*, Arte Johnson; *Analyst*, Ruth Storey; *Bartender*, Bert Freed; *Joshua Hoskins*, Gerry Mulligan; *Carmen McRae*, herself; André Previn, Shelly Manne, Red Mitchell, Art Farmer, Dave Bailey, Buddy Clark, Russ Freeman, Art Pepper, Bob Enevoldsen, William R. Perkins, Frank Hamilton—themselves. MINOR BITS: *Poet*, Paul Sand; *Society Woman*, Nanette Fabray.

MUSIC. VISUAL: "Wanderin'," "Leo in Bar," "Roxanne at Ariel's" Original Jazz interpolations (Previn); "Should I" (Brown-Freed); "Coffee Time" (Warren-

Freed) NONVISUAL: Original Jazz Interpolations in underscoring (Previn).

Running time: 89 minutes.

SUMMER HOLIDAY (1386) (June 17–October 14, 1946) April 16, 1948. Adapted by Irving Brecher and Jean Holloway from the screenplay by Frances Goodrich and Albert Hackett; based on Eugene O'Neill's play, *Ah, Wilderness!* music by Harry Warren; lyrics by Ralph Blane; musical direction, Lennie Hayton; orchestrations, Conrad Salinger, dance direction, Charles Walters; (vocal arrangements, Robert Tucker and Ralph Blane); photographed in Technicolor; director of photography, Charles Schoenbaum; color director, Natalie Kalmus, associate, Henri Jaffa; art direction, Cedric Gibbons and Jack Martin Smith; film editor, Albert Akst; recording director, Douglas Shearer; set decorations, Edwin B. Willis, associate Richard Pefferle; costume supervision, Irene; costumes designed by Walter Plunkett; make-up created by Jack Dawn; hair styles by Sydney Guilaroff; directed by Rouben Mamoulian.

CAST: *Richard Miller*, Mickey Rooney; *Muriel*, Gloria De Haven; *Mr. Nat Miller*, Walter Huston; *Uncle Sid*, Frank Morgan; *Tommy*, Butch Jenkins; *Belle*, Marilyn Maxwell; *Cousin Lily*, Agnes Moorehead; *Mrs. Miller*, Selena Royle; *Arthur Miller*, Michael Kirby; *Mildred*, Shirley Johns; *Wint*, Hal Hackett; *Elsie Rand*, Ann Francis; *Mr. McComber*, John Alexander; *Miss Hawley*, Virginia Brissac; *Mr. Peabody*, Howard Freeman; *Mrs. McComber*, Alice MacKenzie; *Crystal*, Ruth Brady.

MUSIC. VISUAL: "Our Home Town," "Afraid to Fall in Love," "Dan-Dan-Dannville High," "The Stanley Steamer," "Independence Day," "While the Men Are All Drinking," "You're Next," "Weary Blues," "The Sweetest Kid I Ever Met" (Warren-Blane). DELETED: "Never Again," "Omar and the Princess" (song and ballet sequence), "Spring Isn't Everything" (Warren-Blane).

Running time: 92 minutes.

TAKE ME OUT TO THE BALL GAME[10] (1432) (July 28–October 26, 1948) April 1, 1949. Screenplay by Harry Tugend and George Wells (Harry Crane); story by Gene Kelly and Stanley Donen; lyrics and music by Betty Comden, Adolph Green and Roger Edens; vocal arrangements by Robert Tucker; musical direction, Adolph Deutsch; musical numbers staged by Gene Kelly and Stanley Donen; color by Technicolor; director of photography, George Folsey; color director, Natalie Kalmus, associate, James Gooch; art directors: Cedric Gibbons and Daniel B. Cathcart; film editor, Blanche Sewell; recording director, Douglas Shearer; set decorations, Edwin B. Willis and Henry W. Grace; special effects, Warren Newcombe; montage sequence, Peter Ballbusch; women's costumes by Helen Rose; men's costumes by Valles; hair styles designed by Sydney Guilaroff; make-up created by Jack Dawn; associate producer, Roger Edens; directed by Busby Berkeley.

CAST: *Dennis Ryan,* Frank Sinatra; *K. C. Higgins,* Esther Williams; *Eddie O'Brien,* Gene Kelly; *Shirley Delwyn,* Betty Garrett; *Joe Lorgan,* Edward Arnold; *Nat Goldberg,* Jules Munshin; *Michael Gilhuly,* Richard Lane; *Slappy Burke,* Tom Dugan; *Salinka,* Murray Alper; *Nick Danford,* Wilton Graff; *Two Henchmen:* Mack Gray, Charles Regan; *Steve,* Saul Gross; *Karl,* Douglas Fowley; *Dr. Winston,* Eddie Parkes; *Cop in Park,* James Burke; *Specialty,* the Blackburn Twins; *Senator Catcher,* Gordon Jones.

MUSIC. VISUAL: "Take Me Out to the Ball Game" (Von Tilzer-Norworth); "The Right Girl for Me," "O'Brien to Ryan to Goldberg," "Yes, Indeedy," "It's Fate Baby, It's Fate" (Edens-Comden-Green); "Strickly, U.S.A." (Edens); "The Hat My Dear Old Father Wore Upon St. Patrick's Day" (Schwartz-Jerome). DELETED: "Boys and Girls Like You and Me" (Rodgers-Hammerstein); "Sand Man" (Edens-Comden-Green); "Hayride," "Baby Doll" (Warren-Mercer);

[10] Released in the United Kingdom as *Everybody's Cheering.*

NOT USED: Previous planned production score by Harry Warren and Ralph Blane (February 1947): "Someone Like You,"[11] "Me-O-My," "If It Weren't for the Irish," "Puttin' on Airs,"[12] "I've Got a Funny Feeling,"[13] "The Boy in the Celluloid Collar" and "Ride-Ride-Ride."

Running Time: 93 minutes.

TILL THE CLOUDS ROLL BY (1369) (October 8–November 7, 1945, December 11, 1945–February 12, 1946, February 21–March 12, 1946, March 29–April 3, 1946, April 19–May 23, 1946) January 3, 1947. Story by Guy Bolton; adapted by George Wells; screenplay by Myles Connolly and Jean Holloway (Fred F. Finklehoffe, John Lee Mahin, Lemuel Ayers, Hans Willheim); based on the life and music of Jerome Kern; musical direction, Lennie Hayton; orchestrations, Conrad Salinger; vocal arrangements, Kay Thompson; musical numbers staged and directed by Robert Alton; photographed in Technicolor; directors of photography, Harry Stradling and George J. Folsey; color director, Natalie Kalmus, associate, Henri Jaffa; film editor, Albert Akst; recording director, Douglas Shearer; art direction, Cedric Gibbons and Daniel B. Cathcart; set decorations, Edwin B. Willis and Richard Pefferle; special effects, Warren Newcombe; costume supervision, Irene; costumes designed by Helen Rose; men's costumes, Valles; hair styles created by Sydney Guilaroff; make-up created by Jack Dawn; directed by Richard Whorf (George Sidney).

CAST: *Jerome Kern,* Robert Walker; *Marilyn Miller,* Judy Garland; *Sally,* Lucille Bremer; *Sally as a girl,* Joan Wells; *James I. Hessler,* Van Heflin; *Oscar Hammerstein II,* Paul Langton; *Mrs. Jerome Kern,* Dorothy Patrick; *Mrs. Muller,* Mary Nash; *Charles Frohman,* Harry

[11] Used in *My Dream Is Yours* (Warner Brothers).
[12] Originally written for *Huckleberry Finn.*
[13] Used in *Skirts Ahoy* (M-G-M).

550

Hayden; *Victor Herbert*, Paul Maxey; *Cecil Keller*, Rex Evans; *Hennessy*, William "Bill" Phillips; *Band Leader*, Van Johnson; *Guest Stars:* June Allyson, Angela Lansbury, Ray McDonald; *Dance Specialty:* Maurice Kelly, Cyd Charisse and Gower Champion; *Orchestra Conductor*, Ray Teal; *Specialty*, Wilde Twins; *Frohman's Secretary*, Byron Foulger; *Show Boat* number: *Captain Andy*, William Halligan; *Ravenal*, Tony Martin; *Magnolia*, Kathryn Grayson; *Ellie*, Virginia O'Brien; *Julie*, Lena Horne; *Joe*, Caleb Peterson; *Steve*, Bruce Cowling. Finale; Kathryn Grayson, Johnny Johnston, Lucille Bremer, Frank Sinatra, Virginia O'Brien, Lena Horne, Tony Martin.

MUSIC. VISUAL: Opening, Act 1, *Show Boat:* "Life Upon the Wicked Stage," "Can't Help Lovin' That Man," "Ol Man River," "Make Believe," "Who?," "Sunny," "One More Dance," "The Last Time I Saw Paris," "All the Things You Are," "Why Was I Born?" (Kern-Hammerstein); "Ka-lu-a" (Kern-Caldwell); "How'd You Like to Spoon With Me" (Kern-Laska); "They Didn't Believe Me" (Kern-Reynolds); "Till the Clouds Roll By" (Kern-Wodehouse-Bolton); "Leave It to Jane," "Cleopatterer," "Land Where the Good Songs Go" (Kern-Wodehouse); "Look for the Silver Lining" (Kern-De Sylva); "Try to Forget," "Yesterdays" (Kern-Harbach); "Long Ago (and Far Away)" (Kern-Gershwin); "A Fine Romance" (Kern-Fields). NONVISUAL: "The Touch of Your Hand," "Siren's Song," "Why Do I Love You," " 'Twas Not So Long," "Mark Twain Suite" (Polka); "Go Little Boat," "Sun Shines Brighter," "La Jeunne Fille," "Passionate Pilgrim," "You Never Knew About Me," "Pal Like You," "You Are Love," "Crickets Are Calling," Opening, Act 2, *Sally:* "In the Egern of the Tegern Sea," "I Dream Too Much," entr'acte: "Cat and the Fiddle," "Don't Ever Leave Me," "Smoke Gets in Your Eyes." DELETED: "Bill," "Lovely to Look At," "I've Told Ev'ry Little Star," "The Song Is You," "D' Ye Love Me?," "Dearly Beloved."

Running time: 137 minutes.

THE WIZARD OF OZ (1060) (October 13, 1938–March 16, 1939) August 18, 1939. Screenplay by Noel Langley, Florence Ryerson and Edgar Allan Woolf; adaptation by Noel Langley, from the book by L. Frank Baum; musical adaptation by Herbert Stothart (and Roger Edens); lyrics by E. Y. Harburg; music by Harold Arlen; associate conductor, George Stoll; orchestral and vocal arrangements by George Bassman, Murray Cutter, Paul Marquardt, Ken Darby (Roger Edens); musical numbers staged by Bobby Connolly; photographed in Technicolor; directors of photography, Harold Rosson (color), Allen Darby (black/white); color director, Natalie Kalmus, associate, Henri Jaffa; recording director, Douglas Shearer; art directors, Cedric Gibbons, William A. Horning (associate, Jack Martin Smith); set decoration, Edwin B. Willis; special effects, A. Arnold Gillespie; costumes designed by Adrian; character make-up created by Jack Dawn; film editor, Blanche Sewell; (associate producer, Arthur Freed); produced by Mervyn LeRoy; directed by Victor Fleming (King Vidor, Richard Thorpe).

CAST: *Dorothy*, Judy Garland; *Professor Marvel/The Wizard*, Frank Morgan; *Hunk/The Scarecrow*, Ray Bolger; *Zeke/The Cowardly Lion*, Bert Lahr; *Hickory/The Tin Man*, Jack Haley; *Miss Gulch/The Wicked Witch*, Margaret Hamilton; *The Good Witch*, Billie Burke; *Uncle Henry*, Charley Grapewin; *Auntie Em*, Clara Blandick; *Toto*, Toto; *Nikko*, Pat Walshe; The Singer midgets as *The Munchkins* with Jerry Maren.

MUSIC. VISUAL: "Over the Rainbow," "Munchkinland," "Ding Dong the Witch Is Dead," "Follow the Yellow Brick Road," "We're Off to See the Wizard," "If I Only Had a Brain/a Heart/the Nerve," "If I Were King of the Forest," "The Merry Old Land of Oz" (Arlen-Harburg); "Munchkinland ⚡1–4" (Arlen-Harburg-Edens); "Threatening Witch," "Into the Forest of the Wild Beast," "The City Gates Are Open," "At the Gates of Emerald City," "Magic Smoke Chords," "Toto's Chase," "On the Castle

Wall," "Delirious Escape" (Stothart); "The Cornfields" (Stothart-Stoll-Bassman); "Poppies" (Stothart-Stringer); "Optimistic Voices" (Arlen-Stothart-Harburg); "The Witch's Castle" (Stothart-Mendelssohn); "March of the Winkies" (Stothart-Edens); "Dorothy's Rescue" (based on Mussorgsky's "Night on Bald Mountain"; arranged by Edens). NONVISUAL: "In the Shade of the Old Apple Tree" (Van Alstyne). DELETED: "The Jitterbug" (Arlen-Harburg).

Running time: 101 minutes.

WORDS AND MUSIC (1427) (April 4–July 14, 1948, August 7, 1948, October 1, 1948) December 31, 1948. Screenplay by Fred Finklehoffe; story by Guy Bolton; adaptation by Ben Feiner, Jr. (Jean Holloway, Guy Bolton, Isabel Lennart, Jack Mintz); based on the lives and music of Richard Rodgers and Lorenz Hart; associate producer, Ben Feiner, Jr. (Roger Edens); musical direction, Lennie Hayton; orchestrations, Conrad Salinger; vocal arrangements, Robert Tucker; musical numbers staged and choreographed by Robert Alton; color by Technicolor; directors of photography, Charles Rosher and Harry Stradling; color director, Natalie Kalmus, associate, James Gooch; art directors, Cedric Gibbons and Jack Martin Smith; film editors, Albert Akst and Ferris Webster; recording director, Douglas Shearer; set decorations, Edwin B. Willis and Richard A. Pefferle; special effects, Warren Newcombe; women's costumes by Helen Rose; men's costumes by Valles; hair styles created by Sydney Guilaroff; make-up created by Jack Dawn; directed by Norman Taurog.

CAST: *Eddie Lorrison Anders,* Perry Como; *Lorenz "Larry" Hart,* Mickey Rooney; *Joyce Harmon,* Ann Sothern; *Richard "Dick" Rodgers,* Tom Drake; *Peggy Lorgan McNeil,* Betty Garrett; *Dorothy Feiner,* Janet Leigh; *Herbert Fields,* Marshall Thompson; *Mrs. Hart,* Jeanette Nolan; *Ben Feiner, Jr.,* Richard Quine; *Shoe Clerk,* Clinton Sundberg; *Dr. Rodgers,* Harry Antrim; *Mr. Feiner,* Emory Parnell; *Mrs. Feiner,* Helen

Spring; *James Fernby Kelly,* Edward Warle; *Margo Grant,* Cyd Charisse; *Guest Stars:* Judy Garland, June Allyson, the Blackburn Twins, Gene Kelly, Vera-Ellen. MINOR BITS: Allyn Ann McLearie, John Butler, Dee Turnell, Sig Frohlich.

MUSIC. VISUAL: "Lover," "Mountain Greenery," "Manhattan," "There's a Small Hotel," "Way Out West on West End Avenue," "A Tree in the Park," "Where's That Rainbow," "On Your Toes," "You Took Advantage of Me," "Blue Room," "Someone Should Tell Them," "Thou Swell," "With a Song in My Heart," "Where or When," "Lady Is a Tramp," "I Didn't Know What Time It Was," "I Wish I Were in Love Again," "Johnny One Note," "I Married an Angel," "Blue Room," "Spring Is Here," "My Romance," "Slaughter on Tenth Avenue" (Rodgers-Hart). NONVISUAL: "We'll Be the Same," "Here in My Arms," "You Took Advantage of Me," "Yours Sincerely," "This Can't Be Love," "The Girl Friend," "Ship Without a Sail," "March of the Knights," "Nothing but You," "Hollywood Party," "Dancing on the Ceiling" (Rodgers-Hart). DELETED: "You're Nearer," "Give It Back to the Indians," "Mimi," "This Can't Be Love," "The Poor Apache," "It Never Entered My Mind," "Lover," "It's Got to Be Love," "My Heart Stood Still," "Falling in Love With Love," "You Took Advantage of Me," "My Funny Valentine" (Rodgers-Hart).

Running time: 121 minutes.

YOLANDA AND THE THIEF (1347) (January 15, 1944–May 21, 1945) November 20, 1945. Screenplay by Irving Brecher; based upon a story by Jacques Thiery and Ludwig Bemelmans (Joe Schrank, George Wells, Robert Nathan); songs by Arthur Freed and Harry Warren; musical directions, Lennie Hayton; orchestration, Conrad Salinger; dances staged by Eugene Loring; photographed in Technicolor; director of photography, Charles Rosher; color director, Natalie Kalmus, associate, Henri Jaffa, film editor, George White; recording director,

Douglas Shearer; art direction, Cedric Gibbons and Jack Martin Smith; set decorations, Edwin B. Willis and Richard Pefferle; special effects, A. Arnold Gillespie; Miss Bremer's gowns by Irene; costumes designed by Irene Sharaff; make-up created by Jack Dawn; directed by Vincente Minnelli.

CAST: *Johnny Parkson Riggs,* Fred Astaire; *Yolanda,* Lucille Bremer; *Victor Budlow Trout,* Frank Morgan; *Aunt Amarilla,* Mildred Natwick; *Duenna,* Mary Nash; *Mr. Candle,* Leon Ames; *Schoolteacher,* Ludwig Stossel; *Mother Superior,* Jane Green; *Puppeteer,* Remo Bufano; *Padre,* Francis Pierlot; *Taxi Driver,* Leon Belasco; *Gigi,* Ghislaine Perreau; *Police Lieutenant,* Charles La Torre; *Major-domo,* Michael Visaroff. MINOR BIT: *Dilettante,* Andre Charlot.

MUSIC. VISUAL: "This Is a Day for Love," "Angel," "Will You Marry Me," "Yolanda," "Coffee Time" (Warren-Freed). NONVISUAL: "Dream Ballet," "Fred Takes the Money," "Procession," "Fiesta," "Good-bye" (Hayton). DELETED: "By Candlelight." NOT USED: "Feminine Fashions," "Made in the U.S.A." (Warren).

Running time: 108 minutes.

ZIEGFELD FOLLIES (1325) (March 1–August 24, 1944; May–July 8, 1944; January 18–January 30, 1945) March 15, 1946. Writers, E. Y. Harburg, Jack McGowan, Guy Bolton, Frank Sullivan, John Murray Anderson, Lemuel Ayers, Don Loper, Kay Thompson, Roger Edens, Hugh Martin, Ralph Blane, William Noble, Wilkie Mahoney, Cal Howard, Erick Charell, Max Liebman, Bill Schorr, Harry Crane, Lou Holtz, Eddie Cantor, Allan Boretz, Edgar Allan Woolf, Phil Rapp, Al Lewis, Joseph Schrank, Robert Alton, Eugene Loring, Robert Lewis, Charles Walters, James O'Hanlon, David Freedman, Joseph Erons, Irving Brecher, Samson Raphaelson, Everett and Devery Freeman; dance direction, Robert Alton; composers, George and Ira Gershwin, Harry Warren and Arthur Freed, Roger Edens and Kay Thompson, Roger Edens-Hugh Martin-Ralph Blane; musical direction, Lennie Hayton; orchestrations, Conrad Salinger, Wally Heglin; vocal arrangements, Kay Thompson; photographed in Technicolor; directors of photography, George Folsey, Charles Rosher, Ray June; color director, Natalie Kalmus, associate, Henri Jaffa; recording director, Douglas Shearer; art direction, Cedric Gibbons, Jack Martin Smith, Merrill Pye, Lemuel Ayers; puppet sequence photographed by William Ferrari; puppets, Bunin; puppet costumes, Florence Bunin; set decorations, Edwin B. Willis, Mac Alper; costume supervision, Irene; costumes designed by Irene Sharaff and Helen Rose; make-up created by Jack Dawn; hair styles created by Sydney Guilaroff; film editor, Alberto Akst; directed by Vincente Minnelli (George Sidney).

RUNNING ORDER OF FILM: "Ziegfeld Days," *Ziegfeld,* William Powell; and the Bunin Puppets; directed by Norman Taurog / "Here's to the Ladies" (Edens-Freed), Fred Astaire, Lucille Ball, Cyd Charisse, Ensemble; directed by George Sidney / Esther Williams in "A Water Ballet," "This Heart of Mine," (Warren-Freed); directed by Merrill Pye / Keenan Wynn in "Number, Please" (Peter Barr); directed by Robert Lewis / James Melton and Marion Bell in "Traviata" (Verdi); costumes by Irene Sharaff; set design by Merrill Pye; directed by Vincente Minnelli / Victor Moore wants Edward Arnold to "Pay the Two Dollars" (George White-William K. Wells); directed by George Sidney; *Victor Moore,* himself; *Edward Arnold,* himself, *Special Officer,* Roy Teal; *Judge,* Joseph Crehan, *Presiding Judge,* William B. Davidson; *Warden,* Harry Hayden; *Officer,* Eddie Dunn; *Second Officer,* Garry Owen / Fred Astaire and Lucille Bremer in a dance story, "This Heart of Mine" (Warren-Freed); staged by Robert Alton; directed by Vincente Minnelli; *The Imposter,* Fred Astaire; *The Princess,* Lucille Bremer; *The Duke,* Count Stefenelli; *The Duchess,* Naomi Childers; *The Countess,* Helen Boice; *Retired Dyspeptic,* Robert Wayne; *The Major,* Charles Coleman; *The Lieu-*

tenant, Feodor Chaliapin; *The Flunky,* Sam Flint; *Show Girls,* Shirlee Howard, Natalie Draper, Noreen Roth, Dorothy Van Nuys; Katherine Booth, Lucille Casey, Eve Whitney, Elaine Shepard, Frances Donelan, Helen O'Hara, Aina Constant, Aileen Haley / Fanny Brice Wins "A Sweepstakes Ticket" (David Freedman); directed by Roy Del Ruth; staged by Charles Walters; *Norma,* Fanny Brice; *Monty,* Hume Cronyn; *Martin,* William Frawley; *Telegraph Boy,* Arthur Walsh / "Love" (Martin-Blane) with Lena Horne; directed by Lemuel Ayers / Red Skelton will show you what happens "When Television Comes" (Edna Skelton); directed by George Sidney / "Limehouse Blues" (Graham-Furber); prologue and epilogue staged by Robert Lewis; written and choreographed by Robert Alton; costumes and decor by Irene Sharaff; directed by Vincente Minnelli; *Tai Long,* Fred Astaire; *Moy Ling,* Lucille Bremer; *Chinese Gentleman,* Robert Lewis; *Ensemble:* Dante Dipaolo, Robert Chetwood, Jack Purcell, Herb Luri, Walter Stane, Edward Brown, Milton Chisholm, Jack Regas, Bert May, Richard D'Arch, Alex Romero, Don Hulbert, Ricky Ricardi, Robert Trout, Bill Hawley, Rita Dunn, Charlotte Hunter, Patricia Lynn, Ruth Merman, Melba Snowden, Patricia Jackson, Marilyn Christine, Wanda Stevenson, Judi Blacque, Virginia Hunter, Sean Francis, Dorothy Gilmore, Doreen Hayward; *Four Couples:* (*with parasols*) Ellen Ray, Billy Shead, (*with branches*) Eleanor Boiley, Ronnite Stanton, (*with banners*) Jean Ashton, Rod Alexander, (*with birds*) Mary Jo Ellis, James Barron; *Four Men with Masks:* Charles Lunard, Robert Ames, Jack Regas, Sidney Gordon; *Chicken,* Cyd Charisse; *Rooster,* James King; *Costermonger,* Eugene Loring; *Singer in Dive,* Harriet Lee / "A Great Lady Has An Interview," played by Judy Garland (Thompson-Edens); staged by Charles Walters; directed by Vincente Minnelli; *The Butler,* Rex Evans / Fred Astaire and friend (Gene Kelly) in "The Babbitt and the Bromide" (George and Ira Gershwin) (written by Robert Alton and Irving Brecher); staged by Robert Alton; directed by Vincente Minnelli / "Beauty" (Warren-Freed), with Kathryn Grayson and the Ziegfeld Girls. DELETED: "If Swing Goes, I Go Too" (Astaire), Fred Astaire and ensemble; directed by George Sidney / "The Pied Piper," Jimmy Durante in "Start Off Each Day With a Song"; directed by Charles Walters / Fanny Brice in "Baby Snooks and the Burglars" (Everett and Devery Freeman; directed by Roy Del Ruth / James Melton in "A Bit of the West"; directed by Merrill Pye / Lena Horne as "Liza" (George and Ira Gershwin) with Avon Long; staged by Eugene Loring; decor by Jack Martin Smith; directed by Vincente Minnelli / "We Will Meet Again in Honolulu" (Brown-Freed), Esther Williams and James Melton; directed by Merrill Pye / "There's Beauty Everywhere" (Warren-Freed), Fred Astaire, Lucille Bremer, James Melton, Cyd Charisse and the ensemble; directed by Vincente Minnelli / "Death and Taxes" (David Freedman), with Jimmy Durante and Edward Arnold; directed by Vincente Minnelli. PRERECORDED: "Will You Love Me in Technicolor As You Do in Black and White," with Judy Garland and Mickey Rooney. NOT USED: "Fireside Chat," Judy Garland, Ann Sothern and Lucille Ball / "Pass That Peace Pipe" (Edens-Martin-Blane), June Allyson, Gene Kelly, Nancy Walker and ensemble / "Reading of the Play" (Freedman), Judy Garland and Frank Morgan / "As Long as I Have My Art" (Edens-Martin-Blane), Judy Garland and Mickey Rooney / "Glorifying the American Girl," Lucille Ball, Marilyn Maxwell, Lucille Bremer, Lena Horne and Elaine Shephard / "A Trip to Hollywood," Jimmy Durante, Lucille Ball, Marilyn Maxwell and others / "Fairy Tale Ballet" (Loring), Katharine Hepburn, Margaret O'Brien, Jackie Jenkins / "You're Dreamlike" (Dietz-Schwartz).

Running time: 110 minutes.

UNPRODUCED FILMS OF ARTHUR FREED

Year indicates when project was first initiated; parenthesis within project indicates when manuscript was delivered and termination of writer's assignment.

1939

TWENTY LITTLE WORKING GIRLS
Screenplay by Marguerite Roberts (October 9, 1939).

1941

VERY WARM FOR MAY
Based on the musical by Jerome Kern and Oscar Hammerstein II; new songs, "Contrary Mary," "Mary My Girl" (Kern-Hammerstein); first draft screenplay by Jack McGowan (July 2, 1941). Turned over to Jack Cummings and produced as *Broadway Rhythm* (1944).

1942

BABES IN HOLLYWOOD
Story outline by Sid Silvers (February 16, 1942).

BATHING BEAUTY
Story outline; first, second and final draft of screenplay by Virginia Kellogg (*Sing or Swim,* July 16, 1942); first draft screenplay by Hy Kraft (August 27, 1942); first and final draft screenplay by Walter DeLeon and Frank Tarloff (February 3, 1943). Turned over to Jack Cummings and produced under the same title (1944).

HIGH KICKERS
Based on the musical by George Jessel, Bert Kalmar and Harry Ruby (September 23, 1942); outline, first and final draft screenplay by Guy Bolton (December 17, 1942); treatment, first and final draft screenplay by Harry Ruby and James O'Hanlon (July 17, 1943).

THE HUMAN COMEDY
Original screenplay by William Saroyan (February 4, 1942); first draft screenplay by Howard Estabrook (August 12, 1942). Turned over to Clarence Brown, who directed the film (1943).

HONEY BOY
Novel by Daily Paskman (July 28, 1942); screenplay by Jack McGowan (December 12, 1942). For Mickey Rooney, adaptation by Nat Perrin (May 1, 1943); screenplay by George Wells (August 12, 1946). For Frank Sinatra, final draft screenplay by Jack McGowan (May 27, 1948).

1943

HOT TIME IN THE OLD TOWN
Outline by Jack McGowan (July 12, 1943); outline by Sig Herzig and Fred Saidy (December 12, 1943); final draft screenplay by Jack McGowan (February 2, 1944).

THE STORY OF GABY DESLYS
Treatment by Irving Guttman (March 12, 1943); treatment by Robert Thoeren (May 2, 1948). For Judy Garland.

MELODY MAN
Treatment by Joseph Schrank and Paul Jerrico (July 2, 1943). For Mickey Rooney.

1944

RED SHOES RUN FASTER
Original screenplay by Robert Nathan (July 2, 1944); Jules Dassin, Robert Nathan and Hagar Wilde (June 12, 1944); treatment by Edith Fitzgerald (February 2, 1945); Samson Raphaelson (April 2, 1945); first draft by Paul Green (July 10, 1945); revised screenplay by Jean Holloway (March 29, 1946); final screenplay by Harriet Frank, Jr. (November 11, 1946). For Lucille Bremer.

1945

PAPA WENT TO CONGRESS
Based on the novel by Kenneth Horan (October 2, 1945); treatment by Irving Brecher (November 12, 1945).

HUCKLEBERRY FINN
Treatment by Sally Benson (January 2, 1945); musical score by Hugh Martin and Ralph Blane (January 1945): "The Cockebur Song," "Ah' Bin Rich," "There Were Others Passing By," "It Must Be Spring," "I'm

the First Man," "My Old Home Town"; "Pass That Peace Pipe" (Edens-Martin-Blane); additional song by Harry Warren and Ralph Blane, "Puttin' on Airs." New first draft screenplay by Donald Ogden Stewart (May 23, 1950); new musical score by Burton Lane and E. Y. Harburg: "That Real Sunday Feeling," "Don't Run Mirandy" and "Jumpin' Jubilee." New screenplay by Alan Jay Lerner (July 12, 1951); new musical score by Burton Lane and Alan Jay Lerner: "I'm From Missouri," "Huckleberry Finn," "The World's Full o' Suckers," "I'll Wait for You by the River," "I'll Meet You Down by the River," "Pittsburgh Blue," "Asparagus Is Served" and "When You Grown Up You'll Know." Some of the Lerner-Lane score was used in *The Adventures of Huckleberry Finn* produced by Samuel Goldwyn, Jr. (1960).

1946

FOREVER Based on the novella by Mildred Kram; screenplay by Miriam Stuart and Robert McElwaine (October 12, 1946). For Judy Garland.

1947

PRIDE AND PREJUDICE First draft screenplay by Sally Benson (April 2, 1947); new first draft musical screenplay by Sidney Sheldon (August 12, 1947).

LUST FOR LIFE Based on the book by Irving Stone; screenplay written by Irving Stone (February 26, 1947). Turned over to John Houseman and produced under the same title (1956).

1948

EXCURSION Based on the play by Victor Wolfson; first and final draft screenplay by Robert Nathan (January 13, 1948).

1949

HOW TO WIN FRIENDS AND INFLUENCE PEOPLE Based on a title by Dale Carnegie; original screenplay by Harry Ruskin (October 2, 1949). To star Red Skelton as a comedy with music; song: "How to Win Friends and Influence People" (Rodgers-Hart) from *I Married an Angel*.

1951

JUMBO Based on the musical by Richard Rodgers and Lorenz Hart; final screenplay by Joseph Fields (October 2, 1951). Turned over to Joe Pasternak and Roger Edens and produced under the title *Billie Rose's Jumbo* (1962).

THE ROMBERG STORY Based on the life and music of Sigmund Romberg; original screenplay by Joseph Fields (December 2, 1951). Turned over to Roger Edens and produced, with a new screenplay, as *Deep in My Heart* (1954).

1952

TRIBUTE TO A BAD MAN Original screenplay by Charles Schnee (March 26, 1952). Turned over to John Houseman and produced under the title *The Bad and the Beautiful* (1953).

ATHENA Treatment and first draft screenplay by Leonard Spigelgass (July 18, 1952). Turned over and produced by Joe Pasternak as a musical with a score by Hugh Martin and Ralph Blane (1954).

1953

ST. LOUIS WOMAN Based on the musical by Arna Bontemps and Countee Cullen; music by Harold Arlen and lyrics by Johnny Mercer; first, second and final draft screenplay by Fred Finklehoffe (March 12, 1953); continuity script by Helen Deutsch (October 1, 1953).

1954

GREEN MANSIONS First and final draft screenplay by Alan Jay Lerner (October 11, 1954). Dropped by Freed and produced, with a new screenplay, by Pandro S. Berman (1959).

1955

WONDERLAND Based on the music and lyrics of Cole Porter; first, second, revised and final screenplay by Betty Comden and Adolph Green (January 19, 1956).

1960

THE DAY BEFORE SPRING Based on the Broadway musical; book and lyrics by Alan Jay Lerner; music by Frederick Loewe; original screenplay by George Oppenheimer and I. A. L. Diamond for Jack Cummings (1946); new musical score by Johnny Green and Frank Loesser: "The Statue Song," "Opening," "My Sentimental Nature," "Bing, Bang," "Who Could Forget You," "It's Time for the Love Scene," "Ibbedy Bibbedy Sibbedy Sab," "You're So Reliable." Adaptation of Broadway musical libretto by Joseph Stein (November 2, 1960); Lerner-Loewe score "The Day Before Spring," "A Jug of Wine," "You Haven't Changed At All," "My Love Is a Married Man," "God's Green World," "I Love You in the Morning," "This Is My Holiday," "Ballet I and II," "Friends to the End," "Interlude," "Where's My Wife" and "Invitation."

1962

A LIKELY STORY Based on the play *Odd Man In* by Robin Maugham; first, revised and final screenplay by Julius J. Epstein (August 7, 1962). To star Gina Lollibrigida and Tony Curtis; to be directed by Charles Walters.

1963

CARNIVAL Based on the Broadway musical by Michael Stewart; music and lyrics by Bob Merrill; first, second and final draft screenplay by Julius J. Epstein (February 22, 1963). To be directed by Gower Champion.

SAY IT WITH MUSIC Original screenplay by Arthur Laurents (November 26, 1963); original score by Irving Berlin; screenplay by Leonard Gershe (May 20, 1965); screenplay by Betty Comden and Adolph Green, first, second and final draft (February 14, 1966). To star Julie Andrews and Fred Astaire. Screenplay by George Wells (May 15, 1967); coproducer Blake Edwards (1968); new treatment by George Axelrod (May 10, 1968). To be directed by Vincente Minnelli (1962–67), Blake Edwards, (1968–69); new songs by Irving Berlin: "(It's) Always the Same," "A Guy on Monday," "A Man to Cook for," "One Man Woman," "Outside of Loving You, I Like You," "The P.X.," "The Ten Best Undressed Women in the World," "Whisper It," (1963); "Let Me Sing" (1964); "I Used to Play It by Ear" (1965); "Who Needs the Birds and the Bees," "Long as I Can Take You Home,." "Wait Until You're Married," "I Used to Be Color Blind" (1966).

1967

THE BOY FRIEND First, second and final draft screenplay by George Kirgo (March 23, 1967). Dropped and eventually made by Ken Russell (1972).

ARTHUR FREED'S SONG CATALOGUE

MOTION PICTURES

Title	M-G-M Film[1]	Year	Composer
After Sundown	*Going Hollywood*	1933	Nacio Herb Brown
All I Do Is Dream of You	*Sadie McKee*	1934	Nacio Herb Brown
	Broadway Melody of 1936 (in French)	1935	
	Andy Hardy Meets Debu-tante (d)[2]	1940	
	Singin' in the Rain	1952	
	The Boy Friend	1971	
	That's Entertainment!	1974	
Alone	*A Night at the Opera*	1935	Nacio Herb Brown
Angel	*Yolanda and the Thief*	1945	Harry Warren
Beautiful Girl	*Stage Mother*	1933	Nacio Herb Brown
	Going Hollywood (d)	1933	
	Singin' in the Rain	1952	
Blondy	*Marianne*	1929	Nacio Herb Brown
Born to Dance	*Yours and Mine* (un-p)[3]	1935	Nacio Herb Brown

[1] All songs were written for Metro-Goldwyn-Mayer musicals or feature films (unless indicated) with lyrics by Arthur Freed. Many appeared in films other than originally written. Only those used as complete vocals and/or instrumental-visual are listed in this instance. The year, in most instances, only refers to the release of the film and not when the song was first written.

[2] Indicates song was deleted from release print.

[3] Unproduced film.

Title	M-G-M Film[1]	Year	Composer
Boy Friend, The	*The Broadway Melody*	1929	Nacio Herb Brown
Broadway Melody, The	*The Broadway Melody*	1929	Nacio Herb Brown
	Singin' in the Rain	1952	
	That's Entertainment!	1974	
Broadway Rhythm	*Broadway Melody of 1936*	1935	Nacio Herb Brown
	Broadway Melody of 1938	1937	
	Babes in Arms[4]	1938	
	Singin' in the Rain	1952	
	That's Entertainment!	1974	
Bundle of Old Love Letters, A	*Lord Byron of Broadway*	1930	Nacio Herb Brown
Busy Body	*Yours and Mine* (un-p)	1935	Nacio Herb Brown
By the Taj Mahal	*Student Tour*	1934	Nacio Herb Brown
Call to Arms, The	*Good News*	1930	Nacio Herb Brown
Candlelight	*Yolanda and the Thief*	1945	Harry Warren
Carlo, The[5]	*Student Tour*	1934	Nacio Herb Brown
Chant of the Jungle[6]	*Untamed*	1929	Nacio Herb Brown
China Seas[7]	*China Seas*	1935	Nacio Herb Brown
Cinderella's Fella	*Going Hollywood*	1933	Nacio Herb Brown
Coffee Time	*Yolanda and the Thief*	1945	Harry Warren
	The Subterraneans[8]	1960	
College Hymn	*Good News*	1930	Nacio Herb Brown
Dream Was So Beautiful, The	*Hideout*	1934	Nacio Herb Brown
Etiquette	*Pagan Love Song*	1950	Harry Warren
Everybody Sing	*Broadway Melody of 1938*	1937	Nacio Herb Brown
Fight 'Em	*Good News*	1930	Nacio Herb Brown
Fit as a Fiddle	*College Coach* (WB) (d)	1932	Al Hoffman and Al Goodhart
	Singin' in the Rain	1952	
	That's Entertainment!	1974	
Follow in My Footsteps	*Broadway Melody of 1938*	1937	Nacio Herb Brown
Football	*Good News*	1930	Nacio Herb Brown
From Now on	*Student Tour*	1934	Nacio Herb Brown
Going Hollywood	*Going Hollywood*	1933	Nacio Herb Brown
	That's Entertainment!	1974	
Good Morning	*Babes in Arms*	1939	Nacio Herb Brown
	Singin' in the Rain	1952	Nacio Herb Brown
	That's Entertainment! (d)	1974	
Got a Pair of New Shoes[9]	*Thoroughbred's Don't Cry*	1937	Roger Edens, Nacio Herb Brown and Arthur Freed
Here Comes the Sun	*March of Time* (RKO)	1930	Harry Woods

[4] Part of Roger Edens' adaptation, "Opera Vs. Jazz."

[5] Based on Brown's composition, "American Bolero."

[6] On the 24-sheet billboard outside the sound stage during Gene Kelly and Debbie Reynolds' appearance in *Singin' in the Rain,* in which "All I Do Is Dream of You" is performed, this song title is depicted as a feature film.

[7] Same tune as "By the Taj Mahal."

[8] New lyrics written by Freed.

[9] Same music as "A Pair of New Shoes," new lyrics by Roger Edens.

Title	M-G-M Film[1]	Year	Composer
Here in Tahiti We Make Love	Pagan Love Song	1950	Harry Warren
Hold Your Man	Hold Your Man	1933	Nacio Herb Brown
Hot Chocolate Soldiers	Hollywood Revue (d)	1933	Nacio Herb Brown
House of Singing Bamboo[10]	Pagan Love Song	1950	Harry Warren
I Cried for You	Babes in Arms	1939	Arthur Freed, Gus Arnheim and Abe Lyman
If You're Not Kissing Me	Good News	1930	Nacio Herb Brown
I Hear Your Voice	A Lady's Morals	1930	Oscar Strauss; lyrics by Arthur Freed and Clifford Gray
I'll Remember Only You	Peg O' My Heart	1933	Nacio Herb Brown
I Looked in Your Eyes	Sadie McKee	1934	Nacio Herb Brown
I Loved That Man	The Torch Song	1931	Martin Broones
I'm Dancing on a Rainbow	Stage Mother	1933	Nacio Herb Brown
I'm Feeling Like a Million[11]	Broadway Melody of 1937	1937	Nacio Herb Brown
Island of Love	Never the Twain Shall Meet	1931	Arthur Freed
It Was So Beautiful	Blondie of the Follies	1932	Harry Barris
I Got a Feeling You're Fooling	Broadway Melody of 1936 Singin' in the Rain	1935 1952	Nacio Herb Brown
Life Is a Dream	The Prodigal	1931	Oscar Strauss
Life Is a Merry-Go-Round	Dancing Lady	1933	Nacio Herb Brown
Light in the Piazza[12]	Light in the Piazza	1962	Mario Nascimbene
Love Boat	The Broadway Melody	1929	Nacio Herb Brown
Lovely Lady	The Broadway Melody (d)	1929	Nacio Herb Brown
Love Songs of the Nile	The Barbarian	1933	Nacio Herb Brown
Love Was in the Air	Montana Moon (d)	1930	Nacio Herb Brown
Make 'Em Laugh[13]	Singin' in the Rain That's Entertainment!	1952 1974	Nacio Herb Brown
Meet Me in the Gloaming	College Coach (Warner Bros.)	1933	Al Hoffman and Al Goodhart
Moon Is Low, The	Montana Moon	1930	Nacio Herb Brown
Music on the Water	Pagan Love Song	1950	Harry Warren
My Wonderful One, Let's Dance	Two Girls on Broadway	1940	Nacio Herb Brown, Arthur Freed and Roger Edens
New Moon Is Over My Shoulder, A	Student Tour	1934	Nacio Herb Brown
Night Our Love Song Was Born, The		1931	Harry Woods

[10] Same music as "Hayride" (written by Harry Warren and Johnny Mercer) for *The Harvey Girls* (1945), but deleted from the release print.

[11] Film changed title to *Broadway Melody of 1938*.

[12] Last song written by Arthur Freed.

[13] Last song written by Brown and Freed.

Title	M-G-M Film[1]	Year	Composer
Oh, Why	*A Lady's Morals*	1930	Herbert Stothart and Harry Woods
On a Sunday Afternoon	*Broadway Melody of 1936*	1935	Nacio Herb Brown
Only Love Is Real	*Lord Byron of Broadway*	1930	Nacio Herb Brown
Our Big Love Scene	*Going Hollywood*	1933	Nacio Herb Brown
	Paid to Laugh	1933	
Our Love Affair	*Strike up the Band*	1940	Arthur Freed and Roger Edens
Pagan Love Song	*The Pagan*	1929	Nacio Herb Brown
	That's Entertainment!	1974	
Pair of New Shoes, A	*Broadway Melody of 1938* (d)	1937	Nacio Herb Brown
Please Make Me Care	*Sadie McKee*	1934	Nacio Herb Brown
Right Way to Love, The	*Those Three French Girls* (d)	1930	Joseph Meyer
Say Ah	*The Devil Is a Sissy*	1936	Nacio Herb Brown
Sea of the Moon	*Pagan Love Song*	1950	Harry Warren
Sequoia	*Sequoia*	1934	Nacio Herb Brown
Should I	*Lord Byron of Broadway* *Singin' in the Rain* *The Subterraneans* (inst)	1930	Nacio Herb Brown
Sing Before Breakfast	*Broadway Melody of 1936*	1935	Nacio Herb Brown
Singin' in the Rain	*Hollywood Revue of 1929*	1929	Nacio Herb Brown
	Little Nellie Kelly	1940	Herb Brown
	Hi, Beautiful (Universal)	1944	
	Singin' in the Rain	1952	
	Clockwork Orange, A	1972	
	That's Entertainment!	1974	
Singing in the Sun	*Pagan Love Song*	1950	Harry Warren
Six Poor Mortals	*Those Three French Girls*		
Smoke Dreams	*After the Thin Man*	1930	Joseph Meyer
Somethin's Gotta Happen Soon	*Ice Follies of 1939*	1936	Nacio Herb Brown
		1939	Nacio Herb Brown
Sun Showers	*Broadway Melody of 1937*	1937	Nacio Herb Brown
Tahiti	*Pagan Love Song*	1950	Harry Warren
Tell Me That You Love Me	*Pair o' Fools*	1926	Arthur Freed
Temptation	*Going Hollywood*	1933	Nacio Herb Brown
	Paid to Laugh (d)	1933	
There's Beauty Everywhere	*Ziegfeld Follies*	1945	Harry Warren
This Heart of Mine	*Ziegfeld Follies*	1945	Harry Warren
This Is the Day for Love	*Yolanda and the Thief*	1945	Harry Warren
This Is the Night	*Broadway Melody of 1936* (d)	1935	Nacio Herb Brown
Tommy Atkins on Parade	*Hollywood Revue of 1929*	1929	Nacio Herb Brown
Wedding of the Painted Doll, The	*The Broadway Melody* *Singin' in the Rain*	1929 1952	Nacio Herb Brown
		1933	Nacio Herb Brown
We're Together Again	*Riptide*	1933	Nacio Herb Brown
We'll Make Hay While the Sun Shines	*Going Hollywood*	1933	Nacio Herb Brown
We Will Meet Again in Honolulu	*Ziegfeld Follies* (d)	1945	Nacio Herb Brown

Title	M-G-M Film[1]	Year	Composer
What Will Become of Me	*A Lady's Morals* (d)	1930	Harry Woods and Herbert Stothart
Where I Ain't Been Before	*Wells Fargo*	1937	Nacio Herb Brown
Why Is Love So Crazy	*Pagan Love Song*	1950	Harry Warren
Will You Marry Me	*Yolanda and the Thief*	1945	Harry Warren
Woman in the Shoe, The	*Lord Byron of Broadway*	1929	Nacio Herb Brown
Would You?	*San Francisco*	1936	Nacio Herb Brown
	Singin' in the Rain	1952	
Yolanda	*Yolanda and the Thief*	1945	Harry Warren
You and I	*Meet Me in St. Louis*	1944	Nacio Herb Brown
You Are My Lucky Star	*Broadway Melody of 1936*	1935	Nacio Herb Brown
	Babes in Arms	1939	
	Born to Sing	1942	
	Singin' in the Rain	1952	
	The Boy Friend	1971	
You're in a Class by Yourself	*Good News* (d)	1930	Nacio Herb Brown
You Were Meant for Me	*The Broadway Melody*	1929	Nacio Herb Brown
	Hollywood Revue	1929	
	Show of Shows (WB)	1929	
	You Were Meant for Me (20th-Fox)	1948	
	Singin' in the Rain	1952	

STAGE SHOWS

PAIR O' FOOLS (opened Curran Theatre, San Francisco, January 25, 1926, continued to Chicago with its two stars, C. William Kolb and Max M. Dill); a musical comedy, based on Grant Mitchell's *The Whole Town's Talking;* book by John Emerson and Anita Loos; lyrics and music by Arthur Freed: "Honky Tonk Toodle," "In a Taxi Cab," "Isn't It Strange," "Hello, Hello, Sandy"; staged by George Cunningham.

THE HOLLYWOOD MUSIC BOX REVUE (spring edition, 1925), starring Fanny Brice; produced by Carter De Haven; music and lyrics by Arthur Freed: "Hold Me in Your Arms Again," "Quack, Quack," "Who's Who With You?"

HARRY CARROLL'S PICKINGS (a musical comedy presented at Arthur Freed's Orange Grove Theatre, Los Angeles, March 2, 1925); book and lyrics by Ballard MacDonald; music by Harry Carroll and Arthur Freed: "A Portion of Caviar," "California Here We Go," "Charleston Time," "Chop Sticks," "The Cuckoo Clock," "Hay Foot, Straw Foot," "He Had to Pay the Piper," "Hollywood," "Hot Steps," "I'm a Pickford Nobody Picked," "It Happened in 1600," "Mission Bells," "Next Tuesday," "Oriental Pearl," "Rosie Posie's," "Sing Me a Song," "Sweet Pickings," "The Wedding Bells Were Ringing."

ALL FOR YOU (opened at Mason Opera House, Los Angeles, August 24, 1925; San Francisco, December 25, 1925); based on George V. Hobart's play *Up the Line, John Henry;* a musical comedy produced by Thomas Wilkes, starring William

Gaxton; book by George V. Hobart and Charles Grapewin; music and lyrics by Arthur Freed: "All for You," "At the Hotel," "Capering Coopers," "Church Around the Corner," "Cover Me With Kisses," "Dance It Again With Me" (music by Oliver Wallace), "Egypt's No Place for a Lady," "Fidgety Feet," "Fu Ji," "Hold Me in Your Arms Again," "Housekeeping," "If You Love Her (Tell Her So)," "In a Happy Home for Two," "Keep That School Girl Complexion," "Keepin' Out of Trouble," "Little Raindrop," "Mr. Cozy Corner Man" (music by Arthur Freed and Byron Gay), "My Oriental Symphony," "Naughty Little Raindrop," "Osculation," "Remember Me," "Stay at Home," "There's a Little Bit of Spain in California," "They Don't Look the Same in the Morning," "When the Day Is Ended," "You've Got to Dance to Win the Prince of Wales"; staged by Frank Smithson.

THE HOLLYWOOD MUSIC BOX REVUE (fall edition, 1927), produced by Carter De Haven; music by Nacio Herb Brown and lyrics by Arthur Freed: "A Hollywood Relief" (Arthur Freed, lyrics by Leonard Levinson and Robert Lord), "Loose Ankles" (music by Arthur Freed, lyrics by Blanche Merrill), "Singin' in the Rain" (music by Nacio Herb Brown, lyrics by Arthur Freed), "We Don't Know Why—But" (music by Arthur Freed, lyrics by Robert Lord).

ARTHUR FREED'S ORANGE GROVE THEATRE REVUE (1927), music and lyrics by Arthur Freed: "In Our Orange Grove."

NOTE: All songs have lyrics written by Arthur Freed except where indicated. Freed in some instances wrote the music and lyrics; his name, therefore, appears as composer.

MISCELLANEOUS SONGS

Indiana Home (1919), music by Oliver Wallace
After Every Party (1920), music by Arthur Freed and Earl Burtnett
I Found the Heart for You (1920), music by Louis Silvers
Take Me in Your Arms (1921), music by Nacio Herb Brown and King Zany
When Buddha Smiles (1921), music by Nacio Herb Brown and King Zany
Apple Sauce (1922), music by Gus Arnheim, Abe Lyman and Arthur Freed
Cairo (1922), music by Harold Weeks
In the Garden of Other Days (1922), music by Gus Arnheim, Abe Lyman and Arthur Freed
Little Church Around the Corner, The (1922), music by Gus Arnheim, Abe Lyman and Arthur Freed
Longing for You (1922), music by Gus Arnheim and Arthur Freed
Louisiana (1922), music by Oliver Wallace
Peggy Dear (1922), music by Gus Arnheim and Arthur Freed
When Winter Comes (1922), music by Arthur Freed and Harry Carroll
I Was So Romantic (1923), music by Joseph Meyer
My Old Home Town (1924), music by Paul Riese
Closer to Heaven (1930), music by Arthur Freed
Dare Me Lovely Lady (1930), music by Joseph Meyer

When Your Hand First Touched Me (1930), music by Oliver Wallace and Arthur Freed

Hell's Loose (1930), music by Joseph Meyer

It Looks Like Love (1930), music by Harry Woods

Our Love (1930), music by Joseph Meyer

Rattling Along (1930), music by Joseph Meyer

Reaching for the Moon (1930), music by Oliver Wallace

So Near, So Dear (1930), music by Harry Woods

Whispering Through the Pines (1930), music by Harry Woods

A Cowboy's Serenade (1931), music by Richard Whiting

What Can I Do, I Love That Man (1931), music by Arthur Freed and Martin Broones

Because I Worship You (1931), music by Arthur Freed

Between You and Me (1931), music by Arthur Freed

Look in My Eyes (1931), music by Arthur Freed

Night Our Love Song Was Born, The (1931), music by Harry Woods

A Moment in the Dark (1932), music by Carmen Lombardo

Instead of a Million Dollars (1932), music by Arthur Freed and Harry Akst; lyrics by Harold Weeks

Make Me Yours (1932), music by John N. Scott and Tom Gerun

Sun's in My Heart, The (1932), music by Abel Baer

Somewhere in the West (1932), music by Arthur Freed and Peter Tinturin

We're Alone (1932), music by Harry Barris

When the Lights Are Soft and Low (1932), music by Arthur Freed and Peter Tinturin

Music and Moonlight (1932), music by George Meyer

With My Sweetie in the Moonlight (Under Dreamy Southern Skies) (1932), music by Arthur Freed, Sidney Clare and Peter Tinturin

Come Out, Come Out, Wherever You Are (1933), music by Al Hoffman and Al Goodhart

Lovey (1933), music by Al Hoffman and Al Goodhart

Acknowledgments

I must start this important page by thanking Roger Edens for inspiring me to write this book and Lela Simone, who was responsible for making it a reality.

For their valuable assistance while I was researching this book I am grateful to: Professor Robert Knutson, curator of special collections, University of Southern California, Los Angeles, where the Arthur Freed and Roger Edens Archives are housed; Edward Waters, music division, Library of Congress; Academy of Motion Pictures Arts and Sciences Margaret Herrick Library, Mildred Simpson, librarian, staff members Bonnie Rothbart, Alice Mitchell, Judy Polansky, Verna Ramsey, Marlene Medwin, Pat Ishii, Tamera Crombie, Midori Martin and Robert Cushman; American Cinematographers Society, courtesy of ASC Museum of Cinema, Oral History Tapes; Columbia University, Oral History program; Don Fowle, Library of Performing Arts, Theatre Collection, Lincoln Center; Sheila Whittacker and her staff of the National Film Archives at the British Film Institute, London; Stanley Adams and Herb Gottlieb of ASCAP; Jacques Ledoux, curator, the Royal Film Archives of Belgium, Brussels; Janue Barford, Danske Filmmuseum, København, Denmark; Cahiers du Cinema, Paris; Jack Haley, Jr., Norman Kaphan, Dor Freeman and Mike Scrimenti of M-G-M; Producers Guild, Writers Guild, and Directors Guild.

For their various courtesies and generous co-operation, I wish to thank the following individuals: Fred Astaire, Alan Jay Lerner, André Previn, Irene Sharaff, Oliver Smith, Sir Cecil Beaton, E. Y. Harburg, Harold Arlen, Kay Thompson, Joseph Ruttenberg, Larry Blyden, Harry Warren, Betty Comden, Adolph Green, Alex Romero, Rouben Mamoulian, Johnny Green, Oscar Levant, Lena Horne Hayton, Mrs. Dorothy Hammerstein, Irving Berlin, Mary and Richard Fleischer, Hugo Freed, Ruth Freed Akst, Ralph Blane, Stanley Donen, Mrs. Arthur Freed, Gene Kelly, Harold Rosson, George Sidney, Leonard Spigelgass; Charles Walters, Preston Ames, Fred Finklehoffe, Irving Brecher, Adrienne Fazan, Saul Chaplin, George Folsey, George Gibson, Robert Nathan, Merrill Pye, Sidney Sheldon, Emily Torchia, Ben Thau, Randall Duell, George Wells, Ralph Winters, Guy Green, Leo Arnaud, Conrad Salinger, Robert Alton, Myron Fox, Hermes Pan, Julius J. Epstein, Margaret O'Brien, Elizabeth Kern Miller, Nanette Fabray, Ranald MacDougall, Tony Duquette, Alexander Courage, Skip Martin, Al Jennings, Irving Berlin, Jack Cole, Burton Lane, Jack Hefton, Johnny Mercer, Gloria Safier, Busby Berkeley, Keogh Gleason, Irving Lazar, Lillie Messinger, John Lee Mahin, Kathryn O'Brien, Dore Schary, Ralph Freed, Richard Brooks, Lee and Ira Gershwin, Lilly and Eddie Carter, Nacio Herb Brown, Jr., Adolph Deutsch, Vincente Minnelli, Howard Strickling, Stephen Saltzman, Natalie Nostrand, Hilary Knight, Didier Deutsch, Leonard Gershe, Mary Ann Nyberg, Jack Martin Smith, Eugene Loring, Robert Tucker, George Wells, Jesse Kaye, Harry Lojewski, Ruby Armstrong, Walter Plunkett, Arthur Schwartz, Albert Hackett and Francis Goodrich, Howard Dietz, George Sidney, Charles Walters, Helen Auer (Arthur Freed's secretary) and Belva Lannan (Roger Edens' secretary). And, of course, Larry Ashmead, who first was interested in this book, and to my editor, Michele Tempesta.

FILM	DIRECTOR	COST*	DAYS	DOMESTIC*	FOREIGN*	TOTAL*
THE WIZARD OF OZ	Fleming	2,777	108	(39)2,048 (48)1,009 (54) 465	969 555	3,017 1,564 465
BABES IN ARMS	Berkeley	748	44	2,311	1,024	3,335
STRIKE UP THE BAND	Berkeley	854	35	2,265	1,229	3,494
LITTLE NELLIE KELLY	Taurog	718	41	968	1,078	2,946
LADY BE GOOD	McCleod	863	46	1,048	644	1,692
BABES ON BROADWAY	Berkeley	955	53	2,363	1,496	3,859
PANAMA HATTIE	McCleod	1,121	59	1,798	528	2,326
FOR ME AND MY GAL	Berkeley	841	44	2,894	1,477	4,371
CABIN IN THE SKY	Minnelli	679	44	1,719	234	1,953
DUBARRY WAS A LADY	Del Ruth	1,296	52	2,522	924	3,496
BEST FOOT FORWARD	Buzzell	1,162	48	2,051	653	2,704
GIRL CRAZY	Taurog	1,469	67	2,608	1,163	3,771
MEET ME IN ST. LOUIS	Minnelli	1,185	70	5,016	1,550	6,566
MEET THE PEOPLE	Reisner	1,302	59	670	290	960
THE CLOCK	Minnelli	1,560	58	2,173	610	2,783
YOLANDA & THE THIEF	Minnelli	2,444	88	1,221	570	1,791
THE HARVEY GIRLS	Sidney	2,931	89	4,112	1,063	5,175
ZIEGFELD FOLLIES	Minnelli et al	3,403	75	3,569	1,775	5,344
TILL THE CLOUDS ROLL BY	Thorpe	3,316	75	4,748	1,976	6,724
GOOD NEWS	Walters	1,715	48	2,545	411	2,956
SUMMER HOLIDAY	Mamoulian	2,237	67	1,208	401	1,609

FILM	DIRECTOR	COST*	DAYS	DOMESTIC*	FOREIGN*	TOTAL*
THE PIRATE	Minnelli	3,768	67	1,874	782	2,656
EASTER PARADE	Walters	2,503	42	4,144	1,659	5,803
WORDS AND MUSIC	Taurog	2,799	50	3,453	1,099	4,552
TAKE ME OUT TO THE BALL GAME	Berkeley	2,025	41	3,366	978	4,344
THE BARKLEYS OF BROADWAY	Walters	2,250	51	2,987	1,434	4,421
ANY NUMBER CAN PLAY	LeRoy	1,363	43	2,466	739	3,205
ON THE TOWN	Kelly-Donen	2,133	47	2,940	1,500	4,440
ANNIE GET YOUR GUN	Sidney	3,734	46	4,710	3,150	7,860
CRISIS	Brooks	1,581	44	895	520	1,415
PAGAN LOVE SONG	Alton	1,920	55	2,160	1,210	3,370
ROYAL WEDDING	Walters	1,661	33	2,550	1,375	3,925
SHOW BOAT	Sidney	2,389	42	5,300	2,350	7,650
AN AMERICAN IN PARIS	Minnelli	2,724	52	3,755	3,250	7,005
BELLE OF NEW YORK	Walters	2,563	54	1,343	650	1,993
SINGIN' IN THE RAIN	Kelly-Donen	2,593	54	3,265	2,400	5,665
THE BAND WAGON	Minnelli	2,873	55	2,305	1,250	3,555
BRIGADOON	Minnelli	3,019	52	1,985	1,400	3,385
IT'S ALWAYS FAIR WEATHER	Kelly-Donen	2,771	56	1,385	1,100	2,485
KISMET	Minnelli	3,015	46	1,220	800	2,020
INVITATION TO THE DANCE	Kelly	2,822	66	200	415	615
SILK STOCKINGS	Mamoulian	2,581	52	1,740	1,060	2,800
GIGI	Minnelli	3,447	59	6,500	3,200	9,700
				(TV)2,500		
				(TV)1,000		
BELLS ARE RINGING	Minnelli	3,246	58	2,825	800	3,725
THE SUBTERRANEANS	MacDougall	1,407	31	340	425	765
LIGHT IN THE PIAZZA	Green	847	55	1,200	1,000	2,200

*Cost in Thousands